Designing Interactive Systems

THIRD EDITION

Designing Interactive Systems

A comprehensive guide to HCI, UX and interaction design

David Benyon

Harlow, England • London • New York • Boston • San Francisco • Toronto • Sydney • Auckland • Singapore • Hong Kong
Tokyo • Seoul • Taipei • New Delhi • Cape Town • São Paulo • Mexico City • Madrid • Amsterdam • Munich • Paris • Milan

PEARSON EDUCATION LIMITED
Edinburgh Gate
Harlow CM20 2JE
United Kingdom
Tel: +44 (0)1279 623623
Web: www.pearson.com/uk

First published 2005 (print)
Second edition published 2010 (print)
Third edition published 2014 (print and electronic)

© Pearson Education Limited 2005, 2010 (print)
© Pearson Education Limited 2014 (print and electronic)

ISBN: 978-1-4479-2011-3 (print)
      978-1-292-01384-8 (PDF)
      978-1-292-01383-1 (eText)

British Library Cataloguing-in-Publication Data
A catalogue record for the print edition is available from the British Library

Library of Congress Cataloging-in-Publication Data
A catalog record for the print edition is available from the Library of Congress

10 9 8 7 6 5 4 3 2 1
16 15 14 13

Print edition typeset in 9.25/12.5 CharterITC Std by 75
Print edition printed and bound by L.E.G.O. S.p.A., Italy

NOTE THAT ANY PAGE CROSS REFERENCES REFER TO THE PRINT EDITION

Brief contents

Contents

Part I
Essentials of designing interactive systems

1 Designing interactive systems: a fusion of skills

2 PACT: a framework for designing interactive systems

3 The process of human-centred interactive systems design

4 Usability

5 Experience design

Companion Website

For open-access **student resources** specifically written to complement this textbook and support your learning, please visit **www.pearsoned.co.uk/benyon**

Lecturer Resources

For password-protected online resources tailored to support the use of this textbook in teaching, please visit **www.pearsoned.co.uk/benyon**

Guided tour

Student notes: simply scan the QR code icon with your smartphone or tablet to reveal further information and links about each topic.

Linked resources direct you to a selection of the author's chosen resources, including videos, lectures and presentations.

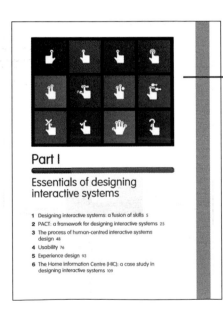

Part I

Essentials of designing interactive systems

Parts: the book is split into four parts, each with a part opener describing the main themes and links between chapters within that part.

Chapter aims introduce topics covered and summarize what you should have learnt by the end of the chapter.

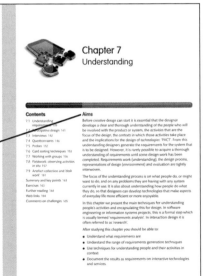

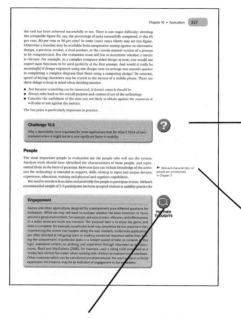

Challenges encourage students to apply their understanding by completing practical tasks and asking questions about topics discussed.

Chapter linking arrows highlight the connections between chapters and indicate where you can find further details about a topic or concept.

Further thoughts invite you to think in more depth about certain topics.

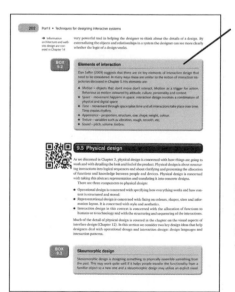

Boxes provide real-world examples to further illustrate topics and issues. These entertaining applications help to clarify and extend a student's understanding.

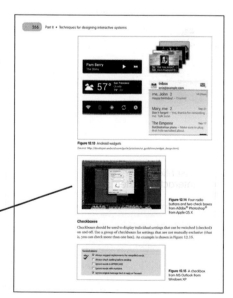

Screenshots, figures and photos feature throughout the text to illustrate key points and clarify topics discussed.

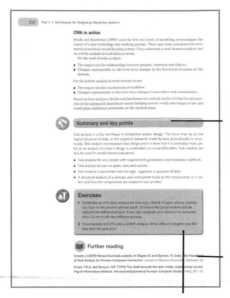

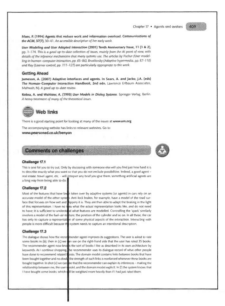

Summary and key points pulls together the main issues addressed in the chapter to provide a useful reminder of topics covered.

Further reading offers sources of additional information for those who wish to explore a topic further.

Exercises, practical challenges and tasks feature at the end of every chapter to test students' understanding and encourage them to apply their knowledge.

Comments on challenges provide guideline answers to chapter challenges.

Preface

Designing Interactive Systems is aimed squarely at the next generation of user experience (UX) and interactive system designers. This book presents a comprehensive introduction to the practical issue of creating interactive systems, services and products from a human-centred perspective. It develops the principles and methods of human–computer interaction (HCI) and Interaction Design (ID) to deal with the demands of twenty-first-century computing and the demands for improved user experience (UX). UX and ID are concerned with the design of websites, desktop applications, smartphone apps, ubiquitous computing systems, mobile systems, wearable systems and systems to support cooperation between people. UX and ID are concerned with the development of novel apps, visualizations, auditory displays and responsive environments. HCI is about how to design for these experiences in a human-centred way that takes account of human abilities and preferences and ensures that systems are accessible, usable and acceptable.

This book aims to be the core text for university courses in HCI, ID and UX design. It contains the core material for introductory courses and advanced material and links to other resources for final-year undergraduate and masters-level students and to meet the needs of usability and UX professionals working in industry.

HCI established itself as an important area of study in the early 1980s and by the early 1990s there was a coherent syllabus and several textbooks. In the early 1990s the 'world wide' Web appeared, opening up website design as a new area. Information architecture and information design emerged as important areas of study and new issues of usability became important in the open and untamed world of the Web. By the late 1990s mobile phones had become a fashion statement for many people; style was as important as function. With colour displays and better screens, mobile phones became increasingly programmable. Interaction designers were needed along with software engineers to create exciting experiences for people. Smartphones, tablet computers and other information appliances made further new demands on software developers. User interfaces became tangible, graspable and immediate and software systems had to be engaging as well as functional. So, came the era of user experience (UX) design. Digital technologies, wireless communications and new sensing devices provided new media for a new generation of artist–designers involving whole installations, new modalities of interaction and wearable computing.

All this has brought us to where we are today: a dynamic mix of ideas, approaches and technologies being used by lots of people doing very different things in different contexts. *Designing Interactive Systems* aims to focus this emerging discipline by bringing together the best practice and experience from HCI, UX and ID. *Designing Interactive Systems* presents a human-centred approach to interaction and experience design. The strength and tradition of HCI has been in its human-centredness and usability concerns. HCI has evolved methods, guidelines, principles and standards to ensure that systems are easy to use and easy to learn. ID has come from design schools, applying traditional approaches to design that emphasize research, insight and critical reflection. UX has emerged during the Internet era to emphasize the enjoyment and engagement of the whole interactive experience.

Practitioners of HCI, website designers, usability experts, user experience designers, software engineers – indeed all those concerned with the design of interactive systems in all their forms – will find much that they recognize in this book. It is concerned with how to design engaging interactions between people and technologies to support the activities that people want to do and the contexts in which they act.

Organization of the book for the 3rd edition

The second edition of *Designing Interactive Systems: a comprehensive guide to HCI and interaction design* established itself as the key text for students and professionals of interaction design (ID), user experience (UX) and human–computer interaction (HCI). It has been translated into Chinese, Portuguese and Italian, ensuring it has real international coverage. This new edition aims to bring the material right up to date and to set the agenda for the future.

The previous edition established a clear structure for presenting the curriculum for HCI, ID and UX. The material was organized into four parts.

- Part I focused on the **essentials** of designing interactive systems.
- Part II covered the key **techniques** for human-centred interaction design that a good designer should master.
- Part III focused on the different **contexts** for interaction design.
- Part IV provided the psychological and sociological **foundations** of the subject.

I reviewed this structure and overall reviewers and students liked it. Some argued that foundations should come first, but providing the essentials first makes the book more accessible. Some argued that the structure of the book should follow the structure of a design project, but interactive systems design projects are so various that there is no one structure that reflects this variety. Others felt that there were too many different techniques and that the book should be more prescriptive.

Taking all these issues on board and looking at the changes that have happened in the subject since the second edition has resulted in this current edition. The four-part structure – essentials, techniques, contexts and foundations – remains. This allows professors and tutors to pick the combination that suits their classes best. Some suggestions are given below. The two chapters on the contextual design method have been removed, with the most important techniques from that method distributed across the relevant chapters. As the contexts in which designing interactive systems takes place continue to change so all the chapters in Part III have been thoroughly revised and a new chapter on wearable computing has been added. Every chapter has been revised in the light of this rapidly changing subject and all the examples have been updated to reflect changing technologies.

Thus *Designing Interactive Systems* now has the following structure.

Part I provides an essential guide to the issues of designing interactive systems – the main components of the subject, key features of the design process and how these are applied to different types of system. The unifying idea is encapsulated by the acronym PACT: designers should strive to achieve a harmony between the needs of different people who undertake activities in contexts using technologies. It is the very large amount of variation in these components that makes designing interactive systems such a fascinating challenge. A key concept throughout is the idea of 'scenarios'. Scenarios are stories about interactions. They provide an effective representation for reflecting on a design throughout its development. All the material has been updated and new material has been added to Chapter 4 on accessibility. The chapter on experience design has been extended to cover gamification and service design.

Part II pulls together all the main techniques arising from HCI, ID and UX that are used for understanding, designing and evaluating interactive products, services and experiences. Part II presents techniques for understanding the requirements of interactive systems, probing people for ideas, getting people to participate in the design process, card sorting to develop information architectures and investigating similar systems for ideas. Part II includes a chapter on ways of envisioning ideas, prototyping and evaluating design ideas. A more formal approach to conceptual and physical design is included along with a chapter on the key HCI technique of task analysis and a detailed presentation of user interface design in two chapters. One chapter focuses on design of visual interfaces and the other on multimodal interfaces that include sound, touch and gesture.

Part III considers interaction and experience design in the different contexts that are dominating the subject today. There is a chapter on website design and another on social media. But ID and UX go way beyond displays on a desktop computer. People are using mobile devices and interacting with interactive environments. Accordingly, Part III includes chapters on designing for mobile and ubiquitous computing. There is also a new chapter on wearable computing. Collaborative environments and agent-based interaction are also important emerging contexts for UX, ID and HCI.

Part IV provides a deep treatment of the psychological foundations of HCI, ID and UX. One chapter deals with memory, attention, and human capacities that influence interaction. There is a chapter on understanding human emotion and how this affects interaction. A central chapter on theories of cognition and action brings together the latest ideas on embodied cognition, conceptual blending and how these impact the UX. Social interaction is increasingly important to UX and ID and there is a chapter devoted to the key issues from this area. Hearing, haptics (touch) and other ways of perceiving the world are considered alongside the psychology of navigation in Chapter 25. This is fundamental knowledge that the professional should seek to acquire. This part provides material aimed at the specialist student or students studying HCI and ID in psychology or design schools.

Topics in HCI, UX and ID

The organization of the book does have a clear logic to it; however, I do not expect many people will start at the beginning and read the book from cover to cover. Accordingly I have provided a number of routes through the text for different people with different needs (see below). The book also contains a comprehensive index so that people can find their own ways in to areas of interest. I have also provided a list of intermediate-level topics at the beginning of each Part. These are shown below in alphabetical order. The topic number indicates which Part it appears in. Numbered topic lists appear in the introduction to each Part.

Readership

There is a wide range of people involved in the design and development of interactive systems in the twenty-first century. *Software engineers* are developing new applications for their organizations. They redesign systems to take advantage of developments in technologies and add on extra features to legacy systems. Software engineers working for software companies develop new generic software products or new releases of existing systems. *Systems analysts and designers* work with clients, end-users and other stakeholders to develop solutions to business problems. *Web designers* are increasingly in demand to organize and present content and new functionality for websites. People are developing applications for new media such as interactive television, 'third-generation' (3G) mobile phones, personal digital assistants and other information appliances. *Product designers* are increasingly finding themselves working with interactive features in their products. Many other people with job titles such as *User Experience Designers, Information Architects* and *Interaction Designers* are involved in this rapidly changing business. All these people need education and training, and require ready access to proven methods and techniques of design and evaluation and to the key theoretical concepts.

Just as the range of people involved in the development and deployment of interactive systems is increasing, so is the range of activities. The basic components of design – establishing requirements and developing systems – are common across all these types of interactive products and systems, but detailed activities vary. For example, the analyst–designer working in an office environment would be likely to use traditional requirements generation techniques such as interviewing, whereas the developer of a new smartphone app might use focus groups and 'future workshops'. A website designer would make use of navigation maps, whereas an application developer might produce a prototype in a programming language such as Visual Basic to show to potential users. An evaluation of a mobile phone might focus on aesthetics, style and 'teenage appeal', whereas an evaluation of a shared diary system in a large bank might concentrate on efficiency and time-saving and acceptance issues.

Contexts of interaction are increasingly diverse. Large organizations such as hospitals are introducing smartphones and tablets for consultants and nurses. Universities are introducing purpose-built shared intranet systems to control development of course materials. Oil-rigs have three-dimensional 'virtual reality' training programs and electricity companies are using text messaging to record meter readings. A start-up software company wants to introduce quality and usability control through its software development process and a new media company is developing a Web-based service for its customers. Household environments, on-line communities, mobile computing, offices and remote 'virtual organizations' are just a few of the contexts for twenty-first-century human–computer interaction design. Most importantly, we are seeing technologies bringing people into contact with people. The design of on-line communities and other systems to support the social aspects of life is a move away from the retrieval of information that characterized older systems.

Finally, technologies are changing. Software development is moving from top-heavy methodologies based on object-oriented techniques with the Unified Modeling Language (UML) dominant, to agile development methods. Websites often include Java programming and have to interface with databases. Phones run under new operating systems such as Android and new network protocols are needed for voice applications through mobile phones and remote control of other devices such as heating controllers. Geographical positioning systems and complete in-car navigational systems have to be seen alongside new concepts in digital entertainment through interactive television and home information centres. Mobile phones converge with digital cameras and MP3 music systems. Multitouch surfaces and gesture recognition are poised to make significant changes to the way we interact with technologies.

So, how do educators and practitioners cross these diverse areas and combinations of people, activities, contexts and technologies? We need to train software engineers to know about and apply principles of usability, Web designers to produce creative designs that are accessible to all, and systems analysts to be sympathetic to the situated nature of work. We need product developers who design for the elderly and infirm, engineers who understand people, their capacities and limitations, and creative people who understand the constraints of software engineering. We need information architects, user experience designers and service design professionals to understand the principles of HCI, accessibility and usability. *Designing Interactive Systems* aims to meet the educational and practical needs of this diverse group by providing the variety of perspectives that is necessary.

How to use this book

HCI, UX and the design of interactive systems take place in a wide variety of contexts, by individuals working alone or in design teams of various sizes. The systems or products to be produced vary enormously in size and complexity and utilize a range of technologies. There is no 'one size fits all' approach that can deal with this variety. In this book and its associated website I provide a variety of perspectives to match the variety inherent in the design of interactive systems. A professional interactive system designer will need to achieve a competence in all the methods and techniques described in this book and will need to understand all the issues and theories that are raised. To achieve this level of competence would take three years of study for an undergraduate student. But not everyone needs to achieve this level, so I have organized the material to make different types of understanding available.

It is an ambitious task to write a complete guide to the design of interactive systems when the area is still evolving. However, I have made an effort to mention all the currently important issues and the further reading at the end of each chapter provides directions on where to go next for more detailed coverage of specific issues. There is also a comprehensive website with student notes, further exercises and tags (keywords) for each chapter subsection to allow for easier searching for additional material.

Of course, the very nature of books is itself changing rapidly and this too is reflected in this new edition. Using a phone running a suitable app, readers can instantly access the Web material associated with each section and get the up-to-date detail directly from the Web. There are also video links in the text so that readers can watch videos related to their studies. So whether you are reading this on a Kindle or iPad or as a printed book, the interactive experience of the text will be as engaging as any other.

The pedagogic style adopted by the text ensures that it meets the needs of students and teachers alike. Boxes are used to highlight significant examples of the subject under discussion and to point readers to interesting diversions. Forward and backward references help to show how topics are linked. Case studies that the author has been involved with have been included to illustrate the issues and to provide a rich source of examples for students and teachers.

The book can be used in part or in total on a wide variety of courses, from specialist degrees in Human–Computer Interaction to a minor part of a degree in Software Engineering to specialist modules on Design or Engineering degrees, Psychology, Communication and Media degrees or other programmes where the design of interactive systems and products is important. Most importantly, this book has been designed with its accompanying website in mind. In the book are the things that I do not expect to change over the next period (up until 2016). The structure should remain stable over this period and the content will remain relevant. All the details that I expect to change are on the website and this will be maintained to ensure it is up to date. Indeed readers are encouraged to e-mail if they find better examples, broken links or out-of-date material. The accompanying website (at **www.pearsoned.co.uk/benyon**) should be considered part of the book.

I and my colleagues have been using this book for several years now and I meet and talk to others who use the book at their universities. The material is highly accessible and flexible. Chapters 1–4, for example, provide the basis of a 200-hour course for first-years and Chapters 1–10 provide a 200-hour course for masters students. Chapters 2, 3, 4 and 10 provide a 16-hour course for on-line financial product developers. To explain how the material can be used, I refer to a first- or second-year undergraduate course of study as 'level 2' material, third-year as 'level 3' and fourth or masters as 'level 4'.

Part I would form the basis of a level 2 course and indeed this is what I teach to our second-year computing students. They study Processing as a prototyping language and I include a number of 'motivational' lectures on current topics in addition to delivering Topics 1.1 to 1.6 and 1.8 to 1.12 (Chapters 1–5) as a series of six two-hour lectures.

Part I material is also suitable for courses on interaction design and as introductory material to a wide variety of level 3 modules. For example, with the materials from Part II it would form a user-centred design module; with more material on psychology from Part IV it would make a level 3 module on human–computer interaction. Chapter 3 and Part II can be used as a course on scenario-based design. Part IV is also suitable at this level where the theoretical background for human–computer interaction is required. In the past I have run an advanced module on navigation (Chapter 25) and cognition (Chapter 23), applied to website design (Chapter 14) and mobile and ubiquitous computing (Chapters 18 and 19). Part II provides a wealth of examples that students can be pointed to that illustrate design issues or to learn specific design techniques as they need them.

Our 'rule of thumb' for a typical course or module unit is 10–15 hours of student time per week. This would be composed as follows and constitutes one 'credit'. Over the period of a year, full-time students study eight 15-credit modules or six 20-credit modules.

Activity	Hours
Primary exposition of material (e.g. lecture)	1–2
Secondary presentation (e.g. seminar)	1–2
Unmoderated, informal student discussions	2
Practical exercises and activities	2
Research and further reading, based on the student notes and further reading suggested	2–3
Revision and assessment	2–4

The following are examples of modules and courses that illustrate how the material in this book could be used. These are just a few of the many variations that are possible.

Course/module	Material, chapter numbers
Level 2 Introduction to HCI (15 credits).	
A basic-level course intended to equip computing students with an appreciation of HCI issues and a set of practical skills.	Most of Chapters 1–5 (Topics 1.1–1.6 and 1.8–1.12) plus basic introduction to prototyping.
Level 3 Interaction Design (15 credits).	
A more advanced module aimed at developing the issues concerned with designing useful and engaging interactions. Based around the development of paper prototypes, it encourages students to focus on design issues rather than programming issues.	Quickly revise material in Chapters 1–4, but base the module around Chapters 7–10, 12 and 13 supplemented with chapters from Part III according to the interest of the lecturer and students. The focus here is on scenarios and developing the skills of envisionment, prototyping and the evaluation of ideas. A critical study of Chapter 6 case study is useful.
Level 3 User-centred Design (15 credits).	
A module focusing on industrial-strength, human-centred design process. Fits nicely alongside Interaction Design.	This can be based on Chapter 3 using a formal scenario-based design as the design method. The conceptual and physical design described in Chapter 9, based on object-action analysis would supplement this, along with task analysis methods (Chapter 11) and further evaluations (Chapter 10).

Course/module	Material, chapter numbers
Level 4 Advanced Interactive Systems Design Concepts (20 credits)	A masters-level module that looks at advanced and modern interfaces such as wearable and tangible computing. Look at experience design in detail (Chapter 5), multimodal interaction (Chapter 13), theories of action (Chapter 23), perception and navigation (Chapter 25). Apply to issues of collaborative environments and gestural interaction (Chapter 16) and blended spaces (Chapter 18).
Level 2 Web Design (15 credits).	Part I material supplemented with Chapters 14 and 15. Include evaluation (Chapter 10) and visual interface design (Chapter 12)
Level 3 or 4 Module on Psychological Foundations of Human–Computer Interaction (20 credits).	In-depth coverage of Part IV materials. Examples from Part III with some introductory material from Part I.

Other resources

The text highlights other important resources where appropriate. Here are some pointers to a few general resources. The Usability Professional Association (UPA) is a good place for interested people to look for examples of good practice and links to other resources: **www.upassoc.org**. The American Institute of Graphic Arts (AIGA, **www.aiga.com**) is increasingly involved with interaction and information design. The Association of Computing Machinery (ACM, **http://acm.org**) has an active special interest group in computer–human interaction (SIGCHI) and the British Computer Society also has an excellent group for both academics and professionals (**www.bcs-hci.org.uk**). Both of these have extensive resource libraries and organize many relevant conferences. There are many good websites devoted to aspects of usability, human–computer interaction and interaction design that can be found by following links from the sources on the companion website at **www.pearsoned.co.uk/benyon**. Finally, there are two international standards that deal with usability. They are ISO 9241-11 and 13407. The European resource centre, 'usability net', has details at **www.usabilitynet.org**.

The author

David Benyon is Professor of Human–Computer Systems at Edinburgh Napier University. He began his career as a systems analyst working for a number of 'software houses' and industrial companies. After several years he moved into academia where he developed a more formal understanding of issues of HCI. The first US conference on computer–human interaction took place in the same year that David began an MSc in Computing and Psychology at Warwick University and in 1984 he published his first paper on the subject. Since then he has continued to publish and now has over 150 published papers and 12 books. He obtained his PhD in Intelligent User Interfaces in 1994 when he also co-authored one of the first HCI textbooks, *Human–Computer Interaction* (by Preece, Rogers, Sharp, Benyon, Holland and Carey, published by Addison-Wesley) and *Usability Now!* (1993). He continues to take an active part in the HCI and ID communities, organizing and presenting at conferences including CHI (Computer Human Interaction),

DIS (Designing Interactive Systems), Interact conferences and Interactions (British Computer Society).

During his career David has worked on twenty European-funded research and development and UK-funded research projects and ten knowledge transfer projects. He has supervised twenty-six PhD students, examined forty-three and undertaken a number of consultancy projects. This wide and extensive experience of all manner of HCI, ID and UX puts David in a unique position within the world of interactive systems design. All this experience and knowledge has fed into this book. In the Persona project David worked with Kristina Höök from the Swedish Institute of Computer Science on ideas of navigation of information spaces and on 'social navigation'. He worked with Bang & Olufsen of Denmark on concepts for a Home Information Centre (HIC) and with NCR, UK on personalization of interfaces to self-service machines. He worked with the University of Dundee and others on technologies for older people, with partners across Europe on projects concerned with ideas of presence and with a large consortium of Scottish universities on interacting with wireless sensor networks. He spent four years exploring concepts of 'Companions' – advanced personalized multimodal interfaces to the Internet – with Telefonica, France Telecom and others in a large integrated research project and working with a number of Indian Institutes of Technology on gesture-based interaction and multitouch displays. Most recently he has been working on applications of multitouch surface computing and augmented reality for tourism applications.

Acknowledgements

This book has been developing for over seven years and in that time many friends and colleagues have helped with ideas, comments and evaluations of materials. Draft materials have been used with students and I would like to acknowledge their help in producing the finished text. Methods and techniques have been developed and used on a variety of research and development projects and I would like to thank all the students and researchers who helped in this respect. In particular all the people who worked on the European FLEX project helped to produce the case study in Chapter 6 and many of the examples used in Part II. These included Tom Cunningham, Lara Russell, Lynne Baillie, Jon Sykes, Stephan Crisp and Peter Barclay. The researchers on Companions, Oli Mival, Brian O'Keefe, Jay Bradley and Nena Roa-Seiler, deserve acknowledgements for their contributions. Other past and present students who have contributed to the ideas and examples in this book include Bettina Wilmes, Jesmond Worthington, Shaleph O'Neil, Liisa Dawson, Ross Philip, Jamie Sands, Manual Imaz, Martin Graham, Mike Jackson, Rod McCall, Martin Clark, Sabine Gordzielik, Matthew Leach, Chris Riley, Philip Hunt and David Tucker. Thanks also to Richard Nesnass, Aurelien Ammeloot and Serkan Ayan.

I would like to thank all my colleagues at Edinburgh Napier University and those who have moved on. In particular Catriona Macaulay was involved in many of the early discussions and contributed much through her innovative teaching and curriculum development. Michael Smyth, Tom McEwan, Sandra Cairncross, Alison Crerar, Alison Varey, Richard Hetherington, Ian Smith, Iain McGregor, Malcolm Rutter, Shaun Lawson, Gregory Leplatre, Tom Flint, Emilia Sobolewska and Ingi Helgason have all contributed through discussions, criticisms and chance remarks. The contribution of other members of the School of Computing is also acknowledged.

David Benyon
Edinburgh Napier University, Edinburgh

Publisher's acknowledgements

We are grateful to the following for permission to reproduce copyright material:

Figures

Figure 3.2 after The rich picture: a tool for reasoning about work context, *Interactions,* 5(2), pp. 21–30, Figure 1 and Figure 2 (Monk, A. and Howard, S. 1998) © 1998 ACM, Inc., reprinted by permission, http://doi.acm.org/10.1145/274430.274434; Figure 3.3 after John M. Carroll, *Making Use: Scenario-based Design of Human-Computer Interactions* Figure 3.2, p. 69 © 2000 Massachusetts Institute of Technology, by permission of the MIT Press; Figure 4.1 after Individual differences and inclusive design, in Stephanidis, C. (ed.), *Interfaces for All: Concepts, Methods and Tools,* Lawrence Erlbaum Associates (Benyon, D. R. et al 2001), copyright 2000 by Taylor & Francis Group LLC – Books, reproduced with permission of Taylor & Francis Group LLC – Books in the format Textbook via the Copyright Clearance Center, Inc; Figure 4.5 after *User-Centered System Design: New Perspectives on Human-Computer Interaction,* Lawrence Erlbaum Associates (Norman, D.A. and Draper, S. (eds) 1986) reproduced with permission of Taylor & Francis Group LLC – Books; permission conveyed through Copyright Clearance Center, Inc; Figure 4.7 after Norman, Donald A., *The Invisible Computer: Why Good Products Can Fail, the Personal Computer Is So Complex, and Information Appliances Are The Solution,* Figure 2.5 © 1998 Massachusetts Institute of Technology, by permission of The MIT Press; Figure 5.6 from The Customer Journey Canvas, *This is Service Design Thinking,* BIS Publishers (Stickdorn, M. and Schneider, J. 2011), This work is licensed under the Creative Commons Attribution-ShareAlike 3.0 Unported Licence. To view a copy of this license, visit http://creativecommons.org/licenses/by-sa/3.0/; Figure 6.9 adapted from *The Scotsman,* August 1998, Scotsman Publications Ltd; Figure 7.6 from http://www.interaction-design.org/images/encyclopedia/card_sorting/groups_chart_26_participants.jpg, with permission from Interaction Design Foundation; Figure 8.2 from David Benyon; Figure 8.8 (top) from Wireframe Online Store http://www.smartdraw.com/specials/images/examples/wireframe-example-online-store.gif, SmartDraw; Figure 8.8 (bottom) from Wireframe Example Email, http://www.smartdraw.com/specials/images/examples/wireframe-example-email.gif, SmartDraw; Figure 11.3 after *HCI Models, Theories, and Frameworks* (John, B. 2003) p. 89, copyright Elsevier 2003; Figure 11.4 reprinted from *International Journal of Human-Computer Studies,* 44(6) Green, T.R.G. and Benyon, D.R., The skull beneath the skin: entity-relationship models of information artefacts, pp. 801–828, Copyright 1996, with permission from Elsevier; Figure 12.5 Apple Inc; Figure 12.34 after *Visual Explanations,* Graphics Press (Tufte, E.R. 1997) pp. 110 and 111, courtesy of Edward R. Tufte and Seth M. Powsner; Figure 13.1 adapted from Augmented Reality: A class of displays on the reality-virtuality continuum, *Proceedings of SPIE,* 2351, p. 282 (Milgram, P., Takemura, H., Utsumi, A. and Kishno, F. 1995), with permission from SPIE; Figure 14.2 from *The Elements of User Experience: User-centered Design for the Web* (Garrett, J.J. 2003) © 2003 Jesse James Garrett, reproduced by permission of Pearson Education, Inc. publishing as New Riders Publishing, all rights reserved; Figure 14.3 after http://www.jjg.net/ia/visvocab, courtesy of Jesse James Garrett; Figure 14.11 after *Information Architecture for the World Wide Web* (Rosenfeld, L. and Morville, P. 2002) p. 187 © 2002, O'Reilly Media, Inc., http://www.oreilly.com; Figure 16.1 from Jetter, Hans-Christian; Geyer, Florian; Schwarz, Tobias; Reiterer, Harald: Blended Interaction – Toward a Framework for the Design of Interactive Spaces. Workshop Designing Collaborative Interactive Spaces (DCIS 2012) at AVI 2012, Human-Computer Interaction Group, Univ. of Konstanz, May 2012. http://hci.uni-konstanz.de/downloads/dcis2012_Jetter.pdf; Figure 17.7 after Adaptive hypermedia, *User Modeling and User-adapted Interaction,* 11 (1–2), Figure 1, p. 100 (Brusilovsky, P. 2001), Kluwer Academic Publishers; Figure 18.10 from *The Home Workshop. A Method for Investigating the Home,* published PhD Thesis, Napier

University, Edinburgh (Baillie, L. 2002) p. 109, Figure 5.8 reproduced by permission of Lynne Baillie; Figure 18.11 from Exploring and enhancing the home experience, *Cognition, Technology and Work,* 5(1), p. 20, Figure 3 (Eggen, B., Hellemans, G. and van de Sluis, R. 2003), Springer-Verlag G,bH & Co. KG; Figure 21.2 after Human memory: a proposed system and its control processes, in Spence, K.W. and Spence, J.T. eds, *The Psychology of Learning and Motivation,* Vol. 2 (Atkinson, R.C. and Shiffrin, R.M. 1968), copyright Elsevier 1968; Figure 21.9 after Cognition underspecification: Its variety and consequences, in Baars, B.J. ed., *Experimental Slips and Human Error: Exploding the Architecture of Volition,* Plenum Press, Fig 15.24 (Reason, J. 1992), with kind permission from Springer Science+Business Media B.V.; Figure 22.1 after Plutchik, Robert, *Emotion: A Psychoevolutionary Synthesis 1st* © 1979 Printed and Electronically reproduced by permission of Pearson Education, Inc. Upper Saddle River, New Jersey; Figure 24.5 from Why distance matters: effects on cooperation, persuasion and deception, *Proceedings of CSCW'02 Conference,* New Orleans, LA, 16–20 November, pp. 226–35 (Bradner, E. and Mark, G. 2002) © 2002 ACM, Inc. Reprinted by permission, http://doi.acm.org/10.1145/587078.587110; Figure 24.8 from The Layers of Presence: a biocultural approach to understanding presence in natural and mediated environments, *Cyberpsychology and Behavior,* 7(4), pp. 402–416 (Riva, G., Waterworth, J.A. and Waterworth, E.L. 2004), Mary Ann Liebert, Inc; Figure 25.11 from *Psychology: The Science of Mind and Behaviour,* (Gross, R. 2001) p. 221, Copyright © 2001 Richard Gross. Reproduced by permission of Hodder Education; Figure 25.19 from Perceptual user interfaces: haptic interfaces, *Communications of the ACM,* 43(3), pp. 40–41 (Tan, H.Z. 2000) © 2000 ACM, Inc., reprinted by permission, http://doi.acm.org/10.1145/330534.330537; Figure 25.21 from Massachusetts Institute of Technology, Kevin Lynch papers, MC 208, box 2. Massachusetts Institute of Technology, Institute Archives and Special Collections, Cambridge, Massachusetts; Figure 25.22 from *The Concise Township,* Architectural Press, Butterworth-Heinemann, copyright Elsevier 1961 (Cullen, G., 1961, re-issued 1994).

Screenshots

Screenshots 1.3, 24.12 from http://secondlife.com, Linden Lab; Screenshots 4.2, 4.3, 12.2, 12.7, 12.9 12.11, 12.12, 12.14, 12.16, 12.23, 12.27, 12.28, 12.29, 12.30, 12.32, 13.7, 14.6, 21.8, 21.12, 23.5, 25.7 Apple Inc; Screenshots 4.8, 9.9, 12.1, 12.3, 12.8, 12.10, 12.15, 12.16, 12.20, 12.21, 12.22, 12.24, 12.25, 12.26, 12.30, 12.33, 16.4, 21.10, 22.9 Microsoft product screenshot frame reprinted with permission from Microsoft Corporation; Screenshot 5.5 from Measuring emotion; development and application of an instrument to measure emotional responses to products, in M.A. Blythe, A.F. Monk, K. Overbeeke and P.C. Wright (eds), *Funology: from usability to enjoyment,* Dordrecht: Kluwer Academic Publishers, pp. 111–123 (Desmet, P.M.A. 2003), with permission from Pieter Desmet; Screenshot 7.2 from http://surveymonkey.com/Home_FeaturesDesign.aspx, SurveyMonkey.com; Screenshot 8.5 from Lucero, A. (2009) Co-designing Interactive Spaces for and with Designers: Supporting Mood-Board Making, PhD Thesis, Eindhoven University of Technology, with permission from Andrés Lucero; Screenshot 12.6 from the Xerox Star user interface, courtesy of Xerox Ltd; Screenshots 12.7, 12.14 Adobe product screenshot reprinted with permission from Adobe Systems Incorporated; Screenshot 12.13 from Figure 1. Example app widgets in Android 4.0, http://developer.android.com/guide/practices/ui_guidelines/widget_design.html, this content is licensed under the Creative Commons Attribution 2.5, license, http://creativecommons.org/licenses/by/2.5/; Screenshot 12.18 from RealOne Player® courtesy of Real Networks, Inc; Screenshot 12.31 from http://www.easyjet.co.uk/en/book/index.asp, easyJet Airline Company Limited; Screenshot 12.35 (top left) from London Underground map by H.C. Beck (1933), © TfL from the London Transport Museum collection; Screenshot 12.35 (top right), 25.24a from London Underground map, 2009. © TfL from the London Transport Museum collection; Screenshot 12.37 from Visual information seeking: Tight coupling of dynamic query filters with starfield displays, *CHI'94 Proceedings of the SIGCHI Conference on Human Factors in Computing Systems* pp. 313–17 (Ahlberg, C. and Shneiderman, B. 1994), Colour plates 1, 2, 3, 4. © 1994 ACM, Inc. Reprinted by permission, http://dx.doi.org/10.1145/191666.191775; Screenshot 12.39 from www.smartmoney.com/map-of-the-market © SmartMoney 2004. All rights reserved. Used with permission. SmartMoney is a joint venture of Dow Jones & Company, Inc. and Hearst Communications, Inc; Screenshot 12.40 from www.plumbdesign.com/thesaurus, Visual

Thesaurus™ (powered by Thimkmap®) © 2004 Plumb Design, Inc., all rights reserved; Screenshot 13.3 from http://wearables.unisa.edu.au/uploads/2010/05/icon-quake26-hf.jpg, used with permission of Dr. Bruce H. Thomas, Wearable Computer Lab, University of South Australia; Screenshot 14.1 (top left) from adidas shop United Kingdom, http://www.shopadidas.com, 'adidas', '3-Bars', '3-Stripes mark', 'The Globe logo', 'The Trefoil Logo', 'ADICOLOR', 'SLVR', and 'SUPERNOVA' are trade marks of the adidas Group, used with permission; Screenshot 14.1(top right) from edutopia © 2009, The George Lucas Educational Foundation (GLEF), www.edutopia.org. All Rights Reserved; Screenshot 14.1 (bottom) from WHITEvoid Portfolio, http://whitevoid.com, WHITEvoid Interactive art & design, Kastanienallee 89, D-10435 Berlin; Screenshot 14.5 from Yahoo! UK and Ireland TV – Listings, Yahoo!; Screenshot 14.7 from www.expedia.co.uk, reproduced with permisssion; Screenshot 14.8 from www.pricegrabber.co.uk, Courtesy of PriceGrabber.com, LLC; Screenshot 14.12 from cheese – Yahoo! Search results, Yahoo!; Screenshot 14.13 from Vincent Flanders' Web Pages That Suck, http://www.webpagesthatsuck.com; Screenshot 14.14 from Edinburgh Napier University School of Computing http://www.napier.ac.uk; Screenshot 14.15 from http://www.easyjet.co.uk, easyJet Airline Company Limited; Screenshot 14.16 from http://www.google.com, Google™ is a trademark of Google Inc. Reproduced with permission of Google Inc; Screenshot 14.17 from Robert Louis Stevenson website, www.unibg.it/rls, with permission from Robert Dury; Screenshots 14.20, 14.21, 14.22 from http://www.robert-louis-stevenson.org; Screenshot 15.2 from http://en.wikipedia.org/interaction_design, this article is licensed under the terms of the GNU Free Documentation License, http://www.gnu.org/Interaction_design; Screenshot 15.3 from http://www.sics.se/~espinoza/documents/GeoNotes_ubicomp_final.htm, Figure 2, Frederick Espinoza; Screenshot 15.5 from http://movielens.umn.edu/login, Joseph A. Konstan; Screenshots 15.6, 17.6 from www.amazon.co.uk. © 2013 Amazon.com Inc. and its affiliates. All rights reserved; Screenshot 15.8 from Socially translucent systems: social proxies, persistent conversation, and the design of 'babble', *Proceedings of the SIGCHI conference on Human factors in computing systems: the CHI is the limit*, May, pp. 72–9, Figure 3 (Erickson, T.M., Smith, D.N., Kellogg, W.A., Laff, M., Richards, J.T. and Bradner, E.

1999) © 1999 ACM, Inc. Reprinted by permission, http://doi.acm.org/10/1145/302979.302997; Screenshot 15.9 from Listio for Web 2.0, http://www.listio.com, with permission from Listio; Screenshot 15.10 from http://www.orkut.com/Main#AppDirectory.aspx, Orkut™ is a trademark of Google Inc; Screenshot 15.11 from www.tweetag.com, with permission from Tweetag; Screenshot 15.12 from http://press.linkedin.com/logo-images, with permission from LinkedIn; Screenshot 15.13 from http://www.freshnetworks.com, built by FreshNetworks; Screenshot 15.14 from WordPress Web Hosting, http://en.wordpress.com/features/, with permission from WordPress.com; Screenshot 15.15 from www.digg.com, Courtesy of Digg; Screenshot 15.16 from https://addons.mozilla.org/en-US/firefox/, Copyright 2005–2009 Mozilla. All Rights Reserved. All rights in the names, trademarks, and logos of the Mozilla Foundation, including without limitation, Mozilla®, mozilla.org®, Firefox®, as well as the Mozilla logo, Firefox logo, and the red lizard logo are owned exclusively by the Mozilla Foundation. All other trademarks, service marks and trade names appearing in this document are the property of their respective owners; Screenshot 15.17 from http://www.cooliris.com, Cooliris, Inc; Screenshot 15.18 from http://www.google.com/google-d-s/intl/en/tour1.html, Google™ is a trademark of Google Inc; Screenshot 16.2 from Google Calendar, Google™ is a trademark of Google Inc; Screenshot 16.3 from https://plus.google.com/+GoogleDrive#; Google™ is a trademark of Google Inc; Screenshot 16.5 from http://bscw.fit.fraunhofer.de, Copyright FIT Fraunhofer and OrbiTeam Software GmbH. Used with permission; Screenshot 16.8 from http://www.billbuxton.com/portholes, courtesy of Bill Buxton; Screenshot 16.11 from www.discover.uottawa.ca/~mojtaba/Newbridge.html, DISCOVER Laboratory, S.I.T.E., University of Ottawa; Screenshot 17.9 from http://www.ananova.com/video/, Ananova Ltd; Screenshot 18.1 from http://www.ambient.media.mit.edu/projects.php?action=details&id=35, Siftables were developed by David Merrill, Jeevan Kalanthi and Pattie Maes at the MIT Media Lab; Screenshot 18.2 from http://hehe.org3.free.fr/images/nv_postcard_hehe.tif, Nuage Vert, Helsinki 2008, copyright HeHe; Screenshot 18.4 from http://www.media.mit.edu/resenv/portals/, Joseph A. Paradiso; Screenshots 19.6, 19.7 from Activity-based serendipitous recommendations with the Magitti mobile leisure guide,

Proceedings of the Twenty-sixth Annual SIGCHI conference on Human Factors in Computing Systems, 5–10 April, Florence, Italy © 2008 ACM, Inc. Reprinted by permission, http://doi.acm.org/10.1145/1357054. 1357237, the research and development behind the Magitti system was sponsored by Dai Nippon Printing Co. Ltd. 'Media Technology Research Center' and 'Corporate R & D Division'; Screenshot 19.8 from Escape: a target selection technique using visually-cued gestures, *Proceedings of the Twenty-sixth Annual SIGCHI Conference on Human Factors in Computing Systems,* 5–10 April (Yatani, K., Patridge, K., Bern, M., Newman, M.W. 2008) © 2009 ACM, Inc. Reprinted by permission, http://doi.acm.org/10.1145/1357054. 1357104; Screenshot 21.11 from Jon Kerridge; Screenshot 22.5 from EU Funded Project (IST-2201-39192) EMMA Project; Screenshot 24.10 from Stress OutSourced, MIT Media Lab, Tangible Media Group; Screenshot 25.24d from Pearson Education.

Tables

Table 9.1 from Marshall Lapham, *Understanding Media: The Extensions of Man,* 1 Table from introduction © 1994 Massachusetts Institute of Technology, by permission of The MIT Press; Table 10.2 adapted from A survey of user-centred design practice, *Proceedings of SIGCHI conference on Human factors in computing systems: Changing our world, changing ourselves*, pp. 471–78, Table 3 (Vredenburg, K., Mao, J.-Y., Smith, P.W. and Carey, T. 2002) © 2002 ACM, Inc. Reprinted by permission, http://doi.acm.org/10.1145/503376.503460; Table 10.3 terms and definitions taken from *ISO 9241–11:1998 Ergonomic requirements for office work with visual display terminals (VDTs),* extract of Table B2, reproduced with the permission of the International Organization for Standardization, ISO, this standard can be obtained from any ISO member and from the website of the ISO Central Secretariat at the following address: www.iso.org, copyright remains with the ISO; Table 12.1 after Marcus, Aaron, *Graphic Design for Electronic Documents and User Interfaces, 1st,* © 1991. Printed and Electronically reproduced by permission of Pearson Education, Inc., Upper Saddle River, New Jersey; Table 13.1 Apple Inc; Table 17.1 from Stereotypes and user modelling, in Kobsa, A. and Wahlster, W. eds, *User Models in Dialog Systems,* Figure 4, p. 41 (Rich, E. 1989), Springer-Verlag and Elaine Rich; Table 21.2 from Wickens, Christopher D.; Hollands, Justin G.,

Engineering Psychology and Human Performance, 3rd, © 2000. Printed and Electronically reproduced by permission of Pearson Education, Inc., Upper Saddle River, New Jersey; Table 22.1 adapted from Picard, Rosalind W., *Affective Computing* Table 1.1 © 1997 Massachusetts Institute of Technology, by permission of The MIT Press; Table 22.2 reprinted from *International Journal of Human-Computer Studies,* 59(1–2), McNeese, M.D., New visions of human-computer interaction: making affect compute, pp. 33–53, Copyright 2003, with permission from Elsevier; Tables 24.1, 24.2 from Distance matters, *Human-Computer Interaction,* 15(2), p. 149, p. 160 (Olson, G.M. and Olson, J.S. 2000), reprinted by permission of the publisher (Taylor & Francis Ltd, http://www.tandf.co.uk/journals).

Text

Box 1.1 Copyright © 1993 by Donald Norman, *Things That Make Us Smart: Defending Human Attributes in the Age of the Machine,* Reprinted by permission of Perseus Books, an imprint of the Perseus Books Group; Box 4.1 from *Principles of Universal Design,* North Carolina State University (Connell, B.R., Jones, M., Mace, R., Mueller, J., Mullick, A., Ostroff, E., Sandford, J., Steinfield, E., Story, M. and Vanderheiden, G. 1977) © Centre for Universal Design, College of Design, North Carolina State University; Extract on pages 96–97 from Digital ground: fixity, flow and engagement with context, *Archis,* 5 (special 'flow' issue, Oct/Nov) (McCullough, M. 2002), with permission from the author; Box 5.1 adapted from on-line interview, http://infodesign. com.au/uxpod/ludicdesign, with permission from William G. Gaver; Box 7.4 from Grounding blue-sky research: how can ethnography help?, *Interactions,* 4(3), pp. 58–63 (Rogers, Y. and Bellotti, V. 1997), © 1997 ACM, Inc., reprinted by permission, http://doi.acm.org/10.1145/255392.255404; Extract on page 278 Apple Inc; Extract on page 279 Apple Inc; Box 12.3 Apple Inc; Box 14.4 from Strategies for Categorizing Categories, www.uie.com, 7 May 2003, User Interface Engineering; Extract on page 332 from email from RA to team; Box 16.3 from Council bans emails to get staff to talk, *The Guardian,* 10 July 2002 (Ward, D.), Copyright Guardian News & Media Ltd 2002; Extracts on page 441, pages 442–3 from Activity-based serendipitous recommendations with the Magitti mobile leisure guide, *Proceedings of Twenty-sixth Annual SIGCHI conference on Human*

Factors in Computing Systems, 5–10 April, Florence, Italy © 2008 ACM, Inc. Reprinted by permission, http://doi.acm.org/10.1145/1357054.1357237, the research and development behind the Magitti system was sponsored by Dai Nippon Printing Co. Ltd. 'Media Technology Research Center' and 'Corporate R & D Division'; Extract on pages 505–6 reprinted from *International Journal of Human-Computer Studies,* 59(1–2), Hollnagel, E. Is effective computing an oxymoron?, pp. 65–70, Copyright 2003, with permission from Elsevier.

Picture Credits

The publisher would like to thank the following for their kind permission to reproduce their photographs:

(Key: b-bottom; c-centre; l-left; r-right; t-top)

6 Science Photo Library Ltd/Hannah Gal. **7** Alamy Images/Keith Morris. **8** Getty Images/Kiyoshi Ota (tr), ChinaFotoPress (bl). **12** Alamy Images/D. Hurst (tr), Fujitsu (tl), Microsoft Limited (br), Pearson Education Ltd/Gareth Boden (bl). **16** Alamy Images/Comstock Images (bl), Getty Images/Justin Sullivan (tl), Bryan Bedder (r). **17** Courtesy of IDEO. **27** DK Images/Susanna Price (tc), Pearson Education Ltd/Mike van der Wolk (tr), Press Association Images (tl). **28** Pearson Education Ltd/Jules Selmes. **29** Getty Images/Patrick Fife/AFP (b), Microsoft Limited (t). **35** DK Images/Rob Reichenfeld (c), Peter Wilson (l), Eddie Lawrence (r). **37** Reuters/Robert Sorbo (bl), Science Photo Library Ltd/Volker Steger (br). **38** Alamy Images/Alan Mather (tl), Microsoft Limited (tr), Phil Turner (b). **39** Getty Images/Red Huber/Orlando Sentinel/MCT (b), David Becker (t). **40** Science Photo Library Ltd/Volker Steger. **41** Reuters/Gustau Nacarino. **58** Companions project (t) (b). **59** Companions project. **60** Companions project. **61** Companions project. **62** Companions project. **84** DK Images/Steve Gorton and Karl Shone. **94** William G. Gaver/Copyright the Interaction Research Studio, Goldsmiths (br) (bl). **97** © Cyan Worlds, Inc. Used by permission. **99** Alamy Images/Hugh Threlfall. **101** © ACM, Inc. Reprinted by permission. **116** David Benyon. **153** © ACM, Inc. Reprinted by permission. **154** Corbis/Henglein and Streets/cultura. **161** David Benyon. **177** David Benyon. **179** Companions project. **181** David Benyon. **192** © ACM, Inc. Reprinted by permission. **203** Getty Images/Mandy Cheng/AFP. **215** Sony Ericsson. **230** Courtesy of Jim Mullin. **231** With permission from IOS Press. **233** David Benyon. **260** Getty Images/Ivary. **268** Alamy Images/© B. O'Kane. **282** Richard Saul Wurman/designed by Joel Katz. **290** Mixed Reality Lab, National University of Singapore. **292** Phil Turner (br) (bl). **293** image courtesy www.5DT.com. **298** Sphere Research Corporation. **301** © ACM, Inc. Reprinted by permission. **304** Pufferfish Ltd. **334** Alamy Images/Katharine Andriotis Photography, LLC (tl), John Cooper (br). **371** Corbis/Ingo Wagner/dpa. **373** Dr. Oli Mival. **375** Norbert Streitz. **379** Science Photo Library Ltd/VR Context/Eurelios. **380** Dr. Oli Mival. **381** Dr. Oli Mival. **382** Dr. Oli Mival. **387** Carnegie Mellon University, Human-Computer Interaction Institute (b), iRobot Corporation (t). **400** Science Photo Library Ltd/Jimmy Kets/Reporters. **415** Reuters/Luke MacGregor. **416** Argo Information Centre. **417** DK Images/Joe Cornish. **431** David Benyon. **436** Getty Images/David Paul Morris/Bloomberg (br), David Becker (bl, bc). **437** Getty Images/James Looker/Future Publishing. **439** © 2004 IEEE/Florian Michahelles. **442** Lancelhoff.com. **452** Photo of Prateek Arora by Kristen Sabol, Carnegie Mellon/QoLT Center, location courtesy of Voyager Jet, Pittsburgh. **451** Photo courtesy Google UK (r), Nike (l). **453** The Museum of HP Calculators, http://hpmuseum.org (tr), © Sun Microsystems, Courtesy of Sun Microsystems, Inc (tl). **456** Maggie Orth. **457** Institut für experimentelles Bekleidungs-. und Textildesign, copyright design: Max Schath, in cooperation with the Frauenhofer IZM, Photo: Özgür Aibayrak. **460** Sarah Kettley Design. **461** Corbis/Peter Ginter/Science Faction (b), Christian Zachariasen/Sygma (tr), Getty Images/Stephane de Sakutin/AFP (tl). **500** Frank Dabek (br) (bl), Elsevier (t). **502** Science Photo Library Ltd/Sam Ogden. **503** Elsevier. **504** © ACM, Inc. Reprinted by permission. **515** Science Photo Library Ltd/Mike Miller. **517** Phil Turner. **531** Alamy Images/Geo Icons (t), Science Photo Library Ltd/Peter Menzel (b). **533** Alamy Images/Trinity Mirror/Mirrorpix. **542** Alamy Images/Marmaduke St. John/Alamy. **544** NASA/JPL-Caltech/Solar System Visualization Project. **545** Alamy Images/Image Source Pink (r). **552** Phil Turner. **554** DK Images/Steve Gorton. **556** Phil Turner. **568** DK Images/Philip Enticknap.

Cover images: *Front:* **Getty Images; Shutterstock.com**

In some instances we have been unable to trace the owners of copyright material, and we would appreciate any information that would enable us to do so.

Apple, Apple logo, Finder, iPhone, iPad, Mac, Mac OS, OS X are trademarks of Apple Inc., registered in the U.S. and other countries.

Adobe, the Adobe logo, Acrobat, the Acrobat logo, Distiller, PostScript, and the PostScript logo are trademarks or registered trademarks of Adobe Systems Incorporated in the U.S. and/or other countries.

IOS is a trademark or registered trademark of Cisco in the U.S. and other countries and is used under license.

QR Code is a registered trademark of DENSO WAVE INCORPORATED.

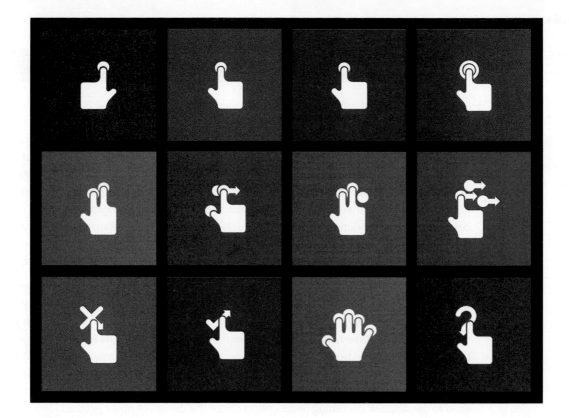

Part I

Essentials of designing interactive systems

Introduction to Part I

Our goal is to design interactive systems that are enjoyable to use, that do useful things and that enhance the lives of the people who use them. We want our interactive systems to be accessible, usable and engaging. In order to achieve this we believe that the design of such systems should be human-centred. That is, designers need to put people rather than technology at the centre of their design process. Unfortunately, the design of inter-active systems and products in the past has not always had a good record of considering the people who use them. Many systems have been designed by programmers who use computers every working day. Many designers are young males. Many designers have been playing computer games for years. This means that they forget just how difficult and obscure some of their designs can be to people who have not had these experiences.

In the days of the Web, issues of usability are critical to e-commerce. Before the imme-diacy of e-commerce, usability problems were discovered only after purchase. If you bought a nice-looking smartphone and brought it home only to find it was difficult to use, you could not take it back! The shop would say that it delivers its functions; all you had to do was to learn how to operate it properly. On the Web, customers look at usabil-ity first. If the system is hard to use, or if they do not understand it, they will go some-where else to make their purchase. People are learning that systems do not have to be hard to use and are becoming more critical about the design of other products too.

This first part of the book provides a guide to the essence of the human-centred design of interactive systems. Chapter 1 focuses on the main elements of interactive systems design. It considers the nature of design, the features of interactive systems and what it means to be human-centred. The chapter provides a brief history of human–computer interaction and interaction design and a glimpse of the future, before focusing on why designing interactive systems is important. Chapter 2 introduces the key components of interaction – people, activities, contexts and technologies (PACT). This proves to be an insightful construct not just for understanding the breadth of interaction design, but also for doing design. The chapter describes and illustrates a first design method: PACT analysis.

Alongside this view we need to consider the products we are designing: what they will do, how they will do it and what information content they will manipulate. In Chapter 3 we look at the processes involved in designing interactive systems. We see why the eval-uation of ideas is central to the process if we are going to be focused on people: 'being human-centred'. The requirements for products, early designs and prototypes of systems all need to be evaluated to ensure that they meet the needs of the people who will use them. But people will make use of technologies in many different contexts, to under-take different activities. The chapter introduces key abstractions for helping designers in their tasks: personas and scenarios. We give examples of personas and offer practical advice on how they can be developed and used. The chapter goes on to provide a whole scenario-based design method, providing advanced treatment of this important idea.

In Chapter 4 we look at principles of design: how to ensure systems are accessible, usa-ble and acceptable. As interactive systems become increasingly embedded in society, they stop being a luxury. Accessibility is about ensuring that the benefits of interaction design are available to all. Another key concept in interaction design that has long been the central focus of human–computer interaction (HCI) is usability. Chapter 4 provides a detailed consideration of usability and acceptability. Finally the chapter provides some high-level design guidelines that will help designers ensure that designs are accessible and usable.

When people use the devices we have designed, what do they feel? Do they have a sense of satisfaction, enjoyment and engagement? Chapter 5 looks at these issues and at aesthetics and designing for pleasure. Once again this serves to illustrate the wide scope of interactive systems design. The chapter also includes some discussion of service design as increasingly designers need to design services as well as products. The final chapter is an extended case study of a design, showing how and why decisions were made and illustrating many of the ideas developed in the first five chapters.

After studying this part you should understand the essential features of designing interactive systems. In particular:

- What interactive systems design is
- Who is involved
- What is involved
- How to develop systems that are human-centred
- Principles of interactive systems design to ensure systems are usable and engaging.

Case studies

The concepts and ideas are illustrated throughout through a number of case studies. Chapter 1 introduces several modern devices that have made a big impact on the world of interaction design. Chapter 2 uses the development of a swipe-card system to illustrate the PACT method. Chapter 3 introduces the MP3 player case study. This involves the development of an MP3 function for the Home Information Centre (HIC) which is itself the focus of the extended case study in Chapter 6. Both the MP3 and the overall HIC case studies are also used in Part II.

Teaching and learning

With some supplementary material showing examples, following up on the Web links and further reading and doing some assessed exercises, the material in this part would make an ideal introductory course on human–computer interaction or interaction design. The list of topics covered in this part is shown below, each of which could take 10–15 hours of study to reach a good general level of understanding, or 3–5 hours for a basic appreciation of the issues. Of course, each topic could be the subject of extensive and in-depth study.

Topic 1.1	Overview of designing interactive systems	Chapter 1
Topic 1.2	Characteristics of people	Section 2.2
Topic 1.3	Activities, contexts and technologies	Sections 2.3–2.5
Topic 1.4	Doing a PACT analysis	Sections 2.1, 2.6
Topic 1.5	The design process	Section 3.1
Topic 1.6	Personas and scenarios	Section 3.2
Topic 1.7	Scenario-based design	Sections 3.3–3.4
Topic 1.8	Accessibility	Sections 4.1–4.2
Topic 1.9	Usability and acceptability	Sections 4.3–4.4
Topic 1.10	Interaction design principles	Section 4.5

Chapter 1
Designing interactive systems: a fusion of skills

Contents

Aims

Designing interactive systems is concerned with developing high-quality interactive systems, products and services that fit with people and their ways of living. Computing and communication devices are embedded in all sorts of everyday devices such as washing machines and televisions, ticket machines and jewellery. No self-respecting exhibition, museum or library is without its interactive component. We carry and wear technologies that are far more powerful than the computers of just a few years ago. There are websites, on-line communities, 'apps' for mobile phones and tablets and all manner of other interactive devices and services that need developing. Interactive systems design is about all this.

In this chapter we explore the width and breadth of designing interactive systems. After studying this chapter you should be able to:

● Understand the concepts underlying the design of interactive systems

● Understand why being human-centred is important in design

● Understand the historical background to the subject

● Understand the skills and knowledge that the designer of interactive systems needs to draw upon.

1.1 The variety of interactive systems

Designing interactive systems is concerned with many different types of product. It is about designing software systems that will run on a computer at work. It is about designing websites, games, interactive products such as MP3 players, digital cameras and applications for tablet PCs (personal computers). It is about designing whole environments in which phones, tablets, laptop computers, digital projectors and other devices and services communicate with one another and through which people interact with one another. It is about designing interactive systems, products and services for the home, for work or to support communities.

Here are some examples of recent interactive products and systems.

Example 1: The iPhone

In 2007 Apple Inc. changed the face of mobile technologies when they introduced the iPhone (Figure 1.1). The iPhone had a carefully crafted, purpose-designed interface to make use of the finger as the input device. It had a revolutionary touch-sensitive screen that allowed for multi-touch input. This facilitated new interaction techniques such as pinching an image and drawing it in to make it smaller, or pinching and moving the fingers out to make an image larger. Many mobile devices and larger screen systems have now adopted this technology, but the iPhone started it. The iPhone also included sensors that could register how the phone was being held and whether it was vertical, horizontal or sloping. This allows for other novel interaction methods. For example, the display would automatically adjust from portrait style to landscape. In 2008 the 'app store' was launched, turning the iPhone into an open platform for developers to design and produce their own software. Combined with the iTunes delivery service, this turned the iPhone into a versatile, multimedia device with hundreds of thousands of applications, from sophisticated games to trivial pieces of entertainment to useful information applications. This created new experiences and new services for a new set of customers that has now spread to many other devices running the Android operating system (from Google) or Windows (from Microsoft). The most recent iPhone has introduced a speech recognition system called Siri that allows people to call or text their friends, enter appointments in a calendar or search the Web just by speaking into the phone.

Figure 1.1 iPhone
(Source: Hannah Gal/Science Photo Library)

Example 2: The Nintendo Wii

Also in 2007 Nintendo introduced the Wii (Figure 1.2). The Wii was a revolutionary new games concept that used infra-red sensors attached to a TV or other display device to track a wand that transmitted infra-red signals. The new system could, therefore, register different gestures such as a 'bowling' action, a 'tennis shot' action or a host of other movements. The notion of computer games changed radically, from a young person shooting at imaginary monsters, or driving imaginary cars, to a family-wide entertainment. When the Wii Fit was introduced it appealed to a new audience of people wanting to keep fit at home. In 2011 Microsoft introduced their Kinnect system that combined infra-red detection and cameras so that users could interact with software using gestures with no need for a wand. Originally aimed at people playing games on the Xbox games machine, the Kinnect was quickly adapted to work with any software that could make use of its application program interface (API).

Figure 1.2 Wii Fit
(Source: Keith Morris/Alamy Images)

Example 3: Virtual worlds

Second Life (Figure 1.3) is a huge on-line community populated by animated virtual people (called avatars). It consists of thousands of simulated buildings, parks, seasides, factories, universities and everything else one could find in the real world (and much else besides). People create avatars to represent themselves in this virtual world. They can determine their size, shape, gender and what they want to wear. They are controlled by their creators using the Internet, interacting with other avatars, and visiting virtual places. Other examples of virtual

Artificial life

Artificial life (often abbreviated to 'Alife') is a branch of artificial intelligence (AI), the discipline that looks at whether intelligent software systems can be built and at the nature of intelligence itself. The tradition in AI has been to represent knowledge and behaviours through rules and rigid structures. Alife tries instead to represent higher-level features of the things in an environment, such as the goals that a creature has and the needs that it must satisfy. The actual behaviour of the artificial creatures is then more unpredictable and evolves in the environment. Increasingly, characters in computer games are using Alife techniques.

FURTHER THOUGHTS

Figure 1.3 Second Life
(Source: http://secondlife.com, Linden Lab)

Figure 1.4 Sony Vita
(Source: Kiyoshi Ota/Getty Images)

worlds include highly popular games such as World of Warcraft and the Sony Home environment that is played on their Playstation platform and Vita handheld device (Figure 1.4). Many of these games include playing on-line with others, a key part of the social side of designing interactive systems.

Example 4: i Robo-Q domestic toy robot

The i Robo-Q domestic toy robot is an example of the new children's toys that are increasingly available (Figure 1.5). Toys are using all manner of new technologies to enhance the experiences of children at play. They use robotics, voice input and output, and a variety of sensors to provide novel and engaging interactions.

Example 5: Facebook

Facebook (Figure 1.6) is a highly popular website that allows people to keep in contact with their friends. Known as social networking sites, there are many similar systems around. Facebook is the most popular with nearly 1 billion users worldwide. Facebook is increasingly becoming an important platform for a wide variety of activities and it allows people to add applications (apps) in a similar way to the Apple and Android platforms. People can store and share digital

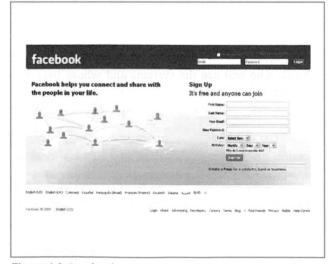

Figure 1.5 i Robo-Q domestic toy robot
(Source: Getty Images/ChinaFotoPress)

Figure 1.6 Facebook
(Source: Facebook, Inc.)

photos, write notes to each other and get regular updates about what their friends are doing. Facebook will probably have its own mobile handset soon as it moves from being just a website into being an important platform for the delivery of all sorts of interactive systems.

Summary

These five examples of interactive systems capture many of the features that the interactive systems designer has to work with. The designer of interactive systems needs to understand the possibilities that exist for new forms of interaction, with fixed devices or mobiles, for people on their own or for connecting people to each other through text messages or through animation and video. It is a fascinating area to work in.

Challenge 1.1

Find five interactive products or systems that you use – perhaps a coffee machine, a cellular phone, a fairground ride, a TV remote control, a computer game and a website. Write down what it is that you like about each of them and what it is that you do not like. Think about the whole experience and not just the functions. Think about the content that each provides: Is it what you want? Is it fun to use?

If possible, find a friend or colleague to discuss the issues. Criticism and design are social activities that are best done with others. What do you agree on? What do you disagree on? Why?

1.2 The concerns of interactive systems design

The design of interactive systems covers a very wide range of activities. Sometimes designers will be working on both the hardware and the software for a system, in which case the term 'product design' seems to be most appropriate to describe what they are doing. Sometimes the designer will be producing a piece of software to run on a computer, on a programmable device or over the Internet. In these cases the terms 'system design' and 'service design' seem more appropriate. We switch between these expressions as appropriate. However, the key concerns of the designer of interactive systems are:

- *Design*. What is design and how should you do it?
- *Technologies*. These are the interactive systems, products, devices and components themselves.
- *People* who will use the systems and whose lives would we like to make better through our designs?
- *Activities and contexts*. What do people want to do? What are the contexts within which those activities take place?

Design

What is design? It's where you stand with a foot in two worlds – the world of technology and the world of people and human purposes – and you try to bring the two together.

Mitch Kapor in Winograd (1996), p. 1

The term 'design' refers both to the creative process of specifying something new and to the representations that are produced during the process. So, for example, to design a website a designer will produce and evaluate various designs, such as a design of the page layout, a design of the colour scheme, a design for the graphics and a design of the overall structure. In a different field of design, an architect produces sketches and outlines and discusses these with the client before formalizing a design in the form of a blueprint.

Design is rarely a straightforward process and typically involves much iteration and exploration of both requirements (what the system is meant to do and the qualities it should have) and design solutions. There are many definitions of 'design'. Most definitions recognize that *both* problem and solution need to *evolve* during the design process; rarely can you completely specify something before some design work has been done.

One thing that is useful is to distinguish the amount of formality associated with a design:

- At one end of a spectrum is engineering design (such as the design of a bridge, a car or a building) where scientific principles and technical specifications are employed to produce formal models before construction starts.
- At the other end of this spectrum is creative or artistic design where innovation, imagination and conceptual ideas are the key ingredients.
- Somewhere in the middle lies 'design as craft' which draws upon both engineering and creative approaches.

Most design involves aspects of all of these. A fashion designer needs to know about people and fabrics, an interior designer also needs to know about paints, lighting and so on, and a jewellery designer needs to know about precious stones and the properties of metals such as gold and silver. The famous design commentator Donald Schön has described design as a 'conversation with materials', by which he means that in any type of design, designers must understand the nature of the materials that they are working with. Design works with, and shapes, a medium; in our case this medium consists of interactive systems. Others emphasize that design is a conscious, social activity and that much design is often undertaken in a design team.

People and technologies

Interactive system is the term we use to describe the technologies that interactive system designers work with. This term is intended to cover components, devices, products and software systems that are primarily concerned with processing information. Interactive systems are things that deal with the transmission, display, storage or transformation of information that people can perceive. They are devices and systems that respond dynamically to people's actions.

This definition is intended to exclude things such as tables, chairs and doors (since they do not process information) but to include things such as:

- Mobile phones (since they transmit, store and transform information)
- Websites (since they store and display information and respond to people's actions)
- Computer game controllers.

Increasingly, interactive components are being included in all manner of other products (such as clothes, buildings and cameras).

A fundamental challenge for interactive systems designers is to deal with the fact that people and interactive systems are different (see Box 1.1). Of course we take the people-centred view, but many designers still take the machine-centred view because it is quicker and easier for them, though not for the person who finishes up using the product. Another difference between people and machines is that we speak different languages. People express their desires and feelings in terms of what they want to do or how they would like things to be (their goals). Machines need to be given strict instructions.

Machine- and people-centred views

View	People are	Machines are
Machine-centred	Vague Disorganized Distractible Emotional Illogical	Precise Orderly Undistractible Unemotional Logical
People-centred	Creative Compliant Attentive to change Resourceful Able to make flexible decisions based on content	Dumb Rigid Insensitive to change Unimaginative Constrained to make consistent decisions

Source: Adapted from Norman (1993), p. 224

The interface

The interface to an interactive system, also called the user interface (UI), is all those parts of the system with which people come into contact, physically, perceptually and conceptually:

- Physically we might interact with a device by pressing buttons or moving levers and the interactive device might respond by providing feedback through the pressure of the button or lever.
- Perceptually the device displays things on a screen which we can see, or makes noises which we can hear.
- Conceptually we interact with a device by trying to work out what it does and what we should be doing. The device provides messages and other displays which are designed to help us do this.

The interface needs to provide some mechanisms so that people can provide instructions and enter data into the system: 'input'. It also needs to provide some mechanisms for the system to tell people what is happening by providing feedback and mechanisms for displaying the content: 'output'. This content might be in the form of information, pictures, movies, animations and so on. Figure 1.7 shows a variety of interfaces.

→ Chapter 2 discusses input and output devices in more detail

Challenge 1.2

Look at the pictures in Figure 1.7. What does the interface to (a) the remote control, (b) the microwave, (c) the palmtop computer or (d) the Xbox controller consist of?

Designing interactive systems is not just a question of designing interfaces, however. The whole human–computer interaction needs to be considered, as does the human–human interaction that is often enabled through the systems. Increasingly, interactive systems consist of many interconnected devices, some worn by people, some embedded in the fabric of buildings, some carried. Interactive systems designers are concerned with connecting people through devices and systems; they need to consider the whole environment they are creating.

Figure 1.7 Various user interfaces: remote control; microwave; palmtop; and Xbox controller

(Source: (a) Fujitsu; (b) © D. Hurst/Alamy Images; (c) Gareth Boden/Pearson Education Ltd. (d) Microsoft Limited)

Being human-centred

Interactive systems design is ultimately about creating interactive experiences for people. Being human-centred is about putting people first; it is about designing interactive systems to support people and for people to enjoy. Being human-centred is about:

- Thinking about what people want to do rather than what the technology can do
- Designing new ways to connect people with people
- Involving people in the design process
- Designing for diversity.

BOX 1.2

The evolving nature of interactive systems design

The primary discipline contributing to being human-centred in design is human–computer interaction (HCI). HCI arose during the early 1980s, evolving into a subject 'concerned with the design, evaluation, and implementation of interactive computing systems for human use and with the study of major phenomena surrounding them' (ACM SIGCHI, 1992, http://old.sigchi.org/cdg/index.html).

HCI drew on cognitive psychology for its theoretical base and on software engineering for its design approach. During the 1990s the closely related area of Computer Supported Cooperative Work (CSCW) focused on technology support for cooperative activities and brought with it another theoretical base that included sociology and anthropological methods. At the same time, designers in many different fields found that they had to deal with interactive products and components, and in 1989 the first computer-related design course was established at the Royal College of Art in London. In America the designers at Apple were putting their ideas together in a book called *The Art of Human–Computer Interface Design* (Laurel, 1990a) and a meeting at Stanford University in 1992 resulted in the book *Bringing Design to Software* (Winograd, 1996). By the mid-2000s interaction design was firmly established as a discipline in its own right with the first textbooks on interaction design coming out (including the first edition of this book) and leading designers contributing their own insights. All this – coupled with the phenomenal changes in computing and communication technologies during the same period – has brought us to where we are today: a dynamic mix of ideas, approaches and philosophies applied to the design of interactive systems and products.

This book is about human-centred interactive systems design. It is about human–computer interaction (HCI) and interaction design in the twenty-first century.

1.3 Being digital

In 1995 Nicholas Negroponte, head of the Massachusetts Institute of Technology's 'Media Lab', wrote a book called *Being Digital* in which he explored the significance of an era in which we change atoms for bits. We live in a digital age, when all manner of devices represent things using binary digits (bits). The significance of being digital is that bits are transformable, transmittable and storable using digital technologies. Consider the following scenario.

In the morning you get woken up by a digital alarm clock which automatically turns on the radio. To change the radio channel you might press a button that searches for a strong signal. You pick up your mobile, cellular phone and check for messages. You might go to your computer and download a personalized newspaper into a tablet device. As you leave the house you set the security alarm. In the car you adjust the heating, use the radio and attend to the various warning and information symbols that detect whether doors are open, or seat belts are buckled. Arriving at the station, you scan your season ticket through the car parking machine, get a train ticket from the ticket machine and get money from an automated teller machine (ATM). On the train you read the newspaper on your tablet, scrolling through text using your finger. Arriving at your office, you log on to the computer network, check e-mail, use various computer packages, browse the Web and perhaps listen to an Internet radio station broadcasting from another country. You have a video link with colleagues in other cities and perhaps work together on a shared document. During the day you use a coffee machine, make calls on the cellphone, check names and numbers in the address book, download a new ringing tone, photograph a beautiful plant that you see at lunchtime and video the swans on the river. You upload these to your social networking website where they are automatically tagged with the location and time they were taken, and with the names of people whose faces the software recognised. Arriving home, you open the garage doors automatically by keying a number on your phone and in the evening you spend an hour or so on the games machine, watch TV and program the set top box to record a late-night show.

This is the world we are living in and the world that designers of interactive systems are designing for. The huge range of interactions that we engage in and the interfaces that we use offer an exciting if daunting challenge. Moreover, increasingly designers are having to deal with the issue of people engaged in multiple interactions with different devices in parallel. One important commentator, Bruce 'Tog' Tognazinni, prefers the term 'interaction architect' to describe this profession.

How we got here

The revolution that has brought us to where we are today started towards the end of the Second World War, in 1945, with the development of the first digital computers. These were huge machines housed in specially built, air-conditioned rooms. They were operated by scientists and specialist computer programmers and operators, who physically pressed switches and altered circuits so that the electronics could complete their calculations.

During the 1960s computer technology was still dominated by scientific and accounting applications. Data was stored on paper tape or cards with holes punched in them, on magnetic tapes and large magnetic disks, and there was little direct interaction with the computer. Cards were sent to the computer centre, data was processed and the results were returned a few days later. Under the guidance of 'Lick' Licklider, however, things were beginning to change. The first screens and cathode ray tubes (CRTs) were being used as interactive devices and the first vision of a computer network – an internet – was formulated by Licklider. He worked at the Advanced Research Projects Agency (ARPA) at the US Department of Defense. His work also led to the establishment of computer science at four US universities (Licklider, 2003). Licklider was followed by the pioneering work of Ivan Sutherland at MIT, Doug Englebart who is credited with inventing the computer mouse, and Ted Nelson who developed the concept of hypertext, the idea of linking objects and being able to jump directly from one object to the next. In the UK pioneering work on computers was based at Manchester University and in 1959 Brian Shackel had published the paper 'Ergonomics for a computer'.

During the 1970s computing technology spread into businesses and screens linked to a central computer began to emerge. Computers were becoming networked together and indeed the first e-mail was sent over the ARPANET in 1972. The method of interaction for most people in the 1970s was still primarily 'batch'; transactions were collected together and submitted as a batch of work and computing power was shared between different people. Interest in HCI began to grow, with publications in the *International Journal of Man–Machine Studies*. As the decade ended so keyboards and screens became more common, but it was not until 1982 that the first real graphically based interfaces appeared in the form of the Xerox Star, Apple Lisa and Apple Macintosh computers. These used a bit-mapped display, allowing a graphical user interface (GUI) and interaction through pointing at icons and with commands grouped into menus. This style became ubiquitous when, in 1985, the Windows operating system appeared on (what were then usually IBM) personal computers (PCs). The personal computer and Windows-like operating system are attributed to another important pioneer, Alan Kay. Kay obtained his PhD, studying under Ivan Sutherland, in 1969, before moving to Xerox Palo Alto Research Center (PARC). It was here that the object-oriented computer programming language Smalltalk was developed. Many argue that it was the development of the VisiCalc spreadsheet program on the Apple

→ Chapter 12 discusses GUIs

II computer (the 'killer app') in 1979 that really fired the personal computer market (Pew, 2003).

The 1980s was the decade of the microcomputer, with the BBC Micro home computer selling over 1 million units and a whole plethora of home computers being adopted worldwide. Games consoles were also gaining in popularity in the home entertainment market. In business, people were getting networked and the Internet began to grow, based around e-mail. It was during the 1980s that human–computer interaction (HCI) came of age as a subject. In both the USA and Europe the first big conferences on HCI were held: the CHI '83 conference on Human Factors in Computing Systems in Boston, MA, and INTERACT '84 in London. Don Norman published his famous paper 'The trouble with UNIX: the user interface is horrid' (Norman, 1981) and Ben Shneiderman published *Software Psychology* (Shneiderman, 1980).

In the 1990s colour and multimedia arrived on the PC, which had begun to dominate the computer market. In 1993 a new interface was produced that took advantage of a simple mark-up or specification 'language' (called hypertext mark-up language, HTML). Thus the 'World Wide Web' came about and revolutionized the whole process of transmitting and sharing files. Pictures, movies, music, text and even live video links were suddenly available to everyone at work and at home. The growth of personal, community and corporate websites was phenomenal and the vision of a wholly connected 'global village' community began to become a reality. Of course, this growth was primarily in the West and in the USA in particular, where 'broadband' communications enabled a much more satisfying experience of the Web than the slow connections in Europe. Many parts of the world were not connected, but in the twenty-first century connections to the Web are global.

By the turn of the century the convergence of communications and computing technologies was just about complete. Anything could potentially be connected to anything, anywhere. Since all the data was digital, it could all be transmitted over the airwaves or over wired networks, and it could easily be transformed from one form into another. The proliferation of mobile devices, coupled with the wide availability of the Internet, brings us to the age of 'ubiquitous computing', a term first coined by the late Mark Weiser in 1993 when he talked of interaction through 'pads, tabs and boards'. Computing devices are now pervasive amongst people and across the world, providing all manner of services and experiences. Computing power continues to double every 18 months or so (according to Moore's law), producing mobile devices that are more powerful now than the largest computers were even just a few years ago. In the twenty-first century computing is truly ubiquitous and interaction is increasingly through touch and gesture rather than the keyboard that has been the main method of input since the PC revolution began. We now have Weiser's pads, tabs and boards in the form of phones and tablets in various sizes, large public screens and wearable computing (Figure 1.8). They all have access to the Web and run different apps. A huge amount of data is stored, and there are billions of videos on YouTube and photos on Flickr. Everything is synchronized and stored in the 'cloud' (in reality the cloud is a network of vast data centres full of computers) and broadband, wireless connectivity is becoming increasingly fast. The interconnectivity provided by the Web and wireless communications makes this a fascinating time to be an interactive systems designer.

Where are we heading?

It is a brave person who makes any strong prediction about where new technologies are headed as there are so many confounding factors. It is never just a technology that wins, but technology linked with a good business model linked with timing. Don

Figure 1.8 Tabs, pads and boards

(Source: (tl) Justin Sullivan/Getty images; (bl) Comstock/Alamy Images; (r) Bryan Bedder/Getty Images)

Norman delivers an interesting insight into both the past and future of technologies in his book *The Invisible Computer* (1999). Discussing such things as why the VHF video format succeeded over Betamax and why Edison's phonograph was not as successful as Emile Berliner's, he takes us forward to something he calls 'information appliances'. This notion has been taken up by others (Sharpe and Stenton, 2003), providing the following set of characteristics of information appliances:

- Appliances should be everyday things requiring only everyday skills to use.
- Appliances have a clear, focused function that can be used in a variety of circumstances.
- Peer-to-peer interaction. A key idea of appliances is that they work together without the need for central control or uploading and downloading.
- Direct user interface. Appliances need to be simple and intuitive to use.
- Successful appliances are those which support the notion of the swift and simple completion of a task.
- Appliances represent the ability to do something on impulse without having to think hard about how to do it.
- Appliances are personal and portable.

In 2013 this vision has been achieved to some extent with the range of smartphones such as the iPhone and Samsung Galaxy. But rather than the appliance concept being reflected in hardware, it is provided through the thousands of focused applications ('apps') that are available to download on to the iPhone, the Google Android or one of the other mobile platforms. Indeed Google along with Amazon are pioneering the idea of cloud computing where you don't need to carry any applications or data with you; just keep them in the cloud and download them when you need them.

FURTHER THOUGHTS

Whom do you trust?

Wireless connectivity between devices is now common both through the 'Wi-fi' standard called IEEE 802.11 and through Bluetooth. For example, your mobile phone will connect to your laptop computer via Bluetooth, and the laptop may be connected to an internal company network via a wireless network and hence to the Internet through the company's wired connection and hence to any other device in the world. How will you know where any piece of data that you look at actually is? If you look at the address book 'in your phone', you might in reality be accessing an address book on your laptop, or on any computer on the company's network or indeed anywhere on the World Wide Web. If data is duplicated, how will it be kept consistent? Across which devices will the consistency be reliable?

What we do know is that new products, business models, services and a range of other features will rapidly come into the world, and the interactive systems designer has to be ready to cope. Whether information appliances are just one of many directions that the future takes, we will have to see. In Microsoft's vision of HCI in 2020 (Microsoft, 2008) they argue that 'HCI needs to move forward from concerns about the production and processing of information toward the design and evaluation of systems that enable human values to be achieved' (p. 77) – something also emphasized by Cockton (2009) and his call for worth-centred design and Bødker in her consideration of 'third wave' HCI (Bødker, 2006).

The design company IDEO undertakes a wide range of projects in interactive systems design as illustrated through some of their projects illustrated in Figure 1.9 (the project shown in Figure 1.9 dates back to 2001). Some projects explore different ideas of changing concepts such as identity, others aim to produce new products and others look to see how people use technologies in their daily lives.

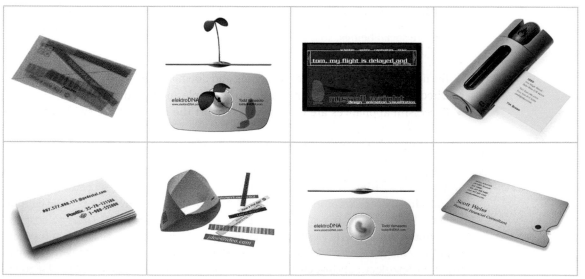

Figure 1.9 Concepts for future business cards and ideas of identity

(Source: IDEO, 2003. Courtesy of IDEO)

> **Challenge 1.3**
>
> *Visit the website of IDEO and look at their projects. Talk about the ideas with a friend.*

1.4 The skills of the interactive systems designer

Designers of interactive systems need a variety of skills and need to understand a variety of disciplines if they are to be able to do their jobs well. They need the mixture of skills that allows them to be able to:

- Study and understand the activities and aspirations of people and the contexts within which some technology might prove useful and hence generate requirements for technologies
- Know the possibilities offered by technologies
- Research and design technological solutions that fit in with people, the activities they want to undertake and the contexts in which those activities occur
- Evaluate alternative designs and iterate (do more research and more design) until a solution is arrived at.

The range of skills and academic disciplines that will contribute to such a person is significant. Indeed, it is often the case that no single person possesses all the skills needed for some design activity, which is why the design of interactive systems is often an affair for a design team. An interactive systems designer may be involved in a community information system project on one occasion, a kiosk for processing photographs on another, a database to support a firm of estate agents on another, and a children's educational game on another! Designers of interactive systems cannot be expert in all these fields, of course, but they must be aware enough to be able to take techniques from different areas, or access research in different disciplines when appropriate. We group the subjects that contribute to the design of interactive systems under the headings of knowledge of people, technologies, activities and contexts, and design, and illustrate the relationships in Figure 1.10 (p. 20).

People

People are social beings, so it is important that the approaches and techniques adopted in the social sciences are used to understand people and technologies. Sociology is the study of the relationships between people in society, the social, political and other groups that they participate in, and the settings in which such relationships take place. Anthropology is similar but focuses also on the study of culture, biology and language and on how these have evolved and changed over time. Both use techniques such as interviews and observation to arrive at their conclusions. A key approach, particularly in anthropology, is 'ethnography', which uses qualitative methods such as observations and unstructured interviews to produce a description of a particular culture or social group and its setting. Also related is cultural studies, which looks at people and their relationship with cultural issues such as identity, but also much more prosaic cultural activities such as shopping, playing computer games or watching TV. Descriptions tend to be from a more literary criticism background, informed by experience and reflection. Psychology is the study of how people think, feel and act. In particular, cognitive psychology seeks to understand and describe how the brain functions, how language works and how we solve problems. Ergonomics is the study of the fit between people and machines. In designing interactive systems, the designer will borrow much from each of these disciplines, including methods to help understand and design for people.

→ Chapter 7 includes a discussion of ethnography

→ Chapter 23 discusses cognitive psychology and embodied cognition

Technologies

The technologies that interactive systems designers need to know about include both software and hardware. Software engineering has developed methods for specifying and implementing computer programs. Programming languages are used to issue instructions to any programmable device such as a phone, computer, robot dog or earrings, shirts and chairs. Designers need to be aware of hardware for sensing different types of data (sensors) and for bringing about some change (actuators, or effectors). There are many different components available that produce many different effects and here designers will draw upon engineering knowledge, principles and methods. Communication between devices uses various communication 'protocols'. Designers need to know how different devices can communicate.

Activities and contexts

Interaction will usually take place in the context of some 'community of practice'. This term is used to denote groups of people who have shared interests and values and engage in similar activities. In business communities and organizations, information systems methods have developed over the years to ensure that information systems are developed that are effective and meet the needs of people who work there. In particular, soft systems theory (Checkland and Scholes, 1999) provides a very useful framework for focusing on the design of interactive systems. Social and organizational psychology are needed to look at the effects of technological change on organizations, and recently knowledge management and social computing have become important areas. Finally, new technologies offer new opportunities as business and interactive systems designers find that they are sometimes creating whole new ways of working with their designs.

Design

Principles and practices of design from all manner of design disciplines are used in designing interactive systems. Ideas and philosophy from architecture, garden design, interior design, fashion and jewellery design all crop up in various ways and different forms. It is not easy to simply pick up ideas from design disciplines, as much design knowledge is specific to a genre. Designers need to know the materials they work with and it is likely that more specialist design disciplines will emerge. One such discipline is product design, which is itself changing as it takes on board the nature of interactivity. Product design is an important contributing discipline to the skills of the designer of interactive systems. Graphic design and information design are particularly important for issues of information layout and the understandability and aesthetic experience of products. Human–computer interaction has itself evolved many techniques to ensure that designs are people-focused.

→ Chapter 12 discusses information design

Challenge 1.4

Imagine that you are put in charge of a design team that is to work on a project investigating the possibility of a new set of Web services for a large supermarket. These services will allow connection from any fixed or mobile device from any location, allowing food items to be ordered and delivered. The client even wants to investigate the idea of a 'smart refrigerator' that could automatically order items when it ran out. What range of skills might you need and which subject areas would you expect to draw upon?

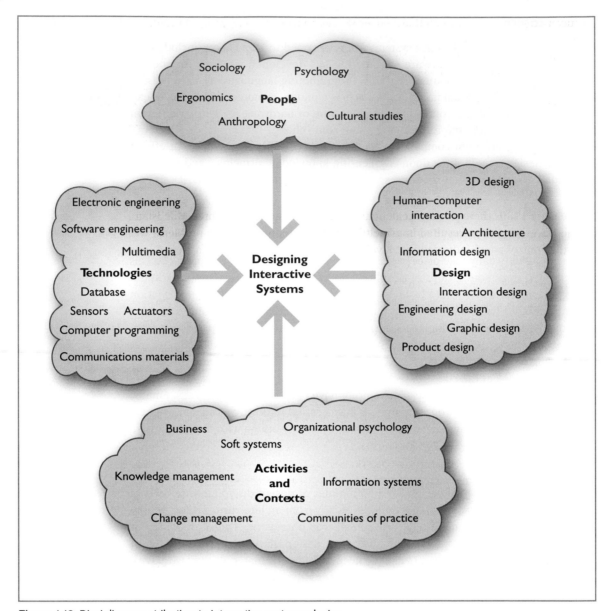

Figure 1.10 Disciplines contributing to interactive systems design

1.5 Why being human-centred is important

Being human-centred in design is expensive. It involves observing people, talking to people and trying ideas out with people, and all this takes time. Being human-centred is an additional cost to any project, so businesses rightly ask whether taking so much time to talk to people, produce prototype designs and so on is worthwhile. The answer is a fundamental 'yes'. Taking a human-centred approach to the design of interactive systems is advantageous for a number of reasons.

Return on investment

Williams *et al.* (2007) provide details of a number of case studies looking at the costs of taking a human-centred approach to interactive systems design and at the benefits that arise. Paying attention to the needs of people, to the usability of the product, results in reduced calls to customer helplines, fewer training materials, increased throughput, increased sales and so on.

Involving people closely in the design of their systems will help to ensure acceptability. Systems will be more effective if they are designed from a human-centred perspective and people will be more productive. Nowhere is the economic argument more pertinent than in Web design and e-commerce sites. Jared Spool and his company User Interface Engineering have a number of reports demonstrating the importance of good design to e-commerce and claim that sales can be increased by 225 per cent by turning 'browsers' into 'buyers'.

Safety

In the early 1980s there was an accident at a nuclear power plant at Three Mile Island in the USA that almost resulted in a 'meltdown'. Reportedly one of the problems was that the control panel indicated that a valve was closed when it was in fact open, and another indicator was obscured by a tag attached to another control: two fundamental design errors – one technical and one organizational – that human-centred design techniques would help to avoid. Other classic horror tales include a number of plane and train disasters that have been attributed to faulty displays or to operators not understanding or interpreting displays correctly. Systems have to be designed for people and for contexts. It is no good claiming 'human error' if the design was so bad in the first place that an accident was waiting to happen.

Ethics

Being human-centred also ensures that designers are truthful and open in their design practice. Now that it is so easy to collect data surreptitiously and to use that data for purposes other than what it was intended for, designers need to be ever more vigilant. As systems are increasingly able to connect autonomously with one another and share data it is vital that people know where the data that they give is going and how it might be used. People need to trust systems and be in a position to make choices about privacy and how they are represented.

The issue of intellectual property is another important aspect of ethical design; it is very easy to take an image from a website and use it without giving proper acknowledgement for its source. There are many issues associated with plagiarism or other dishonest uses of written materials. Privacy, security, control and honesty are all significant features of the interactive systems designer's life. Equality and attention to access are two of the 'political' issues that designers must address.

As technology changes so do traditional views and approaches to big moral and ethical questions. There are standards and legal requirements that need to be met by designs. Fundamentally, ethical design is needed because the systems that are produced should be easy and enjoyable to use, as they affect the quality of people's lives. Designers have power over other people and must exercise that power in an ethical fashion. The ACM (Association of Computing Machinery) code of ethics gives good advice on ethical design.

Sustainability

Interactive systems have a big impact on the world, and designers should approach interaction design from the perspective of what is sustainable. Millions of mobile phones and other devices are thrown away each year and they contain metals that are potentially dangerous to the environment. Large displays and projectors gobble up power. Cultures get swamped by the views and values of the dominant suppliers of hardware and software and local languages die out when all information is in English, Chinese or Hindi. Human-centred design needs to recognize diversity and design to enhance human values.

Summary and key points

Designing interactive systems is a challenging and fascinating discipline because it draws upon and affects so many features of people's lives. There is a huge variety of interactive systems and products, from business applications of computers to websites to dedicated information appliances to whole information spaces. Designing interactive systems is concerned with designing for people using technologies to undertake activities in contexts. Designing interactive systems needs to be human-centred.

● It draws upon many different subject areas, including both engineering design and artistic design.
● It is needed because we live in a digital age when bits are easily transformed and transmitted.
● It is necessary if we are to have safe, effective, ethical and sustainable design.

Exercises

1 Spend some time browsing the websites of corporations such as IDEO, Sony and Apple. Do not just look at the design of the site (though that can be useful); look at the products they are talking about and the philosophy of their design approach. Collect together your favourites and be prepared to spend time discussing them with your colleagues. Think of the whole range of issues about the site: what it looks like, how easy it is to use, how relevant the content of the site is, how clearly the content is organized, what the overall 'feel' of the site is.

2 Being human-centred is about
● Thinking about what people want to do rather than what the technology can do
● Designing new ways to connect people with people
● Involving people in the design process
● Designing for diversity.

Write down how you might approach the design of the supermarket shopping service discussed in Challenge 1.4. Don't do the design; think about how to approach the design. Are there any issues of effectiveness, safety, ethics and sustainability that need to be considered?

 ## Further reading

Laurel, B. (ed.) (1990) *The Art of Human–Computer Interface Design.* Addison-Wesley, Reading, MA. *Although this book is quite old, many of the articles in it are still relevant and many of the authors of those articles are still at the forefront of interaction design today.*

Norman, D. (1999) *The Invisible Computer: Why Good Products Can Fail.* MIT Press, Cambridge, MA. *This is an enjoyable book to read about successes and failures, pasts and futures for technologies.*

Getting ahead

Friedman, B. and Kahn, P.H. (2007) Human values, ethics and design. In A. Sears and J. A. Jacko (eds) *The Human–Computer Interaction Handbook,* **2nd edn.** Lawrence Erlbaum Associates, Mahwah, NJ.

Norman, D. (1993) *Things That Make Us Smart.* Addison-Wesley, Reading, MA.

Norman, D. (1998) *The Design of Everyday Things.* Addison-Wesley, Reading, MA. *These two easy-to-read books provide a wealth of examples of good and bad design.*

 # Web links

The Usability Professionals Association is at **www.upassoc.org**

The Interaction Design Association is at **www.ixda.org**

The on-line material that goes with this chapter is at
www.pearsoned.co.uk/benyon

Comments on challenges

Challenge 1.1

Of course, what you say will be dependent on the product or systems chosen. The important thing is to think in broad terms about the nature of the interaction with the device and at the activities that the device enables, and how good it is at doing them!

I could talk about the coffee machine at work, which is a simple, functional device. A single button press produces a reasonable cup of coffee. It is limited, however, in the variety of coffees that I can get (four types only) so I would ideally prefer a person mixing coffee for me rather than getting it from a machine. If I stay late at work and have to use the other coffee machine, it is a nightmare. The money slots don't work properly, the cups are too thin so the drink burns your hands, and the default is coffee with sugar (which I hate) so I have to remember to press the 'no sugar' button. Which I frequently forget to do!

This simple device can be contrasted with a website. Choose a website you like to visit. Discuss the opening page. Is it nice and clean, is there a site map, or other help to get the visitor oriented? How is the site using images and how does it work with the information? Are things difficult to read or difficult to control? Look at how users have to navigate from one page to another.

Challenge 1.2

The interface to the microwave consists of the various switches on the front that allow programming the time and temperature. There is also an audio part – the 'ping' when the timing is finished. The remote control just uses buttons as the interface and the Xbox controller has various buttons and a 4-way joystick. The PDA uses a pen (pointer) and a touch-sensitive screen. Icons are used on the screen and there are a few buttons on the casing. The PDA accepts 'graffiti' handwriting recognition.

Challenge 1.3

The aim of this challenge is to get you to think beyond user interfaces and beyond human–computer interaction to the changes that new technologies are bringing or could bring. As we create new information appliances and new products such as business cards, we, you, interactive systems designers, change the world. We change what is possible and change how people interact with other people. Reflect on (and discuss with someone else, if possible) the political, moral and ethical issues of these concepts.

Challenge 1.4

This project will demand a wide range of skills. On the technology side there are networking and software engineering issues concerned with how devices can be programmed to do this and how the information about products and orders can be stored. There will be issues of authorization and authentication of payments. Product design may come in if there are to be purpose-built devices created to access the services (e.g. an in-store smart scanner that could be used to record items bought). There will be a lot of information design expertise required and some graphic design to help in the layout of information. On the people side of things, general psychological knowledge will help to inform the design, and sociology may help to understand the social setting and impact that such services would have. Business models may need to be developed and certainly the skills of information systems designers will be needed.

Chapter 2
PACT: a framework for designing interactive systems

Contents

Aims

An essential part of our approach to designing interactive systems is that it should put people first: it should be human-centred. We use the acronym PACT (people, activities, contexts, technologies) as a useful framework for thinking about a design situation. Designers need to understand the people who will use their systems and products. They need to understand the activities that people want to undertake and the contexts in which those activities take place. Designers also need to know about the features of interactive technologies and how to approach designing interactive systems.

After studying this chapter you should be able to:

- Understand the relationship between activities and technologies
- Understand the PACT framework
- Understand the main characteristics of people that are relevant to designing interactive systems
- Understand the main issues of activities and the contexts in which they occur
- Understand the key features of interactive technologies.

2.1 Introduction

People use technologies to undertake activities in contexts. For example, teenagers use mobile (cell) phones to send text messages to their friends while sitting on a bus. Secretaries use Microsoft Word to write documents in a firm of solicitors. Air traffic controllers work together to ensure the smooth operation of an airport. A septuagenarian woman presses various buttons to set the intruder alarms in her house. People use Facebook to make contact with other people when sitting in an Internet café.

In all these settings we see people using technologies to undertake activities in contexts and it is the variety of each of these elements that makes designing interactive systems such a difficult and fascinating challenge. Technologies are there to support a wide range of people undertaking various activities in different contexts. If the technology is changed then the nature of the activities will also change. This issue is nicely summed up in Figure 2.1.

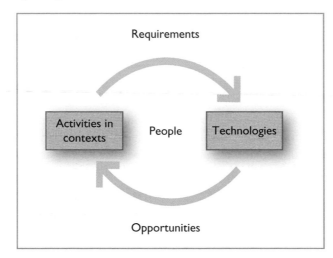

Figure 2.1 Activities and technologies
(Source: Based on Carroll (2002), Figure 3.1, p. 68)

Figure 2.1 shows how activities (and the contexts within which they take place) establish requirements for technologies that in turn offer opportunities that change the nature of activities. And so the cycle continues as the changed activity results in new requirements for technologies and so on. Designers need to keep this cycle in mind as they attempt to understand and design for some domain. (The word 'domain' here means an area of study, a 'sphere of activity'.) For example, as personal computers have become more common so the domain of e-mail has changed. Originally e-mail was all in text only, but now it is in full colour with pictures and video embedded. Other items can be attached to e-mails easily. This has led to a need for better facilities for managing it for organizing pictures, documents and addresses. Software now keeps track of threads of e-mails and links between e-mails. Another example is illustrated in Figure 2.2.

Challenge 2.1

Think of the activity of watching a film. List some ways in which this activity has changed with the introduction of video cassette recorders (VCRs) and digital versatile discs (DVDs) and downloads onto a laptop. How have the contexts changed since the early days of cinema?

To design interactive technologies we need to understand the variety inherent in the four elements of PACT.

Figure 2.2 The changing nature of telephoning activity as technology advances

(Sources: Press Association Images; Susanna Price/DK Images; Mike van der Wolk/Pearson Education Ltd.)

2.2 People

There can be few less controversial observations than that people differ from one another in a variety of ways. The chapters in Part IV of this book deal with these differences in detail. Here we summarize some of the most important features.

Physical differences

People differ in physical characteristics such as height and weight. Variability in the five senses – sight, hearing, touch, smell and taste – has a huge effect on how accessible, how usable and how enjoyable using a technology will be for people in different contexts. For example, colour blindness (usually the inability to distinguish correctly between red and green colours) affects about 8 per cent of Western males, short-sightedness and long-sightedness affect many, and many people are hearing-impaired. In Europe there are 2.8 million wheelchair users, so designers must consider where technologies are placed; and many people have dexterity impairments involving the use of their fingers. All of us have relatively large fingers compared to the small size we can use for buttons. Look at the ticket machine in Figure 2.3. What are the physical aspects of people that need to be taken into account in the design?

Ergonomics

The term 'ergonomics' was coined in 1948 to describe the study of the relationships between people and their environment. At that time, technically advanced weapons systems were being rapidly developed, which required that their design matched human and environmental factors if they were to be used effectively and, paradoxically, safely.

The environment includes the ambient environment (temperature, humidity, atmospheric pressure, light levels, noise and so on) and the working environment too (the design of machines, health and safety issues – e.g. hygiene, toxicology, exposure to ionizing radiation, microwaves, etc.).

Ergonomics is multidisciplinary, drawing on anatomy and physiology, various aspects of psychology (e.g. physiological and experimental), physics, engineering and work studies among others. In everyday life we come across the application of ergonomic design principles in every well-designed interactive system. In the advertisement for a new motor car, we can expect to find reference to its ergonomically designed dashboard

Figure 2.3 Metro ticket machine
(Source: Jules Selmes/Pearson Education)

(a good, desirable feature) or an adjustable, ergonomic driving seat. In the Mercedes-Benz sales literature for its new coupé we find the following ergonomic description:

> Once inside the C-Class Sports Coupé you'll find a wealth of ergonomic detail, designed to live up to the promise of its looks. As if cast from a single mould, the dashboard curves are smooth to the touch.

The term 'ergonomic design' is also extensively used of all manner of office furniture (chairs, desks, lights, footrests and so forth) and office equipment, for example keyboards, monitor stands and wrist rests. Many, if not most, of these principles are now embodied in legally binding design guidelines (see Further reading at the end of this chapter). Figure 2.4 is an illustration of an ergonomically designed keyboard. It is described as ergonomically designed as it reflects the fact that we have two hands – hence the two separate blocks of keys and an integral wrist support. The keyboard has been designed to match the hands and fingers of its intended users.

BOX 2.1

Anthropometrics

Anthropometrics means literally the measurement of man. Anthropometrics can, for example, tell us the limits (diameter and load-bearing characteristics) of the human wrist for the average man and woman. Figures have been compiled from thousands of measurements of different races, different ages and different professions (e.g. office workers vs manual workers) and drawn up as tables. The same body of data will also tell the designer whether the average person can simultaneously press button A while holding down buttons B and C – and whether this is true for both right- and left-handed people.

BOX 2.2

The changing role of the thumb

People who have grown up with mobile phones (or Game Boys) tend to use their thumbs when others are more likely to use their fingers. Sadie Plant from Warwick

Figure 2.4 An ergonomic keyboard

(Source: Microsoft Natural Multimedia Keyboard from www/microsoft.com/press/gallery/hardware/NaturalMultiMedia Keyboard.jpg © 2004 66Microsoft Corporation. All rights reserved. Printed with permission from Microsoft Corporation)

University (*New Scientist*, No. 2315, 3 November 2001) collected data on mobile phone usage in nine cities around the world, including Beijing, Chicago, London and Tokyo. She found that the under-25 age group appear to have experimented with the best way to interact with a mobile phone, one result of which is that now they use their thumbs to ring doorbells, push doors and point.

While ergonomics has a longer history than HCI, it would be a mistake to perceive it as being old and out of touch – quite the reverse. Ergonomics has much to tell us about the design of interactive devices such as a mobile games console, a tablet PC or smartphone. Figure 2.5 shows an example of the former.

Figure 2.5 HP iPAQ Pocket

(Source: Patrick File/Getty Images/ AFP)

Such devices are faced with ergonomic design challenges. For example, we all have relatively fat fingers compared with how small buttons can be made. In the world of mobile computing, small is good but too small is bad (too easily lost, too difficult to use, too easily eaten by the dog). Ergonomics can put numbers on what constitutes small and usable and what is too small and unusable. The best-known example of ergonomic knowledge being applied to HCI issues is Fitts's law (see Box 2.3).

> **BOX 2.3**
>
> ### Fitts's law
>
> Fitts's law is a mathematical formula which relates the time required to move to a target as a function of the distance to the target and the size of the target itself, say moving a pointer using a mouse to a particular button. It is expressed mathematically as follows:
>
> $$T_{(time\ to\ move)} = k \log_2(D/S + 0.5)$$
>
> where $k \sim 100$ ms, D is the distance between the current (cursor) position and the target, and S is the size of the target.
>
> Thus one can calculate the time to move a distance of 15 cm to a button of size 2 cm as
>
> $$T = 100 \log_2\left(\frac{15}{2} + 0.5\right)$$
>
> $$= 0.207 \text{ seconds}$$
>
> Fitts's law describes motor control. The smaller the target and the greater the distance, the longer it will take to hit the target. Fitts's law can also be used to calculate how long it would take to type this sentence or, more importantly, a number of time-critical operations such as hitting the brake pedal of a motor car, or the likelihood of hitting <OK> rather than <Cancel> or, more worryingly, <Fire> or <Detonate>.

Psychological differences

Psychologically, people differ in a variety of ways. For example, people with good spatial ability will find it much easier to find their way around and remember a website than those with poor ability. Designers should design for people with poor ability by providing good signage and clear directions. Language differences are of course crucial to understanding, and cultural differences affect how people interpret things. For example, in the Microsoft Excel spreadsheet application there are two buttons, one labelled with a cross and the other a tick. In the USA a tick is used for acceptance and a cross for rejection, but in Britain either a tick or a cross can be used to show acceptance (e.g. a cross on a voting paper).

> **BOX 2.4**
>
> ### Individual differences
>
> There are often large differences in the psychological abilities of people. Some people have a good memory, others less so. Some people can find their way around environments better than others, or mentally rotate objects more quickly and accurately. Some are good at words, others are good at numbers. There are differences in personality, emotional make-up and ability to work under stress. Many tests have been designed to measure these differences. For example the Myers–Briggs Type Indicator is a series of

tests that results in people being classified as one of 16 personality types. Others classify people as one of five personality types known as OCEAN: Openness to Experience, Conscientiousness, Extraversion, Agreeableness, and Neuroticism. Designers need to consider the range of differences between people and the demands that their designs make on people's psychological abilities.

People also have different needs and abilities when it comes to attention and memory and these can change depending on factors such as stress and tiredness. Most people cannot remember long numbers or complicated instructions. All people are better at recognizing things than they are at remembering things. Some people can quickly grasp how something works, whereas for others it can take much longer. People have had different experiences and so will have different conceptual 'models' of things.

Mental models

The understanding and knowledge that we possess of something is often referred to as a 'mental model' (e.g. Norman, 1998). If people do not have a good mental model of something they can only perform actions by rote. If something goes wrong they will not know why and will not be able to recover. This is often the case with people using software systems, but it is also the case with 'simpler' domestic systems such as central heating systems, thermostats and so on. A key design principle is to design things so that people will form correct and useful mental models of how they work and what they do.

People develop mental models through interacting with systems, observing the relationship between their actions and the behaviours of the system and reading any manuals or other forms of explanation that come with a system. So, it is important that designers provide sufficient information in the interface (and any accompanying documentation) for people to form an accurate mental model.

Figure 2.6 illustrates the problem. As Norman set out in his classic exposition of the issues (Norman, 1986), designers have some conception of the system they have produced. This may or may not be the same as what the system actually does. Moreover, in a system of any large size, no single designer will know everything that the system does.

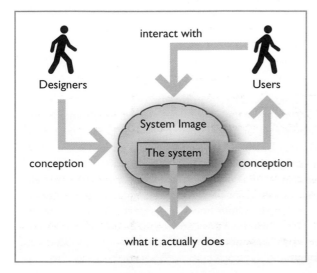

Figure 2.6 The system image

Designers design a system's image that they hope will reveal the designers' conception. The problem is that it is only through the system image – the interface, the behaviours of the system and any documentation – that the designers' conception can be revealed. People interact with the system image and from this have to derive their conception (their 'mental model') of what the system is and what it does. A clear, logical and consistent conceptual design will be easier to communicate to people who use the system and hence they will develop a clearer conception of the system themselves.

Norman has made the following general observations about the nature of mental models of interactive systems (Norman, 1983). He concludes that:

- Mental models are incomplete. People will understand some parts of a system better than others.
- People can 'run' (or try out) their models when required, but often with limited accuracy.
- Mental models are unstable – people forget details.
- Mental models do not have firm boundaries: similar devices and operations get confused with one another.
- Mental models are unscientific, exhibiting 'superstitious' behaviour.
- Mental models are parsimonious. People are willing to undertake additional physical operations to minimize mental effort, e.g. people will switch off the device and start again rather than trying to recover from an error.

→ Chapter 22 discusses the 'mind's eye' in terms of the visuospatial sketchpad of working memory

The psychologist Stephen Payne (1991, pp. 4–6) describes how mental models predict behaviour. The claim is that, in many situations, a great deal of explanatory work can be done by a description of what people know and believe, and how this affects their behaviour. Inferences can be made by 'mental simulation'. Mental models can support reasoning about devices, or the physical world in general, by running simulations in the mind's eye.

Challenge 2.2

What is your mental model of e-mail? How does an e-mail message get from one place to another? Write down your understanding and discuss it with a colleague. What differences are there and why? Think about the level of detail (or level of abstraction) that is present in different models.

BOX 2.5

Device models

Kieras and Bovair (1984) investigated the role of a device model (a person's mental model of a device) in learning how to operate a mock-up of the weapons control panel of the *USS Enterprise* from *Star Trek*. In their first experiment subjects learned how to operate the 'phasers' either by means of rote learning (press this button, then turn that knob to the second position) or by learning the underlying principles (the energy booster takes power from the ship), which required the subjects to infer the procedures. Kieras and Bovair found that learning, retention and use of 'shortcuts' were all enhanced for the group that learned the principles, demonstrating that knowledge of how the system worked enables people to infer how to operate it. Kieras and Bovair concluded by making two key points: first, for a device model to be useful it must support inference about exact and specific control actions, and secondly, the model need not be very complete or thorough.

Social differences

People make use of systems, products and services for very different reasons. They have different goals in using systems. They have different motivations for using systems. Some people will be very interested in a particular system, others will just want to get a simple task completed. These motivations change at different times.

Novice and expert users of a technology will typically have very different levels of knowledge and hence requirements for design features. Experts use a system regularly and learn all sorts of details, whereas a beginner will need to be guided through an interaction. There are also people who do not have to use a system, but who the designer would like to use the system. These people (sometimes called 'discretionary users') are often quickly put off if things are difficult to do. Designers need to entice these people to use their systems.

Designing for homogeneous groups of people – groups who are broadly similar and want to do much the same things – is quite different from designing for heterogeneous groups. Websites have to cater for heterogeneous groups and have particular design concerns as a result. A company's intranet, however, can be designed to meet the particular needs of particular people. Representatives from a relatively homogeneous group – secretaries or managers or laboratory scientists, say – could be made part of the design team and so provide much more detailed input as to their particular requirements.

Challenge 2.3

Look again at the ticket machine in Figure 2.3 and consider the people who will use it. Identify the variety of characteristics, physically, psychologically (including different mental models people might have) and socially, in terms of usage of the system.

2.3 Activities

There are many characteristics of activities that designers need to consider. The term is used for very simple tasks as well as highly complex, lengthy activities, so designers need to be careful when considering the characteristics of activities. Below is our list of the 10 important characteristics of activities that designers need to consider. First and foremost, the designer should focus on the overall *purpose* of the activity. After that the main features are:

- Temporal aspects (items 1–4)
- Cooperation (5)
- Complexity (6)
- Safety-critical (7 and 8)
- The nature of the content (9 and 10).

1 Temporal aspects cover how regular or infrequent activities are. Something that is undertaken every day can have a very different design from something that happens only once a year. People will soon learn how to make calls using a mobile phone, but may have great difficulties when it comes to changing the battery. Designers should ensure that frequent tasks are easy to do, but they also need to ensure that infrequent tasks are easy to learn (or remember) how to do.

2 Other important features of activities include time pressures, peaks and troughs of working. A design that works well when things are quiet can be awful when things are busy.

3 Some activities will take place as a single, continuous set of actions whereas others are more likely to be interrupted. If people are interrupted when undertaking some activity, the design needs to ensure that they can 'find their place' again and pick up. It is important then to ensure that people do not make mistakes or leave important steps out of some activity.

4 The response time needed from the system must be considered. If a website takes two minutes to deliver a response when the server is busy, that may be frustrating for a normal query but it could be critical if the information is needed for some emergency. As a general rule people expect a response time of about 100 milliseconds for hand–eye coordination activities and one second for a cause–effect relationship such as clicking a button and something happening. Anything more than five seconds and they will feel frustrated and confused (Dix, 2012).

 There are many examples of cooperative activities in Chapter 18

5 Another important feature of activities is whether they can be carried out alone or whether they are essentially concerned with working with others. Issues of awareness of others and communication and coordination then become important.

6 Well-defined tasks need different designs from more vague tasks. If a task or activity is well defined it can be accomplished with a simple step-by-step design. A vague activity means that people have to be able to browse around, see different types of information, move from one thing to another and so on.

7 Some activities are 'safety-critical', in which case any mistake could result in an injury or a serious accident. Others are less so. Clearly, where safety is involved designers must pay every attention to ensuring that mistakes do not have a serious effect.

8 In general, it is vital for designers to think about what happens when people make mistakes and errors and to design for such circumstances.

9 It is also important to consider the data requirements of the activity. If large amounts of alphabetic data have to be input as part of the activity (recording names and addresses, perhaps, or word-processing documents) then a keyboard is almost certainly needed. In other activities there may be a need to display video or high-quality colour graphic displays. Some activities, however, require very modest amounts of data, or data that does not change frequently, and can make use of other technologies. A library, for example, just needs to scan in a barcode or two, so the technology can be designed to exploit this feature of the activity.

10 Just as important as data is the media that an activity requires. A simple two-tone display of numeric data demands a very different design from a full-motion multimedia display.

? Challenge 2.4

List the main characteristics of the activity of sending an e-mail. Use the 10 points above to guide you.

2.4 Contexts

Activities always happen in a context, so there is a need to analyse the two together. Three useful types of context are distinguishable: the organizational context, the social context and the physical circumstances under which the activity takes place. Context can be a difficult term. Sometimes it is useful to see context as surrounding an activity. At other times it can be seen as the features that glue some activities together into a coherent whole.

For an activity such as 'withdraw cash from an ATM', for example, an analysis of context would include things such as the location of the device (often as a 'hole-in-the-wall'), the effect of sunshine on the readability of the display, and security considerations. Social considerations would include the time spent on a transaction or the need to queue. The organizational context for this activity would take into consideration the impact on the bank's ways of working and its relationships with its customers. It is important to consider the range of contexts and environments in which activities can take place.

Physical environment

The physical environment in which an activity happens is important. For example, the sun shining on an ATM display may make it unreadable. The environment may be very noisy, cold, wet or dirty. The same activity – for example, logging on to a website – may be carried out in geographically remote environments where Internet access is slow, or with all the facilities of a large city and fast networks.

Social context

The social context within which the activity takes place is also important. A supportive environment will offer plenty of help for the activity. There may be training manuals available, tuition or experts to hand if people get into trouble. There may be privacy issues to consider, and an interaction can be very different if the person is alone compared to being with others. Social norms may dictate the acceptability of certain designs. For example, the use of sound output is often unacceptable in an open-plan office environment, but might be quite effective where a person is working alone.

Organizational context

Finally the organizational context (Figure 2.7) is important as changes in technology often alter communication and power structures and may have effects on jobs such as deskilling. There are many books devoted to the study of organizations and the impact of new technologies on organizations. We cannot do justice to this subject here. The circumstances under which activities happen (time, place and so on) also vary widely and need to be taken into consideration.

Figure 2.7 Different working contexts

(Source: Peter Wilson/DK Images; Rob Reichenfield/DK Images; Eddie Lawrence/DK Images)

BOX
2.6

Interface plasticity

Joelle Coutaz and her colleagues (Coutaz and Calvary, 2012) present the idea of design-ing for interface plasticity. These are interfaces that adapt to different contexts, for example adapting a display of a heating controller from a display on the TV to a display on a small mobile device. Importantly they tie this in with the idea of designing for specific values. Designers should explicitly address the values that are being sought for people in a specific context. The interface should be designed to achieve the required values in the required contexts of use.

2.5 Technologies

The final part of the PACT framework is the technologies: the medium that interactive system designers work with. Interactive systems typically consist of hardware and soft-ware components that communicate with one another and transform some input data into some output data. Interactive systems can perform various functions and typically contain a good deal of data, or information content. People using such systems engage in interactions and physically devices have various degrees of style and aesthetics. Designers of interactive systems need to understand the materials they work with, just as designers in other areas of design such as interior design, jewellery design, etc. have to do.

Of course, interactive technologies change at a fantastic rate and by far the best way for designers to keep abreast of the options available is to subscribe to websites, a number of which are listed on the website that accompanies this chapter. It is also very difficult to classify technologies, as they are continually being packaged in new ways and different combinations facilitate quite different types of interactions. For example, the multi-touch screen on an iPod Touch allows for quite different ways of navigating through your music collection and selecting particular tracks from the trackwheel on an iPod Nano. Designers need to be aware of various possibilities for input, output, com-munication and content.

Input

Input devices are concerned with how people enter data and instructions into a system securely and safely. Switches and buttons facilitate a simple and direct method of issu-ing instructions (such as 'turn on' or 'turn off') but they take up space. On small mobile devices there is not enough room to have many buttons, so designers have to be careful which functions have their own button. On the iPhone, for example, a button on the side of the device is allocated to turning the sound off and on. The designers decided that this was such an important and often-used function that it should have its own button.

Alphanumeric data is usually input to an interactive device through a 'QWERTY' key-board, invented by C.L. Sholes in 1868! At that time, typewriters were relatively crudely manufactured and an alphabetic arrangement of keys tended to result in jams when the keys were struck. By rearranging the keys Sholes solved this problem. The design is still with us today, despite some devices using an alphabetic keyboard where the letters are arranged in alphabetical order.

Touchscreens are sensitive to the touch of a finger. They function through either infra-red sensitivity or electrical capacitance. Because of their lack of moving or detachable parts, they are suitable for applications intended for public places, and provided the interface is well designed they present an appearance of simplicity and ease of use. Many touchscreens only recognize a single touch, but multi-touch screens enable zooming and rotating of images and text. Figure 2.8 shows Microsoft's surface, a multi-touch table.

Touchscreens make use of the person's finger as the input device, which has the obvious benefit that people always have their fingers with them. The light pen (Figure 2.9) was, arguably, the original pointing device. When it is pointed at the screen it returns information about the screen location to a computer which allows the item pointed at to be identified. Light pens are less expensive than touchscreens, can be armoured (made very robust) and can be sterilized. They have a number of industrial and medical applications.

Other forms of pointing device include the stylus which is used on very small displays where a finger is too big to be used as the input device, and on many handheld devices. Being more precise than a finger, a stylus can be used for handwriting recognition. In theory, this is an attractive way of inputting data into an interactive device. Writing with a stylus directly onto a computer's screen or tablet is a natural way of working. However, it is quite slow and can be inaccurate. It requires people to 'train' the device to recognize their handwriting, which improves the recognition accuracy of the software. Many people can type faster than they can write by hand.

One of the most ubiquitous of input devices is the mouse (Figure 2.10), developed at Stanford University Research Laboratory in the mid-1960s. The mouse consists of a palm-sized device that is moved over a flat surface such as the top of a desk. At its simplest (and cheapest) it rests on a rubber-coated ball that turns two wheels set at right angles. These two wheels translate the movement of the mouse into signals that the computer to which it is connected can interpret. One or two buttons sit on top of the mouse and are operated with the person's fingers. The mouse has become the default pointing device. More contemporary mouse design includes a thumbwheel (see Figure 2.11) for scrolling through documents or Web pages. A mouse may be cordless, using infra-red to communicate with the host computer. In 2009 Apple introduced the 'magic mouse' that combined traditional mouse functions with multi-touch capability allowing a range of new touch gestures for interaction.

A trackball is another pointing device, which is best described as a mouse lying on its back. To move the pointer the user moves the ball. Again, like all other pointing devices, there are one or more buttons which can be used to select on-screen items. Trackballs are often found in public-access kiosks because they are difficult to steal and do not require a flat surface to rest upon.

Figure 2.8 Microsoft Surface
(Source: Reuters/Robert Sorbo)

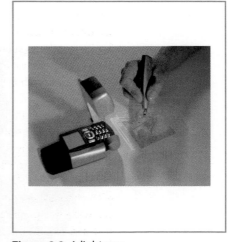

Figure 2.9 A light pen
(Source: Volker Steger/Science Photo Library)

Figure 2.10 A Mac one-button mouse. The single button of the traditional Mac is said to have the advantage of 'you always know which button to press'

(Source: Alan Mather/Alamy Images)

Figure 2.11 A Microsoft two-button mouse with thumbwheel (which is used for scrolling)

(Source: www.microsoft.com/presspass/images/gallery/ hardware/BNMS_mouse_web.jpg. Printed with permission from Microsoft Corporation)

A joystick (Figure 2.12) is a handle which pivots from a central point. Viewing the joystick from above, it may be moved north, south, east and west (and all points between) to control an on-screen pointer, spaceship or any other on-screen object. Joysticks are used mostly for computer games, but they are also found in conjunction with CAD/CAM (computer-aided design/manufacture) systems and VR (virtual reality) applications.

With the introduction of the Nintendo Wii in 2007 a whole new generation of input became possible. The Wii uses infra-red to register the movement of a wand. This allows gestures to be recognized. Other systems, notably the Microsoft Kinnect, recognize gestures through tracking limb and body movements by attaching sensors to the limb or by tracking using cameras (Figure 2.13).

There are many different types of sensor that are now available as input mechanisms. Air pressure sensors, acoustic sensors, vibration detectors, infra-red motion detectors and accelerometers are all readily available for designers to detect specific aspects of an

Figure 2.12 An ergonomically designed games joystick

(Source: Microsoft SideWinder ® Precision 2 joystick. Photo by Phil Turner. Printed with permission from Microsoft Corporation)

Figure 2.13 Microsoft Kinnect
(Source: David Becker/Getty Images)

interaction. Wilson (2012) lists sensors for detecting occupancy, movement and orientation, object distance and position, touch, gaze and gesture, human identity (biometrics), context and affect. There are many proprietary devices used to input specifically to mobile devices, such as jog wheels used for navigation of mobile phone interfaces. Brain activity can also be sensed, allowing for brain–computer interfaces (BCI) – an exciting development for the future.

Speech input is becoming increasingly accurate, particularly if people are willing to spend a few minutes (7–10, say) training a system to recognize their voice. Even without training, the Siri system on the iPhone can be quite impressive. The other day I said to Siri 'Send a text to Linda'. Siri replied 'There are two people called Linda in your address book, Linda and Linda Jane'. I replied 'Send a text to Linda Jane, say Hi'. Siri sent the text and responded, 'A text saying Hi has been sent to Linda Jane'. Speech input for these simple, focused tasks will become an increasingly common option for the interaction designer.

Other forms of input include quick response (QR) codes and augmented-reality (AR) fiducial markers (Figure 2.14). QR codes are used by a general-purpose scanning app on a phone to connect the phone to a website, or to execute a short sequence of operations.

Figure 2.14 QR codes
(Source: Red Huber/Orlando Sentinel/ MCT/Getty Images)

Fiducial markers are used to recognize an object and hence to tailor some interactivity towards it. Markerless AR uses a photo of an object to register a connection allowing graphics, video and other content to be overlaid onto the scene. The Global Positioning System (GPS) can also be used to align views of the real world with digital content to provide an augmented reality.

Challenge 2.5

Which input devices would you use for a tourist information 'kiosk' application to be sited in the arrivals area of an airport? The system allows people to book hotel rooms, etc., as well as to find information about the area. Explain your choices.

Output

Technologies for displaying content to people rely primarily on the three perceptual abilities of vision, hearing and touch. The most fundamental output device is the screen or monitor. Even a few years ago the default monitor used cathode ray tube (CRT) technology that required a large heavy box positioned on a desk or table. Nowadays flat-screen monitors using plasma or TFT (thin-film transistor) or LCD (liquid crystal display) technologies can be mounted on walls. Some of these can deliver very large displays that result in a significantly different interactive experience. Flexible organic light-emitting diode (OLED) displays for screens are just coming onto the market that will enable displays of any shape and size that can bend and hence can be used in clothing (Figure 2.15)

→ Wearable computing is discussed at length in Chapter 20

The physical dimensions of display devices are, however, only one of the factors involved in the resulting output. The output device is driven by hardware – a graphics card – that will vary with respect to the screen resolutions and palette of colours it can support. More generally, designing interactive systems to work with any and all combinations of hardware is very difficult. Typically, applications and games specify minimum specifications.

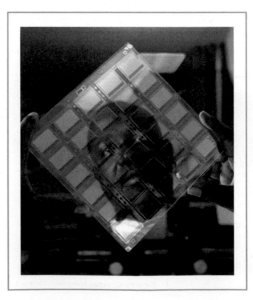

Figure 2.15 Flexible organic light-emitting diode (OLED) display

(Source: Volker Steger/Science Photo Library Ltd)

One way past the problems with restrictive display 'real estate' is to use a data projector (Figure 2.16). While the resolution is usually less than that of a monitor, the resulting projected image can be huge. Data projectors are shrinking in size at a remarkable rate and there are now mobile data projectors. These promise to have a big impact on interaction design as they get small enough to be built into phones and other mobile devices. Images can be projected onto any surface and pointing and other gestures can be recognized by a camera. In this way any surface has the potential to become a multi-touch display.

Besides the visual display of content, sound is an important method of output. Sound is an output medium that is significantly under-used. Speech output is also an increasingly popular option (e.g. in satellite navigation systems). With effective text-to-speech (TTS) systems, simply sending a text message to the system results in clear spoken output.

→ Sound is discussed at length in Chapter 13

A printer is a device that prints text or illustrations on paper, while a plotter draws pictures or shapes. Plotters differ from printers in that they draw lines using a pen. As a result, they can produce continuous lines, whereas printers can only simulate lines by printing a closely spaced series of dots. Multi-colour plotters use different-coloured pens. In general, plotters are considerably more expensive than printers.

Several companies have developed three-dimensional printers. These machines work by placing layers of a powdery material on top of each other to create a real-life model of a digital image. It is thought that with the use of hundreds and perhaps thousands of layers, everything from 'coffee cups to car parts' could be created. Like putting ink on paper, 3D printers print using powder and binder (glue). These printers allow for the rapid prototyping of physical designs for new products.

'Haptics' refers to the sense of touch. However, haptics allows us to be in touch with interactive devices and media in a way that is direct and immediate. Perhaps the most widespread haptic devices are those games controllers that incorporate so-called force-feedback. Force-feedback is typically intended to convey feedback from games environments back to the person engaged. So what are the perceived benefits of force-feedback devices?

→ Haptic interfaces are considered further in Chapter 13

- Sensations can be associated with interactions, such as feeling driving surfaces or feeling footsteps.
- Sensations can also be used to provide feedback as to the location of other players, objects and so forth.
- Force-feedback can allow the player to feel what it would be like to wield a sword, drive a high-speed car, fly a 'speeder' or engage the Empire with a light-sabre.

Figure 2.16 The Samsung i7410 Sirius Projector Phone
(Source: Gaustau Nacarino/Reuters)

A significantly more serious application of force-feedback is NASA's 'Softwalls' initiative in response to the 9/11 terrorist attacks on New York in 2001. Softwalls would be used to restrict airspaces by way of the aircraft's on-board systems. The basic idea, attributed to Edward Lee, would prevent aircraft from flying into restricted airspace (such as city centres) and this would be communicated to the pilot by way of the aircraft's joystick. Other examples include the 'silent alert' vibration of a mobile phone and even the feel of a key when pressed.

Challenge 2.6

Which output devices would you use for a tourist information application as described in Challenge 2.5? Explain your choices.

Communication

Communications between people and between devices is an important part of designing interactive systems. Here, issues such as bandwidth and speed are critical. So too is feedback to people so that they know what is going on and indeed that something is going on! In some domains the transmission and storage of large amounts of data becomes a key feature.

Communication can take place through wired connections such as a telephone line, or an Ethernet network which is often found in offices. Ethernet is the fastest form of communication, but the device has to be plugged into a network to make use of it. Ethernet allows connection to be made to the nearest node on the Internet. Extremely fast communications over fibre-optic cables connect these nodes to each other and hence connect devices to other devices all over the world. Each device on this network has a unique address, its IP (Internet Protocol) address, that enables data to be routed to the correct device. The number of IP addresses available will soon be used up and a new form of address, IPv6, will be needed.

Wireless communication is becoming much more common and often a wireless 'hub' is attached to an Ethernet network. Wireless communications can take place over the wireless telephone network used for mobile phones or over a Wi-Fi connection. Wi-Fi is quite limited in range and you need to be within a few metres of a Wi-Fi hub to get a connection, whereas over the telephone network, coverage is much wider. The new 4G technologies promise to deliver much faster connectivity over mobile devices and superfast broadband will soon be covering cities across the globe. Other forms of wireless communication continue to be developed and WiMax promises to deliver much wider coverage using Wi-Fi. Short-range communications directly between one device and another (i.e. not using the Internet) can be achieved using a technology called Bluetooth. Near-field communication (NFC) is used to connect devices simply by bringing them close to each other. All new mobile phones will soon have NFC capability, a feature which again will change the types of interaction that are possible.

Content

Content concerns the data in the system and the form it takes. Considerations of content are a key part of understanding the characteristics of the activities as described above. The content that a technology can support is also critical. Good content is accurate, up to date, relevant and well presented. There is little point in having a sophisticated information retrieval system if the information, once retrieved, is out of date or irrelevant. In some technologies content is just about everything (e.g. websites are usually all about content). Other technologies are more concerned with function (e.g. a remote control for a TV). Most technologies have a mixture of function and content.

Content can be retrieved when required (known as 'pull technology') or it can be pushed from a server to a device. Push e-mail, for example, is used on the BlackBerry system so that e-mail is constantly updated. RSS feeds on websites provide automatic updates when a website's content is changed.

The characteristics of the data are important for choosing input methods. Barcodes, for example, are only sensible if the data does not change often. Touchscreens are useful if there are only a few options to choose from. Speech input is possible if there is no noise or background interference, if there are only a few commands that need to be entered or if the domain is quite constrained.

'Streamy' outputs such as video, music and speech have different characteristics from 'chunky' media such as icons, text or still photographs. Most important, perhaps, is that streamy media do not stay around for long. Instructions given as speech output, for example, have to be remembered, whereas if displayed as a piece of text, they can be read over again. Animations are also popular ways of presenting content; 2D animation is generally produced using Adobe's Flash program and 3D-style animation can be produced with Papervision or games 'engines' such as 3D Studio Max and Maya.

2.6 Scoping a problem with PACT

The aim of human-centred interactive systems design is to arrive at the best combination of the PACT elements with respect to a particular domain. Designers want to get the right mix of technologies to support the activities being undertaken by people in different contexts. A PACT analysis is useful for both analysis and design activities: understanding the current situation, seeing where possible improvements can be made or envisioning future situations. To do a PACT analysis the designer simply scopes out the variety of Ps, As, Cs and Ts that are possible, or likely, in a domain. This can be done using brainstorming and other envisionment techniques and by working with people through observations, interviews and workshops. There are many techniques for this (these are described in Part II of this book). A PACT analysis is also useful for developing personas and scenarios (see Chapter 3). The designer should look for trade-offs between combinations of PACT and think about how these might affect design.

For people, designers need to think about the physical, psychological and social differences and how those differences change in different circumstances and over time. It is most important that designers consider all the various stakeholders in a project. For activities they need to think about the complexity of the activity (focused or vague, simple or difficult, few steps or many), the temporal features (frequency, peaks and troughs, continuous or interruptible), cooperative features and the nature of the data. For contexts they think about the physical, social and organizational setting, and for technologies they concentrate on input, output, communication and content.

As an example, let us assume that we have been asked by a university department to consider developing a system controlling access to their laboratories. A PACT analysis might include the following.

People

Students, lecturers and technicians are the main groups. These are all well educated and understand things such as swipe cards, passwords and so on. People in wheelchairs need to be considered, as do other design issues such as colour blindness. There may be language differences. Both occasional and frequent visitors need to be considered. However, there are other stakeholders who need access to rooms, such as cleaning staff and security personnel. What are the motivations for management wanting to control access in the first place?

Activities

The overall purpose of the activity is to enter some form of security clearance and to open the door. This is a very well-defined activity that takes place in one step. It happens very frequently, with peaks at the start of each laboratory session. The data to be entered is a simple numeric or alphanumeric code. It is an activity that does not require cooperation with others (though it may be done with others, of course). It is not safety-critical, though security is an important aspect.

Contexts

Physically the activity takes place indoors, but people might be carrying books and other things that makes doing anything complicated quite difficult. Socially it may happen in a crowd, but also it may happen late at night when no one else is about. Organizationally, the context is primarily about security and who has access to which rooms and when they can gain access. This is likely to be quite a politically charged setting.

Technologies

A small amount of data has to be entered quickly. It must be obvious how to do this in order to accommodate visitors and people unfamiliar with the system. It needs to be accessible by people in wheelchairs. The output from the technology needs to be clear: that the security data has been accepted or not and the door has to be opened if the process was successful. Communication with a central database may be necessary to validate any data input, but there is little other content in the application.

Challenge 2.7

Write down a quick PACT analysis for the introduction of a 'point of sale' system (i.e. where goods are priced and paid for) for a café at a motorway service station. Discuss your ideas with a colleague.

Summary and key points

The design of interactive systems is concerned with people, the activities they are undertaking, the contexts of those activities and the technologies that are used: the PACT elements. There is considerable variety in each of these and it is this variety – and all the different combinations that can occur – that makes the design of interactive systems so fascinating.

- The design of interactive systems requires the analyst/designer to consider the range of PACT elements and how they fit together in a domain.

- People vary in terms of physical characteristics and psychological differences and in their usage of systems.
- Activities vary in terms of temporal aspects, whether they involve cooperation, complexity, whether they are safety-critical and the nature of the content they require.
- Contexts vary in terms of physical, social, organizational aspects.
- Technologies vary in terms of the input, output, communication and content that they support.
- Undertaking a PACT analysis of a situation is a useful way of scoping a design problem.

Exercises

1 You have been asked to design the information system for a new cycle path network that is to run through part of your town. The aim of the system is to provide information on directions and distances for leisure cyclists to the main points of interest in the town. It also needs to provide information on other things, such as bus and train times for those cyclists who are commuting to and from work. Undertake a PACT analysis for this application.

2 For the same application produce a project development plan. You should detail what sort of requirements work will be needed to understand the domain, the people or skills that will be needed in the project team, and the approach that will be taken. Identify any milestones that you would have in the project.

 ## Further reading

Norman, D. (1998) *The Design of Everyday Things.* Doubleday, New York. *Donald Norman discusses the ideas of mental models in several of his publications. This is probably the best.*

Getting ahead

Murrell, K.F.H. (1965) *Ergonomics – Man in his Working Environment.* Chapman & Hall, London.

Payne, S. (2012) Mental models. In J.A. Jacko (ed) *The Human–Computer Interaction Handbook: Fundamentals, Evolving Technologies and Emerging Applications,* **3rd edn.** CRC Press, Taylor and Francis, Boca Ratun, FL.

Wilson, A. (2012) Sensor and recognition-based input for interaction. In J.A. Jacko (ed) *The Human–Computer Interaction Handbook: Fundamentals, Evolving Technologies and Emerging Applications,* **3rd edn.** CRC Press, Taylor and Francis, Boca Ratun, FL.

 ## Web links

The accompanying website has links to relevant websites. Go to
www.pearsoned.co.uk/benyon

Comments on challenges

Challenge 2.1

With VCRs came the video hire shop and so the activity of watching a film moved from the cinema into the home. VCRs also allowed films to be recorded from the television so people could watch them whenever they wanted. With DVDs people are given more options than just watching the film, so now the activity includes watching pieces that were cut out of the original film, slightly different versions, interviews with the actors and director and so on. The activity of watching a film is now more interactive: the people watching have more control over what they see.

Challenge 2.2

How an e-mail actually gets from one place to another is surprisingly complicated! It is much more like sending a letter by post than like making a telephone call. The e-mail is sent as one or more 'packets' of data which may be routed across the world by any of a host of different routes. The e-mail travels from your computer through the computer providing the Internet connection, then to a major 'hub' where it joins a high-capacity 'backbone' cable. As it comes closer to its destination this process is reversed as it moves off the main cables into more remote areas. A sophisticated database of addresses and routeing information is used to find the best way.

Challenge 2.3

Physically the siting is important so that people in wheelchairs, children, etc. can reach the buttons. Buttons must be easy to press so that the elderly are not excluded from their use. Psychologically the machine should not make undue demands on people. It is difficult to say anything certain since we do not know the complexity of the machine. Some ticket machines are very simple – designed just to select the destination and deliver the ticket. Others try to offer the whole range of functions, different ticket types, groups, period return tickets and so on. These machines tend to become very complicated and hard to use. From the usage perspective the design needs to support both those people who are in a hurry and perhaps use the machine every day and those people who have never encountered such a machine before, perhaps speak a different language and are trying to do something quite complex. It is difficult to design optimally for both of these types of use.

Challenge 2.4

Sending e-mails is a fairly frequent activity that is often interrupted. It is a straightforward activity in itself but it can become very complex when it is interleaved with other things such as finding old e-mails, finding addresses, attaching documents and so on. It is not necessary to coordinate the activity with others. The tasks of finding and entering addresses are made much easier if the e-mail program has an embedded address book, as the person only has to remember and type small amounts of data. Otherwise long e-mail addresses have to be typed in.

Challenge 2.5

For reasons of durability, we would suggest a touchscreen or ordinary monitor with tracker ball and a robust keyboard (for entering data such as name of hotel guest) or an on-screen version (rather tiresome to use). Other options are possible.

Challenge 2.6

The touchscreen used as an output device, plus a small printer embedded in the casing for confirmation of bookings, etc. would probably be more reassuring than just a confirmation number. Sound output (and indeed input) would be possible but is likely to be impractical in the noisy environment of the airport.

Challenge 2.7

There are many complex issues involved, of course. Here are just a few to start with. People – the whole range! From a coachload of football supporters or elderly people on an outing to individuals wandering around late at night. The key thing to consider is how to deal with crowds at one time and just a few people at another. The activities are simple and well defined. The items have to be identified, priced and totalled. The money has to be taken and a receipt printed. Occasionally there will be a question to be answered that goes outside this simple task structure, such as 'how much would this cost if I . . . ?', or disputes over prices need to be settled. There are also other stakeholders involved: the serving staff, the managers and so on. They also need information from the system. As for technologies, items could have a barcode on them, but for meals this is difficult, so usually individual items need to have the price typed in. This takes time. The interface design will be quite critical – e.g. there could be specific keys for things like tea and coffee, but whether it is a good idea to have a specific key for everything is another matter. Now you have had a chance to think about this, spend some time looking at all the different solutions that different cafés and restaurants use.

Chapter 3
The process of human-centred interactive systems design

Aims

Design is a creative process concerned with bringing about something new. It is a social activity with social consequences. It is about conscious change and communication between designers and the people who will use the system. Different design disciplines have different methods and techniques for helping with this process. Approaches to and philosophies of design change over time. In mature disciplines, examples of good design are built up and people can study and reflect upon what makes a certain design great, good or awful. Different design disciplines have different constraints, such as whether the designed object is 'stand-alone' or whether it has to fit in and live with legacy systems or conform to standards.

In this chapter we look at what is involved in interactive systems design and how to go about designing interactive systems. After studying this chapter you should be able to:

- Understand the nature of interactive systems design
- Understand the four processes involved in design: understanding, design, envisionment, evaluation
- Understand the centrality of evaluation in human-centred design
- Understand the scenario-based design approach
- Develop scenarios and personas
- Understand the scenario-based design method.

3.1 Introduction

There are many different ways of characterizing the activities involved in the design process. For David Kelley, founder of the product design company IDEO, 'Design has three activities: understand, observe and visualize'. He says:

> Remember, design is messy; designers try to understand this mess. They observe how their products will be used; design is about users and use. They visualize which is the act of deciding what it is.   Kelley and Hartfield (1996), p. 156

In this chapter we provide methods and processes to help designers deal with the 'messy' problems of designing interactive systems. We characterize the overall design process in terms of the four activities illustrated in Figure 3.1. The key features of this representation are as follows:

- Evaluation is central to designing interactive systems. Everything gets evaluated at every step of the process.
- The process can start at any point – sometimes there is a conceptual design in place, sometimes we start with a prototype, sometimes we start with understanding.
- The activities can happen in any order, for example understanding might be evaluated and a prototype built and evaluated and some aspect of a physical design might then be identified.

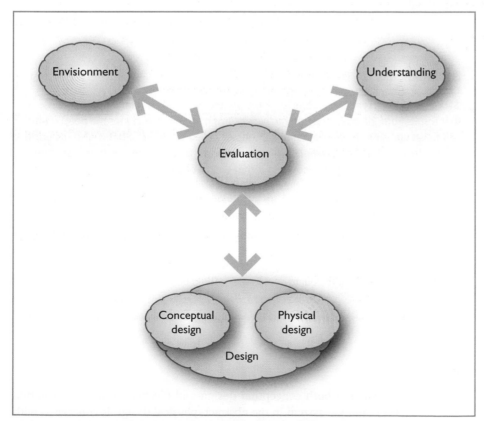

Figure 3.1 Understanding, design, evaluation, envisionment

Understanding

Understanding is concerned with what the system has to do, what it has to be like and how it has to fit in with other things: with the requirements of the product, system or service. Designers need to research the range of people, activities and contexts relevant to the domain they are investigating so that they can understand the requirements of the system they are developing. They need to understand the opportunities and constraints provided by technologies.

There are both functional and non-functional requirements to consider. Functional requirements are concerned with what the system should be able to do and with the functional constraints of a system. It is important for the designer to think about the whole interaction experience in an abstract way. Deciding who does what, when something should be displayed or the sequence in which actions are undertaken should come later in the design process. A good analysis of an activity will strive to be as independent of current practice as possible. Of course, there are always functional constraints – the realities of what is technically possible – which render certain ordering, sequencing and allocation of functions inevitable. There are also logical and organizational constraints that may make particular designs infeasible.

→ Chapter 7 gives a detailed treatment of methods for understanding

Requirements are generated through discussions and interactions with people who will use or be affected by the proposed system – the stakeholders (see Box 3.1). Requirements are also generated through observations of existing systems, research into similar systems, what people do now and what they would like to do. Requirements can be generated through working with people in focus groups, design workshops and so on, where different scenarios can be considered (see Section 3.4). The aim is to collect and analyse the stories people have to tell. Requirements are essentially about understanding.

BOX 3.1

Stakeholders

'Stakeholders' is a term that refers to all the people who will be affected by any system that results from the process of interactive systems design. This includes the people who will finish up using the new system (sometimes called the 'users'), but it also includes many other people. For example, the organization that the system is being designed for will probably have many people in it that will not be using the system, but will be affected by it as it might change their job. For example, introducing a new website into an organization often changes working practices as well as simply providing information. There may be stakeholders outside the organization, such as government authorities, that need to verify some procedures. The number and type of people affected by a new interactive system will vary greatly according to what sort of system it is. An important part of the understanding process is to consider all the different stakeholders and how they might be affected, to decide who should be involved in discussions about the design.

Design

Design activities concern both conceptual design and physical design. Conceptual design is about designing a system in the abstract, physical design is concerned with making things concrete.

Conceptual design

Conceptual design is about considering what information and functions are needed for the system to achieve its purpose. It is about deciding what someone will have to know to use the system. It is about finding a clear conceptualization of a design solution and how that conceptualization will be communicated to people (so that people will quickly develop a clear mental model).

← Chapter 2 discusses mental models

There are a number of techniques to help with conceptual design. Software engineers prefer modelling possible solutions with objects, relationships and 'use cases' (a semi-formal scenario representation). Entity–relationship models are another popular conceptual modelling tool. Flow can be represented using dataflow diagrams and structure can be shown with structure charts. The conceptual design of a website, for example, will include a site map and a navigation structure.

→ Methods for modelling are discussed in Chapter 9

One way to conceptualize the main features of a system is to use a 'rich picture'. Two examples are shown in Figure 3.2. A rich picture captures the main conceptual relationships between the main conceptual entities in a system – a model of the structure of a situation. Peter Checkland (Checkland, 1981; Checkland and Scholes, 1999), who originated the soft systems approach, also emphasizes focusing on the key transformation of a system. This is the conceptual model of processing. The principal stakeholders – customers, actors, system owners – should be identified. The designer should also consider the perspective from which an activity is being viewed as a system (the *Weltanschauung*) and the environment in which the activities take place. (Checkland proposes the acronym CATWOE – customers, actors, transformation, *Weltanschauung*, owners, environment – for these elements of a rich picture.) Most importantly, the rich picture identifies the issues or concerns of the stakeholders, thus helping to focus attention on problems or potential design solutions.

The key feature of conceptual design is to keep things abstract – focus on the 'what' rather than the 'how' – and to avoid making assumptions about how functions and information will be distributed. There is no clear-cut distinction between conceptual and physical design, but rather there are degrees of conceptuality.

Physical design

Physical design is concerned with how things are going to work and with detailing the look and feel of the product. Physical design is about structuring interactions into logical sequences and about clarifying and presenting the allocation of functions and knowledge between people and devices. The distinction between conceptual and physical design is very important. The conceptual design relates to the overall purpose of the whole interactive system. Between the people and the technologies there has to be enough knowledge and ability to achieve the purpose. Physical design is concerned with taking this abstract representation and translating it into concrete designs. On one side this means requirements for hardware and software and on the other it defines the knowledge required by people and the tasks and activities that people will have to do. There are three components to physical design: operational design, representational design and design of interactions.

Operational design is concerned with specifying how everything works and how content is structured and stored. Taking a functional view of an activity means focusing on processes and on the movement, or flow, of things through a system. *Events* are occurrences that cause, or trigger, some other functions to be undertaken. Sometimes these arise from outside the system under consideration and sometimes they arise as a result of doing something else. For example, some activity might be triggered on a particular day or at a particular time; another might be triggered by the arrival of a person or document.

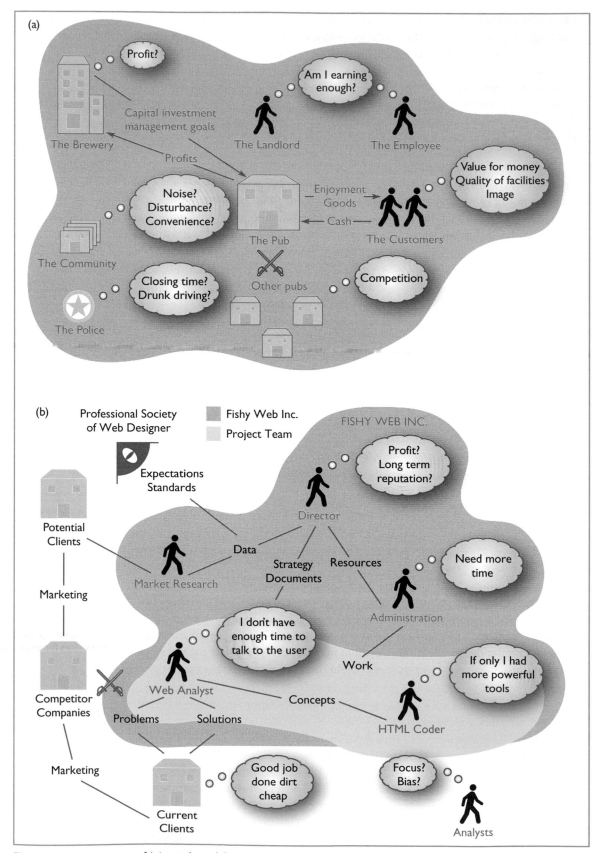

Figure 3.2 Rich pictures of (a) a pub and (b) a Web design company

(Source: After Monk, A. and Howard, S. (1998) Methods & Tools: the rich picture: a tool for reasoning about work context, *Interactions*, 5(2), pp.21–30. © 1998 ACM, Inc. Reprinted by permission)

Representational design is concerned with fixing on colours, shapes, sizes and information layout. It is concerned with style and aesthetics and is particularly important for issues such as the attitudes and feelings of people, but also for the efficient retrieval of information.

→ See Section 12.5 on information design

Style concerns the overall 'look and feel' of the system. Does it appear old and 'clunky' or is it slick, smooth and modern? What mood and feelings does the design engender? For example, most Microsoft products engender an 'office' and 'work' mood, serious rather than playful. Many other systems aim to make the interaction engaging, some aim to make it challenging and others entertaining. In multimedia and games applications this is particularly important.

Interaction design, in this context, is concerned with the allocation of functions to human agency or to technology and with the structuring and sequencing of the interactions. Allocation of functions has a significant impact on how easy and enjoyable a system is to use. Designers create tasks for people by the way they allocate functions.

For example, consider the activity of making a phone call. Conceptually speaking, certain functions are necessary: indicate a desire to make a phone call, connect to the network, enter the phone number, make connection. Years ago a telephone exchange was staffed by people and it was these people who made connections by physically putting wires into connectors. In the days of wired phones, picking up the receiver indicated the desire to make a call, the full number had to be dialled in and then the telephone exchange would automatically make the connections. Nowadays a person just has to press the connect button on a cellular phone, choose someone's name from the phone's address book and the technology does the rest.

Recall the activity–technology cycle (see Chapter 2). The allocation of knowledge and activities between people and technologies is a significant part of how experiences change over time.

Challenge 3.1

Find a colleague and discuss the activity of watching pre-recorded films on TV. Focus on the way the allocation of function changes with the technology such as VCR, DVD and PVR (personal video recorder). How has it changed now that on-line films are easily available on your TV or PC?

Envisionment

Designs need to be visualized both to help designers clarify their own ideas and to enable people to evaluate them. Envisionment is concerned with finding appropriate media in which to render design ideas. The medium needs to be appropriate for the stage of the process, the audience, the resources available and the questions that the designer is trying to answer.

→ Chapter 8 presents techniques for envisionment

There are many techniques for envisionment, but they include any way in which abstract ideas can be brought to life. Sketches 'on the back of an envelope', fully functioning prototypes and cardboard mock-ups are just some of the methods used. Scenarios, sometimes represented in pictorial form as storyboards, are an essential part of prototyping and envisionment. They provide a way of working through a design idea so that the key issues stand out. Scenarios are discussed below.

Evaluation

Evaluation is tightly coupled with envisionment because the nature of the representation used will affect what can be evaluated. The evaluation criteria will also depend on who is able to use the representation. Any of the other design activities will be followed by an evaluation. Sometimes this is simply the designer checking through to make sure something is complete and correct. It could be a list of requirements or a high-level design brief that is sent to a client, an abstract conceptual model that is discussed with a colleague, or a formal evaluation of a functional prototype by the future system users.

→ Chapter 10 provides detail on evaluation

Techniques for evaluation are many and various, depending once again on the circumstances. Expressing the design ideas in terms of a concrete scenario that people have to work their way through can be very effective. The important thing to keep in mind is that the technique used must be appropriate for the nature of the representation, the questions being asked and the people involved in the evaluation.

Challenge 3.2

If you were to have a new room built onto your house – or have a room converted from one use to another – consider the processes that you would have to go through, starting with:

- *A conceptual design*
- *A physical design*
- *Some requirements*
- *A prototype or other envisioned solution.*

Implementation

Figure 3.1 does not include the implementation or production of the design (nor all the planning and management stages of a project). But, of course, ultimately things have to be engineered and software has to be written and tested. Databases have to be designed and populated and programs have to be validated. The whole system needs to be checked to ensure that it meets the requirements until finally the system can be formally 'launched' and signed off as finished. Since this book is primarily about design, we do not spend a lot of time on issues of implementation, but they can account for a significant portion of total development costs. Clients will often want extra features when they see a system nearing completion, but these will have to be costed and paid for. On the other hand, the developers need to ensure that their system really does meet the specification and does not contain any 'bugs'.

→ Chapter 9 provides a number of semi-formal models

If interactive systems designers were architects they would have well-understood methods and conventions for specifying the results of the design process. They would produce various blueprints from different elevations and engineering specifications for particular aspects of the design. In interactive systems design there are a variety of formal, semi-formal and informal methods of specification. The best known of the formal methods is the Unified Modeling Language (UML) (Pender, 2003).

BOX 3.2

Agile development

Over the past few years there has been a move away from large software engineering approaches to the development of interactive systems towards 'agile' development methods. These are designed to produce effective systems of high quality that are fit for purpose, but without the huge overhead associated with the planning and documentation of a large IT (information technology) project.

There are a number of competing methods, but probably the best known comes from DSDM, a not-for-profit consortium of software development companies. Their system, called Atern, is fully documented, showing how software can be developed in small teams. There is still plenty of debate about how well these methods, such as extreme programming (Beck and Andres, 2004), fit in with human-centred approaches, but many of the methods do promote participation between developers and stakeholders. In particular, Obendorf and Finck (2008) describe a method bringing together agile methods and scenario-based design.

3.2 Developing personas and scenarios

In order to guide the design process, designers need to think about the PACT elements (introduced in Chapter 2). The people who will use the system are represented by personas: profiles of the different types, or archetypes, of people the designer is designing for. Activities and the contexts in which they will occur are envisioned through scenarios of use. Different concrete scenarios can be used to envision how different technologies could function to achieve the overall purpose of the system. Personas and scenarios are developed through the understanding process, using any of a wide range of methods (discussed in Chapter 7), and through undertaking a PACT analysis. Almost inevitably, personas and scenarios evolve together as thinking about people involves thinking about what they want to do, and thinking about activities involves thinking about who will be undertaking them!

Personas

Personas are concrete representations of the different types of people that the system or service is being designed for. Personas should have a name, some background and, importantly, some goals and aspirations. Alan Cooper introduced the idea of personas in the late 1990s (Cooper, 1999) and they have gained rapid acceptance as a way of capturing knowledge about the people the system or service is targeted at. In the latest edition of his book (Cooper et al., 2007), he links personas very closely with his ideas of goal-directed design. Personas want to be able to do things using your system. They want to achieve their aims, they want to undertake meaningful activities using the system that the designer will produce. Designers need to recognize that they are not designing for themselves. Designers create personas so that they can envisage whom they are designing for. They create personas so that they can put themselves in other people's shoes.

As any new system is likely to be used by different types of people, it is important to develop several different personas. For example, in designing a website for people interested in the author Robert Louis Stevenson (described in more detail in Chapter 14), we developed personas for a school teacher in Germany, a university lecturer from the UK, a child in Africa and a Stevenson enthusiast from the USA. Such a diverse group of people have very different goals and aspirations, and differ in all the ways – physically, psychologically and in terms of the usage they would make of the site (see Chapter 2).

Scenarios

Scenarios are stories about people undertaking activities in contexts using technologies. They appear in a variety of forms throughout interactive systems design and are a key component of many approaches to design.

Scenarios have been used in software engineering, interactive systems design and human–computer interaction work for many years. More recently, scenario-based design has emerged as an important approach to the design of interactive systems in the twenty-first century (Alexander and Maiden, 2004).

One of the main proponents of scenario-based design is John Carroll, and his book *Making Use* (2000) remains an excellent introduction to the philosophy underlying the approach. In it he illustrates how scenarios are used to deal with the inherent difficulty of doing design. Drawing on the activity–technology cycle (Figure 2.1) to show the position in product development, he argues that scenarios are effective at dealing with five key problems of design (Figure 3.3):

- The external factors that constrain design such as time constraints, lack of resources, having to fit in with existing designs and so on.
- Design moves have many effects and create many possibilities, i.e. a single design decision can have an impact in many areas and these need to be explored and evaluated.

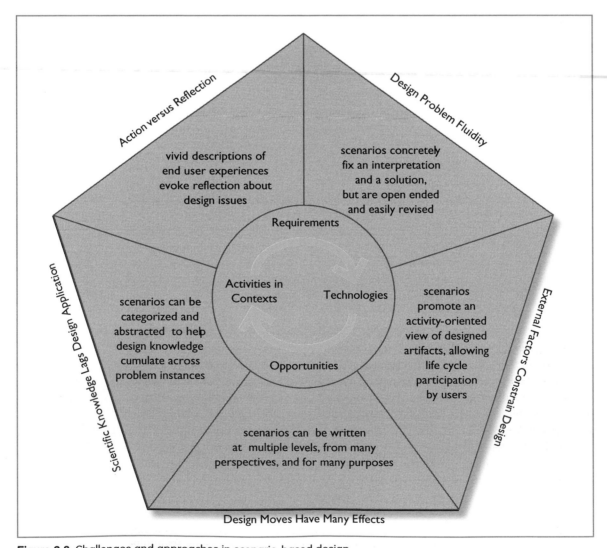

Figure 3.3 Challenges and approaches in scenario-based design

(Source: After John M. Carroll. *Making Use: Scenario-based Design of Human-Computer Interactions*. Fig. 3.2, p. 69 © 2000 Massachusetts Institute of Technology, by permission of the MIT Press)

- How scientific knowledge and generic solutions lag behind specific situations. This point concerns generalities. In other design disciplines, general design solutions to general design problems have evolved over the years. In interactive systems design this does not happen because the technology changes as soon as, or even before, general solutions have been discovered.
- The importance of reflection and action in design.
- The slippery nature of design problems.

Our scenario-based design method is presented in the next section. Below are a few examples of how we have used personas and scenarios in a recent project. Some are quite detailed, others are single snapshots of interactions used to explore design options.

Example: Companions

We have recently been looking at a novel form of interaction that goes under the title of 'companions'. Companions are seen as an intelligent, personalized, multimodal interface to the Internet. Companions know their 'owners' and adapt the interaction to personalized interests, preferences and emotional state. In investigating the companions concept we have developed a number of persons and scenarios.

A health and fitness companion (HFC), for example, would help provide advice and companionship for people in the domain of health and fitness. We explored the idea in a two-day workshop attended by a number of the project partners. During and subsequent to this workshop, three personas were developed to explore the various needs of people with differing lifestyles, levels of fitness and exercise regimes. These are shown in Figures 3.4, 3.5 and 3.6.

One central theme of the explorations concerned the motivational approaches that would be suitable for different scenarios and personas. The Sandy persona (Figure 3.4), for example, would need more encouragement and persuasion to exercise than the Mari persona (Figure 3.5), perhaps by preventing a recorded television programme from being shown until training is completed. Another aspect, concerning social networking, was explored through the Bjorn persona (Figure 3.6). Thus the personas were developed to reflect particular design issues and values. The whole issue of persuasion technologies is a difficult one for interaction design.

BOX 3.3

Captology

B. Fogg introduced the idea of persuasion technologies, or 'captology' as he terms it, in the late 1990s. It is a controversial idea. The basic aim of captology is to persuade people to do things they otherwise would not do. At first sight this looks somewhat immoral. Who are we, as designers, to persuade people to do something they don't want to do? However, we can see examples, such as the Sandy persona, where persuading him to exercise is for his own good. We also need to persuade people to take precautions if things are dangerous. I am quite happy that a software system persuaded me to save my work before the system crashed (on the other hand, why did the system not just save it for me?). Persuasion is 'a non-coercive attempt to change attitudes or behaviors of people' (Fogg *et al.* 2007). However, if this is persuading me to buy something that I cannot afford, then it is not good at all, whether it is non-coercive or not. This is an area of HCI where ethics and values must be taken seriously.

In another exploration we looked at the concept of a companion to deal with digital photos. Such a companion would be functional in helping organize, edit and share photos, but would also be a conversational partner. We envisaged a companion that could discuss photos with its owner and perhaps reminisce about events and people.

Sandy

- age 46
- drives a lot
- drinks and eats too much
- recently divorced
- children in early 20s
- had recent health scare (suspected heart attack which was actually angina)
- kids have bought him a HFC

1. We meet Sandy in a hospital room, he's being visited by his kids.
2. They are worried about his health, he does little exercise and since his wife left him his diet has become appalling.
3. They give him a HFC (what is this?!) which will combine with his current home system. They explain that it's intended to help raise his general level of fitness, monitor his health and set and maintain a healthy balanced diet.
4. They all leave the hospital and Sandy starts the configuration.
5. Being ex-army Sandy decides that a tough-love drill instructor personality would suit him best (he's on board with the fact that he needs to get healthy), so he selects Alf, a no-nonsense archetype companion character.
6. He opens his exercise regime to be accessible by his children, on their request, as he feels this will be an added incentive for him to exercise.
7. Configuration involved biometrics such as weight, height, etc., allowing Alf to suggest appropriate training and diet.
8. It's aim is to understand whether the owner is in bad condition needing to get better, wanting to maintain current health or aim for high performance.
9. Alf reprimands bad behaviour (such as buying unhealthy food), nags when he doesn't exercise, but offers positive motivation when he does.

Figure 3.4 The Sandy persona for HFC scenario

Mari

- age 23
- aerobics instructor
- training seriously for first marathon
- her usual training partner has moved away
- she leads a wild social life and tends to burn the candle at both ends
- she's got a targeted schedule
- companion is very proactive in pace making and motivation

1. She's set up a long-term schedule with her HFC to enable her to run her first marathon in under 4 hours.
2. This includes target goals such as what times she should be running long distances by which stage of the regime.
3. The HFC adapts to maintain the regime when Mari's social circumstance impacts her ability to train.
4. If she runs too far or too fast the companion will advise that this may have a negative impact on her training and may result in potential injury.
5. Explicit instructions in real time run ('ok, now we're gonna push hard for 2 minutes....ok, well done, let's take it easy for the next 5....etc.').
6. The HFC has access to her social schedule (through social companion?) and suggests going to a party the night before a long run may not be a great idea.
7. At the actual marathon her HFC becomes a motivating force and gives her real-time advice (eg, 'there's a hill coming up, pace yourself', it knows this from a run plug-in she bought for the HFC).

Figure 3.5 The Mari persona for HFC scenario

Bjorn

- Age 32
- Office worker (ad account manager)
- No children, lives alone
- Dog died (used to walk it for exercise)
- Starting to put on weight
- Used to play football at university, much less active now
- Active social life
- 'I want to stay fit, but on my own time and fitting in to my own schedule'

1. Home from work, he was meant to go out the previous evening but got invited out to a dinner party instead. This evening is now free, so he decides to go for a run.
2. He's in his living room and sets up for his run. This involves:
   - route choice
   - exercise level, eg easy jog or hard run (specific pacing feedback choice, eg within PB)
   - music choice
   - disturbability status (eg, open to contact/running partner)
   - weather
   - (warm up/stretching?)
3. He gets changed and leaves the house, the handover is transparent from living room companion to mobile device-based companion and is aware of all Bjorn's choices regarding run setup.
4. Just as he's about to begin, the sun breaks through the clouds and Bjorn decides he'd rather go for a longer run than initially selected in his living room; this change must be facilitated through his mobile companion device. Selective rather than creative process (eg, chose run three on route 2).
5. He starts running hard.
6. Asked whether he's warmed up as he's running above a warm-up rate.
7. He slows down to a more gentle jog and reaches his start point.
8. A touch of the device indicates he's starting his run.
9. Music begins.
10. Pace-setting tactile feedback begins.
11. Midway through run he's informed that Julie is also running in the woods and has set her HFC at open to running partners (this is a closed list of the pre-set social network that Bjorn belongs to).
12. He slows down and runs on the spot and sends her a greeting, asking if she'd like to join him; she says yes.
13. She catches up and the companion automatically reconfigures his pacing settings to match hers.
14. After a circuit they part ways and Bjorn heads home.
15. On entering the house Bjorn warms down and stretches which induces a brief summary on his mobile device whilst the detailed data from his run is transparently transferred to his home network.
16. He walks into the kitchen to grab a glass of water and plan what to make for dinner. His home companion notes that he went for a long run today so he must be hungry, and suggests some recipes based on what he has in his fridge: 'how about the steak, it goes out of date tomorrow'. Nothing takes his fancy so he asks the companion to search online whilst he has a shower. Takes shower, comes down and is presented with some new recipes and the fact that Julie called and asked him for a drink that night.
17. At a later time he asks for an overview of his past three months' exercise. His companion notes that his heart rate is recovering quicker which suggests he's getting fitter, but for the past two weeks he's not been running for as long.

Figure 3.6 The Bjorn persona for HFC scenario

Figure 3.7 illustrates a scenario in which a person has a large collection of photographs and wishes to search for a specific image from a recent trip. One feature of this scenario was to explore different modalities for the companion. The interaction employs both speech and touch depending on the activity being undertaken. For example, it is much quicker to specify specific search parameters through speech than by typing or clicking a series of check boxes (part 2 in the scenario). However, when it comes to flicking through the search-generated group or applying certain other editorial functional tasks such as scaling and cropping, touch

1. The user is moving from a standard view of their photos to a search mode. This is a **voice** driven function.

> OK, I need to find the perfect picture to email. **Open search.**

2. Here the user narrows down the field by establishing a search parameter again by voice. Note that the user could search for any metadata parameter or combination of parameters that the system has established. Indeed the system could proactively suggest additional ones.

> **Show me all my photos from my trip to Rome.**

3. Having used voice to establish the smaller field, the user now applies **touch** to quickly flick through the pictures. Additional touch functionality could include scaling, cropping or editing.

> Hmm, there's a few here, good job I can flick through quickly!

4. Having found the photo they want to send, the user now combines speech with touch to indicate that the gesture of flicking to the left means email that specific image to the user's uncle.

> Aha, that's perfect! **Send this to my uncle** please.

Figure 3.7 An scenario of multimodal interaction with a photo companion

becomes the more natural interaction. For example, it's quicker to drag a finger back and forth to resize an image in a serendipitous or haphazard fashion than it is to say, 'Make that image a little bigger . . . bit bigger . . . bit bigger . . . no, that's too big . . . bit smaller . . . too small' and so on. However, for specific categorial edits speech may be best, for example 'Make this image 4 by 6 inches and print'. The true power of the interaction experience comes from the considered use of both in conjunction.

In another scenario we were looking at environmental influence on the interaction. For example, Figure 3.8 shows the potential for moving between displays. Small displays (e.g. digital photoframes) have a more limited touch capability than a larger display (in the case of Figure 3.8 an interactive coffee table). Figure 3.9 illustrates a further option, namely that of using a display that is simply too far from the person to be touched. This in many ways most fairly reflects the current living-room environment. In such a situation physical gesture becomes an appropriate option, either by using one's hands or by wielding an object, such as is used in the Nintendo Wii games console. This allows for parameters such as speed, direction and shape of movement.

Figure 3.8 An example of a multimodal interaction moving between displays from a digital photoframe to a smart coffee table

Figure 3.9 An example of a gesture-based multimodal interaction with a remote screen

3.3 Using scenarios throughout design

Scenarios (and their associated personas) are a core technique for interactive systems design. They are useful in understanding, envisioning, evaluation, and both conceptual and physical design: the four key stages of interactive system design (Figure 3.1). We distinguish four different types of scenario: stories, conceptual scenarios, concrete scenarios and use cases. Stories are the real-world experiences of people. Conceptual scenarios are more abstract descriptions in which some details have been stripped away. Concrete scenarios are generated from abstract scenarios by adding specific design decisions and technologies and, once completed, these can be represented as use cases. Use cases are formal descriptions that can be given to programmers. At different stages of the design process, scenarios are helpful in understanding current practice and any problems or difficulties that people may be having, in generating and testing ideas, in documenting and communicating ideas to others and in evaluating designs.

The place of the different types of scenario and the processes and products of the design process are illustrated in Figure 3.10. The lines joining the types of scenario indicate the relationships between them. Many stories will be represented by a few conceptual scenarios. However, each conceptual scenario may generate many concrete scenarios. Several concrete scenarios will be represented by a single use case. The difference between these types is elaborated below.

Figure 3.10 also illustrates three critical processes involved in design and how they interact with the different scenario types. Designers abstract from the details of stories to arrive at conceptual scenarios. They specify design constraints on conceptual scenarios to arrive at concrete scenarios. Finally they formalize the design ideas as use cases.

Stories

→ Chapter 7 discusses techniques for getting stories

Stories are the real-world experiences, ideas, anecdotes and knowledge of people. These may be captured in any form and comprise small snippets of activities and the contexts in which they occur. This could include videos of people engaged in an activity, diary entries, photographs, documents, the results of observations and interviews and so on. People's stories are rich in context. Stories also capture many seemingly trivial details that are usually left out if people are asked to provide more formal representations of what they do.

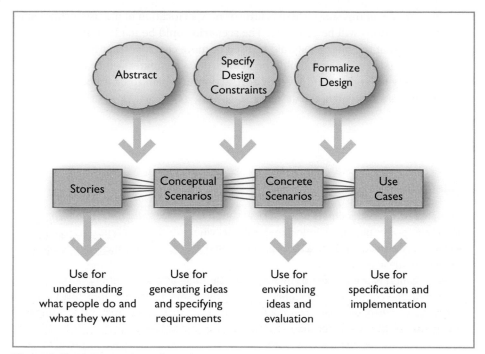

Figure 3.10 Scenarios throughout design

Example

Here is a story from someone describing what happened last time he made an appointment to see his local doctor.

> 'I needed to make an appointment for Kirsty, my little one. It wasn't urgent – she had been having a lot of bad earache every time she had a cold – but I did want to see Dr Fox since she's so good with the children. And of course ideally it had to be when Kirsty was out of school and I could take time off work. I rang the surgery and the receptionist told me that the next appointment for Dr Fox was the next Tuesday afternoon. That was no good since Tuesday is one of my really busy days, so I asked when the next one was. The receptionist said Thursday morning. That meant making Kirsty late for school but I agreed because they sounded very busy – the other phone kept ringing in the background – and I was in a hurry myself. It was difficult to suggest a better time without knowing which appointments were still free.'

Conceptual scenarios

Conceptual scenarios are more abstract than stories. Much of the context is stripped away during the process of **abstraction** (see Box 3.4) and similar stories are combined. Conceptual scenarios are particularly useful for generating design ideas and for *understanding* the requirements of the system.

Example

Once the designer has accumulated a collection of stories, common elements will start to emerge. In this case a number of stories such as the one above result in the conceptual scenario below, describing some requirements for a computerized appointments system.

Booking an appointment

People with any degree of basic computer skills will be able to contact the doctors' surgery at any time via the Internet and see the times which are free for each doctor. They can book a time and receive confirmation of the appointment.

As you can see, at this stage, there is little or no specification of precise technologies or how the functions will be provided. The scenario could be made more abstract by not specifying that the Internet should be used or more concrete (that is, less abstract) by specifying that the booking should be made from a computer rather than a mobile phone. Finding an appropriate level of abstraction at which to describe things for a given purpose is a key skill of the designer.

BOX 3.4

Abstraction

The process of abstraction is one of classification and aggregation: moving from the details of specific people undertaking specific activities in a specific context using a particular piece of technology to a more general description that still manages to catch the essence of the activity.

Aggregation is the process of treating a whole thing as a single entity rather than looking at the components of something. In most domains, for example, one would aggregate a screen, processor, disk drive, keyboard and mouse and treat this as a single thing – a computer – rather than focusing on the components. However, in another situation one of the components – processor speed, or disk size, say – may prove to be critical and so it would be better to have two aggregations: fast computers and slow computers, say.

Classification is the process of recognizing that things can be collected together, so that dealing with the class of things is simpler (more abstract) than dealing with the individual things. There are no set ways to classify things, so the analyst has to work with the stories that have been gathered and with the people themselves to decide which things belong together and why.

Between them, aggregation and classification produce abstractions. Of course, there are different degrees of abstraction and it is one of the skills of a designer to settle upon an appropriate level. The most abstract level is to treat everything simply as a 'thing' and every activity as 'doing something', but such an abstract representation is not usually very useful.

Concrete scenarios

Each conceptual scenario may generate lots of concrete scenarios. When designers are working on a particular problem or issue they will often identify some feature that applies only under certain circumstances. At this point they may develop a more specific elaboration of the scenario and link it to the original. Thus one reasonably abstract scenario may spawn several more concrete elaborations which are useful for exploring particular issues. Notes that draw attention to possible design features and problems can be added to scenarios.

Concrete scenarios also begin to dictate a particular interface design and a particular allocation of functions between people and devices. Concrete scenarios are particularly useful for prototyping and envisioning design ideas and for evaluation because they are more prescriptive about some aspects of the technology. However, there is not a clean break between conceptual and concrete scenarios. The more specific the scenario is about some aspects, the more concrete it is.

Example

In this example, decisions have now been taken concerning drop-down menus, the fact that the next two weeks' details are to be shown, and so on. However, the notes following the scenario show that there are many design decisions still to be taken.

Booking an appointment/01

Andy Dalreach needs a doctor's appointment for his young daughter Kirsty in the next week or so. The appointment needs to be outside school-time and Andy's core working hours, and ideally with Dr Fox, who is the children's specialist. Andy uses a PC and the Internet at work, so has no difficulty in running up the appointments booking system. He logs in [1] and from a series of drop-down boxes, chooses to have free times for Dr Fox [2] displayed for the next two weeks [the scenario would continue to describe how Andy books the appointment and receives confirmation].

Notes to booking an appointment/01

1 Is logging in necessary? Probably, to discourage bogus access to the system, but check with the surgery.
2 Free times can be organized by doctor, by time of day, or by next available time. Drop-down boxes will save screen space but may present problems for less experienced users or those with poor eyesight.

Use cases

A use case describes the interaction between people (or other 'actors') and devices. It is a case of how the system is used and hence needs to describe what people do and what the system does. Each use case covers many slight variations in circumstances – many concrete scenarios. The lines in Figure 3.10 indicate how many concrete scenarios result, after the process of specification and coding, in a few use cases.

Before use cases can be specified, tasks and functions have to be allocated to humans or to the device. The specification of use cases both informs and is informed by the task/ function allocation process. This is the interaction design part of physical design.

Finally, all the design issues will be resolved and the set of concrete scenarios is then used as the basis of the design. A set of use cases can be produced which specifies the complete functionality of the system and the interactions that will occur. There are a number of different ways of representing use cases – from very abstract diagrams to detailed 'pseudo code'. Figure 3.11 shows the 'booking an appointment' use case in a typical format.

→ See also Chapter 11 on task analysis

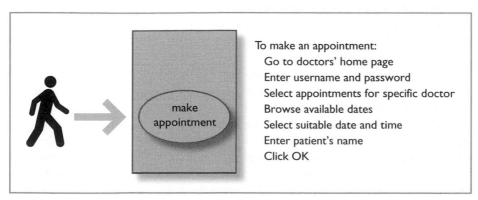

To make an appointment:
  Go to doctors' home page
  Enter username and password
  Select appointments for specific doctor
  Browse available dates
  Select suitable date and time
  Enter patient's name
  Click OK

Figure 3.11 Use case for booking an appointment

Use cases

Despite the fact that use cases have been a core element of software engineering meth-ods since the late 1980s, the concept remains elusive and different authors define a use case in different ways. In a section called 'use cases undefined', Constantine and Lockwood (2001) rage against the lack of clear definition for such a critical term. The definition used in the Unified Modeling Language (UML) – an attempt to provide com-monly agreed specification concepts and notation for software engineering – is too lengthy and obscure to repeat here. Constantine and Lockwood also point out that how the use case is specified – in a sort of pseudo programming code as we have done, or simply using the diagrammatic ellipse and named role as some do, or otherwise – also varies considerably between authors and methods.

It is also the case that use cases are used at different levels of abstraction. Constantine and Lockwood's 'essential use cases' are similar to the conceptual scenarios described here and there are others who base a whole design method on use case modelling. We reserve the term 'use case' for describing an implementable system, i.e. enough inter-face features have been specified, and the allocation of functions between people and the system has been completed, so that the use case describes a coherent sequence of actions between an actor and a system. The term 'actor' is used here because some-times we need to specify use cases between one part of the system (a 'system actor') and another, but usually the actor is a person.

Challenge 3.3

Find a vending machine or other relatively simple device and observe people using it. Write down their stories. Produce one or more conceptual scenarios from the stories.

3.4 A scenario-based design method

The use of the different types of scenario throughout design can be formalized into a scenario-based design method. This is illustrated in Figure 3.12 with, once again, prod-ucts of the design process shown as boxes and processes shown as clouds. Besides the four different types of scenario, four other artefacts are produced during the design process: requirements/problems, scenario corpus, object model and design language. The specification of a system is the combination of all the different products produced during the development process.

Each of the main processes – understanding, envisionment, evaluation and design – is the subject of a chapter in the next part of the book. An important thing to notice is the relationship between specifying design constraints and the use of scenarios. For envisionment and most evaluation, the scenarios have to be made more concrete. This means imposing design constraints. However, this does not mean that the designer needs to design a new physical, concrete scenario each time he or she wants to envision a possible design. It may be that designers imagine a scenario with particular design constraints imposed and this helps them evaluate the design. This sort of 'what if?' gen-eration and evaluation of concrete scenarios is a common and key aspect of design.

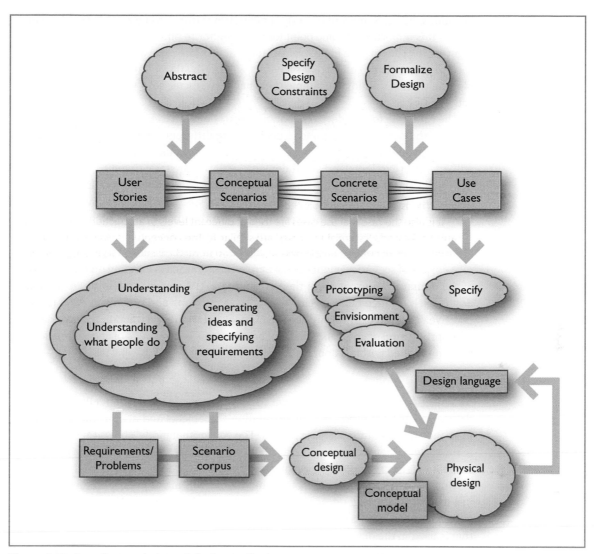

Figure 3.12 Overall scenario-based design method

The key products that have not been discussed so far are: requirements and problems; scenario corpus; conceptual model; and design language. These are briefly introduced below for completeness, but a full understanding will require more in depth study.

→ Further details are given in Chapters 7–10.

Requirements and problems

In the gathering of people's stories and during the analysis and abstraction process, various issues and difficulties will come to light. These help the analyst/designer to establish a list of requirements – qualities or functions that any new product or system should have. For example, in the HFC example, the companion had to be available both at home and when exercising. It needed information about routes and personal preferences. The requirements and problems product is a prioritized list of issues that the system to be designed needs to accommodate.

→ See Chapter 7 on understanding for requirements

Scenario corpus

In our approach we seek to develop a representative and carefully thought-through set, or corpus, of scenarios. Having undertaken some analysis activities designers will have gathered a wide range of user stories. Some of these will be very general and some will be quite specific. Some will be fairly simple, straightforward tasks; others will be more vague. It is important at some point for the designer to pull these disparate experiences together in order to get a high-level, abstract view of the main activities that the product is to support. These conceptual scenarios will often still be grounded in a real example; the trick is to find an example that shares characteristics with a number of other activities.

The rationale for the development of a corpus of scenarios is to uncover the 'dimensions' of the design situation and to demonstrate different aspects of those dimensions. Dimensions include characteristics of the various domains within which the product will operate (e.g. large and small domains, volatile or static domains, etc.), the various media and data types that need to be accommodated and the characteristics of the people who will be using the system. The corpus of scenarios needs to cover all the main functions of the system and the events that trigger the functions. Different types of interaction need to be present along with any key usability issues. The dimensions include different types of content and how that can be structured, issues of style and aesthetics.

➜ The HIC case study is in Chapter 6

A corpus of scenarios might consist of several scenarios depending on the complexity of the domain. For example, in the HIC study we had eleven, and for an MP3 application (which is much more specific – just playing, sorting and organizing MP3 files) we had five. The aim is to specify the scenarios at a level of abstraction that captures an appropriate level of generality that will be useful across the range of characteristics that is demonstrated within a domain.

Conceptual model

➜ Conceptual modelling is covered in Chapter 9

An object or data model results from the process of conceptual modelling, including developing the scenarios and understanding the objects and actions that are evident from the analysis of the scenario corpus. The conceptual model shows the main objects in the system, their attributes and the relationships that exist between them. Conceptual modelling is a very important part of interactive systems design that is often overlooked. Having a clear, well-designed conceptual model will make it easier to design so that people can develop a good, accurate mental model of the system. The conceptual model will also form the basis of the information architecture of a system and of any metaphor that is used in the design.

Design language

➜ We return to this in Chapter 9

The design language produced consists of a set of standard patterns of interaction and all the physical attributes of a design – the colours, shapes, icons and so on. These are brought together with the conceptual actions and objects, and the 'look and feel' of the design is completed. A 'design language' defines the key elements of the design (such as the use of colour, style and types of buttons, sliders and other widgets, etc.) and some principles and rules for putting them together. A consistent design language means that people need learn only a limited number of design elements and then they can cope with a large variety of different situations.

Challenge 3.4

Take a look at the operating system that you use on your computer and identify some key elements of the design language that is used.

Documenting scenarios

Scenarios can become messy, so in order to control the scenarios a structure is needed. We use the PACT framework (people, activities, contexts, technologies) to critique scenarios and to encourage designers to get a good description of the scenario. For each scenario the designer lists the different people who are involved, the activities they are undertaking, the contexts of those activities and the technologies that are being used. We also structure scenario descriptions. Each scenario should be given an introduction. The history and authorship can be recorded, along with a description of how the scenario generalizes (across which domains) and the rationale for the scenario. Each paragraph of each scenario should be numbered for ease of reference and endnotes included where particular design issues are raised. Endnotes are particularly useful in documenting issues raised during the development of the scenario. They are a way of capturing the claims being made about the scenarios (Rosson and Carroll, 2002). Examples of relevant data and media should be collected.

← Chapter 2 describes PACT

Trade-offs and claims analysis

BOX
3.6

Rosson and Carroll (2002) describe an approach to scenario-based design in which scenarios are used throughout the design process and how they help designers to justify the claims that they make about design issues. Design is characterized by trade-offs. There is rarely a simple solution to a problem that solves all the issues. Usually the adoption of one design will mean that something else cannot be achieved. Designers need to document their design decisions so that the trade-offs can be evaluated. Scenarios help by making the rationale for the design explicit. Designers can record the claims that they make about their designs. Claims analysis is an important part of scenario-based design and is used in identifying problems or in thinking through possible future designs (Rosson and Carroll, 2002). The process is simply to identify key features of a scenario and to list good and bad aspects of the design. Rosson and Carroll use a technique of putting a '+' beside good features and a '−' beside bad features. Claims analysis makes the rationale behind a design explicit.

A similar method is to list the design questions, design options and criteria used to make choices, the QOC method (MacLean *et al.*, 1991).

Challenge 3.5

Take a device or system that you have to hand – a mobile phone, a website, a vending machine – and critique the design, focusing on the aspects that are central to its use. Make a list of claims about the design.

When working in a large design team, it is useful to accompany scenarios with real data. This means that different team members can share concrete examples and use these as a focus of discussion. Another key feature of writing scenarios is to think hard about the assumptions that are being made: to make assumptions explicit or deliberately avoid making things explicit in order to provoke debate. In particular, the use of personas can help to focus on specific issues. For example, an elderly woman with arthritis might be one of the personas, thus foregrounding issues of access and the physically impaired interacting with technology.

Finally, with scenarios it is important to provide a very rich context. The guiding principles for scenario writing are people, activities, contexts and technologies.

Example: Scenario MP3/01 – 'How does that song go again?'

This example illustrates how scenarios can be structured and used to think about designs and become part of a corpus. The context for this scenario was the development of a Home Information Centre (HIC). The HIC was envisaged as a new type of information, communication and entertainment device that would look good in the home and, whilst providing similar functions to a computer, would have a novel interface making it far more enjoyable and natural to use.

→ The HIC case study is in Chapter 6

In developing the MP3 player function for the HIC, we explored a number of different scenarios, finally finishing with five that defined the MP3 function corpus. The example here shows the scenario being used to explore requirements and concepts for the HIC. Notice that whilst being quite abstract, it is concrete enough to bring design issues to the fore. Figure 3.13 shows a QOC claims analysis for this scenario.

SCENARIO MP3/01

Title
'How does that song go again?'

Scenario type
Activity scenario

Overview
People = Anne, a single female, computer-literate. Works at home.
Activities = Searching for MP3 tracks.

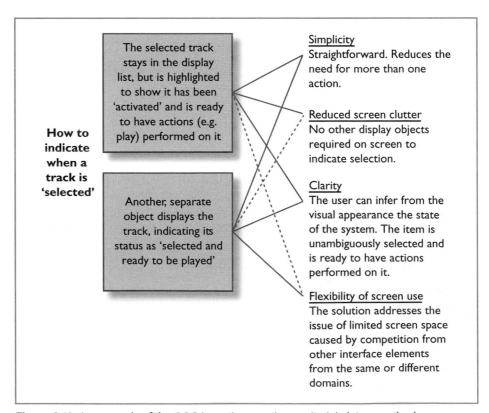

Figure 3.13 An example of the QOC (questions, options, criteria) claims method

Context = Apartment with office/study space where user works from home. HIC is in the kitchen, which is adjacent to the study.

Technology = The HIC and a PC.

Rationale

The substantive activity here is the use of the search function to find a specific MP3 track. The use of different search parameters is described. The user interrogates the HIC using keyboard input; future elaborations might deal with other modalities such as voice input.

P1. Anne is a freelance arts journalist who works mainly from home. She's writing a piece for a national newspaper about singer-songwriters, and is irritated to find she can't remember the lyrics of a particular well-known song she wants to quote in her article. She knows the name of the singer and the song title, but beyond that, her memory is failing her.

P2. She leaves her desk, hoping a break and a cup of coffee will dispel the block. While in the kitchen, she decides she'll check the HIC for new messages [1]. While she is doing this, she realizes the HIC's MP3 player [2] can help her out.

She remembers she has downloaded the song [3] she needs at some time in the past two months or so, and knows it's still in the HIC's memory [4].

P3. She selects the 'play' function (Level 1 of the HIC's actions bar) [5], which takes her down one level in the HIC interface, to where she can see 'MP3 search' [6]. She selects this and the familiar Rolodex interface comes up, asking her to enter some search details. She can search by entering an artist name, track title or music genre – these are all elements of an MP3 track's identity which the HIC can recognize. She is about to enter the artist's name, but realizes she has stored several of this singer's tracks in the HIC; to get a unique search result first time, she enters the track name instead, using the keyboard [7].

P4. The HIC quickly finds the track and asks her [8] if she wants to play it now. She does, and selects this option by touching the screen [9]. The MP3 controller appears on the screen, with the selected track already loaded and ready to play.

P5. She touches the 'play' button and listens. She increases the volume [10]. The lyrics she wants come back to her straight away – she can now go back to her desk. She leaves the HIC on [11] (without thinking).

P6. Later on, she has finished her piece and e-mailed it to her editor. But she wants to hear the song again, as it has sentimental memories for her. Fortunately, she has left the HIC on in MP3 mode. All she needs to do is select 'replay' and the song plays again.

P7. She decides she has put in enough time at the computer for the day, and feels like watching some TV. She chooses the TV device on the HIC and settles down to watch the early evening news [12].

Notes to scenario MP3/01

1 Checking messages is peripheral to the MP3 domain, but it is interesting to consider how MP3-related activities fit in with other domains of the HIC. Multiple screen objects will soon start to compete with each other for screen space.

2 'MP3 player' is meant here in the general sense of the MP3 domain – that is, all the functions relating to MP3.

3 How she has done this is not described here – but see scenario MP3/02 for a more detailed account of this activity.

4 The question of how the HIC stores MP3 and other files is a significant one. One of the popular features of the MP3 format is the ease with which files can be shuffled from one platform to another; this will involve frequent use of saving, copying, deleting and other functions. This may imply the need for some sort of 'File Manager' function in the HIC (cf. scenarios MP3/02, /03, /04).

5 The Actions Bar is now a well-established part of the HIC prototype. Here, Anne goes one level down the HIC's navigation hierarchy to get to the MP3 domain, and her point of entry is the 'play' icon, found on the Actions Bar. But there may be other points of entry too – say, from a 'Favourites' menu or similar.

6   The MP3 domain may be made up of different modules – a 'player' with functional controls, a search function, track lists, and so on. Some or all of these may be present on screen at one time; this raises the question of what the 'default' configuration will be: only the basic functional controls? All the different modules? And how will the user call these up or dismiss them as required?

7   Consider other modalities too: handwritten using a stylus and pressure pad? Voice input?

8   How is the search result presented to Anne? It may be in the form of a list, with the results containing the parameters she gave the HIC. The search may return several results, and there should be a way for her to unambiguously select a track from a list. This could be tricky unless the text is at a good size and spacing for touching on a screen – unless some other selection method is used.

9   She is close to the screen – but could she select the option remotely too?

10   Perhaps the HIC could sample the level of background noise in the area, and adjust the playback volume automatically.

11   Is there a screen saver?

12   What happens to the MP3 interface when the TV comes on? Presumably the whole of the HIC's information space will be filled by the TV image. Other functions and controls will need to be cleared from the screen (perhaps returning automatically when the TV is turned off). Or they could be reduced greatly in size, and put onto a display bar on the periphery of the screen. Perhaps there could be a 'bring to front' command (operated remotely, or by voice?) to make other controls available while the TV was still active.

Cross-referencing scenario types

Another aspect of documentation that is useful is to cross-reference the stories to the conceptual scenarios, through the concrete examples and finally to the use cases. A simple Web-based system can be developed, as illustrated in Figure 3.14.

Other researchers have suggested similar ideas that capture the multiple views necessary to see how scenarios and claims work together to provide a rich understanding of how a design finished as it did.

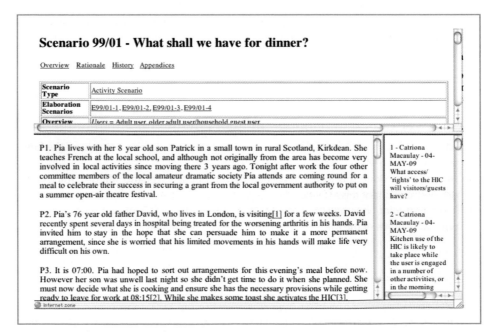

Figure 3.14 The scenario web

Summary and key points

The design of interactive systems is concerned with people, the activities they are undertaking, the contexts of those activities and the technologies that are used. This chapter has introduced the main elements of design – understanding, envisionment, design and evaluation – and how scenario-based design and the development of personas can be used to guide the designer. Scenarios and their different uses in this process have been explored.

- Scenarios are stories about the interactions between people, activities, contexts and technologies.

- Scenarios offer an effective way of exploring and representing activities, enabling the designer to generate ideas, consider solutions and communicate with others.

- Scenarios are used throughout the design process and, along with the requirements and problems, conceptual design and design language can form part of the specification of the system.

Exercises

1 Find someone using some technology to do something and observe what they do. Now write down the story associated with that activity. Abstract a conceptual scenario from this one experience, by removing the contextual detail and other details about the specific interface to the technology. Now think of an alternative design for a device that would allow someone to undertake a similar activity and generate a concrete scenario based on these design constraints. Finally, specify this as a use case.

2 Develop a scenario corpus for people using a vending machine. Consider the dimensions of the usage, the contexts for the interaction and the range of people that you would want to consider.

 ## Further reading

Cooper, A., Reiman, R. and Cronin, D. (2007) *About Face 3: The Essentials of Interactive Design.* **Wiley, Hoboken, NJ.** *Cooper et al. give an insightful and enjoyable tour through some of the worst aspects of interactive systems design and introduce their approach, which focuses on developing personas and taking a goal-oriented approach to design.*

Rosson, M.-B. and Carroll, J. (2012) Scenario-based design. In J.A. Jacko (ed.) *The Human-Computer Interaction Handbook: Fundamentals, Evolving Technologies and Emerging Applications,* **3rd edn.** CRC Press, Taylor and Francis, Boca Raton, FL.

Winograd, T. (ed.) (1996) *Bringing Design to Software.* **ACM Press, New York.** *This book contains a number of interesting articles from interactive systems designers and is essential reading for all would-be interactive systems designers.*

Getting ahead

Interactions is an excellent journal focusing on interactive systems design.

Carroll, J.M. (ed.) (1995) *Scenario-based Design.* Wiley, New York.

Carroll, J.M. (2000) *Making Use: Scenario-based Design of Human–Computer Interactions.* MIT Press, Cambridge, MA.

Rosson, M.-B. and Carroll, J. (2002) *Usability Engineering.* Morgan Kaufmann, San Francisco, CA.

John (Jack) Carroll has been hugely influential in the area of human–computer interaction over many years and with his wife, Mary-Beth Rosson, has written extensively on scenario-based design. The first of his books is a collection of papers showing how the scenario concept appears in a variety of guises throughout human–computer interaction and software engineering. The second is compiled from many of his writings and presents a thoughtful and coherent approach to developing systems using scenarios. It illustrates how scenarios are appropriate in all the stages of systems development. The third is a practical design book.

 Web links

There are some good white papers on Jared Spools' website, some of which cover personas. See **www.uie.com**

The accompanying website has links to relevant websites. Go to **www.pearsoned.co.uk/benyon**

 **Comments on challenges**

Challenge 3.1

When watching a movie on a VCR, the TV would often automatically select the appropriate TV channel and the VCR would start playing automatically. Thus the function of 'start film' was allocated to the device, and often the function of 'select VCR channel' was allocated to the device. With DVDs the human often has to select the appropriate channel and has to select 'start film', or 'play movie', from a menu. So people now have extra tasks to perform. Moreover, the default option on DVDs is often not 'play movie', so the person has to navigate to the appropriate option, giving them even more tasks. PVRs are different again, requiring people to undertake several tasks to watch a film. With huge numbers of films, clips and longer parts of films, YouTube requires people to undertake much more searching and selecting. When allocating functions to people or to devices, think hard about what tasks you are forcing people to undertake.

Challenge 3.2

A conceptual design would focus on the idea for the room. You may think it would be nice to have a conservatory or a downstairs toilet and proceed from there. You would evaluate the idea, perhaps by looking at some physical prototypes at a large store or at a friend's house. This might help to define the requirements, such as the size of the conservatory, where you would locate it and so on. Starting with a physical design, you might see something at a friend's or on television and this might trigger the idea that it would be a nice thing to have. Once you have the concept, proceed as above. Seeing a picture in a book is another example of an envisioned solution starting the process off. On other occasions the process might be started by some requirements. You may feel that you need a study, a new room for a baby, or somewhere to sit in the sun in the winter and it might be these requirements that begin the process. Notice how, wherever the process starts from, the next step will be some evaluation.

Challenge 3.3

A man wearing an overcoat and carrying a backpack came up to the machine and stared at it for two or three minutes. Whilst he was doing this two younger men came up behind him and were trying to look over his shoulder. Finally, he put his hand in his pocket and inserted some money. He pressed two buttons, B and 7, and watched as a packet of crisps was deposited in the tray.

You can imagine a few more stories such as this, resulting in a conceptual scenario along the lines of 'A person comes up to the machine, studies the instructions and what is available, inserts money, presses two buttons and retrieves the goods'.

Challenge 3.4

Key aspects of the design language are standard features of things such as windows and the different types of windows (some that are resizable, some that are not, etc.). Other features include the design of menus, dialogue boxes, alert boxes and so on. The colours are also consistent and chosen to evoke different feelings in people.

Challenge 3.5

Of course, this will depend on the device you have chosen and on how you approach the critique. The design principles (Chapter 4) are a good way to think about designs. A critique of a vending machine, for example, might include the claims:

✓ Useful for out-of-hours sales

✗ Limited selection of goods

✓ Quick interaction

✗ Does not always give change

✗ Mis-operation results in lengthy and time-consuming complaints

✓ High service costs.

Chapter 4
Usability

Contents

Aims

Usability has always been the central pursuit of human–computer interaction (HCI). The original definition of usability is that systems should be easy to use, easy to learn, flexible and should engender a good attitude in people (Shackel, 1990). As the variety of people, activities, contexts and technologies of interactive system design has increased, so this definition, whilst still being valid, hides many important issues. For example, accessibility is now a key design aim, as is sustainability. The goals of usability are now primarily seen as concerned with efficiency and effectiveness of systems.

After studying this chapter you should be able to:

- Understand the key issues and concepts of access
- Understand the principles underlying usability
- Understand the key issues of acceptability
- Understand the general principles of good interactive systems design.

4.1 Introduction

Good design cannot be summed up in a simple way and nor can the activities of the interactive systems designer, particularly one who takes a human-centred approach to design. One view might say, 'The interactive systems designer aims to produce systems and products that are accessible, usable, socially and economically acceptable'. Another view might say, 'The interactive systems designer aims to produce systems that are learnable, effective and accommodating'. A third view could be, 'The aim of the interactive systems designer is to balance the PACT elements with respect to a domain'. All of these views are valid. In this chapter we explore these complementary views of good design. We also develop some high-level design principles that can guide designers and be used to evaluate design ideas. Finally, we put these ideas into practice by looking at some examples of good and bad design across different design contexts.

Accessibility concerns removing the barriers that would otherwise exclude some people from using the system at all. Usability refers to the quality of the interaction in terms of parameters such as time taken to perform tasks, number of errors made and the time to become a competent user. Clearly a system must be accessible before it is usable. A system may be assessed as highly usable according to some usability evaluation criteria, but may still fail to be adopted or to satisfy people. Acceptability refers to fitness for purpose in the context of use. It also covers personal preferences that contribute to users 'taking to' an artefact, or not.

4.2 Accessibility

Access to physical spaces for people with disabilities has long been an important legal and ethical requirement and this is now becoming increasingly so for information spaces. Legislation such as the UK's Equality Act 2010 and Section 508 in the USA now requires software to be accessible. The United Nations and the World Wide Web Consortium (W3C) have declarations and guidelines on ensuring that everyone can get access to information that is delivered through software technologies. With an increasingly wide range of computer users and technologies, designers need to focus on the demands their designs make on people's abilities. Designers have to design for the elderly and for children. Newell (1995) points out that the sorts of issues that face an ordinary person in an extraordinary environment (such as under stress, time pressures, etc.) are often similar to the issues that face a person with disabilities in an ordinary environment.

People will be excluded from accessing interactive systems for any of a number of reasons:

- Physically people can be excluded because of inappropriate siting of equipment or through input and output devices making excessive demands on their abilities. For example, an ATM may be positioned too high for a person in a wheelchair to reach, a mouse may be too big for a child's hand or a mobile phone may be too fiddly for someone with arthritis to use.
- Conceptually people may be excluded because they cannot understand complicated instructions or obscure commands or they cannot form a clear mental model of the system.
- Economically people are excluded if they cannot afford some essential technology.

- Cultural exclusion results from designers making inappropriate assumptions about how people work and organize their lives. For example, using a metaphor based on American football would exclude those who do not understand the game.
- Social exclusion can occur if equipment is unavailable at an appropriate time and place or if people are not members of a particular social group and cannot understand particular social mores or messages.

Overcoming these barriers to access is a key design consideration. Two main approaches to designing for accessibility are 'design for all' and inclusive design. Design for all (also known as universal design) goes beyond the design of interactive systems and applies to all design endeavours. It is grounded in a certain philosophical approach to design encapsulated by an international design community (see Box 4.1). Inclusive design is based on four premises:

- Varying ability is not a special condition of the few but a common characteristic of being human and we change physically and intellectually throughout our lives.
- If a design works well for people with disabilities, it works better for everyone.
- At any point in our lives, personal self-esteem, identity and well-being are deeply affected by our ability to function in our physical surroundings with a sense of comfort, independence and control.
- Usability and aesthetics are mutually compatible.

→ Aesthetics in interaction design is discussed in Chapter 5

BOX 4.1

Principles of universal design*

Equitable use. The design does not disadvantage or stigmatize any group of users.

Flexibility in use. The design accommodates a wide range of individual preferences and abilities.

Simple, intuitive use. Use of the design is easy to understand, regardless of the user's experience, knowledge, language skills, or current concentration level.

Perceptible information. The design communicates necessary information effectively to the user, regardless of ambient conditions or the user's sensory abilities.

Tolerance for error. The design minimizes hazards and the adverse consequences of accidental or unintended actions.

Low physical effort. The design can be used efficiently and comfortably, and with a minimum of fatigue.

Size and space for approach and use. Appropriate size and space are provided for approach, reach, manipulation, and use, regardless of the user's body size, posture, or mobility.

* Compiled by advocates of universal design, listed in alphabetical order: Bettye Rose Connell, Mike Jones, Ron Mace, Jim Mueller, Abir Mullick, Elaine Ostroff, Jon Sanford, Ed Steinfeld, Molly Story, Gregg Vanderheiden.
© Centre for Universal Design, College of Design, North Carolina State University

---

Inclusive design is a more pragmatic approach that argues that there will often be reasons (e.g. technical or financial) why total inclusion is unattainable. Benyon *et al.* (2001) recommend undertaking an inclusivity analysis that ensures that inadvertent exclusion will be minimized and common characteristics that cause exclusion and which are relatively cheap to fix will be identified. Distinguishing between fixed and changing user characteristics, they present a decision tree (see Figure 4.1). We all suffer from disabilities from time to time (e.g. a broken arm) that affect our abilities to use interactive systems.

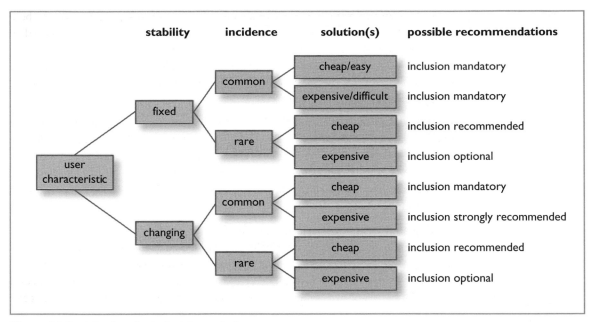

Figure 4.1 Decision tree for inclusivity analysis
(Source: after Benyon *et al.* (2001), Figure 2.3, p. 38)

As a way of ensuring an accessible system, designers should:

- include people with special needs in requirements analysis and testing of existing systems;
- consider whether new features affect users with special needs (positively or negatively) and note this in the specification;
- take account of guidelines – include evaluation against guidelines;
- include special needs users in usability testing and beta tests.

There are a number of assistive technologies, such as Web browsers that read Web pages, and screen enlargers which allow people to set and move the area of focus. Voice input is increasingly available not just for text entry but also as a substitute for mouse/keyboard control, and keyboard filters can compensate for tremor, erratic motion and slow response time. Indeed, there are many highly specialist methods for input and output for people with various disabilities. For example, Majaranta *et al.* (2009) describe a system for typing input through gazing at particular letters.

In the MS Windows operating system there is an Accessibility Option (under the control panel) that allows the setting of keyboard, sound, visual warnings and captions for sounds. The display can be altered, including setting a high contrast, and mouse settings can be adjusted. The Universal Access control panel on the Mac offers similar options (Figure 4.2). A screen reader produces synthesized voice output for text displayed on the computer screen, as well as for keystrokes entered on the keyboard. Voice-based browsers use the same technology as screen reading software, but are designed specifically for Internet use (Figure 4.3).

Web accessibility is a particularly important area as many websites exclude people who are not fit and able. The W4A conference and ACM's SIGACCESS group contain many specialist papers and discussions. Bobby is an automated tool that checks Web pages for conformance to the W3C standards. However, in a study of university websites, Kane *et al.* (2007) found serious accessibility problems, showing that there is still some way to go before these issues are overcome.

To a large extent, design for all is just good design. The aim is to design to cater for the widest range of human abilities. By considering access issues early in the design

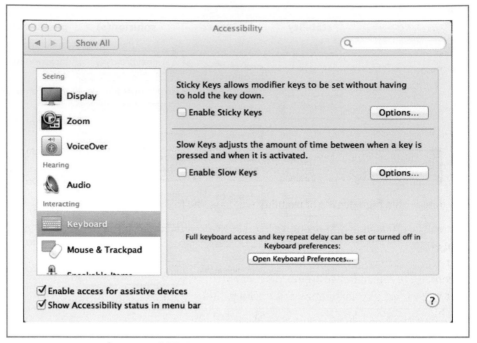

Figure 4.2 Options for accessibility keyboard settings

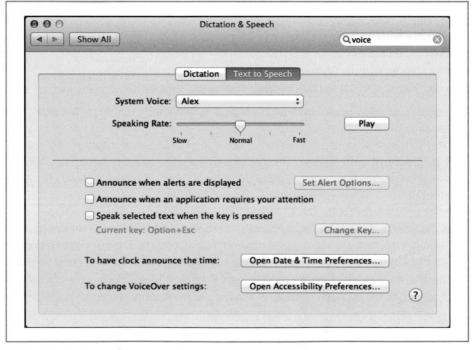

Figure 4.3 A choice of voices (OS X)

process, the overall design will be better for everyone. Stephanidis (2001) provides a range of views on how this can be accomplished, from new computer 'architectures' that can accommodate different interfaces for different people, to better requirements generation processes, consideration of alternative input and output devices and the adoption of international standards.

Challenge 4.1

The UK government is considering introducing electronic access to a variety of social benefits (such as unemployment benefit, housing benefit, etc.). What are some of the access issues involved with this?

4.3 Usability

A system with a high degree of usability will have the following characteristics:

- It will be efficient in that people will be able to do things using an appropriate amount of effort.
- It will be effective in that it contains the appropriate functions and information content, organized in an appropriate manner.
- It will be easy to learn how to do things and remember how to do them after a while.
- It will be safe to operate in the variety of contexts in which it will be used.
- It will have high utility in that it does the things that people want to get done.

Achieving usability requires us to take a human-centred approach to design and to adopt a design approach in which evaluation is central. Some early pioneers of usability, Gould *et al.* (1987), developed the message kiosks for the 1984 Olympic Games. They based their approach on three key principles that Gould and Lewis (1985) had evolved over the previous three years. Their principles were:

← See Section 3.1

- *Early focus on users and tasks*. Designers must first understand who the users will be, in part by studying the nature of the expected work to be accomplished, and in part by making users part of the design team through participative design or as consultants.
- *Empirical measurement*. Early in the development process, intended users' reactions to printed scenarios and user manuals should be observed and measured. Later on they should actually use simulations and prototypes to carry out real work, and their performance and reactions should be observed, recorded and analysed.
- *Iterative design*. When problems are found in user testing, as they will be, they must be fixed. This means design must be iterative: there must be a cycle of design, test and measure, and redesign, repeated as often as necessary. Empirical measurement and iterative design are necessary because designers, no matter how good they are, cannot get it right the first few times (Gould *et al.*, 1987, p. 758).

As a result of their experiences with that project they added a fourth principle, integrated usability:

> All usability factors must evolve together, and responsibility for all aspects of usability should be under one control.   (p. 766)

The development of the Olympic Message System (OMS) is described in detail in Gould *et al.* (1987) and it still makes interesting reading in terms of the different types of testing that were done, from written scenarios of use to 'try-to-destroy-it' tests! However, these classic principles are not advocated by everyone. Cockton (2009), for example, argues that designers need to understand the values that their designs are aiming at and that the sort of advice offered by Gould and Lewis (1985) is dangerous and out of date. Whilst not going as far as that, we would certainly agree that designers need to consider what worth their designs bring to the world!

← PACT is covered in
Chapter 2

BOX 4.2

Value Sensitive Design

Value Sensitive Design is a design approach that aims to account for human values in a principled and comprehensive manner emphasizing the moral perspective, usability and personal preferences. It focuses on three types of investigations.

1 Conceptual investigations concern philosophically informed analyses of the central constructs and issues under investigation.
2 Empirical investigations focus on the human response to the technical artefact, and on the larger social context in which the technology is situated.
3 Technical investigations focus on the design and performance of the technology itself, involving both retrospective analyses of existing technologies and the design of new technical mechanisms and systems.

Based on http://www.vsdesign.org/

One way to look at usability is to see it as concerned with achieving a balance between the four principal factors of human-centred interactive systems design, PACT:

● People
● Activities people want to undertake
● Contexts in which the interaction takes place
● Technologies (hardware and software).

The combinations of these elements are very different in, for example, a public kiosk, a shared diary system, an airline cockpit or a mobile phone; and it is this wide variety that makes achieving a balance so difficult. Designers must constantly evaluate different combinations in order to reach this balance.

Figure 4.4 illustrates an important feature of human–computer interaction. There are two relationships that need to be optimized. On the one hand there is the interaction

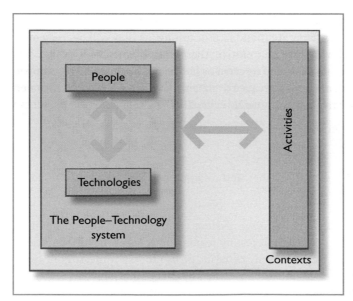

Figure 4.4 Usability aims to achieve a balance in the PACT elements

between people and the technologies that they are using. This focuses on the user interface. The other relationship is the interaction between the people and technologies considered as a whole (the people–technology system), the activities being undertaken, and the contexts of those activities.

The idea of a people–technology system optimized for some activities is nicely illustrated with an example from Erik Hollnagel (1997). He discusses the difference between a person on a horse travelling across open countryside and a person in a car travelling along a road. The combinations of technologies are balanced for the different contexts of travelling; neither is better in all circumstances. It is important to remember that the people–technology system may consist of many people and many devices working together to undertake some activities.

Challenge 4.2

Think of the activity of writing and all the various contexts in which we undertake this activity. For example, you might be writing a report for a student assignment, writing a postcard from a poolside chair on holiday, writing down some thoughts on a train, taking notes in a lecture and so on. Now think about the different technologies that we use for writing: ballpoint pens, felt-tipped pens, computers, palmtop devices and so on. Which combinations are most usable in which circumstances? Why?

Don Norman (Norman, 1988) focuses on the interface between a person and the technology and on the difficulty of people having to translate their goals into the specific actions required by a user interface. Norman's characterization is as follows:

- People have goals – things they are trying to achieve in the world. But devices typically only deal with simple actions. This means that two 'gulfs' have to be bridged.
- The gulf of execution is concerned with translating goals into actions, and the gulf of evaluation is concerned with deciding whether the actions were successful in moving the person towards his or her goal.
- These gulfs have to be bridged both semantically (does the person understand what to do and what has happened?) and physically (can the person physically or perceptually find out what to do or what has happened?).

A key issue for usability is that very often the technology gets in the way of people and the activities they want to do. If we compare using an interactive device such as a remote control to using a hammer or driving a car, we can see the issue more clearly. Very often when using an interactive system we are conscious of the technology; we have to stop to press the buttons; we are conscious of bridging the gulfs (Figure 4.5). When hammering or driving we focus on the activity, not the technology. The technology is 'present to hand' (see Further thoughts box).

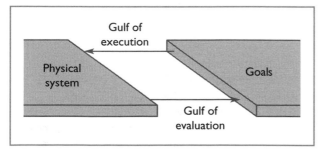

Figure 4.5 Bridging the gulfs
(Source: after Norman and Draper (eds) (1986))

**FURTHER
THOUGHTS**

Technological breakdown

When using a hammer, driving or writing with a pen we will usually focus on the activity itself: we are hammering, driving or writing. It is only when something happens to interfere with the smooth operation of these technologies that we become aware of them. If you hit your finger whilst hammering, if you have to swerve to avoid a hole in the road, or if the pen stops working, then the unconscious use of the technology turns into a conscious interaction with the technology. Winograd and Flores (1986) refer to this as a 'breakdown'. One aim of interactive systems design is to avoid such breakdowns, to provide people with a way of undertaking activities without really being aware of the technologies that enable them to do what they are doing.

← Mental models are discussed further in Chapter 2

Another important aspect of usability is to try to engender an accurate mental model of the system. A good design will have adopted a clear and well-structured conceptual design that can be easily communicated to people. A complex design will make this process much more difficult. Striving for a clear, simple and consistent conceptual model will increase the usability of a system.

Challenge 4.3

The remote control for my TV is shown in Figure 4.6. Yes, all the numbers have got rubbed off the buttons! Write down the processes that a user of this device goes through if they want to enter a code number, 357998, say.

Figure 4.6 My TV remote control
(Source: Steve Gorton and Karl Shone/
DK Images)

4.4 Acceptability

Acceptability is about fitting technologies into people's lives. For example, some railway trains have 'quiet' carriages where it is unacceptable to use mobile phones, and cinemas remind people to turn their phones off before the film starts. Apple's iMac computer was the first computer designed to look good in a living room. A computer playing loud music would generally be considered to be unacceptable in an office environment.

→ Evaluation is covered in Chapter 10

An essential difference between usability and acceptability is that acceptability can only be understood in the context of use. Usability can be evaluated in a laboratory (though such evaluations will always be limited). Acceptability cannot.

BOX
4.3

The Technology Acceptance Model

The Technology Acceptance Model (TAM) is a way of looking at technologies and whether they will be accepted by communities. It has its origins in business studies rather than in computing or psychology. TAM looks at technology acceptance from two perspectives: ease of use and effectiveness. Each of these is further broken down into more specific characteristics of the technology. There are many variants of TAM as it gets adapted to the particular characteristics of a technology. Some of our own work involved looking at the acceptance of biometrics. We felt that a third aspect was important to the acceptance of biometric technology, namely trust.

The key features of acceptability are:

- *Political.* Is the design politically acceptable? Do people trust it? In many organizations new technologies have been introduced for simple economic reasons, irrespective of what people may feel about them and the ways that people's jobs and lives might change. In the broader environment human rights might be threatened by changes in technologies.
- *Convenience.* Designs that are awkward or that force people to do things may prove unacceptable. Designs should fit effortlessly into the situation. Many people send documents electronically nowadays, but many people find reading on-screen unacceptable. They print out the document because it is more convenient to carry and read.
- *Cultural and social habits.* If political acceptability is concerned with power structures and principles, cultural and social habits are concerned with the way people like to live. It is rude to disturb other people, for example. 'Spam' e-mail has become such an unacceptable aspect of life that some companies have given up on e-mail altogether.
- *Usefulness.* This goes beyond the notions of efficiency and effectiveness and concerns usefulness in context. For example, many people have found the diary function on their phone perfectly usable, but not sufficiently useful in the context of everyday living.
- *Economic.* There are many economic issues that render some technology acceptable or not. Price is the obvious one and whether the technology offers value for money. But the economic issues go further than that as the introduction of new technologies may completely change the way businesses work and how they make money. A new 'business model' is often a part of economic acceptability. Don Norman characterizes the situation for a successful technology as a stool with three legs: user experience, marketing and technology (Figure 4.7).

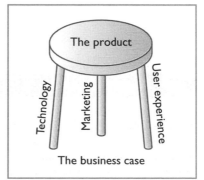

Figure 4.7 The three legs of product development

(Source: after Norman, Donald A., Fig. 2.5, *The Invisible Computer: Why Good Products Can Fail*, © 1998 Massachusetts Institute of Technology, by permission of The MIT Press)

4.5 Design principles

Over the years many principles of good interactive system design have been developed. Don Norman in his book *The Design of Everyday Things* (Norman, 1998) provides several, as does Jacob Nielsen in *Usability Engineering* (Nielsen, 1993). However, the level of abstraction provided by different people at different times is sometimes rather inconsistent and confusing. Design principles can be very broad or they can be more specific. There are also good design principles that derive from psychology, such as 'minimize memory load', i.e. do not expect people to remember too much. (We discuss many of these principles in Chapters 12 and 13 on interface design.) Apple, Microsoft and Google all provide user interface design guidelines for the development of products that run on their platforms.

The application of design principles has led to established design guidelines and patterns of interaction in certain circumstances such as the 'Undo' command in a Windows application, the 'Back' button on a website or the greying-out of inappropriate options on menus.

→ Memory and attention are discussed in Chapter 21

Design principles can guide the designer during the design process and can be used to evaluate and critique prototype design ideas. Our list of high-level design principles, put together from Norman, Nielsen and others, is shown below. All the principles interact in complex ways, affecting each other, sometimes conflicting with each other and sometimes enhancing each other. But they help to orientate the designer to key features of good design and sensitize the designer to important issues.

For ease of memorizing and use we have grouped them into three main categories – learnability, effectiveness and accommodation – but these groupings are not rigid. Systems should be learnable, effective *and* accommodating.

- Principles 1–4 are concerned with access, ease of learning and remembering (learnability).
- Principles 5–7 are concerned with ease of use, and principles 8 and 9 with safety (effectiveness).
- Principles 10–12 are concerned with accommodating differences between people and respecting those differences (accommodation).

Designing interactive systems from a human-centred perspective is concerned with the following.

Helping people access, learn and remember the system

1 *Visibility.* Try to ensure that things are visible so that people can see what functions are available and what the system is currently doing. This is an important part of the psychological principle that it is easier to recognize things than to have to recall them. If it is not possible to make it visible, make it observable. Consider making things 'visible' through the use of sound and touch.

2 *Consistency.* Be consistent in the use of design features and be consistent with similar systems and standard ways of working. Consistency can be something of a slippery concept (see the Further thoughts box). Both conceptual and physical consistency are important.

→ Metaphors are discussed in Section 9.3

3 *Familiarity.* Use language and symbols that the intended audience will be familiar with. Where this is not possible because the concepts are quite different from those people know about, provide a suitable metaphor to help them transfer similar and related knowledge from a more familiar domain.

4 *Affordance*. Design things so it is clear what they are for; for example, make buttons look like push buttons so people will press them. Affordance refers to the properties that things have (or are perceived to have) and how these relate to how the things could be used. Buttons afford pressing, chairs afford sitting on, and Post-it notes afford writing a message on and sticking next to something else. Affordances are culturally determined.

Giving them the sense of being in control, knowing what to do and how to do it
5 *Navigation*. Provide support to enable people to move around the parts of the system: maps, directional signs and information signs.
6 *Control*. Make it clear who or what is in control and allow people to take control. Control is enhanced if there is a clear, logical mapping between controls and the effect that they have. Also make clear the relationship between what the system does and what will happen in the world outside the system.
7 *Feedback*. Rapidly feed back information from the system to people so that they know what effect their actions have had. Constant and consistent feedback will enhance the feeling of control.

Safely and securely
8 *Recovery*. Enable recovery from actions, particularly mistakes and errors, quickly and effectively.
9 *Constraints*. Provide constraints so that people do not try to do things that are inappropriate. In particular, people should be prevented from making serious errors through properly constraining allowable actions and seeking confirmation of dangerous operations.

In a way that suits them
10 *Flexibility*. Allow multiple ways of doing things so as to accommodate people with different levels of experience and interest in the system. Provide people with the opportunity to change the way things look or behave so that they can personalize the system.
11 *Style*. Designs should be stylish and attractive.
12 *Conviviality*. Interactive systems should be polite, friendly and generally pleasant. Nothing ruins the experience of using an interactive system more than an aggressive message or an abrupt interruption. Design for politeness (see Box 4.4). Conviviality also suggests joining in and using interactive technologies to connect and support people.

Consistency

Consistency is a slippery concept because consistency is always relative. A design will be consistent with respect to some things but may be inconsistent with respect to others. There are also times when to be inconsistent is a good thing because it draws people's attention to something that is important. The difference between conceptual consistency and physical consistency is important. Conceptual consistency is about ensuring the mappings are consistent, that the conceptual model remains clear. This involves being consistent both internally to the system and externally as the system relates to things outside it. Physical consistency is ensuring consistent behaviours and consistent use of colours, names, layout and so on.

One famous example of the difficulty of maintaining conceptual consistency in a design comes from the design of the Xerox Star interface (described in Smith *et al.*, 1982).

FURTHER THOUGHTS

→

To print a document, the document was dragged onto a printer icon. This was consistent with the overall style. The question then arose as to what to do with it after it had been printed. The options considered were (1) the system deletes the icon from the desktop, or (2) the system does not delete the icon, but (a) replaces it on the desktop in its previous location, (b) places it at an arbitrary location on the desktop, or (c) leaves it on the printer for the user to deal with. Discuss!

Kellogg (1989) quotes the designers as saying that in this example the trade-off was between the external consistency of not deleting the icon, as it behaved more like a real-world object (a photocopier), against the internal consistency of behaving like other actions in the interface, such as dragging the icon to the wastebasket or to a folder icon. They opted for option 2a. Whether designers would do that nowadays, when more people are much more familiar with these types of interface, is another matter.

BOX 4.4

Polite software

Alan Cooper (1999) argues that if we want people to like our software we should design it to behave like a likeable person. Drawing on work by Reeves and Nass (1996), who found that people interacting with new media were treating the media like a person ('The Media Equation'), they argue that the essentials of polite behaviour are quality, quantity, relevance and clarity. Cooper continues with his list of characteristics:

Polite software:

is interested in me	is taciturn about its personal problems
is deferential to me	is well informed
is forthcoming	is perceptive
has common sense	is self-confident
anticipates my needs	stays focused
is responsive	is fudge-able
gives instant gratification	is trustworthy

Design principles in action

In Part III of this book we look at design in a number of specific contexts including the Web, cooperative systems, mobile computing and ubiquitous computing systems. Specific design issues and principles for those contexts are discussed there. There are also related issues discussed in Chapter 12 on interface design. Here we look at some general examples of the design principles in action.

The computer 'desktop' is likely to remain with us for some time, with its familiar combination of windows, icons, menus and pointer, called a WIMP interface. This form of interaction – the graphical user interface (GUI) – is as ubiquitous as information and communication technologies are becoming and appears on handhelds and other mobile devices as well as on desktop computers.

Designing for GUIS, is still dominated primarily by issues of usability. In particular, the key issue is **consistency**. There are clear guidelines for issues such as menu layout, ordering, dialogue boxes and use of the other 'widgets' associated with graphical user interfaces. There are standards for providing **constraints** such as greying out items on a menu that are not relevant at a particular point. A toolkit, or a design environment such as Visual Basic, will probably be used that will help to ensure that the design conforms to an overall style.

Screen design is a key issue in such environments and attention needs to be paid to the layout of objects on a screen. Avoiding clutter will help to ensure **visibility**. Attention needs to be paid to the use of appropriate, non-clashing colours and the careful layout of information using tables, graphs or text as appropriate. However, on mobile applications visibility is very difficult to achieve.

Often in the design of GUI applications, the designer can talk to the actual future stakeholders of the system and find out what they want and how they refer to things. This will help the designer to ensure that **familiar** language is used and that the design follows any organizational conventions. It can be fitted in with preferred ways of working. Participatory design techniques – involving people closely in the design process – can be used, and stakeholders can participate in the design process through workshops, meetings and evaluation of design ideas. Documentation and training can be given.

A good design will ensure that there is easy error **recovery** by providing warning signs for drastic actions such as 'Are you sure you want to destroy the database?'. A good example of designing for recovery is the Undo command.

Affordances are provided by following GUI design guidelines. People will expect to see a menu at the top of the screen and will expect the menu items to be displayed when the header is clicked on. Items that are not greyed out will afford selecting. The various 'widgets' such as check boxes, radio buttons and text entry boxes should afford selecting because people familiar with the standards will know what to expect. However, care needs to be taken to ensure that opportunities are easily and correctly perceived. On mobile devices the physical buttons afford pressing, but because of the limited screen space the same button has to do different things at different times. This leads to problems of **consistency**.

Menus are also the main form of **navigation** in GUI applications. People move around the application by selecting items from menus and then by following dialogue structures. Many applications make use of 'wizards'. These provide step-by-step instructions for undertaking a sequence of operations, allowing users to go forwards and backwards to ensure that all steps are completed.

Control is usually left in the hands of the users. They have to initiate actions, although some features that provide security are undertaken automatically. Many applications, for example, automatically save people's work to help with recovery if mistakes are made. **Feedback** is provided in a variety of ways. A 'bee' symbol or an 'egg timer' symbol is used to indicate that the system is busy doing something. Counters and progress bars are used to indicate how much of an operation is complete. Feedback can be provided through sound, such as a beep when a message is received on an e-mail system or a sound to indicate that a file has been safely saved.

Flexibility is provided with things such as shortcut keys, allowing more expert users to use combinations of keyboard controls in place of using menus to initiate commands and navigate through the system. Many windows applications allow the user to set their own preferences, to configure features such as the navigation bars and menu items and to disable features that are not often used.

In terms of **style** and **conviviality**, GUI applications are rather limited as they should remain within the standard design guidelines (although Windows 8 is certainly more aesthetic than previous versions). Error messages are one area where the designer can move towards a more convivial design by thinking hard about the words used on the messages. However, all too frequently messages appear very abruptly and interrupt people unnecessarily.

Challenge 4.4

Look at Figure 4.8, an example of a typical 'windows'-type application. Critique the design from the perspective of the general design principles and from design for OS X in particular.

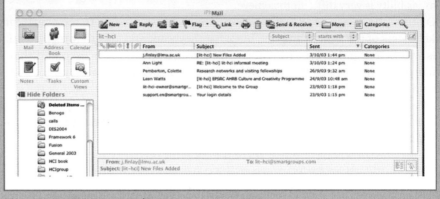

Figure 4.8 'Entourage' on the Mac

(Source: Screenshot frame reprinted by permission of Microsoft Corporation)

→ See Section 14.3 on Information architecture for websites

Navigation is a central issue in website design. Even if a site is well focused, it will soon get large and so issues of how to move around a website become important. Designers need to provide support to enable people to discover the structure and content of the site and to find their way to a particular part of the site. Information architecture is an established area of study devoted to designing websites.

A key feature of **consistency** is the use of standard Web features such as a blue underline for showing a link. Many sites confuse people by not making links sufficiently visible and distinguishable from other text on the site. **Flexibility** of navigation can be enabled by providing alternatives for people; different routes though the site and having a variety of links. Having a site map will **afford** people getting oriented.

Issues of **recovery**, **feedback** and **control** figure most highly in shopping sites. There are often long pauses when processing things such as a payment transaction. Feedback is critical here and statements such as 'this action may take 45 seconds to complete' are used to persuade people not to do anything while the transaction is processed. However, there is no way of enforcing **constraints** in these circumstances.

Conviviality can be provided by allowing people to join in, to support and create communities. Unlike standard GUI applications, websites can easily connect people with one another. **Style** is also key to websites and offers the most opportunities for designers to demonstrate their creative flair. The use of animation, video and other design features can really develop a whole sense of engagement with the site.

→ See Section 5.2 on engagement

Summary and key points

Good design is about usability. It is about ensuring that systems are accessible to all and that designs are acceptable for the people and contexts in which they will be used. Designers need to evaluate their designs with people and involve people in the design process. Paying attention to design principles can help sensitize the designer to key aspects of good design.

- Access to interactive systems for all people is an important right.
- Usability is concerned with balancing the PACT elements in a domain.
- Acceptability is concerned with ensuring that designs are appropriate to contexts of use.
- Twelve design principles are particularly important. They can be grouped into three main design issues of learnability, effectiveness and accommodation.

Exercises

1 Suppose that the designers of the laboratory access system described in Chapter 2 have settled on a system that uses a swipe card and a card reader to access laboratories. How would you set about evaluating this design? Use the design principles to discuss the key issues.

2 Describe how design principles could be used to help in the design of the bicycle route information system described in Chapter 2. How would this be evaluated for accessibility, usability and acceptability?

 ## Further reading

Gould, J.D., Boies, S.J., Levy, S., Richards, J.T. and Schoonard, J. (1987) The 1984 Olympic Message System: a test of behavioral principles of system design. *Communications of the ACM,* 30(9), 758–69.

Norman, D.A. and Draper, S. (eds) (1986) *User-Centred System Design: New Perspectives on Human–Computer Interaction.* Lawrence Erlbaum Associates, Mahwah, NJ.

Stephanidis, C. (ed.) (2001) *User Interfaces for All: Concepts, Methods and Tools.* Lawrence Erlbaum Associates, Mahwah, NJ. *A good collection of papers on accessibility.*

Getting ahead

Kellogg, W. (1989) The dimensions of consistency. In Nielsen, J. (ed.), *Coordinating User Interfaces for Consistency.* Academic Press, San Diego, CA.

Smith, D.C., Irby, C., Kimball, R., Verplank, B. and Harslem, E. (1982) Designing the Star user interface. *BYTE,* 7(4), 242–82.

 ## Web links

The W3C's Web accessibility project is at **www.w3.org/WAI**

The accompanying website has links to relevant websites. Go to **www.pearsoned.co.uk/benyon**

Comments on challenges

Challenge 4.1

This, of course, is a real problem not just for the UK government but for authorities worldwide as they seek to save costs by making use of electronic methods of delivery. The potential barriers include fear of computers amongst some people (often the most vulnerable and in need of support). If this can be overcome then physical access to a computer is necessary, or via other technologies such as interactive TV. However, the interface to interactive TV is still quite poor and the functionality is also limited. Access can be provided in public buildings such as libraries and at social security offices where staff could be on hand to help people enter their details. There are also factors such as privacy where people may not want to provide the sort of detail that is required, or they may distrust the gathering of this information and may need clear reassurance on how any personal data would be used.

Challenge 4.2

The postcard needs a pen to write it – a felt-tipped pen would be too big. But I like writing with felt-tipped pens when I am playing around with some ideas in a notebook – sitting on a train, perhaps. A laptop computer is quite good and saves the trouble of having to transfer things from a book to the computer, but you cannot use a laptop when taking off or landing in a plane whereas you can still write in your book. I have tried the palmtops and handwriting, but have not found it a very satisfying way of working. Perhaps it is better for people who have to write short amounts of material.

Challenge 4.3

There is a lot of bridging of gulfs! Since the display is on the TV, feedback is very poor. In my case I need to take my glasses off to see the remote and put them on again to see the TV. There is a lot of taking my glasses on and off! With no numbers on the remote, the feedback that would usually come from this source is no longer there.

Challenge 4.4

Aesthetically the display is quite pleasant. There is not much clutter, which ensures that most things are visible. Parts of the display can be made larger and smaller, allowing the sort of flexibility that is needed for different people doing different things. Of course, the design is wholly consistent with the Macintosh guidelines. One interesting problem with Entourage is that it does not let people recover easily from inadvertently moving e-mails. For some reason 'Undo' does not relate to transferring e-mails into folders. The use of different font styles for read and unread messages affords focusing on the unread ones, and constraints on allowable actions are enforced – e.g. if you try to move an e-mail message to an inappropriate place it springs back.

Overall this system demonstrates the implementation of many of the design principles recommended in Section 4.5.

Chapter 5
Experience design

Contents

Aims

Designers of interactive systems are increasingly finding themselves going beyond the design of usable systems and are instead expected to design systems that provide people with great experiences. Of course games designers have been doing exactly this for years, but more recent platforms such as the iPhone and Wii are blurring the distinction between games and regular applications. A shopping list application on the iPhone, for example, needs to be much more than functional; it needs to be fun to use, engaging and enjoyable. Websites have to attract and keep customers if they are to be profitable and, once they provide appropriate functionality and content, they will do that only if people enjoy using them. Ubiquitous computing environments need to be responsive to people's needs, but also need to provide engaging and aesthetic experiences.

In this chapter we explore the factors that contribute to creating high-quality experiences for people using interactive systems. This area of HCI and interaction design is often called user experience (UX), though terms such as customer experience (CX) are also used and help us move away from the term 'user'.

After studying this chapter you should be able to:

- Discuss ideas of experience and the different traditions from which concepts come
- Understand Nathan Shredroff's model of experience
- Understand 'designing for pleasure'
- Understand the importance of aesthetics
- Understand service design.

5.1   Introduction

Contributions to an understanding of experience design come from many different areas. Nathan Shedroff (2001) published a very engaging book on the subject and McCarthy and Wright explore the wider issues of experiences through their book *Technology as Experience* (2004), drawing on the philosophy of John Dewey, an American Philosopher and psychologist writing in the mid twentieth century. Patrick Jordan and Don Norman have both published books on the importance of designing for pleasure and others talk about 'ludic' design, 'hedonomics' and 'funology'. Work on aesthetics has a long history and has recently been applied to interactive systems design.

BOX 5.1

Homo Ludens

Homo Ludens was the title of a book by Johan Huizinga written in 1938 concerning the importance of play in culture. In it he explores the concept of play in different cultures. Play is about freedom, it is extraordinary. It has been popularized in interaction design through Bill Gaver's work on what he calls 'ludic' design. In an online interview, Gaver says:

> I don't mean joining in a set of arbitrary rules to see who can win some situation. On the contrary, I mean by 'play' something more fluid and self-motivated. So examples of play are anything from fooling around with friends and taking on imaginary roles when you are having a chat, to stacking up things to see how many you can balance on one another before they all tumble down, or taking a new walk on the way home from work just to see where you get. But also I tend to allow the category to extend beyond the obviously playful to take in things like enjoyment of the scenery, or staring out the window and wondering about how the wind is moving around the leaves and trees and so forth.

(www.infodesign.com.cu/uxpod/ludicdesign)

Gaver has expressed these ideas through a number of playful household objects, including the drift table and history tablecloth (Figure 5.1). The drift table was a coffee table that tilted and showed maps of the UK. The history tablecloth displayed imprints of the objects that had been recently placed on it.

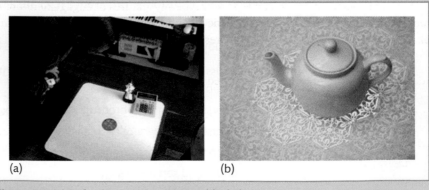

(a)   (b)

Figure 5.1 (a) Drift table and (b) History tablecloth
(Source: Copyright the Interaction Research Studio, Goldsmiths)

Experience design is about recognizing that interactive products and services do not just exist in the world, they affect who we are. They influence our culture and identity. As Dewey says, 'experience is the irreducible totality of people acting, sensing, thinking, feeling and meaning-making including their perception and sensation of the artifact in context' (quoted in McCarthy and Wright, 2004). For Jodi Forlizzi experience is 'the constant stream of self-talk that happens while we are conscious'. In addition to experience, Forlizzi stresses the importance of the social side of things in co-experience (Forlizzi and Batterbee, 2004).

Experience is concerned with all the qualities of an activity that really pull people in – whether this is a sense of immersion that one feels when reading a good book, or a challenge one feels when playing a good game, or the fascinating unfolding of a drama. It is concerned with all the qualities of the interactive experience that make it memorable, satisfying, enjoyable and rewarding. Emotion is a very important part of experience as experience is about feeling.

In their treatment of technology and experience, McCarthy and Wright highlight the need to take a holistic approach to experience. Their approach is holistic, constructionist and pragmatic. The argument is that experiences have to be understood as a whole and cannot be broken down into their constituent parts, because experience lies in the relations between the parts. Interactivity, as we have seen, involves the combination of people, technologies, activities and the contexts in which the interaction happens. This context includes the wider social and cultural context as well as the immediate context of use.

McCarthy and Wright take a stance that emphasizes the rights of people to have the experiences they need and desire rather than having experiences thrust upon them by poor designs. Through experiences we live our lives and this is how we develop our values and sense of self-worth. Experiences are about how we bring artefacts and services into our lives and accept them. Ross *et al.* (2008) develop similar ideas through their notion of enchantment.

Experiences, therefore, cannot really be designed. Designers can design *for* experience, but it is individuals and groups who have the experience.

5.2 Engagement

Engagement is about ensuring that the interaction flows. If usability is concerned with optimizing or balancing the PACT elements in some domain, engagement is when the PACT elements are truly harmonized.

There is, of course, much debate as to what the key features of engagement are and, arguably, this is really the domain of artistic creation. However, Nathan Shedroff in his book *Experience Design* (Shedroff, 2001) presents a 'manifesto' for what he sees as a new discipline. From his work we identify as the key elements:

- *Identity*. A sense of authenticity is needed for identity and expression of the self. The sense of authenticity is often only noticed when it breaks down. If you are engaged in some experience and something happens that suddenly reminds you that it is not real, then the authenticity of the experience can be lost. Shedroff is also getting at the idea of identifying with something as a key element of engagement. Are you a Mac or a Windows person or don't you care?
- *Adaptivity* is to do with change and personalization, with changing levels of difficulty, pace and movement. Musical instruments are often cited as examples of great interaction design. Engagement is not about making things easy; it is about making things that can be experienced at many levels of skill and enjoyment.

- *Narrative* is to do with telling a good story, with convincing characters, plot and suspense. Narrative is not just about fiction, however. Good narrative is just as important for a company's promotional video, a lecture on interaction design, a menu structure on a mobile phone or any other design problem.
- *Immersion* is the feeling of being wholly involved within something, with being taken over and transported somewhere else. You can get immersed in all manner of things (such as reading a book) so immersion is not about the medium; it is a quality of the design.
- *Flow* is the sense of smooth movement, the gradual change from one state to another. Flow is an important concept introduced by the design philosopher Mihaly Csikszentmihalyi (1990) (see the Further thoughts box on this).

A medium is engaging if it draws the person in, if it seems to surround the activity, if it stimulates the imagination. Malcolm McCullough in his book *Abstracting Craft* (McCullough, 2002a) argues that an engaging medium allows for continuity and variety, for 'flow' and movement between many subtle differentiations of conditions. The medium can take many slightly different positions along a spectrum that are just discernible by a person. Think of the way the lights go down in a cinema just before the movie starts. The sense of anticipation, satisfaction and being drawn in is created by the just discernible change in lighting. Interactive technologies are the medium that the interactive system designer shapes.

Challenge 5.1

Think about your favourite activity. It may be talking to a friend on your mobile phone, driving your car, riding your bike, playing a computer game, going to the cinema, shopping or attending a lecture. Using Shedroff's five features above, analyse what it is about the activity that makes it engaging. Could it be more engaging if the design were different?

FURTHER THOUGHTS

Digital ground: fixity, flow and engagement with context

'Flow needs contexts. A river, for example, needs riverbanks otherwise it spreads out in every direction until it becomes a brackish swamp. Similarly, cars need highways, capital needs markets and life's energy needs bodies through which to course.

Flows influence one another. For example, we know that telecommunication generates transportation at least as often as it substitutes for it, starting with Alexander Graham Bell whose first words on his new telephone were 'Watson, please come here'. Similarly, when you order a book from Amazon, the flow of data on the web has an effect outside the web, namely it causes a package to be put on an airplane. This in turn has geographic consequences: the warehouse where your order is filled is probably located near an airport.

Where regular crossovers between flows occur, places emerge.

Here we arrive at Mihaly Csikszentmihalyi's often-cited expression: Flow is the sense of engagement that emerges, between boredom and anxiety, when practiced abilities are applied to challenges that are just about manageable. This notion of engaged tacit knowledge grounds much interaction design. We tend to be familiar with psychological notions of "activity theory", "situated actions" and "persistent structures". We know how possibilities for action are perceived especially amid engaged activity (and we over-use the word "affordance" to describe this). Increasingly, we understand how that per-ception depends on persistent structures, both mental and physical, that surround and give meaning to those activities. We recognize how such response to context is not necessarily deliberative. We find the phenomenology of engagement at the roots of interactivity.

So this is the heart of the matter: Flow needs fixity. Persistently embodied intentional settings, also known as architecture, provide a necessary context for Flow.'

Source: McCullough (2002b)

Gamification

Computer games have to be designed to be engaging and many of the principles of engagement can be seen in the design of games. Increasingly these principles are being applied to various interactive systems. Websites need to hold people's attention and principles of games ('gamification') can be used to interest and motivate people.

An engaging animated computer game will allow for subtle differentiations of con-ditions. An important feature here is also the integration of media. A boring computer game relies on too little change and flow and too little depth in the media components. Computer games illustrate all the other features of engagement above – a feeling of immersion, the need for a good story line, the authenticity of the game play and identi-fication with characters, the different levels accommodating different abilities and the gradual smooth change of scenes: the flow. One of the most engaging games was *Myst* which appeared on the Macintosh in the early 1990s and remains a bestseller today with versions on the iPhone and Nintendo DS. Figure 5.2 shows some of the images from the game, but the atmosphere was considerably enhanced by excellent use of sound and by character and the slow pace of the movement.

Figure 5.2 Pictures for the game Myst

(Source: http://sirrus.cyan.com/Online/Myst/GameShots. © Cyan Worlds, Inc. Used by permission)

Nicole Lazzaro (Lazzaro, 2012) draws the link between fun and emotion in her contribution to understanding what makes interactive activities engaging. She identifies five ways that emotions impact the gaming experience:

→ Chapter 22 covers emotion, or 'affect' as it is also known

1 *Enjoy*. Emotions create strong shifts in internal sensations.
2 *Focus*. Emotions help gamers to focus effort and attention.
3 *Decide*. Emotions are central to decision making in games.
4 *Perform*. Emotions increase appeal to enhance performance.
5 *Learn*. Emotions are important for motivation and attention.

Lazzaro presents the Four Fun Key model in which she distinguishes four different types of fun — hard fun, easy fun, serious fun and people fun — each of which goes on to unlock emotions such as curiosity, relaxation, excitement and amusement, that contribute to a good player experience. More generally we can see these as key emotions in contributing to a high-quality user experience.

(a) Hard fun is concerned with overcoming adversity, the emotion that Lazzaro calls Fiero. It relates to the gamification effects of mastery, challenge and strategy. For example, in a car racing game it is no fun if it is hard to start the car and start the race. However, it is fun if it is hard to avoid the obstacles or keep the car on track whilst driving fast. The hard fun comes from mastering the driving.

(b) Easy fun evokes the key emotion of curiosity. Gamification mechanics such as novelty, ambiguity, fantasy and role play make people curious to explore the interaction. It is more open-ended interaction than the focused, goal-centred interaction of hard fun.

(c) Serious fun is about relaxation. It arises when an interactive experience provides rewards that increase people's self-worth and allow them to focus on activities. Serious fun is about doing work!

(d) People fun concerns the emotion of amusement. It arises when people are connected to one another in cooperative or competitive activities. It is the social side of gamification, connecting into people's social networks and desire to share.

Using these four fun keys helps the interaction designer to produce a UX that moves the user through different emotions, helping to create engaging experiences. In terms of the design process, interaction designers need to consider what type(s) of experience(s) they are trying to create for users of their systems. The four fun keys provide a good way into thinking about this. Subsequently designers can consider the mechanisms that they are going to use to try to evoke those experiences. These include:

● Deciding what challenges to include in the product and whether these are short-term challenges or longer-term 'quests'
● Deciding how to deal with the different skill levels of different users and how to accommodate changing skill levels
● Deciding what rewards to provide people with and how rewards relate to challenges and skill levels
● Deciding if people can collect things, or complete things like puzzles, and if they do collect things how they relate to rewards, abilities and skills
● Deciding how people will relate to other people through competition such as league tables and posting achievements or through cooperation and working with others to achieve a common goal.

5.3 Designing for pleasure

Product designers have long been concerned with building in pleasure as a key marketing point. Pleasure is a focus for many design situations that were once much more dominated by the more functional aspects of usability. The Apple MacBook Air is advertised as being lightweight and elegant (it is only 3 cm thick), with a distinctive and attractive titanium shell (Figure 5.3). While all of these features contribute to the laptop's usability, they also contribute to the pleasure of owning, using and (perhaps) being seen with it.

Figure 5.3 Apple MacBook Air
(Source: Hugh Threlfall/Alamy Images)

Patrick Jordan's book *Designing Pleasurable Products* (2000) argues effectively that designing for pleasure can be as important as ensuring that an interactive device is usable. Jordan describes pleasure as being 'the condition of consciousness or sensation induced by the enjoyment or anticipation of what is felt or viewed as good or desirable: enjoyment, delight, gratification'. In the context of interactive devices or products, designing for pleasure contributes to 'emotional, hedonistic and practical benefits' (Jordan, 2000, p. 12).

Jordan's approach draws heavily on the work of Lionel Tiger, who is an anthropologist and has developed a framework for understanding and organizing thinking about pleasure. This framework is discussed at length in Tiger's book *The Pursuit of Pleasure* (Tiger, 1992). Tiger has argued that there are four dimensions or aspects of pleasure. These are *physio*-pleasure, *socio*-pleasure, *psycho*-pleasure and *ideo*-pleasure.

Physio-pleasure

This is concerned with the body and the senses. Physio-pleasure arises from touching or handling devices or from their smell – think about the smell of a new car, or the pleasingly solid but responsive feel of a well-designed keyboard. This sort of pleasure is also derived from using devices which fit seamlessly with the human body – although this is more usually noticed when the fit is less than ideal. The physical fit of technology to people has long been a central concern for ergonomists working on the design of new products.

← There is more about ergonomics in Chapter 2

Socio-pleasure

Socio-pleasure arises from relationships with others. Products and devices which have a socio-pleasurable aspect either facilitate social activity or improve relationships with others. A very obvious example is the key role which text messaging has rapidly acquired in enhancing social communication for many people, the use of Twitter to keep in touch, or the popularity of social networking websites such as Facebook. Pleasure derived from enhanced status or image is also considered a socio-pleasure, and of course is much exploited by the vendors of successive generations of small personal technologies.

Psycho-pleasure

Psycho-pleasure (short for psychological pleasure) refers to cognitive or emotional pleasure in Tiger's framework. This dimension of pleasure is useful for pulling together sources of pleasure such as the perceived ease of use and effectiveness of a device and the satisfaction of acquiring new skills. For some people, learning a complex programming language generates a degree of satisfaction which would never be obtained from moving icons around the screen in a GUI.

Ideo-pleasure

Ideo-pleasure (ideological pleasure) concerns people's values – things one holds dear or meaningful – and aspirations. We are more likely to enjoy using items that fit our value system. Aspects which come readily to mind here might include a respect for careful craftsmanship and design, the desirability or otherwise of having an obviously expensive device, and our perceptions of the trading ethics of the supplier (for example, commercial software as against free shareware).

The four dimensions in practice

It should be remembered that these four dimensions are simply a method of structuring design thought rather than a description of the nature of pleasure itself.

Let's see how they work by returning to the example of the MacBook Air laptop and analysing it against Tiger's four pleasures.

1 *Physio-pleasure*. The machine is light, the texture of the titanium shell is pleasing and the keyboard is responsive.
2 *Socio-pleasure*. Certainly when first released, owning a MacBook Air might be thought to enhance image as it distinguishes the owner as someone with the discernment to adopt a stylish remodelling of the laptop. There is also a certain socio-pleasure in being part of a small group of Apple devotees among a much larger community of PC users in our particular workplace.
3 *Psycho-pleasure*. The MacBook Air provides relatively seamless integration between different media and so generates satisfaction from streamlining many work tasks.
4 *Ideo-pleasure*. For some consumers, Apple products remain an embodiment of independence, creativity and free-thinking – attributes inherited from the early image of the corporation. Whether this is still an accurate perception is not the point: it is enough that people feel that it is so.

→ Culture and identity are discussed in Chapter 24

Challenge 5.2

Using Tiger's classification, what do you consider is the main pleasure evoked by the design of one of the interactive devices/systems you enjoy owning or using? If possible, compare your response to those of one or more colleagues for a similar device.

Product attachment theory

Zimmerman (2009) discusses how to bring product attachment theory into interaction design. Product attachment concerns the feelings that people have for products and the ways in which the products take on meanings for them. He reflects on a number of products from the perspective of 'designing for the self', by which he means designing for other people to realize themselves through interacting with the product. He looked specifically at six products (Figure 5.4) and at the characteristics they possessed in terms of design patterns. Design patterns are regularities in designs that capture some aspects of successful design. Design patterns are an important part of interactive systems design and are discussed in Chapter 9 as part of our design approach.

The products examined by Zimmerman included Cherish, a smart photoframe (top left in Figure 5.4), a smart bag for organizing and carrying athletic kit that is connected to the family's calendar (top middle, Figure 5.4) and the reserve alarm clock (bottom middle in Figure 5.4) that aimed to stop children waking their parents at night. From his analysis he arrived at six 'framing constructs' that captured important elements of product attachment:

1 Role engagement concerned support for the different roles that people play in their lives. It arises from the observation that people have to switch roles depending on the context, such as the time of day, or relationship required for a particular activity.
2 Control concerned empowering people, giving them control over the product. This could be control over the 'look and feel' of the product, personalizing it to their tastes, or it could be control over the functionality of the product.
3 Affiliation concerns how people develop feelings for a product by ensuring that the product meets a real need for them.
4 Ability and bad habit is a construct concerned with enhancing people's abilities and preventing them making mistakes or engaging in their bad habit. The smart bag, for example, stopped people forgetting things.
5 Long-term goals need supporting as well as short-term functions. People build their attachment by recognizing that the product supports their long-term goals.
6 Ritual concerns how the product fits in with important ritual aspects of the person's life.

Zimmerman encourages designers to keep these framing constructs in mind during the understanding, envisioning, designing and evaluation processes of the whole design process. In doing so they will focus more on designing for the self, and on developing products that people will form an attachment to.

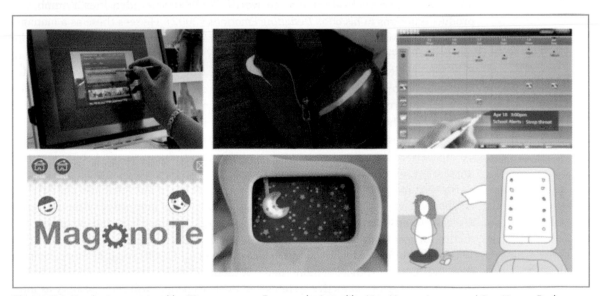

Figure 5.4 Products examined by Zimmerman – Ensure, designed by Hee Young Jeong and Sun Young Park; Smart Bag, designed by Min-Kyung Lee; Cherish, designed by Jeong Kim; Share Moments, designed by Rhiannon Sterling Zivin; Magonote, designed by Mathew Forrest; Reverse Alarm Clock, designed by Kursat Ozenc

(Source: Zimmerman, J. (2009) Designing for the self: making products that help people become the person they desire to be, *CHI '09: Proceedings of the SIGCHI Conference on Human Factors in Computing Systems*, pp. 395–404. © 2009 ACM, Inc. Reprinted by permission. doc.acm.org/10.1145/1518701.1518765)

**FURTHER
THOUGHTS**

Kansei

Kansei engineering is concerned with bringing an emotional and aesthetic element to engineering. It is used across all manner of engineering design practices in order to try to understand and embody what it is that will get people really involved in a design. To date it has been applied very little in interaction design.

Kansei sits alongside Chinsei as one of two threads of the design and engineering process, Kansei dealing with the emotional and Chinsei with the functional.

Schütte, S. (2005). Engineering Emotional Values in Product Design – Kansei Engineering in Development. Doctorate Thesis, Institute of Technology, Linköping University.

5.4 Aesthetics

Aesthetics is a large area of study concerned with human appreciation of beauty and how things are sensed, felt and judged. Aesthetics takes us into the world of artistic criticism and the philosophy of art itself. The perennial debate here is whether aesthetics can ever be inherent in something, or whether 'beauty is in the eye of the beholder'.

In terms of the design of interactive systems, aesthetics has become increasingly important over the past few years from a number of different directions. From the perspective of work on emotion, both Don Norman and Pieter Desmet emphasize the importance of taking emotions into consideration in design. Norman's book *Emotional Design* (2004) discusses people's experiences in terms of visceral, behavioural and reflective elements. At the visceral level lies the perceptual aesthetics of an experience. At the behavioural level a positive emotional response will come from feeling in control and from the understanding that comes through use. At the reflective level are issues of personal values and self-worth. Pieter Desmet identifies a number of product emotions in his book *Designing Emotions* (2002). He sees these as a manageable set of emotions, such as boredom, inspiration, amusement and so on that are particularly relevant for product designers. This work has resulted in a database of anecdotal evidence about products and emotions, the product and emotion navigator and a non-verbal method for measuring people's response to product features, called PrEmo. PrEmo consists of fourteen animations of a cartoon character, each expressing an emotion. There are seven positive emotions, i.e. inspiration, desire, satisfaction, pleasant surprise, fascination, amusement, admiration, and seven negative emotions, i.e. disgust, indignation, contempt, disappointment, dissatisfaction, boredom and unpleasant surprise (Figure 5.5).

Hassenzahl (2007) discusses aesthetics in terms of pragmatic attributes and hedonic attributes. Lavie and Tractinsky (2004) see the aesthetics of interactive systems in terms of classical aesthetics (clean, clear, pleasant, aesthetic, symmetrical) and expressive aesthetics (original, sophisticated, fascinating, special effects, creative). They assert that 'what is beautiful is useable'. However, Hartman *et al.* (2008) see it as more complex than this. Certainly, there is more than traditional usability at work in people's judgements of quality of interactive systems, but at times people will rate usability as most important. Content, services and brand are also factors to be taken into consideration.

For Boehner *et al.* (2008) the issue is to make products not just right, but meaningful. They seek to intimately couple the codification necessary in design with the ineffable nature of human experience.

Challenge 5.3

Go to a website you particularly like and critique the aesthetics of it. Could they be improved?

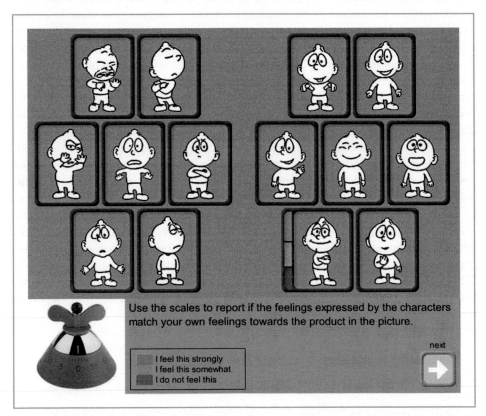

Use the scales to report if the feelings expressed by the characters match your own feelings towards the product in the picture.

next

I feel this strongly
I feel this somewhat
I do not feel this

Figure 5.5 PrEmo
(Source: Desmet, P.M.A. (2003), pp. 111–23)

Brand

The development of a brand identity is an important part of people liking and enjoying a system. Some people are 'Nokia' people, others are 'Apple' people. Some people love Nike and others Reebok. These companies spend a great deal of effort and money developing, refining and promoting their brand. They like to be associated with certain events, or to sponsor certain football or baseball teams, as these associations help to develop the brand. A brand will often deliver consistent guidelines for designers, such as colours, use of particular fonts and so on. Brand immediately leads to a sense of identity, one of the key aspects of experience. And conversely, experience will affect the brand. People's experiences in interacting with branded products and services create the feelings and values they have for the brand.

5.5 Service design

Gillian Crampton-Smith (2004) has argued that 'The job of the designer is now not just to design the device, the software, and the way you interact with it, but to design the whole experience of the service so it is coherent and satisfying' (p. 3). Dan Saffer (2008) defines a service as 'a chain of activities that form a process and have value' (p. 175). The key thing about service design is that there are multiple 'touch points' where people encounter a service and the interactions with services happen over time. To be well designed these touch points need to demonstrate a consistent look and feel, and present consistent values (e.g. Live | Work in Moggridge, 2007, pp. 412–29). A great example of service design in the early 2000s was Orange, with a consistent approach to bills, adverts, shops, the online presence and the mobile presence. Interactions with services typically happen intermittently and take place from different locations and devices. The PACT elements describe services just as well as any other interaction, but the focus of the activities needs to accommodate how the service is created, structured and delivered.

Brand is typically an important aspect of service design (see Further thoughts box). People need to recognize that they are interacting with the same entity (the service provider) even though they are using different technologies and different environments to do so. In service design, designers are concerned with providing resources to enable people-to-provider interactions. Services are more intangible and flexible than products. People do not walk away carrying a service, they take away the results of a service. Services are co-created to a large extent, negotiated between consumer and provider. Figure 5.6 illustrates the concept of a customer journey through the various touch points of a service and how these relate to different aspects of social media. These customer journey maps help the designer view the whole service from the user's perspective.

→ Social media are discussed in Chapter 15

FURTHER THOUGHTS

The end of the seven-layer model

These changes in the person–technology environment have a number of implications for software engineering and interaction design. Firstly, the application no longer governs and the seven-layer Open Systems Interconnection (OSI) model that has dominated software since its inception becomes inadequate. Data and interaction history now have to be shared across applications. In the past the application as the top layer of the OSI model controlled interaction, the context of functions and the overall quality of service. In the next generation of software such details will need to be shared by applications and there is no standard protocol for doing this.

A consistent and engaging service must fit in with people's lifestyles. Interactivity in the next generation is distributed in time and place, the touch points. Saffer highlights the importance of service moments that these touch points provide and the need to design for these moments. Moments come together as service strings, as short paths of an overall process description. To2 achieve this the interface and the history of interactions have to be transmitted between touch points, carried by the individual so that quality of service, security, privacy and quality of interactive experience are all maintained across places and across time. There are both short-term and long-term interactions and the service needs to know what is mine, what I am interested in and who I am willing to share what with; and how this changes depending on how I am feeling. In short, the service needs to know about my lifestyle.

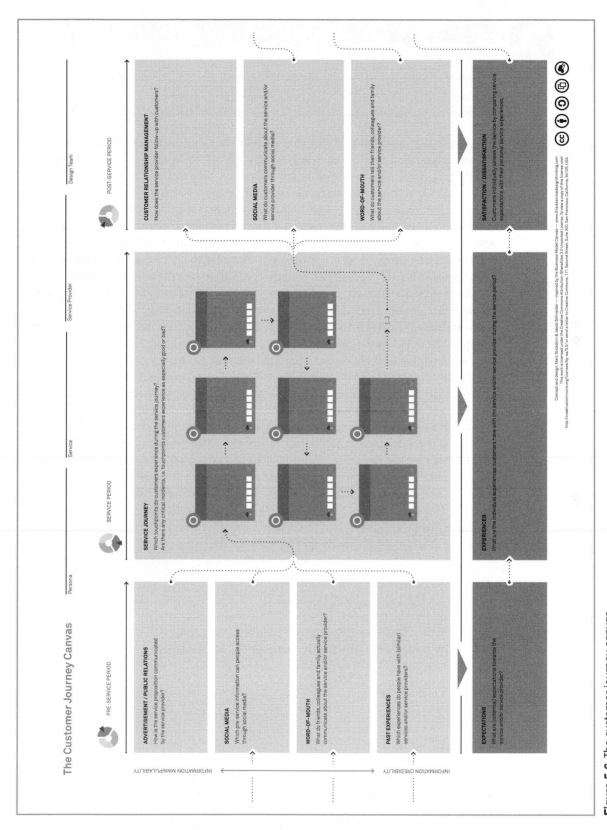

Figure 5.6 The customer journey canvas

(Source: http://files.thisisservicedesignthinking.com/tisdt_cujoca.pdf)

Challenge 5.4

Think about the changing nature of the telephone service – from the days when everything went through an operator to the combination of texts, calls and Web access you get nowadays. How do you rate the service you get?

The developing importance of lifestyles, and the changing nature of interactions in the twenty-first century, have led us to explore an approach to design that we call Designing by Lifestyles (DbL). DbL is an approach to design that aims to deal with service HCI in the 2010s. A key feature of designing for the new environments is that designers cannot 'gather' requirements from observing people or interviewing people using existing systems. There are no existing systems and, moreover, there are no requirements in the sense that the systems are aiming to meet a particular need. Designers are required to create experiences and new services. However, as we know, designers also need to understand the characteristics of the people who will use their new services and engage with the new experiences.

The notion of a 'lifestyle' is deliberately constructed to be more abstract than personas and scenarios. Lifestyle focuses on the ways in which people lead their lives, on their aspirations rather than their intentions, on their values and on their search for identity. There are details of lifestyles and activities associated with lifestyles, but these vary across different domains and environments. There is a presence of services (touch points) and the presence of others (both real and virtual) and interactions appropriate to time, place and circumstance. We characterize this as shown in Figure 5.7 where the keystones of presence, interaction, domain and environment come together to define a lifestyle at the levels of characteristics, activities and aspirations.

→ Section 24.4 covers presence

Besides these different concepts, DbL makes use of four enabling envisionment techniques that allow for rapid prototyping of ideas and engagement of people with evolving designs: video scenarios, style sketches, software demos and Wizard of Oz. Video scenarios allow designers to envision future interactions in video, style sketches are similar to mood boards and Wizard of Oz systems replace not yet available technology by a human (discussed further in Chapter 8). These four forms of representation provide the overall framework for the DbL approach, moving from the conceptual to the concrete much as in a scenario-based design approach, where we move from stories to conceptual scenarios to concrete scenario and use cases. The constructs used in DbL are pitched at a more

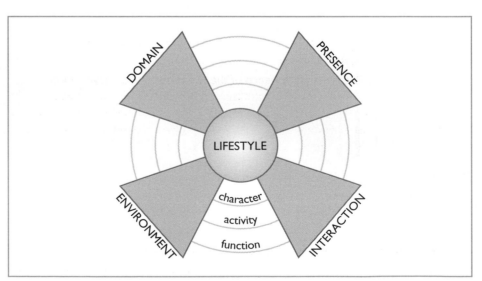

Figure 5.7 Key constructs of Designing by Lifestyles

abstract level to help designers think in the wider context of the heterogeneous, distributed interactions that characterize lifestyles and the services they require.

One key design ambition of service design is to achieve a recognizable consistency and branding across experiences. Interactions must be transferable across applications. There is also a need for aesthetic and emotional interaction. Lifestyles are concerned with how people feel about things, with values and with changes in feelings over time as a result of interactions. Experiences between people and technology need to develop over time, and move from interactions to relationships.

Summary and key points

Experience design is concerned with all the issues that go into providing an engaging and enjoyable experience for people in both the short and longer term. This includes aesthetics, pleasure and emotional engagement in terms of both the product and the service provided. In particular, it is important to consider experiences at a physical, behavioural and social level and in terms of the meanings people derive from their experiences. Experience design draws on:

- Theories of experience
- Theories of emotion
- Theories of aesthetics
- Theories of games.

Exercises

1 How far is it necessary to understand the theory of human emotions in order to design affective technologies? Illustrate your answer with examples.

2 Develop a storyboard showing the proposed use of an affective operating system designed to respond when it detects frustration and tiredness in its user.

3 Consider a standard desktop PC and a small interactive device such as a palmtop, mobile phone or digital camera. Choose recent examples.

   (a) Analyse each device against Tiger's four principles, attempting to determine which (if any) the designers were intending to evoke, and note the results of your analysis.

   (b) Conduct a PACT analysis for each of the two products you have chosen. (PACT – people, activities, contexts and technologies – was introduced in Chapter 2.) Taking account of the results of this, discuss whether pleasure should be an important design feature for the technologies in question. Explain your reasons.

 ## Further reading

McCarthy, J. and Wright, P. (2004) *Technology as Experience,* MIT Press, Cambridge, MA.

Norman, D. (2004) *Emotional Design: Why We Love (or Hate) Everyday Things.* Basic Books, New York.

Getting ahead

McCullough, G. (2002) *Abstracting Craft: The Practiced Digital Hand.* MIT Press, Cambridge, MA.

Shedroff, N. (2001) *Experience Design.* New Riders, Indianapolis, IN.

 **Web links**

AIGA, the professional association for design is at **www.aiga.org**

The accompanying website has links to relevant websites. Go to
www.pearsoned.co.uk/benyon

 Comments on challenges

Challenge 5.1

The computer game *Myst* was a huge success when it first appeared in the mid-1990s. I spent several years playing it off and on with my son until we had finally solved all the puzzles and travelled to all the different worlds.

- *Identity* – the game soon developed a dedicated following of people who identified with the mysterious worlds in which the game took place.
- *Adaptivity* was key to the success of the game. Like many games, there were levels that became harder and harder. Once the challenges of one level had been completed, the players were ready for the next. But also like many games, without the 'cheats' many players would not progress past level 1!
- *Narrative* was also keenly observed in *Myst*. All the game's players knew was that something terrible had happened to two brothers. The purpose of the game was to discover what had happened. Snippets of information were carefully revealed as the players progressed through the game to maintain the momentum of the narrative.
- *Immersion* was remarkable given the tiny screen of the early Mac computers. However, the speakers on our machine were good and the sound in *Myst* excellent and very evocative, with chilling winds blowing and the sounds of water trickling in the distance. Turn off the light on a dark winter's afternoon and you were transported into the *Myst* worlds.
- *Flow* was present, as the scenes shifted gently from one to another and as vistas one saw from a distance gradually came into view. It is much better in later, animated versions of the game.

Challenge 5.2

As you will probably find, in our context, Tiger's classification is a useful guide to thinking about pleasure rather than a hard-and-fast set of categories. You are likely to find that people's responses vary – even for an identical product – so think about how such information could be used to guide design choices.

Challenge 5.3

You will need to debate the issues of whether beauty is in the eye of the beholder, or whether there are good general rules. Discuss the site in terms of classical aesthetics (clean, clear, pleasant, aesthetic, symmetrical) and expressive aesthetics (original, sophisticated, fascinating, special effects, creative).

Challenge 5.4

There are many general issues to think about as services change from being provided by people to being provided automatically – and hence losing the 'personal touch'. Services on phones now cover a lot more than just making calls, of course. And the type of service and the brand identity are key aspects of deciding which provider to use.

Chapter 6
The Home Information Centre (HIC): a case study in designing interactive systems

Aims

In this chapter we will use a case study to illustrate many of the features of the design and evaluation of interactive systems that you have encountered. The case concerns the development of a new concept for a device known as the Home Information Centre (HIC). It was a real project in which our research centre was leading the interaction design component. We were a design team of a full-time designer and two full-time PhD students, and several students who worked on specific aspects of the design. Elsewhere in this book we have included examples that arose from the project. We used the scenario-based design method discussed in Chapter 3 and many of the specific techniques described in Chapters 7–13. The aim of the chapter is to illustrate the process we went through and to highlight the types of decisions and issues that arise during an interaction design project.

After studying this chapter you should be able to:

● Understand how to undertake an interaction design project

● Discuss how design decisions are made in an interaction design project

● Understand the trade-offs that are inherent in such a project

● Appreciate the central role of evaluation in design.

6.1   Introduction

The concept for the HIC came from the observation that there are two typical situations in the home. The TV, video, DVD and music centre are in the living room. It is a 'lean-back' situation, where people are being entertained and where they relax. In the home office there is a PC (personal computer). It is a 'lean-forward' situation where people are actively engaged with and focused on producing things. The relatively poor uptake of devices such as WebTV (which provided Internet access through the television) suggests that neither the lean-forward situation of a PC nor the lean-back situation of a TV in a living room will be the right context or the right device for new services such as home banking, shopping and so on. Instead, a new device, the Home Information Centre, HIC, is proposed. This should be a device where people can get at and provide information while they are occupied with other household activities. The industrial partner characterized this as 'a move-around situation for infotainment'.

BOX 6.1

Infotainment

Infotainment is a term intended to convey a mixture of information and entertainment and is one example of how traditional activities and technologies are increasingly converging. Other terms such as 'edutainment' (education and entertainment) and 'infomercial' (information and commercial, or advertising) are increasingly common. Technologies similarly converge: a phone and a camera, for example, or a PDA and an MP3 player. One of the challenges for interactive systems designers is to understand when and where it is appropriate to converge technologies. Is it better – simpler, more convivial, etc. – to put technologies together or is it better to keep them apart in separate devices?

The project was established to explore the concept of an HIC to see whether full-blown manufacture of such a device was sensible. There were many parallel activities going on in the project to do with issues such as market analysis, hardware costs and so on. There were also many other aspects of the whole software system that were investigated by different partners. In this chapter we focus on the initial design of the overall concept and on the key features of the user interface and human–computer interaction.

The abstract concept of an HIC as a device to deal with 'a move-around situation for infotainment' was initially translated into a number of high-level features and functions. The HIC would need to employ software to address the problems of complexity, difficult navigation and query formulation that bedevil the Web and other large information spaces. Two key features were required: an intuitive navigation support system and a flexible query system. The software should provide the following:

- An abstract representation of the contents of information sources that should be extracted and maintained semi-automatically
- Speech, pen, touch and keyboard as input
- Sound, images, text and animation as output
- Speech recognition (SR)
- Natural language (NL) queries
- An intuitive user interface.

The industrial partner on the project who was most likely to subsequently build and market the device also imposed a key constraint on the project: *the HIC should not look or behave like a PC*. They were keen to explore alternative interface designs in the project – particularly having a design that did not include scrolling or window management. This was a tough design challenge.

The development approach that was adopted was based on the iterative model of design activities (see Figure 3.1), beginning with mock-ups and 'Wizard of Oz'-style experimentation and finally ending with experiments in real homes. The project plan specified that the HIC would be developed as a series of prototypes, leading to a final pilot-like complete system. Four prototypes were planned:

→ Chapter 7 discusses the Wizard of Oz approach

1 *Prototype P0* should be delivered by the end of month 6, and was to be used for the very first 'discount' engineering experiments with the HIC system to aid in the design specification. P0 would not contain software.
2 *Prototype P1* would be delivered by the end of month 13, and would be used for the first laboratory experiments collecting data on usage, including interactions and usage of the natural language query system. The prototype would include full monitor set-up in the laboratory, a PC simulating the HIC client, the content server, a first version of the display visualization, a simple interaction model, a control module and simple or dummy versions of the other modules. An operator at the PC (hidden from the user) would start computer actions requested orally by the user, but not yet handled by the software (the Wizard of Oz approach).
3 *Prototype P2* would be delivered at the end of month 19 and used for full laboratory experiments at first and then in real user homes. The prototype would be used for the final user validation of the HIC and its associated concepts. This prototype would include full monitor set-up, including a PC running the client modules and connected to a second PC running the server modules. All modules should be present in full. The prototype would be improved according to the laboratory experiments and the user site experiments.
4 *Prototype P3* was to be the final official version of the HIC, usable for demonstrations and for the possible basis of further exploitation. It would correspond to P2 but with corrections and enhancements made following the experiments.

It is fair to say that this was an ambitious plan and the project did not succeed in following it in detail. With so much new technology and so many 'unknowns', there were always going to be difficulties. Indeed, in the end two P3 prototypes were produced – one for the functionality of the system and one for the interface concepts. They were never robust enough to be used in people's homes.

Challenge 6.1

Discuss the development approach taken.

6.2 Scenarios for the HIC

As we have seen (Chapter 2), a useful structure for thinking about interactive systems design is the PACT approach: people, activities, contexts and technologies. This can be used to help think about conceptual scenarios of use. Conceptual scenarios are abstract descriptions of the PACT elements in some domain. For the HIC design, we brainstormed

ideas at a number of internal workshops about how the HIC might be used. We finished up with three general, highly abstract uses for the HIC – informational, communicational and entertainment. Early ideas about communication centred on how the HIC might be used as a sort of 'Post-it' system. One member of the family might leave a message for another to buy cat food, get some milk or whatever. The HIC would also be used as a video phone and an e-mail system, and for social networking.

The informational scenarios concerned activities such as finding a recipe. This in turn leads to 'What's in the fridge? What else do we need? What can we cook?' The HIC would be able to calculate the quantities in a recipe for one, two or three people. Other scenarios concerned activities such as going sailing, hence the need to get information on the tides, going skiing (finding out about the weather), going out (getting information about pubs, restaurants and concerts), etc.

The entertainment scenario led to ideas that users might like to play a game, find some sport, watch TV on demand or automatically record preferred programmes. It would be possible to have a chat room running alongside a TV programme and so on.

Other scenarios included integration with other devices, such as heating control, home security and so on. Children doing homework was another, investigating, finding out, doing crosswords and quizzes, ordering videos, photographs and surfing the Web. Often the issue came back – how to accommodate large amounts of data, large visualizations, and the multitude of media that would be needed. Remember that the project was exploring a new device – a home information centre – which was not to be a PC. It was to be different in its look, feel and usage.

In developing the various, more concrete versions of the abstract activities, we were aware from a high-level PACT analysis of the need to cover the different people – children, people with disabilities (e.g. arthritis, short-sightedness), as well as the young and wealthy who would be the early adopters of such technology. We also needed to cover a variety of domains and information spaces – e.g. those with rapidly changing information against those with static information, different media such as maps, voice, sound output and so on. Eleven scenarios constituted the final scenario corpus that was used in the project:

→ Information spaces are discussed in Sections 18.2 and 18.3

- What shall we have for dinner?
- What shall we do now?
- News and e-books
- Entertain me
- Message board
- Traffic
- New users
- Housekeeping
- Payment
- I cannot get my phone to work because . . .
- Planning ahead.

Challenge 6.2

Take one of the scenario ideas above, undertake a PACT analysis and brainstorm how the scenario might unfold.

Note that no decision has been made as to how to deliver these scenarios as yet. The HIC could be an integrated platform designed specifically for the 'move-around infotainment' context or it could be an open platform in which third-party producers would develop apps. The aim was to explore the concept of the HIC first before settling on the physical design. The scenario corpus constituted the first prototype, P0. We were reluctant to fix too soon on a physical design, being wary of early 'design fixation', and felt that it was much better to explore contexts and activities of the HIC at this point. In thinking about scenarios of use for the HIC, we were aware that we needed a suitable variety of domains, interaction styles, media and modalities, people and contexts of use.

One way of learning more about how people might use such a device as the HIC would be to undertake naturalistic studies of people using existing media in their 'infotainment' activities. However, at this early stage in the project we were under considerable time pressure and hence the opportunity to gather real stories of use would have to wait. Accordingly, we began by identifying some conceptual scenarios.

Home technologies

Subsequently we did undertake such studies of people and technologies in their homes and this led to a number of interesting findings regarding technologies in the home and how people use them within the social and physical spaces. A special issue of the journal *Cognition, Technology and Work* (volume 5, number 1, May 2003) is devoted to home technologies and includes a description of these findings. Baillie and Benyon (2008) describe a method for investigating technology in the household, the Home Workshop.

**FURTHER
THOUGHTS**

A future workshop

One important thing about developing prototypes is using them. The scenario corpus was used internally within the project team to generate ideas and discuss the details of functionality. The scenarios were also taken outside the team and used as the basis of 'future workshops'. Future workshops are one of the design methods advocated in the participative design approach to the design of interactive systems. This approach has a long tradition, particularly in Scandinavia, going back to the late 1970s.

→ See Section 7.2 on participative design

A future workshop comprises three stages:

1 *Critique*. This is a group brainstorming session that tries different approaches to the activities/problems being addressed by the proposed system. A set of themes arising out of this stage is used in stage 2, fantasy.
2 *Fantasy*. The emphasis here is on creative solutions/ideas, no matter how unrealistic. From these a number of fantasy themes are generated and these are then used to drive stage 3.
3 *Implementation*. The groups work out what would be necessary in order to produce a real solution to some of the fantasy themes generated (e.g. by producing a mock-up or a storyboard).

Using the 'What shall we do now?' scenario as a basis (see below), we spent a morning working with four groups of high-school students through these three stages. The scenario was supplemented with introductory presentations and written materials and adapted to make it more relevant to the participants; the students were asked to imagine that they and a group of friends had won a trip to the city for the day and had to plan their activities.

→ The prototypes from this are presented in Chapter 8

The results of this session were quite telling. The group focused on the need for the HIC to be personalized. They wanted mobility in the system and they emphasized the communication function over the informational function of the HIC.

A more concrete scenario

At this stage in the project it was important to pick one of these scenarios to orient the various project teams around (ultimately, more fully detailed versions of the scenarios would drive specification of the HIC interface). We suggested that the informational scenario 'What shall we do now?' was the best one to start with because it covered lots of different data types which would help all the project partners. A key feature of the scenario-based design approach that we were following was that all partners in the project would be required to use the scenario and they would need appropriate data to work with. There had to be data for the people doing the data mining, data for the people developing the interface, data for the speech recognition people, and so on. Additionally, the 'What shall we do now?' scenario covered various types of people (young/old, etc.) rather well. Another of the informational scenarios, 'What shall we have for dinner?', was far less applicable to children, for example, and we saw children as potentially significant users of the HIC. The range of activity types (finding out something, communicating with others, booking tickets online, etc.) in the scenario also provided the opportunity for a variety of interaction possibilities to be investigated. The remaining scenarios would allow us to investigate other data types (e.g. pictures/video), use contexts (e.g. hands and eyes occupied elsewhere), activity types (e.g. games, controlling another device such as a TV) and input/output devices not covered in the first scenario.

Developing the scenario

At one of the workshops, one group took the 'What shall we do now?' scenario and discussed it in more detail. The extract below is taken from the notes of this meeting and gives an idea of how the scenario discussion generated ideas and questions. The overall context for the scenario was the large arts festival that takes place in Edinburgh every August. It was envisaged that the HIC would be an ideal device for finding out what was going on so that people could decide 'What shall we do now'.

Early on there was a need to make it more concrete, to focus on a specific context of use. The discussion at the workshop switched rapidly between high-level concerns and the details of a concrete interaction. This also resulted in the development of more detailed personas. It is summarized below.

← See Section 3.2 on personas and scenarios

1 The couple should be aged 20–30. They lived in Edinburgh. It was August and the Edinburgh Festival was in full swing. The couple knew about the Edinburgh Festival and wanted to check out what was on that evening. They did not have much time.

2 What sort of a query would they enter? Broad categories of shows such as 'comedy', time constraints such as 'starting after 6 pm', specific artists or shows or a specific venue (because a venue might have a particular specialism)?

3 What would be on the HIC? For example, would there be text only, or pictures/icons? Would there be advertising? Would people enter a free-form query or browse through an online catalogue? This was an issue that the content or service provider would need to deal with. If this is the case then set-up issues are raised. Perhaps people would select a favourite provider, then they would need to be able to add and remove them.

4 The modality of the input was considered. Would the HIC have handwriting recognition? Should it be an iPad or tablet PC? Should there be voice input for free-form queries, a keyboard, remote keyboard or on-screen keyboard?

5 Once the name of the actor/venue, etc. had been input, people would get some display on the HIC which was dependent on the number of results of the query and the list of categories. Would the categories be generated automatically, or be preset?

6 Queries would need a response time of 5–10 seconds. People would make a selection 'check out show times' – perhaps by touching an icon, perhaps by saying 'show times'. They might be using a remote control – how far could the person be from the screen?

7 Once the HIC had displayed the show time, venue, names of actors, any reviews of the show, etc., the person might want to make a booking. The display would be dependent on the history of the interaction and the visualization of the query history (or at least this should be accessible). Then all the issues of how to go back, up, etc. through the interaction history would need to be addressed.

8 The booking of tickets would probably require a different service or content provider. Would the HIC then 'lose control' of the interface or could the HIC provide its own to someone else's (e.g. the Festival Theatre's) website and online booking facility? How would the person input their name, credit card, address, etc.? Preferably this would be automatic.

9 Would the HIC be able to show the number of seats remaining for a show? Would the tickets be printed on a local printer? There was a need for a function of the HIC that automatically kept people informed of a changing situation: an interface agent perhaps, or just part of the interface?

10 The brainstorming continued – what if there was a need to contact friends about the show, send them details of the location, etc.? They might want to meet for a drink nearby – in which case, could the HIC access a webcam in the pub to see how busy it was?

11 Issues of traffic then arose. How long would it take to get there? What about providing bus or taxi information? The need to have the HIC provide a map or print instructions was recognized – and this should be able to happen from different locations.

12 The group changed the context to explore other areas such as going skiing or sailing, but apart from the issue of scale – the information space of skiing is much larger than the information space of the Edinburgh Festival – few new issues arose. How to update the service or content providers was important and there was some discussion about security, personalizing the HIC, etc.

The results of these discussions were taken away from the workshop and put alongside some real data from the previous year's festival. Flyers for shows, brochures advertising events and the details from the whole Festival programme were used to provide real examples of the sort of data that the HIC in this scenario would have to deal with (Figure 6.1). The final version of the scenario is shown in the next section.

The Edinburgh Festival scenario

The ideas that had been developed finally finished up as the scenario shown below. Although it is quite concrete, with some interface features described and a wealth of context, there are many design features that have not been agreed. These are recorded as footnotes to the scenario. One of the features of the design method is that these footnotes force the designers to consider further design issues. The scenario below illustrates the recommended formal way of presenting scenarios.

Scenario name

What shall we do now?

Scenario history

Version	Date	Author	Description
1	20 April 2009	D. Benyon	Discussed at Struer meeting
1.1	4 May 2009	D. Benyon	Modified following discussions at Struer

Figure 6.1 Example flyers from the Edinburgh Festival
(Source: David Benyon)

Scenario type

Activity scenario

PACT

People – young, wealthy, no children

Activities – searching for information, making bookings, meeting friends

Context – flat in Edinburgh, assume fast Internet connection

Technology – HIC as currently specified.

Rationale

This scenario has been developed as part of the prototype P0 deliverable. It is intended to provide a rich description of a general context of use of the HIC. The scenario is deliberately vague with respect to a number of features such as input and output media and modalities, how the content is provided, etc., in order to stimulate discussion about such things. More concrete forms of the scenario are expected to be produced to illustrate a range of media/ modalities. The scenario is also intended to provide a rich source of data so that issues concerning the semantics of the information space may be considered.

Scenario

1 Jan and Pat are a couple in their mid-thirties. Pat is a university lecturer in Cultural Studies and Jan is an accounts manager at Standard Life insurance. They live in the Stockbridge area of Edinburgh in a two-bedroom flat overlooking the river. It is 12.00 noon on 15 August. Jan and Pat are sitting in their large, airy kitchen/dining room. The remains of pizza and mixed salad mingle with a pile of newspapers on the kitchen table. Jan and Pat have recently returned from a holiday on the island of Zante and, apart from checking their e-mail, have not gone back to work. They decide that they would like to go to see one of the events that is happening as part of the Edinburgh Festival.

2 The Edinburgh Festival is a large arts festival that takes place in the city for three weeks in August. It consists of two arts festivals – the Edinburgh International

Festival and the Edinburgh Festival Fringe – a book festival, a film festival, a jazz festival and a variety of related events. The International Festival is the original, and up until the mid-1980s was the bigger of the two. This is the official festival, which features prestigious performers from around the world, world-class orchestras, composers, ballet troupes, etc. The Fringe, on the other hand, started as an unofficial adjunct to the festival, traditionally more informal and adventurous. It featured new theatres like the Traverse, or the work of artistic mavericks like Demarco. Gradually over the years it has become larger than the official International Festival. In total the Edinburgh Festival consists of some 1200 distinct events that take place at 150 different venues spread throughout the city.

3 Jan activates the HIC[1] and chooses 'Edinburgh Festival'.[2] The HIC connects to the different content providers who are registered as providing content about the festival. The display shows five categories of information – Times of Events, Specific Artists, Specific Events, Specific Venues, Types of Events – a catalogue and a query facility.[3]

4 'What sort of thing do you fancy doing?' asked Jan. 'Hmmm, something funny, perhaps,' Pat replied. 'Richard Herring, maybe, or Phil Kay? Stewart Lee? I guess we ought to check out the International Festival as well.' Jan entered the query 'What do we have for Richard Herring, or Stewart Lee?'.

5 The HIC displays *Excavating Rita*, *King Dong vs. Moby Dick* and *This Morning with Richard not Judy II*[4] along with a display[5] of categories of further information: TV Reviews, Newspaper Reviews, and Times of Events.[6] Jan makes the selection[7] of Times of Events. The HIC responds with details of the events it has retrieved, displaying the data Title, ShortDescription, Venue, FromDate, ToDate, ExceptDates, Days, StartTime, Duration, Cost, ConcessionCost.[8] 'What do you think?' said Jan. 'Check out *Excavating Rita* and *This Morning with Richard not Judy II*,' replied Pat. 'Well, there may not be any tickets left for *This Morning with Richard not Judy II*, I'll check.' Jan specifies that the HIC should monitor the number of tickets left for *This Morning with Richard not Judy II*.[9] The display shows 24 tickets left. 'You had better check *Excavating Rita* as well.' 'OK.' Jan instructs the HIC to monitor TicketsLeft for *Excavating Rita* as well. The display shows 45. The display highlights that the value of TicketsLeft for *This Morning with Richard not Judy II* has changed to 20, then to 18. 'Hmmm, *This Morning with Richard not Judy II* is selling fast, I don't think we are going to make that. Is there anything else?' says Pat.

6 'Well, hundreds of things, actually,' Jan responded: 'Let's see. At 1 pm we have 'Verdi's Macbeth', a lunchtime talk at the Queen's Hall, or an archive recording of

---

[1] How the HIC is activated is not considered here. Different methods may lead to different versions of the scenario.

[2] So, 'Edinburgh Festival' is a 'thing' in, or accessed by, the HIC. It could be some sort of plug-in provided by a third-party content provider. For example, the *Guardian* newspaper might provide a free CD-ROM for its readership, Jan and Pat may have downloaded the data from a website, or the data may be physically resident on some remote machine, or on Pat and Jan's computer.

[3] Again the modality of these are not specified. The query facility could be spoken, typed on a remote keyboard or an on-screen keyboard, written by hand or in some other form such as a query agent. The catalogue facility could be represented in a number of different ways.

[4] How this data is presented is a major issue. We do not know how far our users are from the display.

[5] There are a number of issues concerned with things such as response time here. Will the HIC display some sort of 'busy' icon, provide information on how long the result of the query will take, present data gradually, etc.?

[6] There are many possible categories and ways of presenting and interrelating the data. Ideally the categories will be automatically generated.

[7] Once again, modality is not specified – Jan could touch an icon on the screen, say 'Show Times', use a remote control and click the 'Go' button, etc.

[8] See data dictionary for more details about these data items. (Not included here.)

[9] This raises the whole issue of agent-based interaction. Will the HIC have an agent (anthropomorphic or not) or will it be possible to specify these sorts of things through the general 'intelligence' of the HIC technology? Jan could instruct an agent to monitor some attribute of the data – TicketsLeft in this case – or the system could facilitate this type of facility in other ways.

→ See Chapter 17 on agent-based interaction

Sir John Barbirolli at 2.15. The Nimmo Twins in 'Posh Spice Nude' at the Gilded Balloon, that's at 1.30. . . .' Jan continues to browse the listings, jumping to read reviews, watching snippets of TV Reviews, checking times and so on.[10] The display highlights changes in the TicketsLeft for *Excavating Rita*, now down to 35. At 12.30 the display indicates that *This Morning with Richard not Judy II* has started. 'Well, we had better do something,' said Pat. 'Let's go for *Excavating Rita* and book our tickets now.' Jan selects *Excavating Rita* and 'booking' and the Booking Office at the Pleasance Theatre is displayed.[11]

7   The booking form has fields for Name, Address, PhoneNumber, PostCode and CreditCard type, ExpiryDate and Number. Jan selects 'personal profile' on the HIC,[12] confirms that the details should be Jan's, and the data is entered onto the booking form.[13] 'Just a minute,' says Pat, 'Kat and Toni might like to come. Why don't you check?' Jan activates the phone[14] and selects Kat and Toni.[15] The number is dialled and Toni answers. 'We are going to see *Excavating Rita* with Richard Herring at the Pleasance. Do you fancy coming? It starts at 3.30 and there are only 35, sorry 32 tickets left.' 'Sure,' says Toni, 'We'd love to. I'll come online.'[16] Jan returns to the booking form and specifies four tickets. The total credit card amount is calculated and displayed. Jan confirms the transaction and receives a confirmation number.

8   Jan sees that Toni is online and changes to the conferencing system that they both use. Jan enters the message[17] that they have the tickets and suggests meeting for a drink beforehand. There is some discussion about the location, pubs versus restaurants versus cafés, food or not, etc.[18] Toni indicates that the area is not familiar. 'I'll see if there is a map,' says Jan.

9   Jan selects the Specific Venues category, selects the Pleasance Theatre,[19] and selects map. A map showing the area is displayed. All the restaurants, cafés, pubs, etc.[20] are shown. Jan selects Pubs and the display changes to remove the other eating and drinking places. The pubs are highlighted and referenced.[21] Jan selects three or four pubs in turn and gets information about the pub type, distance from the Pleasance, etc. Jan returns to the conference and sends the message to Toni that there is the Pleasance Courtyard, but it will be packed,[22] or the Southsider. It's a 10-minute walk, but it serves Maclays which is a nice beer.

10   Toni says that some help getting there would be useful. Jan attaches the map to a message and sends it to Toni. When Toni gets it, the HIC at Toni's end is able to provide instructions about how to get to the Southsider. 'See you in the pub in an hour, then,' says Pat, 'but you had better get started. I just checked the traffic on the Dalkeith Road and it's terrible.'

---

[10] An issue here is how the display builds up and how a trace of the various queries and browsing is presented. It would or might be desirable to have some way of showing links between artists, shows, venues, type of event and so on.

[11] Note that at this point we have 'gone outside' the HIC and are at the mercy of the Pleasance Theatre's interface design for their booking system.

[12] Again this could be a personal agent or other way of providing profile data.

[13] This happens automatically, presumably.

[14] This is probably part of the HIC, but could be the regular phone, of course. How it is activated is up for debate.

[15] By Name from an address book, through their personal profile, or whatever.

[16] Or perhaps Toni is automatically 'online' in answering the phone.

[17] This may be spoken interaction, it does not have to be typed.

[18] Ideally the HIC will be able to pick up on keywords used in such conversations and use these in subsequent searches.

[19] Again this would probably be the default given the history of this interaction.

[20] As per their conversation, earlier.

[21] There's another issue about categories here. Maxine's is categorized as a wine bar, but could just as easily be classified as a pub.

[22] Or perhaps looks at the Courtyard in real time through the Pleasance cam.

Challenge 6.3

Using the footnotes recorded against the Edinburgh Festival scenario, discuss possible design decisions, or design trade-offs, that will have to be made.

6.3 Evaluating early interface prototypes

In order to evaluate some interface concepts, three prototype design solutions, each taking one of the scenarios as a starting point, were produced. These draft prototype designs were developed as working solutions to some of the questions that had arisen from three of the scenarios. This section discusses the three prototypes produced and analyses the decisions made by the three designers in response to the design of the HIC as a whole. This work then served as the basis of the development of the second interface design.

Usability principles

The design principles introduced in Chapter 4 were used as a basis for the evaluations. The principles outline the three main categories of usability that interface design should encompass and this can provide the basis for an early high-level 'discount' evaluation. This is a high-level 'walkthrough' of a design undertaken by an expert, guided by design principles. We used our principles of learnability, effectiveness and accommodation.

→ Expert evaluation is discussed in Section 10.2

- *Learnability*. Can people guess easily what the system will do, based upon previous experience? This covers the usability principles of visibility, consistency, affordance and familiarity.
- *Effectiveness*. Can people correct or change previous decisions, and complete their desired task easily, effectively and safely? This covers the usability principles of navigation, control, feedback, recovery and constraints.
- *Accommodation*. Is the system designed to afford a multiplicity of ways in which people can accomplish their goals? Is it pleasant to use? This covers the usability principles of flexibility, style and conviviality.

In order to illustrate this process we report on the evaluation of prototype B which concerned the issue of presentation of huge amounts of information, which will be accessible through the HIC. Figure 6.2 shows a screenshot from this draft prototype illustrating the use of conceptual categories relevant for a 'festival' content provider. An issue at this point was who would define such categories and how many categories are appropriate. This question continued to be extremely important for the project.

The prototype defines multiple levels of information available through the use of a colour-coded history top bar. It also provides a solution for the many actions and operations to be presented on screen only when required, by means of hidden docks. It deals with the issues involved with utilizing the HIC from a distance in connection with speech input or remote control with the implementation of 'Near' and 'Far' buttons which magnify the contents on the screen.

Analysis

- *Learnability*. The interface was easy to follow. The inclusion of 'hotspot' rollovers on certain areas of the interface confirms to the user that these areas are clickable

Figure 6.2 Prototype B – festivals screen snapshot
(Source: David Benyon)

buttons. The animated arrow at the bottom of the interface indicates that there is a hidden dock available at the bottom of the screen. When someone clicks on a button on the main interface and is taken to the next level, their 'route' through the information space is recorded on the history bar at the top of the screen. The separate levels have backgrounds of different colour to separate them. A problem here is that they do not correspond to the colours on the history bar, which is slightly confusing. The history bar contains a group of rainbow-coloured cells that at some points could be completely empty or contain no history, which could confuse. The question also arises as to what would happen to the history bar when the person had gone through more than six pages of information, as the bar has only six cells.

- *Accommodation.* In terms of flexibility, this interface solution offers people a number of ways in which to complete the same task. For example, they could search for a particular event in the Edinburgh Festival, look through a number of events on a certain date, or look for events in a certain area of the city. People can access previous levels of information through the history bar, or through the Back button on the hidden navigation bar, but cannot then return to the level they were on without searching for it again. The Near and Far buttons also provide some kind of solution to the problem of a small 15-inch screen being viewed from the other side of the room by someone who is using voice activation or a remote control as a means of operating the HIC. The buttons on the screen were also well proportioned for using with the touchscreen facility.

- *Effectiveness.* The design is fairly successful concerning effectiveness. People are able to go back to previous levels easily via the history bar or Back button. The design contains a Forward button, which is non-functional, indicating that it was intended to be included in the design. However, its functionality is not clear, and what would the history bar show if people were to go back? How would it indicate that they might also go forward?

Conclusions

After evaluation this solution provided a great many ideas and questions that needed answering. Although not perfect, this design gave a good starting point for providing an effective solution to the many problems that the HIC poses.

In particular, a history bar was an effective idea, but the colour coordination, representation of the bar with no history or huge amounts of history, and representation of the bar when people are moving backward through the information all needed to be looked at further.

Colour coordination of the different levels was also a good idea, but it was not really used to good effect and could be confusing. Used in another way, it could provide a powerful tool for navigating the HIC's huge information space. The allocation of colour to the levels of information needed to be investigated further.

The hidden navigation bar was also an effective idea, and would solve the problem of a large number of actions or facilities having to be available to the user quickly and easily without cluttering and confusing the screen. This was also an idea that would be looked at further.

Challenge 6.4

Put yourself in the place of the industrial partner and offer a brief critique of this interface. Remember that the company was interested in high-quality, novel, 'intuitive' user interfaces and escaping from the PC look and feel.

Outcome of the evaluation

The outcome of this evaluation, taking on board the industrial partner's comments and the views of the design team, is set out in Table 6.1. The activity was very beneficial in highlighting some key interface design issues. In Part III a number of design features that build upon these concepts are illustrated.

Table 6.1 Outcome of the evaluation

Problem or issue	Suggested solutions
History of navigation ideas need to be developed further	Use of animated rectangles, utilization of partner's remote-control button shapes, recording the user's path, providing a bar along the top of the screen, or recording the direction of navigation
Utilization of colour to categorize the huge amount of information stored within the HIC	Define categories and subcategories within the information space and allocate colour accordingly
Attention needs to be paid to the multimodal element	All design decisions must accommodate the multimodal element. Text must be readable from a distance, and any selections regardless of mode of input must confirm user interactions
Separation of the various navigational aspects	Navigational elements must be organized according to definable groupings. Navigation should be available as needed; hidden docks could be used for those least utilized so as not to clutter screen
Formalization and order of the functionality of the system	The actions and activities, as well as the information which needs to be navigated, have to be ordered. Generic actions of the system must therefore be classified
Utilization of the industrial partner's design concepts where possible	Existing style and design of remote controls could be integrated into the design

6.4 A first design

Having evaluated the existing prototypes, it was evident that before finalizing any design ideas it was necessary to understand the HIC and the generic actions of the system. That is, it was important to establish some high-level functional requirements: what the system had to do. As we discuss in Chapter 9, a good method of establishing requirements is to undertake an object–action analysis of the scenarios.

The idea in doing this analysis was to acquire a more in-depth understanding of the HIC. By identifying the activities, actions and objects within the scenarios it was hoped to give an outline of the potential utilization of the HIC. By listing these activities, it also gives an indication of how often particular activities and actions could be carried out and how many objects require being present on the screen at the same time.

The initial object–action analysis resulted in four categories of object:

- *Information display objects* – display-only data which has been searched for or queried. The data is non-editable and provided by content providers, etc.
- *Category objects* – includes lists and catalogues, changeable dependent on the providers that are subscribed to on the HIC. Restrictions or enhancements may also be applied to individual users' preferences.
- *Functions/control objects* – controls and tools which are basic to the HIC and enable functionality of the system, i.e. preferences, payment, set-up, etc.
- *Physical objects* – devices which are displayed on screen or controlled by the HIC.

Details of the objects and actions in the different categories were extracted from all the scenarios, not just the Edinburgh Festival scenario. From the data collected through an analysis of the scenarios, a list of the actions was made, with a count of the number of times these actions occurred in the scenarios. This helped to identify repetition in actions, actions that represent a series of actions rather than singular actions, and any actions that are performed by the system rather than by the user.

Three iterations and consolidations of the actions were undertaken. For example, 'Answers', 'Enters', 'Writes', 'Inputs' and 'Specifies' in the context of the scenarios all describe the action of 'inputting' information into the HIC in a variety of modal forms. The action 'Inputs' therefore best describes the generic action performed. Table 6.2 shows the results of this process.

→ Section 9.4 gives a detailed example of object–action analysis

Table 6.2 Simplification of the data – stage 3

Action	No.	Action	No.
Inputs	12	Down	
Confirms	10	Up	
Selects	21	Back	
Instructs	13	Forward	
Plays	1	Navigate	
Connects	1		
Sends	2		
Attaches	1		
Records	1		

Conceptual design

The results of the analysis of the scenarios and evaluations of the early interface prototypes resulted in a number of conceptual and physical design decisions. A number of important decisions were made, including the concept of a category bar described below. Notice that although the design is primarily conceptual at this point (i.e. we are concerned with what is required rather than how it will look and behave), it is natural to undertake some physical design as part of this process.

The category bar

The wealth of information that was going to be included in the HIC, probably from third-party content providers, had to be categorized to give it some form of order. In interface prototype C (*Recipes*, not included here) the designer had utilized categorization to develop four headings in the history. These categories now needed to be looked at further. The designer had listed 'work', 'household', 'email & web' and 'entertainment'. However, it was not clear why these were chosen, nor how they related to the general domains in which the HIC would be used. The use of the standard terminal colours – red, blue, yellow and green – was liked by the industrial partner, and these seemed to be the most effective colours to use in categorizing the information. This meant that all domains would have to be grouped into four categories. The domains listed in the scenarios were as follows:

Recipes
Travel Planner
Traffic
Culture
Find a Place
News
TV/Radio Programmes
On-line Shopping

The following categories were defined from this list:

- *Culture* – includes the Culture and TV/Radio Programmes domains.
- *News* – includes the News domain.
- *Household* – includes the Recipes and On-line Shopping domains.
- *Travel* – includes the Travel Planner, Traffic and Find a Place domains.

Each of the categories listed above was now colour-coded and represented as buttons on a bar, as shown in Figure 6.3. To aid association for people, the information contained within these categories would also incorporate the colour chosen to identify that category.

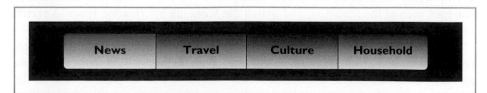

Figure 6.3 Colour-coded category bar

An interface design

The various design ideas were then brought together into the first comprehensive interface prototype. The category bar and a history bar were devised to occupy the top part of the interface, and the navigation controls needed to be central for people to get easy feedback whilst utilizing the system – an important design principle.

An idea of all the control being allocated to the border of the screen meant that the two sliding hidden docks containing the functions and auxiliary objects (such as access to the TV, radio, PVR (personal video recorder), etc.) were placed to the left and right of the screen to slide out when needed (see Figure 6.4).

The idea of the sliding docks was a good one, but the two slide bars intruded somewhat into the main space. There was also the possibility of applying all of these objects to one location rather than splitting them up into groupings. This was another idea worth mocking up. However, when it was designed an immediately obvious problem was its use of pop-up menus that were not intended to be used within the HIC interface, as they are too reminiscent of a PC interface.

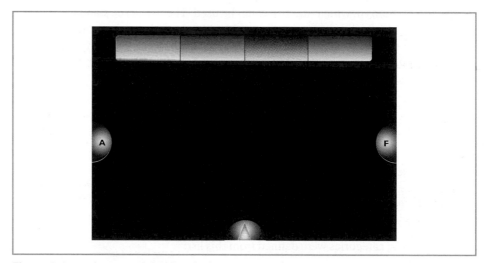

Figure 6.4 First layout with hidden docks

Evaluation of first solutions

These designs were brought back to the main interface design team who met and discussed the ideas. The group was not sure about the categorization of objects. One of the designers suggested that the activities Search and Print, which were allocated to the bottom bar, should be grouped at the left side of the interface. This seemed a much more coherent separation of the objects. He also suggested that the right-hand bar could include the lists of the content providers subscribed to on the HIC. This would allow people to click on an activity, for example Search, and then to click on a content provider, such as the *Scotsman*, and search the *Scotsman* information space. A sketch produced at this meeting is shown in Figure 6.5.

This design decision turned out to be fundamental to the HIC concept. The separation of objects and actions and the provision of a central information space was felt to provide a clear and simple conceptual model: objects on one side and actions on the other. Such a simple and clear model should go a long way to ensuring that the interface was 'intuitive'.

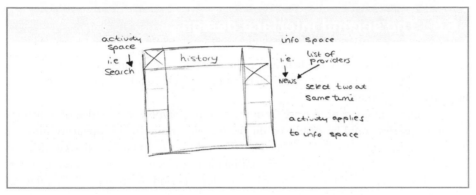

Figure 6.5 Activity and providers bar sketch

The question then arose of what to do if there are lots of content providers that the HIC owner subscribed to. How could they be shown on a bar without the use of scrolling of lists? The use of a rotating bar was suggested to deal with this. A number of alternatives for the side bars, finally resulting in two spinning 'Toblerones' that were also hidden docks (the activity and provider bars on the left and right), was the next stage of development (Figure 6.6). The bottom navigation button was also included.

After development of this prototype it was realized that the idea of a three-sided Toblerone would allow the category bar to have a menu on one side which lists the domains within that category for people to choose from. This would mean that when someone clicks on a category, the bar could spin to reveal a menu. With three sides, the category bar could still have the history on one of the sides. Instead of the history bar being only relevant to the category the person was looking at, the bar would show the history of all the pages the person had visited within all of the categories. For example, it could show two blue arrows from the Travel category, one from the yellow News category, a red search arrow from the Culture section and a green arrow from the Household category. The necessity of this bar to be available on screen at all times meant that this bar would not take the form of a hidden dock.

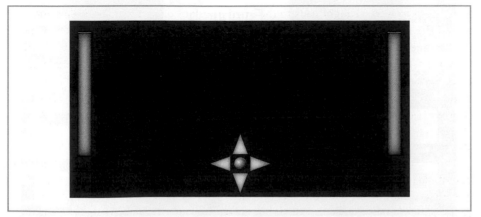

Figure 6.6 Opening HIC sequence showing two 'Toblerones'

6.5   The second interface design

A number of changes were made between the first and second interface designs. These included changing the categories of actions on the left-hand bar and dropping the bottom bar altogether.

One important concept to arise from the first prototype was the idea of a history. Previous queries could be displayed on the screen, gradually disappearing into the distance as they got older. Another member of the design team began to look at this and at the overall concept of searching. The initial ideas for having a novel searching interface had been developed and critiqued over a long period. A number of the relevant sketches are discussed in Part III.

The final design was based on the concept of a 'Rolodex' (Figure 6.7 shows a sketch of the idea). This design avoided the PC-centric design feature of having scrolling windows with all the concomitant window management activities and we felt that it was a more engaging design, suitable for a relaxed home environment. The concept behind the finalized Rolodex is such that the user may 'flip' page by page through results until the required item is found. This is done by simply touching the 'Prev' or 'Next' icons to the left of the Rolodex or by using a 'flicking' gesture on the cards. At any stage the user may select an item by touching the page of the Rolodex or by selecting 'Go!'.

Bringing together the concept of history and the concept of the Rolodex resulted in the idea of having a history of previous searches represented with smaller Rolodexes. When the person selects 'Go!' an animation of the Rolodex shrinking in size and moving to the bottom left-hand corner of the screen is provided. A new Rolodex is presented with the items relevant to the previously selected item, and searching through the information may be performed in exactly the same manner with the new data.

Figure 6.7 Second interface prototype

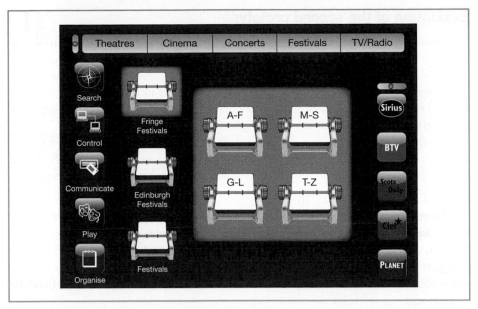

Figure 6.8 Rolodex history and Rolodex tree

One further concept was added. If any category of the search returns more than 20 results the system then presents the person with a number of Rolodexes (Figure 6.8 illustrates this). Another version was based on the idea of a cone tree (see Section 12.5).

In this case the Rolodexes are categorized alphabetically and any miniature Rolodex may be touched for selection. This then fades the display and a new full-size Rolodex is again presented with the information contained in it.

Once the required item has been found, the page of the Rolodex is pressed to see the article in more detail. An expanding page appears from within the Rolodex, looking like a card from a card index in order to maintain the visual metaphor, offering a complete description of the item selected (Figure 6.9). To return to the items in the Rolodex, the user would press the small Rolodex titled 'Items' at the top-left corner of the screen.

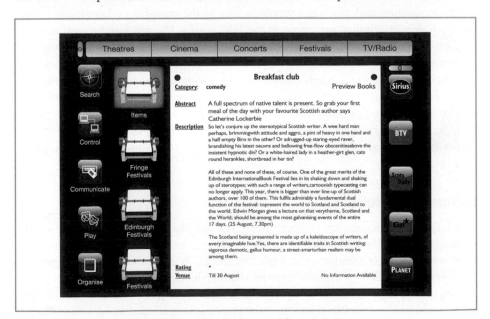

Figure 6.9 Result of search displayed as 'index card' from Rolodex
(Source: *Scotsman*, August 1998)

Evaluation of the second prototype

The second prototype embodied a number of key concepts that would now have to be evaluated with some real people. Designers can only come up with their best ideas. As soon as these are in a coherent form, they need to be evaluated with potential users of the system. A full working visual prototype from which the screenshots in Figures 6.8 and 6.9 were adapted was developed. This included a real database of articles from the *Scotsman* newspaper on the Edinburgh Festival so that people could undertake real searches.

As with the rest of the case study, the evaluation process is not presented as a perfect model to follow, but rather to stimulate discussion of the approaches used. The evaluation was aimed towards the key areas of the interface. In this case the designers were particularly interested in:

- *System learnability*. Does the design of the interface help or hinder people?
- *Toolbars*. Was animation of toolbars effective? Overall concept good?
- *Icons*. Are they understandable? Is their meaning obvious?
- *Logos*. Are the content provider logos effective as identifiers?
- *Rolodex*. Is the general concept of the Rolodex liked? Is it effective? Does it facilitate searching?
- *Categorization*. Is breaking down the search into categories an effective means of searching?
- *Consistency*. Is the system consistent?

A questionnaire was developed to deal with each of the above areas. It included 20 statements for which people could choose from 1 (meaning strongly disagree) to 5 (strongly agree). The questionnaire is explained in Table 6.3.

Questions were mixed – some were expressed in a positive fashion and others in a negative fashion to prevent people simply ticking all the strongly agree or disagree boxes; they had to read and think about each question. A section at the start of the questionnaire established the background of the participant. A further list of three open-ended questions was included at the end of the questionnaire. A comment box was also included for additional suggestions that evaluators could make.

→ Questionnaire design is covered in Chapter 7

The evaluation took place in a vestibule area of the university where many people were passing. A physical prototype of the HIC with a 15-inch touchscreen monitor set into a portable television-sized MDF (medium-density fireboard) casing was programmed with the sample data.

Potential evaluators were approached for their assistance and then taken through the main functions of the HIC. They were then given a concrete scenario to work through in which they were to find a performance from the previous year's Edinburgh Fringe Festival, read an article on it and hence decide if they wished to go and see the show. The evaluations took around 10 minutes each. A total of 50 evaluations were completed over two days.

Evaluation results

Just a few of the results are explored here. The bar chart (Figure 6.10) outlines the responses to each question: whether the person agreed with the question, disagreed with it, or was indifferent (neither agreed nor disagreed). 'N' indicates a negative question, hence if a high proportion disagree it is a good design feature. 'P' indicates a positive question, hence if people agree this is a good feature. The assumption was made that if a person chose agree or strongly agree, then the response was classed as agreeing with the question. If a person chose disagree or strongly disagree, then the response was classed as 'disagree'. This method filtered out all the halfway votes that may have influenced the answer unfairly.

Table 6.3 A brief explanation of the questionnaire

Feature	Question numbers	Question: concept	Question: design	Comments
System	1, 2	Design	To evaluate system as a whole	Do users like the system? Do they find it easy to use?
System integration	3, 4	Consistency	Is system consistent?	Is design too cluttered or ambiguous?
System learnability	5, 6	System should be easy to learn	Does design of interface help or hinder user?	System is designed with ease of use uppermost. These questions will give important feedback on this issue
Searching	7, 8	More than one way to search	Rolodex or content provider logo: any preference?	HIC allows user to search for information in more than one way. Will user even realize this?
Toolbars	9, 10	Animation, i.e. movement idea, sides	Arrows too big or small, colour	Aim: to try to cut out scrolling
Icons	11	To do away with text	Icons understandable and meaning obvious?	Icon meaning may be ambiguous. Do people readily understand them?
Logos	12	Use of pictures to symbolize company	Colour, font, legibility	Aim: to cut out writing and associated problems; to make content providers more recognizable
Touchscreen	13, 14	Touch as in feel, feedback	Design facilitates use of touchscreen	Aim: to reduce amount of peripherals (mouse, keyboard, etc.)
Colours used by the system	15	Colours should be pleasing to the eye, and for categories map onto colours on remote	Aesthetics: shape, colour	Will people like very basic colour used? Makes the design boring?
Rolodex	16	Helps user visualize size of search	Shape, size, legibility of Rolodex itself	To make searches more interesting and help user visualize amount of information returned by their search criteria
Categories	17	Quick way to search, without having to be too specific	Category names, e.g. culture, household	To let user search without having to put in specific search criteria. Aim is also to show some kind of history
Consistency	18–20	Design should be conceptually and physically consistent	Selection/searching mechanism, colours	Also external consistency

It can be seen through this chart that in general all responses were of a positive nature. Some aspects of the system were more positive than others. The data was used for a number of related evaluations. The aspects that this evaluation focuses on are in particular the use of Rolodexes for searching, the Rolodex tree, the categorization of data and the general ease of use of the system.

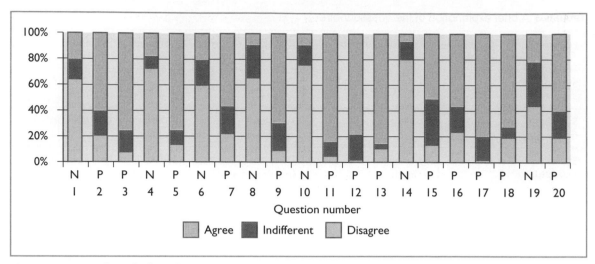

Figure 6.10 Overall results from the questionnaire: averages over 50 evaluations

Results indicated that a general liking was found for the Rolodex concept, although a significant minority felt quite strongly against it. A few negative comments were as follows:

- 'Rolodex too slow, no way to jump through lots of data . . .' (Questionnaire 34)
- 'should be as life-like as possible (putting in markers, taking out cards, leafing through them)' (Questionnaire 36)

Some positive feedback was as follows:

- 'Very intuitive' (Questionnaire 38)
- 'The Rolodexes and menus were very good for browsing' (Questionnaire 41)
- 'The Rolodex idea is very good. Selection of alphabet would improve it.' (Questionnaire 10)

The question that asked whether the Rolodexes helped gain an overview of the information available was posed and the outcome is shown in Figure 6.11.

Through a study of the many comments made regarding the interface by those who took part in the evaluations, it was clear that the first prototype was quite successful and that many of the main concepts of the interface were worth pursuing. Areas of improvement and amendment are necessary, in particular:

- *Larger arrows*. At present the arrows on the toolbars are too small for convenience.
- *Markers*. A point made by many was that a marker system should be introduced to the Rolodex, i.e. some way of holding a page of the Rolodex. Perhaps have a colour-coded tag at the side of the page of the Rolodex.

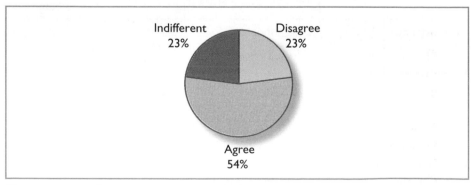

Figure 6.11 Overall response to question whether Rolodexes helped gain an overview

- *Alphabetical search.* It was suggested by a few that displaying an alphabetic search at the top of the Rolodex would be a good idea. This would save searching through each individual item one by one.
- *Order of colours for category buttons.* To conform to a standard they should be red, green, yellow, then blue.

Challenge 6.5

Critique this evaluation. What do you think is good about it? What could have been improved?

Summary and key points

In this case study we have focused on the interface design for a novel device – the Home Information Centre. We have deliberately left the discussions much as they were during the design process so that you can see how discussions move, fluctuating between very detailed concerns and very high-level or conceptual concerns. We have not 'tidied up' the process. Much of what is in this chapter has been taken from reports that were produced at the time. What we have tried to do is to tell a story of a design, the key points being:

- How scenarios were developed to explore the design space of the HIC device
- How the scenarios were analysed in order to understand the main functionality the device required
- How the key design concepts were developed through prototyping ideas, evaluating them and redesigning them
- How key design concepts were realized physically and how the physical design affected the conceptual design and vice versa
- How a physical design was evaluated, focusing on some key aspects of the design.

Exercises

1 Another thorny problem that a device such as the HIC creates is the issue of filing, storing and retrieving data, whether these are e-mail messages, MP3 files, photos or other objects. Consider how to design an effective filing system that does not require people to understand and use a hierarchical system such as on the Mac or PC that uses files and folders.

2 During this project we also investigated how to provide good access to all the content that people would be accessing. We concluded that there would always be a need for content providers to mark up content aimed at a specific audience. Just as news is reported in many different ways, so all the HIC's content would come from subscribing to a content provider. Discuss what a content provider might offer and what the business model might be for providing this service.

Further reading

There are not many books that provide good case studies of doing interactive systems design and it is difficult to get at papers reporting designs. The proceedings of the **ACM Designing Interactive Systems (DIS) conferences** do contain some design cases and it is also worth looking at the **CHI series of conferences** for design cases. Both are available from the **ACM digital library.**

Getting ahead

Mayhew, D. (1999) *The Usability Engineering Lifecycle: a Practitioner's Handbook for User Interface Design.* Morgan Kaufmann, San Francisco, CA. *This is a comprehensive book on Mayhew's commercial approach to ensuring usability in systems.* See also Mayhew and Follansbee (2012).

Moggridge, B. (2007) *Designing Interactions.* MIT Press, Cambridge, MA.

Saffer, D. (2009) *Designing for Interactions Creating Smart Applications and Clever Devices,* **2nd edn.** New Riders, Indianapolis, IN.

 Web links

The accompanying website has links to relevant websites. Go to **www.pearsoned.co.uk/benyon**

 Comments on challenges

Challenge 6.1

The overall approach was sound, but turned out to be far too ambitious. There was planned prototyping and evaluation was central to the approach (see Chapter 3). It adopted a scenario-based design, with P0 being a corpus of scenarios. Developing scenarios and prototypes allows for consistent and early testing with real people. The Wizard of Oz approach allowed us to simulate technologies before they had been developed.

Challenge 6.2

Of course, you will have chosen different examples, but you should have thought about the variety inherent in any of these scenarios. For example, the 'What shall we have for dinner?' scenario might include

- *People* – a young girl with her grandmother who is visiting for a while
- *Activities* – investigating recipes, finding out what could be cooked with the food that is in the house, dealing with allergies to particular foods and finding alternatives, finding simple or complex recipes, finding particular types of food
- *Contexts* – making something quickly, cooking for lots of people, cooking for just one or two
- *Technologies* – the basic HIC design is a constraint, but there is a need to consider the content (i.e. information about recipes). Is there a video showing how to make things, are there links to on-line chat rooms, recommendations from others or from famous chefs, etc.?

Challenge 6.3

There are, of course, many design issues that are raised and hence many design options that can be considered to deal with them. One issue, for example, concerns how much the system can know about the different people – e.g. where they live, what the roads are like, how you can travel from one place to another. Such data is available (e.g. for in-car travel systems), but how the different content from different providers can be linked together by the HIC is a challenge. There would presumably have to be some standard 'mark-up' language used, such as XML. This would allow interoperability between the different applications.

Challenge 6.4

The menu bar or 'history' bar was thought to be a good idea, although the text on the buttons was unclear. The use of colour in the 'history' bar was ineffective, as was the presence of all of the buttons when they had no labels. Use of highlighting of the main screen buttons obscured the text. The animation included in the arrival of the hidden dock on screen was very much approved of, and was seen as a device which should be looked at further.

The organization of buttons in a semi-circle around a topic was liked as a concept for the organization of information and would interpret well for use with the touchscreen. The idea of the Near and Far buttons was a good one. The interaction was felt to be too spread out all over the screen.

Challenge 6.5

The evaluation was quite effective, though probably could have been better. All too frequently these things are rushed near the end, but for its purpose – to get general feedback on the interface concepts – it was probably sufficient. Importantly, it was undertaken with real potential users and there was a good spread of people who used the system. The task was relatively quick to do, which is important from the pragmatic perspective, and the results provided both qualitative and quantitative data.

Part II

Techniques for designing interactive systems

Introduction to Part II

The aim of this part of the book is to bring all the relevant techniques for designing interactive systems into one place. Part I introduced the key processes that are involved in designing interactive systems – understanding, envisionment, design and evaluation – but we have not really explored how to go about these processes. Part I also introduced PACT, scenarios and personas, some useful constructs, and a useful framework for thinking about designing interactive systems. Part I has also covered the principles of designing for accessibility and usability, and described a method for design based on scenarios.

Part II will provide techniques to enable designers to do all these things. If you want to know about people, and to develop personas, you should know about how to interview them, or get them to participate in design. If you want to evaluate some design ideas you need to know how to sketch, prototype and evaluate. If you want to design good products, you need to understand methods for conceptual design and for physical design. This part provides a thorough treatment of all of these.

Chapter 7 discusses methods for understanding the world of interactive systems design. Many of these are also applicable to evaluation. Further techniques more closely associated with evaluation are discussed in Chapter 10. A particular form of analysis that is popular in interactive systems design is task analysis, which is covered in Chapter 11.

The more design-oriented methods, for envisioning physical designs and for exploring the conceptual space of designs, are presented in Chapters 9 and 10. The background for these, and the key issues of interface design are covered in Chapter 12, on the visual aspects, and Chapter 13 on multimodal interaction.

The aim of this part is to be comprehensive in our coverage of the issues. There are many proprietary methods that are provided by design companies and agencies, but they are all based on the examples provided here. As we discuss briefly in Chapter 9, the form of the construct, or modelling method, that designers use will affect which aspects of the design stand out and which are played down. So the choice of method can be critical to the insight provided. A task analysis, for example (Chapter 11), will focus on how easy it is to undertake specific tasks, but will not say much about the overall navigational structure of an interactive system. A focus group may provide useful ideas early on in a project, but may not provide so much insight when designing the detail of a pop-up menu. Designers need to understand the wide range of techniques that are applicable in interactive systems design and where and when they are best used.

Case studies

There are several interesting case studies that are used to illustrate the material in this part. Chapter 8 uses the HIC case study and Companions to explore and illustrate many of the issues. Chapter 9 returns to the MP3 scenario from the HIC project and presents a detailed object–action analysis of the scenario, showing how such an analysis can lead to an effective conceptual design. The same case is used to illustrate the development of a design language and an interaction pattern. Chapter 10 uses the HIC to illustrate aspects of evaluation. A detailed look at an edit function on a photo CD is also included.

Teaching and learning

This is not a part to be read completely in sequence. You should get to know the overall structure by dipping into each chapter and reading the introduction, aim and summary. Flip through the detail to get a high-level picture of the sort of things that are covered. If you are doing an in-depth report on techniques for understanding, or evaluation, say – perhaps to select appropriate methods for a particular project – then do read the appropriate chapter in detail and study the further reading and the Web links that go with the chapter.

Topics should be mixed in with an understanding of the overall design process provided in Part I to give a feel for what is involved in design and how to do it. The list of topics covered in this part is shown below, each of which could take 10–15 hours of study to reach a good general level of understanding, or 3–5 hours for a basic appreciation of the issues. Of course, each topic could be the subject of extensive and in-depth study.

Topic 2.1	Participative design	Section 7.2
Topic 2.2	Requirements	Section 7.1
Topic 2.3	Interviewing people	Section 7.3
Topic 2.4	Developing questionnaires	Section 7.4
Topic 2.5	Probes	Section 7.5
Topic 2.6	Card sorting	Section 7.6
Topic 2.7	Observation and ethnographic studies	Section 7.8
Topic 2.8	Ideas development	Sections 7.7, 8.1, 9.1–9.2
Topic 2.9	Sketching and wireframes	Section 8.2
Topic 2.10	Prototyping	Section 8.3
Topic 2.11	Envisionment in practice	Section 8.4
Topic 2.12	Conceptual design	Section 9.4
Topic 2.13	Metaphors and blends	Section 9.3
Topic 2.14	Design languages	Section 9.5
Topic 2.15	Interaction patterns	Section 9.5
Topic 2.16	Expert evaluation	Section 10.2
Topic 2.17	Participative evaluation	Section 10.3
Topic 2.18	Evaluation in practice	Sections 10.1, 10.4, 10.5
Topic 2.19	Task analysis	Chapter 11
Topic 2.20	Graphical user interfaces (GUIs)	Section 12.3
Topic 2.21	Interface design	Section 12.4
Topic 2.22	Information design	Section 12.5
Topic 2.23	Visualization	Section 12.6
Topic 2.24	Multimodal interaction	Sections 13.1–13.2
Topic 2.25	Mixed reality	Section 13.2
Topic 2.26	Auditory interfaces	Section 13.3
Topic 2.27	Tangible user interfaces	Section 13.4
Topic 2.28	Gestural interaction	Section 13.5
Topic 2.29	Surface computing	Section 13.5

Chapter 7
Understanding

Contents

Aims

Before creative design can start it is essential that the designer develops a clear and thorough understanding of the *people* who will be involved with the product or system, the *activities* that are the focus of the design, the *contexts* in which those activities take place and the implications for the design of *technologies*: 'PACT'. From this understanding designers generate the requirements for the system that is to be designed. However, it is rarely possible to acquire a thorough understanding of requirements until some design work has been completed. Requirements work (understanding), the design process, representations of design (envisionment) and evaluation are tightly interwoven.

The focus of the understanding process is on what people do, or might want to do, and on any problems they are having with any system currently in use. It is also about understanding how people do what they do, so that designers can develop technologies that make aspects of everyday life more efficient or more enjoyable.

In this chapter we present the main techniques for understanding people's activities and encapsulating this for design. In software engineering or information systems projects, this is a formal step which is usually termed 'requirements analysis'. In interaction design it is often referred to as 'research'.

After studying this chapter you should be able to:

- Understand what requirements are
- Understand the range of requirements generation techniques
- Use techniques for understanding people and their activities in context
- Document the results as requirements on interactive technologies and services.

7.1 Understanding requirements

A requirement is 'something the product must do or a quality that the product must have' (Robertson and Robertson, 1999). Designers will study current activities and gather stories of use and soon will have generated a great deal of information about the current situation and about people's goals and aspirations. The task now is to turn this into requirements for a new product, system or service. Sometimes this is straightforward, but often it will need a creative leap. This is why the analysis–design–evaluation process is so iterative. The accuracy of the guess can only be judged when people review the requirements, something that is best done with the aid of scenarios and early designs or a prototype. Just to further complicate matters, additional requirements will emerge as the design process continues.

There has always been much debate about which of the following terms should be used for the requirements activity:

- Requirements *gathering*, which suggests requirements are lying around waiting to be picked up with little interaction between designer and stakeholders
- Requirements *generation*, which suggests a more creative activity, that tends to de-emphasize links to current practice
- Requirements *elicitation*, which suggests some interaction between stakeholders and designers
- Requirements *engineering* – often used in software engineering projects, usually a very formal approach.

This is one of the reasons we have moved to the term 'understanding', as it encapsulates ideas of gathering and generation. Many interaction design projects start from a 'design brief' which may be quite a vague description of something they want. Often clients will require a requirements specification – a formal written document that contains the requirements. Developers also need a clear requirements specification at some point in the development process so that they can cost the project and manage it successfully. Requirements

---

FURTHER THOUGHTS

Requirements templates

The use of a standard format, or template, for specifying requirements is useful, particularly in larger projects. The exact presentation of the information is not important, but at a minimum it should include for each requirement:

- A unique reference number, ideally also coding whether the requirement is functional or non-functional
- A one-sentence summary
- The source(s) of the requirement
- The rationale for it.

As Robertson and Robertson (1999) suggest, there are additional elements which will greatly add to the value of the requirements specification. The most significant of these are:

- The criteria for measuring whether the requirement has been satisfied
- A grade for the importance of the requirement, e.g. on a scale of 1–5
- Dependencies and conflicts with other requirements
- Change history.

specifications increasingly include prototypes, screenshots and other media. When written they should be expressed in clear, unambiguous language, and worded so that it will be possible to test whether the requirement has been met in the final system.

Conventionally, requirements are divided into two types, functional and non-functional. Functional requirements are what the system must do. Non-functional requirements are a quality that the system must have. These qualities may be crucial factors in the acceptability, sales or usage of a product. Non-functional requirements cover a number of aspects of design, including image and aesthetics, usability, performance, maintainability, security, cultural acceptability and legal restrictions. Also important are the data, or media requirements of any system – the type of content that it has to deal with and the various media that will be used.

For both types of requirements, note that how the technology will meet the requirement is not specified. This is a later part of the design activity. It is best to supplement the list of requirements with some supporting evidence – interview or observation reports, photographs of artefacts, video snippets if practicable. This helps readers of the requirements specification to understand the reason behind items in the list.

Prioritizing requirements

Requirements should be reviewed with customers and clients and modified as necessary. Decisions will almost always be made about the relative priority of the requirements, since few design projects have unlimited resources. One way of doing this is by using the '**MoSCoW rules**'. These classify requirements into:

- **M**ust have – fundamental requirements without which the system will be unworkable and useless, effectively the minimum usable subset
- **S**hould have – would be essential if more time were available, but the system will be useful and usable without them
- **C**ould have – of lesser importance, therefore can more easily be left out of the current development
- **W**ant to have but **W**on't have this time round – can wait till a later development.

The MoSCoW method is part of the Atern development method (see Box 3.2 on agile development). The method takes a very business-focused view of prioritizing requirements, tying in the specification of priorities with the overall business costs of developing a system.

Challenge 7.1

The Home Information Centre (HIC, the focus of the case study in Chapter 6) aims to be a new device for the home. Which of these requirements on the HIC are functional and which non-functional? Discuss issues of prioritizing the requirements.

1 *Unobtrusive in the home environment*
2 *Option to print out details*
3 *Fast download of information*
4 *Direct 'panic' link to the emergency services*
5 *Volume control/mute features*
6 *Customizable to support choice of languages, including those with different character sets*
7 *Provides e-mail*
8 *Security for each individual user.*

7.2 Participative design

Research work involves using a variety of techniques to understand and analyse someone else's needs, goals and aspirations. The key thing for designers to remember is that they are not the people who will be using the final system. Designers need to understand the requirements of other people. This is not easy, but talking to people using interviews, observing people and recording their activities on video, organizing focus groups, workshops, etc. will all help the designer to understand both the requirements for the new design and the problems people are having with existing ways of doing things. By engaging with people using various techniques that encourage the participation of people in the design process, designers will acquire a large number of stories that form the basis for the analysis work. Recasting several similar stories into more structured conceptual scenarios will also help the designer to understand and generate requirements.

Throughout this book we emphasize the need to take a human-centred approach to design. First, it is important that human characteristics and activities are taken into account. But beyond this, wherever possible, it is right that the people who will use new interactive technologies have an input to the design process itself. We include the qualification 'wherever possible' not because we think that it is ever proper to exclude the interests of the widest range of stakeholders from the design process, but because in large-scale commercial products it is feasible to involve only a tiny proportion of those who will use the eventual system. The situation is very different from the development of custom-made systems for a small group of people, where it is genuinely feasible for the people concerned to act as co-designers and so acquire ownership of the technology to be introduced.

FURTHER THOUGHTS

The socio-technical tradition

This design philosophy of involving people in the design of their systems is usually attributed to the Scandinavian tradition of worker participation in the management of the workplace. There are also links to the British socio-technical design movement and to the social informatics movement in the US (Davenport, 2008). This started with an emphasis on human considerations in the design of systems to support manual work, such as coal mining, but later evolved methods for user involvement in the design of computer-based systems. The work of Enid Mumford at Manchester, and Ken Eason, Leela Damodoran, Susan Harker and their colleagues at Loughborough University and elsewhere, is central to this development of the socio-technical approach. Methods embodying the socio-technical philosophy included Mumford's ETHICS (Mumford, 1983, 1993), the HUFIT toolkit (Taylor, 1990), which provided a comprehensive, practical set of techniques for working with users, and ORDIT (Eason *et al.*, 1996), which aimed to incorporate organizational considerations into systems design.

The Scandinavian participatory design movement of the early 1980s was also important. This was very much a politically informed initiative, with the emphasis on workplace democracy and empowering workers as co-designers of work practice and the tools supporting it. Techniques such as paper prototyping were invented so that workers were not disadvantaged in working with technologists. The most influential of such initiatives was the work of Pelle Ehn and colleagues in the UTOPIA project (Bødker *et al.*, 1987; Ehn and Kyng, 1987). More recently, Pekkola *et al.* (2006) have reviewed these earlier approaches and suggested how the demands of information systems development and participative design can be brought together. Their method uses an iterative approach to design, bringing in participative methods and prototyping in order to ensure stakeholder

→

involvement throughout the process. Stakeholders were able to evaluate prototypes as a normal part of their work. Deborah Mayhew's Usability Engineering is another well documented and structured human-centred approach (Mayhew, 2007) as is the rapid contextual design of Karen Holtzblatt (Holtzblatt, 2007).

Challenge 7.2

Incorporating input from those who will be affected by a changed system into the requirements process helps to ensure that the eventual technologies have a good fit with the people, activities and contexts they are designed to support. There is also a strong ethical argument for user involvement. Can you think of another reason for doing this?

BOX 7.1

Acting out requirements

Alan Newell and his colleagues (e.g. Newell *et al.*, 2007) have developed methods for acting out requirements in order to make them more understandable to the groups of people they are designing for – primarily older people. The technique requires the designers to work with a professional script writer to develop a short stage play based on the requirements that have been generated. This is acted out by trained actors with the stakeholders making up the audience. Following the play a trained facilitator leads an audience discussion on the play and the issues that it raised. These discussion feed back into the understanding process, helping to provide a rich understanding of the hopes, fears and concerns of the people.

7.3 Interviews

One of the most effective ways of finding out what people want and what problems they have at the moment is to talk to them! Interviews with all the various stakeholders in the domain are a vital way of gathering stories. Designers employ a range of different styles of interview. The *structured* interview uses questions that are developed before-hand. The interview follows the wording exactly. Public opinion polls, for example of the sort produced in great numbers before elections, are normally based on structured interviews. Structured interviews are reasonably easy to carry out, simply because of the degree of pre-structuring. However, people are limited to very restricted replies, and it is difficult for the interviewer to follow up the unexpected response. Here is an extract from a structured interview pro forma about a student information system.

Thinking about the Department's website, about how often would you say that you have used the following during the last week:			
Timetable information	not at all ☐	most days ☐	every day ☐	more than once a day ☐
Staff home pages	not at all ☐	most days ☐	every day ☐	more than once a day ☐
Module information	not at all ☐	most days ☐	every day ☐	more than once a day ☐

Designers very frequently use *semi-structured* interviews. Sometimes, the interviewer is armed with pre-prepared questions, but can reword these as appropriate and explore new topics as they arise. Often, the interviewer simply prepares a checklist, sometimes with suitable prompts such as 'Tell me about the first things you do when you get into the office in the morning'. Clearly, this free-form approach is more demanding for the interviewer, but the data obtained does generally repay the effort.

An example of such an interview is shown in Figure 7.1, with some annotations about interviewing technique. The interview is designed to start at a high level, then to probe at a greater level of detail. The analyst's checklist of topics to cover for this example included the type of information needed, current sources (paper or on-line), and specific examples of information needs.

Completely *unstructured* interviews are sometimes used where it is particularly important to minimize designers' preconceptions, or where very little background information is available beforehand. As the term suggests, there are no preset questions or topics beyond the general subject of the project in question.

FURTHER
THOUGHTS

Contextual inquiry

Contextual Inquiry (CI) is a first-stage design method by Holtzblatt and Beyer (Beyer and Holtzblatt, 1998; Holtzblatt, 2012). They observe, 'The core premise of CI is very simple: go where the customer works, observe the customer as he or she works, and talk to the customer about the work. Do that, and you can't help but gain a better understanding of your customer.'

CI brings together a number of techniques including artefact collection and observation under one unifying theme or philosophy.

There are four guiding principles of Contextual Inquiry:

1 *Context.* Here the advice is to go to the customer's workplace and observe how work is actually carried out. This allows the analyst to experience the rich everyday detail of work. It is best to focus on concrete data and tasks (i.e. user stories) rather than generalized abstraction.

2 *Partnership.* One of the core premises of CI – and of its Scandinavian ancestors – is that analyst and customer are expert in their different fields. The analyst should be looking for patterns and structure in the work while the customer contributes her knowledge of how the work really gets done. As redesign ideas occur, they can also be discussed. Thus customers can genuinely influence the analyst's interpretations of the work and design ideas based upon it. The relationship is characterized by Beyer and Holtzblatt as the 'master–apprentice model'.

3 *Interpretation.* It is not enough simply to observe and document: the analyst must interpret workplace data so that it is properly understood. The analyst abstracts from the stories, producing a more conceptual interpretation. The analyst should reflect her interpretations back to the customer and listen to the response. Be prepared to be wrong.

4 *Focus.* Each site visit and interview needs a focus, though concentrating on one part of the work helps to see detail, but at the expense of other aspects. Be clear about the focus and try to make neither too broad nor too narrow.

Challenge 7.3

What sort of information is likely to be missed by interviews? Why?

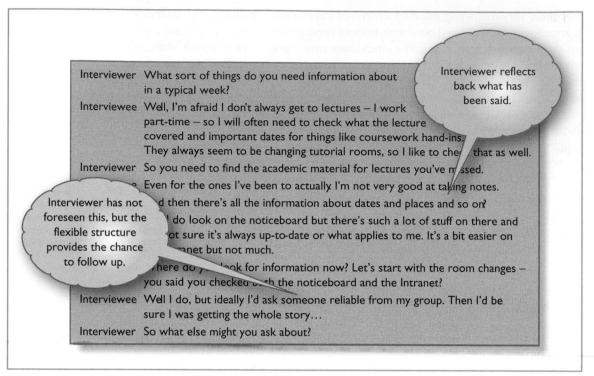

Figure 7.1 Extract from a semi-structured interview

Stories, scenarios and early prototyping in interviewing

← Stories and scenarios have already been introduced in Chapter 3

Scenarios and stories are helpful aids to understanding activities and help avoid having people imagine (or reconstruct) situations in the abstract. For example, people can be asked to recall a typical 'day in the life' or incidents when the current technology does not support what they need to do. This will identify circumstances that the new design must take into account.

Once there is a rough idea of what the new technology might do, discussing a scenario will highlight many issues, from the naming of individual functions to the impact of changes in work practice. Prototypes – anything from paper sketches to semi-functioning products – are very often used to embody scenarios in possible technology. For example, in the later stages of analysis for a shared notebook for engineers, we used simple prototypes created in PowerPoint coupled with small usage scenarios. These were projected on a screen and discussed in a small group meeting, prompting discussion about the match between our design ideas and the way the engineers currently disseminated information.

Whether or not a prototype is used, the analyst and the customer 'walk through' the scenario, while the analyst probes for comments, problems, possible alternatives and suggestions in general. Depending on the outcome of the scenario/prototype walk-through, modifications and further iterations may be desirable. Where many new issues emerge, it may be the case that the early concepts underlying the scenario or prototype are misconceived, and should be radically rethought.

Think-aloud commentaries

When it is necessary to know a good deal of low-level detail about current technology, users can be asked to talk through the operations concerned – including their internal cognitive processes – as they use the technology in question. This data, properly termed a 'verbal protocol' (Ericsson and Simon, 1985), can provide helpful indications of current problems. It is important to remember, however, that by imposing the requirement to generate a commentary you are interfering with the very process you are attempting to study. Further, not all cognitive processes can be accessed by the conscious mind. The description of the 'contextual interview' in Beyer and Holtzblatt (1998) suggests some ways of alleviating this problem.

Practical considerations in interviewing

This section contains some practical 'hints and tips' from our experience of interviewing in a variety of analysis situations.

Preparation

Get to know the background. 'Idiot questions' can uncover unspoken assumptions, but use them deliberately, not by accident. Be careful about using people's own jargon until you are sure that you have it right. For work activities, background research might include studying company reports, brochures, websites and organization charts or scanning through software manuals and promotional materials. For home and leisure activities, what is relevant depends very largely on the context.

Keeping track of the interview

Interviewing is hard work and more effective if carried out by a pair of interviewers. One person can take the lead while the other makes notes. Of course, the note-taking burden is relieved if the interview is audio- or video-recorded. In this case, make sure you check the equipment before each session and periodically during the interview. Even when the interview is recorded, notes are still useful, especially if they include regular records of the time, which will help to find key points – it will take you one hour at the least to watch one hour of videotape even without any analysis or transcription. In addition, your notes will be vital if (for example) building work outside has muffled a section of the audio, or the heavy regional accent that was understandable face-to-face proves impenetrable on tape. A full transcription is rarely needed, but if it is, an audio-typist can save hours of your time. The typist will need briefing about any technical terms.

Telling stories

Just because telling stories and listening to them is such a natural thing to do, they can be misleading. As listeners, designers are looking for current problems, scope for improvements or endorsements of early design ideas. As storytellers, people may respond by giving such things disproportionate emphasis. You need to be aware of this in analysing interview data.

Reflection and exploration

Reflecting back during the interview helps confirm that you have understood what has been said. It is often a good idea to have the interviewee review a summary of the interview. This might be because the interviewee's knowledge is central to the new design, sensitive material is involved or the context is very unfamiliar. You should also look over the notes of the interview yourself to identify any points that need clarification.

General-purpose exploratory questions

These help the interview along, especially in the early stages or with a taciturn interviewee. Some we have found useful are:

'Tell me about your typical day.'

'Tell me three good things about . . .'

'and three bad things.'

'What if you had three wishes to make the application better?'

'What has gone wrong with the application recently? How did you cope?'

'What else should we have asked about?'

When to stop

Deciding when to stop interviewing means balancing practical constraints against the comprehensiveness of the data. Certainly, all significant stakeholder groups must be covered. In the case of generic product development, Beyer and Holtzblatt (1998) suggest two or three interviewees per role (or type of stakeholder) across three or four different types of organization. In many cases, client resources limit the process. With unlimited resources, the general rule is to stop once no new insights are being obtained.

7.4 Questionnaires

Most of the methods we discuss in this chapter involve working with people face-to-face. However, there are ways of obtaining requirements information at a distance. The most common of these is the questionnaire, but there are more ingenious, novel techniques as well.

Questionnaires are one way of streamlining the understanding process if a large number of people are to be surveyed and resources are not available to interview them individually. However, constructing a workable questionnaire is surprisingly difficult and time-consuming. It is a skilled task to devise the wording of questions when there are no opportunities to detect and clear up misunderstandings as they happen. Questionnaires need to be designed, prototyped and evaluated in the same way as any other form of interaction design. For small numbers of people – up to 10 or so – an interview will obtain the same information, and more, in a manageable way. This will consume little or no extra resource if the time required to construct a questionnaire is taken into account.

Challenge 7.4

Consider the following items from a questionnaire about use of the Internet. Are there any problems with the wording? How could the items be improved?

(a) How often do you access the Internet? (tick one)

Every day ❑

Most days ❑

About once a week ❑

> About once a month   ❑
> Less than once a month   ❑
> (b) Please list all types of material which you access frequently using the Internet.

Questionnaires are ideally suited to gathering a large amount of quantifiable data, or to capture responses from people who cannot be involved more directly. With the proliferation of on-line questionnaire services such as Survey Monkey (Figure 7.2), quite complex questionnaires can be constructed and made available on the Web. Another technique for gathering data is 'crowd sourcing'. Here, small specific tasks are put on the Web and volunteers sign up to take the tasks in return for a small payment. Amazon's 'Mechanical Turk' is the best-known example, but needs careful design of the task if it is to be effective.

A good questionnaire is time-consuming to construct so that all the items:

● are understandable
● are unambiguous
● collect data which actually answers evaluation questions
● can be analysed easily.

Response rates to questionnaires can be very low indeed – return rates of under 10 per cent are common if the intended respondents have no particular stake in the design of the technology or incentive (being entered into a prize draw, for example) to participate. Where questionnaires are administered as part of a face-to-face evaluation session most people will complete them, but people who take them away to finish in their own time, or who do the questionnaire on the Web, very often don't.

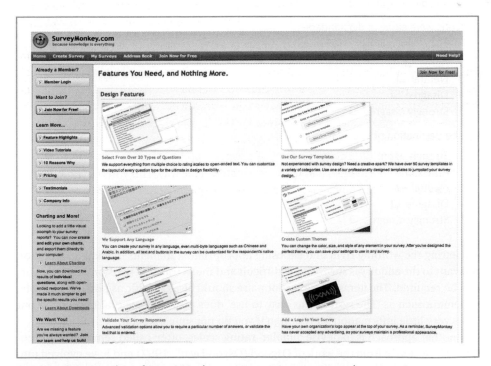

Figure 7.2 Screenshot of SurveyMonkey.com see www.surveymonkey.com/Home_FeaturesDesign.aspx

Finally, analysing the data requires thought and time. If most respondents have awarded feature 'A' 5 out of 7 for usefulness but feature 'B' 6 out of 7, does this really mean that feature B is better? Or is it enough that both features score above the mid-point? Maybe feature A was misunderstood – without a follow-up question the data is difficult to interpret. This is easy to do in an interview, but would add significantly to the length of a questionnaire. Where respondents have been given the opportunity to express opinions as unstructured answers, you will need to devise a scheme for classifying this material so that it is usable.

Perceptions of system design are often collected through rating scales, known as Likert scales (Likert, 1932). The Likert scale is the most common of a number of methods for eliciting opinion. People are asked to indicate their agreement with a statement using a five-point scale:

Strongly agree

Agree

Neutral

Disagree

Strongly disagree

or a seven-point, four-point or ten-point scale. The scale is attached to each of a number of statements such as:

I always knew what I should do next. (*Tick one box*)
1 Strongly agree ❑
2 Agree ❑
3 Neutral ❑
4 Disagree ❑
5 Strongly disagree ❑

Icons were easily understandable.
1 Strongly agree ❑
2 Agree ❑
3 Neutral ❑
4 Disagree ❑
5 Strongly disagree ❑

The destination of links was clear.
1 Strongly agree ❑
2 Agree ❑
3 Neutral ❑
4 Disagree ❑
5 Strongly disagree ❑

Getting the wording right and choosing appropriate statements to elicit information relevant to the enquiry is surprisingly difficult and much trial and revision of statements will be required. The items on a questionnaire should be as specific as possible. A probe statement such as 'The system was easy to use' does provide a general impression but gives very little information for redesign if you do not supplement it.

Another approach is to devise 'bipolar' rating scales, often called semantic differentials. These derive from the work of Osgood (Osgood *et al.*, 1957) and have evolved into a very powerful way of uncovering the feelings people have towards ideas, products and brands. For example, Brian Lawson (2001) used semantic differential to find out

what people liked about pubs and we have used similar methods to explore what people liked about places and how they were represented in a virtual environment (VE).
The 'place probe' (Benyon *et al.*, 2006) was designed to obtain people's responses to a
photo-realistic VE, of different places. Deriving from the work of Relph and others about
the sense of place (Relph, 1976), the probe contained semantic differentials about the
quality of the images, the sense of freedom people had to move around and their overall visual perception and subjective feelings of the place. Figure 7.3 is an example of a
semantic differential. Web-based questionnaire services will often give clear and good
advice on types of question and how to design questionnaires.

Key features of the place

On the tables provided in each question below, please mark a cross in the box that
best describes your experience in relation to the adjectives provided at either side.
Below is an example for an experience that was 'quite bad' and 'very light'.

Example

	Very	Quite	Neither	Quite	Very	
Good				x		Bad
Light	x					Dark

Did the images that were displayed seem?

	Very	Quite	Neither	Quite	Very	
Grainy						Clear
Realistic						Unrealistic
Unbelievable						Believable
Distorted						Accurate

Did the movement of the images seem?

	Very	Quite	Neither	Quite	Very	
Smooth						Jerky
Broken						Unbroken
Slow						Fast
Consistent						Erratic

Did you feel that you were?

	Very	Quite	Neither	Quite	Very	
Passive						Active
Free						Restricted
Disorientated						Oriented
Inside						Outside
Mobile						static

Figure 7.3 Semantic differential

Did you feel that the environment was?

	Very	Quite	Neither	Quite	Very	
Small						Big
Empty						Full
Light						Dark
Enclosed						Open
Permanent						Temporary
Colourless						Colourful
Static						Moving
Responsive						Inert
Far						Near
Untouchable						Touchable

Did you feel that the environment was?

	Very	Quite	Neither	Quite	Very	
Ugly						Beautiful
Pleasant						Unpleasant
Stressful						Relaxing
Harmful						Harmless
Exciting						Boring
Interesting						Uninteresting
Memorable						Forgettable
Meaningful						Meaningless
Confusing						Understandable
Significant						Insignificant

Figure 7.3 Continued

To gather requirements and opinions about system features several ready-made and validated usability questionnaires are available, for example QUIS (Questionnaire for User Interface Satisfaction) from the University of Maryland and SUMI (Software Usability Measurement Inventory) from the University of Cork. These are 'industrial strength' instruments and there is normally a fee for their use. Others may be found in textbooks and on the Web, but in the latter case be sure that their source is a reliable one.

The 'hints and tips' in Box 7.2 (an edited version of Robson, 1993, pp. 247–52) should help you to produce more worthwhile questionnaires. If the questionnaire is very lengthy, however, or targeted at a very large group, then we strongly recommend you consult a reference such as Oppenheim (2000) or an expert in questionnaire design.

Perhaps the most important piece of advice is to pilot the questionnaire in draft form with a few people who are similar to the target group. It is always surprising how an apparently simple question can be misunderstood.

BOX
7.2

Hints and tips for design of questionnaires

Specific questions are better than general ones

General questions (a) tend to produce a wider variety of interpretation by respondents; (b) are more likely to be influenced by other questions; and (c) are poorer predictors of actual behaviour.

> *General*: List the software packages you have used.
>
> *Specific*: Which of these software packages have you used?
>
> Visual Basic ❑   Word ❑   Excel ❑   PowerPoint ❑

Closed questions are usually preferable to open questions

Closed questions help to avoid differences in interpretation. Open questions are more difficult to analyse, but can be useful, for instance, when seeking comments in the respondent's own words, when not enough is known to construct closed questions, and for potentially sensitive items.

> *Open*: People look for different things in a job; what sort of things are important to you in your job?
>
> *Closed*: People look for different things in a job; which one of the following five things is most important to you?
>
> Good pay   ❑
> A feeling of achievement   ❑
> Ability to make your own decisions   ❑
> Good people to work with   ❑
> Job security   ❑

Consider a 'no-opinion' option

If there is no such option people may manufacture an opinion for the questionnaire.

> Mobile communications technology has made life easier. Do you agree, disagree or not have an opinion?
>
> Agree ❑   Disagree ❑   No opinion ❑

However, a middle choice may encourage a non-committal response. One strategy is to omit the middle choice and follow up with an 'intensity item' which separates out strong from mild feelings.

> Do you think mobile communications technology has made life easier or more difficult? Please tick the number which reflects your opinion.
>
> Easier   1   2   3   4   More difficult
>
> How strongly do you feel about this?
>
> Extremely strongly   1   2   3   4   5   Not at all strongly

Vary the orientation of rating scales or intersperse with other questions

If a questionnaire contains a lot of similar scales, all of which have, say, the 'good' end at the left and the 'bad' end at the right, people may go down the page ticking each scale in the same place. Either reverse some scales or put some other types of question in between.

Appearance, order and instructions are vital

The questionnaire should look easy to fill in, with plenty of space for questions and answers. Initial questions should be easy and interesting. Middle questions cover the more difficult areas. Make the last questions interesting to encourage completion

→

and return of the questionnaire. Keep the design simple and give clear instructions, repeating them if confusion seems possible. Ticking boxes is less confusing than circling answers.

Add introductory and concluding notes

The introduction should explain the purpose of the survey, assure confidentiality and encourage reply. The concluding note can ask respondents to check they have answered all questions, encourage an early return of the questionnaire with the deadline date (and return details, if not using a pre-addressed envelope), offer to send a summary of the findings, if appropriate, and thank them for their help.

Make return easy

Using internal mail is often easiest (include a pre-addressed envelope). Or arrange for a box to be placed in a convenient place to be collected by you. For people who habitually use e-mail, an e-mail questionnaire can be one of the easiest ways to get a good response rate. The Web is also worth considering. Postal returns should of course include a pre-paid return envelope.

7.5 Probes

Probes are collections of artefacts designed to elicit requirements, ideas or opinions in specific contexts. 'Cultural probes' were developed by Bill Gaver and colleagues (Gaver *et al.*, 1999) in working with elderly people located in three European cities. The overall aim was to design technologies that would foster greater participation in the community by older people. The designers first got to know the groups in person, then introduced them to the cultural probes packages. Each person received a collection of maps, post-cards, a disposable camera and booklets – each item being carefully designed to stimulate interest and curiosity, and suggesting ways in which people could use it to send ideas back to the designers. They were 'designed to provoke inspirational responses' (*ibid.*, p. 22). Postcards such as that shown in Figure 7.4, for example, asked people to list their favourite devices. The disposable cameras had customized covers which suggested scenes to be captured, such as 'the first person you will see today' or 'something boring'. Over a period of weeks, many of the probe materials were sent back to the designers, carrying rich data about the lives of the elderly people. Not all items worked out as planned – the authors do not specify which – and the materials were selectively redesigned before being distributed to subsequent participants. All in all, the exercise was highly successful in capturing the general sense of what it meant to be elderly in the communities involved, although it is noted that the results did not have a direct impact on design.

The philosophy behind cultural probes was rather different than trying to gather requirements and illustrates well the difference between requirements elicitation and requirements generation. Gaver argues that probes are meant to confront, they are intended to provide inspiration for designers rather than elicit specific requirements.

Technology probes are another form of probe that were used to gather requirements for home technologies and the area has now evolved into a whole area of 'probology'. In discussing the use of mobile probes (Hulkko *et al.*, 2004) it is argued that probes

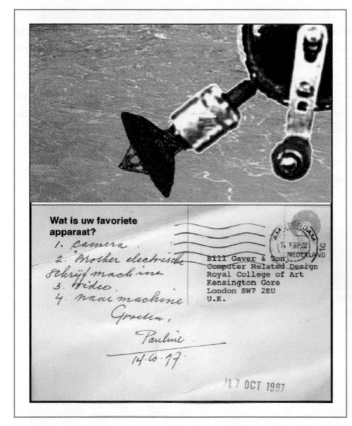

Figure 7.4 Postcard used as a 'cultural probe'

(Source: Gaver, W.W., Dunne, T. and Pacenti, E. (1999) Design: Cultural probes, *Interactions*, 6(1), pp. 21–29 © 1999 ACM, Inc. Reprinted by permission. http://doi.acm.org/10.1145/291224.291235)

are humane, they create fragments of understanding and insight and use uncertainty through providing stories. Probes inspire and provoke designers to engage with the lives of others. Another analysis of probes (cultural, mobile, domestic, urban) by Graham *et al.* (2007) concludes that probes represent the 'turn to the personal' in a direct reference to the 'turn to the social' that happened in HCI at the beginning of the 1990s (see Chapter 18 for more on this). Probes are an amalgam of social science methods (such as photography, diaries, life documents, etc.) that enable designers to focus upon the individual's everyday life, going beyond the general.

7.6 Card sorting techniques

Card sorting refers to a number of techniques concerned with understanding how people classify and categorize things. It has been said that trying to find things on a website is like looking for the scissors in someone else's kitchen. You know there are some, but finding them can be another matter altogether. How people organize things is a very personal matter. Card sorting is particularly relevant in website design as the structure of the content is critical.

→ Information architecture is the study of how to design digital structures and we return to this in Chapter 14.

As a method of understanding, card sorting can be used in a number of ways. At its most basic card sorting involves writing concepts onto cards and then grouping them in different ways. A group of people work with a facilitator to structure data, concepts, objects or other artefacts, trying to understand what categories are most appropriate to group them together. This results in a taxonomy (a classification) and a set of high-level concepts known as an ontology.

Where the results from a large number of people are available, various mathematical grouping techniques can be used. Card sorting can be conducted face to face or using an on-line tool. Hudson (2012) gives the example of a supermarket checkout vegetable pricing machine (Figure 7.5). If a customer has bought some onions, which category should they select? How about if they have some courgettes, broccoli, aubergines? If customers have to spend a long time searching for the right category (and any casual observation of supermarket checkouts suggests they do) queues will build up, people will get dissatisfied and go elsewhere next time they want to shop.

Figure 7.5 Supermarket vegetable weighing machine
(Source: Henglein and Streets/cultura/Corbis)

As a method of understanding, card sorting can be a very effective method of gaining insight into how people think about things and classify them. There are two types of card sort:

1 An open card sort starts with blank cards and participants are asked to write down the objects or actions they think are important in some domain. These are then gathered together into categories
2 A closed card sort starts with predefined categories and asks participants to place objects into the categories.

As with most methods for understanding it is likely that the analyst will move between these different types depending on the questions being addressed. In the question of understanding what problems people are having using the checkout display, you would use a closed card sort because you already have the categories (the pictures on the display). If you are trying to understand what categories different people would choose for vegetables, give them a list of vegetables and ask them how they would like to group them. Hudson did this with 26 participants and got the results shown in Figure 7.6.

You can also look at all the pairs of items that different people put in the same category, and once again look for agreement or disagreement across different people. Different classifications may suggest that there are distinct types of user who may need different classifications. A cluster analysis such as this can be used to produce a

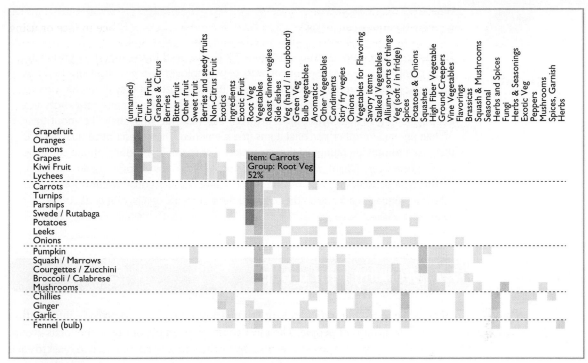

Figure 7.6 Results of card sorting exercise

(Source: www.interaction-design.org/images/encyclopedia/cardsorting/groups chart 26 participants.jpg)

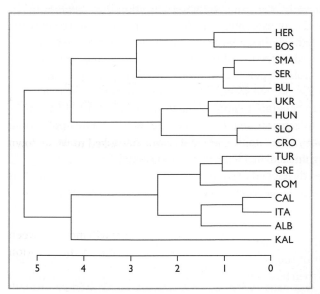

Figure 7.7 Dendogram

(Source: http://dienekes. blogspot.co.uk/2005/08/ haplogroup-frequency-correlations-in.html)

dendrogram (Figure 7.7) which shows the hierarchical clustering of objects (or actions). Representations such as these can then be used in a reverse card sorting (or tree sorting) method to see how the hierarchy is traversed for different tasks.

Analysts really need to practise card sorting to understand the type of insight it can provide and when best to use the technique. A hard part of this is knowing what to sort, which objects or actions to include and when in the overall understanding process the technique will be most helpful.

**FURTHER
THOUGHTS**

Semantic understanding

The dendrogram representation in Figure 7.7 is also used in the repertory grid technique (RepGrid), which is based on the work of psychologist George Kelly (Kelly, 1955). In
this method participants are asked to describe the concepts that they think characterize
some topic. For example you might be investigating the qualities of personal devices and
ask people to give adjectives (the constructs) that describe what they like about their
mobile phone and other personal items (the elements). These descriptive qualities are
then used to provide ratings of the constructs. For example a mobile phone could be
rated as heavy versus light, slim versus fat, comfortable versus uncomfortable and so on.

This type of analysis is also related to the semantic differential (Section 7.4) and to
other techniques that focus on the measurement of meaning (Osgood *et al.*, 1957).

7.7   Working with groups

An alternative to asking individuals or stimulating individuals to provide information
is to work with groups of people. The most common example of this is the focus group.
Here a group of people are posed questions by facilitators and encouraged to react to each
other's comments. If they are part of a group, people can be asked to describe how they
cooperate to manage activities. Members of the group can stimulate each other's memories, and discussion may flow more naturally than in the single-person interview. The
approach is widely used – the early stages of the Joint Application Development (JAD)
method (Wood and Silver, 1995), for example, employ a type of focus group comprising
customers and developers in defining the scope and requirements for a new system.

Focus groups can be enhanced by the use of scenarios, prototypes and other stimuli.
For example, we have used a robotic pet as a stimulus for talking about companionship with groups of older people, printed scenarios and screenshots of a mock-up automatic teller machine (ATM) to generate requirements for personalized ATM services,
and maps and visitor guides to generate requirements for a mobile guide application.
However, group discussion may also inhibit comment about sensitive issues, and can
have the effect of highlighting unusual incidents disproportionately.

Many techniques have been developed to support focus groups. One such example is
CARD (Collaborative Analysis of Requirements and Design, Tudor *et al.*, 1993; Muller,
2001). Used by Microsoft and Lotus among others, CARD uses physical playing cards
with which a group can lay out, modify and discuss the flow of an activity. In the analysis phase, each pre-formatted card contains people's accounts of what is done and why
for an individual component of the activity. Requirements on innovations in human
practices or technologies can then be discussed around the cards. CARD is also intended
to support design and evaluation.

**BOX
7.3**

IDEO Method cards

This is a collection of 51 cards representing different ways that design teams can understand the people they are designing for. The cards can be used by researchers, designers,
engineers and mixed groups to think about design issues and generate debate. The cards
are classified as four suits – Ask, Watch, Learn, Try – that describe various types of activity.

Brainstorming

Another important group activity is brainstorming. Once again there is a wealth of good advice from management consultants and system designers about how to organize and structure brainstorming sessions. Brainstorming sessions should be fun to participate in, but to achieve this they require an experienced facilitator. They also require some stimuli, whether as pictures, text or video, to get the ideas flowing. Participants will need some way of recording their thoughts and ideas; a whiteboard, flip chart, paper and coloured pens. Post-it notes in different colours can be used to capture ideas. This can be useful if the brainstorming session is followed by an affinity analysis where ideas are grouped together using different criteria.

An important point about brainstorming is not to dismiss ideas too soon. The sessions should begin with an 'anything goes' approach. Generate plenty of ideas. These can then be filtered in a part of the session that tries to look at the feasibility of the ideas and their practical impact. A good technique for helping brainstorming sessions is to get different members of the group to adopt different roles – the ideas generator, the critic, the sceptic, the pragmatic, the documenter, and so on.

← The future workshop (Jungk and Müllert, 1987) is a brainstorming technique (see Chapter 6)

7.8 Fieldwork: observing activities *in situ*

Observing people's activities as they happen is another excellent, though time-consuming, method of understanding and requirements generation. Interviews and questionnaires provide one side of the story, but it is difficult for people to describe all the details of the relevant aspect of everyday life or work. Sometimes this is because the activity is intrinsically difficult to describe in words – many manual procedures fall into this category – or because it requires complex and subtle cooperation with other people or events. In other cases, an interviewee may describe the 'official' procedure rather than how something is actually done in practice. They might be embarrassed to admit to some difficulty they are having, or may just tell the designer something to get rid of them.

Data from observation helps to get round these problems. In its simplest form, the designer can simply ask 'Can you show me how you do that?' during an interview. More complex or larger activities will require someone to spend some time on site observing as unobtrusively as possible. This is best done after some initial interviewing, so you have some idea what it is you are looking at. Everyone at the scene must be informed of what is happening and grant their permission in advance, even though they may not be your main focus. Ideally you need to see a range of variations on the normal activity and situations where things go wrong, but this may not be possible in many situations. Here the important point is to identify what you have *not* observed, so you do not over-generalize from your data. If you are lucky enough to be able to choose what you observe, then, just as with interviews, the time to stop is when no new information appears. As in interviews, notes should be taken and video recording is very useful, particularly for sharing the observation with other design team members.

Of course, observation is not without its difficulties. Being unobtrusive is a skill of its own, and your very presence will naturally tend to make people self-conscious and may alter their behaviour. With time, this effect will decrease. It is much less of a problem where the activity you are observing absorbs all the participants' attention, or if you can find a task to carry out which does not interfere with your data collection. It is also hard to observe effectively where the activity is simply one of people processing data at computers with little or no interaction with other people or artefacts. Here it would be more productive to ask people to demonstrate aspects of interest rather than waiting for them to occur in real time. There are also ethical issues associated with observing people, permissions need to be obtained and anonymity of who said and did what should be ensured.

Challenge 7.5

Practise your observational skills next time you are working in a small group on a joint task, obtaining the agreement of the rest of the group first. Ideally, the task should involve working with papers, on-line material or some other tangible artefacts. Imagine that you are designing new technology to improve group working. Note how the group interact with each other and the artefacts. Review your notes afterwards from the point of view of identifying requirements on the new design.

Workplace studies

Workplace studies have become the most widely practised requirements method in the area of Computer Supported Cooperative Working (CSCW). By studying work as it actually happens in its real-world setting, researchers and practitioners aim to overcome many of the difficulties inherent in CSCW. Another factor in their popularity has been the high proportion of CSCW researchers who come with backgrounds in sociology and anthropology, where ethnography – the key approach in workplace studies – has long

→ Chapter 16 discusses collaborative work

been practised. (Strictly speaking, an 'ethnography' is the output of observational fieldwork rather than the fieldwork itself.)

In the early twentieth century, pioneering ethnographic anthropologists endeavoured to understand an unfamiliar way of life through what has become known as 'participant observation' – learning about language, activities and culture through spending months or years living in the community under study. The anthropologists talked to people, observed day-to-day life in detail, and collected not just physical artefacts but stories, myths and so on. Eventually, the resulting personal experience and field data were analysed and recorded as an ethnography. Sociologists, notably those from the University of Chicago in the 1930s, employed similar techniques in the study of societies and groups closer to home. In both domains, the basic approach continues to be used, including the core principle that the ethnographer should not interpose his or her own theoretical or cultural frameworks or expectations between the field data and the resulting ethnography.

**FURTHER
THOUGHTS**

Ethnomethodology and other theoretical difficulties

Following the work of Suchman (1987), most ethnography for technology design adopts a particular flavour of sociology termed 'ethnomethodology'. In short, ethnomethodologists hold that social rules, norms and practices are not imposed externally on everyday life, but that social order is continuously and dynamically constructed from the interactions of individuals. As a corollary of this it is philosophically unsound to generalize beyond the setting where the ethnomethodological ethnography has been undertaken, or to analyse the findings from a theoretical standpoint.

Ethnographic work in human-centred design projects is not always the preserve of specialist 'ethnographers'. As the approach has gained popularity, technologists and HCI practitioners frequently 'do some ethnography' for themselves. Their sometimes casual adoption of the techniques has attracted some adverse comment from those trained in the field (Forsythe, 1999), and more cautious practitioners often refer to their work as 'ethnographically informed'.

Design ethnography is a growing area of research and activity in interaction design. It recognizes the difference between undertaking ethnographies from an anthropologist's perspective (where natural understanding is central) and the ethnographies practised by designers (where the aim is to inform design). Specialist degrees are now offered that present the theory and practice of design ethnography.

Workplace studies consist of ethnographies and field studies of the workplace. These workplaces have included control rooms in the London Underground, the Paris Metro, air traffic control rooms, and financial institutions, to name but a few. The aim of these studies is to describe in fine detail (often called *richly descriptive*) the day-to-day work of these workplaces. The objectives for the ethnographer are very much determined by those of the design project in hand. They often focus on elucidating the role and high-level requirements for a proposed new technology through a deep understanding of work in practice. For instance, Pycock and Bowers (1996) found that ambitious proposals for virtual reality to support fashion design had ignored the mundane but essential work that in fact occupied much of the designers' time. In other projects, the ethnographer's 'added value' is in the definition of usage stories and scenarios, the identification of practical issues for implementation and as a focus for a higher degree of stakeholder involvement (although in some instances, the ethnographers themselves have acted as proxy users). The discussion in the final chapter of Heath and Luff (2000) is a particularly clear account of moving from ethnography to requirements using video-based studies of medical consultations. These contributed to requirements definition for a patient records system. In explicitly requirements-oriented work, a set of guiding questions can be useful, such as those shown in Box 7.4.

A guide to practising workplace ethnography

Resource limitations in many projects can support only a limited amount of ethnographic work. There are also 'political' issues that are raised by the very nature of an ethnographic intervention. With these considerations in mind, Simonsen and Kensing (1997) suggest four preconditions for the use of ethnography in commercial projects:

- Both analysts and user organization must have a positive attitude to investing significant resources.
- Stakeholders must be content with the overall purpose of the new system. Ethnographic approaches, with their emphasis on close work with people, are unlikely to succeed if there are aims to deskill or replace them.
- Analysts must be prepared to handle the 'political' issues which can arise from such an intervention.
- Areas of focus must be identified (ideally, after an initial period of more opportunistic immersion in the environment).

> **Rogers and Bellotti's 'reflective framework' for ethnographic studies**
>
> **BOX 7.4**
>
> - Why is an observation about a work practice or other activity striking?
> - What are the pros and cons of the existing ways technologies are used in the setting?
> - How have 'workarounds' evolved and how effective are they?
> - Why do certain old-fashioned practices, using seemingly antiquated technologies, persist, despite there being available more advanced technologies in the setting?

Envisioning future settings

- What would be gained and lost through changing current ways of working or carrying out an activity by introducing new kinds of technological support?
- What might be the knock-on effects (contingencies arising) for other practices and activities through introducing new technologies?
- How might other settings be enhanced and disrupted through deploying the same kinds of future technologies?

Source: Rogers, Y. and Bellotti, V. (1997) Grounding blue-sky research: how can ethnology help?, *Interactions* 4(3), pp. 58–63. © 1997 ACM, Inc. Reprinted by permission.

So, how can resources best be organized to maximize the potential of the ethnographically informed work? A review of workplace studies and our own experience suggests the following:

- Most can be gained in the early stages when the main design issues are unclear; later work can be focused by data from interviews and other techniques.
- Most information is obtained where people collaborate in some observable way, and share information artefacts in real time.
- Multiple analysts can be valuable, both in observing different activities and in combining perspectives on the same activity.
- Video and audio recording is valuable in capturing data, but field notes remain a vital resource.

The key to (relatively) economical ethnographic work is to recognize when enough data has been collected. One indication of 'enough' may be that no new details are emerging. Another is being able to identify what has *not* been observed, but will not happen within the span of the current work.

Of course, time is required not just to acquire the data but to analyse it. Video is intensely time-consuming to analyse – at least three times the length of the raw sequence and frequently more, depending on the level of detail required. The process can be streamlined by having an observer take notes of significant points in the 'live' action; these notes then act as pointers into the video recording. Software tools such as Atlas.ti and Ethnograph help in analysing pages of text notes (not just of observations, but also transcripts of interviews and group sessions) and, in some cases, audio and video data. For large projects, material can be organized into a multimedia database or Web-based repository.

BOX 7.5

Analysis software

There are a number of software packages that help with the analysis of the rich data that is gathered through ethnographic studies. Atlas.ti, for example, allows the analyst to tag pieces of text or video with key words and then to group these key words into higher-level constructs. This 'grounded theory' approach to analysis aims to let the concepts arise from within the data rather than be imposed top-down by the analyst or designer. Grounded theory was introduced in 1967 (Glaser and Strauss, 1967), but there continues to be considerable work in the area.

Communicating ethnographic results can be challenging. One approach is to encapsulate the findings in 'vignettes' – short descriptions of typical scenes. A vignette is very similar to a scenario but less structured than the format we have proposed – perhaps more like the text of a scene in a play script, complete with stage directions. The vignettes are usually accompanied by a transcript of the accompanying dialogue. Vignettes are often supplemented by video extracts and sample artefacts. Another possibility is for the ethnographer to act as an evaluator of early concepts or prototype designs, before the requirements are finalized and while the design is too immature to benefit from user feedback. A still closer link between workplace studies and system design has been attempted by the COHERENCE project (Viller and Sommerville, 1998, 2000). This takes the output from the study and expresses its findings in the UML notation (UML is the Unified Modeling Language). By contrast, Heath and Luff (2000) and Dourish (2001) argue that the purpose of workplace ethnography is to construct a reservoir of experience that allows designers to uncover how people make sense of technology in use, and so to design tools which support the improvised, situated and continually reconstructed nature of real-world activity.

7.9 Artefact collection and 'desk work'

Data from interviews, questionnaires and observation will have identified a range of artefacts in the form of things that support an activity. It is often possible to supplement this by collecting artefacts – such as documents, forms or computer printouts, in office settings – or to video or photograph items that cannot be removed.

Figure 7.8 shows the sort of photograph which might be taken and annotated to capture the range of information artefacts used in everyday work in an academic's office. These include:

1 Laptop used for file archiving, calendar, document production, e-mail and Internet
2 Paper notebook – notes of *ad hoc* meetings, also holds currently important papers
3 Printouts of journal articles

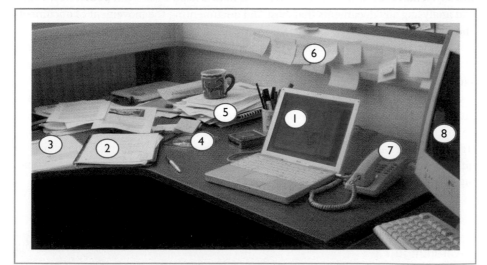

Figure 7.8 Artefacts on and around an office desk
(Source: David Benyon)

4   CD – current backup
5   (Under mug) miscellaneous documents
6   Sticky notes with 'to do' items, important phone numbers, IP address of laptop
7   Telephone – internal and external calls
8   Desktop PC – older file archive, connection to network backup, used for e-mail/ Internet if laptop connection fails
9   Sometimes it can be helpful to track a document through a system, noting everyone who interacts with it and how the document is amended at each stage – a technique sometimes known as a 'tracer study'.

In a study of a health benefits claim processing system, for example, we collected copies of blank claim forms, standard letters sent to claimants, inter-office memos and the public information leaflet about the benefit. By chance, we also found a copy of an article that provided a valuable insight into health professionals' views in a local newsletter. These artefacts helped to ensure that we had a complete understanding not only of the data processed through the system, but also of their relative importance and significance (what information requests are in bold type, what details have to be verified by a medical practitioner or pharmacist, etc.) and how annotations on the original documents were used as notes of progress through the system. In another medical example, this time in a hospital, Symon *et al.* (1996) show how the very appearance and style of a doctor's handwritten notes on patients' records revealed valuable background details to other staff, such as whether the consultation had been carried out in a hurry. All such informal features of the way artefacts are used in practice will make demands on the design of supporting technology.

Understanding activities does not just involve working directly with the people who are doing the activity now or who will be in the future. The designer will need to do plenty of 'desk work' as well. Where the brief is to redesign existing technology such as office systems or home technology products, records of requests for help or user support can be rewarding sources of data about what is confusing or difficult. Similarly, records of bugs reported and change requests often reveal gaps in functionality or presentation. All this can contribute to the new design, but will require interpretation as to which items represent a genuine need for change. Other desk work involves reading procedure manuals and other material about the organization. It involves studying existing software systems to see how they work and what data is kept. Desk work involves collecting and analysing any documents that exist and documenting the movement of documents and the structure of objects such as filing cabinets and ledger books.

Looking at similar products is another way of getting ideas. A market analysis looks at similar products that have been produced. This can be useful because the designer can see the product being used *in situ* and can consider the design solutions that others have proposed. This might highlight good and poor solutions for particular design problems. Looking at similar activities complements such an analysis. An activity might be in quite a different setting from the one under scrutiny, but might have a similar structure. For example, looking at a video hire shop might provide inspiration for a car hire application, or looking at an automatic coffee machine might help in understanding an ATM activity.

Challenge 7.6

What artefacts might you collect or photograph relating to people's use of communications technologies in the home? (Hint: think about non-electronic media as well.)

Summary and key points

In this chapter we have focused on some widely used techniques for understanding people and activities in context, so we can identify requirements on the design of new technologies. However, there is no firm distinction between requirements, design and evaluation, so many of the techniques described here could be used at various stages of the design process. Design starts with researching and understanding the situation at hand, but in the course of achieving that understanding, designers iterate between the exploration of new concepts and understanding and evaluation of ideas, designs and opinions. Using the techniques described here should ensure that designers undertake a human-centred process.

- Techniques for understanding people's activities in context include interviews, observation and collecting samples of artefacts, complemented by background research away from the domain of interest.

- Using more than one technique helps to compensate for their individual limitations.

- Requirements work must be documented for communication and use in design; one way of doing this is a requirements specification supported by illustrative materials, another is in developing a scenario corpus.

- The use of scenarios starts early in the design process, with the construction of conceptual scenarios for exploring requirements and illustrating their application.

Exercises

1 You have been commissioned to design an on-line shopping and home delivery system for a new supermarket chain. Your clients want the system to somehow reproduce the best aspects of real shopping without the drawbacks. They want the system to appeal to all adults with access to a home computer. What techniques would be suitable for carrying out a requirements analysis for the shopping application? Explain the reasons for your choices and any potential limitations on the conclusions you could draw from their use.

2 You are defining functionality and interactivity for the next generation of mobile phones. Find a colleague and interview them for up to 15 minutes about the way they use their current mobile phone and what enhanced functionality they might like. You should make notes of points to cover beforehand. Have them demonstrate the way they use the most useful features with and without a running commentary. Take written notes of your interview; also use an audio- or video-recorder if you have one available. (Ask the interviewee's permission first before recording.) Review the data you have collected as soon as possible after the interview.

    (a) Which questions elicited the most useful data? Why?
    (b) Did the running commentary provide extra information or did it obstruct the demonstration? Did your interviewee seem comfortable with the process?
    (c) If you have recorded the interview, how much is missing from your written notes when compared to the recording?

    If you have time, carry out a second interview with someone else after reflecting on the results of the first.

→

> **3 (More advanced)** It is sometimes argued that understanding people's existing activities does not really help to design future technologies, since activities may change radically once the technology is in use.
>
> **(a)** Do you agree or disagree with this view? Provide supporting arguments for your position.
>
> **(b)** Which requirements elicitation techniques are most likely to be effective in helping users and designers to create the future? Why?
>
> **4 (More advanced)** Read Lundberg *et al.* (2002) 'The Snatcher Catcher' – an interactive refrigerator, *Proceedings of NordiCHI '02* (available on-line through the ACM digital library – www.acm.org/dl). Outline a design for a similarly provocative domestic device which is aimed at stimulating people to think about the future directions for home technologies. Explain how your design would facilitate the process.

 Further reading

A number of general-purpose requirements engineering texts have sound advice on the more user-centred techniques as well as a strong grounding in the software engineering process. In particular we recommend:

Robertson, S. and Robertson, J. (1999) *Mastering the Requirements Process.* Addison-Wesley, Harlow (Chapters 5 and 11).

Sommerville, I. and Sawyer, P. (1997) *Requirements Engineering: a Good Practice Guide.* Wiley, Chichester (Chapter 4).

Wixon, D. and Ramey, J. (eds) (1996) *Field Methods Casebook for Software Design.* Wiley, New York. *An excellent, readable introduction to gathering information from fieldwork at user sites, containing many case studies which show how various techniques have been applied and adapted. Unfortunately, at the time of writing it is not easy to obtain a copy to purchase, but your library should be able to track down a copy.*

Getting ahead

Kuniavsky, M. (2003) *Observing the User Experience – a Practitioner's Guide to User Research.* Morgan Kaufmann, San Francisco, CA. *Contains much sensible, pragmatic material about working with people. Note, however, that most of the examples are oriented towards the design of websites.*

Rogers, Y. and Bellotti, V. (1997) Grounding blue-sky research: how can ethno-graphy help? *Interactions,* 4(3), 58–63. *A short introduction to ethnography, a theoretically informed approach to observation, in this case adapted to the design process.*

 Web links

There are many on-line tutorials for things such as card sorting that are included on the web-site associated with this chapter at **www.pearsoned.co.uk/benyon**

Also see Boxes and Arrows site at **www.boxesandarrows.com**

Comments on challenges

Challenge 7.1

Requirements 1, 3, 6 and 8 are all non-functional – they are all *qualities* which the HIC must have, rather than something it actually does. The functional requirements are 2, 4, 5 and 7. Of course, many non-functional requirements do necessitate some underlying functionality – password-controlled entry, for example.

Challenge 7.2

Think about whether it makes a difference to you personally if you are involved in decisions which affect your everyday work or home life. We would expect that you would be more enthusiastic about a holiday, for example, if you have helped to decide whether it should include relaxing on the beach or visiting ancient ruins, staying in a hotel or camping, etc. If people take part in the specification and design of a system, they are more likely to use it effectively once it is implemented. There is strong research evidence to support this.

Challenge 7.3

There are several limitations to interviewing. They include:

- People can only tell the interviewer about aspects of current activities of which they are aware. This excludes parts of the job (or whatever) which are so familiar that they no longer penetrate into consciousness, aspects beyond the interviewees' direct experience, etc.
- Emphasis on correct, official procedures
- Memory
- Difficult-to-describe complex operations.

Challenge 7.4

(a) The focus may not be clear to everyone. E-mail (and older utilities such as FTP – file transfer protocol) run over the Internet, but many people may simply think of the WWW. The question should make it obvious what is intended: perhaps 'How often do you access the WWW (World Wide Web) or use e-mail?'. Better still, use separate questions for each, since usage levels are likely to be different.

   The word 'typically' or 'normally' should be included when asking about usage, unless you are interested in a snapshot of a specific time period.

   There is no provision for 'never'.

(b) - 'Frequently' is likely to be interpreted in different ways.
   - It is much easier for people to check items on a list of possibilities rather than recall them.
   - Providing a list also makes it easier to analyse the responses. You can include an 'other – please specify' item to catch any types of material you had not expected.
   - You may well have identified additional points.

Challenge 7.5

No specific comments – the idea is to gain experience in observation. This variant, where the observer is also part of the group being observed, is termed 'participant observation'.

Challenge 7.6

Possible artefacts to be collected: printouts of typical day's e-mail and e-mail address book, with notes of the contact's relation to the owner of the address book, screen printout showing WWW favourites, etc. And to be photographed: landline phone(s) and fax machines in normal location(s) with any directories, address books, notepads and so on kept near the phone; similarly the home PC if used for communications, etc. Mobile phones are probably only worth photographing if novel features are used which can be captured in the photograph. It would also be useful to draw a sketch plan showing the location of the various communication devices within the home.

Chapter 8
Envisionment

Contents

Aims

Envisionment is concerned with making ideas visible; with externalizing thoughts. Externalization can take all manner of forms: stories and scenarios, presentations, sketches, formal models, software prototypes, cardboard models and so on. Different forms of representation will be more or less useful at different stages in the design process and more or less effective for doing different things. A formal presentation of a design concept for a potential client will look quite different from a sketch of a screen layout intended to explore what something will look like. Envisionment is needed to represent design work to ourselves and to others. It occurs throughout development as the designer generates multiple design solutions and whittles them down to a final product.

In this chapter we consider the principal envisionment techniques, various forms of prototyping used to explore and evaluate ideas and the presentation of ideas to clients. But first of all we review ways of thinking about the ideas to be externalized.

After studying this chapter you should be able to:

- Use a variety of techniques for envisioning design problems and possible solutions
- Understand the role of concrete scenarios in envisioning design
- Select and use appropriate prototyping techniques
- Understand the main factors in communicating designs effectively.

8.1 Finding suitable representations

Envisionment is fundamental to effective human-centred design, to enable designers to see things from other people's perspectives and to explore design concepts and ideas with others. Different representations of design ideas are useful at different stages for different people. They help with generation, communication and evaluation of ideas. A sketch 'on the back of an envelope' might be useful for generating an idea and expressing it to a colleague – but it is not so good for giving to a client.

There are many techniques that can be used to help develop an understanding of the design problem and to envision possible solutions. None of these techniques in themselves will lead to the perfect design, but they will all generate some kind of document or representation that can be used in the process of communicating with clients, customers and colleagues. It is through communication that design solutions will arise, be evaluated, and (eventually) be transformed into a final product.

Which techniques are used on a particular project will depend on a number of factors: the working style of the development team, the type of project, the resources available and so on. In an ideal world, developers would use a wide variety of representations, but in a two-person company working on a project with a deadline of four weeks this may not be possible.

Choosing suitable representations for the task at hand is one of the skills of a designer; another is making good use of that representation. Representations work by suppressing unnecessary detail, thus ensuring that the significant features of some artefact or activity stand out. A good representation is accurate enough to reflect the features of the system being modelled, but simple enough to avoid confusion. It adopts a style of presentation that is suitable for its purpose.

Consider the following example:

> A car designer has been commissioned to produce a new luxury sports car. He or she doodles a few designs on paper and shows them to other designers on the team. They make some comments and criticisms and as a result changes are made. Finally the designer is satisfied with one of the designs and draws up detailed blueprints that are given to the firm's model maker. Scale models are produced and sent to Marketing and Sales for customer reaction. The scale models are also subjected to wind tunnel experiments to investigate the aerodynamics of the design and the results are used in a computer program that will calculate the car's speed and fuel efficiency.

The designer is using four different representations in at least four different ways:

1 The original representations focus on clearing the mind. In this case they are doodles and sketches that are used to generate new ideas, examine possibilities and prompt for questions.
2 The blueprints given to the model maker and the scale model given to the Marketing and Sales departments are suitable for accurately expressing ideas to others.
3 The wind tunnel experiments show representations being used to test ideas.
4 The computer model is used to make predictions.

Challenge 8.1

Which representations in the example above are being used to explore the problem? Which are being used to communicate ideas?

An outline envisionment process

Here is a suggested series of steps for the envisionment process, pulling together the wide-ranging material in this chapter.

1 Review requirements and conceptual scenarios.
2 Develop representations of your design ideas. At a minimum these should include concrete scenarios, storyboards developing the main interaction sequences, and snapshot sketches of key screens or other aspects of the product.
3 If your product is a new one, experiment with different metaphors and design concepts through your representations (see Chapter 9).
4 Explore design ideas with the people who will be using the system wherever possible (using techniques described in Chapter 7).
5 Develop wireframes to provide more detail on the proposed structure and navigation (this chapter).
6 Iterate and gradually formalize the design (making it more concrete) through prototypes and further evaluations.

8.2 Basic techniques

Envisionment is about bringing abstract ideas to life. It is easy to have great ideas in your head, but it is only by envisioning them that the flaws and difficulties will be exposed. There are a number of basic techniques that can help.

Sketches and snapshots

The art of sketching is something that all designers should practise. Ideas and thoughts can be quickly visualized – either to yourself, or to others – and explored. The Millennium Bridge across the River Thames in London was reputedly designed on a paper napkin in a restaurant. Designers do well to carry a sketchbook with them so that inspiration can be quickly captured and preserved.

Figure 8.1 shows two visualizations of the Edinburgh Festival scenario from the HIC case study. A key design requirement for this system was to display large amounts of data without the need for scrolling (in order to move away from the personal computer paradigm). In the sketches we can see that the designer has been exploring different ideas for displaying and searching through results of a search. The design principle underlying the designs is often referred to as 'focus and context'. Ben Shneiderman has a mantra for visualizations of large amounts of data that he encourages designers to use: 'overview first, zoom and filter, then details on demand' (Shneiderman, 1998, p. 523). On the left is a 'hyperbolic tree' representation of the Festival scenario and on the right is a 'cone tree' representation. Notice how the hyperbolic tree is better for capturing the focus and context principles.

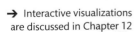
← The full scenario is in Chapter 6

Individual snapshots of a design can be provided to show key moments in an interaction (e.g. Figure 8.2) and are particularly useful for exploring the impact of a certain style or design. Snapshots can be single sketches, or frames, from a storyboard (see below) or they can be produced using software.

→ Interactive visualizations are discussed in Chapter 12

> **Challenge 8.2**
>
> *Sketch two different ways in which you might present information about tourist sites on a town's website.*

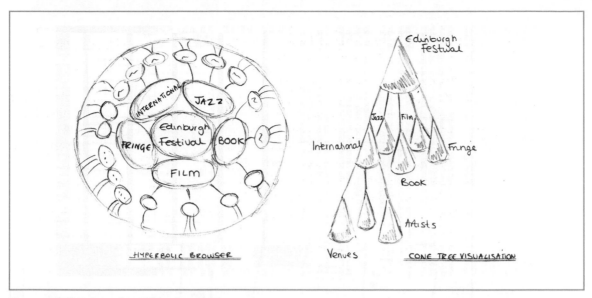

Figure 8.1 Sketches of possible visualization

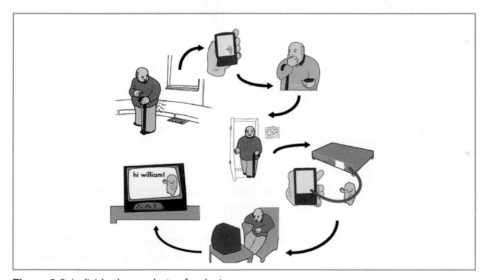

Figure 8.2 Individual snapshots of a design
(Source: David Benyon)

Storyboards

Storyboarding is a technique taken from filmmaking – using a simple cartoon-like structure, key moments from the interactive experience are represented. The advantage of storyboarding is that it allows you to get a feel for the 'flow' of the experience. It is also a very economical way of representing the design – a single page can hold 6–8 'scenes'. It is often helpful to sketch out a storyboard based around a concrete scenario. The two together are very helpful in working through design ideas with customers.

Three main types of storyboarding are commonly found in interactive media design:

- *Traditional storyboarding.* A storyboard for a film would usually have some notes attached to each scene expanding on what will happen – this helps overcome the limitations of representing a dynamic experience in a static medium. For interactive systems, notes below each sketch usually contain the relevant steps from a scenario,

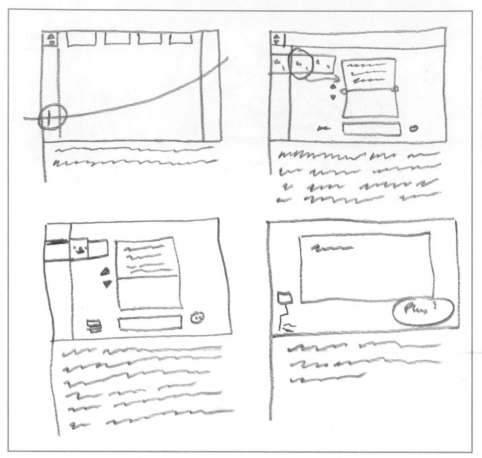

Figure 8.3 Sketched storyboard for the HIC

and the sketches themselves are annotated to indicate interactive behaviour. This is the most usual form of storyboard if there is not a strongly multimedia flavour to the application.

- *Scored storyboards*. If the application has a lot of motion graphics the storyboard can be annotated – a sketch is annotated with appropriate notation and notes about, for example, type, colours, images, sound and other issues are attached underneath.
- *Text-only storyboards*. These are useful if the application has a lot of very complex sequences. You can specify what images appear, what text accompanies them, any accompanying media, general notes about tone, flow, etc.

Figure 8.3 shows a sketched storyboard for an application of the HIC to playing MP3 music files. The storyboard shows how an interaction might take place. It exploits some ideas of marking movement using arrows and lines to indicate change. Figure 8.4 shows part of another storyboard, this time for a website designed to showcase a photographer's portfolio.

Mood boards

Mood boards are widely used in advertising and interior design. Quite simply you gather visual stimuli that capture something of how you feel about the design – photographs and other images, colours, textures, shapes, headlines from newspapers or magazines, quotations from people, pieces of fabric and so on. Attach the stimuli to a pinboard.

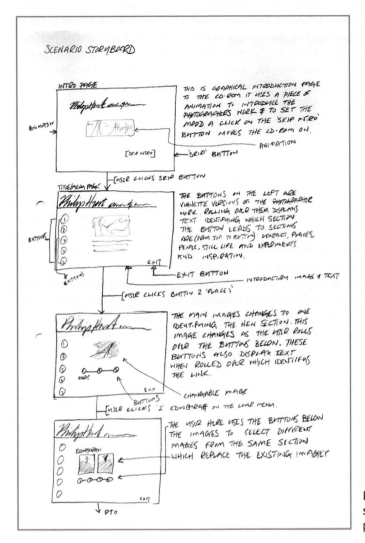

Figure 8.4 Part of a storyboard for a photographer's website

Even thinking about their arrangement can stimulate ideas. You can put pages from websites you like on mood boards. If you use Blu-Tack or something similar then you can add and delete items as your thinking changes. Figure 8.5 shows an example from Lucero (2009) of an interactive system that supports the presentation of mood boards, the 'Funky Wall'.

Figure 8.5 Funky Wall

(Source: Lucero)

The rule with mood boards is that 'anything goes'. The point of the board is not to formally represent some aspect of the design, simply to act as inspiration – perhaps promoting a particular line of thought, or providing inspiration for a colour scheme. One technique is to get the client to create a mood board. This can give you an insight into the kinds of aesthetics that are likely to appeal to them. As a variation on the mood board concept, writing down adjectives that describe some aspect of the system can be useful.

Navigation maps

→ Chapter 14 discusses navigation for websites

→ Chapter 25 discusses navigation in general

Navigation is a key feature for many systems. Navigation maps focus on how people move through the site or application. The aim is to focus on how people will experience the site. Each page in the site, or location in the application, is represented with a box or heading and every page that can be accessed from that page should flow from it. A useful tip is to put in all flows possible (i.e. back and forwards from a page) as this will highlight sections where people might get stranded. Navigation maps can usefully be redrawn many times through the project life cycle, as poor navigational structure is one of the main reasons people turn off a website, for example. The maps can be used with scenarios to 'walk through' particular activities and are a very good way of spotting poor aspects of design such as 'orphan pages' (pages which are not accessible) or dead ends.

Navigation is important in all manner of applications and products, not just websites. Figure 8.6 shows the navigation map for a mobile phone. More formal and more fully annotated maps can also be developed as illustrated in Figure 8.7. Arrows can be added to lines if the direction of a link is important.

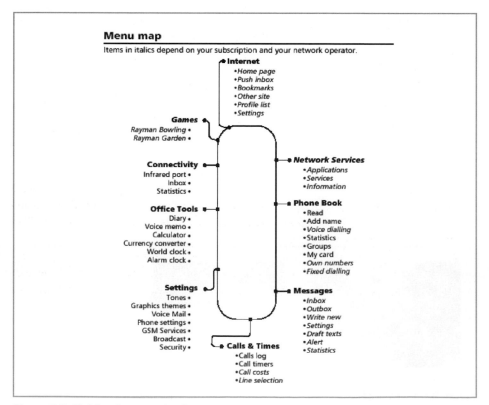

Figure 8.6 Mobile phone navigation map

(Source: Trium phone manual, Mitsubishi)

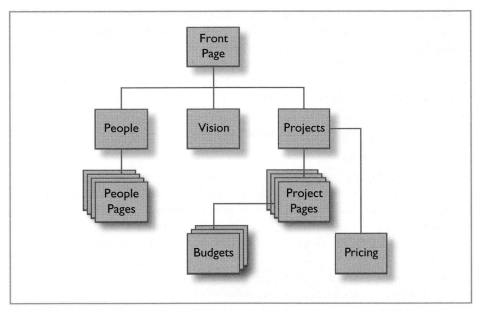

Figure 8.7 Navigation map for a website

Wireframes

Wireframes are outlines of the structure of a software system. They used to be concerned principally with website design, but with the proliferation of small-scale apps for handheld and tablet devices, wireframing has become a mainstream technique. With the developments of Cascading Style Sheets (CSS) and the specification language HTML5, the development of websites and the development of apps are becoming increasingly blurred

Just as navigation maps focus on how pages are structured and linked together, so wireframes focus on the structure of particular types of pages. Use the two together and you have the basics of an app or website design.

Wireframes work because they focus on the general elements of a design without worrying about the final detail. For example in a mobile phone app there are buttons, menu items, selections. Certain events cause certain behaviours such as a button click moves the user to the next page. Wireframing makes use of these generic design features for both apps and websites to create quick designs often for quick evaluation. The storyboard in Figure 8.3 is an informal wireframe.

Software packages are available to help with developing wireframes. The best known is Axure (www.axure.com) but there are a number of other alternatives. These provide templates that constrain the design to the particular size and style of a particular delivery platform such as an iPhone. Good advice on interface design for the iPhone and iPad are provided on the Apple website.

→ Chapter 12 deals with visual interface design

Wireframes sit in between the informal sketching of this section and the development of prototypes described in the next section as there are several software packages that will generate working prototypes from the wireframe. Some examples of wireframes are shown in Figure 8.8.

Challenge 8.3

Construct a navigation map for a website with which you are familiar – perhaps that of your university/college or employer. (If the site is very large, draw a partial map.) Are there any 'dead ends' or complicated routes to important information?

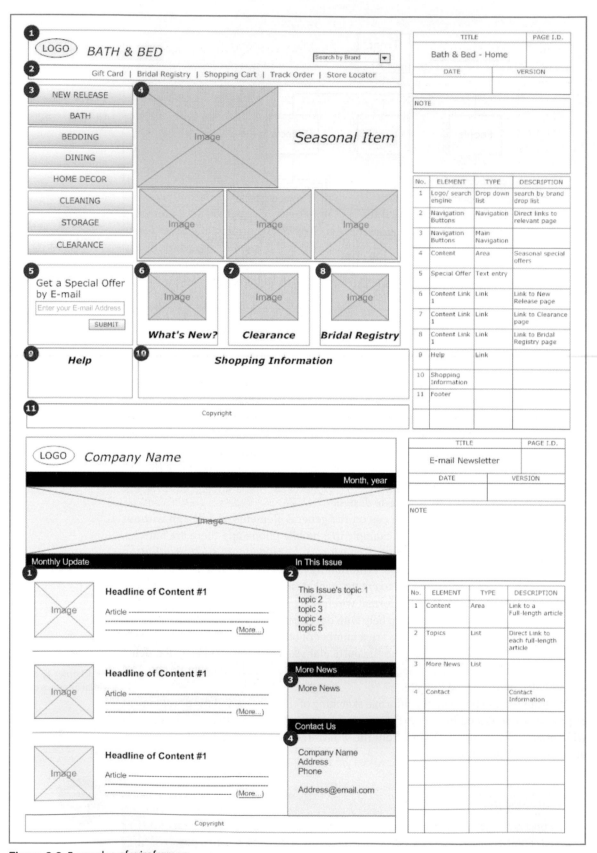

Figure 8.8 Examples of wireframes

(Source: http://www.smartdraw.com, SmartDraw)

Summary

These are just a few of the many possible envisionment techniques. These techniques are filtering mechanisms for the designer, effectively screening out parts of the design space that the designer does not want to explore in order to focus on the parts that are of interest. There are books full of interesting and novel ways of representing aspects of design. For example, 'mind maps' list the main concepts of a design, showing links between them, flow diagrams show the movement of some items or some information through a design, and transition diagrams show how a system changes from one state to another. We discussed an example of a car designer who used sketches, and others in the design process who used scale models, blueprints and so on. We also argued that getting an appropriate representation – appropriate for a particular purpose in a particular context – is important. The different representations will be used alongside other techniques for helping to generate ideas such as brainstorming and other forms of collaborative design. For example, we have found sketching on a whiteboard very effective for a design meeting, as is using a flip chart where pages can be torn off and stuck to the wall. Writing ideas on Post-it notes and sticking them on the walls of a design room is another technique. They can be rearranged to show different collections and 'affinities'. Collaborative writing, where a group all work on a single document using a computer and data projector to display the results on a screen, can be very effective in producing draft documents.

A key feature of design and of the techniques described here is *not* to sit staring at a blank piece of paper. Getting inspiration from magazines, websites, software systems, other people, similar systems or products and so on (the importance of examples in design (Herring *et al.*, 2009)), and externalizing ideas through envisionment techniques, are the first steps in design.

8.3 Prototypes

A prototype is a concrete but partial representation or implementation of a system design. Prototypes are used extensively in most design and construction domains. Lim *et al.* (2008) present a view of prototypes as 'tools for traversing a design space where all possible design alternatives and their rationales can be explored . . . Designers communicate the rationales of their design decisions through prototypes. Prototypes stimulate reflections, and designers use them to frame, refine, and discover possibilities in a design space' (p. 7:2).

Prototypes may be used to demonstrate a concept (e.g. a prototype car) in early design, to test details of that concept at a later stage and sometimes as a specification for the final product. A prototype may be made of something as simple as paper, cardboard or other suitable material, or it may be developed using a sophisticated software package.

Prototyping the lunar lander

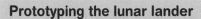

The engineers in the Apollo missions built a full-size cardboard prototype of the lunar landing module to test the position and size of the windows in relation to the field of view of the astronauts. This experimentation led to the design decision that the astronauts would stand (not sit) inside the lander – thus allowing windows to be smaller and saving crucial weight.

BOX
8.1

In our domain of interactive systems design, representations such as screen sketches and simple early prototypes blend into each other. But the main distinguishing characteristic of a prototype is that it is interactive. Something happens when a person 'presses' a 'button' – even if the button is drawn on paper and the action consists of a menu on a Post-it note being added by the designer. The appropriateness of a prototype will depend on a number of factors such as whom the prototype is aimed at, the stage of the design process and what features the designer is looking to explore.

For the design team, representations like navigation maps and flow charts might be meaningful, but for clients and ordinary people some form of prototype is crucial for capturing the outcomes of the envisioning techniques we have discussed so far. The prototype might seek to highlight just the interface, or some crucial aspect of the functionality. Prototypes are first and foremost a way of involving people and clients in evaluating your design ideas. There are two main kinds of prototyping – low-fidelity (lo-fi) and high-fidelity (hi-fi). We also include a section on video prototypes, a medium that is becoming increasingly useful and common in interaction design.

Hi-fi prototypes

Hi-fi prototypes are similar in look and feel, if not necessarily in functionality, to the anticipated final product. They are produced in software, whether in the development environment which will be used for implementation or in packages that will allow interactive effects to be mocked up easily. Hi-fi prototyping has the following features:

- It is useful for detailed evaluation of the main design elements (content, visuals, interactivity, functionality and media) – for example, hi-fi prototypes can be used in usability studies to establish whether people can learn to use the system within a specified amount of time.
- It often constitutes a crucial stage in client acceptance – as a kind of final design document which the client must agree to before the final implementation.
- It is generally developed fairly well into the project when ideas are beginning to firm up, unless there is some crucial issue that needs to be resolved before any other work can proceed.

A problem with developing hi-fi prototypes is that people believe them! This is dangerous if the designer has not checked details and thought through ideas clearly beforehand. A simple error – perhaps in the name of a customer, or of a product – can completely ruin a prototype because clients or employees will get confused. If everything else seems real, why aren't the customers our real customers? It is no good saying 'we were going to fix that' or 'that is just a place holder'. For hi-fi prototyping, accurate detail is vital. Another problem with hi-fi prototyping is that it suggests such a system can be implemented. We have found it impossible to implement in Java some effects that were prototyped using Macromedia Director, for example. Inevitably a degree of effort and time is consumed in producing the prototype. If this is in the eventual development environment, developers can be understandably reluctant to discard work on features rejected in exploring the prototype.

Lo-fi prototypes

Lo-fi prototypes – often termed paper prototypes, since that is what they are usually made from – on the other hand, have the following features:

- They are more focused on the broad underlying design ideas – such as content, form and structure, the 'tone' of the design, key functionality requirements and navigational structure.

- They are designed to be produced quickly, and thrown away as quickly.
- They capture very early design thinking and should aid, not hinder, the process of generating and evaluating many possible design solutions.

The products of some of the envisioning techniques discussed previously are kinds of lo-fi prototypes in some respects. However, the most usual form of this sort of prototype is a series of 'screenshots' that people can 'walk through' (for example, a button on screenshot 1 can be 'clicked' and this is followed by screenshot 6, etc.). How the prototype is implemented is limited only by your imagination, by time and the materials readily to hand. Very flexible prototypes can be produced simply and quickly using screen-sized pieces of stiff paper and index cards or Post-its in different colours. Permanent features of each screen are drawn on the card; dynamic items such as dialogue boxes or menus use the cards or Post-its, cut to size as necessary. Overlays of acetates can simulate dynamic features, or allow people to write comments using wipe-off pens. But it is really important not to spend too much time doing this – the whole point is the low investment in the prototype build. If you are spending a good deal of time trying to replicate design details on paper, you should probably be using a hi-fi software prototype instead.

Figure 8.9 illustrates a lo-fi prototype developed to explore ideas for a tool to allow households to communicate directly with local government. One feature to note here is the small acetate just visible at top left, which allows people to record suggested changes.

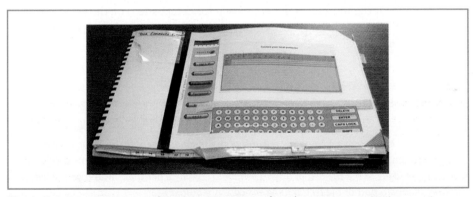

Figure 8.9 Paper prototype of a messaging screen for a home communications centre
(Source: David Benyon)

Paper prototypes

BOX
8.2

Paper prototypes are widely used in practice. A survey of 172 usability professionals conducted in 2002 asked how important they considered the technique to be in their work (Snyder, 2003). The responses are shown in the chart below – a 'useless' option was included but no one chose it. (The percentages do not sum to 100 per cent because of rounding.)

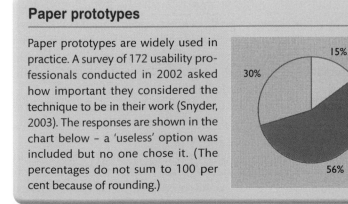

The main practical issues with designing paper prototypes are as follows:

- *Robustness*. If a paper prototype is to be handled by lots of people it needs to be tough enough to survive.
- *Scope*. Focus on broad issues and key elements; if you are trying to tell too detailed a story it can be hard for users to understand.
- *Instructions*. There is a trade-off between adding enough detail for someone to be able to use the prototype without the designer helping (in which case the boundary between the design ideas and the supplementary information can be hard to see) and adding so much detail that it needs someone to talk the person through it (which may affect their responses).
- *Flexibility*. Have parts of the paper prototype adjustable so that people viewing it can 'redesign it' on the fly, e.g. by using sticky notes to represent parts of the screen where the user can move elements around or add new items.

Video prototypes

For over 20 years researchers have highlighted the potential of video as a tool within the participatory design process, from initial observation, through ideas generation and design exploration, what Mackay *et al.* called 'video brainstorming' and 'video proto-typing' (2000). Vertelney's method (1989) involves the creation of a physical mock-up model of the product; a video is then shot with an actor interacting (or 'acting') with the model as though it were fully functional. The product's display dynamics are simulated in an animation program, and are superimposed (or composited) on the video, ensuring synchronization to give the appearance that the product is actually responding to the person's actions.

Challenge 8.4

You are a designer working on a new interface to a supermarket's on-line shopping system. The client wants a complete revamp of the site. Your team leader in your own organization, a software developer, is unconvinced of the value of using lo-fi prototypes to explore ideas. Write the text of a short e-mail to convince her that this is a good idea. (Only the main part of the text arguing the case is required.)

The second method suggested by Vertelney is what is sometimes referred to as the 'weatherman' technique, where a video image is superimposed onto computer graphics. Actions are captured against a blue screen (typically a green screen is used now), allowing removal of the background (via chromakey colour removal) and the superimposition of the video image onto a pre-modelled 3D environment. With appropriate real-world camera movement synchronized with parallel movement within the virtual environment, the resulting composite can have a powerful effect.

What has changed in video prototyping are the tools used to create the video material. The technology and computing power used for the production of ground-breaking Hollywood visual effects, such as the liquid metal T1000 in 1991's *Terminator 2*, are now available to the sub-£1000 consumer market. The software tools used in professional film and television production, such as Final Cut Pro (editing and post-production) and Shake (compositing) as well as Adobe's After Effects (3D animation and rendering) are all well within educational budgets (all are available below £500 with higher education discounts). Furthermore, the advent of technologies such as HDV (High Definition Video), the successor to the ubiquitous mini-DV tape format, has brought high-definition capability at consumer price. The bottleneck is not with the video production hardware or software now, but rather with the skill of the production team. As the Australian film critic Shane Danielsen said at the opening of the Edinburgh Film Festival in 2006, 'The emergence of digital filmmaking puts the tools in the hands of anyone, but not the talent'. And, of course, the ability to put films into the public arena on sites such as YouTube can elicit wide-ranging reactions to design ideas.

An example of video prototyping comes from a project investigating embodiment issues of the concept of a companion based on the following conceptual scenario:

> Lexi is a 3D projected figure that helps its guardian, Tom, by scheduling his personal and work life, keeping him up to date with relevant news articles and being first point of contact for e-mails, phone calls, text messages and the like. Lexi is a mobile companion who can 'leap' from technology to technology as necessary but is most fully realized when projected as a 3D figure on Tom's tablet.

Using a modelling application such as e-Frontier's Poser 7, it is possible to apply multiple figures to a baseline video track in identical fashion. Because the animation uses the same underlying kinematics and basic bone structure, it is possible to investigate the impact of the single variable of character embodiment. As can be seen in Figure 8.10, it is possible to composit different characters onto the baseline video of the companion's owner (actor) Tom, all of which behave identically but look completely different – in this example, a penguin, a man and a woman. In parallel to this is the ability to alter the vocal characteristics of Lexi, for example pitch, tone, naturalness, etc. By applying this multi-layered approach it is possible to produce extremely quickly multiple videos which have only one variable changing from the base line.

Different approaches to functionality in prototypes

There are several other types of prototype that it is useful to distinguish. A full prototype provides full functionality, but at a lower performance than the target system. A horizontal prototype aims to go across the whole system, but deals only with top-level functions, so much of the detail is omitted. In contrast, a vertical prototype implements the full range of features, from top to bottom, but is applied to only a small number of functions of the overall system. Combinations of these are common. Evolutionary and incremental (a more step-wise version of evolutionary) prototypes eventually develop into the full system.

Figure 8.10 Different embodiments of a companion

8.4   Envisionment in practice

In using the prototype, designers sit alongside the people who will use the final system to make the prototype 'work' if it is a lo-fi version. It helps to have two designers, one to 'play computer' and one to make notes. Whatever the type of prototype, record comments and design issues as they arise. Videotape can sometimes be useful if there is likely to be a substantial quantity of detailed feedback for other members of the team.

People find it difficult to react to a prototype if it is just placed in front of them devoid of any context. Some sort of structuring narrative is required. The most common strategy is to have people step through a scenario using the new application or to try carrying out one of their current tasks if the application is to replace an earlier system. For interface design details, set the scene by suggesting what someone would be trying to do with the software at that particular point, for example 'You are interested in buying the shirt shown on this screen but want to know more about the material – show me what you would do now'. It is always best if people interact with the prototype themselves, even if only by pointing to a paper button. This promotes engagement with the questions to be explored, and avoids any danger of the person running the prototyping session misinterpreting responses. But there will be cases where this is not feasible. Perhaps the prototype software is fragile, or the prototype is at a very early stage with very little genuine interactivity. Here designers can run a video prototype produced in software such as Director, Keynote, PowerPoint or Flash to simulate a usage session. The movie can be paused for discussion as appropriate. (What is happening here is, of course, early evaluation, so many of the techniques discussed in Chapter 10 are appropriate.)

Prototypes and participatory design

Lo-fi prototypes are an essential part of participatory design because people cannot always understand formal models, but they can explore and evaluate ideas through engaging with prototyped systems. People can also be directly involved in prototype design. During the development of the HIC we ran a workshop with schoolchildren from a school in Dumfries and Galloway in Scotland. It was decided to use the existing scenarios as stimuli in a participatory design workshop with a group of 20 high-school students. Using the 'what will we do tonight' scenario as a basis, we spent a morning working with the students. The scenario was adapted to make it more relevant to the participants – the students were asked to imagine that they and a group of friends had won a trip to the city for the day and had to plan their activities.

← Chapter 6 describes the HIC case study

We asked participants to use a range of supplied craft materials and information examples to create a mock-up of how they thought the HIC would look and operate. A number of lo-fi prototypes were quickly produced (Figures 8.11 to 8.13).

Trade-offs in prototyping

As with so many aspects of design, the designer has to consider the trade-offs in terms of time, resources, the aim of the evaluation, the stage of the project and so on. Indeed, when reflecting on how and what to prototype, the designer should think in terms of the PACT elements – people, activities, contexts and technologies. Who is the prototype aimed at? What is the designer trying to achieve with the prototype? What stage of the project are things at and what is the context for the use of the prototype? What technologies (hi-fi or lo-fi) are appropriate?

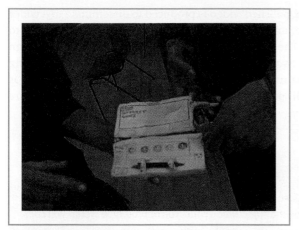

Figure 8.11 HIC mock-up in clay (and pencil!)
(Source: David Benyon)

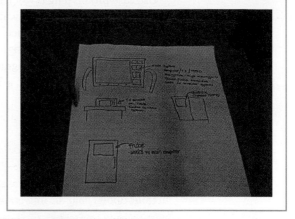

Figure 8.12 Storyboard
(Source: David Benyon)

Figure 8.13 Remote control mock-up
(Source: David Benyon)

Rosson and Carroll (2002) highlight some of these trade-offs:

- High-quality graphics and animation can be used to create convincing and exciting prototypes *but* may also lead to premature commitment to some design decision.
- Detailed special-purpose prototypes help to answer specific questions about a design, *but* building a meaningful prototype for each issue is expensive.
- Realistic prototypes increase the validity of user test data, *but* may postpone testing, or require construction of throw-away prototypes.
- Iterative refinement of an implementation enables continual testing and feedback, *but* may discourage consideration of radical transformations.

Prototyping is used throughout the design process.

'Requirements animation' is a term used to describe the use of prototyping to illustrate requirements. Used at an early stage, a quick prototype can be developed and shown to the client/users for comment on the general design.

Rapid prototyping (also known as 'throw-it-away' prototyping) is common in user interface design where software such as PowerPoint or Keynote is used to illustrate concepts. The prototype will be 'thrown away' because implementation will be in a different language. However, as one famous quotation in software development has it, 'You will throw away your first few designs, so you might as well plan to throw them away in the first place'.

Use case prototyping is when a 'polished' video is produced to disseminate to a wider audience and also to the software and hardware development teams whose job it is to bring the product into existence. The power of this type of video to communicate design requirements in product design as well as software engineering is extremely strong (Mival, 2004). In certain designs this use case will employ a technology beyond what is possible (in the Lexi example, a 3D projection smart pad); we have coined these *'Future Now'* movies.

← Use cases are introduced in Chapter 3

Challenge 8.5

Imagine you are presenting your ideas for a diary tool on a smartphone to a small team of developers from the smartphone manufacturer. What type of prototype would you use?

Prototyping tools

Given the wide range of uses for prototyping and the large number of occasions when it is used, it is not surprising that there are a wealth of software 'tools' that can be used. A good prototyping tool should:

- Allow easy, rapid modification of interface details or functionality
- For designers who are not programmers, allow direct manipulation of prototype components
- For incremental and evolutionary prototypes, facilitate reuse of code
- Not constrain the designer to default styles for interface objects.

Useful tools for requirements animation include paper, PowerPoint (e.g. for illustrating main screens) and drawing packages. Data manipulation languages such as SQL can be effective in animating the functionality of a system, and vertical or horizontal prototypes can be built using simple application builders such as Visual Basic, the Borland development environment, the Java development environment and so on. User Interface Design Environments (UIDEs) are collections of tools that help designers rapidly prototype aspects of the interface.

Throw-it-away (rapid) prototyping emphasizes rapid evaluation and changing requirements. Useful software here includes InDesign and similar tools, Visual Basic, PowerPoint, hypermedia tools and Web tools such as Dreamweaver or Flash. For evolutionary and incremental prototyping there is a compromise between production and prototyping and a long-term view of system development, so a development environment that can be used for implementation is needed. Reuse of code is likely and hence object-oriented languages are suitable.

Prototyping functionality in software has its own pitfalls. For example, if the interface prototype diverges from the functional prototype it may not be possible for them to be brought together. Indeed this is what happened in the HIC case study and we finished up with an interface prototype that was low in functionality and a functional prototype that had a pretty poor interface! Other dangers include people being unable to evaluate functionality because the interface is distractingly difficult. In one project participants in an evaluation of an early prototype of a virtual environment found it so difficult to move around that reviewing the functionality was practically impossible. People found it impossible to find their way around fixtures and fittings (as in the virtual bridge in Figure 8.14), became irretrievably stuck midway up a virtual staircase or entangled themselves with railings. We recovered the situation by refocusing the early evaluation

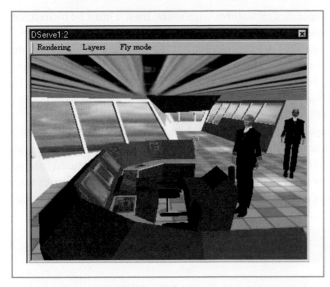

Figure 8.14 The virtual bridge in a training simulator

sessions on interaction mechanisms and considering functionality much later, when the worst problems had been resolved. Incidentally, this illustrates the value of prototyping with people as early as possible in the process. The software designers themselves had naturally experienced no problems with virtual movement.

> **Challenge 8.6**
>
> *What are the advantages and disadvantages of prototyping software at the very early stages of development?*

Presenting designs

Presenting design ideas clearly and appropriately is a key skill of the designer. The design process is a long one, with many different stages, there are many different people involved and there are many different reasons for giving a presentation. The combination of these will affect what sort of presentation and what sort of representation are suitable.

If the ideas are aimed at senior management, for example, then it is likely that the focus is on vision, concepts and key features of design. People in this position are generally concerned with strategic issues rather than detail, so a presentation to management should focus on impact, image and concept. If the presentation is aimed at the client then one would expect a bit more detail and some idea of how it works. If the presentation is aimed at end-users then it is most likely to concentrate on the detail of the design and the workings of the system. If presenting to the people who will be using the system it is important to beware of misconceptions about current activities. It is very easy for people to lose credibility with such an audience if an unrealistic scenario or example is used.

The purpose of the presentation is equally important. If the aim is getting the contract then the presentation should focus on the big selling point and what it is that distinguishes your design from the others. If the contract is organized and the aim is agreeing the concept, then the focus will be on restating the client's brief, clarifying requirements and scoping the area. Where the presentation is concerned with evaluating a general design idea, or with testing major design features with users, then it must be focused on eliciting an appropriate response.

If the prototype or design is still at the concept stage, broad images of the system are appropriate, with little functionality except in key areas. An early design will emphasize the design principles and the basis of the design language. It will show how the parts fit together, basic navigational features and so on. If it is a detailed design then the correct size is important, along with the proposed shapes, colours and text.

Finally it is important to be clear about what is being highlighted by the presentation. Is it the functionality and events, or is it the interactions and usability with the focus on look and feel, or ease of use? If the focus is on content and structure, then attend to what information is there, and how it is organized, whereas if it is style and aesthetics then the focus is on features such as enjoyability, visual and tangible design and use of media.

→ Chapter 9 discusses design languages

Summary and key points

Envisionment and prototyping bring designs to life for both designers and the people who will use the new designs. Prototypes can be anywhere along the spectrum of technical sophistication, be put together in half an hour or take several days of programming. The point is to explore ideas, not to build an entire parallel system or product. Prototyping is at the heart of a human-centred design process.

- Envisionment – the making concrete of design ideas – is a key feature of design. All aspects of the system can and should be envisioned: concepts, functions, structure, interactions.
- Envisionment aids the generation, communication and evaluation of ideas.
- People should take an active part in envisionment wherever possible – the process allows essential feedback from customers and clients.
- Basic techniques include storyboards, different forms of sketch, mood boards, navigation maps, wireframes and concrete scenarios.
- Prototyping may focus on a vertical or horizontal slice through the system, or cover the whole system, and may evolve into a final product or be thrown away and re-engineered.

Exercises

1 You have been asked to develop a website for a local radio station and have gone to meet the radio station manager and one of their leading DJs. What envisionment techniques would you use during and after this meeting? Outline some initial ideas for alternative design concepts.

2 Mood boards are usually constructed out of physical materials, but they can also be made in software. Using any software application that allows the inclusion of visual, audio and text components, make a mood board to explore the following concepts:

(a) a website for seaside holidays targeted at one-parent families
(b) a website for adventure holidays targeted at active, affluent over-sixties.

This can be done as a single-person exercise, but works best as a small group project.

3 (More advanced) We argue strongly in this book for stakeholders to be involved as closely as possible in the envisionment process. Develop some bullet points setting out a counter-argument – that designers 'know best'.

 Further reading

Browsing the design section of a good bookshop, you will find numerous books containing ideas to stimulate creativity – which you find helpful is very much an individual preference. Equally, the business section will offer a wide range of published material for enhancing the generation of ideas in group meetings.

Rosson, M.-B. and Carroll, J. (2002) *Usability Engineering*. Morgan Kaufmann, San Francisco, CA. *Chapter 6 covers prototyping.*

Rudd, J., Stern, K. and Isensee, S. (1996) Low vs. high fidelity prototyping debate. *Interactions,* 3(1), 76–85. *A readable exploration of the issues.*

Snyder, C. (2003) *Paper Prototyping: The Fast and Easy Way to Design and Refine User Interfaces.* Morgan Kaufmann, San Francisco, CA. *Everything you always wanted to know about paper prototyping. A great source of ideas and practical tips.*

Getting ahead

Beaudouin-Lafon, M. and Mackay, W. (2012) Prototyping Tools and Techniques. In Jacko, J.A. (ed) *The Human–Computer Interaction Handbook,* Fundamentals, Evolving Technologies and Emerging Applications, 3rd edn. CRC Press, Taylor and Francis, Boca Raton. FL.

 Web links

The accompanying website has links to relevant websites. Go to
www.pearsoned.co.uk/benyon

 **Comments on challenges**

Challenge 8.1

The sketches and doodles are being used to explore the problem space. The computer simulation is also being used in this way and so the scale model put into the wind tunnel is an essential part of that representation. Both the blueprints and the scale model sent to Marketing are being used to communicate ideas. The blueprints and the scale model are both used for communication, but the blueprints are inappropriate for communicating with Marketing. Marketing people are interested in the physical shape of the design, but the model maker requires a more precise description of the designer's ideas in the form of blueprints. Also notice that the representations must be accurate enough for their purpose, highlighting the important features but ignoring the irrelevant aspects. In the wind tunnel, the interior design of the car is unimportant, so the scale model takes no account of this.

Challenge 8.2

Many different ideas are possible here. Examples could include a simplified interactive map, a text listing by category, a montage of clickable images, etc. Remember that what you are doing here is trying out ideas, so don't spend time adding too much detail or creating a work of art.

Challenge 8.3

No specific comments here, but make sure that you have shown the direction of links on the map where they are important. If there are multiple links to the same target, the map can be simplified by adding a note such as 'all pages link back to home page' and omitting the links themselves.

Challenge 8.4

It would be a good idea to emphasize how the paper prototype would allow radically different concepts to be explored – and eliminated – cheaply and quickly, rather than rejecting weak ideas only when they had been realized in software.

Challenge 8.5

Presumably the idea here is to impress the management with the quality of the design work and to 'get the contract'. The prototype is probably going to be hi-fi with respect to size. Management will want to see how the ideas work on the small screen of a smartphone. The prototype will also have to get over the principles of the design effectively. This might be a novel way of interacting – turning the 'pages' using a pen, for example. Or there might be some special functionality that the designer wants to get over: a facility to zoom to the next appointment, perhaps. The designer should identify these key elements that need to be communicated and prototype them using a hi-fi tool such as Director or Flash. The designer might also take along some paper prototypes of other concepts and designs in order to get more involvement and feedback on ideas. It is all a matter of judgement and resources, trying to 'sell' some of the ideas and concepts (so that the contract can be secured) and exploring others.

Challenge 8.6

Advantages:
- Can gather good feedback from users when there is still plenty of time to modify the design
- Fosters a sense of user involvement
- Can provide a realistic impression of the end-product
- May be possible to develop the prototype into the final product.

Disadvantages:
- May have distracting usability problems
- Developers may be reluctant to discard software to accommodate redesigns
- Can inhibit some more technophobic users
- Can appear too 'finished' to generate comment.

You will probably have thought of others.

Chapter 9
Design

Contents

Aims

As we said in Chapter 2, design is messy. Design problems are usually poorly formed and continue to evolve as solutions are suggested. This results in more ideas, more problems and more solutions. In design we distinguish conceptual design – design in the abstract – from physical design – where ideas are made concrete. Our aim in this chapter is to provide methods and techniques to help designers deal with design situations.

This chapter assumes that you know about techniques for understanding and envisioning ideas (Chapters 7 and 8). It assumes that you know about scenario-based design (Chapter 3), about developing personas (Chapter 3) and PACT analysis (Chapter 2) and that the aim of design is to achieve a high degree of usability (Chapter 4) and to create engaging experiences (Chapter 5). This chapter is concerned with a more abstract view of design and with thinking conceptually and metaphorically about your design. It also provides some more formal ways of capturing and representing designs.

After studying this chapter you should be able to:

● Understand the nature of conceptual and physical design
● Understand how metaphor works in design
● Undertake an object–action analysis to inform design and to produce a conceptual model of a new system
● Describe how the system will look and behave through specifying the design language and interaction patterns
● Specify a design in a form that can be implemented by programmers using use cases.

9.1 Introduction

Figure 9.1 is the lower part of Figure 3.12, which we used earlier to illustrate the whole of the design process. It shows the processes of conceptual and physical design (processes represented as clouds) and the products of design that are produced at this stage (represented as boxes). The minimum system specification is a conceptual model, a set of use cases and a design language. Conceptual design is concerned with arriving at an abstract description of the system – its logic, functions, structure and content – but not with how the structure and functions are to be physically realized. Physical design is concerned with who does what (with the allocation of functions between people and artefacts), how the artefacts will look and how they behave.

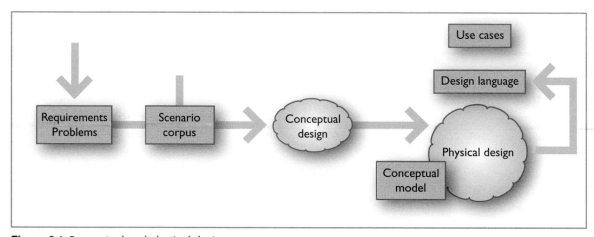

Figure 9.1 Conceptual and physical design

The distinction between conceptual and physical design does not dictate that conceptual design should be finished before physical design starts. Analysts and designers will iterate between these two levels of design description and will fix on some physical design decisions in order to understand the conceptual level better. A good deal of early physical design happens during the envisionment process. This iteration will involve various kinds of evaluation with people so that we can check that the design really does meet their needs. The advantage of designing at the conceptual level before details of the physical design are fixed, however, is that it avoids the problem of 'design fixation' and maintains a wide design space in which alternatives can be considered for as long as possible.

9.2 Conceptual design

Clear conceptual design is central to developing systems that are understandable. Designers need to ensure that their conception of the system is easily learnt by people and fits with their expectations and preferences. This is so that people can develop a clear 'mental model' of the system.

← Mental models were introduced in Chapter 2

For example, in any GUI application most of us would expect to find a menu that allows us to open files, close files and create new files. Moreover, we might expect it to be called 'File'. Logically we would expect to find these functions grouped together somewhere, and if the designer has understood and applied sensible design principles (Chapter 4) then this should be the case. But often we have to spend a long time looking for some function, or we do not know about the existence of some function, because the designer has put it somewhere unexpected. The lack of standards for the menus of mobile phones, for example, results in the need to search the whole structure for an expected command.

A good conceptual model will come from considering the underlying metaphor that is being used to provide the structure for the design (Section 9.3), and by considering how things are classified and organized. Techniques such as card sorting (Chapter 7) will help to get a good classification scheme in place and to develop a clear ontology. The object–action analysis described in Section 9.4 is another good technique for this.

A vital part of design work is to explore the design space in the abstract – to think about what the design is trying to be. Sometimes this will be quite straightforward. If the system is a website, people will expect it to be like other websites, but for the innovative applications and systems now appearing on platforms such as the iPhone or in ubiquitous computing environments this is not the case.

Exploring design concepts

Bill Verplank (Verplank, 2007) is an interaction designer who has been sketching and designing for many years. He argues that interaction design is 'design for human use' and focuses on three main things, which he characterizes as:

- How do you do?
- How do you feel?
- How do you know?

How do you do?

'How do you do?' is concerned with the ways in which we affect the world. Do you poke it, manipulate it, sit on it? For example, one distinction he highlights is between handles and buttons. Handles are better for continuous control (e.g. a trombone), but buttons are better for discrete control (e.g. a piano keyboard). Handles leave you in control (e.g. opening a car door) whereas buttons are more likely to trigger something automatic (e.g. opening an elevator door).

How do you feel?

'How do you feel?' concerns how we make sense of the world and the sensory qualities that shape media. One distinction is Marshall McLuhan's 'hot' versus 'cool'. Marshall McLuhan wrote *Understanding Media* in 1964 and is famed for coining the phrases 'global village', 'age of information' and 'the medium is the message'. The book, which was reprinted in 1994, is a whirlwind tour through the media of his time and has much insight into how media would develop in our time. He introduced a distinction between 'hot media' which are more authoritative and exact and 'cool media' which are fuzzy and incomplete. Cool media invite more participation; they require the audience to fill in the gaps, to interpret. Hot media extend a single sense in high definition; they are filled with data. Photography is a hot medium because it is high-fidelity, whereas a cartoon is a cool, low-definition medium where we fill in the gaps. McLuhan's book is a fascinating if difficult read and he extends the ideas of hot and cool to all manner of concepts such as an axe (hot), the 'city slicker' (hot), rural life (cool). Focusing on 'how do you feel' takes us into the areas of satisfaction, affect, enjoyment, involvement and engagement. In his introduction to the 1994 MIT Press edition of *Understanding Media*, Lewis Lapham characterizes McLuhan's ideas as illustrated in Table 9.1. Do not worry

→ Chapter 22 discusses affect and emotion

Table 9.1 Leitmotifs from McLuhan's *Understanding Media*

Print	Electronic media
Visual	Tactile
Mechanical	Organic
Sequence	Simultaneity
Composition	Improvisation
Eye	Ear
Active	Reactive
Expansion	Contraction
Complete	Incomplete
Soliloquy	Chorus
Classification	Pattern recognition
Centre	Margin
Continuous	Discontinuous
Syntax	Mosaic
Self-expression	Group therapy
Typographic man	Graphic man

Source: Lapham (1994) in McLuhan, Marshall, *Understanding Media: The Extensions of Man*, Table 1 from Introduction, © 1994 Massachusetts Institute of Technology, by permission of The MIT Press

too much about understanding these dichotomies; use them as ways of thinking about 'how do you feel'.

How do you know?

'How do you know?' concerns the ways that people learn and plan; how designers want people to think about their system. For example, Verplank suggests that one choice is between maps and paths. Paths are good for beginners as they provide step-by-step instructions on what to do. Maps are good for understanding alternatives. They take longer to learn but are more robust and are good for expert skill. Maps offer the chance to take shortcuts. Very often, of course, a given system or product will have to accommodate both.

Challenge 9.1

What characteristics do you feel belong to the text message as a medium? Be creative!

Exploring the design space

Design can be thought about through the concept of a design space. A design space constrains a design in some dimensions whilst allowing exploration of alternatives in others (Beaudouin-Lafon and Mackay, 2012). Designers always work within constraints, whether these are financial or functional, but they need to take care not to impose too many constraints too early in the process. This is when they can ignore ideas for designs because of design fixation – settling on a design idea or a design constraint that prevents them from exploring possible alternatives. Brainstorming is a good way of expanding the design space. When writing, thinking about or using scenarios, issues will arise about design features. This is particularly so when reviewing scenarios and other design envisionment with clients. It is vital to do this. Very often it is only when people see some sort of concrete representation of the new system and how it will fit (or not) with their lives that they are able to comment meaningfully. Issues may concern the current state of affairs or a future designed position. We have seen how these issues can be highlighted through adding endnotes to the scenario descriptions, and notes can also be appended to storyboards and so on. In many cases it will be necessary to revisit the requirements, which in turn may entail further analysis of the current situation.

John Carroll (e.g. Carroll, 2000) points out that in design work there are often trade-offs to consider and a design feature may lead to both positive and negative outcomes. He recommends listing positive and negative features of a design alongside a feature, as 'claims'. We have found it useful to identify neutral design features too. Claims are concerned with explaining the design rationale – why design decisions were taken. One way of highlighting design issues is to undertake a walkthrough using the concrete scenarios to drive the thinking of the designer. Scenarios are very effective at forcing issues into the open, so that claims about designs can be articulated, documented and evaluated.

In Chapter 3 we introduced the MP3 scenario for the HIC case study. In paragraph P4 and endnotes 8 and 9, a key design decision was how search results should be displayed and selected. Just one of the many decisions associated with this activity is the size of the font used to display artists' names and track titles. The MP3 domain demands that quite a lot of text is displayed so that people can make a selection. So font size is a key design issue.

Some of the positive and negative features of using a large font size are:

- It can be seen from further away (positive).
- It takes up valuable screen space (negative).
- It means fewer tracks can be displayed (negative).

There are many variations of techniques that can be used to focus attention on design issues. Listing the actions that people will have to take in order to accomplish a goal using a specific design and identifying the positive and negative aspects of a prototype is one way. Another is to list the options against the design criteria, the QOC technique described in Chapter 3.

Warr and O'Neil (2007) describe the envisionment and discovery collaboratory (EDC) that aims to support social creativity and collaborative design through the use of shared 'boundary objects' (Figure 9.2). Boundary objects (or representations) 'talk back' to the design team through the externalization of stakeholders' concepts.

9.3 Metaphors in design

Metaphor is generally seen as taking concepts from one domain (called the source domain, or the vehicle) and applying them to another (the target, or tenor). Recall your schooldays and how you studied 'The ship ploughed through the waves', or 'The President marshalled his arguments to defend his position'. The first of these likens a ship moving through the sea to a plough moving through a field. It suggests the waves

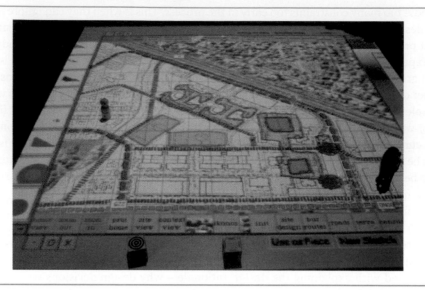

Figure 9.2 The EDC

(Source: Warr, A. and O'Neill, E. (2007) Tool support for creativity using externalizations, *Proceedings of the Sixth ACM SIGCHI Conference on Creativity and AMP: Cognition*, Washington, DC, 13–15 June, C&G '07, ACM, New York, pp. 127–36. © 2007 ACM, Inc. Reprinted by permission. http://doi.acm.org/10.1145/1254960.1254979)

are like the furrows. It has connotations of strength and how the ship is pushing aside the sea. For some people it connotes speed of movement. In the second we see arguments likened to a battle, arguments being marshalled as if they were soldiers, the President's position being analogous to a castle or other physical place that needs defending.

In the development of interactive systems we are constantly trying to describe a new domain (a new application, a different design, new interactive facilities) to people. So we have to use metaphor to describe this new domain in terms of something that is more familiar. Blackwell (2006) gives a comprehensive treatment of the role of metaphor in interactive systems design. After a while the metaphorical use of a term becomes entrenched in the language to such an extent that people forget it ever was a metaphor.

Paths and maps may be thought of as metaphors for the design of interactions. Different metaphors will lead to different conceptions and designs. Think of the idea of navigating an interactive system, for example. Many people immediately think that navigation is trying to get somewhere specific, but this is only one view (often called 'wayfinding'). We also browse around and explore. If we think of navigation as in a city then we think of roads and signposts, metros that take us invisibly from one part of the space to another, taxis to transport us, or buses that we have to learn about.

→ See Chapter 25 on navigation

Considering one metaphor can stimulate creative leaps into other ways of thinking. For example, during a collaborative design meeting to look at the HIC interface as a 'Rolodex' (Figure 9.3), a manual card index device that allowed people to rapidly flip through standard-sized cards, a 'gun barrel' design emerged (illustrated in the left-hand part of Figure 9.4). Although the gun barrel idea was rejected, the Rolodex concept seemed to capture the idea of searching and retrieving results with an intuitive navigational style of flicking through the 'cards'. In this case the conceptual metaphor of the Rolodex translated nicely into a visual representation. So here an interface metaphor seemed wholly appropriate and indeed was implemented as part of the first functional prototype.

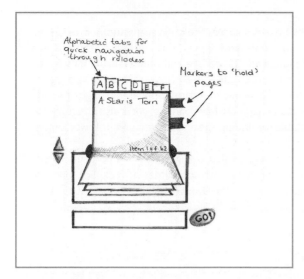

Figure 9.3 Sketch of a Rolodex interface metaphor in HIC project

(Rolodex is a registered trade name, but we use the term in this book to indicate the concept rather than the product)

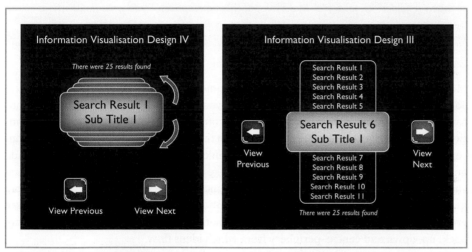

Figure 9.4 Snapshots of alternative designs for searching the HIC

Navigation metaphors

BOX 9.1

Metaphors that might be useful for thinking about navigation have different associations. A wilderness, for example, is frightening, confusing, enchanting. A desert is intimidating and beautiful but has no landmarks. Such metaphors might encourage forging a path, enjoying the scenery and getting out. Wilderness and desert can be included in an overall landscape metaphor where different types of terrain represent different types of information. These metaphors encourage exploration by the user; the system provides a high-level metaphor, but users provide the more detailed structure themselves.

The night sky offers a different sort of space. To the human eye, it contains objects, clusters and patterns and it is very big. It supports the activities of mapping and identifying objects. However, there are relatively few types of object in the night sky (galaxies, stars, planets). It is the configurations and subtypes of these objects that are of interest. Science fiction concepts such as warp drives and worm holes can be used for quick and magic transportation to distant parts of space. The open sea is another metaphor. It encourages a distinction between surface and depth. Thus it is natural to think of a lot of information as being hidden beneath the surface and only available for viewing if the user dives down. Currents can link continents and islands and take people to unexpected places. People can look for islands of information; archipelagos provide clusters. A museum has been structured to allow free roaming, yet is also structured to facilitate learning. A library is suitable for finding specific information. It is well organized and structured.

These metaphors are not meant to suggest that the interface to a particular product looks like a desert, wilderness or library (though sometimes such explicit interface metaphors can be useful); the idea here is to think about activities in different ways.

Challenge 9.2

Consider some of the familiar computing concepts: 'windows', 'cut and paste', 'bootstrap', 'open' a 'folder', 'close' a 'file'. Make a list of these metaphors. Try to write down where they came from.

Metaphor is not just a literary thing, it is fundamental to the way we think. Lakoff and Johnson (1981, 1999) and their colleagues have worked on their theories of metaphor for over 20 years. They describe a philosophy of 'experientialism' or cognitive semantics. They argue that all our thinking starts from the metaphorical use of a few basic concepts, or 'image schemas', such as containers, links and paths. A container has an inside and an outside and you can put things in and take things out. This is such a fundamental concept that it is the basis of the way that we conceptualize the world. A path goes from a source to a destination. The key to experientialism is that these basic concepts are grounded in spatial experiences. There are other basic 'image schemas' such as front–back, up–down and centre–periphery from which ideas flow.

An important contribution from this view is that a metaphor is much more than a simple mapping from one domain to another. It is a much more complex affair. Take the idea of a window as it appears in a computer operating system. We know a computer window is different from a window in a house. It shares the idea of looking into a document, as you might look into a house, but when you open it, it does not let the fresh air in. It is only ever a window into, or onto, something. Moreover, it has a scroll bar, which a window in a house does not. In a similar fashion we know that the trash can, or the recycling bin, on a computer screen is not a real trash can. The connotations of recycling files are really quite complex.

The contribution that Fauconnier and others have made (e.g. Fauconnier and Turner, 2002) is to point out that what we call 'metaphors' in design are really blends. A blend takes input from at least two spaces, the characteristics of the domain described by the source and the characteristics of the target that we are applying it to. So a computer window takes elements from the domain of house windows and elements of the functioning of a computer trying to get a lot of data onto a limited screen display. The metaphor of a folder is a blend from the domain of real folders that you keep papers in and the domain of computer files which have a physical location on a disk.

Figure 9.5 illustrates this idea of a blend. The blend that results from bringing two domains together in this way will have some features that were not in the original domains.

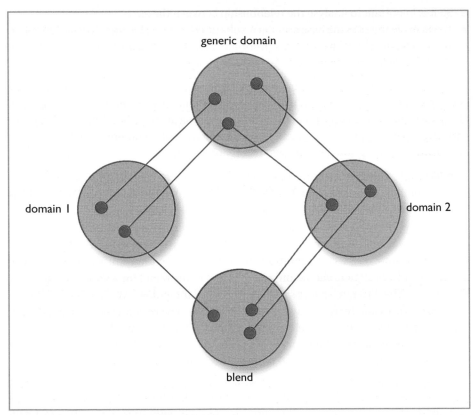

Figure 9.5 Illustrating the concept of a blend

Blends have an emergent structure that results from bringing two sets of concepts (from the source and target domains) together. So, the computer window has different features from both a real window and the computer commands that preceded it. The Rolodex concept that arose during the HIC case study (Chapter 6) had emergent properties. These concerned how people could navigate in the 'virtual' Rolodex (as opposed to a real, physical one) and how the search results were presented as opposed to how they were presented following a traditional query. It is exactly these emergent properties that make one design better than another.

For metaphors and blends to work, there must be some correspondences between the domains that come from a more generic, or abstract, space. So, for example, the metaphor 'the ship ploughs through the waves' works, but the metaphor 'the ship ran through the forest' does not. In the second of these there is not sufficient correspondence between the concepts in the two domains. Of course, the generic space is itself a domain and hence may itself be using metaphorical concepts. This process works its way back until we reach the fundamental image schemas that are core to our thinking. These include the container, path, link and others such as colours (red is hot, blue is cool, red is stop, green is go) and those bodily schemas that come from experience and perception (up, down, in, out, central, peripheral, etc.).

Thinking figuratively is fundamental to both the design and use of computer systems. One job of the interaction designer is to come up with a good metaphor that will help people in learning and using the system and in understanding the content. Metaphor design works as follows:

- The source domain has some features (concepts and functions).
- The target domain has some concepts and features.

- So it is important to analyse the relationship between these.
- Too many features in the base domain results in 'conceptual baggage' of the metaphor.
- Too few features, or too many inappropriate features, may lead to confusion.
- Aim for people deriving appropriate expectations.

Note that metaphor design does not imply a physical resemblance. The important thing about metaphor is to get a good conceptual correspondence. Sometimes it is appropriate to carry through a conceptual metaphor to a physical metaphor, but not always. As with any aspect of interactive system design, evaluation of metaphor is essential. There are, however, a few principles for good metaphor design:

- *Integration.* This is to do with coherence and not mixing metaphors. The aim here is to manipulate the whole blend, maintaining the web of relationships. The blend has its own structure and it is this that needs to have consistency maintained.
- *Unpacking.* People should be able to unpack the blend and understand where the inputs have come from and why they work. Of course, this will often be a case of interpretation. With consideration, reflection and evaluation the designer can achieve this. Designers should only have things in the blend for a good reason.
- *Topology.* The different spaces should have a similar topology. We saw how the structures of waves and furrows have a similar topology, whereas waves and trees do not. Topology is about how the concepts are organized and structured.
- *Analysis.* When undertaking an analysis the designer should concentrate on getting the appropriate functionality and concepts, exploring the ramifications of the metaphor, evaluating how people will interpret it.
- *Design.* At the design level designers should consider how to represent objects and actions. They do not have to be realistic visual representations (e.g. names of menu items are often metaphorical).

Designers cannot avoid metaphors in interaction design, so they need to consider them explicitly. Metaphors are really blends between two or more input spaces and have their own emergent structure. Using metaphors that exploit the fundamental domains such as bodily and perceptual schemas may help people to understand them and to form an accurate mental model. Designers should consider principles of good blends. Imaz and Benyon (2005) develop these ideas as 'designing with blends'.

Challenge 9.3

Think of three different metaphors (or ways of thinking about) that could be used for a diary function on a tablet.

9.4 Conceptual design using scenarios

In Chapter 3 we illustrated how scenarios can be used throughout the design process. Stories aid understanding, conceptual scenarios abstract from stories to provide generic activities. Fixing certain design constraints leads to concrete scenarios that may finish up as functional specifications expressed as use cases. A scenario corpus is developed that should be discussed and evaluated at design team sessions and with the participation of stakeholders. There are degrees of concreteness in scenarios. The most concrete forms are used to envision or evaluate specific interactions. While they are superficially easy to construct, there are a number of ways in which scenarios can be made more effective:

- Complement the scenarios with some of the more visual envisioning techniques.
- In a large design team, include real data and materials so that people not directly involved can appreciate concrete details.
- Think hard about underlying assumptions.
- Include good characterization and develop a number of personas. If this is done well, members of the team start talking about the characters – 'If you design it like that, what will happen when the grandmother tries to use it?'
- Provide a rich contextual background – this grounds design decisions in real life, forcing the designer to think about practicality and acceptability.
- Team members can write their own concrete version of a conceptual scenario that reflects their particular concerns. These can be brought together and overlaps removed.

The aim is to come up with a collection of scenarios that covers all the major uses and functionality of the product. It would be impossible to write scenarios for all possible variations in use, but those produced should cover:

- Interactions that are typical of a number of similar use situations
- Design issues that are particularly important for the focus of the project
- Areas where requirements are unclear
- Any aspects that are safety-critical.

A good way of doing conceptual design is to undertake an object–action analysis of the scenario corpus. For each of the scenarios in the corpus the analyst works through the scenario descriptions, identifying the various objects that are mentioned and the various actions that are performed. Objects are often indicated by nouns or noun phrases and activities and actions by verbs.

Challenge 9.4

Look through the following paragraph from the Edinburgh Festival scenario (described in detail in Chapter 6). Ignoring common verbs such as 'was', 'is', etc. and ignoring duplicates, list the main nouns and verbs and hence the main objects and actions.

The Edinburgh Festival is a large arts festival that takes place in the city for three weeks in August. It consists of two arts festivals – the Edinburgh International Festival and the Edinburgh Festival Fringe – a book festival, a film festival, a jazz festival and a variety of related events. The International Festival is the original, and up until the mid-1980s was the bigger of the two. This is the official festival, which features prestigious performers from around the world, world-class orchestras, composers, ballet troupes, etc. The Fringe, on the other hand, started as an unofficial adjunct to the festival, traditionally more informal, and adventurous. It featured new theatres like the Traverse, or the work of artistic mavericks like Demarco. Gradually over the years it has become larger than the official International Festival. In total the Edinburgh Festival consists of some 1200 distinct events that take place at 150 different venues spread throughout the city.

Working with a corpus of scenarios in this way requires four stages:

1 Analyse the individual scenarios, distinguishing between specific actions and more general, higher-level activities.
2 Summarize objects and actions from each scenario, merging similar or identical actions where necessary.
3 Bring together the analyses from the individual scenarios, collating them into summarized objects, actions and more generic activities.
4 Merge actions and objects where they are identical and give them a single name.

Objects and actions in MP3 example

Table 9.2 shows how part of Scenario MP3/01 – 'How does that song go again?' – is analysed. Activities are shown in the far left column referencing the paragraph number. Where these appeared to be made up of a sequence of individual sub-activities, these are identified in column 2. Actions and objects derived from these appear in columns 3 and 4. Comments are included in column 5. Of course, this is only a fraction of the analysis of the MP3/01 scenario analysis used here to illustrate the idea.

← Scenario MP3/01 is in Chapter 3, Section 3.4

Table 9.3 shows a portion of the collated results across all the scenarios. A tally of the number of occurrences of each action (column 1) and object (column 2) is kept. Various notations are used to indicate questions, slightly different views or uses of the terms and so on. The aim of this analysis is to understand the objects and actions in a domain. It is vital to note that there is no definitive or 'right' answer here. The object–action analysis is just another way of exploring the design space.

Actions that could be thought of as generically similar can now be grouped together, prior to the final distillation stage. This requires careful attention, to avoid mistakenly

Table 9.2 Object–action analysis of part of scenario MP3/01

Activity	Consists of sub-activities	Action	Object	Comments
Search for MP3 track by name P3	Go to Search function **P3**	Go to	Search object	'Search object' – may need revision?
	Enter query (track name) **P3**	Enter (*user input*) Confirm	Search object Query	
Play track P4	Select search result (MP3 track) **P4**	Select	Search result (*track*)	= MP3 track. There is no 'browse search result' formula here, as it is specified that search result contains only one object (track)
	Play track **P4**	Play (*start play*)	Track	'Play' does not imply playing complete track – track may be paused, stopped, fast-forwarded, etc. 'Start Play' may be the better term

Table 9.3 Portion of consolidation of objects and actions in MP3 domain with number of occurrences in parentheses

Scenarios MP3/01 to MP3/05: activities and objects decomposition – stage 3 (A) (all actions and objects collated)	
All actions	**All objects**
. . .	. . .
Go to (21)	Playlist (30)
[Go to] (1)	Playlist catalogue (2)
Load (1)	Playlist catalogue (7)
Modify (4)	Query (4)
Move (1)	Search object (9)
(*Move*) (1)	Search result (Track) (1)
Name (2)	Search result (3)
Name (*user input*) (4)	Set up (1) [scenario MP3/03]
Open (3)	Track (32)
Pause (2)	Track (*MP3 file*) (1)
Play (*start play*) (7)	Track list (1)
Repeat (*replay*) (1)	Tracks (9)
Re-save (*save*) (1)	Tracks (*MP3 files*) (1)
Save (8)	Tracks list (9)
[Select] (1)	[Tracks list] (2)
Select (*specify*) (1)	. . .
[Select (*specify*)] (3)	
. . .	

merging together slightly different actions. The guiding principle is to look for conceptual or functional parallels among the actions, indicating likely candidates for grouping. The table is annotated with comments, documenting the criteria applied in making the groupings. Here, each grouping of actions is merged and given a single name. In each case this is the generic term that will be used from this point on. Table 9.4 illustrates this process with the actions of 'select' and 'choose'.

So, the object–action analysis has resulted in a generic action of select and an understanding of the various objects that can be selected: Track, Playlist, Playlist Catalogue, Query result.

Diagrammatic techniques

The result of the object analysis could be represented as an object model, or entity–relationship model as illustrated in Figure 9.6. This may be read as a Playlist Catalogue consisting of many Playlists, though each Playlist is on just one Playlist Catalogue. A Playlist consists of many tracks. Each track is on just one Playlist and one Tracklist.

Table 9.4 Considering the various uses of actions select and choose

[Select] (1)	7 'Select', '(specify)', 'Choose' all describe a user's action of
Select (*specify*) (1)	• selecting an item or group of items from a list or other display object
[Select (*specify*)] (3)	• selecting an option from a menu of other actions.
	Here, the HIC has determined the list of possible options/interactions available to the user, and is presenting it to the user (in a number of possible forms and modalities).
Choose (1)	1
Choose (*specify*) (1)	1

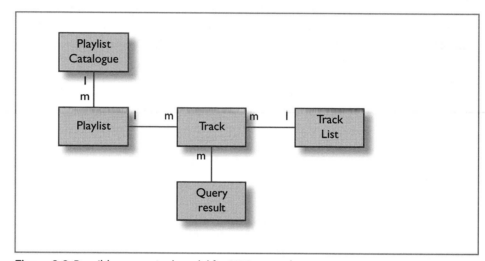

Figure 9.6 Possible conceptual model for MP3 example

A Track may be the result of a Query. Notice how, by developing a conceptual model, we are able to raise and discuss design issues. You may disagree with some of the assertions above. This is fine. This is exactly why making the conceptual model explicit is useful.

Designers will often represent the conceptual model of a system using a diagrammatic technique such as an entity–relationship model or object model. Object models, or entity–relationship models, represent the main objects of interest in a domain and the relationships between them. There are many books devoted to such conceptual models, and the techniques can be used to explore the conceptual structure, not simply to document it. There is an important distinction in conceptual models between the specific instances of an object and the class or type of object. In the MP3 example, an instance of the object type 'Track' might be 'Moondance' and another instance might be 'Gloria' (both songs by Van Morrison as it happens). What makes us group these things together as an object type called Track is that they have certain characteristics in common such as a track name, a duration and so on (classification is discussed briefly in Chapter 7, also see discussion in Chapter 3). Relationships between objects are expressed in terms of how many instances of an object can be related to how many instances of another object. Typically we are not interested in exactly how many instances, but rather whether a relationship exists between one or many instances. The conceptual model is annotated with a 1 if an instance can be related to only one other instance or an m if it can be related to many.

Figure 9.7 shows two alternative conceptual models of the same thing, an ATM. In the upper part is an object model that shows the relationships between the concepts person, card, account and ATM. A person may ask about an account, the card is inserted into the ATM and so on. In the lower part is an entity–relationship model. This is more complex, but captures more of the semantics of the situation. The model distinguishes between the concept of a user and the owner of the card. It distinguishes a usage of the ATM and the accounts that may be accessed.

Such diagrams rarely exist without some further explanation, and entity–relationship diagrams in particular can become quite formalized. For example, the entity–relationship diagram in Figure 9.7 includes a notation showing the participation conditions (optional or mandatory) of entities in relationships and some outline definitions of the entities in terms of the attributes that they contain. Attributes can be shown on the diagram as ovals if required. It is not the intention to explore all the details of conceptual modelling techniques here, but rather to make designers aware that they exist. Books are available on object modelling (e.g. van Harmelen, 2001) and on entity–relationship modelling for interface design (Benyon *et al.*, 1999). Some approaches to information architecture also include formal models. The point to note is that such techniques can be very useful in externalizing the conceptual structure that underlies a design.

In website design it is usual to produce a 'site map' – a conceptual model of the site's structure. Conceptual modelling using a formalism such as an object model can be a

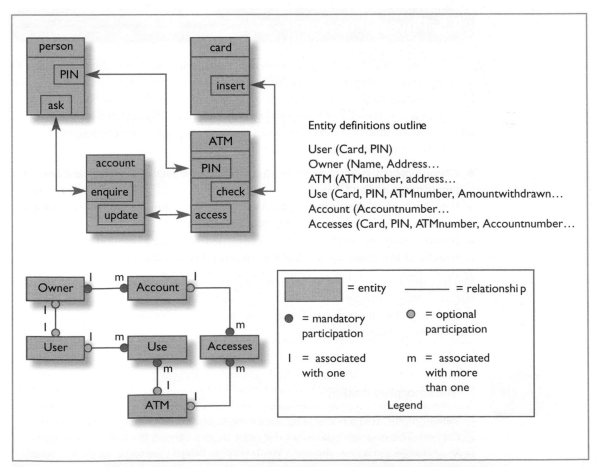

Figure 9.7 Two conceptual models of an ATM: object model above and entity–relationship below

→ Information architecture and website design are covered in Chapter 14

very powerful tool in helping the designer to think about the details of a design. By externalizing the objects and relationships in a system the designer can see more clearly whether the logic of a design works.

BOX 9.2

Elements of interaction

Dan Saffer (2009) suggests that there are six key elements of interaction design that need to be considered. In many ways these are similar to the notion of interaction trajectories discussed in Chapter 5. His elements are:

- *Motion* – objects that don't move don't interact. Motion as a trigger for action. Behaviour as motion coloured by attitude, culture, personality and context.
- *Space* – movement happens in space, interaction design involves a combination of physical and digital space.
- *Time* – movement through space takes time and all interactions take place over time. Time creates rhythm.
- *Appearance* – proportion, structure, size, shape, weight, colour.
- *Texture* – variables such as vibration, rough, smooth, etc.
- *Sound* – pitch, volume, timbre.

9.5 Physical design

As we discussed in Chapter 3, physical design is concerned with how things are going to work and with detailing the look and feel of the product. Physical design is about structuring interactions into logical sequences and about clarifying and presenting the allocation of functions and knowledge between people and devices. Physical design is concerned with taking this abstract representation and translating it into concrete designs.

There are three components to physical design:

- Operational design is concerned with specifying how everything works and how content is structured and stored.
- Representational design is concerned with fixing on colours, shapes, sizes and information layout. It is concerned with style and aesthetics.
- Interaction design in this context is concerned with the allocation of functions to humans or to technology and with the structuring and sequencing of the interactions.

Much of the detail of physical design is covered in the chapter on the visual aspects of interface design (Chapter 12). In this section we consider two key design ideas that help designers deal with operational design and interaction design: design languages and interaction patterns.

BOX 9.3

Skeumorphic design

Skeuomorphic design is designing something to physically resemble something from the past. This may work quite well if it helps people transfer the functionality from a familiar object to a new one and a skeuomorphic design may utilize an explicit visual metaphor in order to build on a conceptual metaphor. But often the use of a skeuo-morphic design seems gratuitous, unnecessary and an out-of-date aesthetic. Apple have come in for a lot of criticism in the Lion operating systems for making the place holder for electronic magazines look like an old-fashioned wooden bookshelf and for making the calendar look like an old leather calendar.

One critic, James Higgis, complains that he finds the skeuomorphic designs from Apple patronizing, particularly compared to the streamlined look of the Metro inter-face (see Box 9.4 and Figure 9.9, p. 204). However, Apple do promote skeuomorphic design in their user experience guidelines, saying 'On iPhone, people instantly know what the Voice Memos app does, and how to use it, because it presents a beautifully rendered focal image (the microphone) and realistic controls'. (See Figure 9.8.)

Figure 9.8 Voice recorder from Apple

(Source: Mandy Cheng/AFP/ Getty Images)

Design languages

A design language consists of the following:

- A set of *design elements* such as the use of colour, styles and types of buttons, sliders and other widgets
- Some *principles of composition* (i.e. the rules for putting them together)
- Collections of *qualifying situations* – contexts and how they affect the rules.

A consistent design language means that people need only learn a limited number of design elements and then they can cope with a large variety of different situations. A design language is how designers build meaning into objects, enabling people to understand what things do and to make distinctions between different types of object.

Any language provides a way of expressing things, and design languages are ways of expressing design concepts. Languages are useful for particular purposes if they have appropriate elements and appropriate organizing principles and use an appropriate medium for both expression and transmission.

Rheinfrank and Evenson (1996) stress that design languages have most impact when they have become deeply embedded and when people use them and exploit them unconsciously. Their method for design includes developing a design language through:

- *Characterization* – the process of describing existing assumptions and any pre-existing design languages
- *Re-registration* – the creation of a new assumption set through exploring trends and needs through field research
- *Development and demonstration* – using storyboards, prototypes and other envisioning techniques
- *Evaluation* of the reactions to the design
- *Evolution* of the language over time. No matter how good a design, it will only last so long – until circumstances force it to be revisited.

BOX 9.4

Microsoft's design language

Starting with the Windows 7 mobile platform and moving onto the desktop in Windows 8, Microsoft have introduced a new design language for their products. The inspiration for the language is described on their website as being Swiss influenced print and packaging and Microsoft software such as Zune and Office Labs, plus games that focus on motion and content over chrome.

The main features of the design language are:

- **Motion.** A system is created to bring the interface to life by developing a consistent set of motions or animations which provide context for usability.
- **Typography.** Aiming for the right balance of weight and positioning can help lead users to more content.
- **Content not Chrome.** Extra chrome is removed so that in the UI, the main focus becomes the content.
- **Honesty.** Design specifically for a hand-held device, incorporating a high resolution screen and using touch. Interaction is expedited and made simple.

Source: www.microsoft.com/design/toolbox/tutorials/windows-phone-7/metro/

Figure 9.9 Microsoft's user interface

(Source: www.microsoft.com/design/toolbox/tutorials/windows-phone-7/metro/)

Design languages help to ensure transparency, helping people to understand what is going on inside a device. They also afford transferability of knowledge from one device to another. The user of one Nokia phone can generally expect to find similar design on another Nokia phone. This also means that people will more readily see opportunities to use a device or function and will expect certain behaviours, structures or functions. Finally, people will identify with a style, which helps to define their identity; they act through the design language.

← Chapter 4, Section 4.5 discusses design principles

Design language for the MP3

← Wireframes are discussed in Chapter 8

The MP3 application would have to fit in with the overall design language of the HIC, but could also have its own features. The key aspect of the HIC's design language was the Rolodex for displaying and accessing search results and the object, action and category bars. In previous work on the HIC, the problem of how to select text items from a Rolodex list had not been considered in depth. This was a significant issue, particularly in a touchscreen environment where serious functional constraints were imposed by the size and proximity of text in the display. Selecting by simple touch was probably the most intuitive solution. However, all but the smallest fingers would find it hard to pick a track unambiguously unless the text was large and widely spaced. One possible solution that was proposed is shown in Figure 9.10.

People can drag the track into the white slot in the module (A) to select it. In this instance, the interaction can take two possible courses: people either drag the track into the slot and take their finger away, resulting in the track being loaded; or they can abort the selection, in which case the track returns automatically to its position in the Rolodex. This 'recoverability factor' is one of the basic design principles.

Whether the interaction is completed or aborted, the text item changes colour from black (B) to orange (C) while it is in transit, to indicate it is 'active'. A dimmed version of the track name (D) remains in the Rolodex while the track is being dragged. Thus the proposed language elements are dimming of selected items, dragging to select, changing the colour to indicate selection and so on.

An important technique for physical design is the wireframe. Wireframes are used in website design and in app design and in general are an important construct in information design. A wireframe is a skeleton, or outline of the information structure of a physical design. It defines the major structural elements of different pages in a design.

Figure 9.10 Possible design for selection action

9.6 Designing interactions

The design of interactions is critical to interactive systems design. The conceptual design should be as independent of an implementation as possible. The move from conceptual to physical design requires designers to allocate functions and knowledge to persons or to devices and hence to create interactions. For example, in the case of the MP3 player there have to be actions that select tracks and that play tracks, that modify playlists or that load playlists. But this does not say who does what. For example, the selection of a track can be left to a random function of the MP3 player. Playlists may be bought from a content provider, or created by the system based on statistics such as how often they are played.

In designing interactions – i.e. allocating functions to people or to devices – designers need to consider the capabilities of people and the constraints on what they can do. People will forget things over time. They will forget things in working memory in a very short time. They are not good at following long lists of instructions, at carrying out boring tasks repeatedly and so on. On the other hand, people are good at improvising and at dealing with ambiguity and incomplete information. On the whole, the capabilities of technology are just the reverse.

But it is not just a question of efficiency. The interaction should be engaging, enjoyable and fulfilling. Moreover, if the system supports working life, it should help to create satisfying and meaningful jobs, while a product for home use has to fit lifestyle and desired image.

Of course, in a very real sense this whole book is about designing interactions, so understanding, evaluation and envisioning design ideas are critical. In this section we aim to provide more formal methods to help in this process. The first of these is interaction patterns and the second reviews a number of models for structuring interactions.

Interaction patterns

The idea of 'patterns' – perceived regularities in an environment – has been adopted by designers of interactive systems and appears as interaction patterns. As with architectural patterns (see Box 9.5), interaction patterns can be identified at many different levels of abstraction. For example, on most PCs if you double-click on something it opens it; if you right-click, it displays a menu of operations you can perform. Macintosh computers have only a single mouse button so the 'right-click' pattern is unknown to Mac users (they have control click instead). Most playing devices such as VCRs, DVDs, cassette players and MP3 players on a computer have a play, stop, fast forward and rewind interaction pattern. Patterns build up into the complex interactions of menus and mice that we are familiar with: patterns of layout of menus, of the highlighting when the mouse rolls over an item, flashing when an item is selected and so on. More recently, people have been developing gesture patterns for interacting with multi-touch displays (Wobbrock et al., 2009).

General usability patterns have been identified which to a large extent are similar to design guidelines, but the advantage that patterns have over guidelines is the rich description and examples that go with them. In the HIC the main interaction pattern was to select an object on the right-hand bar and then select an activity from the activity bar (or vice versa). Another pattern was to touch the scroll buttons and the bars would rotate.

BOX
9.5

Alexandrian patterns

In architecture Christopher Alexander (Alexander, 1979) has been very influential in introducing the idea of architectural patterns. These are regular good design ideas. For example, it is a good idea to have small parking lots in a neighbourhood because very large parking lots are ugly and disrupt the neighbourhood. It is a good idea to have pavement cafés in a city where people can sit outside because it creates a nice atmosphere. It is a good idea to have a low wall next to an open area so people can sit on it.

Alexander's patterns for architectural features are at different levels of abstraction – from patterns for walls to patterns for whole cities. Each pattern expresses a relation between a certain context, a certain system of 'forces' which occurs repeatedly in that context (i.e. a particular problem) and a solution which allows these forces to resolve themselves. Patterns, therefore, refer to other patterns and are part of larger patterns. For example:

- GALLERY SURROUND proposes that people should be able to walk through a connecting zone such as a balcony to feel connected to the outside world.
- OPENING TO THE STREET says that people on a sidewalk should feel connected to functions inside a building, made possible by direct openings.

Patterns are embodied as concrete prototypes rather than abstract principles and tend to focus on the interactions between the physical form of the built environment and the way in which that inhibits or facilitates various sorts of behaviour within it. Pattern languages are not value-neutral but instead manifest particular values in their names and more explicitly in their rationales.

Alexander specified over 200 patterns in his book. Pattern 88 (adapted from Erickson, 2003) is shown below. Notice how it refers to other patterns (numbered) and how there is a wealth of rich, socially based description.

88 Street Café

[picture omitted]

. . . neighborhoods are defined by Identifiable Neighborhood (14); their natural points of focus are given by Activity Nodes (30) and Small Public Squares (61). This pattern, and the ones which follow it, give the neighborhood and its points of focus, their identity.

The street café provides a unique setting, special to cities: a place where people can sit lazily, legitimately, be on view, and watch the world go by.

The most humane cities are always full of street cafés. Let us try to understand the experience which makes these places so attractive. We know that people enjoy mixing in public, in parks, squares, along promenades and avenues, in street cafés. The preconditions seem to be: the setting gives you the right to be there, by custom; there are a few things to do that are part of the scene, almost ritual: reading the newspaper, strolling, nursing a beer, playing catch; and people feel safe enough to relax, nod at each other, perhaps even meet. A good café terrace meets these conditions. But it has in addition, special qualities of its own: a person may sit there for

[nine paragraphs of rationale omitted]

Therefore:
Encourage local cafés to spring up in each neighborhood. Make them intimate places, with several rooms, open to a busy path, where people can sit with coffee or

a drink and watch the world go by. Build the front of the café so that a set of tables stretch out of the café, right into the street.

[diagram omitted]

Build a wide, substantial opening between the terrace and indoors – OPENING TO THE STREET (165); make the terrace double as A PLACE TO WAIT (150) for nearby bus stops and offices; both indoors and on the terrace use a great variety of different kinds of chairs and tables – DIFFERENT CHAIRS (251); and give the terrace some low definition at the street edge if it is in danger of being interrupted by street action – STAIR SEATS (125), SITTING WALL (243), perhaps a CANVAS ROOF (244).

[text omitted]

Patterns are described in some general format. The format used in the HIC case study is illustrated in Table 9.5, which shows the interaction pattern for the Edit function in the MP3 application. Each pattern is described in this standard way, given a name and description, an indication of the problems it addresses, the design rationale or forces that act on the design decision, and the solution that has been adopted. Patterns will typically refer to other patterns and be referenced by other patterns.

Table 9.5 An interaction pattern for the edit action

Interaction pattern: Edit	
Description	Edit the contents of an HIC entity
	(Conceptually associated with 'Sort' – q.v.)
Examples	Adding MP3 tracks to a playlist
	Adding a URL (Web address) to an MP3
	Favourites List
	Moving tracks to different positions within a playlist
	Moving MP3 tracks from one genre list to another
	Removing a track from a playlist
Situation	Some entities – lists and categories, for instance – have constituent objects associated with them. The user will want to change what these are, and the way they are organized within the 'umbrella' entity.
Problem	How does the user know which entities are editable and, if so, how to perform the 'Edit' action on them? How will the user select the components of the entity which are to be the subject of the edit?
	If objects are removed from an entity, will this mean they are permanently deleted from the HIC?
	Is it the 'umbrella object' which is actually edited, or its constituent objects? (For instance, a list, or its entries?)
Forces (i.e. issues affecting the problem and possible solutions)	The object(s) to be edited will be displayed on the screen. If the user requires to move the position of items within an object, or move an item from one object to another, all the relevant objects will have to be on the screen. The size of the objects, and of the screen, presents a limitation.

Interaction pattern: Edit	
	Some items may be difficult to isolate (select) on the screen due to their small size or close proximity to each other, and this may make them difficult to edit – for example, text strings in a list.
	Alternative modalities could be offered other than screen touch.
	Editing may involve more than one step: select > edit > go/confirm.
	There should be clear feedback telling the user the changes they are about to make. There should probably be a means of cancelling or escaping from the action.
Solution	The graphical interface signals to the user (perhaps by means of a familiar or self-explanatory symbol) whether an entity can be edited. It may also be clear from the context which items are likely to be editable (for instance, the user would expect playlists to be editable).
	There are several possible means of editing. The user could select items one by one or in groups, and use a 'Go' action to complete the process (suitable for touchscreen, remote control or perhaps voice activation). Or she could 'drag and drop' objects to edit them (suitable for touchscreen). Items being edited could change their appearance – perhaps change colour.
	If the object being edited (such as a list) is larger than the available screen space, it could be divided into contiguous sections. A suitable device for displaying this might be the scrolling 'Rolodex' device already established in the present HIC prototype.
Resulting situation	It is clear to the user which objects of the HIC can be edited; the interaction pathways for editing them are apparent (if more than one step is involved, the sequence should be apparent). Clear feedback is given during the Edit action, and the screen is updated afterwards to reflect the new situation.
Notes	This pattern is conceptually associated with 'Sort', the important distinguishing factor being that 'Edit' can change the number and identity of the constituent objects in an entity, while 'Sort' simply rearranges (categorizes) them.
	It also has links with 'Delete'. It is unclear at this stage whether removing an MP3 track from, say, a playlist or a track list, actually deletes it from the HIC entirely, or merely from that list (*qua* display object). Is the original file kept in another part of the HIC's file management space?

Challenge 9.5

Look at the interaction patterns on a mobile phone that you have available. What combination of buttons and displays does what? Identify the 'select' key or select pattern. Identify the 'move down' pattern. Does it always work in the same way or are there different patterns for 'move down a menu' and 'move down through some text'? Compare the existence of patterns in phone design to those in the design of car controls.

Diagrammatic techniques

The diagrammatic techniques we presented in Section 9.4 are concerned with representing the structure of a system. By contrast, the design of interactions is concerned with processes. In many design situations there will be a need to provide a structured

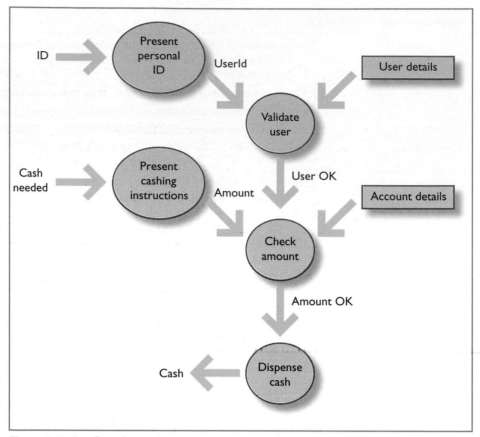

Figure 9.11 Dataflow diagram

'dialogue' between the system and the person using it. The system may need to elicit particular pieces of data in a particular sequence, or to guide people through a series of actions, or to present a number of related options together. Dataflow diagrams are a good way of showing the logical steps required to complete some interaction. The example in Figure 9.11 shows the steps needed to complete a simple transaction with a cash machine. It shows the data needed to go in, the processes (shown as circles) that need to be undertaken and the data that flows out. It also shows the stores of data (boxes) that will be needed. With a logical flow diagram such as this, designers can debate where the human–computer interface should be and where certain functions should take place. Notice that this representation is as independent of technology as possible. Some data, called 'ID', is needed but this representation does not say that this should be a card and PIN. It could be, but it could equally be some new technology such as iris recognition, or fingerprint recognition.

Several other methods are available for representing interactions. Sequence models are one; task structure diagrams are another (Chapter 11). Use cases can be used to describe the interactions, as can simple tabular layouts that show people actions on one side and system responses on the other. Another common diagrammatic technique is the state transition network (STN). This shows how a system moves from one state to another depending on the actions by the user. Figure 9.12 shows an STN for the ATM example. Notice both the similarities and the differences between the two representations. STNs come in a variety of forms and can be powerful techniques for thinking about and creating interactions.

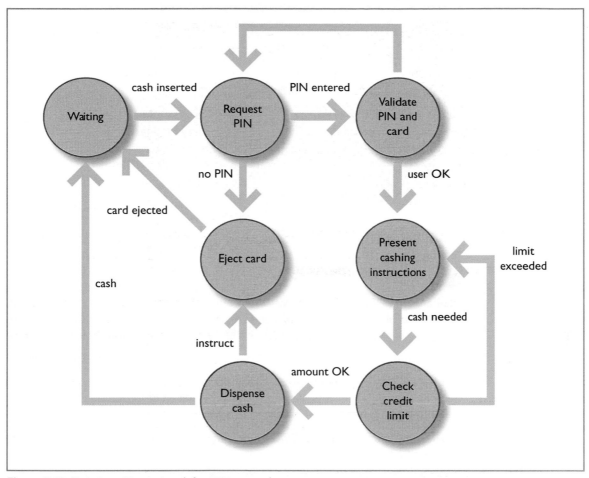

Figure 9.12 State transition network for ATM example

Summary and key points

Conceptual and physical design will happen in any system development, and conceptual modelling, in particular, is a key activity for designers. In this chapter we looked at the importance of conceptual modelling and at conceptual exploration of design spaces. All projects will need to consider the conceptual model and underlying metaphor of the systems, because it is this that leads to people developing their own conceptual model – their mental model – of the system. In addition to developing the conceptual model we have highlighted the need for designing interactions and packaging design ideas into a design language.

- Designers need to explore the concepts and blends in their designs.
- Designers can understand objects and actions in the existing, proposed system by analysing the scenario corpus.
- Designing interactions is concerned with allocating functions to people or devices and hence arriving at a set of interaction patterns.
- Designers should ensure that there is a consistent design language in terms of both the patterns of interaction and representational aspects of design.

Exercises

1 Discuss the underlying conceptual model for the following activities: using an ATM; buying a plane ticket on the Web; using a public information kiosk; setting a VCR to record a programme.

2 In the design of electronic calendars, there are lots of functions such as making regular appointments (say an appointment every Wednesday at 3 pm). In shared calendar systems appointments can be made by other people. There are even some systems that let software 'agents' make appointments. Discuss issues of the allocation of functions between people and software in the context of electronic calendars.

 Further reading

McLuhan, M. (1994) *Understanding Media: The Extensions of Man*. MIT Press, Cambridge, MA. *This is not a book for the faint-hearted, nor for those who want some simple answers. It is something of a psychedelic tour through a 1960s view of the coming age of media. It makes you think.*

Newell, A. and Simon, H. (1972) *Human Problem Solving*. Prentice-Hall, Englewood Cliffs, NJ.

Rheinfrank, J. and Evenson, S. (1996) Design languages. In Winograd, T. (ed.), *Bringing Design to Software*. ACM Press, New York. *A good chapter on design languages and how they have been used in everything from houses in Nantucket to knitting patterns.*

van Harmelen, M. (ed.) (2001) *Object Modeling and User Interface Design: Designing Interactive Systems*. Addison-Wesley, Boston, MA. *This book is a collection of papers providing different methods for conceptual and physical design. Constantine and Lockwood's chapter 'Structure and style in use cases for user interface design' covers much the same ground as presented here but is wholly based around use cases. Constantine and Lockwood define 'essential' use cases that are basically the same as our conceptual scenarios. William Hudson's chapter 'Toward unified models in user-centred and object-oriented design' gives a very comprehensive overview of different methods and how they might all be brought together.*

Graham, I. (2003) *A Pattern Language for Web Usability*. Addison-Wesley, Harlow. *An excellent example of the development of a pattern language, this time to help designers to design good websites.*

Getting ahead

Blackwell, A.F. (2006) The reification of metaphor as a design tool. *ACM Transactions on Computer–Human Interaction (TOCHI)*, 13(4), 490–530.

Imaz, M. and Benyon, D.R. (2005) *Designing with Blends: Conceptual Foundations of Human Computer Interaction and Software Engineering*. MIT Press, Cambridge, MA.

Saffer, Dan (2007) *Designing for Interaction*. New Riders, Indianapolis, IN.

 Web links

Bill Verplank is at **www.billverplank.com**

The accompanying website has links to relevant websites. Go to
www.pearsoned.co.uk/benyon

Comments on challenges

Challenge 9.1

Personal, direct, fun, impromptu, young, quick, pervasive, hot . . . occur to me, but there are almost infinite possibilities here. There are no right or wrong answers; it depends on your own perceptions and feelings.

Challenge 9.2

The window is one of the components of the original 'desktop metaphor' that has led to the current operating systems Windows 8 and OS X. The window allows you to look in on something. 'Cut and paste' comes from journalism where paragraphs of stories were cut up and pasted (with glue) onto paper in a different order. A bootstrap was attached to riding boots so that people would pull themselves up. Most people are familiar with manila folders kept in a filing cabinet that needs to be opened up to see what is inside. Interestingly, since a folder contains many files, a computer folder is more like a drawer in a filing cabinet and a computer file is more like a real folder.

Challenge 9.3

Thinking of physical diaries is one way to come up with possible metaphors: pocket diaries, desk diaries, the diary of personal events that you might keep, the diary of future events in an area such as sports, a diary of events for a local society or club. This might lead to the metaphor of a pocket diary in which the interface had 'pages' that could be 'turned'. The diary of events leads to a wall-chart type of display with the days of the month laid out. The personal diary might lead to ideas such as secrecy and security, being able to write free-flowing text rather than having a regimented date- and event-driven design that a business diary suggests.

Challenge 9.4

Nouns: arts festival, city, three weeks, August, Edinburgh International Festival, Edinburgh Fringe Festival, book festival, film festival, jazz festival, related events, performers, orchestras, composers, ballet troupes, theatres, the Traverse, mavericks, Demarco, events, venues. Verbs: takes place, consists of, features, started.

The main objects are the same as the nouns; there are the different types of festival and events, different types of performers, theatres and venues. We also know a bit more about some of these: 1200 events, 150 venues, etc. The main activities express relationships between the objects. In this way the underlying conceptual model of the domain begins to emerge.

Events take place at a venue/theatre. A festival consists of events and features performers, and so on.

Challenge 9.5

Most phones will have these standard patterns, though exactly how they are implemented varies widely between different makes and varies over time. Preferences shift from four-way rocker keys to arrow keys and back again. Presumably designs will settle down at some stage, as they have done, for example, in the design of car controls, which were highly non-standard but which now have similar patterns of interaction – for signalling, for windscreen washing, turning the lights on, and so on.

Chapter 10
Evaluation

Contents

Aims

Evaluation is the fourth main process of interactive systems design that we identified in Chapter 3. By evaluation we mean reviewing, trying out or testing a design idea, a piece of software, a product or a service to discover whether it meets some criteria. These criteria will often be summed up by the guidelines for good design introduced in Chapter 4, namely that the system is learnable, effective and accommodating. But at other times the designer might be more interested in some other characteristic of the design. The designer is concerned not just with surface features such as the meaningfulness of icons, but also with whether the system is fit for its purpose, enjoyable, engaging and so on.

After studying this chapter you should be able to:

- Appreciate the uses of a range of generally applicable evaluation techniques designed for use with and without users
- Understand expert-based evaluation methods
- Understand participant-based evaluation methods
- Apply the techniques in appropriate contexts.

10.1   Introduction

The techniques in this chapter will allow you to evaluate many types of product, system or service. Evaluation of different types of system, or evaluation in different contexts, may offer particular challenges. (For example, evaluating mobile devices, or services delivered by a mobile device, are explored in more detail in Chapter 19).

Evaluation is closely tied to the other key activities of interactive systems design, understanding, design and envisionment. In particular, many of the techniques discussed in Chapter 7 on understanding are applicable to evaluation. Evaluation is also critically dependent on the form of envisionment used to represent the system. You will only be able to evaluate features that are represented in a form appropriate for the type of evaluation. There are also issues concerning who is involved in the evaluation.

Challenge 10.1

Collect several advertisements for small, personal technologies such as that shown in Figure 10.1. What claims are the advertisers making about design features and benefits? What issues does this raise for their evaluation?

Design
Get the ultimate multimedia experience with Satio.

Figure 10.1 Sony Ericsson T100 mobile phone

(Source: www.sonyericsson.com)

In our human-centred approach to design, we evaluate designs right from the earliest idea. For example, in the case study in Chapter 6, very early ideas for the HIC were mocked up and reviewed, to be followed later by more realistic prototyping and testing of a partially finished system and finally by evaluation of the near-complete device in its intended home setting. There are two main types of evaluation. One involves a usability expert, or an interaction designer, reviewing some form of envisioned version of a design: expert-based methods. The other involves recruiting people to use an envisioned version of a system: participant methods. Where possible these people should be representative of the people at whom the system is aimed (sometimes called 'end-users'). This is the preferred choice for 'in-house' systems where the designer has access to the target population. Alternatively, the participants may be other people (perhaps other designers, students or whoever happens to be around), who are invited to play the part of the people who will use the system. The characteristics of the target population can be captured through personas.

← Personas are described in Chapter 3

Evaluation occurs throughout the interaction design process. At different stages, different methods will be more or less effective. The form of envisionment of the future systems is also critical to what can be evaluated.

Obtaining feedback to inform early design concepts

You may need to evaluate initial concepts, especially if the application is novel. Here, quick paper prototypes can help, or even software if this can be produced rapidly. Evaluations of competitor products or previous versions of technology can also feed into the design process at this stage.

Deciding between different design options

During development, designers have to decide between options, for example between voice input and touchscreen interaction for a shared electronic household wall-planner or between different sequences for order processing functions.

Checking for usability problems

Testing will identify potential problems once a stable version of the technology is available. This needs to respond when a participant activates a function, but it does not require the whole system to be fully operational (a horizontal prototype). Alternatively, the system may be completely functional, but only in some parts (a vertical prototype). What is important is that there is still time to fix problems. What happens all too frequently is that you are asked to check that interaction is 'user-friendly' just before development is completed. Very often all that can be changed are minor issues such as the position, colour or labelling of on-screen buttons. It is best to be helpful in these circumstances. If you make a note of problems that could have been solved easily if identified sooner, you can exploit these examples (tactfully) to justify evaluation work at an earlier stage in the next project.

Evaluation of the types described above is sometimes termed formative evaluation, because the results help to form – or shape – the design.

Assessing the usability of a finished product

This may be to test against in-house guidelines, or formal usability standards such as ISO 9241, or to provide evidence of usability required by a customer, for example the time to complete a particular set of operations. Government departments and other public bodies often require suppliers to conform to accessibility standards and health and safety legislation.

This type of evaluation is often termed summative evaluation.

As a means of involving people in the design process

In the participatory design approach, stakeholders help designers set the goals for the evaluation work. Involving stakeholders has great benefits in terms of eventual uptake and use of the technology. (Of course, this applies only to technology that is tailor-made for defined communities, rather than off-the-shelf products.) For example, in a redevelopment of a Web-based gallery showcasing the work of disadvantaged artists, as many of the artists themselves as possible were involved in evaluating the new designs, thus preserving the sense of community which the site aimed to embody (Macleod, 2002). A number of methods of involving people in the design process were discussed in Chapter 7 on understanding and Chapter 8 on envisionment (prototyping). Susanne Bødker's Design Collaboratium (Bødker and Buur, 2002) is another example.

10.2 Expert evaluation

A simple, relatively quick and effective method of evaluation is to get an interaction design, or usability, expert to look at the system and try using it. As we said in the introduction this is no substitute for getting real people to use your design, but expert evaluation is effective, particularly early in the design process. Experts will pick up common problems based on this experience, and will identify factors that might otherwise interfere with an evaluation by non-experts.

However, to help the experts structure their evaluation, it is useful to adopt a particular approach. This will help to focus the expert's critique on the most relevant aspects for the purpose. The general approach to expert evaluation is that the expert will **walk through** representative tasks or scenarios of use. Additionally they may adopt one of the personas. Thus expert evaluation is tied in to scenario-based design (and central to it).

← Scenario-based design is covered in Chapter 3 and the importance of evaluation in Chapter 2

Heuristic evaluation

Heuristic evaluation refers to a number of methods in which a person trained in HCI and interaction design examines a proposed design to see how it measures up against a list of principles, guidelines or 'heuristics' for good design. This review may be a quick discussion over the shoulder of a colleague, or may be a formal, carefully documented process.

There are many sets of heuristics to choose from, both general-purpose and those relating to particular application domains, for example heuristics for Web design. Below is a brief list of the design principles – or heuristics – that we introduced earlier. (You should refer back to Chapter 4 for the details.)

1	Visibility	7	Feedback
2	Consistency	8	Recovery
3	Familiarity	9	Constraints
4	Affordance	10	Flexibility
5	Navigation	11	Style
6	Control	12	Conviviality

Ideally, several people with expertise in interactive systems design should review the interface. Each expert notes the problems and the relevant heuristic, and suggests a solution where possible. It is also helpful if a severity rating, say on a scale of 1 to 3, is added, according to the likely impact of the problem, as recommended by Dumas and Fox (2012) in their comprehensive review of usability testing. However, they also note the disappointing level of correlation amongst experts in rating severity of problems.

Evaluators work independently and then combine results. They may need to work through any training materials and be briefed by the design team about the functionality. The scenarios used in the design process are valuable here.

Discount usability engineering

The list of design principles above can be summarized by the three overarching usability principles of *learnability* (principles 1–4), *effectiveness* (principles 5–9) and *accommodation* (principles 10–12). If time is very short, a quick review of the design against this triad can produce reasonably useful results. This is known as a discount heuristic evaluation.

← An example of discount heuristic evaluation was provided in the HIC case study in Chapter 6

This approach to evaluation was pioneered by Jakob Nielsen (1993) and enthusiastically followed by many time-pressured evaluation practitioners. It is now used for any 'quick and dirty' approach to evaluation where the aim is to get useful, informed feedback as soon as possible. Once again a number of usability experts 'walk through' concrete scenarios, preferably accompanied by personas, and inspect the design for difficulties.

Challenge 10.2

Carry out a quick review of the controls for a domestic device, e.g. a stove, microwave or washing machine, for learnability, effectiveness and accommodation.

Unless there is no alternative, you should not evaluate your own designs. It is extremely difficult to ignore your knowledge of how the system works, the meaning of icons or menu names and so on, and you are likely to give the design the 'benefit of the doubt' or to find obscure flaws which few users will ever happen upon.

Woolrych and Cockton (2000) conducted a large-scale trial of heuristic evaluation. Evaluators were trained to use the technique, then evaluated the interface to a drawing editor. The editor was then trialled by customers. Comparison of findings showed that many of the issues identified by the experts were not experienced by people (false positives), while some severe difficulties were missed by the inspection against heuristics. There were a number of reasons for this. Many false positives stemmed from a tendency by the experts to assume that people had no intelligence or even common sense. As for 'missing' problems, these tended to result from a series of mistakes and misconceptions, often relating to a set of linked items, rather than isolated misunderstandings. Sometimes heuristics were misapplied, or apparently added as an afterthought. Woolrych and Cockton conclude that the heuristics add little advantage to an expert evaluation and the results of applying them may be counter-productive. They (and other authors) suggest that more theoretically informed techniques such as the cognitive walkthrough (see below) offer more robust support for problem identification. It is very evident that heuristic evaluation is not a complete solution. At the very least, the technique must be used together with careful consideration of people and their real-life skills. Participant evaluation is required to get a realistic picture of the success of a system.

Heuristic evaluation therefore is valuable as *formative* evaluation, to help the designer improve the interaction at an early stage. It should not be used as a *summative* assessment, to make claims about the usability and other characteristics of a finished product. If that is what we need to do, then we must carry out properly designed and controlled experiments with a much greater number of participants. However, the more controlled the testing situation becomes, the less it is likely to resemble the real world, which leads us to the question of 'ecological validity'.

FURTHER THOUGHTS

Ecological validity

In real life, people multitask, use several applications in parallel or in quick succession, are interrupted, improvise, ask other people for help, use applications intermittently and adapt technologies for purposes the designers never imagined. We have unpredictable, complex but generally effective coping strategies for everyday life and the technologies supporting it. The small tasks which are the focus of most evaluations are usually part of lengthy sequences directed towards aims which change according to circumstances. All of this is extremely difficult to reproduce in testing, and often deliberately excluded. So the results of most user testing can only ever be indicative of issues in real-life usage. Practitioners and researchers are not unaware of this problem and a number of solutions have been proposed. They include:

- Ethnographically informed observations of technologies in long-term use (although this is more often undertaken earlier in the design – evaluation cycle) – see Chapter 7
- Having users keep diaries, which can be audiovisual as well as written – there is more about this in Chapter 7
- Collecting 'bug' reports – often these are usability problems – and help centre queries

Cognitive walkthrough

Cognitive walkthrough is a rigorous paper-based technique for checking through the detailed design and logic of steps in an interaction. It is derived from the human information processor view of cognition and closely related to task analysis (Chapter 11). In essence, the cognitive walkthrough entails a usability analyst stepping through the cognitive tasks that must be carried out in interacting with technology. Originally developed by Lewis *et al.* (1990) for applications where people browse and explore information, it has been extended to interactive systems in general (Wharton *et al* ., 1994). Aside from its systematic approach, the great strength of the cognitive walkthrough is that it is based on well-established theory rather than the trial and error or a heuristically based approach.

Inputs to the process are:

- An understanding of the people who are expected to use the system
- A set of concrete scenarios representing both (a) very common and (b) uncommon but critical sequences of activities
- A complete description of the interface to the system – this should comprise both a representation of how the interface is presented, e.g. screen designs, and the correct sequence of actions for achieving the scenario tasks, usually as a hierarchical task analysis (HTA).

→ Hierarchical task analysis (HTA) is discussed in Chapter 11

Having gathered these materials together, the analyst asks the following four questions for each individual step in the interaction:

- Will the people using the system try to achieve the right effect?
- Will they notice that the correct action is available?
- Will they associate the correct action with the effect that they are trying to achieve?
- If the correct action is performed, will people see that progress is being made towards the goal of their activity? (modified from Wharton *et al.*, 1994, p. 106)

If any of the questions is answered in the negative, then a usability problem has been identified and is recorded, but redesign suggestions are not made at this point. If the walkthrough is being used as originally devised, this process is carried out as a group exercise by analysts and designers together. The analysts step through usage scenarios and the design team are required to explain how the user would identify, carry out and monitor the correct sequence of actions. Software designers in organizations with structured quality procedures in place will find some similarities to program code walkthroughs.

Several cut-down versions of the technique have been devised. Among the best documented are:

- The 'cognitive jogthrough' (Rowley and Rhoades, 1992) – video records (rather than conventional minutes) are made of walkthrough meetings, annotated to indicate significant items of interest, design suggestions are permitted, and low-level actions are aggregated wherever possible.
- The 'streamlined cognitive walkthrough' (Spencer, 2000) – designer defensiveness is defused by engendering a problem-solving ethos, and the process is streamlined by not documenting problem-free steps and by combining the four original questions into two (*ibid.*, p. 355):
  - Will people know what to do at each step?
  - If people do the right thing, will they know that they did the right thing, and are making progress towards their goal?

Both these approaches acknowledge that detail may be lost, but this is more than compensated for by enhanced coverage of the system as a whole and by designer buy-in to the process. Finally, the cognitive walkthrough is very often practised (and taught) as a technique executed by the analyst alone, to be followed in some cases by a meeting with the design team. If a written report is required, the problematic interaction step and the difficulties predicted should be explained. Other checklist approaches have been suggested, such as the Activity Checklist (Kaptelinin *et al.* 1999), but have not been widely taken up by other practitioners.

Challenge 10.3

A joint walkthrough session between evaluators and designers can work well, but there can be drawbacks. Suggest what these might be and how you might overcome them.

While expert-based evaluation is a reasonable first step, it will not find all problems, particularly those that result from a chain of 'wrong' actions or are linked to fundamental misconceptions. Woolrych and Cockton (2001) discuss this in detail. Experts even find problems that do not really exist – people overcome many minor difficulties using a mixture of common sense and experience. So it is really important to complete the picture with some real people trying out the interaction design. The findings will always be interesting, quite often surprising and occasionally disconcerting. From a political point of view, it is easier to convince designers of the need for changes if the evidence is not simply one 'expert' view, particularly if the expert is relatively junior. The aim is to trial the design with people who represent the intended target group in as near realistic conditions as possible.

10.3   Participant-based evaluation

Whereas expert, heuristic evaluations can be carried out by designers on their own, there can be no substitute for involving some real people in the evaluation. Participant evaluation aims to do exactly that. There are many ways to involve people that require various degrees of cooperation. The methods range from designers sitting with participants as they work through a system to leaving people alone with the technology and observing what they do through a two-way mirror.

Cooperative evaluation

Andrew Monk and colleagues (Monk *et al.*, 1993) at the University of York (UK) developed cooperative evaluation as a means of maximizing the data gathered from a simple testing session. The technique is 'cooperative' because participants are not passive subjects but work as co-evaluators. It has proved a reliable but economical technique in diverse applications. Table 10.1 and the sample questions are edited from Appendix 1 in Monk *et al.* (1993).

Table 10.1 Guidelines for cooperative evaluation

Step	Notes
1 Using the scenarios prepared earlier, write a draft list of tasks.	Tasks must be realistic, doable with the software, and explore the system thoroughly.
2 Try out the tasks and estimate how long they will take a participant to complete.	Allow 50 per cent longer than the total task time for each test session.
3 Prepare a task sheet for the participants.	Be specific and explain the tasks so that anyone can understand
4 Get ready for the test session.	Have the prototype ready in a suitable environment with a list of prompt questions, notebook and pens ready. A video or audio recorder would be very useful here.
5 Tell the participants that it is the system that is under test, not them; explain and introduce the tasks.	Participants should work individually – you will not be able to monitor more than one participant at once. Start recording if equipment is available.
6 Participants start the tasks. Have them give you running commentary on what they are doing, why they are doing it and difficulties or uncertainties they encounter.	Take notes of where participants find problems or do something unexpected, and their comments. Do this even if you are recording the session. You may need to help if participants are stuck or have them move to the next task.
7 Encourage participants to keep talking.	Some useful prompt questions are provided below.
8 When the participants have finished, interview them briefly about the usability of the prototype and the session itself. Thank them.	Some useful questions are provided below. If you have a large number of participants, a simple questionnaire may be helpful.
9 Write up your notes as soon as possible and incorporate into a usability report.	

Sample questions *during* the evaluation:
- What do you want to do?
- What were you expecting to happen?
- What is the system telling you?
- Why has the system done that?
- What are you doing now?

Sample questions *after* the session:
- What was the best/worst thing about the prototype?
- What most needs changing?
- How easy were the tasks?
- How realistic were the tasks?
- Did giving a commentary distract you?

Participatory heuristic evaluation

The developers of participatory heuristic evaluation (Muller *et al.*, 1998) claim that it extends the power of heuristic evaluation without adding greatly to the effort required. An expanded list of heuristics is provided, based on those of Nielsen and Mack (1994) – but of course you could use any heuristics such as those introduced earlier (Chapter 4). The procedure for the use of participatory heuristic evaluation is just as for the expert version, but the participants are involved as 'work-domain experts' alongside usability experts and must be briefed about what is required.

Co-discovery

Co-discovery is a naturalistic, informal technique that is particularly good for capturing first impressions. It is best used in the later stages of design.

The standard approach of watching individual people interacting with the technology, and possibly 'thinking aloud' as they do so, can be varied by having participants explore new technology in pairs. For example, a series of pairs of people could be given a prototype of a new digital camera and asked to experiment with its features by taking pictures of each other and objects in the room. This tends to elicit a more naturalistic flow of comment, and people will often encourage each other to try interactions that they might not have thought of in isolation. It is a good idea to use people who know each other quite well. As with most other techniques, it also helps to set users some realistic tasks to try out.

Depending on the data to be collected, the evaluator can take an active part in the session by asking questions or suggesting activities, or simply monitor the interaction either live or using a video-recording. Inevitably, asking specific questions skews the output towards the evaluator's interests, but does help to ensure that all important angles are covered. The term 'co-discovery' originates from Kemp and van Gelderen (1996) who provide a detailed description of its use.

BOX 10.1

Living Labs

Living Labs is a European approach to evaluation that aims to engage as many people as possible in exploring new technologies. There are a number of different structures for Living Labs. For example, Nokia has teamed up with academics and other manufacturers of mobile devices to hand out hundreds of early prototype systems to students to see how they use them. Other labs work with elderly people in their homes to explore new types of home technologies. Others work with travellers and migrant workers to uncover what new technologies can do for them.

The key idea behind Living Labs is that people are both willing and able to contribute to designing new technologies and new services and it makes sense for companies to work with them. The fact that the discussions and evaluation take place in the life-context of people, and often with large numbers of people, gives the data a strong ecological validity.

Controlled experiments

Another way of undertaking participant evaluation is to set up a controlled experiment. Controlled experiments are appropriate where the designer is interested in particular features of a design, perhaps comparing one design to another to see which is better. In order to do this with any certainty the experiment needs to be carefully designed and run.

The first thing to do when considering a controlled experiment approach to evaluation is to establish what it is that you are looking at. This is the independent variable. For example, you might want to compare two different designs of a website, or two different ways of selecting a function on a mobile phone application. Later we describe an experiment that examined two different ways of presenting an audio interface to select locations of objects (Chapter 18). The independent variable was the type of audio interface. Once you have established what it is you are looking at, you need to decide how you are going to measure the difference. These are the *dependent* variables. You might want to judge which Web design is better based on the number of clicks needed to achieve some task; speed of access could be the dependent variable for selecting a function. In the case of the audio interface, accuracy of location was the dependent variable.

Once the independent and dependent variables have been agreed, the experiment needs to be designed to avoid anything getting in the way of the relationship between independent and dependent variables. Things that might get in the way are learning effects, the effects of different tasks, the effects of different background knowledge, etc. These are the *confounding* variables. You want to ensure a balanced and clear relationship between independent and dependent variables so that you can be sure you are looking at the relationship between them and nothing else.

One possible confounding variable is that the participants in any experiment are not balanced across the conditions. To avoid this, participants are usually divided up across the conditions so that there are roughly the same number of people in each condition and there are roughly the same number of males and females, young and old, experienced and not. The next stage is to decide whether each participant will participate in all conditions (so-called within-subject design) or whether each participant will perform in only one condition (so-called between-subject design). In deciding this you have to be wary of introducing confounding variables. For example, consider the learning effects that happen if people perform a similar task on more than one system. They start off slowly but soon get good at things, so if time to complete a task is a measure they inevitably get quicker the more they do it. This effect can be controlled by randomizing the sequence in which people perform in the different conditions.

Having got some participants to agree to participate in a controlled experiment, it is tempting to try to find out as much as possible. There is nothing wrong with an experiment being set up to look at more than one independent variable, perhaps one being looked at between subjects and another being looked at within subjects. You just have to be careful how the design works. And, of course, there is nothing wrong with interviewing them afterwards, or using focus groups afterwards to find out other things about the design. People can be videoed and perhaps talk aloud during the experiments (so long as this does not count as a confounding variable) and this data can also prove useful for the evaluation.

A controlled experiment will often result in some quantitative data: the measures of the dependent values. This data can then be analysed using statistics, for example comparing the average time to do something across two conditions, or the average number of clicks. So, to undertake controlled experiments you will need some basic understanding of probability theory, of experimental theory and, of course, of statistics. Daunting as this might sound, it is not so very difficult given a good textbook. *Experimental Design and Statistics* (Miller, 1984) is a widely used text, and another good example is Cairns and Cox (2008) *Research Methods for Human–Computer Interaction*.

Challenge 10.4

You have just completed a small evaluation project for a tourist information 'walk-up-and-use' kiosk designed for an airport arrivals area. A heuristic evaluation by you (you were not involved with the design itself) and a technical author found seventeen potential problems, of which seven were graded severe enough to require some redesign and the rest were fairly trivial.

You then carried out some participant evaluation. You had very little time for this, testing with only three people. The test focused on the more severe problems found in the heuristic evaluation and the most important functionality (as identified in the requirements analysis). Your participants – again because of lack of time and budget – were recruited from another section of your own organization which is not directly involved in interactive systems design or build, but the staff do use desktop PCs as part of their normal work. The testing took place in a quiet corner of the development office.

Participants in the user evaluation all found difficulty with three of the problematic design features flagged up by the heuristic evaluation. These problems were essentially concerned with knowing what information might be found in different sections of the application. Of the remaining four severe problems from heuristic evaluation, one person had difficulty with all of them, but the other two people did not. Two out of the three test users failed to complete a long transaction where they tried to find and book hotel rooms for a party of travellers staying for different periods of time.

What, if anything, can you conclude from the evaluation? What are the limitations of the data?

10.4   Evaluation in practice

A survey of 103 experienced practitioners of human-centred design conducted in 2000 (Vredenburg *et al.*, 2002) indicates that around 40 per cent of those surveyed conducted 'usability evaluation', around 30 per cent used 'informal expert review' and around 15 per cent used 'formal heuristic evaluation' (Table 10.2). These figures do not indicate where people used more than one technique. As the authors note, some kind of cost–benefit trade-off seems to be in operation. Table 10.2 shows the benefits and weaknesses perceived for each method. For busy practitioners, the relative economy of review methods often compensates for the better information obtained from user testing. Clearly the community remains in need of methods that are both light on resources and productive of useful results.

The main steps in undertaking a simple but effective evaluation project are:

1   Establish the aims of the evaluation, the intended participants in the evaluation, the context of use and the state of the technology; obtain or construct scenarios illustrating how the application will be used.
2   Select evaluation methods. These should be a combination of expert-based review methods and participant methods.
3   Carry out expert review.
4   Plan participant testing; use the results of the expert review to help focus this.
5   Recruit people and organize testing venue and equipment.
6   Carry out the evaluation.
7   Analyse results, document and report back to designers.

Table 10.2 Perceived costs and benefits of evaluation methods. A '+' sign denotes a benefit, and a '−' a weakness. The numbers indicate how many respondents mentioned the benefit or weakness.

Benefit/weakness	Formal heuristic evaluation	Informal expert review	Usability evaluation
Cost	+ (9)	+ (12)	− (6)
Availability of expertise	− (3)	− (4)	
Availability of information			+ (3)
Speed	+ (10)	+ (22)	− (3)
User involvement	− (7)	− (10)	
Compatibility with practice			− (3)
Versatility			− (4)
Ease of documentation			− (3)
Validity/quality of results	+ (6)	+ (7)	+ (8)
Understanding context	− (10)	− (17)	− (3)
Credibility of results			+ (7)

Source: Adapted from Vredenburg, K., Mao, J.-Y., Smith, P.W. and Carey, T. (2002) A survey of user-centred design practice, *Proceedings of SIGCHI conference on human factors in computing systems*, MN, 20–25 April, pp. 471–8, Table 3. © 2002 ACM, Inc. Reprinted by permission

Aims of the evaluation

Deciding the aim(s) for evaluation helps to determine the type of data required. It is useful to write down the main questions you need to answer. For example in the evaluation of the early concept for a virtual training environment the aims were to investigate:

- Do the trainers understand and welcome the basic idea of the virtual training environment?
- Would they use it to extend or replace existing training courses?
- How close to reality should the virtual environment be?
- What features are required to support record keeping and administration?

The data we were interested in at this stage was largely qualitative (non-numerical), so appropriate data gathering methods were interviews and discussions with the trainers.

If the aim of the evaluation is the comparison of two different evaluation designs then much more focused questions will be required and the data gathered will be more quantitative. In the virtual training environment, for example, some questions we asked were:

- Is it quicker to reach a particular room in the virtual environment using mouse, cursor keys or joystick?
- Is it easier to open a virtual door by clicking on the handle or selecting the 'open' icon from a tools palette?

Figure 10.2 shows the evaluation in progress. Underlying issues were the focus on speed and ease of operation. This illustrates the link between analysis and evaluation – in this case, it had been identified that these qualities were crucial for the acceptability of the virtual learning environment. With questions such as these, we are likely to need quantitative (numerical) data to support design choices.

Figure 10.2 A trainer evaluating a training system

Metrics and measures

What is to be measured and how? Table 10.3 shows some common usability metrics and ways in which they can be measured, adapted from the list provided in the usability standard ISO 9241 part 11 and using the usability definition of 'effectiveness, efficiency and satisfaction' adopted in the standard. There are many other possibilities.

Such metrics are helpful in evaluating many types of applications, from small mobile communication devices to office systems. In most of these there is a task – something the participant needs to get done – and it is reasonably straightforward to decide whether

Table 10.3 Common usability metrics

Usability objective	Effectiveness measures	Efficiency measures	Satisfaction measures
Overall usability	• Percentage of tasks successfully completed • Percentage of users successfully completing tasks	• Time to complete a task • Time spent on non-productive actions	• Rating scale for satisfaction • Frequency of use if this is voluntary (after system is implemented)
Meets needs of trained or experienced users	• Percentage of advanced tasks completed • Percentage of relevant functions used	• Time taken to complete tasks relative to minimum realistic time	• Rating scale for satisfaction with advanced features
Meets needs for walk up and use	• Percentage of tasks completed successfully at first attempt	• Time taken on first attempt to complete task • Time spent on help functions	• Rate of voluntary use (after system is implemented)
Meets needs for infrequent or intermittent use	• Percentage of tasks completed successfully after a specified period of non-use	• Time spent re-learning functionsNumber of persistent errors	• Frequency of reuse (after system is implemented)
Learnability	• Number of functions learned • Percentage of users who manage to learn to a pre-specified criterion	• Time spent on help functions • Time to learn to criterion	• Rating scale for ease of learning

Source: ISO 9241-11:1998 Ergonomic requirements for office work with visual display terminals (VDTs), extract of Table B.2

the task has been achieved successfully or not. There is one major difficulty: deciding the acceptable figure for, say, the percentage of tasks successfully completed. Is this 95 per cent, 80 per cent or 50 per cent? In some (rare) cases clients may set this figure. Otherwise a baseline may be available from comparative testing against an alternative design, a previous version, a rival product, or the current manual version of a process to be computerized. But the evaluation team still has to determine whether a metric is *relevant*. For example, in a complex computer-aided design system, one would not expect most functions to be used perfectly at the first attempt. And would it really be meaningful if design engineers using one design were on average two seconds quicker in completing a complex diagram than those using a competing design? By contrast, speed of keying characters may be crucial to the success of a mobile phone. There are three things to keep in mind when deciding metrics:

● Just because something can be measured, it doesn't mean it should be.
● Always refer back to the overall purpose and context of use of the technology.
● Consider the usefulness of the data you are likely to obtain against the resources it will take to test against the metrics.

The last point is particularly important in practice.

Challenge 10.5

Why is learnability more important for some applications than for others? Think of some examples where it might not be a very significant factor in usability.

People

The most important people in evaluation are the people who will use the system. Analysis work should have identified the characteristics of these people, and represented these in the form of personas. Relevant data can include knowledge of the activities the technology is intended to support, skills relating to input and output devices, experience, education, training and physical and cognitive capabilities.

← Relevant characteristics of people are summarized in Chapter 2

You need to recruit at least three and preferably five people to participate in tests. Nielsen's recommended sample of 3–5 participants has been accepted wisdom in usability practice for

---

Engagement

Games and other applications designed for entertainment pose different questions for evaluation. While we may still want to evaluate whether the basic functions to move around a game environment, for example, are easy to learn, efficiency and effectiveness in a wider sense are much less relevant. The 'purpose' here is to enjoy the game, and time to complete, for example, a particular level may sometimes be less important than experiencing the events that happen along the way. Similarly, multimedia applications are often directed at intriguing users or evoking emotional responses rather than having the achievement of particular tasks in a limited period of time. In contexts of this type, evaluation centres on probing user experience through interviews or questionnaires. Read and MacFarlane (2000), for example, used a rating scale presented as a 'smiley face vertical fun meter' when working with children to evaluate novel interfaces. Other measures which can be considered are observational: the user's posture or facial expression, for instance, may be an indicator of engagement in the experience.

FURTHER THOUGHTS

over a decade. However, some practitioners and researchers advise that this is too few. We consider that in many real-world situations obtaining even 3–5 people is difficult, so we continue to recommend small test numbers as part of a pragmatic evaluation strategy.

However, testing such a small number makes sense only if you have a relatively homogeneous group to design for – for example, experienced managers who use a customer database system, or computer games players aged between 16 and 25. If you have a heterogeneous set of customers that your design is aimed at, then you will need to run 3–5 people *from each group* through your tests. If your product is to be demonstrated by sales and marketing personnel, it is useful to involve them. Finding representative participants should be straightforward if you are developing an in-house application. Otherwise participants can be found through focus groups established for marketing purposes or, if necessary, through advertising. Students are often readily available, but remember that they are only representative of a particular segment of the population. If you have the resources, payment can help recruitment. Inevitably, your sample will be biased towards cooperative people with some sort of interest in technology, so bear this in mind when interpreting your results.

If you cannot recruit any genuine participants – people who are really representative of the target customers – and you are the designer of the software, at least have someone else try to use it. This could be one of your colleagues, a friend, your mother or anyone you trust to give you a brutally honest reaction. Almost certainly, they will find some design flaws. The data you obtain will be limited, but better than nothing. You will, however, have to be *extremely* careful as to how far you generalize from your findings.

Finally, consider your own role and that of others in the evaluation team if you have one. You will need to set up the tests and collect data, but how far will you become involved? Our recommended method for basic testing requires an evaluator to sit with each user and engage with them as they carry out the test tasks. We also suggest that for ethical reasons and in order to keep the tests running, you should provide help if the participant is becoming uncomfortable, or completely stuck. The amount of help that is appropriate will depend on the type of application (e.g. for an information kiosk for public use you might provide only very minimal help), the degree of completeness of the test application and, in particular, whether any help facilities have been implemented.

The test plan and task specification

A plan should be drawn up to guide the evaluation. The plan specifies:

- Aims of the test session
- Practical details, including where and when it will be conducted, how long each session will last, the specification of equipment and materials for testing and data collection, and any technical support that may be necessary
- Numbers and types of participant
- Tasks to be performed, with a definition of successful completion. This section also specifies what data should be collected and how it will be analysed.

You should now conduct a pilot session and fix any unforeseen difficulties. For example, task completion time is often much longer than expected, and instructions may need clarification.

Reporting usability evaluation results to the design team

However competent and complete the evaluation, it is only worthwhile if the results are acted upon. Even if you are both designer and evaluator, you need an organized list of findings so that you can prioritize redesign work. If you are reporting back to a design/development team, it is crucial that they can see immediately what the problem is, how significant its consequences are, and ideally what needs to be done to fix it.

The report should be ordered either by areas of the system concerned, or by severity of problem. For the latter, you could adopt a three- or five-point scale, perhaps ranging from 'would prevent participant from proceeding further' to 'minor irritation'. Adding a note of the general usability principle concerned may help designers understand why there is a difficulty, but often more specific explanation will be needed. Alternatively, sometimes the problem is so obvious that explanation is superfluous. A face-to-face meeting may have more impact than a written document alone (although this should always be produced as supporting material) and this would be the ideal venue for showing *short* video clips of participant problems.

Suggested solutions make it more probable that something will be done. Requiring a response from the development team to each problem will further increase this probability, but may be counter-productive in some contexts. If your organization has a formal quality system, an effective strategy is to have usability evaluation alongside other test procedures, so usability problems are dealt with in the same way as any other fault. Even without a full quality system, usability problems can be fed into a 'bug' reporting system if one exists. Whatever the system for dealing with design problems, however, tact is a key skill in effective usability evaluation.

An example small-scale evaluation

BOX
10.2

This is the process implemented by a postgraduate student to evaluate three different styles of interface for the editing functions on photo CDs. It is not a perfect example, but rather illustrates making the best use of limited resources.

Four experts reviewed the three interfaces in stage 1. Stage 2 consisted of a small number of short interviews of potential customers designed to elicit typical uses for the software. These were used to develop scenarios and test tasks. Finally, stage 3 was a detailed participant-based evaluation of the interfaces. This focused on exploration of the issues identified by the experts and was structured around the scenarios and tasks derived from stage 2. Stages 1 and 3 are described here.

Each person carrying out the heuristic evaluation had experience of interface evaluation and a working knowledge of interface design. They familiarized themselves with a scenario describing the level of knowledge of real customers and their aims in using the product, together with a list of seven generic usability heuristics, then examined the software. They spent approximately one hour per interface and explored all functions, listing all usability issues discovered.

Participant testing involved a group of three males and three females aged between 25 and 35. Half were students and half were professionals; they had varying degrees of PC experience. With such a small sample, it was impossible to reflect the entire spectrum of the target population, but it was considered that these would provide a reasonable insight into any problems. After drawing up a test plan, scenarios and tasks were derived from background interview data and task analysis (see Chapter 11), supplemented by the results of the expert evaluation. Five main tasks were identified. Since the software was for home use, the tests were carried out in a home environment using equipment equivalent to that identified for the target population. Participants undertook the testing individually and were reassured that the focus was not on their skills but on any problems with the software. Written instructions emphasizing this and listing the five tasks were supplied, together with a scenario to set the scene. Each session lasted no more than 45 minutes to avoid fatigue.

Each participant started with simple tasks to gain familiarity with the interface. The main tasks consisted of selecting an image and performing a number of typical editing tasks. For example, participants were asked to select a specific image and edit it by rotating it the correct way round, switching to black and white, cropping the picture

→

and adjusting the brightness and contrast before saving the new image. The intention was to give an overview of the functionality and a chance to learn the more complicated tools. Parts 3 and 4 of the tests asked the participants to perform almost identical tasks to those already achieved. The aim here was to monitor the 'learnability' of the interface. The test was completed by accessing the slideshow option of each interface. Where possible, the participant was also asked to attempt to import images from the hard disk. No help except that available from the software was provided.

Each sub-task required the participant to rate the functions on a scale from 1 (easy) to 5 (difficult) before proceeding to the next. During the session, the evaluator noted participant behaviour and verbalizations. Participants were prompted to verbalize where necessary.

Finally, the participant undertook a short task based on the operation of a mobile phone – intended as an indicator of competence in operating a commonplace artefact – before completing a brief questionnaire. This collected details of experience of PCs and software packages.

Challenge 10.6

Design a simple one-page pro forma for a usability evaluation summary.

10.5 Evaluation: further issues

Of course, there are lots and lots of specifics associated with evaluation. Many are considered in the chapters on contexts. In this section we look at a number of particular issues.

Evaluation without being there

With the arrival of Internet connectivity, people can participate in evaluations without being physically present. If the application itself is Web-based, or can be installed remotely, instructions can be supplied so that users can run test tasks and fill in and return questionnaires in soft or hard copy. On-line questionnaires and crowd sourcing methods are appropriate here (see Chapter 7).

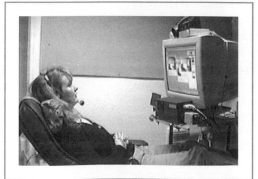

Figure 10.3 A participant being eye-tracked
(Source: Mullin *et al.* 2001, p 42. Courtesy of Jim Mullin)

Physical and physiological measures

Eye-movement tracking (or 'eye tracking') can show participants' changing focus on different areas of the screen. This can indicate which features of a user interface have attracted attention, and in which order, or capture larger-scale gaze patterns indicating how people move around the screen. Eye tracking is very popular with website designers as it can be used to highlight which parts of the page are most looked at, so-called 'hot spots', and which are missed altogether. Eye-tracking equipment is head-mounted or attached to computer monitors, as shown in Figure 10.3.

Eye-tracking software is readily available to provide maps of the screen. Some of it can also measure pupil dilation, which is taken as an indication of arousal. Your pupil dilates if you like what you see. Physiological techniques in evaluation rely on the fact that all our emotions – anxiety, pleasure, apprehension, delight, surprise and so on – generate physiological changes.

→ There is more about the role of emotion in interactive systems design in Chapter 22

The most common measures are of changes in heart rate, the rate of respiration, skin temperature, blood volume pulse and galvanic skin response (an indicator of the amount of perspiration). All are indicators of changes in the overall level of arousal, which in turn may be evidence of an emotional reaction. Sensors can be attached to the participant's body (commonly the fingertips) and linked to software which converts the results to numerical and graphical formats for analysis. But there are many unobtrusive methods too, such as pressure sensors in the steering wheel of a games interface, or sensors that measure if the participant is on the edge of their seat.

Which particular emotion is being evoked cannot be deduced from the level of arousal alone, but must be inferred from other data such as facial expression, posture or direct questioning. Another current application is in the assessment of the degree of presence – the sense of 'being there' evoked by virtual environments (see Figure 10.4).

Typically, startling events or threatening features are produced in the environment and arousal levels measured as people encounter them. Researchers at University College London and the University of North Carolina at Chapel Hill (Usoh *et al.*, 1999, 2000; Insko, 2001, 2003; Meehan, 2001) have conducted a series of experiments when measuring arousal as participants approach a 'virtual precipice'. In these circumstances changes in heart rate correlated most closely with self-reports of stress.

Figure 10.4 A 20-foot 'precipice' used in evaluating presence in virtual environments

(Source: Reprinted from *Being There: Concepts, Effects and Measurement of User Presence in Synthetic Environment*, Inkso, B.E., Measuring presence. Copyright 2003, with permission from IOS Press)

Evaluating presence

Designers of virtual reality – and some multimedia – applications are often concerned with the sense of presence, of being 'there' in the virtual environment rather than 'here' in the room where the technology is being used. A strong sense of presence is thought to be crucial for such applications as games, those designed to treat phobias, to allow people to 'visit' real places they may never see otherwise, or indeed for some workplace applications such as training to operate effectively under stress. This is a very current research topic, and there are no techniques that deal with all the issues satisfactorily. The difficulties include:

- The sense of presence is strongly entangled with individual dispositions, experiences and expectations. Of course, this is also the case with reactions to any interactive system, but presence is an extreme example of this problem.
- The concept of presence itself is ill-defined and the subject of much debate among researchers. Variants include the sense that the virtual environment is realistic, the extent to which the user is impervious to the outside world, the retrospective sense of having visited rather than viewed a location, and a number of others.
- Asking people about presence while they are experiencing the virtual environment tends to interfere with the experience itself. On the other hand, asking questions retrospectively inevitably fails to capture the experience as it is lived.

The measures used in evaluating presence adopt various strategies to avoid these problems, but none are wholly satisfactory. The various questionnaire measures, for example the questionnaire developed by NASA scientists Witmer and Singer (1998) or the range of instruments developed at University College and Goldsmiths College, London (Slater, 1999; Lessiter *et al.*, 2001), can be cross-referenced to measures which attempt to quantify how far a person is generally susceptible to being 'wrapped up' in experiences mediated by books, films, games and so on as well as through virtual reality. The Witmer and Singer Immersive Tendencies Questionnaire (Witmer and Singer, 1998) is the best known of such instruments. However, presence as measured by presence questionnaires is a slippery and ill-defined concept. In one experiment, questionnaire results showed that while many people did not feel wholly present in the virtual environment (a re-creation of an office), some of them did not feel wholly present in the real-world office either (Usoh *et al.*, 2000). Less structured attempts to capture verbal accounts of presence include having people write accounts of their experience, or inviting them to provide free-form comments in an interview. The results are then analysed for indications of a sense of presence. The difficulty here lies in defining what should be treated as such an indicator, and in the layers of indirection introduced by the relative verbal dexterity of the participant and the interpretation imposed by the analyst.

Other approaches to measuring presence attempt to avoid such layers of indirection by observing behaviour in the virtual environment or by direct physiological measures.

Challenge 10.7

What indicators of presence might one measure using physiological techniques? Are there any issues in interpreting the resulting data?

Evaluation at home

People at home are much less of a 'captive audience' for the evaluator than those at work. They are also likely to be more concerned about protecting their privacy and generally unwilling to spend their valuable leisure time in helping you with your usability evaluation. So it is important that data gathering techniques are interesting and stimulating for users, and make as little demand on time and effort as possible. This is very much a developing field and researchers continue to adapt existing approaches and develop new ones. Petersen *et al.* (2002), for example, were interested in the evolution over time of relationships with technology in the home. They used conventional interviews at the time the technology (a new television) was first installed, but followed this by having families act out scenarios using it. Diaries were also distributed as a data collection tool, but in this instance the non-completion rate was high, possibly because of the complexity of the diary pro forma and the incompatibility between a private diary and the social activity of television viewing.

→ Probes described in Chapter 7 are relevant here

An effective example of this in early evaluation is reported in Baillie *et al.* (2003) and Baillie and Benyon (2008). Here the investigator supplied users with Post-its to capture their thoughts about design concepts (Figure 10.5). An illustration of each different concept was left in the home in a location where it might be used, and users were encouraged to think about how they would use the device and any issues that might arise. These were noted on the Post-its, which were then stuck to the illustration and collected later.

Where the family is the focus of interest, techniques should be engaging for children as well as adults – not only does this help to ensure that all viewpoints are covered, but working with children is a good way of drawing parents into evaluation activities.

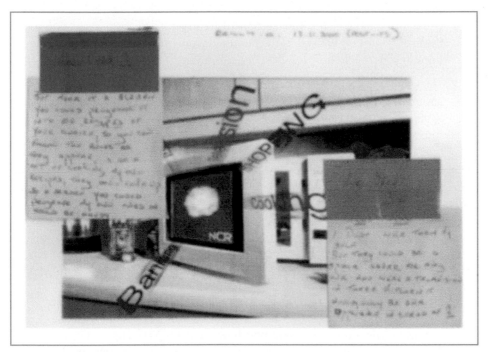

Figure 10.5 Post-it notes
(Source: David Benyon)

Challenge 10.8

Suggest some ways in which 6–9-year-olds could take part in evaluation activities situated in the home.

Summary and key points

This chapter has presented an overview of the key issues in evaluation. Designing the evaluation of an interactive system, product or service requires as much attention and effort as designing any other aspect of that system. Designers need to be aware of the possibilities and limitations of different approaches and, in addition to studying the theory, they need plenty of practical experience.

- Designers need to focus hard on what features of a system or product they want to evaluate.
- They need to think hard about the state that the system or product is in and hence whether they can evaluate those features.
- There are expert-based methods of evaluation.
- There are participant-based methods of evaluation.
- Designers need to design their evaluation to fit the particular needs of the contexts of use and the activities that people are engaged in.

Exercises

1 Using the list of heuristics from Section 10.2, carry out a heuristic evaluation of the features dealing with tables in your usual word processor and the phone book in your cellphone.

2 Think about the following evaluation. A call centre operator answers enquiries about insurance claims. This involves talking to customers on the phone while accessing their personal data and claim details from a database. You are responsible for the user testing of new database software to be used by the operators. What aspects of usability do you think it is important to evaluate, and how would you measure them?

    Now think about the same questions for an interactive multimedia website which is an on-line art gallery. The designers want to allow users to experience concrete and conceptual artworks presented in different media.

3 (More advanced) Identify any potential difficulties with the evaluation described in Box 10.2. What would you do differently?

4 (More advanced) You are responsible for planning the evaluation of an interactive toy for children. The toy is a small, furry, talking animal character whose behaviour changes over time as it 'learns' new skills and in response to how its owner treats it, for example how often it is picked up during a 24-hour period. The designers think it should take around a month for all the behaviours to develop. Children interact with the toy by speaking commands (it has voice recognition for 20 words), stroking its ears, picking it up, and pressing 'spots' on the animal's back which are, in effect, buttons triggering different actions. No instructions will be provided; children are intended to find out what the toy does by trial and error.

    Design an evaluation process for the toy, explaining the reasons behind your choices.

5 How do we know that the criteria we use for evaluation reflect what is important to users? Suggest some ways in which we can ground evaluation criteria in user wants and needs.

6 An organization with staff in geographically dispersed offices has introduced desktop video-conferencing with the aim of reducing resources spent on 'unnecessary' travel between offices. Working teams often involve people at different sites. Before the introduction of video-conferencing, travel was

regarded as rather a nuisance, although it did afford the opportunity to 'show one's face' at other sites and take care of other business involving people outside the immediate team. One month after the introduction of the technology, senior managers have asked for a 'comprehensive' evaluation of the system. Describe what techniques you would adopt, what data you would hope to gain from their use, and any problems you foresee with the evaluation.

7 Critically discuss the strengths and weaknesses of the 'standard' user evaluation techniques of task-based interviews and observation in settings beyond the workplace. What additional methods could be used in these domains?

 ## Further reading

Cairns, P. and Cox, A.L. (2008) *Research Methods for Human–Computer Interaction.* Cambridge University Press, Cambridge.

Cockton, G., Woolrych, A. and Lavery, D. (2012) Inspection-based evaluations. In Jacko, J.A. (ed.), *The Human–Computer Interaction Handbook: Fundamentals, Evolving Technologies and Emerging Applications,* **3rd edn.** CRC Press, Taylor and Francis, Boca Ratun, FL, pp. 1279–98.

Monk, A., Wright, P., Haber, J. and Davenport, L. (1993) *Improving Your Human–Computer Interface: a Practical Technique.* BCS, Practitioner Series, Prentice-Hall, New York and Hemel Hempstead. *This book includes a full description of cooperative usability evaluation. It may now be hard to purchase but should be available through libraries.*

Getting ahead

Doubleday, A., Ryan, M., Springett, M. and Sutcliffe, A. (1997) A comparison of usability techniques for evaluating design. *Proceedings of DIS '97 Conference*, Amsterdam, Netherlands. ACM Press, New York, pp. 101–10. *This compares the results of heuristic evaluation with user testing in the evaluation of an information retrieval interface. A good example of the continuing stream of research into the relative efficacy of different approaches to evaluation.*

Nielsen, J. (1993) *Usability Engineering.* Academic Press. New York. *Nielsen's classic exposition of his 'discount' approach. Highly practical, but as discussed in this chapter and in Chapter 19, later work has suggested that the results obtained can have some limitations.*

Robson, C. (1994) *Experiment, Design and Statistics in Psychology.* Penguin, London.

Willcocks, L. and Lester, S. (1998) *Beyond the IT Productivity Paradox: Assessment Issues.* Wiley, Chichester. *This provides a good overview on the evaluation of workplace information technologies and use from the information systems perspective.*

 ## Web links

The British HCI Group's website **www.usabilitynews.com** often carries current debates about usability evaluation.

The accompanying website has links to relevant websites. Go to **www.pearsoned.co.uk/benyon**

Comments on challenges

Challenge 10.1

The 'answer' to this, of course, depends on the material collected. But you will probably have found adverts appealing to aspirational needs and desires – status, style and so on – which standard usability techniques do not deal with particularly well.

Challenge 10.2

The control panel for our dishwasher is very simply designed. It has four programmes, each of which is listed and numbered on the panel with a brief explanatory label (e.g. 'rinse') and a rather less self-explanatory icon. The dial to set the programme has starting points labelled with the programme numbers. The design is learnable – even without the handbook it is clear what each programme does and how to select it. It is also effective – I can easily select the programme and the movement of the dial shows how far the cycle has progressed. It is accommodating to some extent in that I can interrupt the process to add more dishes, but fails (among other deficiencies here) to cope with the needs of partially sighted or blind users – something that could apparently be done fairly simply by adding tactile labels.

Challenge 10.3

Potential difficulties include over-defensiveness on the part of the designers and consequently lengthy explanations of design rationale and a confrontational atmosphere. It would be a good idea to hold a preliminary meeting to diffuse these feelings from the start. Also, asking the designers the walkthrough questions may help people to identify issues themselves rather than feeling under attack.

Challenge 10.4

It is likely that the three problems found in both evaluations are genuine, not merely induced by the testing procedures. You cannot really conclude very much about the remaining four, but should review the relevant parts of the design. The difficulties with long transactions are also probably genuine, and unlikely to have been highlighted by heuristics. In all these cases you should ideally test the redesigns with real representative users.

Challenge 10.5

Learnability – in terms of time taken to become familiar with functionality – can be less crucial, for example, when the application is intended for intensive, sustained long-term use. Here people expect to invest some effort in becoming acquainted with powerful functionality; also the overall learning time is relatively small compared with that spent using the software productively. Applications for professionals, such as computer-aided design, desktop publishing, scientific analysis software and the myriad of products intended for use by computer programmers, fall into this category. This doesn't mean that overall usability and good design cease to matter, but there will be more emphasis on issues such as fit to activity rather than superficial ease of learning.

Challenge 10.6

Points to consider here:

- A very short summary
- Structure (by topic, severity or some other ordering principle)
- A rating scale for severity
- Brief suggested solutions
- Links to supporting data
- Space for explanations where necessary.

Challenge 10.7

Changes in heart rate, breathing rate and skin conductance (among other things) will all indicate changes in arousal levels. The issues include teasing out the effects of the virtual environment from extraneous variables such as apprehension about the experiment itself, or something completely unrelated which the participant is thinking of.

Challenge 10.8

One technique which has been tried is to have the children draw themselves using the technology in question – perhaps as a strip cartoon for more complicated operations. Older children could add 'thinks' bubbles. Possibilities are limited only by your imagination.

Chapter 11
Task analysis

Contents

Aims

The notion of a 'task' has been central to work in human–computer interaction since the subject started. Undertaking a task analysis is a very useful technique – or rather set of techniques – for understanding people and how they carry out their work. Looking at the tasks that people do, or the tasks that they will have to do because of some redesigned system, is a necessary part of human-centred design. This chapter provides some philosophical background on what task analysis is and where it fits into interactive systems design. It then provides practical advice on doing different types of task analysis.

After studying this chapter you should be able to:

- Understand the difference between goals, tasks and actions
- Undertake a hierarchical task analysis
- Undertake a procedural cognitive task analysis
- Understand the importance of considering a structural view of a domain.

11.1 Goals, tasks and actions

Some authors consider 'task analysis' to encompass all manner of techniques (such as interviewing, observation, development of scenarios, etc.). We do not. We consider task analysis to be a specific view of interactive systems design that leads to specific techniques. This chapter looks more formally at the concept of task, how to undertake task analyses and what benefit designers might get from such analyses. In the final section we look at the importance of understanding a structural perspective of a domain.

The distinction between the key concepts in task analysis – goals, tasks and actions – may be identified as follows:

> *A task is a goal together with some ordered set of actions.*

The concept of task derives from a view of people, or other agents, interacting with technologies trying to achieve some change in an application domain. Taken together, the people and technology constitute what is sometimes called a 'work system', which is separate from the 'application domain'. Dowell and Long (1998) emphasize that the application domain (or simply 'domain') is an abstraction of the real world, i.e. some abstract representation (such as a database, a website or an iPhone app). Importantly, task analysis is concerned with some aspects of the performance of a work system with respect to a domain. This performance may be the amount of effort to learn a system, to reach a certain level of competence with a system, the time taken to perform certain tasks, and so on. This conceptualization is shown in Figure 11.1.

← We called the work system the 'people–technology' system in Chapter 3

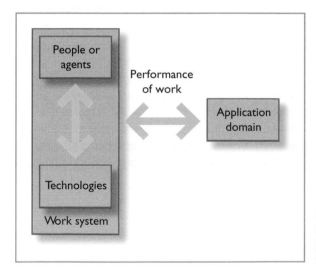

Figure 11.1 Task analysis is concerned with the performance of work by a work system

Diaper's full definition of task analysis (Diaper, 2004) is:

Work is achieved by the work system making changes to the application domain. The application domain is that part of the assumed real world that is relevant to the functioning of the work system. A work system in HCI consists of one or more human and computer components and usually many other sorts of thing as well. Tasks are the means by which the work system changes the application domain. Goals are desired future states of the application domain that the work system should achieve by the tasks it carries out. The work system's performance is deemed satisfactory as long as it continues to achieve its goals in the application domain. Task analysis is the study of how work is achieved by tasks.

This view of the separation of work system and domain is not shared by everyone but this definition does result in some useful task analysis techniques for systems analysis and design. Other definitions are as follows.

Goals

A goal is a state of the application domain that a work system wishes to achieve. Goals are specified at particular levels of abstraction.

This definition allows for artificial entities such as technologies or agents or some combination to have goals. For example, we might be studying the organizational goals of a company, or the behaviour of a software system in terms of its goals. It is not just people who have goals; the work system as a whole may have goals. For this reason the term 'agent' is often used to encompass both people and software systems that are actively and autonomously trying to achieve some state of the application domain. The term 'technology' is used to encompass physical devices, information artefacts, software systems and other methods and procedures.

For example, an agent might have a goal such as to write a letter, to record a programme on TV, or to find the strongest mobile phone signal. The assumption is that the domain is in one state now – no letter written, the TV programme not recorded, the signal not confirmed as the strongest – and the agent has to undertake some activities, i.e. some tasks, in order to get it into the required state.

Usually a goal can be achieved in a variety of different ways. So the first thing the agent has to decide is which technology to use to achieve the goal. For recording a TV programme, for example, an agent could use the following technologies:

← States and transitions were introduced in Chapter 9

- Ask a friend to record it.
- Press 'Rec' on the PVR (personal video recorder).
- Set the timer using a manual setting.
- Set the timer using an on-screen TV guide.

Of course, the agent needs to know quite a lot about each of these technologies and the pros and cons of each and will select different ones at different times depending on the circumstances. The agent may misunderstand some of the technologies and so may not take the optimum course of action. The selection of a technology will depend on the agent's knowledge of the functions, structure and purpose of particular technologies; and this knowledge may be quite erroneous. Once a technology has been decided upon, the tasks can now be defined.

Tasks and actions

A task is a structured set of activities required, used, or believed to be necessary by an agent to achieve a goal using a particular technology. A task will often consist of sub-tasks where a subtask is a task at a more detailed level of abstraction. The structure of an activity may include selecting between alternative actions, performing some actions a number of times and sequencing of actions.

The task is broken down into more and more detailed levels of description until it is defined in terms of actions. Actions are 'simple tasks'. Whereas a task might include some structure such as doing things in a particular sequence, making decisions as to alternative things to do (selection) and doing things several times (iteration), an action does not. This structure is often called a plan or method.

An action is a task that has no problem solving associated with it and which does not include any control structure. Actions and tasks will be different for different people.

For example, in the case of recording a TV programme, if the programme is just about to come on it might be best to press 'Rec' on the PVR which would start recording immediately. This brings its own problems as the PVR might be tuned to the wrong channel depending on the particular connections between the devices. Alternatively, the agent could set the timer manually. Using an on-screen menu system is more laborious as the agent has to turn the TV on to use the on-screen menu. If the agent is not very well informed about the operation of the system, the agent may fiddle around selecting the PVR channel, finally getting to the on-screen programming and so on. The agent may do things that are strictly unnecessary because the agent had a poor conceptualization, their mental model of the device.

> ### Challenge 11.1
>
> *Write down the task structure for manually recording a programme using a PVR. Think about the decisions that an agent would need in order to undertake this task and about the differences between tasks and actions for different agents with different knowledge. Discuss with a friend or colleague.*

Task analysis methods can be divided into two broad categories: those concerned with the logic of the task – the sequence of steps that need to be undertaken by a work system to achieve a goal – and those concerned with cognitive aspects. Cognitive task analysis is concerned with understanding what cognitive processes the work system will have to undertake in order to achieve a goal. Cognition is concerned with thinking, solving problems, learning, memory, and their mental models.

→ Cognition is discussed in Chapter 23

People also have knowledge of how to do things in general and how to do things with specific technologies. People make use of things in the environment (such as displays on a computer screen or notes on a piece of paper) as part of the cognitive processes. Cognitive task analysis has a long-established tradition in human–computer interaction, with a large number of methods coming from a variety of slightly different backgrounds. Most of the theoretical treatments of cognition and action presented in Chapter 23 have resulted in some technique applied to the design or evaluation of interactive systems.

In terms of the goals, tasks and actions, we need to consider both the goal–task mapping (knowing what to do to achieve some goal) and the task–action mapping (knowing how to do it). There is also a need to consider the goal formation stage – knowing that you can do something in the first place. In addition to this procedural knowledge, people have structural knowledge. Structural knowledge concerns knowing about concepts in a domain and knowing how those concepts are related. This sort of knowledge is particularly useful when things go wrong, when understanding the relationships between the components in a system will help with troubleshooting.

11.2 Task analysis and systems design

There are many views on, and methods for, task analysis and task design. As noted previously, some authors equate task analysis with the whole of systems development. Others equate methods of task analysis with methods of requirements generation and evaluation. Yet others distinguish task analysis (understanding existing tasks) from task design (envisioning future tasks). Diaper and Stanton (2004a) provide a comprehensive overview of 30 different views. One thing that people agree upon is that a task analysis will result in a task model, though, as we will see, these models can take very different forms.

Balbo *et al.* (2004) emphasize the expressive power of different methods in their taxonomy of task analysis techniques. For example, they focus on whether a technique captures optionality (is a task mandatory or optional in pursuing a goal?), parallelism (can tasks be performed in parallel?) or non-standard actions such as error handling or automatic feedback. They also classify methods along the following axes:

- *The goal of using the notation.* By this they mean the stage in the development life cycle; is it best for understanding, design, envisionment or evaluation?
- *Its usability for communication.* Some task analysis techniques can be very hard to read and understand, particularly those that are based on a grammar rather than graphical notation.
- *Its usability for modelling tasks.* Task analysis methods have to fit into the software development process and be used and understood by software engineers. It has long been a problem that software engineers do not have ready access to a good task analysis technique. Some methods are intended to assist in the automatic generation of systems (see Further thoughts box).
- *The adaptability of a task analysis technique to new types of system, new aims or new requirements.* To what extent is the technique extensible to other purposes? (e.g. a task analysis technique aimed specifically at website design may not be very adaptable).

Diaper and Stanton (2004b) make an important observation regarding many task analysis techniques, namely that they are usually mono-teleological. That is to say, they assume that the agent or work system has a single purpose which gives rise to its goal. Teleology is the study of purposes, causes and reasons, a level of description of activities that is missing from most task analysis approaches. In reality, of course, people and work systems may be pursuing multiple goals simultaneously.

Task analysis is an important part of systems development, but it is a term that encompasses a number of different views. It is undertaken at different times during systems development for different purposes.

FURTHER THOUGHTS

Model-based user interface design

One particular branch of task analysis concerns the formal representation of systems so that the whole system, or part of it, can be automatically generated by a computer system from the specification or model. Work on model-based design has continued, without much success, in several areas. In user interface design several systems have been tried (see Abed *et al.*, 2004, for a review) that represent systems at the domain level, an abstract level of description and the physical level of different styles of widget such as scroll bars, windows, etc. One aim of the model-based approaches is to enable different versions of a system to be automatically generated from the same underlying model. For example, by applying different physical models an interface for a smartphone, a computer and a tablet could be generated from the same abstract and domain models. Stephanidis (2001) uses this approach to generate different interfaces for people with varying levels of ability.

Model-based approaches have also been tried in software engineering for many years (e.g. Benyon and Skidmore, 1988), again with limited success. The screen-design systems that automate the generation at the physical layer (such as Delphi, Borland and VB) have been highly successful, but automatically linking this to an abstract level of description proves difficult.

- During the understanding process, for example, the task analysis should aim to be as independent as possible from the device (or technology), for the aim is to understand the essential nature of the work in order to inform new designs.
- During the design and evaluation of future tasks, task analysis focuses on the achievement of work using a particular technology (i.e. a particular design) and hence is device-dependent.

During understanding, task analysis is concerned with the practice of work, with the current allocation of function between people and technologies, with existing problems and with opportunities for improvement. During design and evaluation, task analysis is concerned with the cognition demanded by a particular design, the logic of a possible design and the future distribution of tasks and actions between people and technologies.

Task analysis is in many ways similar to scenario-based design, for tasks are just scenarios in which the context and other details have been stripped away. Task analysis is best applied to one or two key activities in a domain. Task analysis is not quick or cheap to do, so it should be used where there is likely to be the best pay-off. In an e-commerce application, for example, it would be best to do a task analysis on the buying-and-paying-for-an-item task. In designing the interface for a mobile phone, key tasks would be making a call, answering a call, calling a person who is in the address book and finding your own phone number.

← Scenario-based design is described in Chapter 3

In the rest of this chapter we look at two analysis techniques. The first is based on **hierarchical task analysis (HTA)** and is concerned with the logic of a task. The second, based on the **goals, operators, methods, selection rules (GOMS)** method, is concerned with a cognitive analysis of tasks, focusing on the procedural knowledge needed to achieve a goal. This is sometimes called 'how to do it' knowledge. Finally we look at understanding structural knowledge, sometimes called 'what it is' knowledge.

11.3 Hierarchical task analysis

Hierarchical task analysis (HTA) is a graphical representation of a task structure based on a structure chart notation. Structure charts represent a sequence of tasks, subtasks and actions as a hierarchy and include notational conventions to show whether an action can be repeated a number of times (iteration) and the execution of alternative actions (selection). Sequence is usually shown by ordering the tasks, subtasks and actions from left to right. Annotations can be included to indicate *plans*. These are structured paths through the hierarchy to achieve particular goals. For example, making a call using a mobile phone has two main routes through the hierarchy of tasks and subtasks. If the person's number is in the phone's address book then the caller has to find the number and press 'call'. If it is not, the caller has to type the number in and press 'call'.

HTA was developed during the 1960s and has appeared in a variety of guises since then. Stanton (2003) gives a detailed account. HTA uses a structured diagram representation, showing the various tasks and actions in boxes and using levels to show the hierarchy. Figure 11.2 shows an example for using an ATM (cash machine).

There are a number of notational conventions that can be used to capture key features of the tasks. We recommend using an asterisk in the box to show that an action may be repeated a number of times (iteration) and a small 'o' to show optionality. The plans are used to highlight sequencing. Others (e.g. Stanton, 2003) like to show decision points as parts of the plans.

HTA is not easy. The analyst must spend time getting the description of the tasks and subtasks right so that they can be represented hierarchically. Like most things in

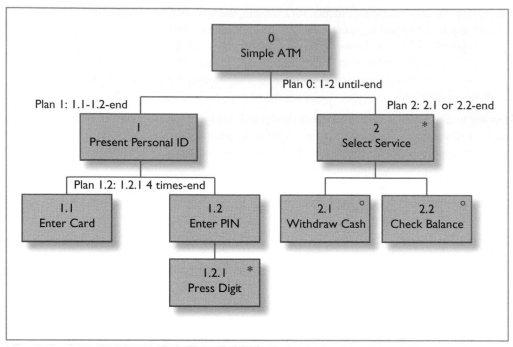

Figure 11.2 Hierarchical task model for a portion of an ATM

interactive systems design, undertaking a hierarchical task analysis is highly iterative and you will not get it right first time. The analyst should return to the task list and try to redefine the tasks so that they can be represented hierarchically.

HTA appears in many different methods for interactive systems design. For example, Stanton (2003) uses it as part of his method for error identification. He develops an HTA model of a system and then works through the model looking for possible error situations. At the action level (bottom level of an HTA), people might make a slip such as pressing the wrong button. What happens if they do this? At the task and subtask levels the analyst can consider what type of task it is and hence what types of error might occur.

Annett (2004) provides a step-by-step guide to how to do an HTA:

➔ Chapter 21 discusses human error and action slips

1 Decide on the purpose of the analysis. This is typically to help with systems design or to design training materials.
2 Define the task goals.
3 Data acquisition. How are you going to collect data? Observation, getting people to use a prototype, etc.
4 Acquire data and draft a hierarchical diagram.
5 Recheck validity of decomposition with stakeholders.
6 Identify significant operations and stop when the effects of failure are no longer significant.
7 Generate and test hypotheses concerning factors affecting learning and performance.

Lim and Long (1994) use HTA slightly differently in their HCI development method, called MUSE (Method for Usability Engineering). They illustrate their approach using a 'Simple ATM' example as shown in Figure 11.2. This shows that the 'Simple ATM' consists of two subtasks that are completed in sequence: Present Personal ID and Select Service. Present Personal ID consists of two further subtasks: Enter Card and Enter PIN. In its turn, Enter PIN consists of a number of iterations of the Press Digit action. Select Service consists of *either* Withdraw Cash *or* Check Balance.

11.4 GOMS: a cognitive model of procedural knowledge

GOMS is the most famous and long-lasting of a large number of cognitive task analysis methods (Kieras, 2012). GOMS focuses on the cognitive processes required to achieve a goal using a particular device. The aim is to describe tasks in terms of the following:

- *Goals*. What are people trying to do using some system (e.g. make a call using a cell phone.)
- *Operators*. These are the actions that the system allows people to perform, such as clicking on menus, scrolling through lists, pressing buttons and so on.
- *Methods*. These are sequences of subtasks and operators. Subtasks are described at a more abstract level than operators – things such as 'select name from address book' or 'enter phone number'.
- *Selection rules*. These are the rules that people use to choose between methods of achieving the same subtask (if there are options). For example, to select a name from an address book a person could scroll through the names or type in the first letter and jump to a part of the address book.

There are many different 'flavours' of GOMS, focusing on different aspects of a task, using different notations, using different constructs. In this book we do not claim to teach GOMS as a method, but just to alert readers to its existence and provide some illustrative examples. Kieras (2004) provides his version and John (2003) provides hers.

Looking at the constructs in GOMS, it is clear that the method is applicable only if people know what they are going to do. John (2003) emphasizes that selection rules are 'well-learned' sequences of sub-goals and operators. GOMS is not a suitable analytical method where people are problem-solving. Also it is mainly applicable to systems being used by a single person where it can give accurate estimates of performance and help designers think about different designs.

John (2003) gives the example of a GOMS analysis in project Ernestine. She and co-worker Wayne Gray constructed 36 detailed GOMS models for telephone operators using their current workstation and for them using a new proposed workstation. The tasks such as answer call, initiate call and so on are broken down into the detailed operations that are required, such as enter command, read screen and so on. Times for these operations are then allocated and hence the overall time for the task can be calculated.

The new workstation had a different keyboard and screen layout, different keying procedures and system response time. The company believed the new workstation would be more effective than the old. However, the results of the modelling exercise predicted that the new workstation would be on average 0.63 second slower than the old. In financial terms this cost an additional $2m a year. Later, field trials were undertaken which confirmed the predicted results.

John (2003) provides much more detail on this story, but perhaps the most important thing is that the modelling effort took two person-months and the field trial took 18 months and involved scores of people. A good model can be effective in saving money. A portion of the model is shown in Figure 11.3.

Undertaking a GOMS analysis shares with HTA the need to describe, organize and structure tasks, subtasks and actions hierarchically. As we have seen, this is not always easy to do. However, once a task list has been formulated, working through the model is quite straightforward. Times can be associated with the various cognitive and physical actions and hence one can derive the sort of predictions discussed by John (2003).

```
GOMS goal hierarchy                    Observed behavior

goal: handle-calls
.   goal: handle-call
.   .   goal: initiate-call
.   .   .   goal: receive-information
.   .   .   .   listen-for-beep               Workstation: Beep
.   .   .   .   read-screen(2)                Workstation: Displays source information
.   .   .   goal: request-information
.   .   .   .   greet-customer                TAO: 'New England Telephone, may I help you?'
.   .   goal: enter-who-pays
.   .   .   goal: receive-information
.   .   .   .   listen-to-customer            Customer: Operator, bill this to 412-555-1212-1234
.   .   .   goal: enter-information
.   .   .   .   enter-command                 TAO: hit F1 key
.   .   .   .   enter-calling-card-number     TAO: hit 14 numeric keys
.   .   goal: enter-billing-rate
.   .   .   goal: receive-information
.   .   .   .   read-screen(1)                Workstation: previously displayed source information
.   .   .   goal: enter-information
.   .   .   .   enter-command                 TAO: hit F2 key
.   .   goal: complete-call
.   .   .   goal: request-information
.   .   .   .   enter-command                 TAO: hit F3 key
.   .   .   goal: receive-information
.   .   .   .   read-screen(3)                Workstation: displays credit-card authorization
.   .   .   goal: release-workstation
.   .   .   .   thank-customer                TAO: 'Thank-you'
.   .   .   .   enter-command                 TAO: hit F4 key
```

Figure 11.3 GOMS analysis
(Source: After John, 2003, p. 89, part of Figure 4.9)

Challenge 11.2

Write a GOMS-type description for the simple ATM (Figure 11.2).

11.5 Structural knowledge

Task analysis is about procedures. But before a person sets about some procedure they need to know what types of things can be accomplished in a domain. For example, if I am using a drawing package I need to know that there is a facility for changing the thickness of a line, say, before I set about working out how to do it. I need some conception of what is possible, or what is likely. So in this section, instead of focusing on the steps that people have to go through to achieve a goal (hence looking at a procedural representation), we can look at the structural knowledge that people have and how an analysis of this can help in designing better systems.

← Chapter 2 discusses mental models

Payne (2012) shows how the concept of a 'mental model' can be used to analyse tasks. He proposes that people need to keep in mind two mental spaces and the relationships between them. A **goal space** describes the state of the domain that the person is seeking to achieve. The **device space** describes how the technology represents the goal space. An analysis of the different representations used can highlight where people have difficulties. If the device space employs concepts that are very different from those that the person uses in the goal space, then translating between them, and explaining why things happen or why they do not, is made more difficult. A good example of this is the history mechanism on Web browsers. Different browsers interpret the history in different ways and some wipe out visits to the same site. If a person tried to retrace their steps through a Web space, this will not be the same as the steps stored in a history (Won *et al.*, 2009).

Payne (2012) also discusses the concept of a 'mental map', which is analogous to a real map of some environment and can be used to undertake tasks. He discusses how an analysis of mental models can be useful in highlighting differences between people's views of a system. In one piece of empirical work he looked at different mental models of an ATM and found several different accounts of where information such as the credit limit resided.

→ Chapter 25 discusses mental maps

Green and Benyon (1996) describe a method called ERMIA (entity–relationship modelling of information artefacts) that enables such discrepancies to be revealed. ERMIA models structural knowledge and so can be used to represent the concepts that people have in their minds. Relationships between the entities are annotated with '1' or 'm', indicating whether an entity instance is associated with one or many instances of the other entity. Figure 11.4 shows the different beliefs that two subjects had about ATMs in a study of mental models undertaken by Payne (1991).

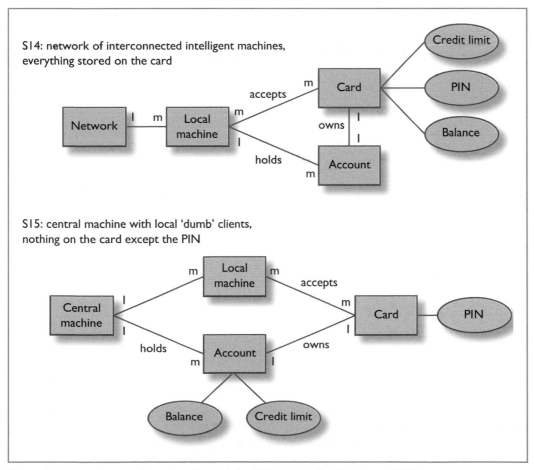

Figure 11.4 Comparison of two mental models of ATMs described by Payne (1991)
(Source: After Green and Benyon, 1996)

ERMIA uses an adaptation of entity–relationship modelling to describe structures. Entities are represented as boxes, relationships by lines, and attributes (the characteristics of entities) by circles. We introduced E–R modelling in Chapter 9 alongside object modelling, which is broadly similar.

In Figure 11.5 we can see a typical menu interface. An important part of this type of analysis is that it helps to expose differences between the designer's model, the system image and the 'user's' model. What are the main concepts at the interface?

← The designer's model and system image are presented in Chapter 3

Menu systems have two main concepts (entities). There are the various menu headings, such as File, Edit and Arrange, and there are the various items that are found under the headings, such as Save, Open, Cut and Paste. More interestingly, there is a relationship between the two kinds of entity. Can we imagine an interface that contains a menu item without a menu heading? No, because there would be no way to get at it. You have to access menu items through a menu header; every item must be associated with a heading. On the other hand, we can imagine a menu that contained no items, particularly while the software is being developed.

This, then, is the basis of ERMIA modelling – looking for entities and relationships and representing them as diagrams (see Figure 11.6). Benyon *et al.* (1999) provide a practical guide to developing ERMIA models, and Green and Benyon (1996) provide the background and some illustrations. A key feature of ERMIA is that we use the same notation to represent the conceptual aspects of a domain and the perceptual aspects. The conceptual aspects concern what people think the structure is and what the designer thinks the concepts are. The perceptual aspects concern how the structure is represented perceptually. In the case of menus we have the concepts of menu header and menu item and we represent these perceptually by the bold typeface and position on a menu bar and by the drop-down list of items. A different perceptual representation is to represent the menu using a toolbar.

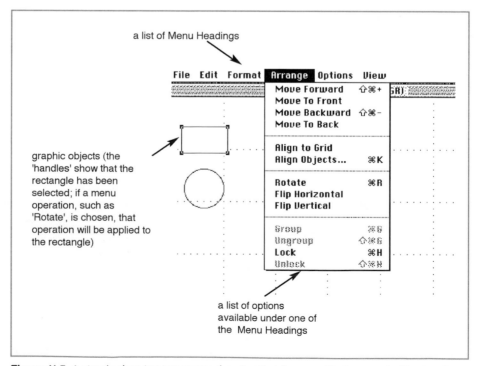

Figure 11.5 A simple drawing program, showing the document being created (a drawing, currently consisting of a rectangle and a circle) and the interface to the application

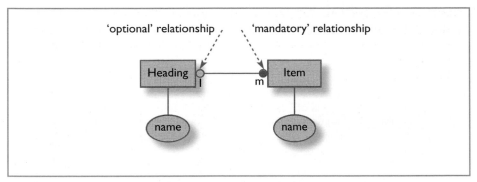

Figure 11.6 ERMIA structure of a menu system containing headers and items. The relationship is between reading and item is 1:m (that is, each can refer to many items, but an item can be associated with only one heading). For items, the relationship is mandatory (that is, every item must have a heading), but a heading can exist with no associated items

Returning to the relationships between menu headers and menu items, each menu heading can list many items, while each item is normally found under only one heading – in other words, the relationship of heading to item is one to many (written 1:m).

Is it strictly true that the relationship between menu items and menu headers is 1:m? Not quite; by being forced to consider the question precisely, we have been alerted to the fact that different pieces of software are based on differing interpretations of the interface guidelines. There is actually nothing to prevent the same menu item being listed under more than one heading. So an item like 'Format' might be found under a Text heading and also under the Tools heading; the true relationship between heading and item is therefore many to many, or m:m as it is written.

Many-to-many relationships are inherently complex and can always be simplified by replacing the relationship with a new entity that has a many-to-one relationship with each of the original entities. This is a surprisingly powerful analytical tool as it forces the designer to consider concepts that would otherwise remain hidden.

Look again at the top diagram in Figure 11.4 and consider the m:m relationship between local machine and card. What is this relationship and does it help us understand anything? The answer is that the relationship represents a transaction: a usage of a local machine by a card. There is nothing particularly interesting in this except perhaps that it means that the local machine will not store long-term details of the card but just deals with transaction details.

ERMIA represents both physical and conceptual aspects of interfaces, which enables comparisons to be made and evaluations to be carried out. Like GOMS and HTA, this enables the analyst to undertake model-based evaluation (see Further thoughts). Because ERMIA presents a clear view of the different models, it can be used as part of the process of reasoning about the models. If we have a designer's model that the designer wishes to reveal, he or she can look at the model of the interface and see to what extent the 'intended' model shows up. Similarly, one can gather different user views, in the manner of Payne's work (1991), and compare them to the designer's view, making the models and their possible differences explicit through ERMIA.

It has to be said that ERMIA modelling has not been taken up by interaction designers, probably because the effort required to learn and understand it is not repaid by the insight it provides. Green has continued to work on other ways of bringing this type of knowledge to HCI through the 'cognitive dimensions' framework (Blackwell and Green, 2003) and the CASSM framework (Blandford *et al.*, 2008).

FURTHER THOUGHTS

Model-based evaluation

Model-based evaluation looks at a model of some human–computer interaction. It can be used either with an existing interface or with an envisaged design. It is particularly useful early in the design process when designs are not advanced enough to be used by real users or when testing with real users is uneconomic or otherwise infeasible. The process involves the designer working through a model of a design, looking for potential problems or areas which might prove difficult. ERMIA can be used like this and GOMS was used in this way in Section 11.4.

ERMIA models can be used to explore how people have to navigate through various information structures in order to retrieve specific pieces of information and even to estimate the number of steps that people will need to take.

Challenge 11.3

Draw an ERMIA model for the World Wide Web. List the major entities that the Web has and begin to sketch the relationships. Spend at least 10 minutes on this before looking at our solution.

11.6 Cognitive work analysis

Cognitive work analysis (CWA) has evolved from the work of Jens Rasmussen and his colleagues (Rasmussen, 1986, 1990; Vicente and Rasmussen, 1992), originally working at the Risø National Laboratory in Denmark. Originally formulated to help in the design of systems concerned with the domain of process control, where the emphasis is on controlling the physical system behind the human–computer interface, it provides a different and powerful view on the design of interactive systems. CWA has been used in the analysis of complex real-time, mission-critical work environments, e.g. power plant control rooms, aircraft cockpits and so on.

The approach is also known as 'the Risø genotype' (Vicente, 1999) and relates closely to ecological interface design (Vicente and Rasmussen, 1992). Flach (1995) provides a number of perspectives on the issues and includes chapters by others originating from the Risø National Laboratory, including Vicente, Rasmussen and Pejtersen. One principle underlying CWA is that when designing computer systems or any other 'cognitive artefact' we are developing a complete work system, which means that the system includes people and artefacts. Seeing the whole as a work system enables designers to recognize that this system is more than the sum of its parts: it has emergent properties.

Another key principle of CWA is that it takes an ecological approach to design. Taking an ecological approach recognizes that people 'pick up' information directly from the objects in the world and their interaction with them, rather than having to consciously process some symbolic representation. In CWA, there is much discussion over the similarities between the ecological psychology of Gibson (1986) and designing systems that afford certain activities. The emphasis is on taking a user-dependent view of the analysis and design, recognizing the skills and knowledge that the user will have.

In the domain in which CWA was formulated, process control, it is vital that the operator has a correct view of the operation and status of the plant and that he or she can correctly identify any component that is malfunctioning. A key feature of the approach is to understand the domain-oriented constraints that affect people's behaviours and to design the environment so that the system easily reveals the state it is in and how that state relates to its purpose. CWA provides a structural representation of a domain.

CWA is quite complex and comprises a set of techniques and models. CWA techniques include such things as task analysis (including sequencing and frequency) and workload analysis (flow of work, identification of bottlenecks).

In short, there is a strong emphasis on work analysis and job design.

Modelling in CWA is made up from six different kinds of modelling, each of which breaks down into further levels. For example, a work domain analysis has five further levels of abstraction, describing

- The functional purpose of the system
- The priorities or values of the system
- The functions to be carried out by the system
- The physical functionality of the system
- The physical objects and devices.

The abstraction hierarchy

CWA describes a system, subsystem or component at five levels of abstraction. At the top level is the system's purpose: the analysis takes an intentional stance. Taking the design stance, CWA distinguishes between the abstract function and the generalized function of the system. The abstract function concerns the capabilities that it must have in order to achieve its purpose, and the generalized function describes the links between the physical characteristics and that abstract function. At the physical level of description CWA distinguishes the physical function from the physical form of the system.

→ See also the discussion of the domain model in Section 17.3

For example, a car's purpose is to transport people along a road. Therefore it must have the abstract functions of some form of power, some way of accommodating people and some form of movement. These abstract functions may be provided by the generalized functions of a petrol engine, some seats and some wheels with pneumatic tyres. Physically the engine might be realized as an eight-cylinder fuel-injected engine, the seats are of a size to accommodate people and the tyres have an ability to take the weight of the car and its passengers. The physical forms of these functions are the features that distinguish one type of car from another and concern the different arrangements of the engine components, the colour and material of the seats and the characteristics of the tyres.

A work domain analysis describes the whole system in these terms and describes each of the subsystems, components and units in these terms. For example, in describing the car, we could describe each of the engine's subsystems (fuel system, ignition system, etc.), its components (the petrol tank, feed tubes, injector mechanism, etc.) and the basic units that make up the components. At each level of the hierarchy the connection going up the hierarchy indicates why some system or component exists, whereas the relationship looking down the hierarchy indicates how something is achieved. The chain of 'hows' describes the means by which something happens and the chain of 'whys' describes the reasons for the design – the ends or teleological analysis. Hence the whole physical functioning of the domain is connected with its purpose.

So, the car can transport people because it has an engine, which is there to provide the power. The engine needs a fuel system and an ignition system because the fuel system and the ignition system provide power. This discussion of means and ends can continue all the way down to an observer looking under the car bonnet, saying 'that pipe takes the fuel from the fuel tank to the fuel injection system but because it is broken this car has no power so it cannot transport us until it is fixed'.

CWA in action

Benda and Sanderson (1999) used the first two levels of modelling to investigate the impact of a new technology and working practice. Their case study concerned an automated anaesthesia record-keeping system. They undertook a work domain analysis and an activity analysis in work domain terms.

For the work domain analysis:

- The output was the relationships between purpose, functions and objects.
- Changes representable at this level were changes to the functional structure of this domain.

For the activity analysis in work domain terms:

- The output was the coordination of workflow.
- Changes representable at this level were changes to procedure and coordination.

Based on these analyses, Benda and Sanderson successfully predicted that the introduction of the automated anaesthesia record-keeping system would take longer to use and would place additional constraints on the medical team.

Summary and key points

Task analysis is a key technique in interactive system design. The focus may be on the logical structure of tasks, or the cognitive demands made by tasks procedurally or structurally. Task analysis encompasses task design and it is here that it is probably most useful, as an analysis of a future design is undertaken to reveal difficulties. Task models can also be used for model-based evaluations.

- Task analysis fits very closely with requirements generation and evaluation methods.
- Task analysis focuses on goals, tasks and actions.
- Task analysis is concerned with the logic, cognition or purpose of tasks.
- A structural analysis of a domain and worksystem looks at the components of a system and how the components are related to one another.

Exercises

1 Undertake an HTA-style analysis for phoning a friend of yours whose number you have in the phone's address book. Of course the actual actions will be different for different phones. If you can, compare your solution to someone else's. Or try it with two different phones.

2 Now translate the HTA into a GOMS analysis. What different insights into the task does this give you?

Further reading

Annett, J. (2004) Hierarchical task analysis. In Diaper, D. and Stanton, N. (eds), *The Handbook of Task Analysis for Human–Computer Interaction*. Lawrence Erlbaum Associates, Mahwah, NJ.

Green, T.R.G. and Benyon, D.R. (1996) The skull beneath the skin: entity–relationship modelling of information artefacts. *International Journal of Human–Computer Studies*, 44(6), 801–28.

John, B. (2003) **Information processing and skilled behaviour. In** Carroll, J.M. (ed.), *HCI Models, Theories and Frameworks.* Morgan Kaufmann, San Francisco, CA. *This provides an excellent discussion of GOMS.*

Getting ahead

Carroll, J.M. (ed.) (2003) *HCI Models, Theories and Frameworks.* Morgan Kaufmann, San Francisco, CA. *This is an excellent introduction to many of the key task analysis methods and includes a chapter by Steve Payne, 'Users' mental models: the very ideas', a good chapter on cognitive work analysis by Penelope Sanderson, and the chapter by Bonnie John on GOMS.*

Diaper, D. and Stanton, N. (eds) (2004) *The Handbook of Task Analysis for Human–Computer Interaction.* Lawrence Erlbaum Associates, Mahwah, NJ. *A very comprehensive coverage of task analysis with chapters from all the major writers on the subject. There is a good introductory chapter by Diaper and two good concluding chapters by the editors.*

 **Web links**

The website for cognitive dimensions work: **www.cl.cam.ac.uk/~afb21/CognitiveDimensions**

The accompanying website has links to relevant websites. Go to
www.pearsoned.co.uk/benyon

Comments on challenges

Challenge 11.1

The overall goal of this activity is to have the PVR record a TV programme. This will involve the following tasks: (1) making sure the PVR is ready to record, (2) programming the right TV channel, (3) programming the right time to start and stop the recording, and (4) setting the PVR to automatically record. Task 1 will involve the following subtasks: (1.1) finding the right remote control for the PVR, (1.2) ensuring the TV is using the PVR, and (1.3) selecting the appropriate channel. Task 1.1 will involve all manner of considerations such as whether the remote is down the back of the sofa, how many other remote controls are on the coffee table and how long ago you last recorded a programme. For someone familiar with the household this might be a simple action, but for someone unfamiliar with the whole set-up, it can be a major task.

Challenge 11.2

GOMS goal hierarchy	Observed behaviour
Goal: present personal ID	
Goal: insert card	
Goal: locate slot	Card inserted
	Screen displays 'enter PIN'
Goal: enter PIN	
Recall number	
Locate number on keypad	Press key
	Beep +*
Repeat 4 times	

Challenge 11.3

The major entities you should have thought of are Web pages and links. Then there are websites. There are many other things on the Web; files are one type of thing, or you may have thought of different types of file such as PDF files, Word files, GIFs, JPEGs and so on. Overall, though, the Web has quite a simple structure, at least to start with. A website has many pages, but a page belongs to just one site. A page has many links, but a link relates to just one page. This is summarized in Figure 11.7.

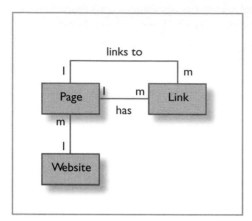

Figure 11.7

As soon as we have this basic structure we start questioning it. What about 'mirror' sites? A link can point to a whole website, so we should include that in our model. How are we defining a page? Or a site? This will affect how we model things. What about within-page links? And so on.

Chapter 12
Visual interface design

Contents

Aims

The design of the interface that mediates the interaction of people with devices is a crucial characteristic of the overall interaction design. This is often referred to as the user interface (UI) and it consists of everything in the system that people come into contact with, whether that is physically, perceptually or conceptually. In this chapter we discuss the issues of interface design focusing on the visual aspects of the design. In the next chapter we focus on issues of design when multiple modalities are involved in an interface.

After studying this chapter you should be able to:

● Understand different types of interaction, command languages and graphical user interfaces (GUIs)
● Understand and apply interface design guidelines
● Understand the issues of information presentation and visualization.

← We first encountered the interface in Chapter 2

12.1 Introduction

The design of the interface that mediates the interaction of people with devices is a crucial characteristic of the overall interaction design. This is often referred to as the user interface (UI) and it consists of everything in the system that people come into contact with, whether that is physically, perceptually or conceptually.

Physically people interact with systems in many different ways, such as by pressing buttons, touching a screen, moving a mouse over a table so that it moves a cursor over the screen, clicking a mouse button, rolling their thumb over a scroll wheel. We also interact physically through other senses, notably sound and touch, but we defer a discussion of these modalities until the next chapter.

Perceptually people interact with a system through what they can see, hear and touch. The visual aspects of interface design concern designing so that people will see and notice things on a screen. Buttons need to be big enough to see and they need to be labelled in a way that is understandable for people. Instructions need to be given so people know what they are expected to do. Displays of large amounts of information need to be carefully considered so that people can see the relationships between data to understand its significance.

Conceptually people interact with systems and devices through knowing what they can do and knowing how they can do it. Conceptually people employ a 'mental model' of what the device is and how it works. People need to know that certain commands exist that will allow them to do things. They need to know that certain data is available and the form that that data takes. They need to find their way to particular pieces of information (undertake navigation). They need to be able to find details of things, see an overview of things and focus on particular areas.

Putting these three aspects together is the skill of the interface designer. Interface design is about creating an experience that enables people to make the best use of the system being designed. When first using a system people may well think 'right, I need to do X so I am going to use this device which means I am going to have to press Y on this keyboard and then press Z', but very soon people will form their intentions in the context of knowing what the system or device does and how they can achieve their goals. Physical, perceptual and conceptual design get woven together into the experiences of people.

The vast majority of personal computers, phones and handheld and tablet devices have graphical user interfaces (GUIs) typically based on one of the main three software platforms: Apple (with its operating systems OS X and iOS), Microsoft Windows and Google's Android. However, underlying these GUIs are user interfaces without the graphical elements, known as command languages.

A command language is simply a set of words with an associated syntax, the rules governing the structure of how commands are put together. To interact with a device using a command language the user types a command such as 'send', 'print', etc., and supplies any necessary data such as the name of a file to be sent or printed. UNIX is the most common command language. Command languages suffer from the problem that people:

- Have to *recall* the name of a particular command from the range of literally hundreds of possibilities
- Have to *recall* the syntax of the command.

Prior to the creation of Microsoft Windows, the vast majority of personal computers ran the operating system MSDOS. On switching on their PC, people were faced with the

```
▣ Command Prompt                                              _ □

(C) Copyright 1985-2001 Microsoft Corp.

C:\>dir
 Volume in drive C is System
 Volume Serial Number is E4AB-3BC8

 Directory of C:\

22/01/2002  13:43                     0 AUTOEXEC.BAT
22/01/2002  13:43                     0 CONFIG.SYS
01/05/2003  09:53       <DIR>           Documents and Settings
30/09/2003  09:27                    80 lconfig.aot
28/07/2003  11:47       <DIR>           My Documents
24/07/2002  16:39       <DIR>           My Music
30/01/2002  13:58       <DIR>           NOVELL
29/09/2003  11:44       <DIR>           Program Files
22/08/2002  15:06                     0 ScreenFlag
25/02/2002  11:13             1,056,768 test.sdb
10/10/2003  11:51       <DIR>           WINDOWS
30/09/2003  09:27                   958 WSREG32.LOG
30/01/2002  14:08                     0 WSREMOTE.ID
               7 File(s)      1,057,806 bytes
               6 Dir(s)   8,687,484,928 bytes free

C:\>_
```

Figure 12.1 The enigmatic c:\> prompt in MSDOS

user interface known as the c:\> prompt (Figure 12.1). People were then required to type in a command such as dir which listed the contents of the current directory (or folder). Anyone who had never encountered MSDOS (or even those who had) was continually faced with the problem of having to recall the name of the command to issue next.

However, command languages are not all bad. They are quick to execute and, particularly if there are only a few of them, people using them frequently will remember them. Commands can be spoken which makes for a very convenient interface, particularly if you are concentrating on something else. Spoken commands are very convenient for in-car systems, for example. The search engine Google has a number of commands such as 'define:' to indicate particular types of search. There are gestural commands such as a three-fingered swipe on an Apple track pad to move to the next item.

Challenge 12.1

In his piece in Interactions *Don Norman (2007) argues that commands have a number of benefits. However, a key issue is that the system must be in the correct mode to recognize and react to the commands. For example, in* Star Trek *people have to alert the computer when they wish to enter a command, e.g. the captain might say 'Computer. Locate Commander Geordie Laforge'. If they did not do this the computer would not be able to distinguish commands intended for it from other pieces of conversation. However, in the 'Turbo Lift' (the elevator), this is not necessary. Why is this?*

12.2 Graphical user interfaces

Graphical user interfaces (GUIs), which are found on every personal computer, on smart phones, on touchscreen displays and so on, have had an interesting though brief history. The Microsoft range of Windows GUIs were broadly based on (perhaps *influenced by* might be better) the Macintosh, which in turn was inspired by work at Xerox PARC, which in turn was developed and built upon early research at the Stanford Research Laboratory and at the Massachusetts Institute of Technology. During the 1980s and 1990s a number of different designs of GUIs were produced, but gradually Windows and Apple Macintosh came to dominate the GUI operating system market. However, Google Chrome OS may be just starting to challenge them.

A direct manipulation (DM) interface is one where objects – usually graphical objects on a screen – are directly manipulated with a pointing device in place of the typed commands of command languages. Ben Shneiderman at the University of Maryland coined the term 'direct manipulation' in 1982. He defined a DM interface as one where there is:

1 Continuous representation of the object of interest.
2 Physical actions or labelled button presses instead of complex syntax.
3 Rapid incremental reversible operations whose impact on the object of interest is immediately visible. (Shneiderman, 1982, p. 251)

The fact that objects are represented as graphics means that people can *recognize* what they want to do rather than having to recall some command from memory. They can also reverse their actions, which means recovering from mistakes is much easier.

WIMPs

The most prevalent of the GUIs is the WIMP interface such as Windows or OS X. WIMP stands for windows, icons, menus and pointers. A **window** is a means of sharing a device's graphical display resources among multiple applications at the same time. An **icon** is an image or symbol used to represent a file, folder, application or device, such as a printer. David Canfield Smith is usually credited with coining the term in the context of user interfaces in 1975, while he worked at Xerox. According to Smith, he adopted the term from the Russian Orthodox Church where an icon is a religious image. A **menu** is a list of commands or options from which one can choose. The last component is a **pointing device** of which the mouse is the most widespread, but fingers are also used, as is the stylus. An important aspect of a WIMP environment is the manner in which we use it. This form of interaction is called **direct manipulation** because we directly manipulate the on-screen objects as opposed to issuing commands through a command-based interface.

BOX 12.1

Direct manipulation

A direct manipulation (DM) interface is one where graphical objects on the screen are directly manipulated with a pointing device. This approach to interaction was first demonstrated by Ivan Sutherland in the Sketchpad system. The concept of direct manipulation interfaces for everyone was envisioned by Alan Kay of Xerox PARC in a 1977 article about the Dynabook (Kay and Goldberg, 1977). The first commercial systems to make extensive use of direct manipulation were the Xerox Star (1981), the Apple Lisa (1982) and Macintosh (1984). However, it was Ben Shneiderman at the University of Maryland who actually coined the term 'direct manipulation' in 1982.

Direct manipulation depends upon having bitmapped screens, so that each picture element or pixel can be used for input and output, and a pointing device. Early mobile phones did not have such a display, so direct manipulation of objects was not possible. Nowadays many of them do, and DM is found on a wide range of devices.

Windows

Windows allow a workstation's screen to be divided into areas which act like separate input and output channels that can be placed under the control of different applications. This allows people to see the output of several processes at the same time and to choose which one will receive input by selecting its window, using a pointing device, such as clicking on it with a mouse, or touching a touchscreen. This is referred to as changing the focus. Early windowing systems were tiled (did not overlap), but overlapping windows were eventually suggested by Alan Kay at Xerox PARC (although MS Windows 1, which was released in 1985, supported only tiled windows).

Windowing systems exist in a wide variety of forms but are largely variations on the same basic theme. Microsoft Windows dominates the personal computer market and in turn exists in a variety of forms, although they appear to be converging (at least in terms of appearance) in an XP-like form. There are two other major windowing systems which are widely used. The current Macintosh OS X is proving to be well received (particularly by academics); the X Window System was originally developed at MIT. X is used on many UNIX systems and X11R6 (version 11, release 6) was originally released in May 1994. X is large and powerful and, above all, complex. Figures 12.2 and 12.3 show examples of an OS X window and a Microsoft Windows 7 window.

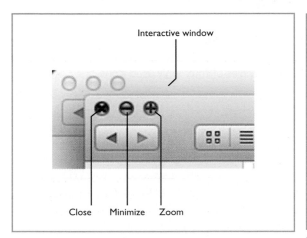

Figure 12.2 OS X window

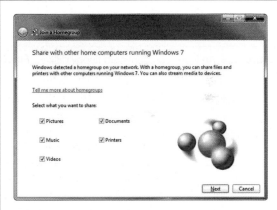

Figure 12.3 Windows 7 window

Icons

Icons are used to represent features and functions on everything from software applications, DVD players and public information kiosks to clothing (as those incomprehensible washing symbols on the back of the label). Icons are generally regarded as being useful in helping people to recognize which feature they need to access. Icons first appeared on the Xerox Star (Box 12.2) and became an important research issue in the 1980s and early 1990s, though since then there has been considerably less interest.

The use of icons is now ubiquitous, but their design, apart from a small number of standard items (see Further reading at the end of this chapter) is rather arbitrary. Icons make use of three principal types of representation: metaphor, direct mapping and convention. **Metaphor** relies on people transferring knowledge from one domain and applying it to another. The use of metaphor can be seen in icons for such things as the cut and paste operations that exist in many applications. These two operations relate to a time when in preparing a text it was not unusual to cut out elements of a document using scissors and then physically paste them into another document.

← Metaphor is discussed in detail in Chapter 9

The use of **direct mapping** is probably the simplest technique in the design of icons and involves creating a more or less direct image of what the icon is intended to represent. Thus a printer icon looks like a printer. Finally, **convention** refers to a more or less arbitrary design of an icon in the first instance, which has become accepted as standing for what is intended over time. This can lead to anachronisms. For example, the icon representing the function *save* on the Mac that I am using to write this is a representation of a floppy disk (Figure 12.4) despite the fact that the machine is not fitted with a floppy disk drive and many people will never have heard of a floppy disk. Figure 12.5 shows further examples of icons.

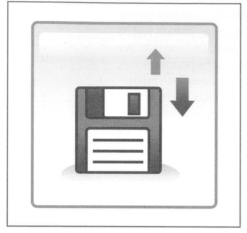

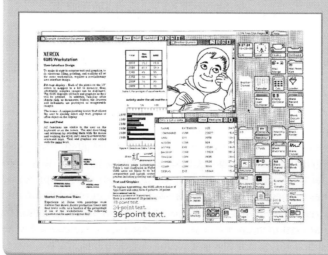

Figure 12.4 An icon representing a floppy disk
(Source: Ivary/Getty Images)

Figure 12.5 Examples of commonly used icons

The Xerox Star

It is widely recognized that every graphical user interface owes a debt to the Xerox Star workstation. Launched as the 8010 Star information system in April 1981, it was designed to be used by office workers and other professionals to create and manage business documents such as memos, reports and presentations. The Star's designers took the perspective that people were primarily interested in their jobs and not in computers *per se*. Thus from its inception a central design goal was to make use of representations of objects that would be easily recognizable from an office environment (Figure 12.6).

Figure 12.6
The Xerox Star user interface
(Source: Courtesy of Xerox Ltd)

However, the two most important design issues for icons are legibility (whether or not one can discriminate between icons) and interpretation (what it is that the icon is intended to convey). The legibility aspect refers to icons not always being viewed under ideal conditions (e.g. poor lighting, screen resolution or the size of the icon itself). Research has indicated that under such conditions it is the overall global appearance of the icon that aids discrimination, so icons should not be designed so that they differ only with respect to one small detail.

The interpretation of the icon is a non-trivial issue. The icon may indeed be recognized as an object but remains opaque as to its meaning. Brems and Whitten (1987) for this reason caution against the use of icons which are not accompanied by a textual label. Do remember, however, that one reason why icons are used is that they are succinct and small (i.e. do not take up too much screen space); adding labels removes this advantage. Solutions to this problem include **balloon help** and **tool tips** which have appeared as effective pop-up labels.

Horton's icon checklist

William Horton (of William Horton Consulting, Inc.) has produced a detailed checklist (1991) designed to help the icon designer avoid a whole raft of common mistakes. We reproduce his top-level headings here together with a sample question for each issue.

Understandable	*Does the image spontaneously suggest the intended concept to the viewer?*
Familiar	*Are the objects in the icon ones familiar to the user?*
Unambiguous	*Are additional cues (label, other icon documentation) available to resolve any ambiguity?*
Memorable	*Where possible, does the icon feature concrete objects in action? Are actions shown as operations on concrete objects?*
Informative	*Why is the concept important?*
Few	*Is the number of arbitrary symbols less than 20?*
Distinct	*Is every icon distinct from all others?*
Attractive	*Does the image use smooth edges and lines?*
Legible	*Have you tested all combinations of colour and size in which the icon will be displayed?*
Compact	*Is every object, every line, every pixel in the icon necessary?*
Coherent	*Is it clear where one icon ends and another begins?*
Extensible	*Can I draw the image smaller? Will people still recognize it?*

Menus

Many applications of interactive systems make use of menus to organize and store the commands that are available. These are often called menu-driven interfaces. Items are chosen from the menu by highlighting them, followed by pressing <Return> or by simply pointing to the item with a mouse and clicking one of the mouse buttons. Menus are also familiar on mobile phones, touchscreen kiosks and, of course, restaurants where the available options for the customer are listed on a menu.

When creating menus, commands should be grouped into menu topics, which are a list of menu items. When a command or option (menu item) is selected from the list, an action is performed. Menus are also used extensively on websites to structure information and to provide the main method of navigation of the site's content. While menus should be simple, there is little to prevent the over-zealous designer from creating very complex and difficult to navigate menus. Figure 12.7 is a screenshot of the Mac version of a typical **hierarchically** organized menu. In this example, the various options are arranged under a top-level topic (filter) and in turn have series of sub-menus. Figure 12.8 is the equivalent Windows XP version. Hierarchical menus are also called

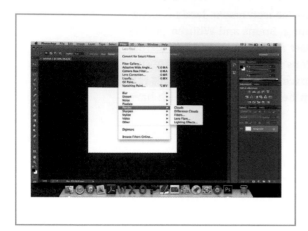

Figure 12.7 An example of a menu taken from the Mac version of Adobe® Photoshop®

Figure 12.8 The jump bar menu from Windows 8

cascading menus. In a cascading menu, the sub-menu appears to cascade out when a choice is made from the higher-level menu.

Another frequently encountered form of menu is the **pop-up**. A pop-up menu is distinguished from a standard menu in that it is not attached to a menu bar in a fixed location (hence the name). Once a selection is made from a pop-up menu, the menu usually disappears. Figure 12.9 is a screenshot of a pop-up menu. In this case it includes a number of options that are not simple commands, so it is more usually referred to as a

Figure 12.9 A screenshot of a pop-up menu (or panel) providing information on the file 'chapters 5 & 6 v03' after clicking on the file and using the context menu

panel. Also, in this case it is also a **contextual menu.** The make-up of contextual menus varies according to the context (hence their name) from which they are invoked. If a file is selected, the contextual menu offers file options. If instead a folder is selected, folder options are displayed.

Finally, to aid experts, it is common practice to associate the most frequently used items with keyboard shortcuts (also known as accelerators in MS Windows systems). Figures 12.10 and 12.11 illustrate shortcuts for both the Windows XP operating system and OS X.

Figure 12.10 Shortcuts (Windows XP)   **Figure 12.11** Shortcuts (OS X)

Pointers

The final part of the WIMP interface is the pointer. These come in many forms, some of which are discussed below. The most common is the mouse, but joysticks are also common, for example in game controllers. On mobile phones and tablets, a stylus is often provided as the pointer and on touchscreen systems the finger is used. Remote pointers include the Wii wand and other infra-red pointers, for example for doing presentations. The arrival of multi-touch surfaces has enabled a wide range of gestures to be recognized in addition to a simple point and select operation.

→ Gestures are discussed in Chapter 13

12.3 Interface design guidelines

Modern graphical user interfaces have as part of their make-up a range of widgets including buttons and radio buttons, sliders, scroll bars and checkboxes. These will often combine several aspects of the basic WIMP objects. Designing a GUI for an application does not guarantee that the finished system will be usable. Indeed, given the ease with which GUIs can be created with modern development tools, it is now very simple to create inelegant, unusable interfaces. This problem is well recognized and has resulted in the creation of **style guides** that provide a range of advice to the interface developer. Style guides exist for the different kinds of windowing systems available and are occasionally written by specific software vendors or companies to ensure that their products are consistent, usable and distinctive.

The Microsoft website offers abundant helpful advice on designing interfaces. Here is a sample:

> Grouping of elements and controls is also important. Try to group information logically according to function or relationship. Because their functions are related, buttons for navigating a database should be grouped together visually rather than scattered throughout a form. The same applies to information: fields for name and address are generally grouped together, as they are closely related. In many cases, you can use frame controls to help reinforce the relationships between controls.

Other advice on interface design operates at a much smaller level of detail, at the level of individual widgets. Interface consistency is an important result of using style guides as is evident on devices such as the iPhone.

The Apple guidelines for the iOS platform provide good advice and guidance on designing for standard items such as a toolbar, navigation bar, etc. See Box 12.3.

BOX 12.3

The Apple toolbar

A toolbar (Figure 12.12) contains controls that perform actions related to objects in the screen or view. A toolbar is typically contained in a navigation controller, which is an object that manages the display of a hierarchy of custom views. To learn more about defining a toolbar in your code, see "Displaying a Navigation Toolbar" in View Controller Programming Guide for iOS and UIToolbar Class Reference.

Figure 12.12 Apple toolbar

Appearance and behavior

On iPhone, a toolbar always appears at the bottom edge of a screen or view, but on iPad it can instead appear at the top edge.

Toolbar items are displayed equally spaced across the width of the toolbar. The precise set of toolbar items can change from view to view, because the items are always specific to the context of the current view.

On iPhone, changing the device orientation from portrait to landscape can change the height of the toolbar automatically. On iPad, the height and translucency of a toolbar does not change with rotation.

Guidelines

Use a toolbar to provide a set of actions users can take in the current context.

● Use a toolbar to give people a selection of frequently used commands that make sense in the current context. An alternative is to put a segmented control in a toolbar to give people access to different perspectives on your application's data or to different application modes (for usage guidelines, see "Segmented Control").

● If appropriate, customize the appearance of a toolbar. If you want the toolbar to coordinate with the overall look of your app, you can specify a custom background image or tint and you can specify translucency. In some cases, it can be a good idea to supply a resizable background image; to learn more about creating a resizable image, see "Tips for Creating Resizable Images."

  Make sure that your toolbar customization is consistent with the look of the rest of your application. If you use a translucent toolbar, for example, don't combine it with an opaque navigation bar. Also, it's usually best to avoid changing the appearance of the toolbar in different screens in the same orientation.

● Note: If you want to design a toolbar that slightly overlaps the main content view, you can supply a custom background image that is taller than the standard bar height. In an iPhone app, you can supply different background images for the different bar heights (in an iPad app, the same custom image is used in both orientations). If you provide a taller background image, it's best to create a translucent image (and to specify that the toolbar itself is translucent) so that users can see the content behind the bar.

● Maintain a hit target area of at least 44 × 44 points for each toolbar item. If you crowd toolbar items too closely together, people have difficulty tapping the one they want.

● Use system-provided toolbar items according to their documented meaning. See "Standard Buttons for Use in Toolbars and Navigation Bars" for more information. If you decide to create your own toolbar items, see "Icons for Navigation Bars, Toolbars, and Tab Bars" for advice on how to design them.

● If appropriate, customize the appearance of toolbar items. If you customize the appearance of the toolbar, you might want to consider creating a coordinating appearance for the toolbar items. You might also want to adjust the selected appearance of the items so that they look good on your customized toolbar background.

● Try to avoid mixing plain style (borderless) and bordered toolbar items in the same toolbar. You can use either style in a toolbar, but mixing them does not usually look good.

● On iPhone, take into account the automatic change in toolbar height that occurs on device rotation. In particular, make sure your custom toolbar icons fit well in the thinner bar that appears in landscape orientation. Don't specify the height of a toolbar programmatically; instead, you can take advantage of the UIBarMetrics constants to ensure that your content fits well . . .

Source: http://developer.apple.com/library/ios/#documentation/userexperience/conceptual/mobilehig/
UIElementGuidelines/UIElementGuidelines.html#//apple_ref/doc/uid/TP40006556-CH13-SW1

Other advice on interface design operates at a much smaller level of detail, at the level of individual widgets. For example Android provide detail advice about how large to make certain widgets and Apple say that any button should be no smaller than 44 pixels square. Android widgets are shown in Figure 12.13.

Radio buttons

Use a series of radio buttons to allow people to make *exclusive* choices – think about the buttons on a radio: you can listen to FM or AM at any one time but not both. Figure 12.14 is a detail from a PhotoShop interface dialogue in which the radio buttons constrain people to choosing a Selection or Image. These choices are exclusive.

Figure 12.13 Android widgets

(Source: http://developer.android.com/guide/practices/ui_guidelines/widget_design.html)

Figure 12.14 Radio buttons and check boxes from Adobe® Photoshop® from Apple OS X

Checkboxes

Checkboxes should be used to display individual settings that can be switched (checked) on and off. Use a group of checkboxes for settings that are not mutually exclusive (that is, you can check more than one box). An example is shown in Figure 12.15.

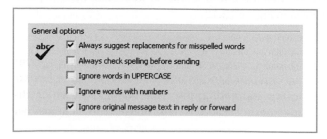

Figure 12.15 A checkbox from MS Outlook from Windows XP

Challenge 12.2

You are designing an e-mail client which – among other things – allows people to:

- Set a series of preferences for incoming mail (download large files on receipt, display first two lines of message body, reject mail from senders not in address book, alert when new mail received . . .)
- Set a colour scheme for the e-mail application (hot colours, water colours or jewel colours).

Would you use radio buttons or checkboxes for these?

Toolbars

A toolbar is a collection of buttons grouped according to function (in this respect they are conceptually identical to menus). The buttons are represented as icons to give a clue as to their function. Passing the mouse pointer over an icon will usually trigger the associated 'tool tip', which is a short textual label describing the function of the button. Toolbars are also configurable: their contents can be changed and one can choose whether or not they are displayed. Hiding toolbars helps make the best use of the display resources (usually described as the screen real-estate). Figure 12.16 illustrates this.

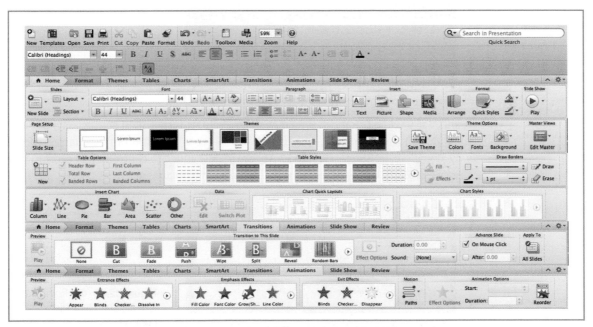

Figure 12.16 Why it is useful to be able to hide the full range of available toolbars (taken from MS PowerPoint)

List boxes

A list box is an accurately named widget as it is a box in which files and options are listed. List boxes take a variety of forms and within these forms they offer different ways of viewing the contents – as lists (with more or less detail), as icons or as thumbnails (little pictures of the files' contents). A list box for the iPhone is shown in Figure 12.17.

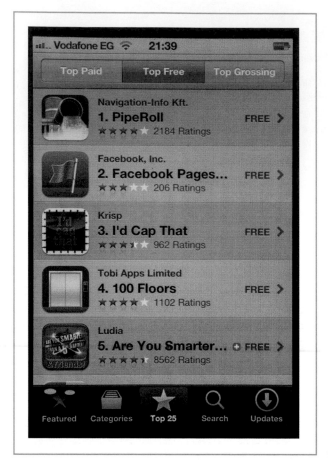

Figure 12.17 iPhone list box
(Source: © B. O'Kane/Alamy Images)

Sliders

A slider is a widget that can return analogue values: rather than setting, say, the volume to 7 on a scale of 10, people can drag a slider to a position three-quarters of the way along a scale. Sliders (Figure 12.18) are ideally suited to controlling or setting such things as volume or brightness or scrolling through a document.

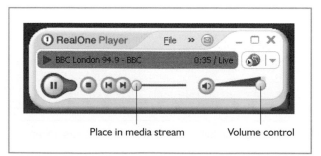

Figure 12.18 The RealOne Player® with two slider controls
(Source: Courtesy of Real Networks, Inc.)

Form fill

Form filling is an interface style that is particularly popular with Web applications. Form fill interfaces are used to gather information such as name and address. Figure 12.19 is a very typical example of a form fill interface. This screenshot is taken from an on-line bookshop. The individual boxes are called **fields** and are frequently marked with an asterisk (*) to indicate that an entry is **mandatory**. This particular interface is a hybrid as it not only has form fill aspects but has other widgets too, including pull-down menus.

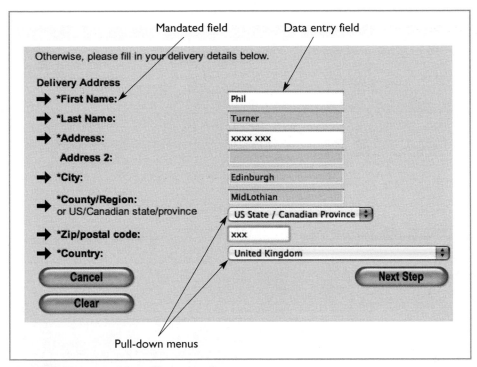

Figure 12.19 A typical form fill user interface
(Source: http://bookshop.blackwell.co.uk)

Form fill interfaces are best used when structured information is required. They can sometimes be automatically updated from a set of structured data stored on a personal computer. Examples of structured information include such things as:

- An individual's name and postal address required for mail order services
- Travel details, e.g. the airport from which one is flying, intended destination, time and date of departure
- Number and type of goods, e.g. 10 copies of the DVD *The Sound of Music*.

Wizards

Wizard is the name given to a style of interaction that leads people by the metaphorical hand (or pointer) step-by-step through a series of questions and answers, picklists and other kinds of widgets to achieve a task. In MS Windows wizards are used to install hardware and applications. This style of interaction is widely used by all windowing systems.

The great strength of wizards is that they present complex tasks in 'bite-sized' pieces. Figure 12.20 is a series of screenshots capturing the steps involved in installing a new item of hardware. This is only one possible route through the process of installing a new item of hardware. Many others are possible.

Alerts

Figure 12.21 illustrates two different approaches (by the same software vendor) to alerting people to the presence of new mail. Figure 12.21(a) is the unobtrusive display of an envelope or mailbox symbol. In this instance one would expect the user to notice the message but in their own time. The second approach, in contrast, may interrupt people's work, so do not display this kind of alert box, which requires interaction, unless it is important, urgent or life-threatening. Allow the person to configure the application to turn off such alerts. Figure 12.21 (b) is an illustration of an unobtrusive alert signalling the delivery of a new e-mail message.

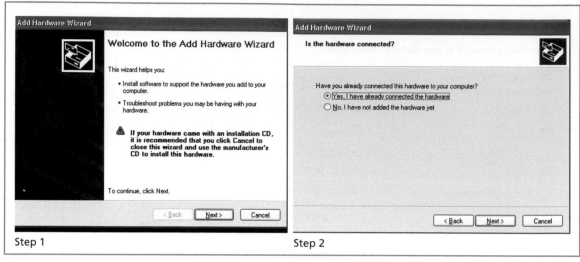

Step 1   Step 2

Figure 12.20 The Microsoft Add Hardware wizard

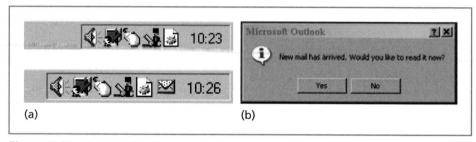

(a)   (b)

Figure 12.21 Attracting attention

→ Chapter 21 discusses attention

Attracting attention is a simple enough matter – flash a light, use some other form of animation, ring a bell, and our attention is directed at that stimulus. It is, of course, possible to alert someone as to where to direct their attention. An air traffic controller's attention, for example, might be directed to a potential collision.

However, the challenge of attracting and holding attention is to do so in a manner which:

● Does not distract us from the main task, particularly if we are doing something important, such as flying an aircraft or operating a complex or hazardous tool
● In certain circumstances *can* be ignored while in other circumstances *cannot* and *should not* be ignored
● Does not overwhelm the user of a system with more information than they can reasonably understand or respond to.

12.4 Psychological principles and interface design

As we mentioned above, there are many sites offering good guidelines to the interface designer. Apple, Android and Microsoft have style guides and many development environments will ensure that designs conform to the standards they are aiming at. There are also many issues applicable to the different contexts of design – websites, mobiles, etc. – that we discuss in Part III. In this section we present some guidelines deriving from the principles of psychology presented in Part IV.

Cooper *et al.* (2007) argues that visual interface design is a central component of interaction design as it combines graphic design, industrial design and visual information design. We deal with information design and the closely related area of visualizations in the next section. Designers need to know about graphic design, such as what shape, size, colour, orientation and texture screen objects should be. Designs should have a clear and consistent style. Recall the idea of a design language introduced in Chapter 3 and discussed in Chapter 9. The design language will be learnt and adopted by people, so they will expect things that look the same to behave the same and, conversely, if things behave differently make sure they look different. Cooper recommends developing a grid system to help to structure and group objects at the interface. In Chapters 8 and 14 we describe wireframes which are used to provide visual structure. However, we cannot hope to teach the whole of graphic design and pointers are given in the Further reading section to comprehensive texts on this. We can, however, provide some guidelines that follow from our understanding of the psychology of people.

Guidelines from perception

Chapter 25 discusses perception and introduces a number of 'laws' of perception that have been developed by the 'gestalt' school of perception. Perception research also provides us with other fundamental aspects of people's abilities that should be considered when designing visual interfaces.

Using proximity to organize buttons

One of the *Gestalt* principles of perception is the observation that objects appearing close together in space or time tend to be perceived together. The usefulness of this law can be seen by contrasting the next two figures. Figure 12.22 is a standard Microsoft Windows XP alert box with the buttons equally spaced. Figure 12.23 is the OS X equivalent. The Mac version makes clear use of proximity. The **Cancel** and **Save** buttons are grouped away from the option **Don't Save**. This has the effect of seeing the two commands – **Save** and **Cancel** – as a pair and clearly separating from the potentially ambiguous **Don't Save**.

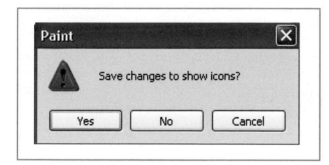

Figure 12.22 Equally spaced buttons – Windows XP

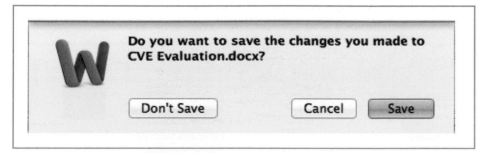

Figure 12.23 Buttons organized by proximity – OS X

Using similarity to organize files

A second *Gestalt* law we consider is that of **similarity**. Figure 12.24 is a screenshot of the contents of a folder. All of the files are ordered alphabetically, starting at the top left.

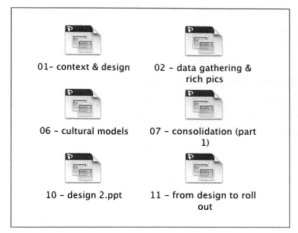

Figure 12.24 Organizing files using similarity

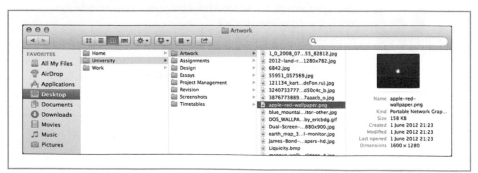

Figure 12.25 Disorganized files

The PowerPoint files are perceived as a contiguous block. This stands in sharp contrast to the file icons in Figure 12.25.

Using continuity to connect disconnected elements

A third *Gestalt* law is **continuity**. Disconnected elements are often seen to be part of a continuous whole. Figure 12.26 illustrates part of an MS Windows scrollbar that indicates that there is more of the document to be seen below the current windowful. The length of the slider is an indication of how much of the total document is visible. The slider indicates that about 80 per cent of the document is visible.

Closure

This particular law refers to the fact that it has been found that closed objects are easier to perceive than those that are open. As evidence of this, we will often unconsciously add missing information to close a figure so that it is more easily perceived against its background.

An example of the use of closure is the Finder application (Figure 12.27) which offers a visual track from the top level of a computer's hard disk (down) to an individual file. We perceive a connection running from *My hard disk* on the far left to the file *MS Scrollbar* on the extreme right, yet the connection is not strictly continuous.

Principles from memory and attention

Our understanding of human abilities in remembering and attending to things also leads to a number of sound guidelines. Memory is usually considered in terms of our

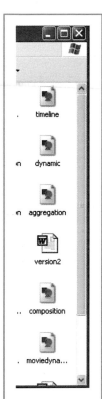

Figure 12.26
A Microsoft
Windows XP
scrollbar

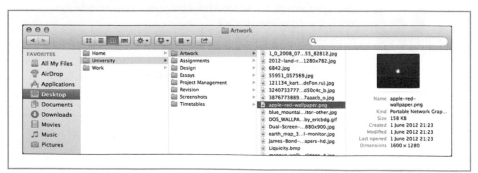

Figure 12.27 The new Finder window (OS X)

short-term or working memory and long-term memory. These are explained in detail in Chapter 21. Attention concerns what we focus upon.

Short-term (or working) memory

There is a widely quoted design guideline based on *Miller and his magic number*. George Miller (1956) found that short-term memory is limited to only 7 ± 2 'chunks' of information. This principle has been used in HCI to suggest that menus should be restricted to about seven items, or Web navigation bars should be seven items. While these are perfectly reasonable heuristics for designers to use, they do not derive from a limitation of short-term memory which is to do with how much most people can remember.

There is also an issue about how true this finding is, and more recent work indicates that the real capacity of working memory is closer to three or four items; indeed, Cowan has argued for 4 ± 1 (Cowan, 2002). The central observation, however, that you should not expect people to remember lots of detail is well made.

Chunking

Chunking is the process of grouping information into larger, more meaningful units, thus minimizing the demands on working memory. Chunking is a very effective way of reducing memory load.

An example of chunking at the interface is the grouping of meaningful elements of a task into one place (or dialogue). Think about setting up a standard template for a document. Among the things we have to remember to do are printing the document on the printer we wish to use, setting document parameters such as its size and orientation, setting the print quality or colour setting, and so on. Another example of chunking can be seen in Figure 12.28. Here a large number of formatting options (font, alignment, border and document setting) have been chunked into a single, expandable dialogue. The ▶ symbol indicates that the selection will expand if selected. Having clicked on the *Alignment and Spacing* button, the chunked dialogue expands to unpack a number of related options.

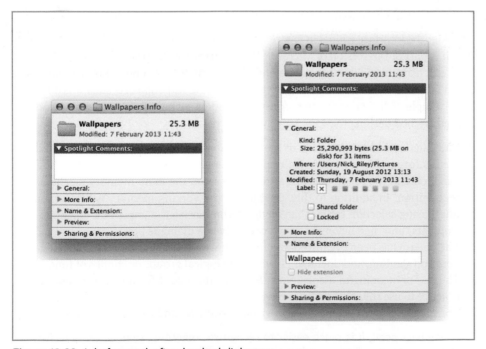

Figure 12.28 A *before* and *after* chunked dialogue

Time limitations

Memories, particularly those in short-term or working memory, are surprisingly short-lived, and even in ideal conditions they will persist for only 30 seconds. So, it is essential to make important information presented persist (Figure 12.29); that is, do not flash an alert such as 'Cannot save file' onto a screen for a second or two and then remove it. Insist that a button, typically 'OK', is pressed. 'OK' in this instance really means 'I acknowledge the message'.

Figure 12.29 An example of a persistent alert box

Recall and recognition

→ Chapter 21 examines these issues more closely

Another guideline derived from our knowledge of memory is to design for recognition rather than recall. Recall is the process whereby individuals actively search their memories to retrieve a particular piece of information. Recognition involves searching your memory and then deciding whether the piece of information matches what you have in your memory store. Recognition is generally easier and quicker than recall.

Challenge 12.3

Find instances of designing for recall and recognition in software you use regularly. Hint: websites requiring form-filling are often good sources of examples.

Designing for memory

Consider the interface widget in Figure 12.30. This is an image of the formatting palette which is part of the version of Microsoft Word current at the time of writing. Microsoft have extensive usability laboratories and the design of this application will have benefited from a sound understanding of the capabilities of people. As such it is an excellent example of designing for memory and embodies a whole series of design principles reflecting good design practice:

● The palette has been designed to use recognition rather than recall. The drop-down menus for style, name and size remove the need to recall the names of the fonts installed and the range of styles available. Instead the main memory mechanism is recognition. In addition to this, the burden on working memory is kept to a minimum using selection rather than having to memorize the name of a font (e.g. Zapf Dingbats) and then having to type it correctly in a dialogue box.
● The palette has been organized into four chunks – font, alignment and spacing, borders and shading, and document – which are logical groups or chunks of functions.
● The use of meaningful associations: **B** stands for bold, *I* for italic. It is good design practice to use these natural mappings.
● The palette also relies on aspects of visual processing and the use of icons.

As we have seen, it is much easier to recognize something than to recall it. Novices prefer menus because they can scroll through the list of options until a particular

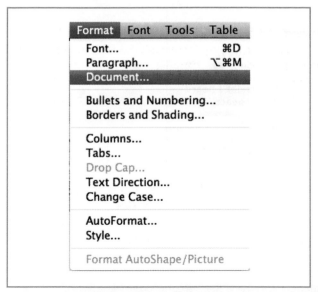

Figure 12.30 Interface widgets in OS X

command is recognized. Experts, however, have been reported as being frustrated in scrolling through a series of menus (particularly nested menus) and often prefer keyboard shortcuts instead (e.g. <alt>-F-P-<return> instead of select File menu / Print / OK). Interactive systems should be designed to accommodate both styles of working.

Further key evidence of the advantage of recognition over recall can be seen in the use of **picklists**. Picklists have two clear advantages over simply asking someone to recall a specific name, or any other piece of data. They offer help when we are faced with trying to recall something that is on the tip of our tongue or something that is ambiguous (as in the example of Figure 12.31 which identifies one of several London airports) or which may be difficult to spell. Consider the next two examples: imagine you are trying to book a flight from Edinburgh to London. You know that the target airport is not London Heathrow but one of the others and are confident that you will be able to recognize the specific airport without difficulty from the list more easily than from unaided memory. Figure 12.31 is an image of a standard Web pull-down picklist.

London Stansted is easier to recognize than trying to remember (a) how to spell it – *Stanstead, Standsted* or *Stansted*? – and (b) the official airline abbreviation (STN). The use of a picklist can also significantly improve the spelling of the documents we produce. Current versions of Microsoft Word identify misspelled words by underlining them with a red wavy line. Left-clicking on the word drops down a picklist of alternative spellings. This approach has also been adopted by modern visual (software) development environments where not only misspelled commands are identified but the syntax of commands is checked. Figure 12.32 is an illustration of this.

The recent use of **thumbnails** is another example of how recognition is more effective than recall. Figure 12.33 is a screenshot of the *My Pictures* of a computer running the Windows 7 operating system. The folder contains a number of thumbnails, that is, very small (thumbnail-sized) images of the contents of the files in the folder. Each is immediately recognizable and reminds the person of the original content.

Figure 12.31 Flying to London

(Source: www.easyjet.co.uk/en/book/index.asp)

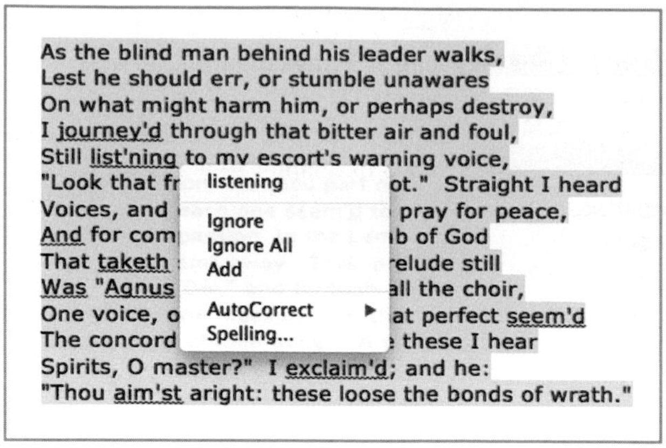

As the blind man behind his leader walks,
Lest he should err, or stumble unawares
On what might harm him, or perhaps destroy,
I journey'd through that bitter air and foul,
Still list'ning to my escort's warning voice,
"Look that fr
ot." Straight I heard
Voices, and
pray for peace,
And for com
b of God
That taketh
relude still
Was "Agnus
all the choir,
One voice, o
at perfect seem'd
The concord
these I hear
Spirits, O master?" I exclaim'd; and he:
"Thou aim'st aright: these loose the bonds of wrath."
listening
Ignore
Ignore All
Add
AutoCorrect
Spelling...

Figure 12.32 Spelling checker

Libraries
Search Libraries
Organize
New library
Favorites
Desktop
Downloads
Recent Places
Libraries
Documents
Music
Pictures
Videos
Homegroup
Phil (PHIL-PC)
Computer
Network
Libraries
Open a library to see your files and arrange them by folder, date, and other properties.
Documents
Library
Music
Library
Pictures
Library
Videos
Library
4 items

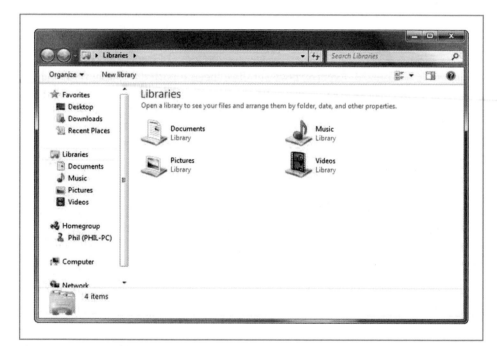

Figure 12.33 Use of thumbnails

BOX 12.4

Colour blindness

The term colour blind is used to describe people with defective colour vision. Red-green colour blindness (i.e. the inability to distinguish reliably between red and green) is the most common form, affecting approximately 1 in 12 men (8 per cent) and 1 in 25 women (4 per cent). It is a genetic disorder with a sex-linked recessive gene to blame – hence the greater number of men being affected. A second and rarer form of colour blindness affects the perception of the colours blue-yellow. The rarest form of all results in monochromatic vision in which the sufferer is unable to detect any colour at all.

Designing with colour

Colour is very important to us. To describe someone as being colourless is to say that they are without character or interest. Designing colour into interactive systems is very difficult. If it were otherwise, why are most domestic electronic devices black? The design language adopted by Microsoft (discussed in Chapter 9) makes use of colourful tiles for its design and Apple have long favoured smooth blue and graphite grey as their livery.

Aaron Marcus's excellent book *Graphic Design for Electronic Documents and User Interfaces* (Marcus, 1992) provides the following rules.

Rule 1   Use a maximum of 5 ± 2 colours.

Rule 2   Use foveal (central) and peripheral colours appropriately.

Rule 3   Use a colour area that exhibits a minimum shift in colour and/or size if the colour area changes in size.

Rule 4   Do not use simultaneous high-chroma, spectral colours.

Rule 5   Use familiar, consistent colour codings with appropriate references.

Table 12.1 holds a number of Western (Western Europe, the United States and Australia) denotations as identified by Marcus. These guidelines are, of course, just that – guidelines. They may not suit every situation but should at the very least provide a sound starting point. One final caveat – colour connotations can vary dramatically even within a culture. Marcus notes that the colour blue in the United States is interpreted differently by different groups – for healthcare professionals it is taken to indicate death; for movie-goers it is associated with pornography; for accountants it means reliability or corporateness (think of 'Big Blue' – IBM).

Table 12.1 Some Western colour conventions

Red	Danger, hot, fire
Yellow	Caution, slow, test
Green	Go, okay, clear, vegetation, safety
Blue	Cold, water, calm, sky
Warm colours	Action, response required, proximity
Cool colours	Status, background information, distance
Greys, white and blue	Neutrality

Source: After Marcus, Aaron, *Graphic Design for Electronic Documents and User Interfaces*, 1st, © 1991. Printed and Electronically reproduced by permission of Pearson Education, Inc., Upper Saddle River, New Jersey.

Error avoidance design guidelines

The following design guidelines have been drawn (and edited) from Reason and Norman's design principles for minimizing error (*cf.* Reason, 1990, p. 236):

→ Human error is covered in Chapter 21

- Use knowledge both in the world and in the head in order to promote a good conceptual model of the system; this requires consistency of mapping between the designer's model, the system model and the user's model.
- Simplify the structure of tasks so as to minimize the load upon vulnerable cognitive processes such as working memory, planning or problem solving.
- Make both the execution and the evaluation sides of an action visible. Visibility in regard to the former allows users to know what is possible and how things should

be done; visibility on the evaluation side enables people to gauge the effects of their actions.

- Exploit natural mappings between intentions and possible actions, between actions and their effects on the system, between the actual system state and what is perceivable, and between the system state and the needs, intentions and expectations of the user.
- Exploit the power of constraints, both natural and artificial. Constraints guide people to the next appropriate action or decision.
- Design for errors. Assume that they will happen, then plan for *error recovery*. Try to make it easy to reverse operations and hard to carry out non-reversible ones. Exploit forcing functions such as wizards that constrain people to use a limited range of operations.
- When all else fails, standardize actions, outcomes, layouts, displays, etc. The disadvantages of less than perfect standardization are often compensated for by the increased ease of use. But standardization for its own sake is only a last resort. The earlier principles should always be applied first.

Error message design guidelines

- Take care with the wording and presentation of alerts and error messages.
- Avoid using threatening or alarming language in messages (e.g. fatal error, run aborted, kill job, catastrophic error).
- Do not use double negatives as they can be ambiguous.
- Use specific, constructive words in error messages (e.g. avoid general messages such as 'invalid entry' and use specifics such as 'please enter your name').
- Make the system 'take the blame' for errors (e.g. 'illegal command' versus 'unrecognized command').
- DO NOT USE ALL UPPERCASE LETTERS as it looks as if you are shouting – instead, use a mixture of uppercase and lowercase.
- Use attention-grabbing techniques cautiously (e.g. avoid over-using 'blinks' on Web pages, flashing messages, 'you have mail', bold colours, etc.).
- Do not use more than four different font sizes per screen.
- Do not over-use audio or video.
- Use colours appropriately and make use of expectations (e.g. red = danger, green = ok).

Principles from navigation

Navigation is discussed in Chapter 25, highlighting the importance of people having both survey knowledge and route knowledge in understanding and wayfinding through an environment. Apple user experience guidelines agree:

Give People a Logical Path to Follow. People appreciate knowing where they are in an app and getting confirmation that they're on the right path. *Make the path through the information you present logical and easy for users to predict.* In addition, be sure to provide markers – such as back buttons – that users can use to find out where they are and how to retrace their steps. *In most cases, give users only one path to a screen.* If a screen needs to be accessible in different circumstances, consider using a modal view that can appear in different contexts.

Source: See source of Further thoughts

Apple's user experience guidelines for iOS apps

Focus on the Primary Task

Elevate the Content that People Care About

Think Top Down

Give People a Logical Path to Follow

Make Usage Easy and Obvious

Use User-Centric Terminology

Minimize the Effort Required for User Input

Downplay File-Handling Operations

Enable Collaboration and Connectedness

De-emphasize Settings

Brand Appropriately

Make Search Quick and Rewarding

Entice and Inform with a Well-Written Description

Be Succinct

Use UI Elements Consistently

Consider Adding Physicality and Realism

Delight People with Stunning Graphics

Handle Orientation Changes

Make Targets Fingertip-Size

Use Subtle Animation to Communicate

Support Gestures Appropriately

Ask People to Save Only When Necessary

Make Modal Tasks Occasional and Simple

Start Instantly

Always Be Prepared to Stop

Don't Quit Programmatically

If Necessary, Display a License Agreement or Disclaimer

For iPad:

Enhance Interactivity (Don't Just Add Features)

Reduce Full-Screen Transitions

Restrain Your Information Hierarchy

Consider Using Popovers for Some Modal Tasks

Migrate Toolbar Content to the Top

Source: http://developer.apple.com/library/ios/#documentation/userexperience/conceptual/mobilehig/UEBestPractices/UEBestPractices.html#//apple_ref/doc/uid/TP40006556-CH20-SW1

12.5 Information design

In addition to designing screens and individual widgets for people to interact with a system or device, interaction designers need to consider how to lay out the large amounts of data and information that are often involved in applications. Once designers have worked out how best to structure and organize the information, they need to provide people with methods to interact with it. The tools and techniques for navigating through large amounts of information have a big impact on the inferences people will be able to make from the data and the overall experience that people will have.

→ See also the discussion of information spaces in Chapter 18

Jacobson (2000) argues that the key feature of information design is that it is design dealing with meanings rather than materials. Information design is essentially to do with sense-making, with how to present data (often in large amounts) in a form that people can easily understand and use. Information designers have to understand the characteristics of the different media being used to present data and how the medium affects how people move through structures.

Information design is traditionally traced back to the work of Sir Edward Playfair in the eighteenth century and to the work of the French semiologist Jacques Bertin (1981). Bertin's theories of how to present information and on the different types of visualizations have been critical to all work since. The work of Edward Tufte (1983, 1990, 1997) shows just how effective good information design can be (see Box 12.5). He gives numerous examples of how, in finding the best representation for a problem, the problem is solved. Clarity in expression leads to clarity of understanding. He describes various ways of depicting quantitative information such as labelling, encoding with colours or using known objects to help get an idea of size. He discusses how to represent multivariant data in the two-dimensional space of a page or a computer screen and how best to present information so that comparisons can be made. His three books are beautifully illustrated with figures and pictures through the centuries and provide a thoughtful, artistic and pragmatic introduction to many of the issues of information design.

BOX 12.5

Edward Tufte

In the introduction to *Visual Explanations*, Tufte (1997, p. 10) writes

My three books on information design stand in the following relation:

The Visual Display of Quantitative Information (1983) is about pictures of numbers, how to depict data and enforce statistical honesty.

Envisioning Information (1990) is about pictures of nouns (maps and aerial photographs, for example, consist of a great many nouns lying on the ground). Envisioning also deals with visual strategies for design: color, layering and interaction effects.

Visual Explanations (1997) is about pictures of verbs, the representation of mechanism and motion, or process and dynamics, or causes and effects, of explanation and narrative. Since such displays are often used to reach conclusions and make decisions, there is a special concern with the integrity of the content and the design.

Figure 12.34 is one of Tufte's designs and shows a patient's medical history involving two medical and two psychiatric problems.

Harry Beck's map of the London Underground is often cited as an excellent piece of information design. It is praised for its clear use of colour and its schematic structure – not worrying about the actual location of the stations, but instead concerned with their linear relationships. The original map was produced in 1933 and the style and concepts have remained until now. However, it is interesting to note how nowadays – with the proliferation of new lines – the original structure and scheme is breaking down. With only a few Underground lines, the strong visual message could be conveyed with strong colours. With a larger number of lines the colours are no longer easily discernible from one another. Figure 12.35 shows the map from 1933 and a recent version.

Another key player in the development of information architecture and information design is Richard Saul Wurman. His book *Information Architects* (Wurman, 1997) provides a feast of fascinating images and reflections on the design process by leading information designers. Wurman's own contribution dates from 1962 and includes a wide variety of information design cases, from maps comparing populations, to books explaining medical processes, to his *New Road Atlas: US Atlas* (Wurman, 1991), based on a geographical layout with each segment taking one hour to drive. Figure 12.36 shows an example from his *Understanding USA* book (Wurman, 2000).

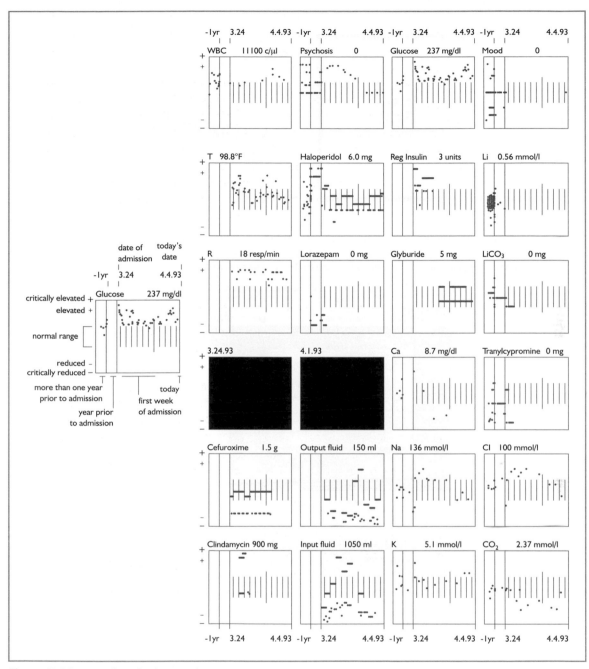

Figure 12.34 Examples of Tufte's work

(Source: After Tufte (1997), p. 110 and p. 111. Courtesy of Edward R. Tufte and Seth M. Powsner)

A number of authors are keen to ground information design in theory – particularly theories of perception and cognition. Indeed, some of these theoretical positions, such as *Gestalt* principles described above, are useful. General design principles of avoiding clutter, avoiding excessive animations and avoiding clashing colours also help make displays understandable. Bertin's theories and modern versions such as that of Card (2012) are useful grounding for anyone working in the area. Card (2012) provides a detailed taxonomy of the various types of visualization and provides details on different types of data that designers can deal with. He also discusses the different visual forms that can be used to represent data.

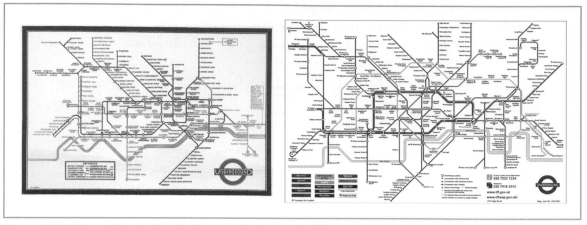

Figure 12.35 Maps of the London Underground rail network: left, in 1933; right, now

(Source: Screenshot (top left) from London underground map by H.C. Beck (1993), © TfL from the London Transport Museum collection; Screenshot (top right) from London underground map, 2009. © TfL from the London Transport Museum collection)

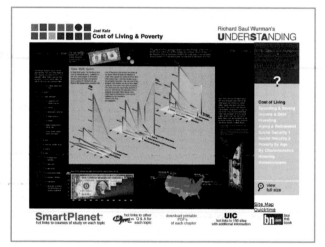

Figure 12.36 Illustration from Richard Saul Wurman's book *Understanding USA*

(Source: Wurman, 2000, designed by Joel Katz)

Essentially, though, information design remains a design discipline rather than an engineering one. There are many methods to help designers understand the problems of information design in a particular context (and taking a human-centred view is the most important), but there can be no substitute for spending time critiquing great designs and looking at the reflection of designers on their creative and thinking processes. Readers are encouraged to follow up the references at the end of this chapter.

← Design languages are discussed in Chapter 9

When developing a scheme of information design in a given context, designers should realize that they are developing visual 'languages'. The visual language of information design is an important part of these. Designers will imbue colours, shapes and layouts with meanings that people have to come to understand.

12.6 Visualization

The other key feature of information design that the modern information architect or designer might get involved with is interactive visualization. With the vast amounts of data that are available, novel ways of presenting and interacting with this are necessary. Card *et al.* (1999) is an excellent set of readings covering many of the pioneering systems. Spence (2001) provides a good introduction to the area and Card (2012) provides a thorough and accessible treatment of the options. Interactive visualizations are concerned with harnessing the power of novel interactive techniques with novel presentations of large quantities of data. Indeed, Card (2012) argues that visualization is concerned with 'amplifying cognition'. It achieves this through:

- increasing the memory and processing resources available to people,
- reducing the search for information,
- helping people to detect patterns in the data,
- helping people to draw inferences from the data,
- encoding data in an interactive medium.

Ben Shneiderman has long been a designer of great visualizations (see www.cs.umd.edu/nben/index.html). He has a 'mantra', an overriding principle for developing visualizations:

Overview first, zoom and filter, then details on demand.

The aim of the designer is to provide people with a good overview of the extent of the whole dataset, to allow zooming in to focus on details when required, and to provide dynamic queries that filter out the data that is not required. Card (2012) includes retrieval by example as another key feature. So rather than having to specify what is required in abstract terms, people request items similar to one they are viewing. Ahlberg and Shneiderman's (1994) Film Finder is an excellent example of this (Figure 12.37). In the first display we see hundreds of films represented as coloured dots and organized spatially in terms of year of release (horizontal axis) and rating (vertical axis). By adjusting the sliders on the

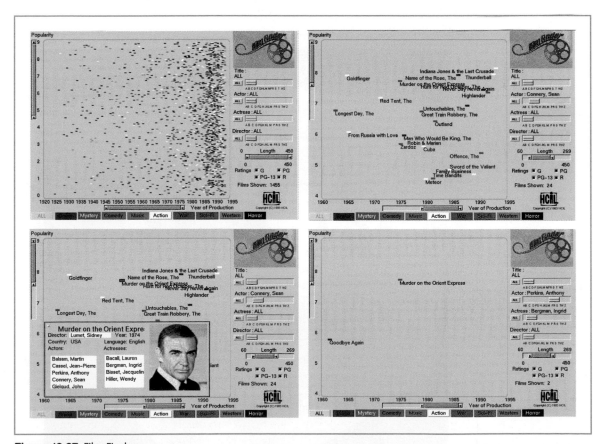

Figure 12.37 Film Finder

(Source: Ahlberg, C. and Shneiderman, B. (1994) Visual information seeking: Tight Coupling of Dynamic Query Filters with Starfield Displays, *Proceedings of the CHI'94 Conference*, pp. 313–317. © 1994 ACM, Inc. Reprinted by permission.)

right-hand side, the display zooms in on a selected part of the first display, allowing names to be revealed. Effectively the sliders provide dynamic queries on the data, allowing people to focus in on the part that is of interest. Clicking on a film brings up the details of a film, allowing this to be used for retrieval-by-example style further searches.

Another classic example of a visualization is ConeTree (Figure 12.38) Various facilities are available that allow people to 'fly' around the display, identifying and picking out items of interest. Once again the interactive visualization allows for overview first, zoom and filter, and details on demand. The key thing with visualizations is to facilitate 'drilling down' into the data.

Figure 12.39 shows the display of the stock market at SmartMoney.com. This display is known as a 'tree map'. The map is colour-coded from red through black to green, indicating a fall in value, through no change to a rise in value. The brightness of colour indicates the amount of change. Companies are represented by blocks, the size of the block representing the size of the company. Mousing over the block brings up the name and clicking on it reveals the details.

Figure 12.40 shows a different type of display where connections are shown by connecting lines. It is an on-line thesaurus that demonstrates the 'fish-eye' capability which again allows for the focus and context feature required by visualizations. This allows users to see what is nearby and related to the thing that they are focusing on. There are many more exciting and stimulating visualizations built for specific applications. Card (2012) lists many and Card et al. (1999) discuss specific designs and their rationale.

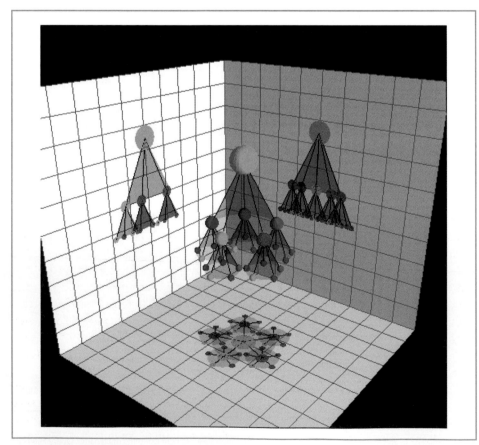

Figure 12.38 ConeTree

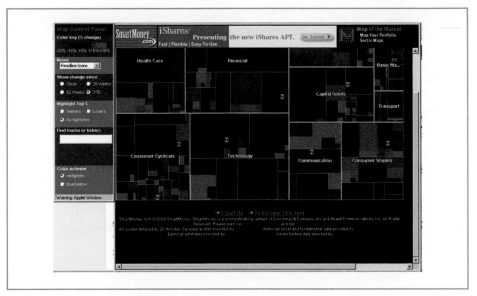

Figure 12.39 SmartMoney.com

(Source: www.smartmoney.com/map-of-the-market © SmartMoney 2004. All rights reserved. Used with permission. SmartMoney is a joint venture of Dow Jones & Company, Inc. and Hearst Communications, Inc.)

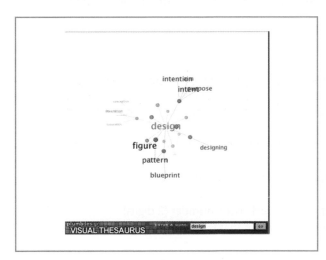

Figure 12.40 The Visual Thesaurus™

(Source: www.plumbdesign.com/thesaurus Visual Thesaurus™ (powered by Thinkmap®) © 2004 Plumb Design, Inc. All rights reserved)

Card (2012) argues that the key decision in any visualization is to decide which attributes of an object are to be used to spatially organize the data. In Film Finder it is rating and year. In SmartMoney.com it is the market sector. Once this has been decided, there are relatively few visual distinctions that can be made. The designer can use points, lines, areas or volumes to mark different types of data. Objects can be connected with lines or enclosed inside containers. Objects can be distinguished in terms of colour, shape, texture, position, size and orientation. Other visual features that can be used to distinguish items include resolution, transparency, arrangements, the hue and saturation of colours, lighting and motion.

There are a number of novel visualization applications that are available to view certain websites and other large datasets such as collections of photos. Cool Iris is one such application, facilitating panning, zooming, and moving through the data in an extremely engaging way. DeepZoom is a zoomable interface based on Silverlight from Microsoft and Adobe market Papervision which provides similar functionality based on Flex.

Summary and key points

The design of visual interfaces is a central skill for interactive system designers. There are principles of aesthetics to consider (we covered aesthetics in Chapter 5), but mostly designers need to concentrate on understanding the range of 'widgets' that they have available and how they can be best deployed. It is how the overall interaction works as a whole that is important.

● Graphical user interfaces use a combination of WIMP features and other graphical objects as the basis of their design.

● Design guidelines are available from work in psychology and perception and from principles of graphic design.

● In information design interactive visualizations need to be considered when there is a large amount of data to be displayed.

Exercises

1 Examine the tabbed dialogue widget shown in Figure 12.30. Which of the major components of human cognition are being addressed in the design?

2 (**Advanced**) I pay my household credit card bill every month using my debit card (which is used for transferring money from my bank account). The procedure is as follows:
   ● I have to phone the credit card company on a 12-digit telephone number.
   ● Then from the spoken menu I press 2 to indicate I wish to pay my bill.
   ● I am instructed to enter my 16-digit credit card number followed by the hash key.
   ● I am then told to enter the amount I want to pay in pounds and pence (let's imagine I wish to pay £500.00 – 7 characters).
   ● Then I am told to enter my debit card number (16 digits) followed by the hash key.
   ● Then I am asked for the debit card's issue number (2 digits).
   ● Then the system asks me to confirm that I wish to pay £500.00, by pressing the hash key.
   ● This ends the transaction. The number of keystrokes totals $12 + 1 + 16 + 7 + 16 + 2 + 1 = 55$ keystrokes on a handset which does not have a backspace key.
   What design changes would you recommend to reduce the likelihood of making a mistake in this complex transaction?

Further reading

Card, S. (2012) Information visualizations. In Jacko, J.A. (eds.) *The Human–Computer Interaction Handbook*, **3rd edn.** CRC Press, Taylor and Francio, Boca Raton, FL, 515–48.

Marcus, A. (1992) *Graphic Design for Electronic Documents and User Interfaces.* ACM Press, New York.

Getting ahead

Cooper, A., Reiman, R. and Cronin, D. (2007) *About Face 3: The Essentials of Interaction Design.* Wiley, Hoboken, NJ. *Provides a wealth of detailed interface design guidance and numerous examples of good design.*

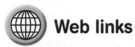 **Web links**

For further information on Horton's approach to icon design see **www.horton.com**

The accompanying website has links to relevant websites. Go to
www.pearsoned.co.uk/benyon

Comments on challenges

Challenge 12.1

Saying 'Computer' puts the computer into the correct mode to receive commands. In the lift the only commands the system responds to are instructions on which deck to go to. Thus the context of the interaction in the lift removes the need for a command to establish the correct mode.

Challenge 12.2

Radio buttons for the colour scheme – only one option can be chosen. The incoming mail preferences use checkboxes since multiple preferences can be selected.

Challenge 12.3

Again, instances abound. An example of design for recognition is the provision of a drop-down list of all airports for a particular city destination in a flight booking site rather than expecting customers to recall which airports exist and type in the exact name.

Chapter 13
Multimodal interface design

Contents

Aims

In the design of interactive systems one thing that is certain is that designers will increasingly be making use of technologies that go far beyond the screen-based systems that used to be their main concern. Designers will develop multimedia experiences using a variety of modalities (sound, vision, touch, etc.) combined in novel ways. They will be mixing the physical and the digital. In this chapter we look at issues of designing for multimodal and mixed reality systems, at designing for sound, touch and at wearable computing. (Related material on design can be found in Chapter 18 on ubiquitous computing and Chapter 19 on mobile computing. Auditory and haptic perception is discussed in Chapter 25.)

After studying this chapter you should understand:

- The spectrum of media, modalities and realities
- The key design guidelines for designing for audition
- The role of touch, haptics and kinaesthetics
- Designing for tangible and wearable computing.

13.1 Introduction

Sutcliffe (2012) distinguishes several key concepts of communication:

- *Message* is the content of a communication between a sender and a receiver.
- *Medium* is the means by which a message is delivered, and how the message is represented.
- *Modality* is the sense by which a message is sent or received by people or machines.

→ Some related ideas of semiotics are discussed in Chapter 24

A message is conveyed by a medium and received through a modality.

The term 'mixed reality' was coined by Milgram *et al.* in 1994 to encompass a number of simulation technologies, including augmented reality (digital information added to the real world) and augmented virtuality (real information added to the digital world). The result was the Reality–Virtuality continuum, as shown in Figure 13.1. The continuum can be described as 'the landscape between the real and the virtual' (Hughes *et al.* 2004), where the two are blended together. Milgram *et al.* (1994) did not see this as an adequate representation of mixed reality and instead proposed a three-dimensional taxonomy. In essence there are three scales covering:

- 'Extent of World Knowledge' (the degree to which the world is modelled in the computer)
- 'Reproduction Fidelity' (the quality of resolution and hence the realism of the real and virtual worlds)
- 'Extent of Presence Metaphor' (the degree to which people are meant to feel present in the system).

→ Presence is discussed in Chapter 24

However, it is the one-dimensional continuum that has been most widely accepted (Hughes *et al.*, 2004; Nilsen, *et al.* 2004).

The Augmented Reality (AR) region of the scale aims to bring digital information into the real world whereas augmented virtuality applications would include Google Earth. By far the most common blending in AR is that of visual stimuli. Here a live video stream can be enhanced with computer-generated objects (rendered so that they appear to be within the actual scene). Methods of presenting this visual information fall into the two main categories: immersive (where people see no view other than that of the mixed reality environment) and non-immersive (where the mixed reality environment takes up only a portion of the field of view). The latter method can make use of a vast range of displays, including computer monitors, mobile devices and large screen displays. For immersive presentations people will generally wear a special helmet which incorporates a display, and which excludes any other view of the outside world. These head-mounted displays (HMDs) are split into two categories: *video see-through* (where the real world is recorded by a video camera and people are presented with a digital display) and *optical see-through* (where the display screens are semi-transparent, allowing a direct view of the real world and only adding computer graphics on top).

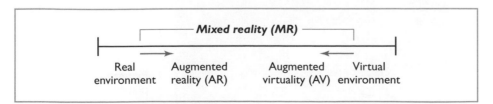

Figure 13.1 Reality–Virtuality (RV) Continuum
(Source: Adapted from Milgram, P. *et al.* (1994))

The second most common (and often used in conjunction with the previous) is auditory simulation. In this case computer-generated sounds can be supplied in such a way that they appear to originate from locations within the real environment. Common methods include the use of headphones or speaker arrangements, but there are more exotic technologies such as a *hypersonic sound device* that can target a specific location and make it appear that the sound is originating from there.

Of the remaining three senses, the sense of touch (or haptics) is the most developed field, with work ranging from the physical sensation of holding objects to simulating the sensation of touching different surfaces (Hayward *et al.*, 2004).

Smell has been simulated, but with limited success. Developments are even being made at the University of Tsukuba in simulating the sensation of eating (Iwata *et al.*, 2004). However, these systems are currently unwieldy and limited in application.

BOX 13.1

Smell, taste and emotion

Smell and taste are challenging senses for digital technologies because scientists have not been able to identify the basic components of these senses. Whereas a particular colour can be made up from a combination of three primary colours red, green and blue, we have no ideas what the primary components are for smell and taste. Moreover, since these are inherently analogue media, we can't digitize them to transmit the information over networks.

People have developed smell projectors that can deliver a burst of a particular perfume smell but it is difficult to keep the smell localized and to get rid of the smell when that part of the interaction is over. It is sometimes said that taste can be described in terms of five basic tastes; sweet, sour, salty, bitter and umami. However, there are many other sensations that can be detected by the tongue that contribute to the overall sensation of a particular taste.

Smell is particularly connected with emotions and will often evoke memories of past events and people. Scientists believe this is because the olfactory system is connected into the limbic system in the body.

Adrian Cheok at the Mixed Reality Lab in Keio University in Japan has been experimenting with a number of different ways of generating and interacting with taste and smell. The food project there is looking at producing digitized foods using a 3D printer and synthetic food material (Figure 13.2).

We can already send hugs and kisses to our loved ones over the Internet using devices such as the hug-me T-shirt. How long is it before we can send digitized birthday cakes or the smell of baking bread?

Figure 13.2 A food printer

(Source: Mixed Reality Lab, National University of Singapore)

13.2 Interacting in mixed reality

Interaction tools used in virtual reality include: 'spacemice', which expand the two degrees of freedom in traditional mice (horizontal and vertical movement) to six degrees of freedom (horizontal, vertical, depth movements and yaw, pitch and roll rotations); 'data gloves', where a glove is fitted with sensors to track hand location and finger positions and allows the grabbing and manipulation of virtual objects; and 'wands', such as the Wii, which are sticks again with six degrees of freedom and various input controls such as buttons and scrollers. These tools offer full three-dimensional input. TACTool has added tactile feedback to a wand device (Schoenfelder *et al.*, 2004), and interaction slippers, which add some functionality of datagloves to feet. Microsoft's Kinect allows for hand, arm and body gestures to interact with the content.

Mixed reality interaction demands the most from interaction designers as they grapple with technological problems and usability issues side by side. One technical issue is that of accurately aligning the real and virtual environments: a process called 'registration' (Azuma, 1997). A number of systems allow the technology used for performing this registration to also offer the kind of 3D input provided by the tools discussed previously. A notable example of this is the ARToolkit (2007), a software library that includes facilities required to optically track images placed in the real world, and align computer-generated graphics based on their position and orientation.

Quick Response (QR) codes can be used to connect the real and virtual worlds as can data from the Global Positioning System (GPS). Images can be used as a marker, so that when a smartphone captures the image it triggers the delivery of some content such as a video. It all depends on the accuracy required. A GPS trigger, for example, could be accurate to 5 metres (and accuracy varies with the actual device used), but this would be no use for a very precise application such as remote surgery when the alignment of real and virtual worlds is a major technological undertaking.

A huge number of applications in the field of AR use the ARToolkit; for example, in the Tangible Hypermedia application (Sinclair *et al.*, 2002), some markers are used for objects (planes in the examples), and others as data sources called 'spice piles'. By moving a spice pile near to an object and shaking it, data is sprinkled onto the object in the form of labels. The longer a person shakes the spice pile, the more detailed the information becomes. People can also shake the object, dislodging some of the spice dust, and reducing the complexity of the labels.

When mixed reality is applied to games the range of input methods becomes more diverse. Some applications use traditional game-controller-style inputs, using augmented reality as a replacement for a computer monitor. Examples include ARWorms (Nilsen *et al.,* 2004) and Touchspace (Cheok *et al.,* 2002).

However, Touchspace also uses full body interaction as a method of input. People navigate around a real-world space (an empty room) with a window onto a virtual world. The first objective in the game is to find a witch's castle, and then to battle her in AR. A number of applications go further with full body interaction, not limiting themselves to a single room. One of the most advanced is the Human Pacman game (Cheok *et al.,* 2003) where participants take one of three roles: a Pacman (collecting spheres from the environment by walking over them); a ghost (aiming to capture the Pacmen by touching their shoulders – where there is a touch sensor); or helper (given an overview of the game through a traditional interface, and given the task of guiding either a ghost or a Pacman). As well as collecting virtual objects (virtual spheres), players also collect ingredients to make 'cookies' (similar to power pills in the original Pacman) by picking up Bluetooth-enabled physical objects. The AR Quake system (Thomas *et al.,* 2000) is

Figure 13.3 AR Quake

(Source: Bruce H. Thomas)

similar to the Human Pacman work in that an outdoor AR game was developed. Players in a real world do battle with virtual monsters (Figure 13.3).

Immersive virtual reality requires people to wear a light-excluding helmet (an HMD – head-mounted display) which houses the display, and a data glove which facilitates the manipulation of virtual objects within virtual reality. An HMD consists of two colour displays located in line with one's eyes and a pair of stereo earphones. An HMD also has a head tracker which provides information about the wearer's position and orientation in space. Figure 13.4 offers a view of the interior of an HMD, while Figure 13.5 shows one in use. Gloves equipped with sensors (data gloves) are able to sense the movements of the hand, which are translated into corresponding movements in the virtual environment. Data gloves are used to 'grasp' objects in virtual environments or to 'fly' through

Figure 13.4 An interior view of an HMD

(Source: Phil Turner)

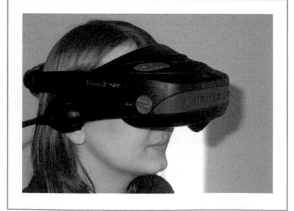

Figure 13.5 An HMD

(Source: Phil Turner)

virtual scenes. Figure 13.6 is an illustration of a force-feedback data glove which uses actuators to 'feed back' an impression of, say, the grasped object.

The main features of immersive VR are:

- Head-referenced viewing provides a natural interface for navigation in three-dimensional space and allows for look-around, walk-around and fly-through capabilities in virtual environments.
- Stereoscopic viewing enhances the perception of depth and the sense of space.
- The virtual world is presented in full scale and relates properly to human size.
- Realistic interactions with virtual objects via data glove and similar devices allow for manipulation, operation and control of virtual worlds.
- The convincing illusion of being fully immersed in an artificial world can be enhanced by auditory, haptic and other non-visual technologies.

The original Computer Augmented Virtual Environment (CAVE) was developed at the University of Illinois at Chicago and provides the illusion of immersion by projecting stereo images on the walls and floor of a room-sized (a pretty small room, it should be said) cube. People wearing lightweight stereo glasses can enter and walk freely inside the CAVE. A panorama is like a small cinema. The virtual image is projected onto a curved screen before the 'audience' who are required to wear liquid-crystal display (LCD) shuttered spectacles (goggles). The shutters on the LCD spectacles open and close over one eye and then the other 50 times a second or so. The positions of the spectacles are tracked using infra-red sensors. The experience of a panorama is extraordinary, with the virtual world appearing to stream past the audience. Panoramas are expensive and far from portable.

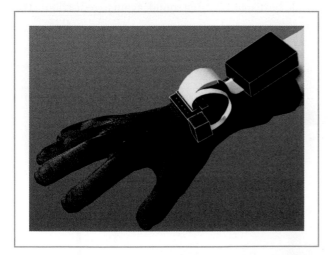

Figure 13.6 A force-feedback data glove

(Source: Image courtesy www.5DT.com)

Non-immersive virtual reality (sometimes called desktop virtual reality) can be found in a wide range of desktop applications and games as it does not always require specialist input or output devices.

Multimodal systems that do not mix realities, but combine gesture, speech, movement and sound, are increasingly common and raise their own issues to do with synchronizing the modalities. One of the earliest systems was 'Put That There' (Bolt, 1980), which combined speech and gesture. More recent examples include the 'Funky Wall' interactive mood board described in Chapter 9, which also includes proximity to the wall as a modality (Lucero *et al*., 2008).

13.3 Using sound at the interface

Sound is an increasingly important part of interface design in both mixed reality and multimodal systems. The following section is based closely on Hoggan and Brewster's chapter on 'Non-speech auditory and crossmodal output' (Hoggan and Brewster, 2012) in *The Human–Computer Interaction Handbook*. The main headings are theirs.

Vision and hearing are interdependent

While comic book superheroes may acquire super-sensitive hearing on the loss of their sight, for the rest of us ordinary mortals our visual and auditory systems have evolved to work together. It is interesting to contrast the kinds and range of information our eyes and ears provide. Sight is a narrow, forward-facing, richly detailed picture of the world, while hearing provides information from all around us. An unexpected flash of light or a sudden movement orients our heads – and hence our hearing – to the source; the sound of a car approaching from behind makes us turn to look. Both sound and vision allow us to orient ourselves in the world.

Reduce the load on the visual system

This design guideline and the next two are very closely related. It is now recognized that modern, large or even multiple-screen graphical interfaces use the human visual system very intensively – perhaps over-intensively (see Figure 13.7). To reduce this sensory overload, key information could be displayed using sound, again to redistribute the processing burden to other senses.

Figure 13.7 A typical visually cluttered desktop

Challenge 13.1

Suggest three different ways in which information belonging to a typical desktop could be displayed using sound.

Reduce the amount of information needed on screen

One of the great design tensions in the creation of mobile and ubiquitous devices is to display a usable amount of information on a small screen – small as in palm-sized, or pocket-sized, or carried or worn without a course in body building. The problem is that we live in an information-rich society. When moving information from one place to another was expensive, the telegram ruled: 'Send money. Urgent'. Now we are likely to send a three-part multimedia presentation complete with streamed video, with the theme of 'send money, urgent'. Mobile and ubiquitous devices have very small screens which are unsuited to viewing large bodies of data. To minimize this problem, information could be presented in sound in order to free screen space.

Reduce demands on visual attention

Again in the context of mobile and ubiquitous devices, there is an uneasy and at present unsatisfactory need to switch from attending to the world – crossing the road, driving a car, following a stimulating presentation – to paying attention to the display of such devices. As we saw earlier, the UK government made it an offence from December 2003 to drive a car while using a mobile phone (hands-free phones excepted). The need for visual attention in particular could be reduced if sound were used instead.

→ Attention is discussed in Chapter 21

The auditory sense is under-utilized

We listen to highly complex musical structures such as symphonies and operas. These pieces of music comprise large complex structures and sub-structures. This suggests that there is, at least, the potential of using music to transmit complex information successfully.

Sound is attention-grabbing

While we can look away from an unpleasant sight, the same is not true of an unpleasant sound. The best we can do is to cover our ears. This makes sound very useful for attracting attention or communicating important information.

To make computers more usable by visually disabled users

While screen readers can be used to 'read' on-screen textual information, they cannot easily read graphical information. Providing some of this information in an auditory form can help alleviate this problem.

Challenge 13.2

Can you think of possible disadvantages to augmenting the interface with sound? Or circumstances where it would be inappropriate?

To date, most research on auditory user interfaces (AUIs) has concentrated on the use of either earcons or auditory icons. **Earcons** are musical sounds designed to reflect events in the interface. For example, a simple series of notes may be used to indicate the receipt of an SMS message on a mobile phone. A different sound is used when an SMS is sent. In contrast, **auditory icons** reflect the argument that we make use of many sounds in the everyday world without thinking about their musical content. The sounds used in these interfaces are caricatures of everyday sounds, where aspects of the sound's source correspond to events in the interface. The sound for an SMS being sent on my phone is a 'whoosh': off it goes.

Earcons

Earcons are abstract, musical tones that can be used in structured combinations to create auditory messages. They were first proposed by Blattner *et al.* (1989) who defined earcons as 'non-verbal audio messages that are used in the computer–user interface to provide information to the user about some computer object, operation or interaction'. Earcons are based on musical sounds.

Numerous studies of the usefulness of earcons in providing cues in navigating menu structures have been conducted. The following study, from Brewster (1998), involved the creation of a menu hierarchy of 27 nodes and four levels with an earcon for each node. Participants in the study were asked to determine their location in the hierarchy by listening to an earcon. Results of this and similar experiments showed that participants could identify their location with greater than 80 per cent accuracy. This suggests that earcons are a useful way of providing navigational information. Given their usefulness, one proposed use for earcons is in telephone-based interfaces where navigation has been found to be a problem.

These design guidelines have been adapted from the work of Brewster, Wright and Edwards (1993). They are quoted more or less verbatim.

- *Timbre*. Use synthesized musical instrument timbres. Where possible use timbres with multiple harmonics. This helps perception and avoids masking.
- *Pitch*. Do not use pitch on its own unless there are very big differences between those used. Some suggested ranges for pitch are maximum 5 kHz (four octaves above middle C) and minimum 125–130 Hz (an octave below middle C).
- *Register*. If this alone is to be used to differentiate earcons which are otherwise the same, then large differences should be used. Three or more octaves difference give good rates of recognition.
- *Rhythm*. Make rhythms as different as possible. Putting different numbers of notes in each rhythm was very effective. Very short notes might not be noticed, so do not use less than eighth notes or quavers.
- *Intensity*. Some suggested ranges are maximum 20 dB above threshold and minimum 10 dB above threshold. Care must be taken in the use of intensity. The overall sound level will be under the control of the user of the system. Earcons should all be kept within a close range so that if the user changes the volume of the system no sound will be lost.
- *Combinations*. When playing earcons one after another, leave a gap between them so that users can tell where one finishes and the other starts. A delay of 0.1 second is adequate.

Auditory icons

One of the most famous examples of auditory icons is the SonicFinder developed for Apple. The SonicFinder was developed as an alternative to the Macintosh Finder (equivalent to Explorer in MS Windows). The SonicFinder used sound in a way that reflects how it is used in the everyday world. Users were able to 'tap' objects in order to determine whether they are applications, disks or folders, and it was possible to gauge their size depending upon how high-pitched they sounded (small objects sounded high-pitched while large objects sounded low-pitched). Movement was also represented as a scraping sound.

Soundscapes

The term 'soundscape' is derived from 'landscape' and can be defined as the auditory environment within which a listener is immersed. This differs from the more technical concept of 'soundfield', which can be defined as the auditory environment surrounding the sound source, which is normally considered in terms of sound pressure level, duration, location and frequency range.

Challenge 13.3

We use background sound to a surprising degree in monitoring our interaction with the world around us. For example, I know that my laptop is still writing to a CD because it makes a sort of whirring sound. If my seminar group are working on problems in small groups, a rustling of papers and quiet-ish murmuring indicates all is well, complete silence means that I have baffled people, and louder conversation often means that most have finished. At home, I can tell that the central heating is working as it should by the background noise of the boiler (furnace) and the approximate time during the night by the volume of traffic noise from the road.

Make a similar – but longer – list for yourself. It might be easier to do this over a couple of days as you notice sounds. Read over your list and note down any ideas for using sound in a similar way in interaction design.

An important issue in designing for sound is that of *discrimination*. While it is easy to talk about discriminating between low- and high-pitched tones, it is quite another to discriminate between quite low and fairly low tones. There are a number of open questions about how well we can distinguish between different tones in context (in a busy office or a noisy reception area) and this is made worse by the obvious fact that sounds are not persistent. One of the strengths of the graphical user interface is the persistence of error messages, status information, menus and buttons. Auditory user interfaces are, in contrast, transient.

Speech-based interfaces

Speech-based interfaces include speech output and speech input. Speech output has developed over the past few years into a robust technology and is increasingly common in such things as satellite navigation systems in cars ('satnavs') and other areas such as announcements at railway stations, airports, etc. Speech output uses a system that converts text to speech, TTS. Sounds are recorded from an individual and are then stitched together through the TTS to create whole messages. In some places TTS is becoming so ubiquitous that is gets confusing hearing the same voice in different locations. The woman telling you something at a railway station is the same woman advising you on your satnav system. TTS systems are readily available and easy to install into a system. They have gone beyond the robotic-type voices of the last decade to produce realistic and emotionally charged speech output when required.

Speech input has not quite reached the level of sophistication of speech output, but it too is becoming a technology that has reached levels of usability such that the interaction system designer can now consider it to be a real option. The best systems require people to train the automatic speech recognizer (ASR) to recognize their particular voice. After only 7–10 minutes of training an ASR can achieve recognition levels of 95 per cent accuracy. This paves the way for natural language systems (NLS) where people can have conversations with their devices. There are still many obstacles to overcome in NLS – it is one thing to understand the speech, it is another to understand what the person means by what they are saying. But in limited domains, where dictionaries can be used to help disambiguate words, they are starting to make a real impact. In 2011 Apple introduced a speech-based 'personal assistant' called Siri to the iPhone which can carry out simple tasks such as sending a text message or finding out information. It has met with a mixed reception, sometimes appearing to be quite impressive and sometimes being very stupid!

→ Haptic perception is covered in Chapter 25

13.4 Tangible interaction

Tangible means being able to be touched or grasped and being perceived through the sense of touch. Tangible interaction is a practical application of haptics and has been used for thousands of years (Figure 13.8). Tangible interaction has given rise to TUIs – tangible user interfaces, which have a structure and logic both similar to and different from GUIs. With the introduction of multi-touch displays, TUIs promise to be increasingly important as they lead to interaction through physical objects and through gesture recognition.

Figure 13.8 An abacus, which combines tangible input, output and the data being manipulated

(Source: www.sphere.bc.ca/test/sruniverse.html. Courtesy of Sphere Research Corporation)

Most of the work to date has been confined to the major research laboratories, for example the Media Lab at MIT, which have constructed advanced prototype systems. Many of these systems have been used in fairly specific domains, for example urban planning (Urp) and landscape architecture among others. Illuminating Clay is described in detail below. While many of these systems may never become commercial products, they do illustrate the state of the art in tangible interaction design.

The Tangible Media Lab at MIT describe their vision for the future of HCI in the following way:

Tangible Bits is our vision of Human Computer Interaction (HCI) which guides our research in the Tangible Media Group. People have developed sophisticated skills for sensing and manipulating our physical environments. However, most of these skills are not employed by traditional GUI (Graphical User Interface). Tangible Bits seeks to build upon these skills by giving physical form to digital information, seamlessly coupling the dual worlds of bits and atoms. Guided by the Tangible Bits vision, we are designing 'tangible user interfaces' which employ physical objects, surfaces, and spaces as tangible embodiments of digital information. These include foreground interactions with graspable objects and augmented surfaces, exploiting the human senses of touch and kinesthesia. We are also exploring background information displays which use 'ambient media'– ambient light, sound, airflow, and water movement. Here, we seek to communicate digitally-mediated senses of activity and presence at the periphery of human awareness.

(http://tangible.media.mit.edu/projects/Tangible_Bits)

So their 'goal is to change the "painted bits" of GUIs (graphical user interfaces) to "tangible bits", taking advantage of the richness of multimodal human senses and skills developed through our lifetime of interaction with the physical world'.

Why tangible interaction?

There are a number of good reasons why we should think about adopting (or at least exploring the possibilities of) tangible interaction. First of all, if we could remove the divide between the electronic and physical worlds we potentially have the benefits of both. We could have all the advantages of computation brought to us beyond the confines of the graphical display unit and have them, as it were, present-to-hand. Present-to-hand could also be taken literally by putting information and computation literally 'in our hands' (we are, after all, discussing tangible interaction). Finally, and this is proving to be a recurrent theme in this chapter, there may be advantages in off-loading some of the burden of our computation (thinking and problem solving) by (a) accessing our spatial cognition and (b) adopting a more concrete style of interaction (like sketching, which provides a more fluid and natural style of interaction). Graspable, physical objects provide stronger (real) affordances as compared to their virtual equivalents.

**FURTHER
THOUGHTS**

Hiroshi Ishii is one of the key people at MIT and a leading light in the world of tangible computing. He notes that

TUIs couple physical representations (e.g. spatial manipulable physical objects) with digital representations (e.g. graphics and audio), yielding interactive systems that are computationally mediated but generally not identifiable as 'computers' per se.

Ullmer and Ishii (2002)

In plain English, if we want to use an on-screen, virtual tool – say a pen – we would use a real, physical pen which in some sense has been mapped onto the virtual equivalent. Picking up the real pen would then be mirrored in the computer by the virtual pen being raised or becoming active. Drawing with the real pen would result in an equivalent virtual drawing which might be displayed on a screen and represented as a data object.

TUIs are different from GUIs in many different ways, but here are three important ones:

- TUIs use physical representations – such as modelling clay, physical pens and so on and physical drawing boards rather than pictures of them displayed on monitors. So, for example, instead of having to manipulate an image on a screen using a mouse and keyboard, people can draw directly onto surfaces using highlighter pens.

- As these tangible, graspable elements cannot, of course, perform computation on their own, they must be linked to a digital representation. As Ullmer and Ishii put it, playing with mud pies without computation is just playing with mud pies.
- TUIs integrate representation and control which GUIs keep strictly apart. GUIs have an MVC structure – Model–View–Control. In traditional GUIs we use peripheral devices such as a mouse or keyboard to control a digital representation of what we are working with (the model), the results of which are displayed on a screen or printer or some other form of output (the view). This is illustrated in Figure 13.9.

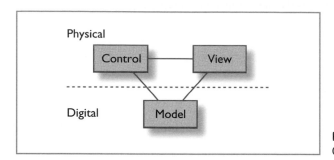

Figure 13.9 Model–View–Control

TUIs in contrast have a more complex model that can be seen in Figure 13.10. This is the MCRpd model. The control and model elements are unchanged but the view component is split between Rep-p (physical representation) and Rep-d (digital representation). This model highlights the tight linkage between the control and physical representation. This MCRpd model is realized in the prototypes described in the section below.

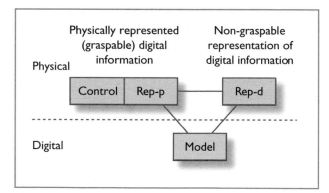

Figure 13.10 MCRpd

Illuminating Clay

Illuminating Clay is an interesting, though specialist, example of tangible computing. Illuminating Clay is introduced and placed in context by its creators with the following scenario:

> A group of road builders, environment engineers and landscape designers stand at an ordinary table on which is placed a clay model of a particular site in the landscape. Their task is to design the course of a new roadway, housing complex and parking area that will satisfy engineering, environmental and aesthetic requirements. Using her finger the engineer flattens out the side of a hill in the model to provide a flat plane for an area for car parking As she does so an area of yellow illumination appears in another part of the model.

The environmental engineer points out that this indicates a region of possible landslide caused by the change in the terrain and resulting flow of water. The landscape designer suggests that this landslide could be avoided by adding a raised earth mound around the car park. The group tests the hypothesis by adding material to the model and all three observe the resulting effect on the stability of the slope.

Piper, et al. (2002)

In the Illuminating Clay system, the physical, tangible objects are made of clay. Piper *et al.* (2002) experimented with several different types of modelling material, including Lego blocks, modelling clay, Plasticine, Silly Putty and so on. Eventually they found that a thin layer of Plasticine supported by a metal mesh core worked best. This clay was then shaped into the desired form by the landscape specialists (see Figure 13.11). The matte white finish also proved to be highly suitable as a projection surface onto which the digital elements of the system were projected. Ordinarily, people working with landscapes would create complex models using computer-aided design (CAD) software and then run simulations to examine, for instance, the effects of wind flow, drainage and the position of powerlines and roads. With Illuminating Clay, the potential consequences of the landscape are projected directly (for example, as in the scenario above, a patch of coloured light) onto the clay itself.

The coupling between clay and its digital representation is managed by means of a ceiling-mounted laser scanner and digital projector. Using an angled mirror, the scanner and projector are aligned at the same optical origin and the two devices are calibrated to scan and project over an equal area. This configuration ensures that all the surfaces that are visible to the scanner can also be projected upon.

Thus Illuminating Clay demonstrates the advantages of combining physical and digital representations for landscape analysis. The physical clay model conveys spatial relationships that can be directly manipulated by the user's hands. This approach allows users to quickly create and understand highly complex topographies that would be time-consuming using conventional computer-aided design (CAD tools).

Figure 13.11 An image from Illuminating Clay

(Source: Piper, B., Ratti, C. and Ishii, H. (2002) Illuminating Clay: a 3D tangible interface for landscape analysis. *Proceedings of the SIGCHI Conference on Human Factors in Computing Systems: Changing our world, changing ourselves*, Minneapolis, MN. 20–25 April, CHI '02 ACM, pp. 355–62. © ACM. Inc. Reprinted by permission. http://doi.acm.org/10.1145/503376.503439)

Challenge 13.4

Suggest other application areas where Illuminating Clay may be useful.

13.5 Gestural interaction and surface computing

With the arrival of multi-touch surfaces – table tops, smartphones, tablets and interactive walls that recognize multiple touch points – a whole new era of interaction design is just beginning. A number of sessions at the CHI2009 conference were devoted to exploring these issues. The iPhone introduced gestures for 'making things bigger' (pinch with two fingers and draw them out) and 'making things smaller' (touch an object with two fingers and draw them in) (see Table 13.1). Experimental systems such as CityWall (http://citywall.org) introduced gestures for rotating objects, 'flicking' gestures to move objects from one location to another. Fiebrink *et al.* (2009) gave people the option of designing gestures, or using virtual controls on a tabletop application for collaborative audio editing. However, we are still some way from having the type of standard widgets that we see in GUIs. Different applications demand different types of gesture according to the different activities that people are engaged in. Interactive surfaces can be interacted with through direct touch, sweeping movements, rotation and flicking, which can be mapped onto specific functions. Interaction can also take place using physical objects that represent functions, or other objects. Similar to earcons these have been called 'phicons'. Combinations of phicons, virtual on-screen buttons, slides and other widgets and natural gestures (such as a tick gesture for 'OK', or a cross gesture for cancel) promise to open up new applications and new forms of operating system that support different gestures.

Table 13.1 iOS gestures

Gesture	Action
Tap	To press or select a control or item (analogous to a single mouse click).
Drag	To scroll or pan (that is, move side to side). To drag an element.
Flick	To scroll or pan quickly.
Swipe	With one finger, to reveal the Delete button in a table-view row, the hidden view in a split view (iPad only), or the Notification Center (from the top edge of the screen). With four fingers, to switch between apps on iPad.
Double tap	To zoom in and center a block of content or an image. To zoom out (if already zoomed in).
Pinch	Pinch open to zoom in. Pinch close to zoom out.
Touch and hold	In editable or selectable text, to display a magnified view for cursor positioning.
Shake	To initiate an undo or redo action.

Source: http://developer.apple.com/library/ios/#DOCUMENTATION/UserExperience/conceptual/
MobileHIG/Characteristics/Characteristics.html#//apple_ref/doc/vid/TP40006556-CH7-SW1

In Windows 8 there are a number of standard gestures for use with touchscreen devices. A swipe from the right-hand side of the tablet to the left brings up the 'charms' menu, which includes icons for Search, Share, Devices, Settings and Start Screen. A swipe from the left brings a list of the apps that are currently running, whereas a slow swipe from the left lets people select an app and position it on the main screen. Windows 8 has gestures for making things larger and smaller and right and left swipes will move between objects such as different sites on Internet Explorer. At the Start Screen, you can swipe down on any tile to select it and bring up additional options.

Surface computing brings its own set of design issues. Orientation has always been an issue in collaborative tabletop workspaces because when people are seated at different locations around a table, they will see the same object with different orientations. This affects comprehension of information, coordination of activities, and communication among participants. Different tabletop systems have found different solutions to this issue. Some systems use one single and fixed orientation where the participants have to sit side-by-side. Some systems use an automatic orientation of artefacts towards the people in the workspace, or use an automatic rotation of the workspace. However, most systems just let participants manually orient digital objects. Various techniques have been developed to facilitate orientation. Dragging and spinning artefacts in the workspace using fingers is one; another consists of a translation by clicking and dragging a digital object and a rotation by selecting, touching a corner, and then turning the object around an axis located at the centre of it (Kruger *et al.*, 2005).

There are a number of user interface issues specific to multi-touch interaction. The 'fat fingers, short arms' problem is just one. Fingers limit the precision of any input gesture such as touching or dragging. Thus, interface objects should have a minimum size, should not be close together and feedback should be given when people succeed in hitting the target (Lei and Wong, 2009; Shen *et al.*, 2006). Similarly short arms mean that targets must be relatively close to people. For example there is no point in having a menu at the top of a screen if people cannot reach it! Another problem is screen occlusion. When people interact with the interface their hands can occlude a part of the interface, especially the part immediately below what they are interacting with. To avoid this problem objects should be large, or gestures should be performed with only one finger (where the palm can be slanted) instead of spreading five fingers (Lei and Wong, 2009). Additionally, information such as a label, instructions or sub-controls should never be below an interactive object (Saffer, 2008).

Shen *et al.* (2006) developed two systems to avoid this occlusion. The first was an interactive pop-up menu that is able to rotate, linked to an object and which can be used for displaying information or performing commands, and the second a tool allowing people to perform operations on distant objects. Another UI issue is that when people perform actions, they might lead to unexpected activation of functionality (Ashbrook and Starner, 2010) such as if the surface records a false positive touch or gesture recognition for example, if someone's sleeve touches the surface as they reach over. Thus the system needs ways to differentiate an intentional gesture from an unintentional gesture.

Saffer (2008) provides good sound advice on gesture design coming from ergonomic principles such as 'avoid outer position, avoid repetition, relax muscles, utilize relaxed and neutral positions, avoid staying in a static position, and avoid internal and external force on joints'. He also warns us to consider fingernails, left-handed users, sleeves and gloves in the design of multi-touch interfaces. On large multi-touch tables, some parts of the display can be unreachable, thus, objects like menus, tools and work surface have to be mobile.

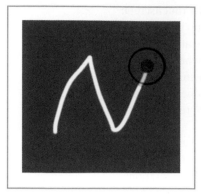

Figure 13.12 The N-wave gesture to open a browser; the red and black circles give feedback on the user's touches

→ We discuss different materials in Chapter 20

We described the design of a multi-touch tabletop application later (Chapter 16). However, on another project we were developing we realized that there was no standard gesture for 'open a browser'. We explored a number of options such as drawing a circle ('o' for open), but the problem here was that different people draw circles in different ways. We tried drawing a square. Just touching the surface led to a large number of false positives when the system detected a touch that was not intended to be an open-a-browser command. Finally we settled on the gesture shown in Figure 13.12 ('N' for new) because most people draw an 'N' from left to right and bottom to top and hence the system could detect the required orientation of the browser.

Surface computing does not just relate to flat surfaces such as tabletops, tablets and walls. Flexible displays are already being developed which can be produced in different shapes, and other materials such as fabrics can be used as interactive devices. These developments will once again change the issues for interaction design.

For example Pufferfish (Figure 13.13) makes large spherical displays and new OLED (organic light-emitting diode) technologies are allowing for curved and flexible displays. These bring new forms of interaction to the world of interaction design.

Gestural interaction does not always mean that users have to touch a surface. Sensors may detect different levels of proximity of people, or hands and can interact based on this information. The Kinect detects distant movement, allowing people to interact with content from a distance. In short, all manner of new forms of interaction with gestures and surfaces will appear in the next few years.

Figure 13.13 An interactive PufferSphere M600 which was used as part of the 'Audi Spheres' experience in Copenhagen July/August 2012, http://www.pufferfishdisplays .co.uk/2012/08/future-gazing-with-audi

(Source: www.pufferfishdisplays.co.uk/case-studies. Courtesy Pufferfish Ltd.)

Haptics meets hearing

A new mobile phone has just been announced which requires the user to put their finger into their ear. The Japanese telecoms company NTT DoCoMo has developed a wearable mobile phone that uses the human body to make calls. Called Finger Whisper, the device is built into a narrow strap worn on the wrist like a watch. To answer a call on the Finger Whisper phone, to make a call or hang up, the user simply touches forefinger to thumb and then puts their forefinger in their ear. Electronics in the wristband convert sound waves into vibrations, which are carried through the bones of the hand to the ear so that the Finger Whisper user can hear the other caller. A microphone in the wristband replaces the cell phone's usual mouthpiece, and instead of dialling a number, the user says it out loud. Voice recognition technology turns the command into a dialled number. The company said it was too early to say when the Finger Whisper phone might go on sale. However, it should be noted that the prototype is currently the size of a kitchen cupboard.

Summary and key points

There is no doubt that sound, touch and mixed reality will play an important role in the design of future interactions. Across the spectrum of virtual worlds mixing with the real world are opportunities for new and novel experiences. The work which has been carried out to make sound useful and usable at the interface is convincing but still has not been adopted by the major user interface designers. TUIs offer a new way of thinking about and interacting with computers. While the keyboard and mouse of the typical PC offer a tangible interface, true TUIs embodying the MCRpd model are still only available as advanced prototypes. Finally, gestural interaction will evolve rapidly over the next few years.

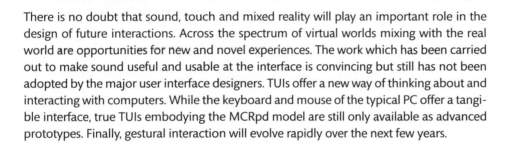

Exercises

1   Design a sonically enhanced interface for a *simple* game in the form of a general knowledge quiz for children. The quiz is presented as a set of multiple-choice questions. If time is short, confine yourself to one screen of the game. This is much more fun done in presentation software such as PowerPoint or any of the multimedia software packages if you are familiar with them.

2   Discuss the advantages and disadvantages of augmenting the user interface with (a) sound and (b) haptics. In your view, which has more potential and why? Support your argument with specific examples.

 ## Further reading

Ullmer, B. and Ishii, H. (2002) Emerging frameworks for tangible user interfaces. In Carroll, J.M. (ed.), *Human–Computer Interaction in the New Millennium*. ACM Press, New York. *A useful introduction to the tangibles domain.*

Getting ahead

Blauert, J. (1999) *Spatial Hearing*. MIT Press, Cambridge, MA.

 **Web links**

The Media Lab is a good place to start looking for examples of mixed reality and multimodal systems. See **www.mit.edu**

The accompanying website has links to relevant websites. Go to **www.pearsoned.co.uk/benyon**

 Comments on challenges

Challenge 13.1

Here are three possibilities. There are, of course, many more. All would need careful design.
1   Voice read-out of calendar reminders.
2   Different audio tones to distinguish levels in the file system hierarchy.
3   Read-out of senders and first lines of incoming e-mail, so one could do other physical jobs around the room while listening to a new batch of messages. Even better with voice command input.

Challenge 13.2

It can be a fascinating experience to attend to the usually unconscious use we make of sound. For example, an ATM does not have to make a noise as it counts out the money, but it is reassuring for people to know that the transaction is nearly complete. In fact lots of machines – kettles, drinks machines, cars, bikes and so on – indicate the state they are in through the sounds they make.

Challenge 13.3

The list you produce will be individual to you and your circumstances. An idea which comes to mind is attaching an unobtrusive humming to a file search or other lengthy operations, perhaps changing in pitch as it nears completion.

Challenge 13.4

Any area where the design of physical objects has to be checked for particular properties or against guidelines is a possibility. One might be the design of car bodies, which – at least until relatively recently – are 'mocked-up' full-size in order to check for wind resistance, etc. Designers make modifications to the mock-up by hand and then check in a wind tunnel.

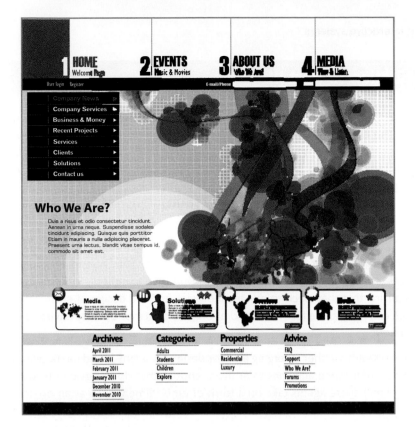

Part III

Contexts for designing interactive systems

Introduction to Part III

In this part we look at a number of different contexts in which interactive systems design takes place. The first of these is website design. The aim of Chapter 14 is to provide a practical approach to website development. Website development needs to take a human-centred approach just as other interactive systems do, so it is necessary to augment the approach described with the principles and practices of good design discussed in Part I and employing the techniques described in Part II. Chapter 15 covers the particular use of websites and mobile applications for social media which emphasizes people working together and sharing digital content.

Chapter 16 covers Computer Supported Cooperative Working (CSCW) and collaborative environments – particularly those making use of multitouch surfaces. Many organizations are realizing that they need to mix technologies and the design of environments to encourage creativity and effective collaboration. The demands of these environments are covered here.

Chapter 17 deals with another emerging area for designers, agent-based interaction. We are increasingly delegating activities to artificial entities that do things on our behalf: agents. Sometimes these agents take on a form of embodiment such as an on-screen avatar, or as a robotic character. Chapter 17 is about agents and avatars and how they provide a distinctive context for interactive systems design. The structure of agents is discussed along with issues of just how difficult it is to make sensible inferences from the limited data that interactive devices have access to.

Chapters 18 and 19 deal with two highly intertwined contexts: ubiquitous computing and mobile computing. Ubiquitous means everywhere and computers are everywhere partly because they are mobile, so design issues of the one get mixed with design issues of the other. However, the two chapters deal with things in a slightly different way. Chapter 18 deals with the more theoretical issues of ubiquitous computing and with the ideas of information spaces and how they can be successfully navigated. Chapter 19 is more practical, discussing how to design for small, mobile devices and taking readers through the design process as applied to mobile devices.

Finally, Chapter 20 introduces the new context of wearable computing. The emergence of interactive fabrics means that people can now wear their computers instead of carrying them! In Chapter 20 we look at the state of the art in wearable computing and where it may go over the next few years.

Case studies

Chapter 14 presents an example of website design, the design of the Robert Louis Stevenson website. This project illustrates many of the issues that all Web designers face. Chapter 16 describes our experiences in developing a multitouch table application for the Norwegian National Museum and how technologies and activities fit together to facilitate collaboration, including a study of the London Underground. Chapter 17 includes a case study of an e-mail filtering agent. Chapters 18 and 19 draw upon some recent project work that we have been involved with, known as Speckled Computing. This is an example of a wireless sensor network (WSN) consisting of potentially thousands and thousands of tiny, possibly mobile devices. Scattered over a physical area they create a cyber-physical system. This is the sort of context that the near future holds. In order to move through this space requires a mobile device.

Teaching and learning

This part contains seven different contexts that have specific requirements for interaction design. Thus each chapter can be studied as an example and used to explore the design processes and techniques discussed in Parts I and II. The list of topics covered in this part is shown below, each of which could take 10–15 hours of study to reach a good general level of understanding, or 3–5 hours for a basic appreciation of the issues. Of course, each topic could be the subject of extensive and in-depth study.

Topic 3.1	Website design	Sections 14.1–14.2, 14.5
Topic 3.2	Information architecture	Section 14.3
Topic 3.3	Navigation design for websites	Section 14.4
Topic 3.4	Social media	Sections 15.1–15.4
Topic 3.5	Future Internet	Section 15.5
Topic 3.6	Cooperative working	Sections 16.1–16.3
Topic 3.7	Collaborative environments	Section 16.4
Topic 3.8	Agent-based interaction	Sections 17.1, 17.3–17.4
Topic 3.9	Adaptive systems	Section 17.2
Topic 3.10	Embodied conversational agents	Section 17.5
Topic 3.11	Ubiquitous computing	Sections 18.1, 18.5
Topic 3.12	Information spaces	Section 18.2
Topic 3.13	Blended spaces	Section 18.3
Topic 3.14	Home environments	Section 18.4
Topic 3.15	Navigation care study sections	Sections 18.5, 19.5
Topic 3.16	Context-aware computing	Sections 19.2, 19.5
Topic 3.17	Mobile computing	Sections 19.1, 19.3–19.4
Topic 3.18	Wearable computing	Chapter 20

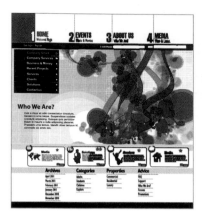

Chapter 14
Designing websites

Contents

Aims

One of the most likely things that interactive system designers will design is a website. There are dozens of books on website design, all offering advice, but some are more focused on the usability and experience than others. Albert Badre (2002) identifies four main genres of websites: News, Shopping, Information and Entertainment. Each of these has several sub-genres (for example, News has Broadcast TV, Newspaper and Magazine), and within a genre certain design features are common. For example, shopping sites will have a fill-in form to collect data on delivery address and payment details; news sites must pay special attention to the presentation of text. The genres also have different ways of arranging the content. News sites will have long scrolling pages whereas shopping sites will have short pages. Combination sites are, of course, common. For example, a site for booking plane flights will often have a news site associated with the destination.

In this chapter we distil the best advice from the world's best website designers, looking at issues relevant to all manner of websites. After studying this chapter you should be able to:

● Understand how to approach website design and the stages you need to go through

● Understand the importance of information architecture

● Understand how to design for navigation in website design.

14.1 Introduction

The development of a website involves far more than just its design. There are a lot of pre-design activities concerned with establishing the purpose of the site, who it is aimed at and how it fits into the organization's overall digital strategy. In larger organizations there will be plenty of disagreement and arguments about all these issues and these internal politics often affect the final quality of the site. Many sites finish up as too large, trying to serve too many issues with the marketing people in charge; usability and engagement come a long way down the list of priorities. At the other end of the process the launch of the site has to be carefully managed and other infrastructure issues will need to be addressed, such as how, when and by whom the content is written and updated, who deals with e-mails and site maintenance, and so forth.

In the middle of these two is the part that interests us – the design and development of a site that is effective, learnable and accommodating. This includes developing the structure of the site: the information architecture. Website design is also concerned with information design (discussed in Chapter 12) and, importantly, with navigation design.

Some example websites are shown in Figure 14.1.

(a)

(b)

(c)

Figure 14.1 Examples of websites: (a) Shopadidas; (b) edutopia; (c) whitevoid

(Source: (a) www.shopadidas.com; (b) www.edutopia.org; (c) www.whitevoid.com)

Writing content

Vital to the success of a website, of course, is the content. In website design the designer has to acquire another skill – that of writing and organizing information content. In many organizations someone else might work with the designer to help. Many websites are seriously overloaded with content and try to serve too many different types of customer. A university website will often try to cater for potential students, existing students, academic staff, administrative staff (its own and from other universities), business partners and so on. Trying to accommodate all these different user groups results in an unruly and rambling site, making it difficult for any one of these groups to be satisfied. The same is true of large corporation and public service sites. A detailed PACT analysis and developing personas will help to identify the needs of different user groups.

Websites are implemented either using the mark-up language, HTML5, and the associated page layouts described in Cascading Style Sheets (CSS) or using a content management system (CMS). There are a variety of CMSs readily available with the most popular being WordPress. Other more sophisticated CMSs include Joomla! and Drupal. It is also important to understand that a website is part of the global World Wide Web, so if designers want the site they are designing to be found by other people, they will need to make it stand out. This involves adding features that will enable search 'engines' such as Google to index the site. The art of search engine optimization (SEO) is somewhat mysterious, but basically involves adding metadata to the site and getting the information architecture of the site right. This is discussed in Section 14.3.

14.2 Website development

The design of websites should follow the principles of good interaction design that have been outlined previously. Designers need to know who is going to use the site and what they are going to use it for. Websites need to be well focused with clear objectives. They should develop personas of the people whom they expect to be visiting the site and understand clearly what goals they will have when using the site. The design phases of understanding, envisionment, design and evaluation need to be undertaken. Scenarios of use should be developed, prototyped and evaluated.

Even if a site is well focused, it will soon get large and so issues of how to move around a website become important; navigation is a central concern here. Support to enable people to discover the structure and content of the site and to find their way to a particular part of the site is the key issue. Information architecture is an area of study devoted to designing websites and helping people to answer questions such as: Where am I? Where can I go? Where have I been? What is nearby? Navigation bars at the top and down the side of the Web pages will help people develop a clear overall 'map' of the site.

It is also vital to pay attention to the design principles outlined in Chapter 4. Consistency is important and a clear design language should be developed, including interaction patterns for the main recurring interactions. If it is not desirable to use the standard blue underlined links then ensure that links are consistent so that people will quickly learn them. Many sites confuse people by not making links sufficiently visible and distinguishable from other text in the site.

Provide people with feedback on where they are in the site and clarify contexts and content. Using meaningful URLs (uniform resource locators, i.e. Web addresses) and familiar titles will help people find what they are looking for and understand what other content is in the site. A good design guideline for websites is to minimize the need for scrolling and plan for entry at (almost) any page, as not all your visitors will go in through the front page.

In general there is a trade-off between designing pages for people who have just arrived there and people who have followed the navigational structure. Having a link to the 'home' (front) page of a site in a prominent position and having a site map will enable people to orient themselves.

The site's home page is particularly important and should feature a directory, a summary of important news/stories and a search facility. Ensure that it is clear what has been searched when designing the search facility. Different people have different strategies on websites. Half of all site visitors are 'search-dominant', 20 per cent 'link-dominant' and the rest mixed (Nielsen, 1993). Search-focused people are task-centred and want to find what they want, whereas others are happy to browse around.

Jesse James Garrett (Garrett, 2003) conceptualizes the development of a website in terms of five elements: strategy, scope, structure, skeleton and surface (Figure 14.2).

● The bottom layer is the 'strategy' plane concerned with understanding the overall objective of the website, the nature of the people who will be using the site and what their requirements of the site are. Strategy is concerned with business goals, the organization's brand and a market analysis.

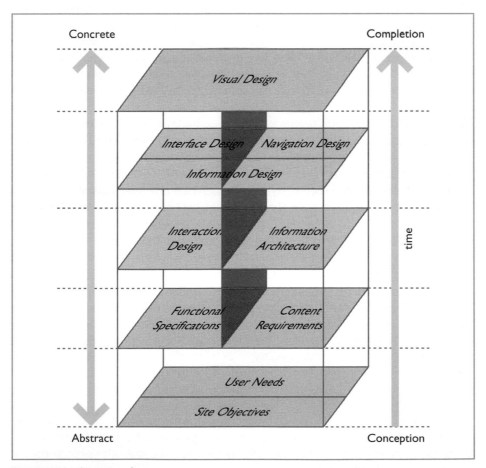

Figure 14.2 Elements of user experience

(Source: *The Elements of User Experience: User-centered Design for the Web* (Garrett, J.J. 2003) © 2003 Jesse James Garrett, reproduced by permission of Pearson Education, Inc. publishing as New Riders Publishing, all rights reserved)

- The next layer is the 'scope' plane where the emphasis is on functionality (what the site will let people do) and on content (the information the site will hold). He argues that spending time on the scope plane is important so that Web designers know what they are designing and what they are not designing! The result of scoping the site is a clear, prioritized set of requirements.
- The third layer is called the 'structure' plane. It covers information architecture but also includes specifying the interaction design. The key feature here is to establish a clear conceptual model.
- The 'skeleton' plane is concerned with information design, navigation design and interface design.
- The final element of Garrett's scheme is the 'surface' plane, concerned with the aesthetics of the site and with ensuring that good design guidelines are followed. For example, links should look like links and things that are not links should not!

Garrett advocates using a simple graphical 'language' to map out the information architecture of a website. The key elements of the language are a representation of pages, files, and stacks of pages and files. These are structured into site maps, showing direction of links if appropriate. Garrett also employs other symbols to represent decisions (a diamond shape), forbidden routes (a cross-bar) and other key concepts. A full explanation can be found at Garrett's website. An example of his site map is shown in Figure 14.3.

The skeleton plane of Garrett's scheme is concerned with information design, navigation design and interface design. A key technique for bringing all these elements together is the 'wireframe'. Wireframes aim to capture a skeleton of a general page layout. They are on the border between information architecture and information design as the various components of a page are assembled into the standard structures described by wireframes.

To construct a wireframe, designers need to identify the key components of the design for each different type of page, then place them on a layout. It is very important to consider not just the type of object – navigation bar, search box, banner headline, advert, text box and so on – but what content that item can have. It is no use having a very small text box, for example, if there is a lot of text to go in it. It is no good having a drop-down menu if the user has to search through hundreds of items. Figure 14.4 (p. 318) shows a typical wireframe.

← Wireframes are discussed in Chapter 8

Visual design is at the top of Garrett's five elements. Consistency and appropriateness of the presentation are critical here. An effective way of achieving this consistency is through the use of style sheets. Style sheets describe how Web documents are displayed, the colours that are used and other formatting issues that will make for a clear and logical layout. Just as the wireframe specifies the structure, so the style sheet specifies the visual language used. The World Wide Web Consortium, W3C, has promoted the use of style sheets on the Web since the Consortium was founded in 1994. W3C is responsible for developing the CSS ('cascading style sheets') language, a mark-up language for specifying over 100 different style features, including layouts, colours and sounds. Different style sheets can be developed for different platforms (so, for example, the same data can be displayed on a computer or a mobile phone) so that the content looks sensible on the particular platform it is aimed at. XSL is an alternative language for specifying the look of XML documents.

Challenge 14.1

Go to the British Airways flight selection website at www.britishairways.com/travel/home/public/en_gb. *Try to produce a wireframe for this site. Go to another airline's site and do the same. Compare them.*

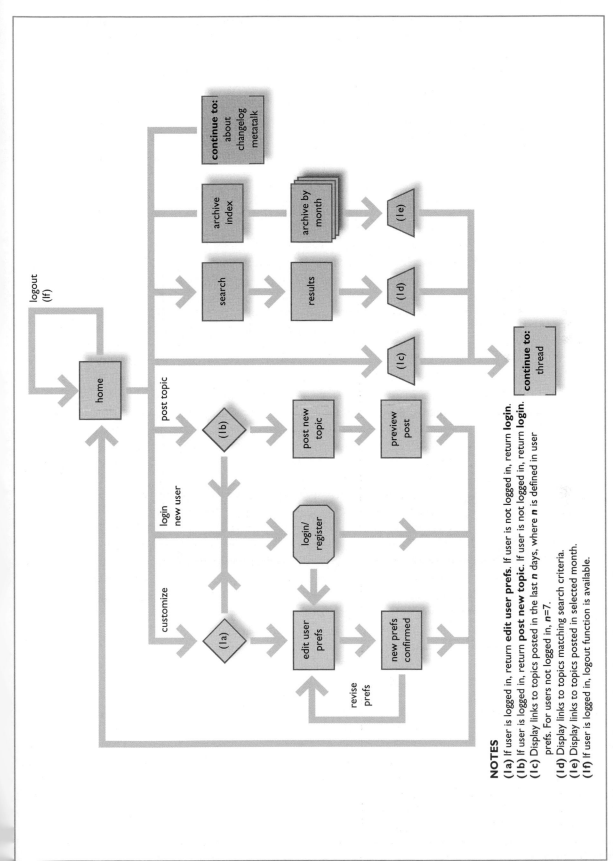

NOTES

(1a) If user is logged in, return **edit user prefs.** If user is not logged in, return **login.**
(1b) If user is logged in, return **post new topic.** If user is not logged in, return **login.**
(1c) Display links to topics posted in the last **n** days, where **n** is defined in user
prefs. For users not logged in, **n=7.**
(1d) Display links to topics matching search criteria.
(1e) Display links to topics posted in selected month.
(1f) If user is logged in, logout function is available.

Figure 14.3 Site map design (continued over three pages)

(Source: After site map from http://www.jjg.net/ia/visvocab/ Courtesy of Jesse James Garrett)

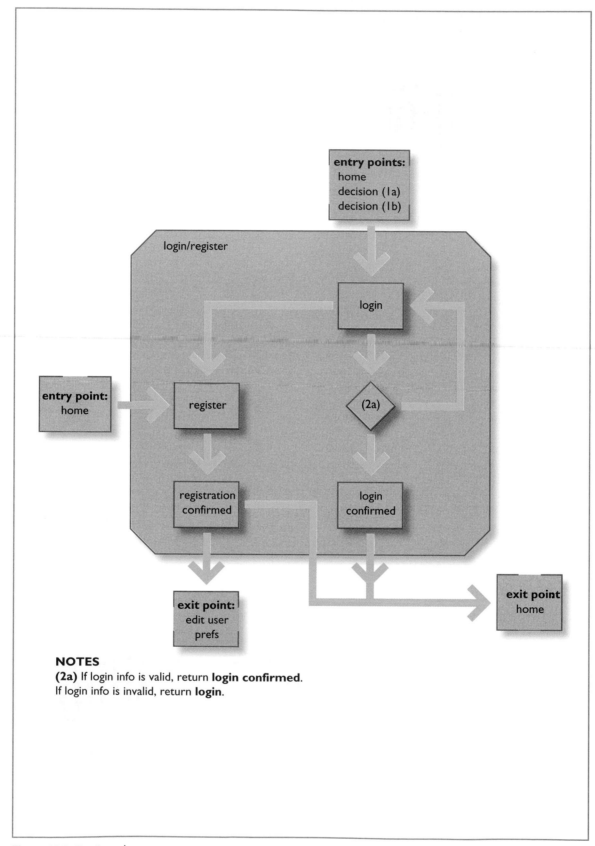

Figure 14.3 Continued

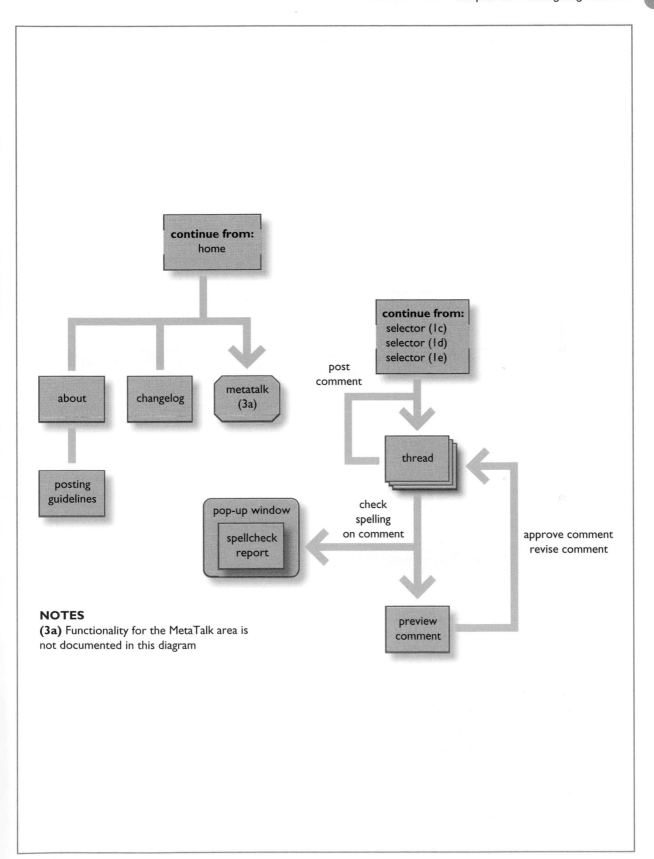

NOTES
(3a) Functionality for the MetaTalk area is
not documented in this diagram

Figure 14.3 Continued

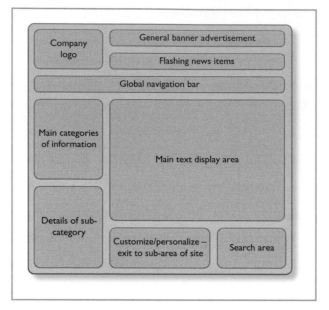

Figure 14.4 Wireframe

14.3 The information architecture of websites

Information architecture is concerned with how the content is classified and organized. Techniques such as affinity diagrams and card sorts (Chapter 7) are used to understand how people conceptualize content.

The difficulty is that different types of site have to serve many different purposes for many different people. Getting an information architecture that is robust enough to serve such multiple interests is difficult and website 'information architects' are in great demand. The features of websites will clearly vary widely.

BOX 14.2

Implementing websites

Websites are implemented on the Internet by specifying the layout of the pages in a language known as the Hypertext Mark-Up Language (HTML) which is itself a variant of the Standard Graphical Mark-up Language (SGML). As a mark-up language HTML suffers from not having much functionality. Essentially it is a publishing language which describes how things are laid out, but not how they should behave. For this reason the Web itself suffers from some awkward interactions when real interactivity is required (such as submitting forms to a database). More recently, dynamic HTML has been developed, which allows functions more commonly associated with a graphical user interface such as a 'drag and drop' style of interaction. It is also possible to embed interactive displays into an HTML page by writing a 'movie' in the programming language Flash. Once again this facilitates new methods of interaction such as drop-down menus. HTML5 is now becoming established as the standard for structuring and presenting content for the Web.

Information architecture for websites is to do with how the content of the site is organized and described: how to organize the content (i.e. create a taxonomy), how to label the items and categories, how to describe the content in the site and how to present the architecture to users and to other designers. To borrow the title of

Christina Wodtke's book, we are engaged in *Information Architecture: Blueprints for the Web* (Wodtke, 2003).

Classification schemes

The choice of an ontology or classification scheme is crucial to how easy it is to retrieve an instance of an object. The ontology is fundamental as it affects how things can be organized. Morville and Rosenfeld (2006) distinguish between exact organization schemes (of which there are three – alphabetical, chronological and geographical) and ambiguous schemes that use subjective categorization. Nathan Shedroff (2001) suggests that there are seven organizational schemes: alphabets, locations, time, continuums (i.e. using some rating scale to rank instances), numbers, categories and randomness.

Alphabetical is a very common organizational scheme, of course, and is exploited in all manner of information artefacts such as phone books, book stores and directories of all kinds. Although at first sight an alphabetical organization is straightforward, it is not always easy, especially where forenames and surnames are muddled up, or where rogue characters can get into the name. Where is a '.' in the alphabet, or a '–'? Another occasion when alphabetical organization breaks down is when the formal title of a company or organization is not the same as the informal name. Looking in the paper-based phone directory for the phone number for Edinburgh City Council recently, I finally found it under 'C' for 'City of Edinburgh'! There was not even an entry under 'E' pointing to the entry under 'City'.

Ontologies, taxonomies and epistemologies

Ontologies have become a popular topic of research in recent years because of issues over the vast amounts of information on how best to conceptualize activities associated with this. Philosophically the concept of an ontology is concerned with what things exist, with the nature of those things that make up our experience. How we choose to group these together is the concern of taxonomies. A taxonomy is a method of classification. Both ontology and taxonomy provide philosophers with plenty to talk about. Even things such as plants are not organized into a single agreed taxonomy, but rather several taxonomies coexist. Epistemology concerns how we come to know things, with the nature of knowledge and of knowing.

Classification is difficult

FURTHER THOUGHTS

These ambiguities, redundancies and deficiencies recall those attributed by Dr Franz Kuhn to a certain Chinese encyclopedia entitled *Celestial Emporium of Benevolent Knowledge*. On those remote pages it is written that animals are divided into (a) those that belong to the Emperor, (b) embalmed ones, (c) those that are trained, (d) suckling pigs, (e) mermaids, (f) fabulous ones, (g) stray dogs, (h) those that are included in this classification, (i) those that tremble as if they were mad, (j) innumerable ones, (k) those drawn with a very fine camel's hair brush, (l) others, (m) those that have just broken a flower vase, and (n) those that resemble flies from a distance.

Source: Jorge Louis Borges (1999), essay: 'The Analytical Language of John Wilkins'

Chronological organization is suitable for historical archives, diaries and calendars, and event or TV guides (see Figure 14.5).

Figure 14.5 Yahoo! TV guide

Geographical organization suits travel subjects, social and political issues and regional organizations such as wine sites, local foods, etc. Problems can arise, of course, when one's geography is not good enough. The time zones on my calendar program are organized geographically (I think), which makes finding certain time zones very difficult (see Figure 14.6).

Organization by *topic* or subject is another popular way to structure information, but here it is important to prototype the names of topics with the potential users of a site. Often a topic structure used by people internal to an organization is different from those from outside.

Task organization structures the website by particular activities that people may want to do ('Buy ticket'; 'Contact us').

Figure 14.6 Time zones feature in MS Entourage, presumably in some geographical sequence

Audience is another popular structuring method. This can be very effective when there are a few well-defined types of user. 'Information for staff', 'Information for students', and so on, helps different users find their part of a site.

Hybrid schemes can be (and often are) used to mix these types of organization together. Other authors suggest that there are other organizational schemes. For example, Brinck *et al.* (2002) include 'department' as a scheme. They give the following example to illustrate the differences:

- Task-based: 'Buy a Car'
- Audience: 'Car Buyers'
- Topic-based: 'Cars'
- Department: 'Sales Department'.

Faceted classification

Any website can be described in terms of three key features: its dimensions, the facets (or attributes) of those dimensions and the values that these facets can take. The dimensions come from the ontology – the major concepts in the site. So, the travel site illustrated in Figure 14.7 has dimensions of cars, flights, hotels and so on that serve as titles for the tabs along the top. Each of these has certain common facets (such as price) but also may have its own unique facets: flights go from one city to another, hotels are located in a single city (but may be part of a chain), cars generally are rented and returned to the same location but may exceptionally be returned elsewhere. Ferries have a different pricing structure from planes which have a different structure from trains. Each of these attributes, or facets, can take certain values. The name of a city, for example, could be just about anything, but the name of an airport could be restricted to a known list of official airports. Classification in terms of the facets of dimensions works particularly well in small, clearly defined spaces. Music sites classify music in terms of its

Figure 14.7 Expedia website

main facets, such as genre, artist and title. Recipe sites will have facets such as country/region, main ingredient, course/dish and so on. Wodtke (2003) points out, though, that once such a site includes things such as cooking utensils, the sharing of facets across such different entities as utensils and recipes is no longer possible. Faceted classification has an important impact on the interface that is provided. With clear and known facets and values the interface can be optimized to exploit the structure.

Challenge 14.2

Consider some classification schemes for a music website.

Organizational structures

One thing that a designer can be quite sure about is that he or she will not be able to fit everything onto one page. Some decisions will have to be taken about how to break up the site to accommodate this constraint. There are a number of standard organizational structures for this. These, of course, tie in with the classification schemes chosen. A **hierarchical** structure (also sometimes called a '**tree**', although it is an upside-down tree) arranges the pages with a single root at the top and a number of branches underneath, each of which has several sub-branches. For example, in a music website, the root page might be called 'home', then branches under that might be 'Classical', 'Rock', 'Jazz' and so on, each of which would be split into sub-genres. Hierarchies are a very common organization and lead naturally to the technique of providing a 'you are here' sign. Figure 14.8 shows a page from a shopping website.

Figure 14.8 Hierarchical organization of a shopping website

(Source: www.pricegabber.co.uk. Courtesy of PriceGrabber.com. LLC)

The impact of ontology

Information architecture is concerned with the structure and organization of objects in an interactive system. The first thing designers must do, then, is to decide how to conceptualize the domain; they need to define an ontology. The ontology – the chosen conceptualization of a domain – is critical and will affect all the other characteristics of the information space.

Deciding on an ontology for some domain of activity is deciding on the conceptual entities, or objects, and relationships that will be used to represent the activity. Choosing an appropriate level of abstraction for this is vital as it influences the number of entity types that there are, the number of instances of each type and the complexity of each object.

A coarse-grained ontology will have only a few types of object, each of which will be 'weakly typed' – i.e. will have a fairly vague description – and hence the objects will be quite complex and there will be a lot of instances of these types.

Choosing a fine-grained ontology results in a structure which has many strongly typed simple objects with a relatively few instances of each. In a fine-grained ontology the object types differ from each other only in some small way; in a coarse-grained ontology they differ in large ways.

For example, consider the ontology that you (acting as an information architect) choose to help with the activity of organizing the files in your office. Some people have a fine-grained structure with many types (such as 'Faculty Research Papers', 'Faculty Accommodation', 'Faculty Strategy', etc.) whilst others have a coarser structure with only a few types (such as 'Faculty Papers'). These different structures facilitate or hinder different activities. The person with the fine-grained ontology will not know where to put a paper on 'Faculty Research Accommodation', but will have less searching to do to find 'Minutes of April Research Committee'.

In my office I have a large pile of papers. This makes filing a new paper very easy – I just put it on the top. But it makes retrieval of specific papers much more time-consuming. My colleague carefully files each paper she receives, so storage takes longer but retrieval is quicker.

The size of an information space is governed by the number of objects which in turn is related to the ontology. A fine-grained ontology results in many object types with fewer instances of each type, and a coarse-grained ontology results in fewer types but more instances. A larger space will result from a finer-grained ontology, but the individual objects will be simpler. Hence the architecture should support locating specific objects through the use of indexes, clustering, categorization, tables of content and so on. With the smaller space of a coarse-gained ontology the emphasis is on finding where in the object a particular piece of information resides. A fine-grained ontology will require moving between objects; a coarser grain requires moving within the object.

Rosenfeld and Morville (2002) point out the need to consider the granularity of the ontology as this leads to the breadth vs depth debate in website design. Often the same material can be organized as a deep structure – only a few main branches but many sub-branches – or as a shallow and broad structure with many branches and only a few sub-branches. As a general rule, six to eight links per category is about right, but the nature of the content and how it would naturally be divided up by the people who will be visiting the site must also be considered.

The problem with a hierarchical structure is that no matter what classification scheme is chosen, some item will not fit nicely into it, and the designer will want to put it under two or more headings. As soon as this happens, the nice clean structure of a hierarchy breaks down. Soon the hierarchy becomes a **network**.

Networks are structures in which the same item may be linked into several different hierarchies. It is a more natural structure but also a more confusing one for people to understand. Often the visitor to a website navigates down through a hierarchy and so develops a reasonably clear view of the site structure. However, in a network they may then go back up another branch or may jump from one part of the site to another. In such cases understanding the overall logic of the site is much more difficult. Organizing pages into a **sequence** is ideal for dealing with a straightforward task structure such as buying a product or filling in a series of questions. The different structures are illustrated in Figure 14.9.

← That is, they develop a clear 'mental model'. See Chapter 2

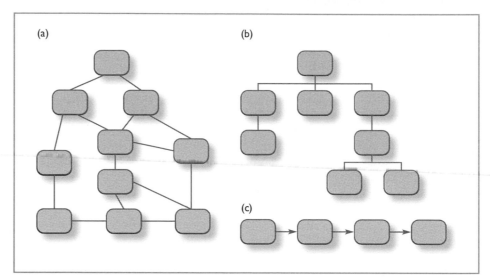

Figure 14.9 Common organizational structures: (a) network, (b) hierarchy, (c) sequence

The importance of classification

This is a portion of an article on Jared Spool's User Interface Engineering website in which UIE investigated different ways of classifying clothes. UIE is a research company that investigates usability issues in websites. Their site contains several interesting articles. Here they describe a study investigating shopping sites with 44 users.

Among the thirteen sites we studied, we found five different department-page designs. Most listed the departments in a left navigation panel, with the galleries for that department listed in the center. (Look at Macy's department pages – http://www.macys.com – by clicking on Women, then Tops.)

However, some got clever. For example, the Gap and Victoria's Secret (http://www.gap.com, http://www.victoriassecret.com) both used a menu-based department that wasn't a separate page, but instead used menus at the top of the screen.

Old Navy (http://www.oldnavy.com) used a combination department and gallery page where sometimes the left nav contains galleries and sometimes it contains products. (Try clicking on Girls, then Accessories. Compare that to clicking on Girls, then Skirts & Dresses.)

Lands' End (http://www.landsend.com) used a design that had both product descriptions and departments. (Click on Women's, then Swimwear to see their department page design.)

Finally, Eddie Bauer (http://www.eddiebauer.com) combined text lists of all the products in the department with a toggle to see the pictures for a gallery. (Click on Women, then Sweaters. Click on View Photos to see a specific gallery.)

After realizing that there were five basic types, we got very excited about seeing if the different types made a difference. While we'd expect differences between individual sites, it wasn't clear that we'd see if an entire type of design outperformed others.

After watching people shopping on the sites, we compared their behaviors. (As with many of our e-commerce studies, these users came to our facilities with a list of products they wanted to buy. We gave them the money to make the purchases and told them to purchase as much on their list as possible. In this particular study, there were 44 users who shopped for a total of 687 products.)

Studying the different designs on apparel and home goods sites turned out to be a good thing. Out of the 687 shopping expeditions that we observed, users only used the search engine 22% of the time. That means that 78% of the time they used the categorization scheme to locate their desired products.

We found the sites with the standard left-nav design, such as Macy's, actually performed the worst, selling the least amount of product. Lands' End's design performed the best, with Old Navy's combination design being second.

It turned out, in our study, that the number of pages that a user visited before they put something into their cart was inversely proportional to purchasing. The more pages they visited, the less they bought. (Remember, our users knew exactly what they wanted and were ready to make a purchase.)

Source: www.uie.com/articles/

Metadata

Metadata means data about data and in the case of websites this means data about the content of the site. Metadata is becoming increasingly important with the ubiquitous use of tags. Here people develop their own *ad hoc* taxonomies, often called 'folksonomies'. We return to discussing this in Chapter 15.

Wodtke (2003) suggests that there are three types of metadata for describing websites:

- Intrinsic metadata describes the factual, technical nature of the data files. It covers things like file size, resolution of graphics, type of file, etc.
- Administrative metadata is concerned with how the content should be treated. It might include details of the author, date of origin, dates of any revisions, security issues and so on.
- Descriptive metadata highlights the facets of the thing, the ways it is classified and so on, so that it can be found and related to other items of content.

Metadata is easily seen and indeed is used by search engines on the Web to locate and rank pages for relevance to a search term entered. Figure 14.10 shows how some metadata is specified in HTML.

For example, an image on a photo library website will have a description below it showing how the picture is categorized. The website will allow users to refine their search based on these keywords. I could, for example, request more images of the person shown in the photograph. There is more on metadata and tagging in Chapter 15.

Vocabularies

A taxonomy is a classification scheme. There are many different types that serve many different purposes. One of the most famous is the Dewey Decimal Classification that is

```
<!DOCTYPE HTML PUBLIC "-//W3C//DTD HTML 4.0
Transitional//EN">
<html>
<head>
    <meta http-equiv="content-type"
content="text/html;charset=iso-8859-1"  />
    <meta name="keywords" content="stock photography, stock
images, digital images, photos, pictures, advertising, gallery,
digital photography, images, sports photography, graphic design,
web design, content" />
    <meta name="copyright" content="All contents © copyright.
All rights reserved."  />
```

Figure 14.10 Example HTML tags

used to classify books in libraries. It is a hierarchical structure that divides books into 10 top-level categories such as:

000   computers, information and general reference
100   philosophy and psychology
200   religion

and so on. Within each classification more levels can be added with decimal points: 005 is computers, 005.7 is information architecture and so on. Of course, all schemes get out of date and it is perhaps strange that religion gets as much space in the scheme as computers. In our university library there are several rows of shelves devoted to the 005 classification, but only part of a row devoted to 200.

One of the problems with devising a taxonomy is that different people use different concepts to organize things. Another is that people use different words and terms to refer to the same thing. There are synonyms and homonyms. There are slight variations of meaning and often it is difficult to find a home for an instance of something. A thesaurus is a book of synonyms and semantic relationships between words. Similarly, in information architecture there is often a need to define a thesaurus to help people find what they are looking for. Rosenfeld and Morville (2002) suggest the structure illustrated in Figure 14.11.

The preferred term is at the centre of the structure. It needs to be chosen carefully so that it will be recognized and remembered by the people using the site. Far too often these terms are chosen by administrative staff and reflect an administrative view of things. Our university has a heading 'Facilities Services' on its website rather than 'Catering', and the library is now a 'Learning Information Service'. Different nationalities will use different words. The preferred term should be linked to any number of variant terms. These are synonyms that people might be expected to use, or follow or type into a search engine. Narrower terms describe sub-categories of the term (sometimes called siblings) and these are related to other terms (sometimes called cousins). Moving up the hierarchy takes us to a broader term.

Specifying all these relationships is a lengthy but important activity for the information architect. This structure will be used to explain the conceptual structure to people using the site and to people administering the site. It will be used in displaying the content on the page, as part of the navigation system and to help people searching. This scheme also helps to provide functionality such as 'may we also suggest' on a shopping site. The scheme will be used to provide category information for people, navigation bars and the 'breadcrumbs' that show where you are on a site. We return to these when discussing navigation. You can see the scheme at work on sites such as Yahoo! (Figure 14.12). Look at the different categories returned when searching for 'cheese' on Yahoo!.

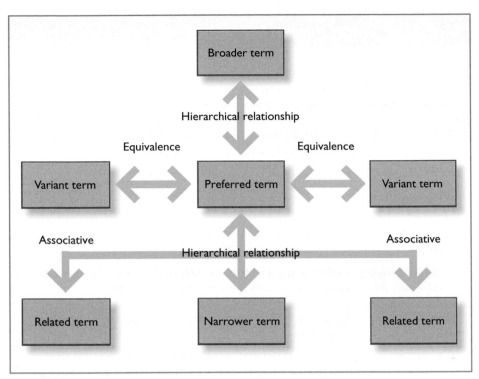

Figure 14.11 Structure of thesaurus

(Source: After Rosenfeld and Morville, 2002, p. 187)

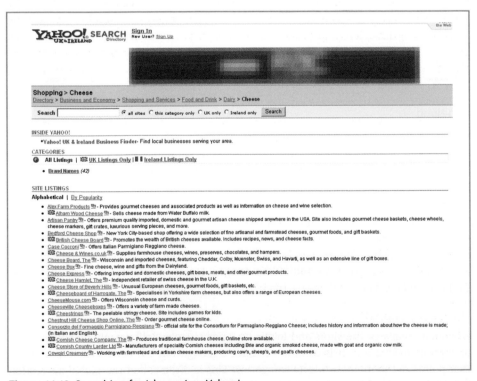

Figure 14.12 Searching for 'cheese' on Yahoo!

14.4 Navigation design for websites

The design of navigation mechanisms is the second main pillar of information architecture. Brinck *et al.* (2002) add to the general ideas of navigation by identifying seven types of navigation (see Box 14.5), from the omniscient user ('they benefit from short, efficient paths') to rote memorization ('use distinctive landmarks and orientation cues'). Along with Morville and Rosenfeld (2006) they identify three key features of a good navigation design for websites: labelling, navigation support and searching mechanisms.

**BOX
14.5**

How people navigate

- *Omniscience.* Users have perfect knowledge and make no mistakes – provide short, efficient paths.
- *Optimal rationality.* Users reason perfectly, but only know what they have seen – make sure links provide adequate cues to the content they lead to.
- *Satisficing.* Users avoid remembering and planning and make decisions on what is immediately perceptible – organize the page to make the most important content and links available immediately.
- *Mental maps.* Users actively use the cues available to try to infer the structure of a website – organize the site simply so that users can easily conceptualize it. Design the navigation bar and site maps to reinforce this mental map.
- *Rote memorization.* When users find a path that works, they tend to remember and repeat it – make sure the most obvious solution is also efficient. Use distinctive landmarks and orientation cues to help people recognize where they have been before.
- *Information foraging.* Users try to get as much as possible at one location – enable spontaneous discovery by providing context, structure and related topics.
- *Information costs.* Users have limited knowledge and reasoning ability – minimize the mental costs of sense making, decision making, remembering and planning.

Source: Brinck *et al.* (2002), pp. 126–7

Labelling

Labels are used for internal and external links, headings and subheadings, titles and related areas. Not all labels are text and iconic labels can be very useful if the context and design are clear. Paying attention to good, consistent, relevant labels is a critical part of information architecture. Information architects must develop a clear and unambiguous preferred vocabulary.

There is nothing more confusing for people than a website changing its own vocabulary, for example referring to 'products' one minute and 'items' the next. The same labels should be used on searching mechanisms as on the main pages, in the names of the pages and in the link names. Figure 14.13 shows the front page of the 'Web Pages That Suck' site. This is a great site full of bad designs. However, I found it quite difficult to find what was on the site, because the labelling is not very clear.

Navigation support

Of course, many of the signs and labels on a website are deliberately placed in order to support navigation. It is common to have a navigation bar across the top of a site that points to the main, top-level categories. This is often called the global navigation bar. Within each of these there will be sub-categories. These might be placed down the left-hand side of the site or may drop down when the main category is selected. These

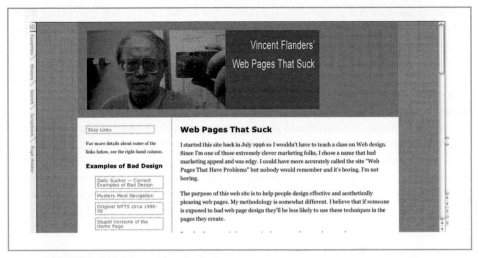

Figure 14.13 The Web Pages That Suck site

(Source: www.webpagesthatsuck.com)

are known as local navigation. It is a good design principle to have the global, top-level navigation bar the same on every page so that people can easily jump back to the home page, to a 'frequently asked questions' page or to one of the other main categories.

An essential feature of the navigation features of any website is to provide a 'you are here' sign. This is often presented by a description showing where people are in the hierarchy of the site. Other devices such as indexes and glossaries are helpful in assisting people find exactly what they are searching for. A site map should be made available that can be called up when needed. The map displays the structure and content headers of the various categories. Figure 14.14 shows a university website where several different types of navigation are used.

Figure 14.14 Edinburgh Napier University School of Computing screenshot

(Source: www.napier.ac.uk)

Global navigation is provided by the tabbed bar across the top and covers the whole site. It is supplemented by a navigation bar that drops down when clicked (on the right-hand side). In Figure 14.14 you can see a 'breadcrumbs' display. (Breadcrumbs comes from the story of Hansel and Gretel who left a trail of breadcrumbs so they could find their way back when they were taken into the forest.) Using breadcrumbs is a common way of showing people where they are. In Figure 14.14 the breadcrumbs tell us that we are at Faculty, School of Computing, Research.

Navigation bars – both local and global – are essential for supporting easy navigation around a site. Site maps and good feedback on where people are in the structure will also help. Another alternative is to provide a clear path through a part of the site. This is particularly important when a number of activities or pages have to be visited in sequence. A site 'wizard' that guides people and explains what each activity is for can help here. Often this is simply a succession of pages, such as when buying a ticket or booking a flight (Figure 14.15).

Figure 14.15 Path through a part of a site

(Source: www.easyjet.co.uk)

Information foraging theory

Peter Pirolli from Xerox PARC has developed a theory of information navigation based on evolutionary theory (Pirolli, 2003). He sees people as 'infovores' eagerly seeking out information, much as we used to forage for food. Information foragers use perceptual and cognitive mechanisms that carry over from the evolution of food-foraging adaptations. People use proximal cues in the environment to help them search out information: 'information scent'. They seek to maximize their information-seeking activities, to yield more useful information per unit cost.

Searching

One of the significant features of the Web as an information space is that many sites support searching. Search engines can be bought; the better ones are quite expensive but are also effective. Once again the preferred vocabulary (Section 14.3) should form the basis of searching, and where the synonyms have been defined they too can be used in defining search terms and in helping people to refine their search.

There are two main problems with searching a website. The first is knowing exactly what sort of documents the search engine is searching. The second is how to express combinations of search criteria. A frequent failing of websites is not to make clear which items are included in the search. Is the content of different documents searched, or is it just the Web pages themselves? Does it include PDF files, or Word files, and in the latter case is it the whole content or just some tagged keywords? Sites should indicate what is searched and provide options to search different types of content.

How to express a search is another key issue. In natural language, if I say I am interested in cats and dogs, I usually mean I am interested in cats, or dogs, or cats *and* dogs. In search engine language 'cats and dogs' can mean only 'cats *and* dogs'. This is because search engines are based on Boolean logic. So to find information about cats and dogs, I need to put in that I am looking for information on cats or dogs. Figure 14.16 shows the search engine Google. Notice how it can make use of a controlled vocabulary to offer alternatives to possibly misspelt words. Also notice how in the second shot it shows the positioning of the structure using breadcrumbs (trail markers).

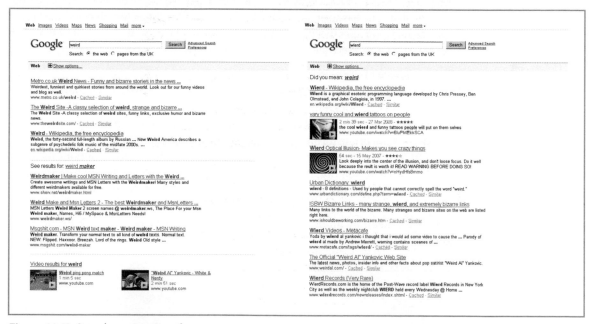

Figure 14.16 Search engine Google

(Source: www.google.com. Google™ is a trademark of Google Inc. Reproduced with permission of Google Inc.)

14.5 Case study: designing the Robert Louis Stevenson website

Whilst we were writing this chapter we were involved in the development of a website for the author Robert Louis Stevenson. Well known for books such as *Treasure Island, Kidnapped* and *The Strange Case of Doctor Jeykyll and Mr Hyde*, Stevenson published 36 works, including novels, short stories, travel writing and poetry. He was an important literary figure in Scotland, but the only existing Web presence for Stevenson was a rich, but rather unstructured site maintained by a Stevenson scholar and enthusiast.

The project leader (PL) had obtained funding from the Carnegie Trust of Scotland to develop a comprehensive website dedicated to the life and works of Stevenson. With this she was able to appoint a part-time research assistant (RA), a website developer (WD) and David Benyon as an adviser (DB). The project began in December 2008.

The first meeting of the project team was mainly concerned with getting to know each other and understanding the different roles members of the project team would play. The PL ultimately had to deliver against the conditions of the grant and wanted the site to be the best site of its genre (a literary website). It should contain material suitable for the academic community it needed to serve, including hosting the *Journal of Stevenson Studies* and academic writing on Stevenson's work. It should be a comprehensive archive for use by students, teachers and schoolchildren. It should include a comprehensive archive of Stevenson memorabilia such as photos, places he visited and so on.

The RA had investigated the existing site and between her and the PL had gained agreement that all this material would be transferred to the new site and that the existing site's owner, RD, would be another adviser to the team, even though he was based in Italy. The RA reported on the existing site. In an e-mail to the team she commented:

> The attached document outlines Dury's site and I occasionally comment on some of the problems with the material. Often information is redundant, under confusing headings or incredibly unwieldy with long, long, long pages of spreadsheets. The information itself is very detailed and useful, but will likely have to be presented in a totally different manner on our own site. If anyone has suggestions about how to make the listing (which marks the bulk of this material) more user friendly and accessible, that would be great! At any rate, I thought it would be useful for everyone to see the material that we already have at our disposal.

The front page of the existing site is shown in Figure 14.17.

Everyone agreed that Dury's site was an excellent resource to have but that the organization was somewhat chaotic, having evolved over a number of years. The WD was keen that the project should identify a suitable URL and domain name as soon as possible and the team brainstormed some possibilities. Stevenson is readily known as RLS, so **www.RLS.org** and **www.RLS.com** were favourite options. Other options included Robert-Louis-Stevenson.org, Robert_Louis_Stevenson.org, RobertLouisStevenson.org, Stevenson.com and so on. It was agreed that team members should go away and look at some possibilities. When we did this, we discovered that RLS.org and RLS.com had already been taken by an organization devoted to helping people with Restless Leg Syndrome!

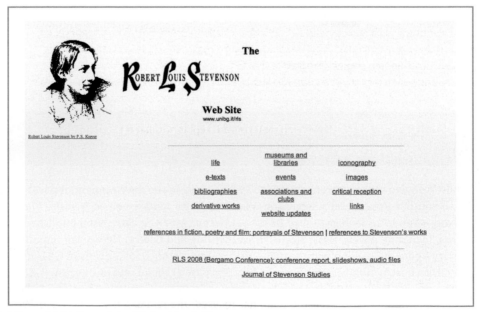

Figure 14.17 The original Robert Louis Stevenson website

DB advised that it was vital to develop personas early on as the site would have to accommodate a range of different types of visitor. This would help to get the information architecture right. The team discussed what information architecture was and how important it was. The WD said that he would use the Joomla development environment for the implementation, as this was an environment he was familiar with, it was flexible and it would be suitable. We also discussed where the site could be hosted, how much this would cost and what impact it might have on the university and on the project funders. There was some early discussion about what the top-level ontology might be.

During the next three weeks there was a lot of e-mail discussion across the whole team. WD and RA met frequently and PL and RA also met frequently. RA spent a significant amount of time making contact with other potential stakeholders in the project. For example, the Writer's Museum in Edinburgh had collections of RLS material, the National Library could be consulted and there was a network of Stevenson scholars worldwide. During this period there was a degree of press coverage and this made its way across the world, resulting in a number of contacts being made with Stevenson museums and other interested parties, and hence stakeholders.

The next formal meeting took place early in January 2009. RA had produced the initial list of personas. There were nine in all: the academic, the PhD student, the undergraduate student, the secondary school student, the primary school student, the teacher, the general interest person, the tourist interested in Scotland, the museum curator. They could be based in different parts of the world since this was intended to be the world's resource for RLS. RA agreed that some of the personas overlapped, but it was a good start. She included some stock photos and general aims and goals that her personas had. The academic and tourist are illustrated below.

The academic

Dr Violet Twinnings is a lecturer in English Literature at McGill University in Montreal, Canada (Figure 14.18). She specializes in the late Victorian period and has recently developed an interest in researching RLS. She hopes to attend some conferences, write some articles on the subject and eventually turn all of the research into a monograph. She also teaches a course, 'English Literature 1880–1930: From Victorianism to Modernism', and plans to include some Stevenson on the syllabus. She will use the website for:

- Publication details: dates of works, numbers of editions
- Sources for a bibliography: lists of critical works that might be useful, recent articles
- Full texts: ability to search full texts for specific material (to find where a passage comes from, to check quotes, to find linking themes)
- Teaching undergrads: giving links to full texts so students can obtain more difficult texts (such as 'Edinburgh: Picturesque Notes') on the syllabus – also so students can get background of Stevenson
- Holdings: where various Stevenson materials are kept for research purposes
- Conferences: list of events and conferences about Stevenson where people might present findings and attend a conference.

The international tourist

Sayan Mitra is from India (Figure 14.19) and has always been a great fan of Stevenson's work. He would love to travel in Stevenson's footsteps. He will use the site for:

- Travelling in the footsteps of Stevenson and visiting his homes and haunts, looking in particular for maps and destinations, itineraries.
- Finding information about Stevenson museums: location, opening hours, entry fee.

At this stage of the project, the team has focused on finalizing the design, structure and navigation aspects of the website. RA circulated a document outlining a site plan,

Figure 14.18 Violet Twinnings

(Source: Katerine Andriotis Photography, LLC/Alamy Images)

Figure 14.19 Sayan Mitra

(Source: John Cooper/Alamy Images)

which the team discussed and changed accordingly. RA also created a mood board to start discussions on the kinds of colours the team wanted to use and to establish the personality of the site. The whole concept of establishing a personality was debated at length. The site should be authoritative, inviting and confident. WD also circulated ideas for colour palettes and pointed the rest of the team to a number of websites where people could look at colour palettes. The team met on 28 January, 13 February and 6 March, and also stayed in touch by e-mail. WD and RA met weekly and PL and RA also met weekly.

During this time there were many debates. One of the largest concerned the information architecture. The biography section was renamed 'Life'. The works section could be ordered by date or by title and there was significant discussion about which was better. Looking at the different personas it was clear that people who already knew about Stevenson would prefer to access by title, but for those who did not, viewing by date would help them to discover the works that he had written.

BOX 14.7

Web analytics

Web analytics refers to the collection and analysis of data concerning how many times a website has been accessed, by whom and what they did once they were there. It is relatively easy to get data about who has accessed your website (by looking at the Internet Protocol (IP) address) and it is easy to follow the clicks that they made on the site (or at least the pages they visited, and the links that they followed). From this the Web designer can gain useful insight into issues such as navigation problems, parts of the site that are not visited and so on.

For example, we were doing some work with a company that seemed to have a good website. It had 48,000 visitors a week with an average of 2.5 pages viewed per visitor. However, the web analytics also revealed that there was a 66 per cent 'bounce rate'. That is, 66 per cent of visitors arrived at the site and immediately went off somewhere else. So our client was actually only getting about 14,000 visitors a week. The good news was that these people viewed on average 7.5 pages on the site. Average time on the site was just over 1 second! So even accounting for the average being skewed by all those bounced visits, people were not spending a long time there. The site was not 'sticky'.

The best known of the analytics software is probably Google analytics. It provides a wide variety of statistics to help the Web designer see what is going on. Of course, interpreting those statistics is often the hard part!

There was also a long discussion about scrolling pages against more clicks. WD produced the first version of the Works>Novels page much as shown in Figure 14.20. This design showed off the visual images of the book covers well and worked fine for parts of the site where there was only a small amount of content (such as Short stories, and Poetry). For Novels, however, it resulted in a very long page as there are 13 novels to accommodate. WD tried various designs to try to fit all the novels on one page. Unfortunately, these made the visual images of the book covers look quite unimpressive. He tried larger images and other layouts, all of which were discussed by the team over e-mail. Finally he finished up with the compromise shown in Figure 14.21. There is enough showing for people to realize that they will have to scroll, the images are large enough to make an impression and the layout is aesthetic for the 13 items that need to be accommodated.

By the end of March there had been significant progress:

- The team had named the site the RLS Website.
- WD had created a logo for the site, so that it could be easily identifiable and have a presence both on and off the site.
- WD had created a banner for the site – we would also make a printed copy to bring to any presentations, conferences etc.
- The team had decided on a colour scheme – largely Victorian muted colours (dull reds, sepias) but also some blues and purples.
- The team had decided that each section would have a quotation from RLS which related to the content of that section.
- WD had worked on the navigation aspects of the site and had begun to upload images so that the site was now beginning to take shape.

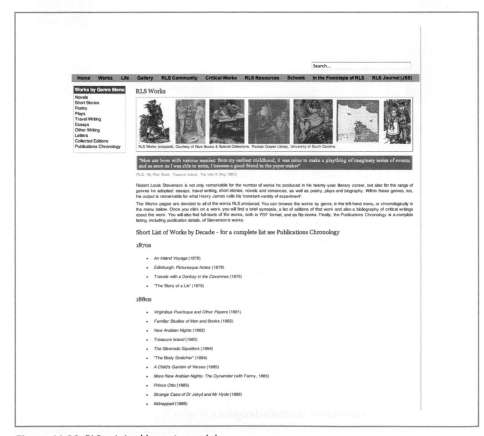

Figure 14.20 RLS original layouts model

The team established the first level of sections as follows:

Home	Gallery	Schools
Works	Community	In the Footsteps of RLS
Life	Resources	Journal

Figure 14.20 illustrates the results of the colour discussion and the banner. RA had spent considerable time working through various photos to select one for the banner that gave the right feeling. Since RLS had written several books associated with the sea, the sailor image at the centre made a key point. The images of RLS used either side captured the young and more mature Stevenson, looking inwards towards the site. The colour scheme worked nicely and would be followed through throughout the site. The RLS website logo can also be seen.

Notice in Figure 14.21 how the titles of the level-one categories have changed since the original list above. In prototyping the design and working through the various informal scenarios suggested by the personas, we had realized that titles such as Resources and Community were too general.

Figure 14.21 Novels' front pages

RA and PL undertook some informal card sorting to ensure that the second-level material did fit clearly into one of the top-level categories. DB had argued for a 'three-click' design where possible, so that visitors to the site could get where they were going in three clicks. This made some sections quite difficult to design. In Figure 14.22 we can see the 'In the footsteps of RLS' section that directs people to places Stevenson had a particular affinity with. WD came up with the double-column design to ensure all the locations could fit on one page. Figure 14.22 also illustrates the use of the quotations that were included on each level-one front page.

During this time RA had been very busy making contacts and finding material for the site. She managed to source a complete set of full-text editions of the RLS novels with an agreement that the RLS website could access them. She had uncovered several hundred previously unseen photos of Stevenson from an archive in the Writer's Museum in Edinburgh and had obtained the following agreements alongside many others.

● Contacted Edinburgh University's special collections about the possibility of digitizing images of Stevenson's records of attendance.
● Received permission to use the Bournemouth/Swearingen images of Stevenson from the Beinecke Library at Yale University.

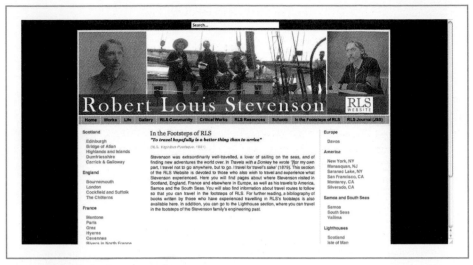

Figure 14.22 In the footsteps of RLS

- Received permission from the University of South Carolina to use the images from their Stevenson exhibit (mostly images of early editions of Stevenson's works).
- Received images of the exterior and interior of the Silverado Museum.
- Received images of the exterior of the Stevenson State Historical Monument, Monterey.
- Received images of the exterior of the cottage at Saranac Lake.

BOX 14.8

Evaluating websites

Once a website is up and running there are many ways to evaluate it. Information provided by software such as Google Analytics can help designers monitor who has accessed the site and when and how long they spent on the site. Measuring the number of clicks taken to arrive at a certain place in the website is another good indication of usability. The click distance is a measure of navigational difficulty.

Many companies such as Google and Microsoft use the A–B method of testing. In this approach a new page design is made available and users are randomly assigned to the old version (A) or the new version (B). Measures of click distance, time taken to complete a task and user surveys such as a simple click star rating can be used to compare the two designs. However, attention should be paid to setting up a well-controlled experiment with no confounding variables, as described in Chapter 10.

During April the main aim was to populate the site and write the content for the site. A colleague in Canada with experience of writing content for the Web was able to provide valuable advice on how to write for the Web. It was also important to plan the site's launch. In June the site was ready for evaluation and Stevenson scholars worldwide were invited to critique the design and content.

An on-line survey was developed and hosted on Survey Monkey. It was based on the design guidelines developed in Chapter 3 and applied to the particular issues of the RLS website. (The questions are shown in Figure 14.23. Compare these with the guidelines from Chapter 3.) The RA developed a sample scenario for each of the personas and mailed this to members of the RLS community. They were invited to explore the site, look at the site from the perspective of different personas and to mail the RA with any general comments.

Overall the general impression of the site was good. Inevitably people had their own prejudices about what was important. This was one reason we had developed so many different

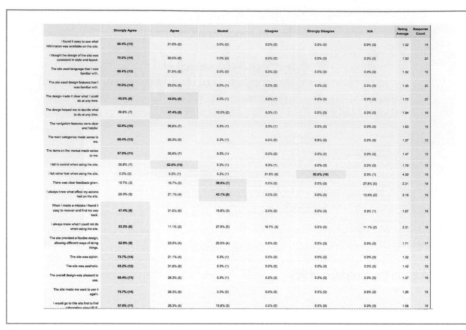

Figure 14.23 Questionnaire

personas: so we as the design team could keep in mind how many different types of people would access the site, and not get bogged down in the needs of one or two specific groups. The power of the personas was well demonstrated by one respondent who commented that she had difficulty finding the information required when working through scenario 7, but found it easily when working through scenario 8. This showed how important the way that people framed their information needs was in making use of the navigational structure.

Another comment concerned making the content more 'Web-friendly'; 'i.e. shorter, tighter, chunkier and keyword-emphasized'. The same respondent suggested looking at the design of the horizontal bar across the pages as, viewing it on his 15-inch screen, the bar was top heavy. It forced him into a lot of unnecessary scrolling.

The results of the survey are shown in Figure 14.23. Of course, it is always difficult to interpret such data as some people will tend to put 'agree' when others would put 'strongly agree', and so with only 18 responses it is difficult to tease apart too much detail. However, it is clear that there is strong support for the first four questions. The following five are less clear-cut and the question concerning control has produced over 50 per cent who can only 'agree' rather than 'strongly agree'. The negative question, 'I felt rather lost when using the site', brought a positive result and helped to ensure that people were paying attention when filling in the questionnaire!

Challenge 14.3

Go through the results of the questionnaire and write your interpretation of what you can say as a result of this survey. What would you focus on when making changes?

A number of key changes were made following this evaluation. The team agreed to work on, and adopt, a particular house style for writing content, much as we had agreed on a colour scheme and overall 'personality' for the site. The team agreed to prioritize the remaining work to ensure that all the site visitors would be accommodated. RA would develop the sections on Life, In the Footsteps and the plot synopses in the house style that had been agreed. WD would concentrate on getting the gallery fully functional and getting all the pictures tagged with event, location, person, relationships and year. Three hundred images had to be uploaded, tagged and made ready for the site. RA would also pay attention to the Community part of the site to ensure that people could comment, rectify any errors and participate in the wider RLS community.

The site officially went live on 13 November, the anniversary of Stevenson's birth.

Summary and key points

In this chapter we have looked at the design of websites. As with the design of all interactive systems, the design of websites requires understanding, envisionment, design and evaluation and a clear view of the purpose of the system.

- Website design needs to follow sound design principles and will include the development of personas, scenarios and a clear design language.
- Information architecture is concerned with understanding the structure and organization of the content of the site.
- Navigation concerns how people move around the site and how they get to know what is on the site and where it is.
- The case study illustrates many aspects of website design, but also shows how much else goes on around the design of a website.

Exercises

1 There is no better way to get good at Web design than by critiquing other sites. Go to a website – your university site, say, or your favourite shop, or an airline. Undertake a structured critique of the site, focusing on the organization scheme used, the navigation bars and the overall look of the site. Develop some personas of typical site visitors and work through some scenarios that they might want to undertake. How easy and effective is the site?

2 Go to the Webby awards website at www.webbyawards.com and look at which sites win. Think about the different categories of sites and the different requirements they have.

 Further reading

Garrett, J.J. (2003) *The Elements of User Experience*. New Riders, Indianapolis, IN. *A very approachable little book that packs a lot of good advice into a small package. It does not go into information architecture in any great detail, but covers the basics of Web design very well.*

Wodtke, C. (2003) *Information Architecture: Blueprints for the Web*. New Riders, Indianapolis, IN. *A highly readable and practical account of information architecture for the Web. A second edition by C. Wodtke, A. Govella (2009) is now available.*

Getting ahead

For information architecture chat and articles: **www.boxesandarrows.com**

Brinck, T., Gergle, D. and Wood, S.D. (2002) *Designing Websites that Work: Usability for the Web.* Morgan Kaufmann, San Francisco, CA. *An excellent book on Web design in general.*

Rosenfeld, L. and Morville, P. (2002) *Information Architecture for the World Wide Web.* O'Reilly, Sebastopol, CA. *A more comprehensive book than Wodtke's but it is less accessible for a general reader. It covers much more ground in terms of thesauri, but sometimes the detail obscures the message. A later edition by Morville, P. and Rosenfeld, L. (2006) is now available.*

 **Web links**

An excellent site for all things about web design is **http://blog.jjg.net/**

Also see **www.boxesandarrows.com/** and **www.uie.com/articles/**
www.pearsoned.co.uk/benyon

 Comments on challenges

Challenge 14.1

Figure 14.24 shows our version of the BA site.

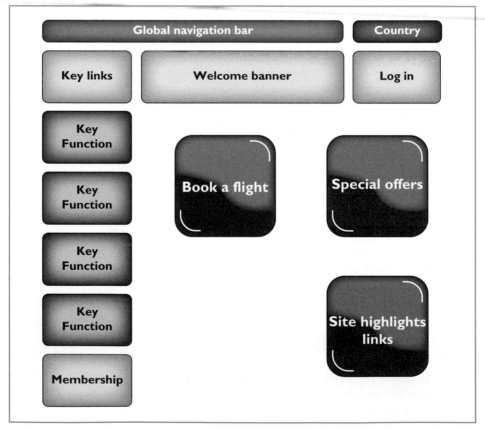

Figure 14.24 BA site

Challenge 14.2

Different genres of music often classify things in different ways. So one way of classifying music is by genre (rock, classical, indie, etc.). Artist is another common category. There could be 'festivals', 'live shows' and other categories such as male, girl bands, acoustic and so on.

Chapter 15
Social media

Contents

Aims

In the twenty-first century there has been an explosion in the use of technologies to connect people with one another. Social networking websites such as Facebook and Google+ are used by millions of people every day to exchange photos, play games and keep up with their friends' activities. Other sites such as eBay or Trip Advisor aggregate the comments and recommendations of other people to give hotels, resorts or eBay traders a quality ranking. Systems designed to support these and related activities are known as social computing, or social media.

In this chapter we look at the rise of social media and at many of the design features that are unique to such systems. Social media is an interesting phenomenon as many systems that started life as purely social become increasingly important to businesses. Where once a system such as Twitter, for example, was mostly about individuals chatting about trivia, now it is used by emergency services and commercial organizations as an important part of their overall business strategy.

After studying this chapter you should be able to:

- Understand the history of social media
- Understand the background to the main types of system that constitute social media
- Understand the future developments of the Web.

15.1   Introduction

The World Wide Web, as we know it, began in 1989 when Tim Berners Lee developed the idea for a hypertext document management system to be used at the nuclear research centre, CERN, Switzerland. He coined the term 'World Wide Web' in 1990 when developing the first browser based on the Next computer and operating system (Figure 15.1).

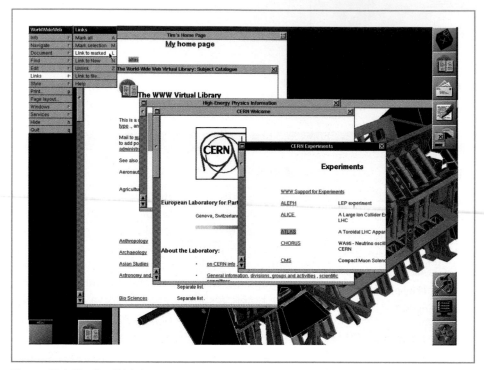

Figure 15.1 The first Web browser

(Source: www.w3.org/History/1994/WWW/journals/CACM/screensnap2_24c.gif)

BOX
15.1

Hypertext

Hypertext is the concept of being able to jump from one piece of text to another through a link embedded in the text. Hypermedia extends the idea to any media. The concept is so familiar through Web links that it seems strange to imagine a world where it did not exist, but of course if was only through the introduction of electronically stored text that automatic links could be automatically enabled. Prior to that, the best one could hope for was the adventure game books you have as children where making a particular decision makes the reader jump to a particular part of the book.

The idea of hypertext is usually traced back to a paper by Vannevar Bush in 1945, but the idea was really popularized by Ted Nelson in the 1960s and through his book *Literary Machines* (1982). The first hypertext conferences began in the 1980s and in the mid-1980s Apple issued their hypertext system, Hypercard, as standard on all Apple Macintosh computers. Presumably this is why Tim Berners Lee wanted a hypertext document management system, and it led to the Web.

In 1993 a cross-platform browser called Mosaic was developed at the National Center for Supercomputing Applications (NCSA) – perhaps the most significant piece of interface design ever undertaken. It revolutionized the world. Prior to 1993 there was plenty of traffic across the Internet, but it was all based on command languages with complex syntax that made using the Internet suitable only for specialists. The advent of the graphical Web browser suddenly made the locating, downloading, viewing of media across the Internet available to everyone. The Web spread rapidly, with millions of people joining every year and with an explosion of websites of shopping, travel, sport, indeed everything. By the later 1990s companies were trading on the stock market at vastly inflated prices. Everyone thought the Web was going to make them millions, but no one could quite work out how to do it. Internet time and Internet logic replaced reality and common sense. In 2001 the market for the Web crashed. The 'dot-com' bubble, as it was known, had burst. But far from this being the end of the Web, it turned out to be the beginning.

The problem with the original Web was that it was primarily a publishing medium. The language used for writing websites was based on a mark-up language that described how to display things and how to move from one place to another. When Berners Lee introduced the Hypertext Mark-up Language or HTML, he used a very much simplified version of the publishers' Standard Graphic Mark-up Language, SGML (1986). HTML, in the period 1994–8, was in a constant state of flux, as competing browsers Netscape (Mozilla – 'Mosaic Killer') and Internet Explorer (based on Mosaic) ran ahead of the attempts to standardize HTML, adding new visual and interactive features, some of which turned out to be dead ends. HTML was particularly unsuited to updating things in real time and HTML and its component technologies, such as the scripting language JavaScript, blurred the distinction between content and how it was displayed.

In the second half of the 1990s many efforts were being made to deal with these restrictions of the Web. By 1998 XML had been developed as a way of separating form and content. XML (extensible mark-up language) simply describes the structure of the contained data, not how it should be displayed. XML describes content by enclosing the content in between a start-tag and an end-tag. For example <Title> Designing Interactive Systems</Title> describes the title of something as 'Designing Interactive Systems'. A specification of how a title should be displayed (e.g. in bold typeface) can then display this as defined. More structure can be added by using multiple attributes of an object. For example, <Book> Author= 'David Benyon'</Book>. These structures required different terms for different areas – for example, the attribute 'element' in Chemistry refers to Oxygen or Carbon, whereas in Physics it refers to an electrical source of heat. Thus different XML ontologies were defined for different areas, such as Extensible Business Reporting Language (XBRL) or Weather Markup Language (WeatherML).

This theme of separating style from content gathered pace during the first years of the new century, and a range of technologies vied to present and interact with XML data. Macromedia (now Adobe) Flash was used to render XML content in a visually attractive way. The programming language Java began to be used to provide more interactivity in websites and the combination of these two became known as AJAX. The continual spread of people using the Web meant that the social side of things became as important as information exchange had been in the early years.

By 2004 it was clear that enough had changed for a new phenomenon to be christened. The first Web 2.0 conference, or summit, was held in 2004, hosted by the O'Reilly organization. Tim O'Reilly explains his rationale for distinguishing Web 2.0

from the Web's previous incarnation. He sees Web 2.0 as a move to much more open services, with application program interfaces (APIs) that allow others to make use of services. Software is no longer a huge application running on your computer, it is a service to be accessed when needed. Web 2.0 is about participation more than publishing; ordinary people, often unpaid, supply the content and the trail of their activities adds value. New business models have evolved through Web 2.0 and continue to do so.

BOX 15.2

The long tail

In his book *The Long Tail: Why the Future of Business Is Selling Less of More (2008)*, Chris Anderson discusses new business models where people sell lots of relatively specialist items required by only a few consumers, rather than selling large numbers of more standardized items. The Internet facilitates businesses that can exploit the long tail. For example, Amazon may sell only a few copies of obscure books, but it is still worth their while to stock them. Other models for businesses include things such as selling rare music albums or personalizing data to the needs of relatively few people.

Thousands of small focused applications, Web apps, such as shopping carts, calendars and subscription services, are freely available to be mixed by enthusiastic consumers. Thus the content of websites can be much more dynamic and much more usable.

The result of all this is a fundamental change to Internet computing. Software engineering processes have changed to be much more agile, with a rapid turnaround of upgrades and new versions of software. Web 2.0 turned the Web into a platform for collective intelligence that crosses devices. Since 2004 the term 'social media' has gradually replaced the term Web 2.0 although the web2 summits (www.web2summit.com/web2011/) did still take place until 2011 and were attended by some very influential people in the field. The future of these conferences remains to be seen.

In 2006 Jeff Howe coined the term 'crowdsourcing' to describe the way the Internet can be harnessed to create a large crowd of people dedicated to solving some problem. Wikipedia (Figure 15.2) is one of the most successful examples of people working together as both providers and consumers (sometimes called 'prosumers') of content. Digital photos are another example, with literally millions of photos covering all subjects being made freely available. Other notable examples of this active participation of people to tackle problems or work together on significant issues include surveys, such as surveys of garden birds and the search for extraterrestrial life.

Challenge 15.1

What do you think the most important characteristic of a site that allows you to provide and consume information is?

Figure 15.2 Wikipedia: people are both providers and consumers

15.2 Background ideas

Of course, social media did not just pop into existence, and there had been several commercial examples of social media applications and related research projects during the 1990s. The whole area of Computer Supported Cooperative Working (CSCW, Chapter 16) concerns cooperation, communication and awareness of others. Our own work during this time went under the name of 'personal and social navigation of information space'. In the introduction to their book, Höök *et al.* (2003) illustrated the ideas of what they called 'social navigation' with an example of a grocery store:

> Consider the design of an on-line grocery store from the perspective of social navigation. First of all, we would assume that other people would 'be around' in the store. Instead of imagining a 'dead' information space, we now see before us a lively space where (in some way) the user can see other shoppers moving about, can consult or instruct specialist agents and 'talk to' the personnel of the grocery store. These are examples of direct social navigation. We also see the possibility of providing information pointing to what groceries one might buy based on what other people have bought, e.g. if we want to help allergic users to find groceries and recipes that work for them, we could use the ideas of recommender systems; pointing people to products that, based on the preferences of other people, the system believes would be suitable. Sometimes we just like to peek into another's basket, or just take the most popular brand of some product. These are examples of indirect social navigation.   (Höök *et al.*, 2003, pp. 5–6)

Social navigation was seen as encompassing a whole collection of techniques and designs that make people aware of others, and of what others had done. Social networking communities, such as those on Facebook, MySpace or Ortuk, exist primarily for the purpose of enabling people to maintain and build links with other people. Other systems are more concerned with making people aware of what others are doing, and yet more, with making aggregate knowledge of others available.

A central theme of the early work was to move away from the 'dead space' of information to bring personal and social issues to the fore. The early Web was characterized by vast amounts of information being rapidly made available. It was, therefore, difficult to find out what was there and what you were interested in. We observed that when we talk to someone else, the information we get back is often personalized to our needs, and the adviser may offer information that changes what we want to do or how we might approach it, making us aware of other possibilities. For example, if you need directions to a part of an unfamiliar city you could use a map, or use a satellite navigation system, or you could ask someone. When you ask someone you will often get stories, additional information about nice places to visit, alternative routes and so on. People may ask for clarification, elaborate details and so on. This personalizing of information comes from the social element of information gathering.

People can judge to what extent the information given can be trusted, depending upon the credibility of the information provider. Even if the information cannot be trusted, it may still be of value as people know where it has come from. In information spaces, using person-to-person communication is an important part of the information architecture that is often overlooked.

A number of experimental systems were developed during the late 1990s that explored some of these ideas. GeoNotes (Persson *et al.*, 2003) is a system for augmenting the geographical world with virtual 'Post-it' notes. Thanks to the advances in GPS, an electronic message can be left associated with a particular place. When another person (suitably technologically equipped) arrives at the place, the system alerts him or her to the message. As Persson *et al.* point out, such attachments of information spaces to geographical spaces go back to cave paintings and people continue to annotate places with graffiti, Post-its and fridge magnets. GeoNotes offers a technologically enhanced version, putting people in contact with other people (Figure 15.3). In 2008 an iPhone app appeared that performed a very similar function.

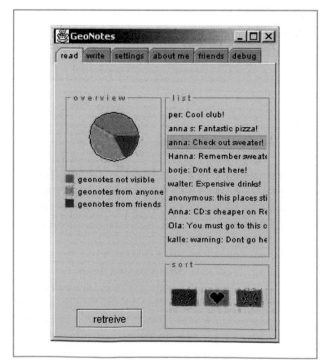

Figure 15.3 GeoNotes

(Source: www.sics.se/~espinoza/ documents/GeoNotes_ubicomp_final. htm, Fig 2.)

If other people are not around to provide help and advice then there are a number of systems that try to filter out uninteresting information and point people to things that they will find relevant (see, e.g., Konstan and Riedl, 2003). Just as a newspaper editor filters news into a form that readers of that newspaper like, so filtering systems aim to tailor information to people. (Conversely, we select a newspaper or TV channel because we like the way that channel filters and presents the news.)

In content-based filtering the information is scanned for specific articles that match some criteria. Based on a statistical analysis the system rates the relevance of the information for the consumer. Usually keyword-matching techniques are used to filter the information. People supply a preference file to the system with keywords that the system should look for in documents. For example, an agent scans a newsgroup for documents that contain the keywords on a regular basis. This is the basis of systems such as MyYahoo! (Figure 15.4).

Figure 15.4 MyYahoo!

Challenge 15.2

Join eBay and browse the site. Decide on something to buy and follow the links on sellers and buyers. What can you learn about people? How reliable do you think the evidence is? Do you think the information provided on buyers and sellers helps you make a decision on what to buy and who to buy it from? How does all this contribute to trust?

Recommender systems make suggestions to people for information based on what other people with similar tastes like or dislike. People using the system are connected to a server that keeps track of what everyone does – the articles they read, the Web pages and blogs that they visit, the videos that they watch and so on – in a personal profile. Personal profiles are matched and the system creates clusters of people with similar tastes. One of the earliest examples of this was Movielens (Figure 15.5). Amazon, the on-line book and media vendor, is probably the best example of a mature recommender system. People who subscribe to Amazon can have the system recommend books based on those that they have bought previously and on those that they rank (Figure 15.6).

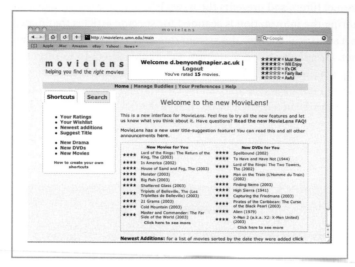

Figure 15.5 Rating preferences with Movielens

(Source: http://movielens. umn.edu/login)

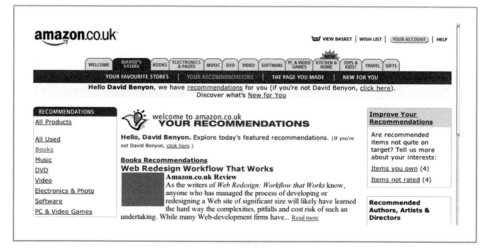

Figure 15.6 Amazon.co.uk recommender system

(Source: www.amazon.co.uk. © 2013 Amazon.com, Inc. and its affiliates. All rights reserved.)

Another method of providing socially based information is to provide a tag so that whenever someone comes upon a new piece of information he or she can see what other people with similar interests think of that particular piece of information. This is sometimes called social searching. People can tag the items discovered by others, thus providing a social tagging system, and tags can also be added automatically according to some criteria. Some sort of rating of the information pieces has to be done by other people using the system so that the system can create and cluster personal profiles. The more people who rate items, the more accurately the system can group others. Ratings can be done explicitly and/or implicitly; implicit ratings are, for example, time spent reading an article; explicit ratings let people score information sources.

Filtering needs some sort of input to work with, and explicit rating of information is not all that simple. How do we judge ratings from someone who has created the information? Explicitly rating information is also an additional burden on people, so sometimes they will not bother.

An excellent and fascinating example of this sort of rating system is eBay (Figure 15.7), the on-line auction site. Here, buyers and sellers have ratings based on the quality of service that they have provided. Buyers rate sellers and sellers rate buyers. Moreover, you can see what both buyers and sellers have been trading. This allows you to build up a picture of the sort of person you are trading with.

Figure 15.7 Ebay

History-enriched environments, or 'readware', is another technique. What other people have done in the past can tell us something about how to navigate the information space. If we get lost in the woods and come upon a trail, a good idea is to follow that trail. Similarly, people take certain paths through information space. By making the activities of others explicit, new visitors to the space can see familiar paths through it. A very familiar technique is to automatically change the colours on the links in a Web page when a person has visited that page, so subtly letting them know where they have already been. In some other systems this may be generalized based on usage of links. Perhaps the main example of this was the Footprints project (Wexelblat, 2003), where ideas of interaction history are associated with an object.

Social translucence was a project based at IBM. It employed three core principles – visibility, awareness and accountability – implemented in a number of prototype systems, so-called 'social proxies'. Erickson and Kellogg (2003) illustrate their concept by telling the tale of a wooden door that opened outwards in their office. If opened too quickly the door would smash into anyone who was walking down the corridor. The design solution to this problem was to put a glass panel in the door. This enabled the three principles of social translucence:

- *Visibility*. People outside were now visible to those inside who were going to open the door. Of course, the transparency of the window meant that people inside the office were also visible!
- *Awareness*. Now people could see what others were doing and could take appropriate action – opening the door carefully, perhaps.
- *Accountability*. This is an important principle. Not only are people aware of others but now they are aware that they are aware of others. If the person inside the office opens the door and smashes into someone in the corridor, the person in the corridor knows that the office person knew this. Hence he or she has to be socially accountable for the action.

The best known of their prototypes was Babble – a social proxy for meetings, chat and e-mail. People are represented by 'marbles' and the space of discussion by the large circle in the centre of the system (see Figure 15.8). The more active people are, the nearer the centre they are, and the marbles gradually move towards the periphery if they do not participate in the chat for some length of time. Other details of the people can be seen in the panes around the edge of the system. This is just one example of a number of visualizations of behaviours that provide awareness of others.

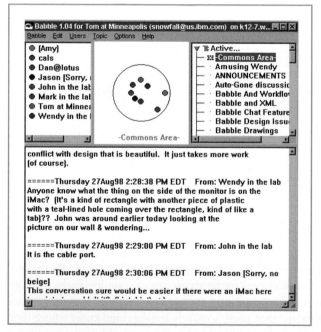

Figure 15.8 Babble

(Source: Erickson *et al.* (1999) pp. 72–9, Fig. 3. © 1999 ACM, Inc. Reprinted by permission)

Since then, research groups have changed and moved on, and the commercial world has taken over much of the work of these prototype systems. There are now thousands of Web apps providing all manner of social media functionality. For example, MovieLens now has a Facebook app. There are directories of social media applications and awards for the best ones. For example, listio.com has listings as illustrated in Figure 15.9. This uses a visualization, popular in social media apps, known as a tag cloud. The larger the typeface the more items there are with that tag.

Figure 15.9 Listio website. www.listio.com/

15.3 Social networking

There are hundreds of different forms of social networking and almost certainly you make use of one of them. Facebook, MySpace and Bebo are popular. Although they are different in style and popularity in different countries, they all provide a mix of updates and functions such as photo sharing.

Figure 15.10 shows the Orkut log-in page. Once a person is logged into their account they can join groups, view messages, play games and share media with their friends. Many social networking sites allow people to make short announcements about their status, what they are doing, or what they are thinking.

Status updates is the whole purpose of Twitter. This application lets people post short messages concerning what they are doing. Twitterers are able to follow the messages ('tweets') of other twitterers. Many of these are simply messages such as 'having coffee in Oxford' or 'lost in Boston', but many other uses have been found for it. Terrorist attacks have become news first on Twitter, as have plane disasters and other events. Businesses use Twitter to promote their interests. Of course, there are millions of people using Twitter and a plethora of Twitter help sites have grown up. For example, tweettag (Figure 15.11) allows people to see the most popular tags.

There are also a number of professional social networking sites such as LinkedIn, Pulse and Namyz. These allow people to present their profile for their professional life. Increasingly these sites add new applications. For example, LinkedIn allows for sharing PowerPoint files and has common interest groups, with regular updates. Twine is another popular example. Figure 15.12 shows LinkedIn.

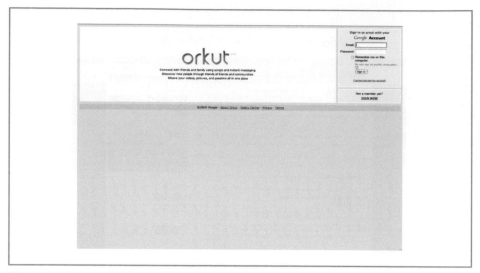

Figure 15.10 Example of a popular networking site: Orkut

(Source: www.orkut.com/Main#AppDirectory.aspx; Orkut™ is a trademark of Google Inc.)

The style and look and feel of the sites reflects the different markets and customers that are the focus of these sites. There are also companies that provide software that allows people to add social networking to their own sites. This allows topic-specific social networks. For example, Freshnetworks.com provides a bundle of 'social media' tools that allow programmers to create member profiles, news feeds, ratings and reviews. People can add their own content and edit that of others (Figure 15.13).

Figure 15.11 Tweetag.com

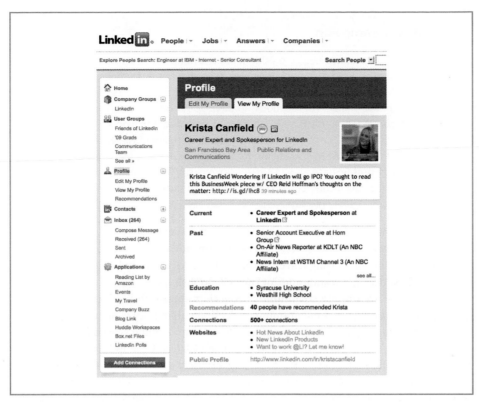

Figure 15.12 LinkedIn.com

Figure 15.13 FreshNetworks.com

(Source: community.lv.com)

The Obama campaign

In 2008 Barack Obama was elected president of the United States of America. During his campaign he and his team made extensive use of social media technologies, with on-line presence on MySpace and Facebook and regular updates on Twitter. He employed Chris Hughes, one of the founders of Facebook, to develop his on-line campaign. He had his own on-line community at My.BarackObama.com, with over 1 million members. During the period August to November 2008 there were 500 million blog entries that mentioned Obama (in contrast to 150 million for his opponent, John McCain). Obama had 844,927 'friends' on MySpace and 118,107 followers on Twitter. Following his election the use of social media technologies continues through the Change.gov website.

There are now thousands of community websites and social networking environments. Some of these revolve around travel, such as TripAdvisor, others focus on activities such as hiking or cycling, or knitting (ravelry.com). Others focus on finding the best pizza in a town, the best bars and restaurants, or the best bookshops.

Indeed, there are on-line communities covering almost all hobbies, interests and social issues. Setting up and maintaining an on-line community is not always straightforward and achieving a critical mass of people with an ongoing shared interest can be difficult. In this, on-line groups share many of the issues of group formation that are discussed in Chapter 24. These include getting a critical mass of people, keeping things up to date and knowing how old some advice is. For example, whilst writing this I was browsing a site offering recommendations for pizzas in San Diego. The largest blob on the map represented just 14 recommendations. This is an example of a 'mashup', bringing together data from a site with Google maps using a few lines of code that exploit the Application Program Interface (API) for each dataset.

Individuals can easily create their own comment websites by using one of the many blog sites such as WordPress (Figure 15.14) or blogspot and contribute to shared discussions and debates using a wiki, a site that allows registered members to add and update content. The most famous, of course, is Wikipedia, the on-line encyclopedia.

Challenge 15.3

Compare the functions and interfaces of two social networking sites.

**FURTHER
THOUGHTS**

Identity 2.0

Sharing and transferring information between people and between sites is all very well, but it introduces its own problems of identity. In current Web systems identity is managed through usernames and passwords. These are checked against a directory to see if you have access to a website. In social media we need a much greater level of management of identity. I might decide to allow you to see just some of my photos, or hear some of my music, but there are other parts that are private. I might want to share some of the places I have visited with you, and some of the details about what I liked, but not all of it.

Identity management is a growing area that strikes at the heart of the social, shared environments that characterize social media. How can systems be open, how can they share and how can we network without compromising security and introducing the possibilities of identity theft? Some Web-based passport or 'driver's licence' is needed that is accepted by all Web services. How that is going to be achieved is another matter.

Figure 15.14 http://en.wordpress.com/features/

15.4 Sharing with others

A second aspect of social media is sharing with others. With the huge amount of information and activity that takes place on the Web, finding what you are interested in and letting others know what you are interested in has become a major issue. The most popular way of keeping track of photos, videos, or indeed any digital assets is through tagging.

Tagging is concerned with adding keywords to assets so that those labelled the same can be grouped, shared or used for navigation. Tag clouds such as those in Figure 15.11 (tweettag) is an example.

The creation of tags is sometimes referred to as a folksonomy. Despite efforts to arrive at a universally agreed set of tags of digital assets (see Box 15.4), informal tagging is most frequently used.

The Semantic Web

BOX 15.4

The Semantic Web is an initiative of the World Wide Web Consortium (W3C) 'to create a universal medium for the exchange of data. It is envisaged to smoothly interconnect personal information management, enterprise application integration, and the global sharing of commercial, scientific and cultural data.' The underlying assumption is that objects on the Web need to be processable automatically by computer. This would enable such things as artificial agents (Chapter 17) to search out objects and exchange information with them.

RDF stands for the 'Resource Description Framework' which aims to provide an application-independent form for processing metadata. Web Ontology is a standard Web classification scheme. Together these are the enabling technologies that would bring about the Semantic Web. The idea behind the Semantic Web is to establish a defined ontology of objects. This would allow programs to automatically locate defined items of content that shared an ontology.

Del.icio.us is a bookmarking application that allows people to store URLs and tags and retrieve them in different ways. In addition to the personal tags that are attached to a site, colleagues and others in a personal network can access your bookmarks and add their own activity. Bookmarks from everyone using del.icio.us can also be accessed by popularity or by how recent they are. Digg.com is another site devoted to helping people share their views of the Web. A simple click allows people to 'digg' a site, video or story and those with the most 'diggs' appear higher up the list. A screenshot from Digg is shown in Figure 15.15.

Figure 15.15 Digg.com

A third example of this is StumbleUpon. StumbleUpon allows people to see recommended websites, blogs and other assets. You indicate whether you like the site and gradually it builds up a picture of your likes and dislikes. Matching that with the ratings of others allows StumbleUpon to recommend sites you might like. As with Digg, a general ontology of types of site is provided (news, technology, sports, science and so on) to help provide a structure. CiteULike is a site for managing references to academic papers, again with the idea of sharing this with others and of joining like-minded groups.

There are many examples of event management applications such as Eventbrite which allows people to organize, publicize and register for public and private events. Shared workspaces make setting up of work spaces easy. (Many of these types of application are discussed further in Chapter 16 on CSCW.)

Another development is in the area of Web browsers where additional functionality is added into a browser. For example, StumbelUpon and del.icio.us both add buttons to the browser so that websites can be quickly and easily bookmarked and there are a host of addins for the Firefox Web browser (Figure 15.16).

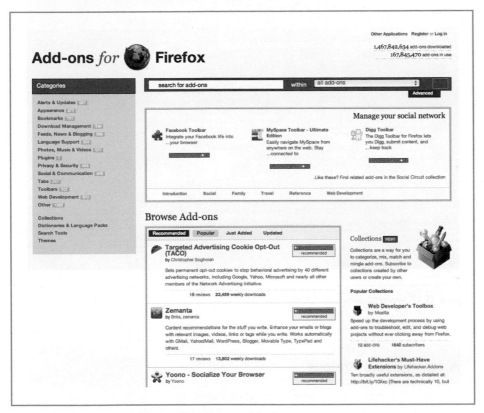

Figure 15.16 https://addons.mozilla.org/en-US/firefox/

As we have seen, one way to visualize tags is through tag clouds. Popular sites such as Flickr also use tag clouds to tag photos and there are various sites that provide advanced searching and refined search through tags. For example, Clusty has some clever search remix functions. Other visualizations include Cooliris (Figure 15.17) and there are many available from Google. Zoomable interface tools such as Papervision or Deep Zoom provide ways of navigating through large collections of tags.

← Visualization was discussed in Chapter 12

Challenge 15.4

Visit a sharing site such as CiteULike and spend some time looking at the different groups and how things are tagged. What do you notice? How might these sites work better?

Figure 15.17 www.cooliris.com/start/

A social media strategy

An essential question nowadays for any organization is what they should do about social media. How much time should be invested in it and what returns can be expected? The use of social media is bound up with the organization's mission, its marketing strategy, branding and business model. Designers need to step outside their comfort zone of creating effective, efficient and attractive digital media and think about how their skills affect the whole business. Social media affects the whole experience of customers, the services that the organization provides and the relationship that the organization is aiming to establish and promote.

The annual Social Media Marketing Industry Report, from Socialmediaexaminer. com reports that 78% of marketers saw increased Internet traffic with six hours a week invested in social media. So, if this increased traffic translates into more business, then it is probably a good investment. The main sites where organizations would have a social media presence include Facebook, Twitter, LinkedIn, YouTube, Google+ and surprisingly (at the time of writing) Pinterest.

Amy Porterfield (www.amyporterfield.com) argues that in developing a social media strategy the three steps are to assess your audience, design and implement the strategy and then monitor, manage and measure the impact. She suggests you assess the audience through short surveys, quizzes, blogs and shared documents. Look at the Google Analytics to see where the visitors to your Web pages come from and how long they stay on your pages. From the surveys, produce reports and post these and links to these on Twitter and LinkedIn. People get interested in some aspect of your work, click on the link and so become aware of your organization and what it does. Make it easy for people to follow your posts and you are suddenly connected into another person's network.

Of course a central part of the social media strategy is understanding what your organization is, what its brand is and what values it stands for. Capturing these in a clear and concise way is necessary before targeting the particular social media platforms that you will use. Decide if the aim of the strategy is to increase loyalty, or raise awareness of your brand, or to more directly increase sales. Once you are up and running you can measure how well your social media strategy is working through a site such as Klout that surveys the influence you are having.

However, it is important to remember that social media take time, and you need to be clear about how much time you can give to them. There are tools for helping people to manage their social media, for example by posting comments to Twitter or LinkedIn automatically at predetermined times. You will also need to coordinate announcements and new additions to your website.

15.5 The developing web

Social media is not the end of the story for the Web and designers need to keep their eye on the next big thing. Location-based services are growing rapidly as more people have GPS in their phone. For example Foursquare is an app that registers your location and posts this information to your social network. There are a number of tourism apps that take advantage of your location to provide relevant information and we can expect location-based group apps and games to become more common.

Indeed gamification of interaction is itself a growing theme. Gamification involves adding incentives, challenges and rewards to activities to try to motivate people to join in. For example an app to help people lose weight and to take more exercise can be greatly enhanced if there are rewards for making progress. Designers can think up different points schemes – 50 points for losing a pound in weight, say – and these can be posted on the person's website. Get them to join with a group of friends and they can all see how well the others are doing. Suddenly a dull website becomes a hub for a social game.

← Gamification is discussed in Chapter 5

Cloud computing is a development of the Web that (at the time of writing) promises to have a big impact over the next few years. It has also arisen from ideas of utility computing and grid computing where the emphasis has been on sharing resources. The argument goes that since there is now so much storage space, so many applications and so much computing power on the Internet, why bother to have your own? Large organizations such as Amazon and Google are pioneering flexible, reliable and personalized complete computing services over the Web (the 'cloud'). This allows their customers to choose what features they want when they want them – and where they want them. The cloud is available anywhere and from any device. To go along with cloud computing, computer appliances are simple devices with no software on them. Just access any application and any data over the Internet. Web services and other software services are provided on a pay-to-use basis. Data is kept on a remote server with all the appropriate security and other management activities also provided as a service. Amazon's Elastic Computer Cloud (EC2) is probably the first real commercially focused example of the full cloud computing concept, but there are many other examples of cloud computing at work.

Google docs is one example of a cloud service that allows people to work on a shared document (Figure 15.18). Google calendar lets people easily set up shared calendars and iGoogle brings it all together into a personalized page – your one stop every time you log on to the Web.

So the Internet continues to evolve. The next development expected is known as the Internet of Things. When the new Internet protocol is introduced, IPv6, there will be enough Internet addresses available for everything to be available on the Web. This could be as radical as every $10 bill, every packet of crisps and every cow. This promises to bring many changes to businesses and to people's social and leisure activities. Exactly what they will be remains to be seen.

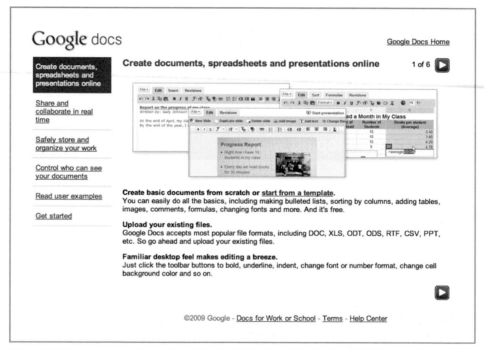

Figure 15.18 www.google.com/google-d-s/intl/en/tour1.html; Google™ is a trademark of Google Inc.

The Internet of Things will bring many of the problems that have already emerged as people try to share things, add to existing things and interface with other things. This is the problem of who owns what and what reward they should get for their part of the overall value chain. Innovative business models have emerged, allowing the costs of providing the free service to be covered by other forms of revenue such as advertising. However, a growing problem is the requirement by social media sites to require contributors not only to supply their content for free, but also to give over to the site many of their intellectual property (IP) rights. Many sites offer you the chance to promote your band but gain the right to do what they want with your songs. When Facebook attempted to change their standard terms and conditions, a storm of protest caused them to reverse at least temporarily that decision. But many users were surprised to find that Facebook now owned rights to the photos they had uploaded.

Summary and key points

Social media is concerned with all aspects of the Web concerned with making it social and making it a platform for development. Social media takes the static, dry, information-based approach to the Web and tries to lighten it with novel features that connect people with people.

- Social media arose out of the ashes of the dot-com bubble.
- The principles underlying much of social media had been developed throughout the previous decade.
- Key aspects of social media include social networking and sharing with others.
- Future developments of the Web include cloud computing and the Internet of Things.

 ## Further reading

The original article from O'Reilly is at **http://oreilly.com/web2/archive/what-is-web-20.html**

Getting ahead

The World Wide Web Consortium has lots of detail on the Semantic Web. See **www.w3.org/2001/sw/**

 ## Web links

See also the Web material that goes with this chapter
www.pearsoned.co.uk/benyon

 ## Comments on challenges

Challenge 15.1

It must be easy to use and it must have a structure that is easy to understand. Unfortunately, many wikis have neither of these characteristics. A wiki can very soon develop a most unwieldy structure and adding information is often not very intuitive as it has to be written using a difficult syntax. Sometimes files are uploaded to strange parts of the site and you can't find them again. Blogs, on the other hand, are very easy to set up and use.

Challenge 15.2

The information about buyers and sellers on eBay provides a very interesting insight into the types of people engaged in trade. Finding out what other people have been buying and selling and over what period certainly helps to build a picture of how reliable they are and the type of business they are interested in. The data has to be quite reliable because otherwise disillusioned buyers and sellers would comment. This does help to build a sense of trust in the virtual marketplace.

Challenge 15.3

Things to look out for include the various types of information that is provided to different types of contact, how easy it is to control access and the overall look and feel of different sites. There is quite a lot of difference between them, and it may take you quite a long time to find out exactly what the differences are as, of course, time is a fundamental part of building and maintaining social networks.

Challenge 15.4

One of the biggest things I have observed is how quickly groups become out of date and how few people can contribute to some groups. Look at groups in HCI, or usability, and see how activity tails off very quickly. There is plenty of discussion about forming and keeping groups in Chapter 24 on social interaction.

Chapter 16
Collaborative environments

Contents

Aims

Collaborative environments comprise spaces and software designed to support people working together. The terms 'groupware' and 'Computer Supported Cooperative Working (CSCW)' are also used to refer to this area of interactive systems design. Groupware is rooted in an understanding of the social features of computing. In this regard, then, it shares a lot with the material covered in the previous chapter. Whilst social media have evolved primarily to support social computing applications in the context of home usage, CSCW focused on the world of work. The overlap comes with many of the applications, such as shared diaries and shared documents, that both social media and CSCW deal with. Indeed many CSCW applications make use of social media technologies, particularly wikis, blogs and software to support social networks, and many social media apps have arisen from earlier groupware systems.

Collaborative environments, however, go beyond the traditional focus on software to include the design of physical spaces to support collaboration and creativity. Collaborative environments support both remote and face-to-face collaboration.

In this chapter we focus on a number of technologies that support collaborative working. Chapter 24 deals with the social psychology of working in groups. After studying this chapter you should be able to:

- Understand the main issues involved in collaboration
- Understand the various types of technological support that can be provided
- Understand collaborative virtual environments.

16.1 Introduction

CSCW – Computer Supported Cooperative Work (or Working) – is a clumsy but accurate description of most modern work. However, in their introduction to the second edition of their article in the Handbook of Human-Computer Interaction, Olson and Olson point out that the term now seems somewhat anachronistic as the area covers devices that are not desktop computers, activities that are not work and relationships that are not cooperative! However, the term CSCW still persists in the titles of many conferences and publications, so it cannot really be abandoned just yet. The term computer-mediated communication (CMC) also covers many related areas.

The history of CSCW usually starts with the mid-to-late 1980s, which witnessed a remarkable conjunction of complementary research work. Technological developments were complemented by fresh perspectives on human activities from researchers with their roots in anthropology and sociology. Since both these fields emphasize the collective and socially based nature of human activities and culture, a 'turn to the social' away from the emphasis on the isolated single person and single computer was not surprising. (The phrase 'turn to the social' was introduced by the ethno-methodologist Graham Button in 1993.)

Paul Cashman and Irene Grief coined the term CSCW to describe the theme of a workshop they had organized to which they invited a group of people who were interested in how people work cooperatively and in the technology to support that work. Since then CSCW has become the focus of a considerable number of research projects, two international conferences (CSCW in America and ECSCW in Europe) and a highly respected international journal. In addition to this academic interest, designing for co-working or collaboration or cooperation (the terms vary with authors) is a source of interest to a number of major software vendors. Add to this the widespread interest in computer-mediated communication (CMC) that includes video-conferencing, video-telephony, on-line chat and mobile phone-based 'txting' (the use of short messaging service (SMS) text messaging) and MMS (multimedia messaging).

BOX 16.1

CSCW early days

The early accounts of CSCW as portrayed by Grudin (1988), Grudin and Poltrock (1997) and Bannon and Schmidt (1991) indicate that CSCW was very much of this time. Following the famous inaugural workshop came Lucy Suchman's *Plans and Situated Actions* in 1987 (with a second edition in 2007). This was her critique of the underlying planning model employed by much of artificial intelligence (AI) research at the time, and it sparked a now famous debate in the journal *Cognitive Science* (see Vera and Simon, 1993). Suchman's work effectively opened the doors to the sociological practice of ethnomethodology that has become the tool of choice in CSCW research.

← Ethnomethodology is discussed in Chapter 7

More recently there have been developments in designing, not just software to support collaboration, but whole physical environments. 'Roomware' (Streitz *et al.,* 1997) is a project that has been ongoing since the late 1990s and more recently there have been environments that take advantage of tabletops and multitouch surfaces. Another related area is collaborative virtual environments (CVEs) where virtual environments such as Second Life are used for collaborative activity.

Jetter *et al.* (2012) introduce the idea of blended interaction as a way of thinking about developing collaborative spaces, based on ideas of designing with blends

(Imaz and Benyon, 2005). They identify four things for designers to focus upon in designing collaborative spaces: the individual interaction, the social interaction, workflow and the physical environment (Figure 16.1).

→ There is also a discussion of blended spaces in Chapter 18

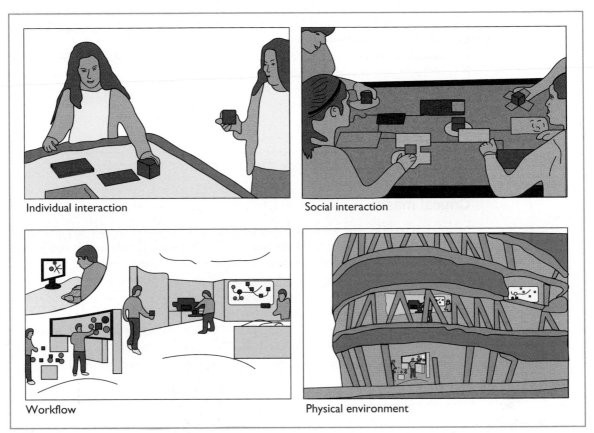

Individual interaction

Social interaction

Workflow

Physical environment

Figure 16.1 Blended interaction

(Source: Jetter, Geyer, Schwarz and Reiterer (2012))

16.2 Issues for cooperative working

Jonathan Grudin (Grudin, 1994), Mark Ackerman (Ackerman, 2000) and Judith and Gary Olson (2012) have identified a number of key challenges for CSCW and for collaborative working in general. Based on their work, here is our list.

The disparity between who does the work and who gets the benefit

People have to contribute additional effort so that others can benefit from the additional information. For example, if there is a shared diary or calendar system in an organization such as Google Calendar (Figure 16.2), then everyone is expected to be disciplined and to put their appointments, etc., in the system. However, some people find it an additional annoyance to have their engagements and free time available for all to see, but for people who need to arrange meetings, the system makes life much easier. Grudin suggests that remedies may be to promote clearly the collective benefits of the system and provide some sort of advantage for everyone.

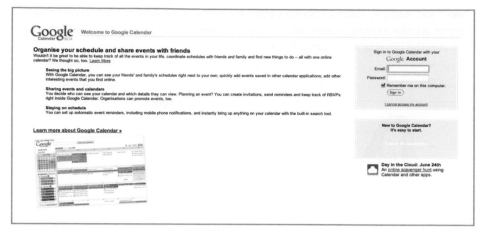

Figure 16.2 Google Calendar; Google™ is a trademark of Google Inc.

Critical mass

In order to be effective, group working needs a critical mass of people to participate. The shared diary we considered above will not be effective if only one or two people contribute to it. This is critical when the application is first introduced, since early adopters may give up before enough people participate to make use worthwhile. With all manner of group activities, it is only when there is a critical mass of people that the benefits of belonging to a group are realized. Groups usually have a dynamic as they go from just starting, to attracting a lot of people, to fading out. There are countless examples of failed groups on the Web. The reverse situation – too many people using a CSCW technology for too many purposes – can also occur. E-mail is the best example of this.

BOX 16.2

The prisoner's dilemma

The prisoner's dilemma refers to a number of situations where cooperation is the best course of action for all, only not for the individuals concerned. Two prisoners are in separate rooms at a police station, accused of a crime. If they both admit to committing the crime they will get 3 months' community service each. If one admits to the crime and the other does not, the one who admits it will get 12 months' community service and the other will go without punishment. If they both deny committing the crime, they each get 6 months' punishment. You can see their dilemma! Do they cooperate and hope the other does the same, or do they go for the selfish option of denial? They could get away with no punishment, or they could finish up with 6 months rather than 3.

There are many varieties of these situations and changing the types and amount of award or punishment changes the way people behave.

Social issues

Work is not just a rational activity, but a socially constructed practice, with all the shifting, conflicting motivations and politicking that this implies. We navigate through this environment using our knowledge of other people, guided by social conventions. Introducing collaborative environments can disrupt the balance between private and public spaces. For example, a person's personal diary is not normally available for inspection. Video-mediated 'shared offices' and similar technologies attempt to support privacy conventions by such devices as alerting people when a video 'glance' is intruding into their space, but still manage to embarrass people from time to time. New group-working technologies may shift delicate power balances through the increased availability of information.

Council bans e-mails to get staff to talk

The following is the text of an article by David Ward in the *Guardian* newspaper, 10 July 2002:

> A city council will ban the use of internal e-mails today in an attempt to persuade staff to start talking to each other. But to ensure that withdrawal symptoms are not too extreme, Liverpool council's chief executive, David Henshaw, has decreed that the ban will only apply one day a week – Wednesdays.
>
> He insists that the ban, described as an experiment, is designed to make council business flow more efficiently. It is not intended to put the brakes on the free exchange of scandal, gossip and mucky jokes, nor to stop Brian in council tax from making a date with Fiona from environmental health. All staff will still be able to communicate electronically with the outside world. But not with each other.
>
> A council spokesman estimated that e-mail now accounted for 95% of internal communications. 'We want people to pick up their phones or even get up from their desks, go down the corridor and talk to someone face to face,' he said. 'This kind of personal contact is infinitely preferable, not least because there can be room for misunderstanding in the written word sometimes.'
>
> The main issue appears to be a concern about whether e-mail is the most efficient way to communicate. 'Without doing anything else, one can just become sucked into the technology – we want people to solve problems rather than bat them off into bureaucratic cyberspace,' said the spokesman. 'They might find they have been given a useful reminder about what human contact is all about.'

Source: David Ward, *The Guardian*, 10 July 2002; copyright Guardian News and Media Ltd, 2002

The space–time matrix

A number of different ways of characterizing technology to support cooperative working have been discussed since CSCW's inception in the mid-1980s. DeSanctis and Gallupe (1987) proposed the space (or place)–time matrix. Their original formulation simply recognized that the two key variables were space and time. This very simply means that people might be co-present while they work or may be located elsewhere, and equally, they may be working together at the same time (*synchronous*) or at different times (*asynchronous*). Since the original version, various suggestions have been made for additional dimensions, of which predictability is perhaps the most important. Table 16.1 maps a selection of old and new technologies (and working practices) against the space–time matrix.

→ Also see the discussion of communication in Section 24.2

A word or two of warning – while the table is a useful heuristic it can be seen that some technologies can be placed in more than one category. Many of us will have experienced the use of e-mail in an almost synchronous fashion, when we have effectively conducted a conversation with it. Similarly, there is no reason why workflow cannot be used between shifts of people working in the same place.

Table 16.1 The space–time matrix

		Time	
		Same	**Different**
Place	**Same**	Face-to-face meetings and meeting support tools	Post-it messages, e-mail, shared information spaces such as Lotus Notes Project management and version control software
	Different	Tele-conferencing Video-conferencing Collaborative text and drawing editors Instant messaging	Traditional letters, e-mail, shared information spaces such as Lotus Notes Workflow Threaded discussion databases

Challenge 16.1

Extending the matrix to n dimensions (which would, of course, make it difficult to draw), what other dimensions do you think might be relevant?

Articulation and awareness

In order for a number of individuals to collaborate in an activity they must organize and divide the activity into individual tasks (articulation) and they have to have some appreciation of what other people are doing or have done (awareness). Awareness makes it possible to evaluate individual actions and the relevance of contributions in order to manage collaborative work. People can be aware of each other visually, audibly and through body positioning. They can also be aware of what other people have done through observations of changes to 'boundary objects' (Lutters and Ackerman, 2007). These are objects that are shared between collaborating individuals.

Articulation refers to how work is broken down into units and subtasks, its delegation among participants and its reintegration towards the goal of the work. It refers to the explicit organization of tasks as plans and schedules, the allocation of informational and interactional resources, and of rights and responsibilities in the group. Articulation also covers how these component tasks are carried through in the physical and conceptual contexts that pertain at a given time. Thus articulation involves the processes by which the boundary objects are worked on and the sequence in which this happens, where they are put and who picks them up next in the process.

Sharing and collaboration inevitably lead to issues of individual and shared territories. These may relate to physical space, where people like to have their own space and a shared space. They also like to distinguish personal spaces from public spaces. Similarly territories may refer to digital spaces whether these are areas of a shared tabletop or whether they are personal laptop computers where individuals can work on something in private before they have to share it with their collaborators.

In a collocated collaboration it is easier for people to see what one another are doing and of course they can talk to each other! In distributed collaborative environments designers need to attend to the design of the interaction to ensure that collaborators are aware of changes that happen. For example, applications such as Dropbox or Google Drive (Figure 16.3) allow people to share files, but the notifications on such systems when modifications are made to a file are not so good. Of course you do not want to receive an e-mail every time a small change is made to a shared document, but you do want to know when a collaborator has made changes and finished working on it. And for this you will have to send an e-mail.

Keep everything. Share anything.   Google Drive

Figure 16.3 Google Drive; Google™ is a trademark of Google Inc.

16.3 Technologies to support cooperative working

There are, of course, many proprietary systems that support cooperation. Large organizations will use a system such as Microsoft SharePoint to provide corporate address books and mailing lists, and manage content for the organization's intranet. Bødker and Buur (2002) describe 'The Design Collabotorium'. Much material that used to be on paper, such as standard forms, is now kept centrally for people to download as they need. This leads to some of the problems identified in Grudin's list of challenges, such as forcing people to work in a particular way to suit the technology, but does provide many benefits to the organization.

There are also many systems that provide support for social computing, which we discussed in Chapter 15. Here we summarize the main types of technology for supporting group work.

Communication

Communication is central to being able to work as a group and a typical example of a CSCW system is Microsoft's NetMeeting (Figure 16.4) which comprises support for video- and audio-conferencing, application sharing and 'chat'. Skype is another popular and free product providing similar services. Such systems provide synchronous (same-time) different-place communications, including voice, video and typed conversation.

Chat systems permit many people to engage in text conferencing, that is, writing text messages in real time to one or more correspondents. As each person types in a message it appears at the bottom of a scrolling window (or a particular section of a screen). Chat sessions can be one-to-one, one-to-many or many-to-many and may be organized by chat rooms that are identified by name, location, number of people, topic of discussion and so forth. Video and speech are also provided, along with support for managing the conversations with optics and threaded discussions.

Figure 16.4 NetMeeting in action

(Source: Screenshot reprinted by permission from Microsoft Corporation)

Shared work spaces

Bulletin boards, together with threaded discussions, news groups and public/shared folders, are a family of related technologies that support asynchronous working by way of access to shared information. Very simply, the option to permit shared folders is checked and then a set of permissions established with those who wish to access the folder.

Figure 16.5 is a screenshot from BSCW – Basic Support for Cooperative Work. BSCW is a very successful product from a EU-funded research project (of the same name) and is available (free of charge for non-commercial users) from **bscw.gmd.de.** It also forms the basis of commercially marketed applications.

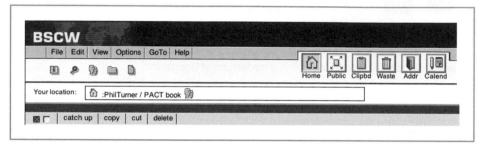

Figure 16.5 Screenshot from BSCW (Basic Support for Cooperative Work

(Source: http://bscw.fit.fraunhofer.de. Copyright FIT Fraunhofer and OrbiTeam Software GmbH. Used with permission)

The BSCW system, in the words of Hoschka (1998), 'offers the functionality of a comfortable and easy to use shared workspace and may be used with all major Web browsers and servers'. While BSCW was originally intended for research communities, its hosts at the Fraunhofer Institute for Applied Information Technology (FIT) state that it is used in a wide range of other domains. Essentially, the system allows teams access to working documents, images, links, threaded discussions, etc., in shared workspaces. The coordination of group working is supported by a raft of version management, access control and notification tools.

There are many other examples of shared spaces. Wikis allow group members to edit documents and contribute files. Facebook supports a variety of group activities, keeping others informed about your status, sharing photos and playing games together.

File sharing can be accomplished through software such as Dropbox (see discussion in previous chapter). A number of other application–sharing products have been created, flowered briefly and been lost to history. Google docs is one particularly successful example.

Challenge 16.2

Imagine you are application-sharing with a group of people and someone presses Undo. What should the Undo undo? The last action, that person's last action? And what if that person's last action has been changed by someone else in the conference?

Shared whiteboards

Shared whiteboards allow people in different places to view and draw on a shared computer-based drawing. The surface of the 'whiteboard' may simply be a window on each individual computer desktop or on a large common display in each location, typically touch-sensitive. The implementation of the parallel with physical whiteboards varies from product to product but users are normally represented as tele-pointers which are colour-coded or labelled. Input is typically by touch or stylus in the case of the large shared display, or by any normal input device for individual workstations. The backdrop of the whiteboard may be blank, as in its physical counterpart, or the contents of another software application. Since the early 1990s large shared whiteboards such as LiveBoard (Elrod *et al.*, 1992) have moved from research labs to commercial products. Their use is now commonplace in business settings, and increasingly in other domains such as education (Figure 16.6).

Figure 16.6 Electronic whiteboard in educational setting
(Source: Ingo Wagner/dpa/Corbis)

Shared workspaces

Shared workspaces have been tailored for specific purposes. Instances include numerous real-time shared text-editing systems, e.g. ShrEdit (Olson *et al.*, 1992), the 'Electronic Cocktail Napkin' described by Gross (1996) which facilitates shared freehand sketching for architectural design using handheld computers, and the page layout design application described by Gutwin *et al.* (1996). The most ambitious shared workspaces support the illusion of collaborating in three-dimensional space with haptic feedback from the manipulation of shared physical objects. Examples of such applications include the work of Hiroshi Ishii, such as Illuminating Clay allowing the manipulation of a 3D landscape.

← Illuminating Clay is described in Chapter 13

Video-augmented shared workspaces combine a shared information space with a video image of other participants. It has generally been shown (e.g. Tang and Isaacs, 1993; Newlands *et al.,* 1996) that although task performance itself is not enhanced, the availability of visual cues improves coordination and creates a greater sense of teamwork. A number of researchers have developed more integrated combinations of shared space and video, such that other participants' gestures and/or faces may be seen in the same visual space as the shared workspace. Applications have been targeted at design tasks, with the aim of supporting the interplay of drawing and gesture observed in many studies of designers at work.

Electronic meeting systems

Electronic meeting systems (EMSs) are technologies that are designed to support group meetings with tools to improve group process, by enhancing communication, individual thought and decision making. GSS (group support systems) and GDSS (group decision support systems) include quite complex facilities to help with decision making such as ranking options and decision criteria, help for brainstorming and so on. More recently these idea have spread to the democratic process and there are a number of systems designed to support teledemocracy. On-line petitioning systems and voting systems are deployed by a number of governments.

The evidence about the effectiveness of meeting support systems is contradictory. Some researchers (e.g. Antunes and Costa, 2003) claim that they have been relatively unsuccessful, for reasons such as the need for skilled meeting facilitators, negative effects on meeting process, cost and usability problems. Other reviews, notably Fjermestad and Hiltz (2000), have found the technology to improve group performance as measured by effectiveness, efficiency, consensus, usability and satisfaction. As these authors propose, one reason for the apparent differences may be that many studies have used short-lived groups in artificial experimental settings. The technology is more likely to bring positive benefits in real organizational settings where task success is of genuine importance and teams are better motivated to succeed as well as generally having a history of co-working.

**BOX
16.4**

The ICE

The ICE is a meeting room, with an interactive boardroom table and five wall-mounted multitouch screens (Figure 16.7). We have been developing and using it over the last 2 or 3 years, first to provide a new type of meeting room for departments at our university and secondly to try to better understand how collaborative technologies and spaces can change the way we work. These include many of the issues raised in the design of collaborative environments, immersive environments (see Section 16.4) and issues of gesture and touch interaction. In physical terms we have been looking at how partitioning of the space and orientation contribute to territoriality (the expressions of ownership towards an object) and issues of control, communication and shared spaces. There are issues of awareness and collaboration, of workflow, articulation of tasks distributed spatially and temporally and coordination of activities. The social affordances of the space are influenced by the physical affordances of the space (Rogers *et al.*, 2009).

Our intention is to make the ICE a functioning meeting room and not simply a demonstration of technology. It is certainly true that the technology was chosen because it was available at the time (2009) and the room is the size and shape it is because it too was available. This real-world combination of opportunities and constraints is another feature of interaction design in the rapidly changing technological environment that we inhabit. Clearly we are not alone in recognizing an emerging design paradigm. Since the ICE has been completed we have had a steady stream of businesses and public-sector organizations coming in to see it, to discuss possibilities and to see the opportunities that may be possible in their own organizations, constrained as ever by cost, by available technology and by the characteristics of available physical locations.

Figure 16.7 The ICE www.futureinteractions.net
(Source: Dr Oli Mival)

Groupware toolkits

The need to prototype different CSCW configurations to investigate such issues as awareness (see below) and the management of collaborative work sessions led to the development of groupware toolkits, of which the best known is GroupKit. This was developed over some five years in the 1990s by Saul Greenberg's team at the University of Calgary. It supports the creation of real-time collaborative applications, such as multi-user drawing tools, text editors and meeting tools. GroupKit was and is widely used in the CSCW research community.

More recently, Gutwin (Hill and Gutwin, 2003) has developed MAUI, a Java-based toolkit with standard GUI widgets and group-specific elements such as telepointers. The toolkit is said to be 'the first ever set of UI widgets that are truly collaboration-aware'. Saul Greenberg's grouplab continues to extend and develop toolkits for a variety of situations including using proximity and movement in interaction design.

Awareness applications

Being aware of what co-workers are doing and whether they are busy or available for discussions is an important part of effective collaboration. In Chapter 15 we described Babble, which showed some of the activities of co-workers at IBM.

The Portholes system was an early example of awareness technology. It is, however, a highly representative example of CSCW research in this area, focusing as it does on the reactions of a group of workers to novel technologies under naturalistic conditions. The work was originally reported by Dourish and Bly (1992), but there have been several later implementations and related studies.

Portholes' main functionality was to provide people with a set of small video snapshots of other areas in the workplace, both other people's offices and common areas (Figure 16.8). These were updated only every few minutes, but were enough to give people a sense of who was around and what they were doing. The original studies were conducted at Rank Xerox research labs in the US and the UK. Users mostly enjoyed the opportunities for casual contact. Examples reported include the following:

- A participant at PARC (the US lab) was spending many late nights working in his office; his presence was not only noted by EuroPARC (UK) participants but also led them to be quite aware of his dissertation progress.

- Another late-night worker at PARC was pleased to tell his local colleagues that he had watched the sun rise in England.
- Enjoying a colleague's message when he sang Happy Birthday to himself.
- Being able to check unobtrusively that someone was in the office before going to speak to them.
- The sense of whether people were around and seeing friends.
- Feeling a connection to people at the other site.

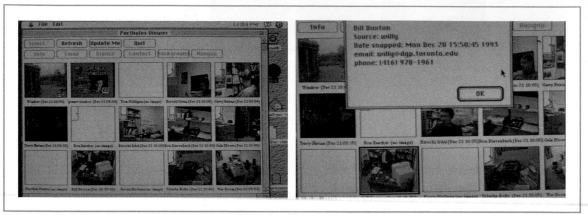

Figure 16.8 Screenshots from the Portholes system
(Source: Courtesy of Bill Buxton)

Disadvantages included the consumption of screen real-estate and the potential for privacy violations. Later versions incorporated the sound of a door opening as a cue that a video snapshot was about to be taken. Portholes raises two of the fundamental trade-offs in designing for awareness:

- Privacy versus awareness
- Awareness versus disruption.

In normal everyday life we have unobtrusive, socially accepted ways of maintaining mutual awareness while respecting privacy. Examples include checking for a colleague's car in the car park or noticing that someone is in the office because their jacket is over the back of a chair even if they are not actually present at the time. In computer-mediated collaboration, many of these cues have to be reinvented, and the consequences of their new incarnations are often unclear until tried out in real life. Experiments have included shadowy video figures, muffled audio, and a variety of mechanisms to alert people that they are being (or about to be) captured on video or audio.

Roomware

Roomware® is defined as the integration of furniture, other room elements such as doors and walls and information and communication devices assembled to support different activities and was trademarked by Streitz *et al.* (1997, 1998, 1999) (see Figure 16.9 and http://www.roomware.de). The ICE described above is an example of roomware. Streitz and his colleagues (Streitz *et al.,* 1997) comment that making comparisons of effectiveness across different configurations of public shared spaces and private spaces is somewhat fruitless because the different combinations of technologies, people's preferences and the activities make generalizations difficult. However, they do show that the combination of a public display and personal workstations was more effective in their design task. Fluidum in Munich is a lab that looks at novel surface-based interactions and the Media space at the University of Aachen in Germany combines multiple devices in media content. The NiCE project (Haller *et al.*, 2010) developed a meeting room with an augmented whiteboard with a projected overlay and tracking capability. The goal was to enable content creation and sharing during group discussion meetings in a cohesive, seamless system enabling work in different media: paper, whiteboard and digital media. It combines and integrates different features and interaction techniques identified and developed in a series of other projects.

Figure 16.9 The second generation of the IPSI Roomware components (DynaWall, InteracTable, CommChair, ConnecTables) developed in 1999
(Source: Norbert Streitz)

As part of the project the team set up a list of design challenges for interactive workspaces. Interactive workspaces should support the multiplicity and diversity of tasks that are inherent in different types of meeting. They quote Plaue and colleagues (Plaue *et al.*, 2009) in arguing for the 'conference room as toolbox' and point to the importance of floor and access control through multiple input and output devices. A second challenge concerns the physical and perceptual aspects of the whole workspace. People need to feel close to collaborate, physically or perceptually, but not so close as to feel uncomfortable in terms of the four proxemic zones (Hall, 1966).

→ Proxemics is discussed in Chapter 24

Challenge 16.3

What other simple (non-technological) cues do you use in everyday life in maintaining awareness of others?

Active badges

Active badges were small wearables that identify people and transmit signals providing location information through a network of sensors. Early uses included the obvious one of locating someone within a building and being able to have one's own set-up and files instantly available from the nearest PC. The growth of wireless technologies has led to wide-ranging and more sophisticated applications such as making tourist information available as locations come into view, navigation information for the visually handicapped and making people with shared interests aware of each other at conferences.

→ Wearable computing appliances are described in Chapter 20

This is well illustrated in Harper's study (Harper, 1992) of the adoption of active badges (a product called the Locator) in research laboratories, using two communities of researchers at Rank Xerox as participants. Harper (a sociologist) wished to explore the social and organizational nature of the research lab through studying technology in use. He concluded that the way people used the badges – reluctantly or with commitment and enthusiasm – 'is determined by what they do, their formal position, and their state of relations – meant here in the broadest sense – with others in the labs. From this view, wearing a badge, viewing the Locator as acceptable or not as the case may be, symbolically represents one's job, one's status, one's location within the moral order.' (Harper, 1992, p. 335). Among many interesting nuggets in the report, the contrast between reactions of receptionists and researchers is (yet again) an example of Grudin's 'challenge' of differential costs and benefits. Receptionists are already in a known, fixed location for most of a regular working day: using a badge to track their whereabouts changes very little. Researchers, by custom and practice, have freedom to work irregular hours, at home, in the office, or walking around thinking through an idea. Tracking their location can be perceived as significantly impinging on this liberty, but makes the receptionist's job considerably easier.

BOX 16.5

An ethnographic study of awareness

Christian Heath and Paul Luff provide a classic study of a London Underground control room (Heath and Luff, 2000). Our summary of the work will focus on the awareness issues, but the original report covers far more than this and would repay reading in full.

The team of researchers from University College London studied the operation of the Bakerloo Line control room on a day-to-day basis. The Bakerloo Line is a busy line serving the London Underground network.

The control room (CR) had been recently upgraded, replacing manual signalling with a computerized system. The CR housed the line controller responsible for the coordination of the day-to-day running of the line, the divisional information assistant (DIA) responsible for providing passenger information via a public address system (PA) and communicating with stations, and two signal assistants who supervised a busy section of track. The controller and the DIA sat together in a semicircular console facing a fixed real-time display of the traffic on the line. Lights on this display indicated the location of trains. The console was equipped with a radio telephone, touchscreen telephones, a PA system, a closed-circuit TV control system and monitors displaying line information and traffic and a number of other control systems. The London Underground system as a whole was coordinated by way of a paper timetable which details the number of trains, crew information and a dozen other items of relevance to the controller. The control room staff aimed overall to support the running of a service which matched the timetable as closely as possible.

While the control room staff have different formal responsibilities, the job was achieved in practice by a cooperative interweaving of tasks requiring close coordination, which in turn depended on a high degree of awareness. Some of the many instances were:

- In the case of service announcements delivered over the PA, information was drawn from the fixed line diagram and tailored to the arrival of trains visible on the CCTV monitor, but crucially from awareness of the activities of colleagues and their conversations with drivers about the state of train traffic.
- Instructions to drivers similarly depended on being aware of colleagues. All staff maintained this level of awareness, but at a level which intruded neither on their

colleagues' work nor on their own, picking up on key words in conversations and significant actions taken, such as instructing trains to turn round, or even glancing towards a particular information resource.

- Temporary changes to the timetable were made using erasable acetate overlays, thus providing the change information to all concerned when it was needed, rather than intruding into current tasks.
- Talking out loud when working through timetable changes, nominally a single-person job, so that others were aware of what was about to happen.

Heath and Luff conclude their analysis by emphasizing the fluid, informal yet crucial interplay between individual and cooperative work and the unobtrusive resources for awareness that support this achievement. The point for designers is that any attempt to design technology which can be used only in either strictly individual or strictly collaborative modes, still less to define formal teamworking procedures to be mediated by technology, is likely to fail.

Challenge 16.4

What collaboration technologies do you use in working with others? List the reasons for your choices. How far do your reasons match the issues raised in the previous material in this chapter? What can you conclude about the fit between the state of design knowledge and real-world conditions?

16.4 Collaborative virtual environments

Collaborative virtual environments (CVEs) allow their participants to interact inside a virtual environment with each other and virtual objects. Normally, people are embodied as 3D graphical avatars of a varying degree of sophistication and detail. CVEs such as Second Life provide a remarkable amount of detail and are being used for virtual meetings and for education and training. Figure 16.10 shows some of these features in the DISCOVER training environment. At top left the window shows the view (from the perspective of the user's avatar) of another avatar operating a fire extinguisher. A plan of the environment can be seen at the bottom, and at top right a window on another part of the virtual ship. The grey buttons at bottom left are difficult to see, but allow the user to communicate with others via virtual telephone or intercom. Communication generally in CVEs is most often via voice or text, although occasionally video is integrated with other media.

CVEs support awareness of other participants' activities in the shared space. Perhaps the most prominent of research CVEs in the 1990s, MASSIVE-1 and MASSIVE-2 (Bowers *et al.*, 1996), had a sophisticated model of spatial awareness based on concepts of *aura* (a defined region of space around an object or person), *focus* (an observer's region of interest) and *nimbus* (the observer's region of influence or projection). While normally designed for synchronous work, there are some asynchronous examples, as described by Benford *et al.* (1997) in an account of an environment which mimics the affordances of documents for everyday coordination in an office setting – for example, indicating whether work has started through the position of a virtual document on a virtual desktop.

Figure 16.10 Extinguishing a fire in the DISCOVER CVE

Many CVEs remain as research tools, but the technology is migrating slowly towards practical applications for collaborative work. Training applications are prominent, allowing people to practise teamwork in situations that may be inaccessible or dangerous, or to enable distributed teams and tutors to train together. Figure 16.11 is a screenshot from a CVE designed to allow tutors and trainees to interact in training to replace ATM switches.

An interesting point here is the video window at the left of the screen which illustrates the correct procedure. The creation of the CVE was motivated by the wide geographical dispersion of trainees and tutors and the fragility and cost of the ATM equipment involved.

Issues in the training arena, aside from the usability of some technologies, relate to the following:

- How far training in the virtual world can transfer to the real
- The validity of training teams to interact with the rather different (but smaller) range of awareness cues available in CVEs – for example, it is often difficult to detect where a fellow avatar is looking
- The inflexibility of even the most sophisticated virtual environments compared to the infinite possibilities of imaginary scenarios in face-to-face training exercises
- Overcoming the perception of employers that CVEs are a just a species of game (although game-like features not surprisingly enhance participants' experience).

Educational CVEs are also becoming commonplace. Among many examples are an application related to museum exhibits that allows people to play an ancient Egyptian game (Economou *et al.*, 2000) and a CVE for fostering social awareness in educational settings (Prasolova-Førland and Divitini, 2003). Among diverse other applications are collaborative information search and visualization, for example the virtual pond filled with data masquerading as aquatic creatures described by Ståhl *et al.* (2002), commercial dispute negotiation, representing evidence as virtual objects in video streams, and

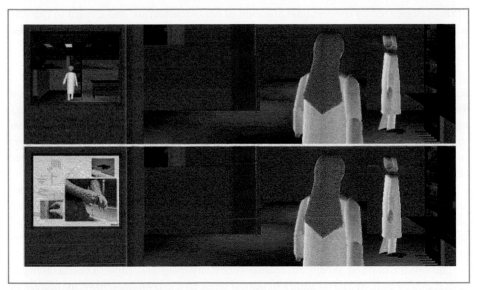

Figure 16.11 An application learning to replace ATM switches
(Source: www.discover.uottawa.ca/~mojtaba/Newbridge.html)

public entertainment (Dew *et al.*, 2002). Several ventures in this last domain are summarized by Benford *et al.* (2002). Finally, of course, very many games can be regarded as a species of CVE. A screenshot from a disaster simulation display for a virtual reality system called 'Walkinside' is shown in Figure 16.12. This was developed to allow people to practise and plan for disasters at sites like oil platforms.

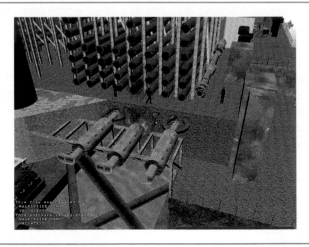

Figure 16.12 A disaster simulation display from 'Walkinside'
(Source: VR Context/Eurellos/Science Photo Library)

16.5 Case study: developing a collaborative tabletop application

Snøkult is a multitouch-enabled educational software tool running on a tabletop surface, created at Edinburgh Napier University to assist secondary school students with the process of ideation in architectural design. The application is one phase in a series of tasks organized by the National Museum of Art, Architecture and Design in Norway, with the intention of enabling students to collaborate over design ideas, then to express them visually.

The scenario that the system was developed for is as follows:

A class of students of average age 14 years is taken to a remote site selected by the Museum for particular geographic characteristics, to discuss architectural issues in groups, collect photographs of the landscape with a digital camera, then return to the classroom to further construct ideas. Activity then involves building a physical model using simple materials, which is also photographed. The entire task is performed in groups collaboratively, with members assigned specific tasks within.

Finally, selected photographs are brought into the Snøkult application for manipulation and layout. Using a multitouch table, Snøkult software enables site images, models, sketches, hotspots and annotations to be combined into a number of 'collages', which are later output to disk or printer.

The tender defined sketching, transparency, layering and camera connectivity as core requirements, with the ability to output work to a screen presentation, images on disk and print media. Aside from satisfying these needs, our design priorities were also to produce something simple and intuitive to use for the intended audience, with minimal steps required from collection input through to collage output.

These goals were achieved successfully, counting however on a significant amount of overtime. A first version of the product containing essential functionality was delivered on time, with updates provided thereafter including some remaining lower-priority features. An evaluation sheet was then delivered to the client, questioning how users perceive the application interface. At the time of writing we still await feedback from the Museum regarding the evaluation, which we hope will confirm our design decisions.

The system is designed around the metaphor of an actual table, with drawers to supply materials and a canvas as the creative surface. The student will upload photos, manipulate and select appropriate ones and compile their ideas. The teacher will guide students and perform occasional administration on Snøkult.

A wooden table (Figure 16.13) was employed of almost equal size to the multitouch screen already in the possession of the Museum, in order to closely simulate environmental circumstances. In fact the virtual 'table' concept with its content can be mapped very effectively with object-oriented design and was utilized throughout the design and development stages. Discussion was undertaken about issues such as reachability, icon size, clutter, multi-sided operation, menu structure and simplicity of presentation to the student audience.

Figure 16.13 Using a table to prototype the interaction
(Source: Dr Oli Mival)

Though the table appears large at first observation, screen pixels and touch sensitivity affect how objects should be sized to appear. This is considered in combination with students' smaller fingers and their arms having lesser reach. The 46″ cell screen resolution of 1920 × 1080 when viewed at a short distance does not give the same level of detail as an equivalent desktop PC screen, meaning a ratio of 20.7 pixels per centimetre is utilized as a guide for sizing features, particularly operational components such as buttons. Icons were set to 40 × 40 pixels for most operations on the main screen, with 64 × 64 used for global menu and drawer category functions.

The number of students operating the system at once is also a concern. Though the users are obviously smaller than adults in stature, limitations on number of concurrent operations are most significantly affected by screen real-estate. Toolbars associated with each object take a specific amount of area, leading to potential overlap of controls when many sets are activated at once. From experiments on the physical table, we estimated six people would be the ideal number of operators at any moment. The general interface shown in Figure 16.14 was designed to make best use of the table space available.

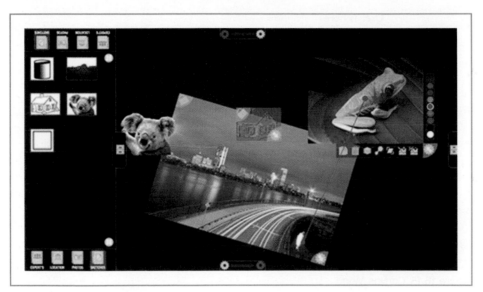

Figure 16.14 General interface
(Source: Dr Oli Mival)

The Drawer is situated at either of two screen sides and pulled out containing categories where source images sit, including camera imports, each item manipulable within. This allows new items to be easily brought onto screen (Canvas), but also limits clutter. Drawers extend to about ⅓ of table width and have dual-sided controls and switchable content orientation.

A decision was made to create two drawers with duplicate content. Each drawer contains duplicated content allowing multiple users to rearrange items in either one or the other, before bringing them onto Canvas. Otherwise there is potential for confusion if the same data is mirrored in multiple places.

As the only other immediately visible item, at adjacent screen sides to the Drawer, the Global Menu gives access to snapshot saving, printing, presenting, screen saver and group/canvas changes. Despite many system-level operations taking place here, we have managed to avoid any need for interaction with the underlying operating system by automating tasks. All file operations are applied within Materials and Work folders in the local Dropbox account, printing and snapshot saving are completed without dialogue. The Global Menu itself was created to separate general tasks from user-specific ones. Other intentions with the target audience in mind were to minimize steps required to perform tasks and remove all reliance on underlying operating system interaction.

The Canvas Menu (Figure 16.15) is displayed at the point of touch with an orientation facing the user within 360 degrees. In the fashion of multiple orientation, it is a created as a circular item with central controller, from which operations used to create new objects are placed equidistant. Though not available directly from the Cornerstone API, orientation information can be calculated using geometry from the Finger and Hand data contained within a touch event, allowing the menu to be displayed at any angle of rotation to suit the direction of the requesting user. Once again, operation of the control prevents accidental activation by requiring the central widget to be dragged across one of the menu targets.

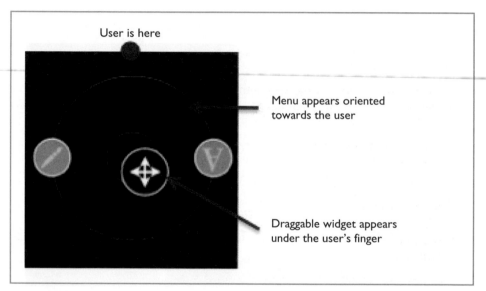

Figure 16.15 Canvas Menu
(Source: Dr Oli Mival)

Summary and key points

This chapter has argued that the most significant aspect of the 'turn to the social' has been the growing interest in studying groups of people – particularly people at work – and the design of CSCW systems to support work activity. CSCW has developed from the original serendipitous convergence of technologies and insights from the social sciences in the late 1980s, and now encompasses many advanced technologies and social media applications.

- CSCW focuses on the social aspect of people working together.
- Different application domains demand different types of support.
- Key issues are cooperation, collaboration and awareness of others.

Exercises

1 Consider the shopping scenario in Section 15.2 and have a look at on-line sites that use recommendations such as Amazon and Netflix (www.netflix.com/). What other forms of awareness of others and of relevant information could you include?

2 Log on to Twitter and browse around. See how easy it is to find what is going on, what is current and what are the dead topics. Do this over several days to see the changes.

 Further reading

Grudin's two classic papers on challenges for CSCW (Grudin, 1988, 1994) repay reading in full as an encapsulation of how the field has developed and the main difficulties for CSCW.

Heath, C. and Luff, P. (2000) *Technology in Action.* Cambridge University Press, Cambridge. *A comprehensive collection of workplace studies.*

Getting ahead

Martin, D., Rodden, T., Rouncefield, R., Sommerville, I. and Viller, S. (2001) Finding patterns in the fieldwork. In Prinz, W., Janke, M., Rogers, Y., Schmidt, K. and Willy, V. (eds), *Proceedings of ECSCW '01 Conference,* Bonn, Germany, 16–20 Sept. Kluwer, Dordrecht, pp. 39–58.

Viller, S. and Sommerville, I. (2000) Ethnographically informed analysis for software engineers. *International Journal of Human–Computer Studies,* 53(1): 169–96.

 Web links

Norbert Strietz has a site devoted to his Roomware and related projects, see **www. smart-future.net/1.html**

The accompanying website has links to relevant websites, Go to **www.pearsoned.co.uk/benyon/chapter16**

Comments on challenges

Challenge 16.1

Some possibilities include:

- Focus on interpersonal communication vs focus on the shared work
- Text and speech only vs mixed modalities (e.g. video, shared graphics workspaces)
- Structured vs unstructured.

Consideration of these and other variations can be found throughout the material in the rest of this chapter.

Challenge 16.2

There is no easy answer to this and actual implementations vary. What is most important is that everyone understands the way it works.

Challenge 16.3

Here are just two examples. For my part, I can hear when my colleague in the next-door office is talking – not enough to overhear the words themselves, but enough to stop me from interrupting unless it's really urgent. Similarly, when someone has headphones on while sitting at their desk it generally means they're busy. These cues are so undemanding of my attention that I normally don't think about them – unlike having a video window sitting on my screen.

Challenge 16.4

The important thing here is to list the wisest range of technologies. You collaborate in all sorts of ways, so do not just think about the obvious software such as Skype or Instant Messenger; think about exchanging files, using shared diaries, or meeting management software. Think about paper, phones, faxes and, of course, talking to people!

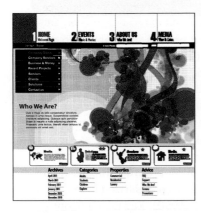

Chapter 17
Agents and avatars

Contents

Aims

Agents are autonomous, active computer processes that possess some ability to communicate with people and/or other agents and to adapt their behaviour. In short, agents are small artificial intelligence (AI) computer programs. The ones that interest us have some impact on the interaction of people with interactive systems. Agent-based interaction has long been seen as a solution to many usability problems, but so far it has not delivered as much as was hoped, something that it shares with all applications of AI. However, there have been some notable successes and many of the systems described in Chapter 15, such as recommender systems, employ some form of agent or agency in the interaction.

After studying this chapter you should be able to:

- Describe the key features of interface agents
- Understand the conceptual model of agents
- Understand the key idea of user modelling
- Describe some agent-based systems.

17.1 Agents

Agents are autonomous, active computer processes that possess some ability to communicate with people and/or other agents and to adapt their behaviour. In some work in artificial intelligence, there is a 'strong view' of agents: they have beliefs, desires and intentions (and maybe emotions) and can plan, learn, adapt and communicate. Much of this work is not concerned with interface issues, but rather with activities such as planning, scheduling and controlling computer networks. In HCI circles there is the 'weaker view' presented above. There is also a large amount of hype surrounding agents and many entities proclaimed as agents are not even 'weak' agents. In human–computer interaction and the design of interactive systems, the move towards utilizing intelligence at the interface through the use of artificial agents was popularized in the 1990s by people such as Brenda Laurel (1990b) and Alan Kay (1990). Kay talked about the move away from direct manipulation of interface objects to the 'indirect management' of interface agents.

Kay's vision was of a world in which more and more activities are delegated to agents. Agents would act as 'talking heads' and attend meetings for us. They could organize our diaries in cooperation with agents acting for members of our work group. Other agents would be guiding us through large information spaces in a variety of personas, acting as tutors and mentors in teaching systems or explaining the complexities of a new piece of software, drawing on our experience with previous similar applications. However, progress towards this situation has been relatively slow. The fundamental difficulty is that computers have access to a very limited view of what people are doing. They can detect mouse movements, typing, the selection of menu items and that is just about all. Making sensible inferences about what people are trying to do from such limited data is very difficult.

Agents can be seen in a number of different ways:

- As guides they would explain the structure and features of an information space.
- As reminder agents they would help us keep appointments and keep us up to date with new developments.
- As monitors they would watch over mailing lists and announcements for relevant information.
- As collaborators they would work with us on problems.
- As surrogates they would stand in for us at meetings.

Generally there are two main types of agent:

- Some act on behalf of and know about an individual person. This, then, allows for personalization and adapting systems to an individual's preferences, habits and knowledge.
- Others know about particular types of work such as indexing, scheduling, spell-checking and so on. They have more domain knowledge, but less knowledge of individuals. Predictive technologies such as the T3 text system and the systems on Web browsers that try to anticipate long URLs are examples.

Of course, robots are examples of agent-based interaction and industrial and domestic robots are becoming more common. Industrial robots include pre-programmed systems, such as are used in car manufacturing, and mobile robots, used in applications such as security monitoring. Domestic robots include lawnmowers and devices for undertaking other menial tasks, such as vacuum cleaners. Figure 17.1 shows a robot vacuum cleaner.

Figure 17.1 Robot vacuum cleaner
(Source: Courtesy of iRobot Corporation)

Human–robot interaction is becoming an increasingly important area of study. There are many social issues that arise as people and robots begin to live together. Robots of the future will give assistance or provide companionship for elderly and disabled people. Figure 17.2 shows the Nursebot, 'Pearl'. Pearl was one of the first prototypes of a robot that would provide home care.

Figure 17.2 The Nursebot 'Pearl'

(Source: Carnegie Mellon University, Human-Computer Interaction Institute)

When thinking about what agents can do it is useful to consider metaphors from real-life agents (see Box 17.1). Some agents can learn about behaviours over time; others can be programmed (end-user programming). All are based, however, on some important principles of adaptive systems. We briefly review the concept of an adaptive system before developing an architecture of agents and looking at some examples.

BOX 17.1

Metaphors for thinking about agents

- Travel agents – the user specifies some fairly high-level goal that they have and some broad constraints. The agent tries to come up with an option that satisfies.
- Estate agents work independently on behalf of their clients, scanning the available options for real estate and picking likely-looking properties.
- The secret agent goes out to find out what is going on, working with and against others to discover important information.
- The agent as friend or companion suggests someone who gets to know your likes and dislikes and who shares your interests – someone who can pick out interesting things when they see them.
- The film star's or basketball player's agent is someone who works on their behalf negotiating the best deals or the best scripts or teams.
- The slave does the jobs for you that you do not want to do.

?

Challenge 17.1

Instructing agents on what you want them to do can be quite difficult. Anyone who has bought a house or rented a flat will know that estate agents seem to send houses that are completely at odds with what the buyer wanted. Try writing down some instructions that would describe which news stories you would like to know about. Exchange the descriptions with a friend and see whether you can find exceptions or whether they would be able to follow your instructions.

17.2 Adaptive systems

Agents are adaptive systems. A system is a more or less complex object that is recognized, from a particular perspective, to have a relatively stable, coherent structure (Checkland, 1981). Systems contain subsystems and are contained within supersystems (or environments). Systems interact with other systems. Systems interact with their environments, with their subsystems and with other systems at the same level of abstraction. A seed interacts with the earth and so obtains necessary nutrients for its growth. A traveller listens to an announcement at Munich airport. A hammer interacts with a nail and drives the nail into a piece of wood.

In order to interact with another system at all, every system requires some representation, or model, of the other system. So a seed embodies a representation of its environment and if this model is inaccurate or inappropriate the seed will not germinate; it will not succeed in its interaction. The interaction of the traveller and the airport announcement can be described at the following levels:

- *Physical.* The announcement must be clear and loud enough for the traveller to hear it.

- *Conceptual*. The traveller must be able to interpret what is heard in terms of airports, travel and the German language.
- *Intentional*. The announcement will relate more or less to some purpose of the traveller.

The hammer has been carefully designed in order to achieve its purpose of banging nails into wood; its physical model must capture the conceptual level (that it is strong enough) which must be suitable for its purpose.

In each case, the systems in question have a 'model' of the interaction which in turn is dependent on two other representations: the model which a system has of itself and the model which it has of the systems with which it can interact – those that it is adapted to. In most natural systems, these models equate with the entirety of the system, but in designed systems the system's model of itself reflects the designer's view. We may represent the overall structure of the representations possessed by a system as shown in Figure 17.3. A system has one or more models of the other system(s) with which it is interacting. A system also includes some representations of itself.

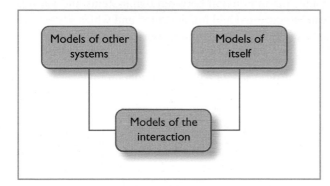

Figure 17.3 Basic architecture of interacting systems

The complexity of the various models defines a number of levels and types of adaptation. Browne *et al.* (1990) identify a number of types of adaptive system in their consideration of adaptivity in natural and computer-based systems:

1. At the simplest level, some agents are characterized by their ability to produce a change in output in response to a change in input. These systems must have some receptor and transmitter functions (so that they can interact with other systems) and some rudimentary, rule-based adaptive mechanism. They have a generally limited variety of behaviour because the adaptive mechanism is 'hard-wired'. These are the stimulus–response systems such as a thermostat: the temperature rises so the thermostat turns the heating off, the temperature falls so it turns the heating on.
2. The simple agent can be enhanced if it maintains a record of the interaction that allows it to respond to sequences of inputs rather than just individual signals. This can be further developed if it keeps a history of the interaction. Predictive text systems fall into this category.
3. A more complex system will monitor the effects of the adaptation on the subsequent interaction and evaluate this through trial and error. This evaluation mechanism then selects from a range of possible outputs for any given input. Many game-playing programs (e.g. chess games, noughts and crosses games, etc.) use this form of adaptation.
4. Type 3 agents have to wait to observe the outcome of any adaptation on the resultant dialogue. In the case of game-playing agents, this might mean that they lose the

game. More sophisticated systems monitor the effect on a *model* of the interaction. Thus possible adaptations can be tried out in theory before being put into practice. These systems now require a model of the other system with which they are interacting (in order to estimate the change of behaviour which will result from the system's own adaptive change). Moreover, these systems now require inference mechanisms and must be able to abstract from the dialogue record and capture a design or intentional interpretation of the interaction. Similarly, the system must now include a representation of its own 'purpose' in its domain model.

5. Yet another level of complexity is in systems which are capable of changing these representations: they can reason about the interaction.

Browne *et al.* (1990) point out that the levels reflect a change of intention, moving from a designer specifying and testing the mechanisms in a (simple) agent to the system itself dealing with the design and evaluation of its mechanisms in a type 5 system. Moving up the levels also incurs an increasing cost that may not be justified. There is little to be gained by having a highly sophisticated capability if the context of the interaction is never going to change.

Dietrich *et al.* (1993) consider the interaction between two systems and various stages at which adaptations can be suggested and implemented and which system has control at the different stages. In any system–system interaction we can consider

- *Initiative*. Which system starts the process off?
- *Proposal*. Which system makes the proposal for a particular adaptation?
- *Decision*. Which system decides whether to go ahead with the adaptation?
- *Execution*. Which system is responsible for carrying out the adaptation?
- *Evaluation*. Which system evaluates the success of the change?

As a very simple example of a human–agent interaction, consider the spellchecker on a word processor. It is up to the person to decide whether to take the initiative (turn on the spellchecker), the system makes proposals for incorrectly spelled words, the person decides whether to accept the proposal, the system usually executes the change (but sometimes the person may type in a particular word) and it is the person who evaluates the effects.

Adaptive systems are characterized by the representations they have of other systems, of themselves and of the interaction. These models will only ever be partial representations of everything that goes on. Designers need to consider what is feasible (what data can be obtained about an interaction, for example) and what is desirable and useful.

Challenge 17.2

Cars illustrate well how more and more functions have been handed over to adaptive systems, or agents. Originally there were no synchromesh gears, the timing of the spark had to be advanced or retarded manually, there were no servo-break mechanisms and people had to remember to put their seat belts on. Using these and other examples, discuss what models the agents have. What do they know about the other systems that they interact with? What do they know about their own functioning?

17.3 An architecture for agents

The simple model of adaptive systems provides a framework or reference model for thinking about agent-based interaction. Agents are adaptive systems – systems that adapt to people. Hence they need some representation of people; the 'model of other

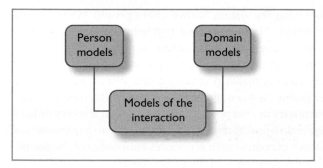

Figure 17.4 Basic architecture for an agent

systems' from Figure 17.3 becomes a 'person model' here (Figure 17.4). The 'model of itself' is the representation that the agent has of the domain, or application. The model of the interaction is an abstract representation of the interaction between the models of people and the models of the domain. Each of these may be further elaborated as indicated in Figure 17.5, which provides the full structural agent architecture. This architecture is elaborated and discussed below.

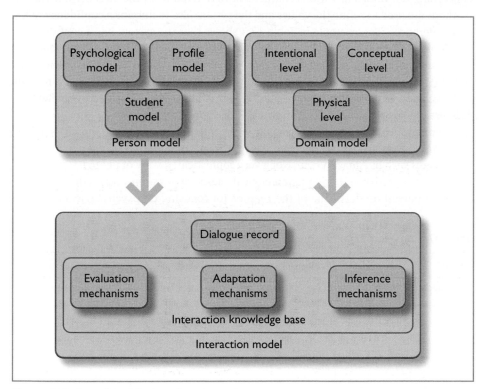

Figure 17.5 Overall architecture for an agent

Person model

The person model is also known as a 'user model', but the term 'user' here seems particularly inappropriate for human–agent interaction where people are not using agents, but are interacting with them. Indeed, some agent-based interaction is aiming to move beyond interaction, with its rather impersonal overtones. In Section 17.5 we describe something called 'personification technology' where the aim is to turn interactions into relationships. This brings in emotional and social aspects to the interaction.

→ Emotion is in Chapter 22 and social interaction is in Chapter 24

The person model describes what the system 'knows' about people. We like to distinguish psychological data from profile data because psychological data, emotional make-up and personality are qualitatively different features of people than their interests, history and habits that make up the profile data. Some systems concentrate on developing models of habits, inferred by monitoring interactions over time (i.e. by keeping a dialogue record). Other profile data can often be most easily obtained by asking people to provide it. Other systems try to infer people's goals, although it is very difficult to infer what someone is trying to do from the data typically available to a computer system (mouse clicks and a sequence of commands). A person's knowledge of the domain is represented in the student model component of the person model.

The pioneering approach to user models comes from Elaine Rich and her system called GRUNDY (Rich, 1989). This work introduced the ideas of stereotypes – sets of characteristics shared by many people. In GRUNDY the system is recommending books to people. A simple set of characteristics is given a value representing the amount of that value and triggers are objects associated with a situation that selects the stereotype. For example, if someone responds to a question asking whether that person is male or female then the answer will trigger a male or female stereotype. A response that the person is athletic will trigger a sportsperson stereotype. The system then makes inferences concerning the values of various characteristics derived from the stereotypes. Various methods are used to refine the values and the system also maintains a confidence rating in its inferences. The example in Table 17.1 shows that the system has a confidence of 900 (out of 1000) in the assumption that the person is a male. If the person is male and a sportsperson then he will like thrills (score 5 out of 5). Again the system is quite confident (900/1000). The system is marginally less confident that the person will tolerate violence and less confident again (760/1000) that he will be motivated by excitement. The justification for the ratings is shown on the right-hand side.

Although such an approach, especially in the rather crude example shown, is politically rather dubious, it can be effective. This is the sort of data that is kept about all of us on websites such as Amazon.com. Not a very sophisticated view of people!

People's cognitive and other psychological characteristics represent a different challenge for person models. One of the reasons for focusing on psychological models is

Table 17.1 An example of stereotype modelling from GRUNDY

Facet	Value	Rating	Justification
Gender	Male	900	Male Name
Thrill	5	900	Man Sports-Person
Tolerate violence	5	866	Man Sports-Person
Motivations	Excitement	760	Man Sports-Person
Character strengths	Perseverance Courage Physical strength	600 700 950	Sports-Person Man Man
Interests	Sport	800	Sports-Person

Source: Rich (1989), p. 41, Fig. 4

that these are characteristics that are most resistant to change in people (van der Veer *et al.*, 1985). If you have a lower spatial ability, you will have more trouble using a virtual reality system than someone who has a higher spatial ability. Kristina Höök, for example, showed that individuals differ considerably in their ability to navigate information spaces. She developed a hypertext system that adapted to different users by automatically hiding some information from people who would not be interested in a particular node (Höök, 2000). Whereas people can learn domain knowledge and may be tolerant of different learning styles, they are less likely to be able to change fundamental psychological characteristics such as spatial ability. Where a high level of such an ability is demanded by an application, many people will be excluded from a successful interaction.

Most person models in practice are just simple pragmatic representations of a very few characteristics of people. Of course, there are important privacy issues to be considered and ethical considerations as to what people should be told about what data is kept on them. Person models can quickly become out of date and need maintaining.

Domain model

The domain model describes the agent's representation of the domain. It may do so at all or any of three levels of description (see Further thoughts box): physical, conceptual and intentional. Physical characteristics of the domain would include things such as colours of a display, and whether data was displayed as a menu or as a list of radio buttons. The physical characteristics are to do with the 'skins' of a system. Conceptually a domain is described in terms of the objects and attributes of the things in that domain.

The intentional description is to do with purpose. For example, an e-mail filtering agent might have a domain model which describes e-mails in terms of the main concepts – header, subject, who it is from, and so on. A physical description of the domain may include font and colour options. An intentional description may have a rule that says 'if the message is classified as "urgent" then display an alarm to the person'.

FURTHER THOUGHTS

Levels of description

These three levels of description are apparent in Rasmussen's consideration of mental models and HCI (Rasmussen, 1986, 1990) and in the philosophical arguments of Pylyshyn (1984) and Dennett (1989). Pylyshyn argues that what 'might be called *the basic assumption of cognitive science* [is] that there are at least three distinct, independent levels at which we can find explanatory principles biological, functional and intentional' (Pylyshyn, 1984, p. 131, Pylyshyn's italics). The levels are distinguishable from each other and necessary because they reveal generalizations which would otherwise not be apparent. A functional description is necessary because different functions may be realized through the same physical states. For example, the physical action of pressing ^D will result in the application performing different functions depending on the system. The intentional level is needed because we interpret behaviours of systems not only through function, but also through relating function to purpose – by relating the representations of the system to external entities. The purely functional view of someone dialling 911 in the USA (or 999 in the UK) does not reveal that that person is seeking help. It is this level – of intentions on the part of the user of a system – that also needs describing.

Dennett also recognizes three levels of description. We can understand the behaviour of complex systems by taking a physical view, a design view or an intentional view.

> The physical view (also called the physical stance or physical strategy) argues that in order to predict behaviour of a system you simply determine its physical constitution and the physical nature of any inputs and then predict the outcome based on the laws of physics. However, sometimes it is more effective to switch to a design stance. With this strategy, you predict how the system will behave by believing that it will behave as it was designed to behave. However, only designed behaviour is predictable from the design stance. If a different sort of predictive power is required then you may adopt the intentional stance which involves inferring what an agent will do based upon what it ought to do if it is a rational agent.

Domain models are needed so that the system can make inferences, can adapt, and can evaluate their adaptations. Systems can only adapt, and make inferences about what they 'know' about the application domain – the domain model. A system for filtering e-mail, for example, will probably not know anything about the content of the messages. Its representation of e-mail will be confined to knowing that a message has a header, a 'from' field, a 'to' field, etc. A system providing recommendations about films will only know about a title, director, and one or two actors. This is quite different from what it means for a human to know about a film. The domain model defines the extent of the system's knowledge.

For example, there are a number of programs available that filter out supposedly unwanted e-mail messages. These typically work by using simple 'IF–THEN' rules to make inferences (see also Interaction model below). IF the message contains <unacceptable word> THEN delete message. Of course, it is the content of the place holder <unacceptable word> that is key. At our workplace one of the 'unacceptable words' was 'XXX' and any message containing an XXX was simply deleted with no notification to either the sender or the receiver. Since there is a relatively common e-mail convention to say things such as 'Find the files XXX, YYY, ZZZ, etc.', many legitimate messages were simply disappearing. The domain model in this case (that XXX is an unacceptable word) was far too crude.

Interaction model

The third component of the framework is the interaction model. This consists of two main parts: an abstraction of the interaction (called the dialogue record) and a knowledge base that performs the 'intelligence'. The knowledge base consists of mechanisms for making inferences from the other models, for specifying adaptations and, possibly, for evaluating the effectiveness of the system's performance. This knowledge base consists of 'IF–THEN' rules, statistical models, genetic algorithms or any of a host of other mechanisms.

The interaction model as expressed through the adaptive, inference and evaluation mechanisms may be extremely complex, embodying theories of language, pedagogy or explanation. A tutoring model, for example, represents a particular approach to teaching concerned with the interaction between the student and the course content (the domain model). A tutoring model component of an intelligent tutoring system would be described through the inference and adaptation mechanisms in the interaction model.

An interaction is a person (or other agent) making use of the system at a level which can be monitored. From the data thus gathered:

● The system can make inferences about the person's beliefs, plans and/or goals, long-term characteristics, such as cognitive traits, or profile data, such as previous experience.

- The system may tailor its behaviour to the needs of a particular interaction.
- Given suitably 'reflective' mechanisms, the system may evaluate its inferences and adaptations and adjust aspects of its own organization or behaviour.

The dialogue record is simply a trace of the interaction at a given level of abstraction. It is kept for as long as is required according to the needs of the adaptive system and is then deleted. The dialogue record may contain details such as:

- Sequence of keystrokes made
- Mouse clicks and mouse movements
- Facial expressions of people using the system
- Timing information such as the time between commands or the total time to complete a task
- Eye movement, pupil size and direction of gaze
- Characteristics of speech such as speed, tone and loudness
- Words spoken as recognized by an automatic speech recognizer (ASR)
- System messages and other system behaviour
- Command names used
- Physiological characteristics of people such as skin conductivity, pressure of grip and so on.

The dialogue record is an abstraction of the interaction insofar as it does not capture everything that takes place. Facial expressions and other gestures are increasingly becoming available to the dialogue record and with new input devices gesture, movement, acceleration and all manner of other features that can be sensed are enriching this whole area of interaction. However, it is still difficult to record any non-interactive activities (such as reading a book) that people may undertake during the interaction (however, with video input it may be possible to infer this). As the variety of input devices continues to increase with the introduction of video recordings of interactions, tracking of eye movements, etc., so the dialogue record will become more subtle.

The person model and domain model define what *can* be inferred. The interaction knowledge base actually does the inferring by combining the various domain model concepts to infer characteristics of people or by combining person model concepts to adapt the system. The interaction knowledge base represents the relationship between domain and person characteristics. It provides the interpretation of the dialogue record. An important design decision which the developer of agent-based systems has to make is the level of abstraction which is required for the dialogue record, the data on the individual and the interaction knowledge base.

Challenge 17.3

The Amazon.co.uk website contains an agent that welcomes returning customers, gives them recommendations for books to purchase and explains its reasoning. Figure 17.6 shows a dialogue with the Amazon.co.uk agent. Speculate about the representations of people, the domain and the interaction that this agent has. Discuss with a colleague and justify your assumptions.

Example: Maxims – an e-mail filtering agent

Some of the most influential work on agents from an HCI perspective has been undertaken at the MIT Media Lab – particularly the Learning Agents (Maes, 1994) and Letizia (Lieberman, 1995; Lieberman *et al.*, 2001). These learn from patterns of behaviour of a single person, from

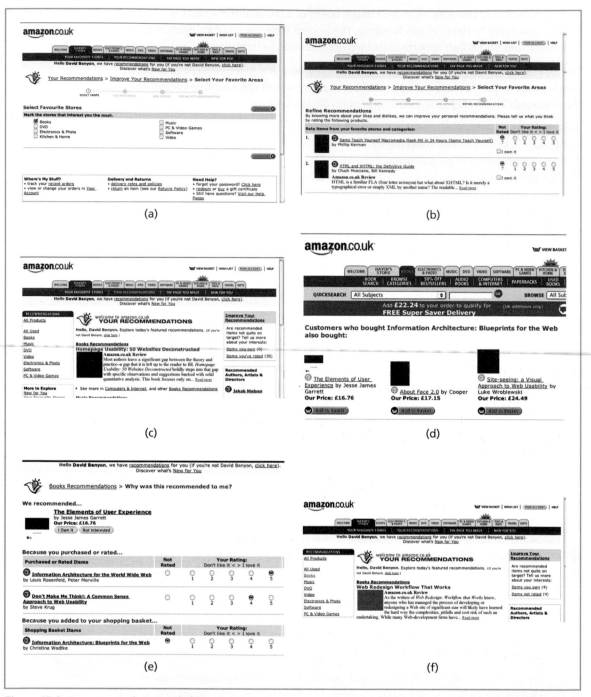

Figure 17.6 Amazon.co.uk agent dialogue

other people and from other agents. Applications have been demonstrated in arranging meetings, filtering e-mail, recommending music and recommending Web pages.

For example, an agent to help with filtering e-mail messages 'looks over the shoulder' of a person as he or she deals with e-mail and records all situation–action pairs. For example, the person reads a message and then saves it in a particular folder, reads another message and deletes it, reads another message, replies and files this. The agent maintains a dialogue record at the level of abstraction of messages and the actions taken.

When a new event occurs, the agent tries to predict the action(s) the person would take based on its library of examples. It finds the closest match between the new situation and its library of examples, using a distance metric based on weighted features of the situations. For example, if a message with the word 'ski-trip' in the header is received, the agent examines previous similar examples (e.g. previous messages with 'ski-trip' in the header) and sees what action was taken. If, for example, every previous message with 'ski-trip' in the header was deleted, then it is quite likely that this will be deleted too.

From time to time the agent compares its predictions with actual actions taken and calculates a confidence level for its predictions. People set confidence thresholds: a 'do-it' threshold when the agent can take the action autonomously and a 'tell-me' threshold when the agent must inform them of its prediction.

Over time the agent gains confidence through experience and through direct instruction (through hypothetical examples). When the agent does not have enough confidence it may send part of the situation description to other agents and request information on what they would do. From this the agent can learn which other agents are 'trustworthy' (i.e. which ones provide advice which most closely matches the subsequent response of the user). In a meeting-scheduling version of this agent it had the 'do-it' threshold at 80 per cent and the 'tell-me' threshold at 30 per cent, i.e. the agent would perform the function automatically if it had an 80 per cent or higher confidence in its prediction.

In terms of the general architecture above:

- The agent has a person model (profile) of preferences (read mail, delete/save, etc.).
- The domain model consists of e-mail conceptual attributes such as keywords in the subject, the 'cc' list, the 'from' line, etc., and the possible actions: read or not read, delete, save, etc.
- The dialogue record consists of the object details and actions.
- The inference mechanisms are a weighted closeness of fit to previous situations.
- The adaptation mechanisms are the actions taken.
- The evaluation mechanisms are expressed in the agent's ability to reflect, review confidence, etc.

It is also interesting to note the distribution of control at the various stages of the interaction. The existence of the user-defined thresholds allows the person to keep control over critical actions.

17.4 Applications of agent-based interaction

The field of agent-based interaction, person (user) modelling and user-adapted interaction is large and is continuing to grow. Personalization is a key aspect of interactive systems design and automatic personalization is particularly sought after. In this section we point to a few of the main areas.

Natural language processing

Natural language processing – in terms of speech input and speech output, but also in terms of typed input – has been the dream of computing since it was invented. Natural language systems adapt by generating text appropriate to the particular query and characteristics of individual people or by recognizing natural language statements. To do this they have to infer the person's needs and focus of attention from the (ambiguous) use of natural language. Anaphoric references (the use of words such as 'it', 'that', etc.) and ellipsis (where information is missing from a statement) offer difficult syntactic problems, but inferring the semantics of an utterance and the intention which the person had in making that utterance are even more intractable problems which have generated a wealth of research studies in both AI and Computational Linguistics. The best results have been obtained in phone-based, flight or cinema ticketing systems. Here indices and dictionaries of known names can be stored to help with detection and recognition of valid input. However, these systems are far from 100 per cent accurate. In these systems the domain is quite restricted, so it can be assumed that the person is saying something relevant to the domain. In other domains that may be much more open and where background noise can easily reduce the recognition of the words to less than 40 per cent, let alone a sensible interpretation of them, the technology is not yet acceptable.

Chatbot or Chatterbot systems take typed input and try to respond to keep the conversation going. They are mainly used for entertainment. Examples include Jabberwocky and Alice. One interesting area of study is to what extent people should be able to abuse these 'social' agents, something that happens frequently on Chatbot sites.

FURTHER THOUGHTS

Wired for speech

In their comprehensive review of studies of speech, Nass and Brave (2005) believe that humans are 'wired for speech'. Understanding language is an innate ability. Even people who score low on intelligence quotient (IQ) scores can speak. From the age of 8 months children learn on average 8–10 new words a day. This continues into adolescence. Speech is fundamental to building relationships. We easily distinguish one voice from another. In short, people are experts at extracting the social aspects of speech and at using speech as the primary means of communication.

Intelligent help, tutoring and advice-giving systems

Help, advice and teaching are natural applications for agent-based interaction. The rationale of intelligent tutoring systems (ITSs) is that, for given students and topics, an intelligent system can alleviate the variance of human-based teaching skills and can determine the best manner in which to present individually targeted instruction in a constrained subject domain. In order to minimize the discrepancy between a student's knowledge state and the representation of an identified expert's knowledge (a 'goal state'), the ITS must be able to distinguish between domain-specific expertise and tutorial strategy. ITSs need to be able to recognize errors and misconceptions, to monitor and intervene when necessary at different levels of explanation, and to generate problems on a given set of instructional guidelines (Kay, 2001).

A 'student model' of the student using an ITS stores information on how much the student 'knows' about concepts and relationships which are to be learnt and about the student's level and achievements. These student models use a method whereby the student's assumed level of knowledge is laid over the expert's; mismatches can then be revealed. An ITS often contains a history of task performance and some detailed representation of the state of an individual's knowledge in a specified subject area. Some of this may be held in the form of a user profile and can have other uses in management and score-keeping.

Another popular application of intelligent interface systems is in the provision of context-dependent 'active' help (Fischer, 2001). On-line help systems track the interaction context and incorporate assistant strategies and a set of action plans in order to intervene when most appropriate or when the user appears to be having difficulty. Intelligent help systems share some characteristics with ITSs, since a diagnostic strategy is required to provide the most appropriate help for that user in that particular situation. However, they also have to be able to infer the user's high-level goal from the low-level data available in the form of command usage. Intelligent help has further developed into 'critiquing systems' (Fischer, 1989), where users must be competent in the subject domain being critiqued, rather than being tutees or learners.

Adaptive hypermedia

With the Web as its laboratory, adaptive hypermedia research has blossomed over recent years. Brusilovsky (2001) provides an excellent review. Figure 17.7 shows his schematic of the different adaptive hypermedia systems. Adaptations in hypermedia systems are divided between adaptive presentation and adaptive navigation support. The systems can add links, change links, add annotations and so on, depending on what nodes people have visited previously and what they did there. One interesting application is in adaptive museum commentaries where the content of the description of an item is adapted to suit the inferred interests of the viewers.

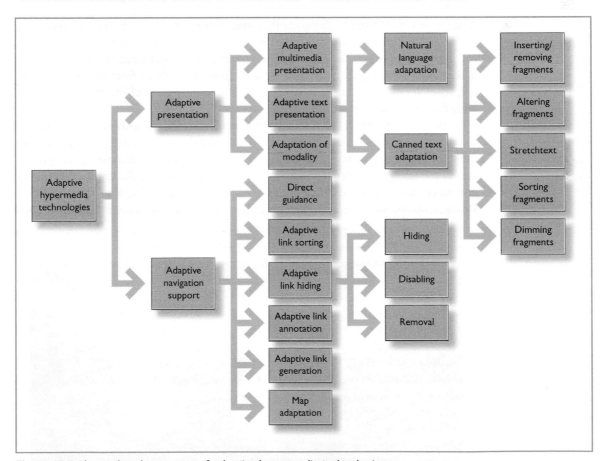

Figure 17.7 The updated taxonomy of adaptive hypermedia technologies
(Source: After Brusilovsky, 2001, p. 100, Fig. 1)

The Loebner Prize

The Loebner Prize Contest in Artificial Intelligence was established in 1990 by Hugh Loebner and was first held at the Boston Computer Museum in 1991. The Loebner Prize Medal and cash award is awarded annually to the designer of the computer system that best succeeds in passing a variant of the Turing test. In accordance with the requirements of the donor (as published in the June 1994 *Communications of the ACM*) the winner of the $100,000 Gold Prize must be prepared to deal with audiovisual input, and appropriate competitions will be held once competitors have reached Turing's 50:50 likelihood level of being mistaken for a human. An intermediate Silver Prize of $25,000 will be offered for reaching this level in a text-only test. There is also an annual Bronze Prize, currently $2000, which is awarded to the designer of the 'most human computer' as rated by a panel of judges.

Sources: www.loebner.net/Prizef/loebner-prize.html

17.5 Avatars and conversational agents

Avatars, or virtual humans, bring another degree of interest to agent-based interaction. Here the agent is represented by a character – either an on-screen character or a physical object. For example, Nabaztag is a plastic rabbit-like object which has flashing lights and rotating ears (Figure 17.8). It takes data from the Web, or from e-mail messages, and reads it out using a text to speech (TTS) system. More sophisticated systems are known as embodied conversational agents (ECAs).

A significant research effort is currently being directed towards embodied conversational agents (e.g. Cassell, 2000) and 'Companions' (see below). This pulls together much of the work that we have presented in this chapter, but includes a representation of the agent and behaviours deliberately designed to make the agent more lifelike and more engaging. Researchers in the area of conversational agents argue that providing a 'talking head' or embodied agent is much more than a cosmetic exercise and

Figure 17.8 Nabaztag

(Source: Jimmy Kets/Reporters/Science Photo Library)

fundamentally changes the nature of the interaction. People believe these agents more. They trust the agent more and they have an emotional engagement with the agent.

The persona effect

In a classic experiment by James Lester and colleagues (Lester *et al.*, 1997), the persona effect was demonstrated. This showed that people were more engaged and learned more in an educational environment where the agent was represented by an on-screen character. Although subsequent studies have (of course) clouded the issues slightly, there still seems plenty of evidence to support the fact that having a character involved in an interaction is generally a positive experience. Whether it will always help to improve comprehension and understanding is a moot point. The persona effect, understood to mean that having a persona has a positive effect, is generally accepted.

Another conversational agent is Ananova (Figure 17.9). This character reads news stories. There is no adaptation to individual viewers but the text-to-speech facility is quite engaging. The synchronization of lips to speech is quite good, but there are still the telltale inflections that do not sound correct. No doubt this technology is set to develop in the next few years.

Figure 17.9 Ananova
(Source: www.ananova.com/video/)

Some of the best work is happening at MIT where they are developing the real-estate agent, Rea (Figure 17.10). Rea tries to handle all the conversational issues such as turn-taking, inflection and ensuring that the conversation is as natural as possible. Conversational agents will still need to build models of the users and they will still have models of the domains in which they operate. Their adaptations and the inferences that they make will only be as good as the mechanisms that have been devised. But in addition, they have the problems of natural language understanding and natural language generation, gesture and movement that go to make the interactions as natural as possible.

Figure 17.10 Rea – a real-estate agent. Rea's domain of expertise is real estate: she has access to a database of available condominiums and houses for sale in Boston. She can display pictures of these properties and their various rooms and point out and discuss their salient features

(Source: www.media.mit.edu/groups/gn/projects/humanoid/)

Companions

Our own work in this area focuses on companions: ECAs that aim to provide support and emotional engagement with people. The aim is to 'change interactions into relationships'. Benyon and Mival (2008) review a number of systems and technologies that aim to get people to personify them. In *The Media Equation* (1996) Reeves and Nass discuss how people readily personify objects, imbuing them with emotion and intention. We shout at our computers and call them 'stupid'. We stroke our favourite mobile phone and talk to it as if it were a person. Companions aim to develop these relationships, so that people will engage in richer and more fulfilling interactions. Companions need to engage in conversations with people, conversations that need to be natural and appropriate for the activity being undertaken. This raises new aspects for research into ECAs and their behaviours and into natural language processing.

Our understanding of companions is summed up in Figure 17.11. We see companions as changing interaction into relationships. Bickmore and Picard (2005) argue that maintaining relationships involves managing expectations, attitudes and intentions. They emphasize that relationships are long-term, built up over time through many interactions. Relationships are fundamentally social and emotional, persistent and personalized. Citing Kelley (1983), they say that relationships demonstrate interdependence between two parties – a change in one results in a change to the other. Relationships demonstrate unique patterns of interaction for a particular dyad, a sense of 'reliable alliance'.

It is these characteristics of relationships as rich and extended forms of affective and social interaction that we are trying to tease apart so that we can provide advice for people designing companions. Digesting all our experience to date we describe companions by looking at the characteristics of companions in terms of utility, form, personality, emotion, social aspects and trust.

Utility

The issue of the utility of companions is a good place to start as there is a spectrum of usefulness for companions. At one end is non-specific purpose (i.e. companions that serve no specific function) while at the other is specific purpose. A cat has no specific

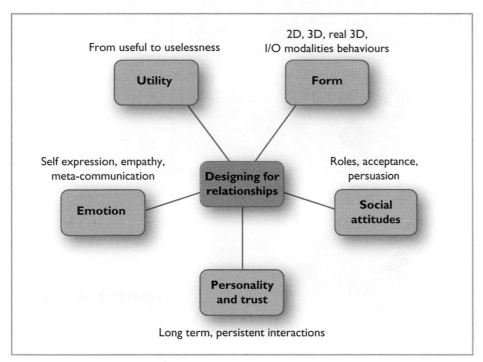

Figure 17.11 Turning interactions into relationships

function other than to be a cat, while a care assistant undertakes specific tasks such as distributing medication, monitoring health and supervising exercise, but both may be considered companions. A companion can be concerned with entertainment and having fun resulting in pleasure, or it can be about providing aid in whatever format is suitable. The Sony AIBO, despite now being discontinued, was one of the most effective robotic 'pets' there have been, but it had no real utility (Figure 17.12).

Utility is also concerned with the allocation of function between the two participants in a relationship. For example, the PhotoPal Companion could send the photo to an identified friend or relation, because PhotoPal can access the necessary addresses and functions to do this. PhotoPal would be able to discard blurred pictures, but would be unlikely to argue that one was a bit too dark (unless it was much too dark). This sort of judgement should rightly come from the human in this relationship. Leave PhotoPal to perform the function of lightening the picture, but leave the human to judge which pictures to lighten.

← PhotoPal was introduced in Chapter 3

← Allocation of functions is discussed in Chapter 9

The 'instrumental support' (Bickmore and Picard, 2005) provided by a companion is a key part of relationship building. A companion might filter large amounts of information and conflicting views. It might take the initiative and be proactive in starting some new activity, or wait for its 'owner' to initiate some activity.

Form

The form that a companion takes refers to all the issues of interaction such as dialogues, gestures, behaviours and the other operational aspects of the interaction. It also refers to the representational aspects such as whether it is 2D, graphical 3D or true 3D, whether it has a humanoid, abstract or animal form, and the modalities that it uses. The many aesthetic issues are also considered under this heading. The form and the behaviours of the companion are likely to vary widely between different owners. We observed in some older people's focus groups that although the detailed behaviours of AIBO, Sony's robotic 'dog', were noted, they were not foregrounded. Utility was the big issue and the details were secondary. This represents a utilitarian view of technology that we might

Figure 17.12 AIBO, model
ERS-7
(Source: Sony Electronics Inc.)

expect of the older generation. Younger people tend to be more relaxed about usefulness and more focused on design details.

Certainly the attention that Sony paid to the behaviours of AIBO led to a stronger emotional attachment. In a number of informal evaluations of AIBO, people would regularly
comment on 'him' being upset, enjoying something, being grumpy and so on. The attribution of beliefs, desires and intentions to an essentially inanimate object is an important
aspect of designing for relationships. For example, people say that AIBO likes having his
ears stroked, when there are no sensors in his ears. The careful construction of a mixture of
interface characteristics – sound, ear movement and lights on the head in this case – result
in people enjoying the interaction and attributing intelligence and emotion to the product.

Emotion

Designing for pleasure and design for affect are key issues for companions. Attractive
things make people feel good, which makes them more creative and more able
(Norman, 2004). Relationships provide emotional support. Emotional integration and
stability are key aspects of relationships (Bickmore and Picard, 2005). There should
be opportunities for each partner to talk about themselves to help self-disclose and to
help with self-expression. Relationships provide reassurance of worth and value and
emotional interchange will help increase familiarity. Interactions should establish common ground and overall be polite. Politeness is a key attribute of the media equation
described by Reeves and Nass (1996).

Emotional aspects of the interaction also come through meta-relational communication, such as checking that everything is all right, use of humour and talking about the
past and future. Another key aspect of an interaction, if it is to become a relationship,
is empathy: empathy leads to emotional support and provides foundations for relation-
ship-enhancing behaviours.

Personality and trust

Personality is treated as a key aspect of the media equation by Reeves and Nass (1996).
They undertook a number of studies that showed how assertive people prefer to interact

with an assertive computer and submissive people prefer interacting with submissive devices. As soon as interaction moves from the utilitarian to the complexity of a relationship, people will want to interact with personalities that they like.

Trust is a 'a positive belief about the perceived reliability of, dependability of, and confidence in a person, object or process' (Fogg, 2003). Trust is a key relationship that develops over time through small talk, getting-acquainted talk and through acceptable 'continuity' behaviours. Routine behaviours and interactions contribute to developing a relationship where they are emphasizing commonalities and shared values.

Social attitudes

Bickmore and Picard (2005) emphasize appraisal support as a key aspect of relationship building and the importance of other social ties such as group belonging, opportunities to nurture, autonomy support and social network support.

Relationships also play a key role in persuasion. The rather controversial idea of 'persuasive technologies' (Fogg, 2003) is based on getting people to do things they would not otherwise do. In the context of companions, though, this is exactly what you would hope a companion would do – providing it was ultimately for the good. A health and fitness companion, for example, should try to persuade its owner to run harder, or train more energetically. It is for their own good after all!

How these ideas are translated into prototypes and systems is another matter. Automatic inference and person modelling are not easy. Representations of emotions will usually be restricted to 'happy', 'sad' or 'neutral'. Many examples in emotion research develop complex models that are simply unusable in any application. Our current application of companions is based on the Samuela avatar (Figure 17.13) from Telefonica and on a complex multi-component architecture shown in Figure 17.14.

Figure 17.13 Samuela

The companions architecture shows the integration of the various components. The TTS (text to speech), ASR (automatic speech recognition), GUI (graphical user

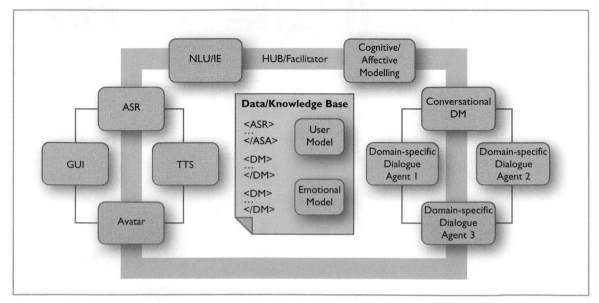

Figure 17.14 Companion architecture

interface) and avatar provide the multimodal input and output mechanisms. On the right-hand side of the figure the conversational dialogue model (DM) is brought alongside domain-specific agents that are trained in knowledge of specific domains; in the companion case of digital photos, health and fitness and general aspects of work such as meetings, relationships and other functions suitable for a 'how was your day' scenario. The natural language understanding (NLU), information extraction (IE, where specific named entities and more complex relationships are extracted from the language that has been understood) and cognitive and affective modelling are shown along the top of the diagram. These components drive the inference that is undertaken from the multimodal input. The lower part of the diagram shows the components concerned with natural language generation (NLG) and fusion of media and modalities to form the output.

Each of these components is itself highly complex, so the overall complexity that needs to be realized if companions are to become a reality is significant. Moreover, each of these components currently has to be hand-crafted; there are no standard units here, with the one exception of the TTS component that is so familiar now on satellite navigation systems.

Another view of the companion architecture is shown in Figure 17.15. This shows the architecture moving from input on the left to output on the right and the order in which components are accessed and information extracted. First, the different modalities of input – GUI and touch, ASR and signal detection – are integrated. Emotion is detected through voice detection software and through an analysis of the sentiment expressed in the words of the utterance. The dialogue is 'understood' based on analysis of the words used, the emotion inferred and the entities that are recognized by the system. This accesses domain and user knowledge to determine the best course of action (the output

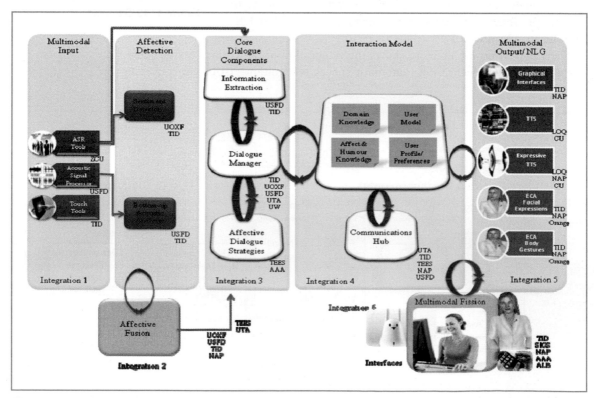

Figure 17.15 Another view of the Companion architecture

strategy) and the best way of presenting this in terms of words spoken, intonation and other aspects of the prosody of the speech and the behaviours of the avatar.

One interesting issue of this project is how to evaluate companions. How do we know if the various components are working well and being successful in what they are trying to achieve? A two-pronged approach was taken to the evaluation drawing upon a user-centric approach of subjective measures of satisfaction and a more objective approach, looking at the accuracy of recognition and at the suitability of responses produced by the companion.

Qualitative surveys were used to acquire subjective opinions from the people who used the companion prototypes, in conjunction with quantitative measures relating specifically to the speech component, the dialogue performance, users' experience and task completion as a whole.

Measures of how people related to the companions were collected through on-line questionnaires based on a five-point Likert scale (strongly agree, agree, undecided, disagree, strongly disagree). The questions were organized around six themes derived from the model above (Figure 17.11):

A. The behaviour of the companion and what it looked like
B. The utility of the companion
C. The nature of the relationship between participant and companion
D. The emotion demonstrated by the companion
E. The personality of the companion
F. The social attitudes of the companion.

The Likert scales asked people to indicate whether they agreed or not with statements such as:

'The dialogue between the Companion and me felt natural.'

'I thought the dialogue was appropriate.'

'Over time I think I would build up a relationship with the Companion.'

'I liked the behaviour of the Companion.'

'The Companion showed empathy towards me.'

'The Companion demonstrated emotion at times.'

'The Companion was compassionate.'

The metrics considered objective measures of the quality of speech, characteristics of the dialogue and task and some 'user satisfaction' metrics.

Vocabulary sizes and utterance lengths (in words) were calculated based on both ASR results and on transcriptions. Word error rate (WER) measures the quality of the speech recognition and has been calculated using a standard formula: (Deletion Errors + Insertion Errors + Substitution Errors) / (number of words actually uttered by user). Concept error rate (CER) of the speech recognition was calculated by seeing which concepts the system retrieved based on the words that had been recognized.

Dialogue measures included number of dialogue turns (sum of both user and system turns), dialogue duration, average length of user utterances measured as number of words and vocabulary size used by people. In some preliminary experiments the vocabulary ranged between 33 and 131 words, and the dialogue duration ranged from 9 to 15 minutes with between 100 and 160 turns.

These measures were used, along with measures such as task completion time, to consider an overall 'appropriateness' metric. This measure must, of course, be appropriate for the type of companion and the activities that the companion is engaged in. This may itself be a highly utilitarian task such as doing something specific with photos, or it might be more non-utilitarian such as having a pleasant conversation. On other occasions it may be more emotionally based, such as making you feel better after a bad day at work.

Summary and key points

Agent-based interaction sits right on the border between human–computer interaction and artificial intelligence. This makes it a particularly difficult area to understand as work has taken place from different disciplines, with the researchers employing different techniques and specialized language to explain their concepts. Moreover, with the increasing importance of the look and behaviour of on-screen avatars, the craft of producing engaging agent-based interactions is indeed challenging and multidisciplinary.

What we have attempted in this chapter is to provide a unifying framework for thinking about agents and avatars.

- All applications of agent-based interaction have the high-level architecture of user, domain and interaction models coupled with a dialogue record, but different applications and different types of system will express this in different ways.

- All agents are adaptive systems in that they automatically alter aspects of the system to suit the requirements of individual users or groups of users – or more generally to suit the needs of other agents in the system.

- Some systems try to infer characteristics of users and agents from the interaction. Others require users to input characteristics explicitly.

- Based on these inferences and other user and domain characteristics, they may adapt the displays or data of a system.

- Currently, few agent-based systems do an evaluation of their adaptations.

- Conversational agents have the additional difficulty of interacting naturally with a human interlocutor.

Exercises

1 A group of research workers in a telecommunications laboratory want to make it easier to share Web pages they have visited with their colleagues. Design a Web browsing agent to help them. Describe it in terms of the agent architecture.

2 One of the social navigation features you might have thought of in considering Exercise 1 in Chapter 17 is an agent that recommends recipes based on the shopping you are doing. Discuss the design of this agent.

Further reading

Benyon, D.R. and Murray, D.M. (1993) **Adaptive systems: from intelligent tutoring to autonomous agents**. *Knowledge-based Systems*, 6(4), 177–217. *This provides a more detailed discussion of the agent architecture presented here.*

Maes, P. (1994) **Agents that reduce work and information overload.** *Communications of the ACM,* **37(7),** 30–41. *An accessible description of her early work.*

User Modeling and User Adapted Interaction **(2001) Tenth Anniversary Issue, 11 (1 & 2),** pp. 1–174. *This is a good up-to-date collection of issues, mainly from the AI point of view, with details of the inference mechanisms that many systems use. The articles by Fischer (User modelling in human–computer interaction, pp. 65–86), Brusilovsky (Adaptive hypermedia, pp. 87–110) and Kay (Learner control, pp. 111–127) are particularly appropriate to this work.*

Getting Ahead

Jameson, A. (2007) **Adaptive interfaces and agents.** In Sears, A. and Jacko, J.A. (eds) *The Human–Computer Interaction Handbook,* **2nd edn.** Lawrence Erlbaum Associates, Mahwah, NJ. *A good up-to-date review.*

Kobsa, A. and Wahlster, A. (1993) *User Models in Dialog Systems.* Springer-Verlag, Berlin. *A heavy treatment of many of the theoretical issues.*

Web links

There is a good starting point for looking at many of the issues at **www.um.org**

The accompanying website has links to relevant websites. Go to **www.pearsoned.co.uk/benyon**

Comments on challenges

Challenge 17.1

This is one for you to try out. Only by discussing with someone else will you find just how hard it is to describe exactly what you want so that you do not exclude possibilities. Indeed, a good agent – real estate, travel agent, etc. – will *interpret* any brief you give them, something artificial agents are a long way from being able to do.

Challenge 17.2

Most of the features that have been taken over by adaptive systems (or agents) in cars rely on an accurate model of the other system. Anti-lock brakes, for example, have a model of the road surface that focuses on how wet and slippery it is. They are then able to adapt the braking in the light of this representation. I have no idea what the actual representation looks like, and do not need to have; it is sufficient to understand what features are modelled. Controlling the 'spark' similarly involves a model of the fuel–air mixture, the position of the cylinder and so on. In all these, the car has only to capture a representation of some physical aspects of the interaction. Interacting with people is more difficult because the system needs to capture an intentional description.

Challenge 17.3

The dialogue shows how the recommender agent improves its suggestions. The user is asked to rate some books in (b), then in (c) we can see on the right-hand side that the user has rated 35 books. The recommender agent now knows the sort of books I like as described in its own architecture by keywords. As I continue shopping, the recommender uses its dialogue record of what other people have done to recommend related books. The domain model contains links between books that have been bought together and no doubt the strength of such links is reinforced whenever these books are bought together. In shot (e) we can see that the recommender can explain its inferences – making the relationship between me, the user model, and the domain model explicit. In (f) the system knows that I have bought some books, which will be weighted more heavily than if I had just rated them.

Chapter 18
Ubiquitous computing

Contents

Aims

Information and communication devices are becoming so common and so small that they can truly be said to be becoming 'ubiquitous' – they are everywhere. They may be embedded in walls, ceilings, furniture and ornaments. They are worn as jewellery or woven into clothing. They are carried. Norman (1999) reminds us of other technologies such as electric motors that used to be fixed in one place. Electric motors are now truly ubiquitous, embedded in all manner of devices. The same is happening to computers – except that they also communicate with each other.

The term 'ubiquitous computing' covers several areas of computing, including wearable computing, mobile computing (sometimes collectively called nomadic computing), computationally enabled environments, also called 'responsive environments', and cyber-physical systems. In many cases people will use a mobile computing device to interact with a computationally enabled environment. But there are many other issues concerned with mobile computing. Consequently we devote a whole chapter (Chapter 19) to discussing the issues of mobile computing. Similarly, wearable computing is covered in Chapter 20. In this chapter we focus on general issues of ubiquitous computing, in particular how information and interaction are distributed across physical environments.

After studying this chapter you should be able to:

- Understand the ideas of distributed information spaces and ubiquitous computing
- Describe and sketch distributed information spaces in terms of the agents, information artefacts and devices that populate them
- Apply the ideas to future homes
- Understand the wider issues of responsive environments and mixed reality systems.

18.1 Ubiquitous computing

Ubiquitous computing (also called ubicomp or pervasive computing) is concerned with 'breaking the box': it anticipates the day when computing and communication technologies will disappear into the fabric of the world. This might be literally the fabrics we wear, the fabric of buildings and of objects that are carried or worn. There may be a mobile phone in your tooth and you might communicate with your distant partner by rubbing your earring. At the other end of the scale we might have wall-sized flat display technologies or augmented physical environments with graphical objects, or physical objects used to interact with sensor-enabled walls and other surfaces. HCI and interaction design in ubicomp environments is concerned with many computing devices interacting with many others.

The original work on ubiquitous computing was undertaken at Xerox PARC (Palo Alto Research Center) in the early 1990s. It is summed up by one of the main visionaries of the time, Mark Weiser.

> Ubiquitous computers will also come in different sizes, each suited to a particular task. My colleagues and I have built what we call tabs, pads and boards: inch-scale machines that approximate active Post-it notes, foot-scale ones that behave something like a sheet of paper (or a book or a magazine), and yard-scale displays that are the equivalent of a blackboard or bulletin board.
>
> Weiser (1991)

The intention was that these devices would be as ubiquitous as the written word, with labels on packaging being replaced by 'tabs', with paper being replaced by 'pads' and walls by boards. Many of these devices will be wearable and many will be portable.

Now of course we have exactly these tabs, pads and boards in the form of phones, tablets and large interactive screens. Whole cities are covered with very high-speed broadband connectivity and 4G, the fourth generation of mobile communications which promises much higher bandwidth than hitherto. So now the technological infrastructure to support ubicomp has arrived, designers need to think how they are going to design services and apps that take advantage of mobility, the ability to use people's physical locations and movement in the context of large, fixed interactive walls and public displays.

Ubicomp is about spaces and movement and blending the physical and the digital. After looking at the technological space, we will look at information spaces (also known as digital spaces) and how these two come together with the physical space to create a blended space. We conclude with a look at ubicomp in the home.

Ubicomp technologies

With appliances embedded in walls, implanted in people and so on, human–computer interaction becomes very different and the design of interactive systems extends to the design of whole environments. We will input data and commands through gestures – perhaps stroking an object, perhaps by waving at a board. Full-body interaction will become possible. Output will be through haptics, sound and other non-visual media. The applications of this technology are many and visions include new forms of learning in the classroom of the future, augmenting the countryside with objects and placing devices in airports, university campuses and other community projects.

BOX 18.1

Full-body interaction

Full-body interaction concerns the wide range of techniques that can be used to track body movement in a space and how those movements can be interpreted. Many games and home entertainment systems make some use of body movement. For example, there are dance games that track the player's dance movements and games for the Kinect and Wii utilize movement. In the case of the Wii the player holds an infra-red sensor that provides input and with the Kinect movement of the body is tracked through cameras and infra-red. Other systems make use of multiple sensors attached to the body, allowing more accurate tracking of movement, and have been used in applications such as physiotherapy at home where the patient matches correct exercises with an on-screen character. More sophisticated systems require a whole room to be equipped with sensors and tracking devices so that complex movements such as dance can be monitored and used as input.

One vision of ubicomp is Ambient Intelligence (AmI), a concept first used by Philips in 1999 to represent their vision of technology 18 years into the future. The principles served as a foundation for the European Commission's Framework programme funding initiative, under the advice of the Information Society Technologies Advisory Group (ISTAG), and as a result has been a strong force in European research over the past decade.

Philips (2005) describes the main characteristics of AmI systems as:

→ Context awareness is discussed in Chapter 19

- *Context awareness* – the ability to recognize current situation and surroundings.
- *Personalized* – devices customized to individuals.
- *Immersive* – improving user experiences by manipulating the environment.
- *Adaptive* – responsive environments controlled through natural interaction.

In the AmI vision, hardware is very unobtrusive. There is a seamless mobile/fixed Web-based communications infrastructure, a natural-feeling human interface and dependability and security.

BOX 18.2

Seamful interaction

In contrast to the idea of seamless ubicomp, Matthew Chalmers (2003) and others have suggested that the opposite may be a better design principle. Unicomp environments inevitably contain a degree of uncertainty. For example, locations can often not be determined with absolute certainty or accuracy. Rather than the system pretending that everything is as it seems, we should design so that the seams of the various technologies are deliberately exposed. People should be aware when they are moving from one area of the environment to another. They should be aware of the inaccuracies that are inherent in the system. This allows people to appropriate technologies to their needs (i.e. take advantage of how the technology works) and to improvise.

← These are examples of mixed reality described in Chapter 13

Cyber-physical systems are another form of these ambient environments where the physical world is augmented with computational devices that are often enabled through wireless sensor networks (WSN). A WSN is an interconnected network of computing devices.

A node on a WSN contains (at least) a computer processor, one or more sensors and some communication ability. Some WSNs are fixed, but others include mobile elements that can quickly join and leave networks and networks that can configure themselves to suit different contexts (*ad hoc* networks). Romer and Mattern give the following definition for a WSN:

> a large scale (thousands of nodes, covering large geographical areas), wireless, ad hoc, multi-hop, un-partitioned network of homogeneous, tiny (hardly noticeable), mostly immobile (after deployment) sensor nodes that would be randomly deployed in the area of interest.
> (Romer and Mattern, 2004)

One of the projects was 'smart-dust', developed by UC Berkeley (Hoffman, 2003). The smart-dust project was pioneering in the field of wireless sensor networks and is currently one of the most advanced projects, reportedly already having achieved the production of a single microchip containing all of the required electronics (processor, A-D converter, transmitter), which had dimensions of under 3 mm (JLH Labs, 2006). Miniature devices of this type are referred to as 'mems' (micro electro-mechanical systems). The smart-dust project has also resulted in the production of commercial wireless sensor nodes called 'motes', which compromise with a larger size to achieve increased robustness and functionality, and appear in both WSN research and industrial applications.

The Speckled Computing project based in Scotland is very much in the same vein as smart-dust. Both focus on miniaturization and both explore the use of optical as well as radio communication. However, while the smallest motes contain only a transmitter, the specks (nodes in a speckled WSN) will have a full transceiver and 'specknets' are intended to be decentralized and *ad hoc,* 'and both explore the use of optical as well as radio communication' in large networks (Specknets) of very tiny nodes (specks).

Other examples of WSNs include 'Smart-Its' developed as part of the EU 'disappearing computer' project. 'SensorTags' and 'Smart Pebbles' use a different form of technology that follows the principles of static radio frequency identification (RFID) tags; they gain power from an external source via electromagnetic induction (SRI International, 2003). When a 'reader' passes in close proximity (handheld, mounted on a vehicle, etc.), the device gains enough power to transmit its unique ID and sensor reading. Siftables from MIT are small bricks that form networks and can be applied to a wide range of applications (Figure 18.1).

Responsive environments is a term used for systems that combine art, architecture and interaction in novel ways at the boundary of new interactive technologies. Lucy Bullivant (2006) surveys the field under chapter headings such as 'interactive building skins', 'intelligent walls and floors' and 'smart domestic spaces'.

Nanotechnologies

The vision of smart-dust and speckled computing ultimately leads to the idea of smart nanotechnologies. These are computing devices that are the size of molecules and could enter the body, repairing damaged functions such as eyesight. Nanotechnologies are already with us, helping to create new self-cleaning fabrics, for example. In the novel *Prey*, Michael Crichton envisages swarms of nanocomputing devices that can self-organize, taking on the shape of people and generally causing chaos when they escape from a secure manufacturing plant.

FURTHER THOUGHTS

Figure 18.1 siftables: http://ambient.media.mit. edu/projects.php?action= details&id=35

The area is dominated by a relatively small group of architect/interaction designers such as HeHe, Usman Haque and Jason Bruges who specialize in novel installations and interactive experiences. Some of these are at a grand scale, for example, buildings that slowly change colour or the illumination of waste gas. Nuage Vert uses a laser and camera-tracking to project a green contour onto the waste cloud, the outline changes in size according to the amount of energy being consumed (Figure 18.2). Another example at the London Stock Exchange uses a matrix of large balls to dynamically display news headlines (Figure 18.3).

Figure 18.2 Pollstream – Nuage Vert
(Source: Nuage Vert, Helsinki 2008, copyright HeHe)

At the MIT Media lab the responsive environments group is more concerned with exploring future environments from a functional rather than artistic perspective. The ubiquitous sensor portals project consists of an array of sensors distributed throughout the physical space of the Media Lab (Figure 18.4). This allows live real-time linking between the Media Lab and a virtual laboratory space in the virtual world, Second Life.

Figure 18.3 LSE system
(Source: Reuters/Luke MacGregor)

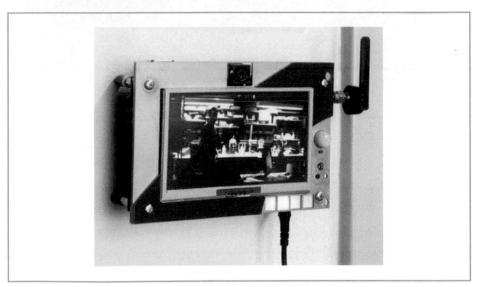

Figure 18.4 Ubiquitous sensor portals.www.media.mit.edu/resenv/portals/

Representations of people in Second Life can see live video of the real world at Media Lab and can communicate across the boundaries of the two realities.

Another project uses RFID tags to monitor the movement of cargo. This approach to automatic monitoring is widely used. For example, cattle can be monitored as they move through field gates.

WSNs and other forms of ubiquitous computing environments offer new and intriguing forms of interaction. Devices can adapt to the specific context of use (and we return to context-aware computing in the next chapter). Devices can spontaneously join networks or form themselves into networks. One application of WSNs was in a vineyard where a network was formed to monitor for diseases. These ideas of 'proactive computing' allow the system to automatically trigger an event, such as turning on sprinklers when soil moisture is low or firing air cannons when birds were detected (Burrell *et al.*, 2004).

Although WSN technology is relatively young, it would be wrong to assume that there are only small-scale deployments. For example, ARGO is a global network with an intended 3000 sensors that will monitor salinity, temperature, fresh water storage, etc. of the upper layers of the oceans, and transmit results via satellite (Figure 18.5). Deployment began in 2000, and now there are thousands of floats in operation (ARGO, 2007). Ubiquitous computing can be on a worldwide scale as well as in local environments.

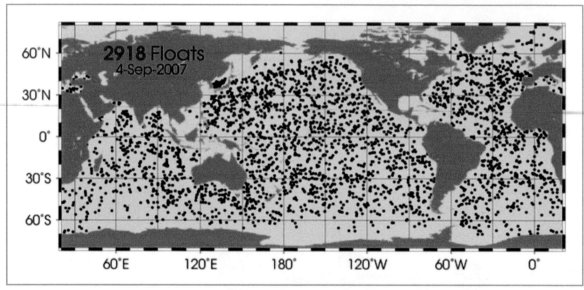

Figure 18.5 ARGO float deployment

(Source: Argo, www.argo.net)

Challenge 18.1

Imagine a building in which all the walls, the floor and ceiling are embedded with specks. What are the interaction design issues that such an environment raises?

18.2 Information spaces

These different varieties of ubiquitous computing offer different opportunities for new forms of interaction. What they all share is that information and interaction are distributed throughout the information space. In physically distributed ubicomp environments information and interaction are distributed through physical space as well. Moreover, many ubicomp environments will include objects that are not computing devices at all. The physical architecture of an environment will affect the interaction, as will the existence of signs, furniture and other people. In order to understand this wider context it is useful to introduce the concept of an 'information space'.

Three types of object are found in information spaces: agents, devices and information artefacts. Devices include all the components of a space that are not concerned with information processing (such as furniture) and those that can only receive, transform and transmit data. Devices do not deal in information. Things like buttons, switches and wires are devices. Communication mechanisms are devices, as are the other hardware components that constitute the network. The power source, aerial and circuits of WSN nodes are devices. However, as soon as devices start dealing with information (or we consider them to be dealing with information), they need to be treated differently. Information artefacts (IAs) are systems that allow information to be stored, transformed and retrieved. An important characteristic of IAs is that the information has to be stored in some sequence and this has implications for how people locate a specific piece of information. We also identify a third type of object that may be present in an information space – agents. Agents are systems that actively seek to achieve some goal.

← Agents are discussed in Chapter 17

People make use of and contribute to information spaces as they pursue their daily activities. Information spaces allow people to plan, manage and control their activities. Information spaces provide opportunities for action. Sometimes information spaces are designed specifically to support a well-defined activity, but often activities make use of general-purpose information spaces and information spaces have to serve multiple purposes.

For example, consider the signage system that might be employed in an airport. This is an information space that could consist of some devices (e.g. display devices, cabling, gates, communication mechanisms, chairs, etc.), some information artefacts (e.g. TV monitors showing the times of departures and arrivals, announcements made over a system of loudspeakers, signs showing gate numbers, etc.) and some agents (e.g. people staffing an information desk, people checking boarding cards). This information space has to support all the activities that go on at an airport, such as catching planes, finding the right gate, meeting people who have landed, finding lost luggage, and so on (Figure 18.6).

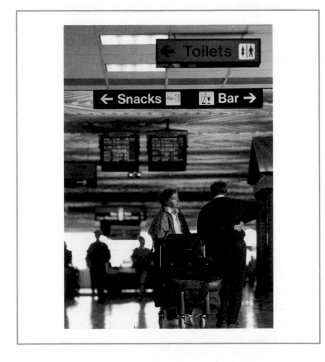

Figure 18.6 Airport information space

(Source: Joe Cornish/DK Images)

Another example of an information space is a university campus, which again makes use of physical signs to provide information along with electronic forms of information on the website and delivered through Wi-Fi communications. A third example of an information space could be the vineyard, described in Section 18.1. Here, sensors are spread around the vineyard, and there is a central database of sensor readings. The manager of the vineyard may use a mobile device to interact with the database or with the sensors *in situ*.

We conceptualize the situation as in Figure 18.7. This shows a configuration of agents, devices and information artefacts and a number of activities. The information space covers several different activities and no activity is supported by a single information artefact. This is the nature of distributed information spaces, and is the case for almost all activities.

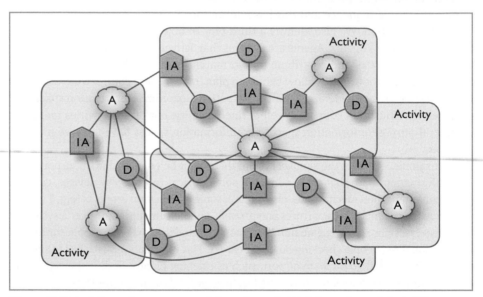

Figure 18.7 An information space consisting of agents (A), information artefacts (IA) and devices (D). Communication is through signs sent along the communication media (illustrated with lines)

→ We return to issues of navigation in Chapter 25

A key feature of information spaces is that people have to move from one IA to another; they have to access devices and perhaps other agents. They have to *navigate* through the information space. In the case of an airport, or other distributed information space, people need to navigate between the different objects: the agents, information artefacts and devices that constitute that space and physically move through the geographical space. This raises many issues for people interacting with ubiquitous computing, particularly as the computational devices become increasingly invisible. It is difficult to know what systems and services exist.

Sketching information space

Sketches of information space can be used to show how the information is distributed through the components of a space. Activities are rarely correlated one-to-one with an information artefact. People will need to access various sources of information in order to complete some activity. Importantly, some of that information may be in the heads of other people and so sketches of information space should show whether this is the case. People can be treated as 'information artefacts' if we are looking at them from the perspective of the information they can provide.

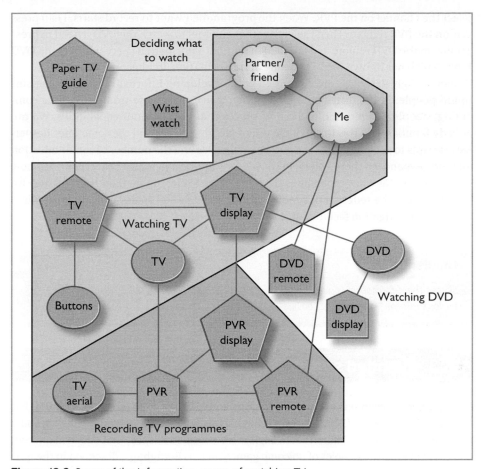

Figure 18.8 Some of the information space of watching TV

Figure 18.8 illustrates some of the information space for watching TV in my house. Developing the sketch helps the analyst/designer think about issues and explore design problems. Notice the overlap of the various activities – deciding what to watch, recording TV programmes, watching TV and watching DVDs.

The space includes the agents (me and my partner), various devices such as the TV, the personal video recorder (PVR), the DVD buttons on the remote controls and so on, and various information artefacts such as the paper TV guide, the PVR, DVD and TV displays and the various remote control units. There are a lot of relationships to be understood in this space. For example, the PVR is connected to the TV aerial so that it can record broadcast TV. The remote control units communicate only with their own device, so I need three remotes. The TV has to be on the appropriate channel to view the DVD, the PVR or the various TV channels.

Looking at the activities, we can see how we move through the space in order to complete them. Choices of programme are discussed with my partner. We will need to check the time using her wristwatch, look at the TV guide and consult until a decision is made. Finally a channel is decided upon. To watch TV, I turn the TV on by pressing a button on the TV; the TV display then shows a green light. Then the channel number has to be pressed on the remote control (though in my case the button labels have become unreadable, so there is an additional process of remembering and counting to locate the required button). Indeed, if I want to record a TV programme later while I watch a DVD, then it is wiser to select the PVR channel at this point, then use the PVR remote to select the channel on the PVR. When the programme I want to record starts, I can press 'rec' on the PVR remote. Then I select another channel to watch the DVD. I need to press 'menu' on the DVD remote and am then in another information space which is the DVD itself, which has its own menu structure and information architecture. Phew!

Increasingly designers are concerned with developing information spaces that surround people. In the distributed information spaces that arise from ubiquitous computing, people will move in and out of spaces that have various capabilities. We are already familiar with this through the use of mobile phones and the sometimes desperate attempts to get a signal. As the number of devices and the number of communication methods expand, so there will be new usability and design issues concerned with how spaces can reveal what capabilities they have. The sketching method is useful and we have used it in the redesign of a radio station's information space, lighting control in a theatre and navigation facilities on a yacht.

Challenge 18.2

Sketch the information space of buying some items at a supermarket. Include all the various information artefacts, devices and agents that there are.

18.3 Blended spaces

Designing for ubicomp is about designing for a mix of the physical and the digital. For example Randell *et al.* (2003) discuss how they designed an augmented reality wood – an environment where children could explore an information space embedded in a wood, and there are many examples of ubicomp games such as Botfighters, described in the next chapter. In designing for ubiquitous computing, interaction designers need to think about the whole experience of the interaction. This means they need to think about the shape and content of the physical space and of the digital space and how they are brought together. See Figure 18.9

We find the principles of designing with blends very useful in these contexts to help designers think about the relationships between physical and digital spaces and the physical

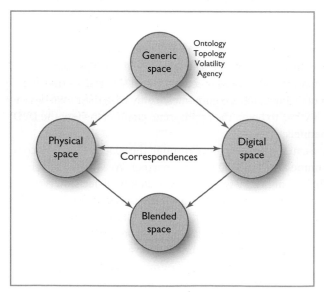

Figure 18.9 Blended spaces

and digital objects in those spaces. Designing with blends was introduced in Chapter 9. The central message is that in ubicomp environments designers are producing a space blended from the characteristics of the physical and the digital spaces. We have found that the key characteristics of spaces that designers should attend to are those characteristics of generic spaces: ontology, topology, volatility, and agency. This is illustrated in Figure 18.9

Designers need to pay attention to the correspondences between the physical and digital spaces and aim to produce a harmonious blend. One particularly important feature here is to attend to the anchor points, or portals between the physical and digital spaces, as these transitions are often clumsy and interrupt the flow of the user experience.

Ontology: conceptual and physical objects

We have seen that any information space will be populated by a variety of objects and devices. For example, a hospital environment has various information artefacts (conceptual objects) such as a patient's personal details, medication, operating schedules and so on. (The design of these conceptual objects is the ontology and is often undertaken by systems analysts and database designers.) In addition to these conceptual objects, there are physical/perceptual devices that are used to interact with this space – monitors, handheld devices used by doctors, RFID tags attached to patients and so on. There is also the physical space of the hospital with the different wards, offices and operating theatres.

The relationship between physical devices and spaces and the conceptual objects is critical to the design of the space. A handheld computer provides a very different display than a 27-inch computer screen and so the interaction with the content will be different. The perceptual devices provided in information spaces also have a big impact on the ease of use of an information space. Large screen displays make it easier to share information, but may compromise on privacy. Nurses will need to access information both at their office desk and when visiting a patient in bed.

A good mapping between conceptual and physical objects generally results in better interaction. This relationship between the conceptual and physical objects and the conceptual and physical operations that are available in the interface objects fundamentally affects the usability of systems. For example, the arrangement of windows showing different applications needs to be controlled in the limited screen space provided by a typical screen display. When this same space is accessed through a handheld device, different aids need to be provided. The way in which objects are combined is also significant.

The physical organization of the information artefacts and the functions provided to manipulate types and instances will determine how effective the design is.

For example, a common design issue in ubicomp environments is deciding whether to put a lot of information on one device (a large display, say) or whether to distribute across many smaller devices and link these together. Navigating within the large display requires people to use scrolling, page turning and so on to find the information they want. On small displays they can immediately see all the information, but only of one part of the whole space.

← See also the discussion of ontology in Chapter 14 on website design

Topology

The topology of spaces concerns how objects are related to one another. The conceptual structure will dictate where conceptual objects are, and how things are categorized. The physical topology relates to the movement between and through physical objects and the physical environment and how the interfaces have been designed.

In a museum, for example, the conceptual structure will dictate whether things are grouped by type of object (china, jewellery, pottery, clothing, etc.) or by period. This is

all down to the conceptual information design of the museum – the conceptual topology. How they are physically laid out relates to the physical topology.

Conceptual and physical distance results from the conceptual and physical topologies chosen by the designer. The notion of distance relates to both the ontology and the topology of the space, with the ontology coming from the conceptual objects and the topology coming from how these are mapped onto a physical structure. Issues of distance in turn relate to how people navigate the information space.

Direction is also important and again relates to the ontology and topology. For example, which way should you go to find a specific item in a museum? Similarly do you swipe right or left on your interactive table to see the next item in a set? It depends how the designer has conceptualized things and how that conceptualization has been mapped onto interface features.

Volatility

Volatility is a characteristic of spaces concerned with how often the types and instances of the objects change. In general it is best to choose an ontology that keeps the types of object stable. Given a small, stable space, it is easy to invent maps or guided tours to present the contents in a clear way. But if the space is very large and keeps changing then very little can be known about how different parts of the space are and will be related to one another. In such cases interfaces will have to look quite different. The structure of physical spaces is often quite non-volatile, but meeting rooms are easily configured and physical devices frequently do get changed around. Many times I have come into a meeting room to find the data projector is not plugged in to the computer or that some other configuration has changed since I last used the room.

Volatility is also important with respect to the medium of the interface and how quickly changes in the conceptual information can be revealed. For example, consider the information space that supports train journeys. The ontology most of us use consists of stations, journeys and times. An instance of this might be 'The 9.10 from Edinburgh to Dundee'. This ontology is quite stable and the space fairly small so the train timetable information artefact can be produced on paper. The actual instances of the journeys such as the 9.10 from Edinburgh to Dundee on 3 March 2012 are subject to change and so an electro-mechanical display is designed that can supply more immediate information. The volatility of the objects (which in itself is determined by the ontology) demands different characteristics from the display medium.

Media

Some spaces have a richer representation that may draw upon visual, auditory and tactile properties, while others are poorer. Issues of colour, the use of sound and the variety of other media and modalities for the interaction are important components of the blended space.

If the space has a coherent design it is easier to convey that structure to people. Museums are usually carefully designed to help people navigate and to show relationships between objects. Other spaces have grown without any control or moderation.

Agency

In some spaces, we are on our own and there are no other people about. In other spaces we can easily communicate with other people or agents and in still other spaces there may not be any people now, but there are traces of what they have done. Agency is concerned with the ability to act in an environment and designers need to consider what people will be able to effect and what they will only be able to observe.

← Agents are discussed in more detail in Chapter 17

Distributed resources

FURTHER THOUGHTS

Wright *et al.* (2000) present a model of distributed information spaces called the Resources Model in which they focus on information structures and interaction strategies. They propose that there are six types of resource that are utilized when undertaking an activity:

- Goals describe the required state of the world.
- Plans are sequences of actions that could be carried out.
- Possibilities describe the set of possible next actions.
- History is the actual interaction history that has occurred – either the immediate history or a generic history.
- Action–effect relations describe the relationships between the effect that taking an action will have and the interaction.
- States are the collection of relevant values of the objects in the system at any one time.

These resources are not kept in any one place, but rather are distributed throughout an environment. For example, plans can be a mental construct of people or they might appear as an operating manual. Possibilities are often represented externally such as in (restaurant, or other) menus, as are action–effect relations and histories. Knowing action–effect relations and the history (e.g. pressing button 3 now on the remote control will select channel 3) allows us to achieve the goal.

Wright *et al.* (2000) identify four interaction strategies that may be used:

- Plan following involves the user coordinating a pre-computed plan, bearing in mind the history so far.
- Plan construction involves examining possibilities and deciding on a course of action (resulting in plan following).
- Goal matching involves identifying the action–effect relations needed to take the current state to a goal state.
- History-based methods rely on knowledge of what has previously been selected or rejected in order to formulate an interaction strategy.

Wright *et al.* (2000) provide a number of examples of distributed information and how different strategies are useful at different times. They argue that action is informed by configurations of resources – 'a collection of information structures that find expression as representations internally and externally'. Clearly in any distributed space these are exactly the issues that we were considering in navigation of information space. There are also strong resonances with distributed cognition.

→ Chapter 23 discusses distributed cognition

Challenge 18.3

Consider your journey from home to university, or your workplace. What information resources do you make use of? How is this different if you are going to an unfamiliar destination?

How to design for blended spaces

The overall objective of blended space design is to make people feel present in the blended space, because feeling present means it is a better user experience (UX). Presence is the intuitive, successful interaction within a medium.

→ Sense of presence is discussed in Chapter 24

Designers should think of the whole blended space as a new medium that the users are interacting with and that they are existing within. It is a multi-layered medium, a multimedia medium with both physical and digital content. In blended spaces people are existing in multiple media simultaneously and moving through the media, at one time standing back and reflecting on some media and at other times engaging in and incorporating other media, moving in and out of physical and digital spaces.

Design approach

1   Think about the overall experience of the blended space that you are trying to achieve and the sense of presence that you want people to have.

2   Decide on the activities and content that will enable people to experience the blended space that you want.

3   Decide on the digital content and its relationship with the physical space in terms of the ontology, topology, volatility and agency of the digital and physical spaces. So think about

   – the correspondences between these characteristics of the spaces

   – design for suitable transitions between the digital and physical spaces

   – the points where people transition between physical and digital spaces; consider these as anchor points, portals or entry points

   – how to make people aware that there is digital content nearby

   – how to help people navigate in both physical and digital worlds; how to navigate to the portals that link the spaces

   – creating narratives to steer people through the blended space

   – how to enable people to effortlessly access and interact with content

   – designing at the human scale rather than the technological scale

   – how to avoid sudden jumps or abrupt changes as these will cause a break in presence

   – the multi-layered and multimedia experiences that weave the digital and physical spaces together.

4   Do the physical design of the digital and physical spaces, considering

   – the user interfaces and individual interactions

   – social interactions (sometimes called the 'information ecology' (Nardi and O'Day, 1999) that combines people, practices, values and technologies within a local environment)

   – flow (movement through the blended space, workflow in a work setting, trajectories in a spectator setting) (see Box 18.3)

   – the physical environment.

We have developed a number of ubicomp tourism apps using the blended spaces approach and thinking about how people would like to experience the physical and digital spaces (Benyon et al., 2012; 2013a, b). In one app we mapped the writings of Robert Louis Stevenson onto the physical locations of Edinburgh where he wrote them, using QR codes to provide the anchors between the physical and digital worlds. In another we used a tourist location in central Edinburgh and augmented it with 'historical echoes' providing an immersive, audio experience. Indeed the ICE meeting room described in Chapter 16 is an example of a blended space, bringing together the physical design of a meeting room with multitouch technology.

BOX
18.3

Hybrid trajectories

Benford *et al.* (2009) introduce the concept of 'interaction trajectories' in their analysis of their experiences with a number of mixed-reality, pervasive games. Drawing upon areas such as dramaturgy and museum design they identify the importance of design for interactions that take place over time and through physical as well as digital spaces. These hybrid experiences take people through mixed spaces, times, roles and interfaces. They summarize the idea as follows:

A **trajectory** describes a journey through a user experience, emphasizing its overall continuity and coherence. Trajectories pass through different **hybrid structures**.

Multiple physical and virtual spaces may be adjacent, connected and overlaid to create a **hybrid space** that provides the stage for the experience.

Hybrid time combines story time, plot time, schedule time, interaction time and perceived time to shape the overall timing of events.

Hybrid roles define how different individuals engage, including the public roles of participant and spectator (audience and bystander) and the professional roles of actor, operator and orchestrator.

Hybrid ecologies assemble different interfaces in an environment to enable interaction and collaboration. Various uses may be intertwined in practice; the experiences that we described were all developed in a highly iterative way, with analysis feeding into further (re)design. (p. 716)

Challenge 18.4

Consider the different modalities that could be used to convey different aspects of such navigational support (refer to Chapter 13 for a discussion of multimodality). What advantages and disadvantages do they have?

18.4 Home environments

The home is increasingly becoming an archetypal ubiquitous computing environment. There are all sorts of novel devices to assist with activities such as looking after babies, keeping in touch with families, shopping, cooking and leisure pursuits such as reading, listening to music and watching TV. The home is ideal for short-distance wireless network connectivity and for taking advantage of broadband connection to the rest of the Internet.

The history of studying homes and technologies is well established – going back to the early impact of infrastructure technologies such as electrification and plumbing. Since the 'information age' came upon us, homes have been invaded by information and communication technologies of various sorts and the impact of these has been examined from various perspectives. Indeed, it may be better to think in terms of a 'living space' rather than a physical house, since technologies enable us to bring work and community into the home and to take the home out with us. Our understanding of technologies and people needs to be expanded from the work-based tradition that has informed most methods of analysis and design to include the people-centred issues such as personalization, experience, engagement, purpose, reliability, fun, respect and identity (to name but a few) that are key to these emerging technologies.

Households are fundamentally social spaces and there are a number of key social theories that can be used. Stewart (2003) describes how theories of consumption, domestication and appropriation can be used.

- *Consumption* is concerned with the reasons why people use certain products or participate in activities. There are practical, functional reasons, experiential reasons which are more to do with having fun and enjoying an experience, and reasons of identity – both self-identity and the sense of belonging to a group.
- *Appropriation* is concerned with why people adopt certain things and why others are rejected. The household is often a mix of different ages, tastes and interests that all have to live side by side.
- *Domestication* focuses on the cultural integration of products into the home and the ways in which objects are incorporated and fit into the existing arrangement.

Alladi Venkatesh and his group (e.g. Venkatesh *et al.,* 2003) have been investigating technologies in the home over many years. He proposes a framework based around three spaces.

- The physical space of the household is very important and differs widely between cultures and between groups within a culture. Of course, wealth plays a huge role in the physical spaces that people have to operate in. The technologies that are adopted, and how they fit in, both shape and are shaped by the physical space.
- The technological space is defined as the total configuration of technologies in the home. This is expanding rapidly as more and more gadgets are introduced that can be controlled by more and more controllers. The ideas of 'smart homes' (see below) are important here.
- The social space concerns both the spatial and temporal relationships between members of a household. The living space may have to turn into a work space at different times. In other households there may be resistance to work intruding on the relaxing space.

It is also useful to distinguish home automation from the various information-seeking and leisure activities that go on. Climate control, lighting, heating, air conditioning and security systems are all important. There are also automatic controls for activities such as watering the garden, remote control of heating and so on. X10 technology has been popular, particularly in the USA, but it is likely that this will be overtaken by connectivity through wireless communications.

Lynne Baillie (Baillie, 2002) developed a method for looking at households in which she mapped out the different spaces in a household and the technologies that were used. Figure 18.10 is an example.

Smart homes

Eggen *et al.* (2003) derived a number of general design principles for the home of the future from conducting focus groups with families. Their conclusions were as follows.

- Home is about experiences (e.g. coming/leaving home, waking up, doing things together, etc.). People are much less concerned with 'doing tasks'. This indicates the importance of the context of use in which applications or services have to run: they should fit into the rhythms, patterns and cycles of life.
- People want to create their own preferred home experience.

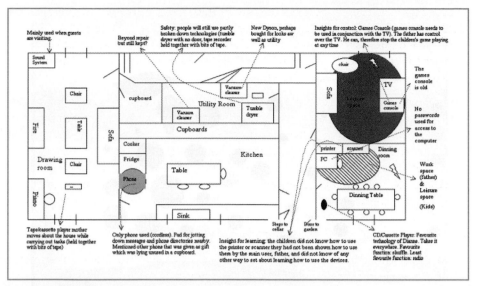

Figure 18.10 A map of the house showing different spaces

(Source: Baillie *et al.* (2003), p. 109, Figure 5.8. Reproduced by permission of Lynne Baillie)

- People want technology to move into the background (become part of the environment), interfaces to become transparent, and focus to shift from functions to experiences.
- Interaction with the home should become easier and more natural.
- The home should respect the preferences of the inhabitants.
- The home should adapt to the physical and social situation at hand. For example, a preference profile can be very different in a social family setting (e.g. watching TV with other family members) compared to a situation where no other persons are present.
- The home should anticipate people's needs and desires as far as possible without conscious mediation.
- The home should be trustworthy. Applications should, for example, adequately take consideration of privacy issues.
- People stress that they should always be in control.

This is an interesting list. Ambience is important: the fabric of the house should contain the technologies so that they are unobtrusive. The house needs to be trustworthy and should anticipate needs. This is going to be very difficult to achieve because of the inherent problems of agent-based interaction (Chapter 17). We might also expect that people will be wearing much more technology (Chapter 20) and the interaction between what is worn, carried and embedded in the fabric of buildings will bring wholly new challenges. Essentially these are the challenges of ubiquitous computing.

Eggen *et al.* describe the 'wake-up experience' that was one concept to arise from their work. This would be a personalizable, multi-sensing experience that should be easier to create and change. It should be possible to create an experience of smelling freshly brewed coffee, listening to gentle music or the sounds of waves lapping on a beach. The only limitation would be your imagination! Unfortunately, people are not very good at programming, nor are they very interested in it. Also, devices have to be designed for the elderly and the young and those in between. In this case the concept was implemented by allowing people to 'paint' a scene – selecting items from a palette and positioning them on a timeline to indicate when various activities should occur (Figure 18.11).

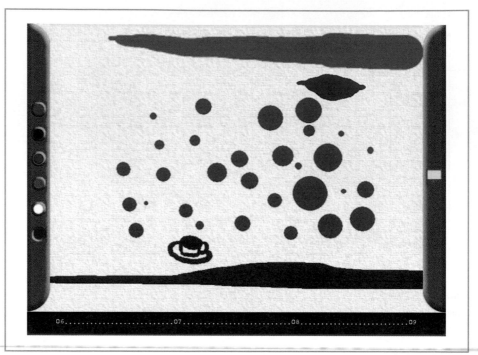

Figure 18.11 Concept for the wake-up experience
(Source: Eggen *et al.*, 2003, p. 50, Fig 3)

Supportive homes

Smart homes are not just the preserve of the wealthy. They offer great promise for people to have increased independence into their old age. With increasing age comes decreasing ability to undertake activities that once were straightforward, such as opening curtains and doors. But technologies can help. In supportive homes controllers and electric motors can be added into the physical environment to ease the way on some of these once routine activities. The problem that arises then is how to control them – and how to know what controls what. If I have three remote controls just to watch television, we can imagine the proliferation of devices that might occur in a smart home. If physical devices do not proliferate then the functionality available on just one device will cause just as many usability problems.

Designers can sketch the information spaces, including any and as much of the information that we have discussed. It may be that designers need to identify where particular resources should be placed in an environment. It may be that ERMIA models can be developed to discuss and specify how entity stores should be structured and how access to the instances should be managed.

← ERMIA is introduced in Chapter 11

In Figure 18.12 we can see a specification for part of a smart home that a designer is working on. The door can be opened from the inside by the resident (who is in a wheelchair) either by moving over a mat or by using a remote control to send an RF signal; perhaps there would be a purpose-made remote with buttons labelled 'door', 'curtains', etc. The remote would also operate the TV using infra-red signals as usual. (Infra-red signals cannot go through obstacles such as walls, whereas radio frequency, RF, can.) A visitor would press a button on the video entry phone. When he or she hears a ring, the resident can select the video channel on the TV to see who is at the front door and then open it using the remote control. The door has an auto-close facility.

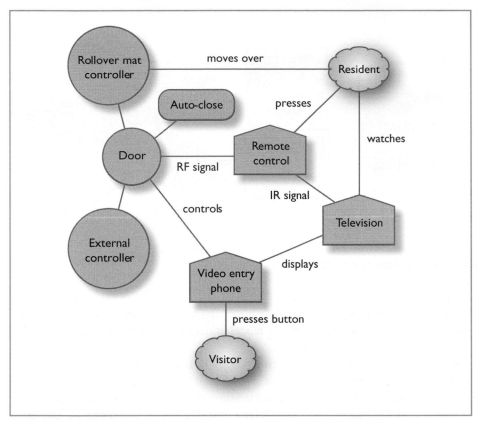

Figure 18.12 Information space sketch of the door system in a supportive home

18.5 Navigating in wireless sensor networks

Besides the work on general blended spaces our own work in this area has been concerned with how people navigate through such mixed-reality environments – particularly in WSNs that are distributed across a physical environment (Leach and Benyon, 2008). Various scenarios have been investigated, such as a surveyor investigating a property that has various sensors embedded in the walls. Some monitor damp, some monitor temperature, some monitor movement and so on. In such an environment, the surveyor first has to find out what sensors exist, and what types of thing they measure. The surveyor then has to move through the physical environment until physically close to the sensors that are of interest. Then the surveyor can take readings using a wireless technology such as Bluetooth.

Another scenario for this class of systems involved an environmental disaster. Chemicals had been spread over a large area. Specks with appropriate sensors would be spread over the area by a crop duster and the rescue teams could then interrogate the network. An overview of the whole situation was provided with a sonification of the data (described further in Chapter 19). Different chemicals were identified with different sounds so that the rescue team was able to determine the types and distribution of the chemicals. Sonification is particularly appropriate for providing an overview of an information space because people can effectively map the whole 360 degrees. This is much more difficult to do visually.

← We introduce specks
in Section 18.1

The overall process of interacting with a ubicomp environment is illustrated in Figure 18.13. The models of data-flow and interaction represent two interconnected

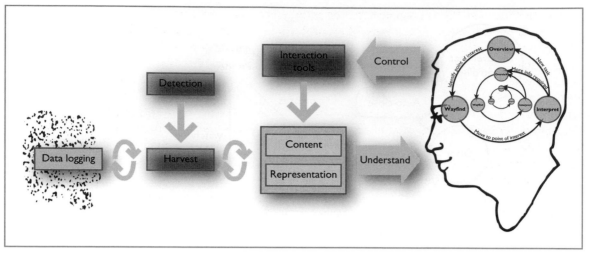

Figure 18.13 Overview of human–Specknet interaction

aspects of Specknet applications. While the model of interaction represents the activities a user may wish to engage in, the model of data-flow can be seen as the practical means of undertaking those activities.

The model of data-flow acts as a conduit of information between the Specknet and people, with understanding of the data coming from its presentation (*content* and *representation*) and control of the system exerted through the *interaction tools*. Figure 18.14 shows a model of human–Specknet interaction. In general situations an individual would start by gaining an overview of the distributed data in the network, physically move to the location where the data was generated (wayfind), and then view the data in the context of the environment to assist them in their task. The model is shown in a spiral form because there may be several resolutions at which data can be viewed: moving through a series of refining searches – physically and digitally shifting perspectives on the network until the required information is discovered.

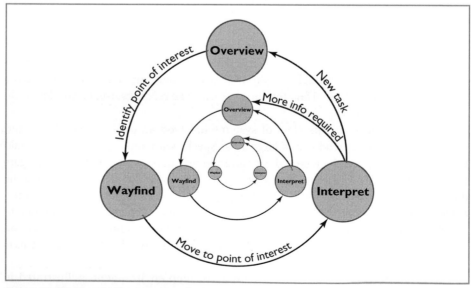

Figure 18.14 Model of human–Specknet interaction

Note that the model is proposed to cover the entire process of direct human interaction with Specknets, but not all stages of the model would need to be implemented in all applications. A clear example could be the use of Specknets in medical applications, where patients could be covered in bio-monitoring sensors. Bedside diagnosis/surgery would involve only the *interpretation* phase; however, if an emergency occurred and the doctor needed to locate a patient then the *wayfind* stage may be required; finally a triage situation could also require inclusion of the *overview* stage to prioritize patients. In contrast, a fire-fighting application would require an *overview* tool to present the distribution of the fire/trapped civilians/hazardous materials, a *wayfind* tool to locate the same, but little in the way of *interpretation* tools – since the firefighter either extinguishes the fire or rescues the person trapped.

→ Navigation is discussed in Chapter 25

The key purpose that the model serves is to allow the assessment of an application and identify the tools required. We postulate that any application requiring *in situ* interaction can be divided into these three activities, and that the application developer can then focus on people at each stage. As mentioned above, overview can be well supported through an auditory interface. There are many examples of systems that aid wayfinding. In our case we used a waypoint system (Figure 18.15). Four directions were supplied: proceed forwards, turn left, turn right and make a U-turn. These directions were conveyed both graphically on the screen and with vocalized audio (as used in satellite navigation systems). The latter addition was to remove the need to look at the screen, but the graphical representation remains for reference.

Once the people reach the required place they face the same problem as the surveyor. How can the data on the specks be visualized? In our case we used an augmented-reality (AR) system, ARTag, where the data was represented with semantically encoded glyphs, with each glyph representing one variable value (either liquid or powder chemical). Glyphs are used to capture several attributes of something and their associated

→ See Chapter 13 on AR

Figure 18.15 Integrated toolkit wayfinding screen
(Source: David Benyon)

values: they provide an economical way of visualizing several pieces of related data. Gaze selection was used to allow the display of actual values, and a menu button was used to make the final selection. Dynamic filtering was also included, using a tilting mechanism to select the value range of interest (Figure 18.16).

Figure 18.16 Integrated toolkit interpretation screen

Summary and key points

Computing and communication devices are becoming increasingly ubiquitous. They are carried, worn and embedded in all manner of devices. A difficulty that this brings is how to know what different devices can do and which other devices they can communicate with. The real challenge of ubiquitous computing is in designing for these distributed information spaces. Home environments are increasingly becoming archetypal ubiquitous computing environments.

- There are a variety of ubiquitous computing environments that designers will be designing
- Information spaces consist of devices, information artefacts and agents
- Blended spaces is a useful way of considering the design of ubicomp environments
- Designers can use a variety of methods for sketching information spaces and where the distributed information should reside
- Navigation in ubiquitous computing environments requires new tools to provide an overview, assist in wayfinding and display information about the objects using techniques such as AR.

Exercises

1 A friend of yours wants to look at an article that you wrote four or five years ago on the future of the mobile phone. Whilst you can remember writing it, you cannot remember what it was called, nor exactly where you saved it, nor exactly when you wrote it. Write down how you will try to find this piece on your computer. List the resources that you may utilize and list the ways you will search the various files and folders on your computer.

2 Go-Pal is your friendly mobile companion. Go-Pal moves from your alarm clock to your mobile phone to your TV. Go-Pal helps you with things such as recording your favourite TV programme, setting the security alarms on your house, remembering your shopping list and remembering special days such as birthdays. Discuss the design issues that Go-Pal raises.

 ## Further reading

Cognition, Technology and Work (2003) volume 5, no. 1, pp. 2–66 Special issue on interacting with technologies in household environments. *This contains the three articles referenced here and three others on issues to do with the design and evaluation of household technologies.*

Weiser, M. (1993) Some computer science issues in ubiquitous computing. *Communications of the ACM*, 36(7), 75–84. See also Weiser (1991).

Getting ahead

Mitchell, W. (1998) *City of Bits*. MIT Press, Cambridge, MA.

Greenfield, A. (2006) *Everyware: The Dawning Age of Ubiquitous Computing*. Pearson, New Riders, IN.

 ## Web links

www.interactivearchitecture.org

The accompanying website has links to relevant websites. Go to
www.pearsoned.co.uk/benyon

Comments on challenges

Challenge 18.1

The key features of interaction in such an environment are (i) enabling people so that they know what technologies exist and (ii) finding some way of letting them interact with them. In such an environment people need to navigate both the real world and the computational world. See Section 18.4.

Challenge 18.2

Figure 18.17 shows just a few ideas.

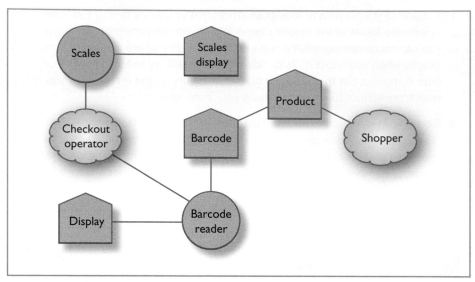

Figure 18.17 Information space for supermarket shopping

Challenge 18.3

You will probably know the route quite well, so you will not need maps or satellite navigation. You will, however, make choices based on the weather. You might need to consult bus or train timetables. You will need information about traffic when you decide where to cross the road. All these resources are distributed throughout the environment. When going somewhere unfamiliar you will consult maps or city guides, use signposts or use a satnav system.

Challenge 18.4

It is really a matter of skill as a designer to get the right combination of modalities. You need to provide an overview, directions to particular objects and information about those objects. Information about some object is probably best provided visually, but peripheral information – about what is nearby, or about things you are passing – is probably best provided aurally so it does not disrupt your attention too much.

Chapter 19
Mobile computing

Contents

Aims

Mobile computing is probably the largest area of growth for designing interactive systems. Mobile computing covers all manner of devices, from mobile phones, to small laptop computers, tablets, e-book readers and tangible and wearable computing. Many of the design principles that we have presented remain true for mobile computing, but the huge variety of different devices that have different controls and different facilities make designing for mobiles a massive challenge.

Mobiles are an essential part of ubiquitous computing, discussed in Chapter 18. There, the emphasis was on integrating mobile technologies with background systems. In this chapter we look at the life cycle of designing for mobiles and at the issues that this particular application of human-centred interaction design raises.

After studying this chapter you should be able to:

- Understand issues of context-aware computing
- Understand the difficulties of undertaking research of mobile applications and specifying the requirements for mobile systems
- Design for mobile applications
- Evaluate mobile systems, applications and services.

19.1 Introduction

Mobile computing devices include the whole range of devices – from laptops to hand-held devices – mobile phones, tablets and computational devices that are worn or carried. A key design constraint with mobile technology is the limited screen space, or no screen at all. Other significant technological features include the battery life and there may be limitations on storage, memory and communication ability. Many of the screens on mobiles are not 'bit-mapped', so GUIs that rely on the direct manipulation of images on the screen cannot be used. All sorts of people will be using the device and, of course, it will be used in all manner of physical and social contexts. This is significant as it means that designers often cannot design for specific people or contexts of use. On the other hand, mobiles offer a whole range of novel forms of interaction, by employing different screen technologies and more sensors than are found on traditional computers.

Because of the small screen it is very difficult to achieve the design principle of visibility. Functions have to be tucked away and accessed by multiple levels of menu, leading to difficulties of navigation. Another feature is that there is not room for many buttons, so each button has to do a lot of work. This results in the need for different 'modes' and this makes it difficult to have clear control over the functions. Visual feedback is often poor and people have to stare into the device to see what is happening. Thus other modalities such as sound and touch are often used to supplement the visual.

There is no consistency in the interfaces across mobiles – even to the point of pressing the right-hand or left-hand button to answer a call on a mobile phone. There are strong brands in the mobile market where consistent look and feel is employed – e.g. Nokia has a style, Apple has a style, etc. Style is very important and many mobile devices concentrate on the overall experience of the physical interaction (e.g. the size and weight of the device). The new generation of smartphones from manufacturers such as Apple, Nokia, Google and BlackBerry have provided better graphical interfaces, with the many devices now including a multitouch display. Netbooks provide more screen space, but lose some of the inherent mobility of phone-sized devices. Other devices use a stylus to point at menu items and on-screen icons.

Many mobile devices have various sensors embedded in them that can be used to provide novel forms of interaction. Many devices include an accelerometer, compass and gyroscope to sense location and orientation and designers can make use of these to provide useful and novel interactive features. For example the iPhone turns the screen off when you bring the phone to your ear. Other devices make use of tilting when playing racing games (Figure 19.1).

(a)   (b)   (c)

Figure 19.1 Some mobile devices: (a) Samsung Galaxy Note II; (b) Motorola Droid 4; (c) Lenovo IdeaPad Yoga

(Source: (a) David Becker/Getty Images; (b) David Becker/Getty Images; (c) David Paul Morris/Bloomberg/Getty Images)

The iPhone also introduced the first touchscreen in 2007 and this allowed them to dispense with a traditional keyboard. The touchscreen provides a pop-up keyboard. While some people love this, others do not, and BlackBerry and Nokia continue to use physical keyboards.

Many mobiles have a Global Positioning System (GPS) that can be used to provide location-specific functions. This allows the device to provide details of useful things nearby, to provide navigation and to automatically record the position of photos, or where messages have been left. And of course many mobiles include cameras, audio players and other functions.

Different devices have different forms of connectivity, such as Bluetooth, Wi-Fi, GPRS and 3G. While these provide various degrees of speed, access and security issues, they also gobble up the battery.

There are also issues concerning the cost of mobile devices and there are a bewildering array of calling plans, add-ons and other features that some people will have and others will not. All this variety makes designing for mobiles a big challenge.

Besides general-purpose mobile devices there are many application-specific devices. E-book readers (Figure 19.2) are mobile devices with a number of hardware and software features optimized to reading e-books. These include different screen technologies that make reading much easier, page-turning functions and the ability to annotate the text by writing with a stylus. There are also applications in laboratories, medical settings and industrial applications.

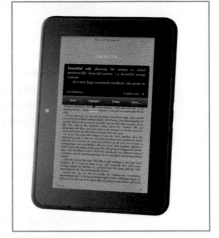

Figure 19.2 Amazon Kindle e-book reader

(Source: James Looker/Future Publishing/Getty Images)

19.2 Context awareness

Mobiles are inherently personal technologies that have moved from simple communication devices to entertainment platforms, to 'information appliances', to general-purpose controllers. It would be impossible to give a comprehensive description of mobile applications as there are so many, ranging from the quite mundane such as note taking, to-do lists, city guides and so on to the novel applications that are being made available day by day. What is more interesting is to look at the new forms of interaction that mobiles offer and at applications where there is a need for mobile devices.

i-Mode

BOX 19.1

i-Mode is a multimedia mobile service first established in Japan through the NTT DoCoMo company in the late 1990s. It differs from most mobile services because it was created as an all-in-one package. NTT DoCoMo coordinated the platform vendors, the mobile handset manufacturers and the content providers through a simple business model to provide a bundle of always-on on-line services. Ease of use is a critical component of i-Mode, along with affordability, and this has proved enormously popular in Japan, in particular, where there are over 50 million subscribers. The content is controlled by DoCoMo, with news from CNN, financial information from Bloomberg, maps from iMapFan, ticket reservations and music from MTV, sports and other entertainment from Disney, telephone directory service, restaurant guides and transactions including book sales, ticket reservations and money transfer. Whether the model transfers to other societies is not yet known, but O_2 have just started offering an i-Mode service in Ireland and the UK.

Mobiles offer the opportunity for interaction to be tailored to the context in which it takes place. Context-aware computing automates some aspects of an application and thus introduces new opportunities for interaction. Context-aware computing is concerned with knowing about the physical environment, the person or persons using the device, the state of the computational environment, the activities being undertaken and the history of the human–computer–environment interaction (Lieberman and Selker, 2000). For example, a spoken command of 'open' could have different effects if the person saying it was staring at a nearby window, if that window was locked or not or if the person had just been informed that a new e-mail had arrived.

If the environment is computationally enabled (see Chapter 18), for example with RFID tags or wireless communications, then the state of the computational environment may deliver information about the physical environment (e.g. what type of shop you are near). If the local environment is not so enabled then the mobile device can take advantage of GPS location. Picture recognition can be used to identify landmark buildings, and sounds can be used to infer context, as can video.

In an excellent case study, Bellotti *et al.* (2008) describe the development of a context-aware mobile application for Japanese teenagers. The aim was to replace traditional city guides with a smart service delivered over a mobile device. Their device, called *Magitti,* knew about the current location, the time and the weather. It also recorded patterns of activity and classified items in the database with tags associated to generic activities (eating, shopping, seeing, doing or reading).

Botfighters 2 is a mobile phone game that uses the player's location in the real world to control their location in a virtual one, and allows them to engage in combat with others nearby (It's Alive, 2004). Botfighters 2 is played on a city-wide scale and uses the mobile phone network to determine proximity to other players (rather than having detection capabilities in the player's device). Figure 19.3(a) shows the interface to Botfighters 2 running on a mobile phone, with the player's character in the centre and nearby opponents to the left and right. Figure 19.3(b) shows a player of the game *Can you see me now?*.

Players of Botfighters were required to wander the city waiting to be alerted to another player's proximity. Several examples of ubicomp games where accurate location was important were produced by Blast Theory (2007) – a group of artists who work with interactive media. A main feature of these games is collaboration between

(a) Java Interface to Botfighters

(b) Chasing players in *Can you see me now?*

Figure 19.3 Mobile and context-aware games

individuals moving through a real city, and individuals navigating through a corresponding virtual city via PCs.

In another example of context-aware mobile computing, Holmquist *et al.* (2004) report on a mobile interface used in their A-Life application, designed as an aid to avalanche rescue workers. Skiers are fitted with a number of sensors monitoring such things as light and oxygen levels, and in the event of an avalanche these readings are used to determine the order in which to help those trapped. The interface shown in Figure 19.4 shows the priority of all skiers within range, and allows access to their specific sensor readings.

There are many examples of context awareness in digital tourism where a mobile device is used to display information about a tourist site, or to provide a guide to the site. Here specific locations can be geo-tagged to indicate to people (through their mobile phone, or other device) that there is some digital content that can be accessed at that location; e.g. the phone may start vibrating when the user is at a certain location. Video or textual information about the location can then be provided.

Wireless sensor networks are another example of where a mobile device is wholly necessary for context-aware applications. When a person is in a WSN they have to be able to detect the devices that are there and the functionality that they have. It is the interaction of people, the computational environment, the physical environment, the history of the interaction and the activities people are engaged in that provides context.

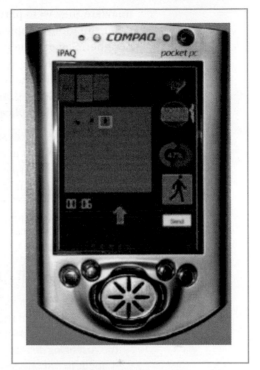

Figure 19.4 PDA interface for A-Life system

(Source: Holmquist *et al.* (2004) Building intelligent environments with Smart-Its, *IEEE Computer Graphics and Applications*, January/February 2004, © 2004 IEEE (Photographer: Florian Michahelles))

19.3 Understanding in mobile computing

Recall that one of the processes in developing interactive systems is 'understanding'. This concerns undertaking research and developing requirements for the system or service to be produced. Undertaking research of people using mobiles and establishing requirements for new mobile applications and devices is the first part of the mobile design challenge. As discussed in Chapter 3, the main techniques for designers are to understand who they are designing for (where the development of personas is particularly useful), and the activities that are to be supported (where scenarios are particularly useful). There is a need to understand current usage and to envision future interactions. The methods adopted must be suitable for the technologies and contexts of use; some of these may be situated in the actual or a future context, other techniques may be non-situated, for example having a brainstorming session in a meeting room.

In the context of mobile computing, observing what people are actually doing can be quite difficult as the device has a small screen that typically cannot be directly observed and the device provides a personal interaction. However, observing wider contextual issues and behaviours is more easily accomplished. For example, one researcher observed teenagers' use of their phones in shopping malls, on buses and in cafés. The aim of this study was to find out what teenagers did with mobile phones. It was not directly concerned with understanding usability issues or for gathering requirements for some new application. Here the teenagers being observed were unaware they were part of a study and so this raises a number of ethical issues. In other situations, people such as travelling sales staff may be explicitly shadowed by a designer. Some of the naturalness of the setting is lost, but the designer can observe in much more detail.

Of course, different methods will be useful for understanding different things. Jones and Marsden (2006) draw on work by Marcus and Chen (2002) to suggest five different 'spaces' of mobile applications:

- Information services such as weather or travel
- Self-enhancement applications such as memory aids or health monitoring
- The relationships space for maintaining social contacts and social networking
- The entertainment space, including games and personalization functions such as ringtones
- M-commerce (mobile commerce) where the emphasis is on commercial transactions.

BOX 19.2

Interacting with a parking meter

The parking meters in Edinburgh and other cities allow people to interact through a mobile phone. After registration of a credit card number, people phone a central number and enter the parking meter number. This enables the parking meter for use, with the cost being debited to the credit card number. Ten minutes before the paid-for time is about to run out, the system sends a text message to the phone, alerting the person that their time is about to expire and so hopefully avoiding a parking fine.

Another method for investigating issues in mobile computing is to get people to keep a diary of their use. Clearly, much use of mobile technologies takes place in quite private settings when the presence of an observer could be embarrassing (e.g. in bed). However, diary studies are notoriously difficult to do well. Participants need to be well motivated if they are to record their activities correctly, it is difficult to validate the diaries and participants may make fictitious entries. However, it can be a suitable way to collect data about current usage. One researcher used diaries in this way, but placed people in pairs in order to help the validation. While the results were informative, there were some notable problems. For example, person X sent a text message to person Y at 2 am, but person Y does not record receiving a message.

Of course, diaries can be cross-referenced to the phone's own record of texts sent and received, but ethics and privacy then become an issue. If these issues can be overcome, then capturing data from the mobile device itself is an excellent way to investigate current usage. There is ample data on number of calls, types of calls, duration, location and so on. What is missed from such data, however, is context. Where the person was, what they were doing and what they were thinking when they engaged in some activity is lost.

High-level conceptual scenarios can be useful to guide understanding. Typically these are abstracted from gathering stories from the target customers. Mitchell (2005) identified wandering, travelling and visiting as three key usage contexts for mobile phone services. Lee *et al.* (2008) identified capturing, storing, organizing and annotating, browsing, and sending and sharing as conceptual scenarios for a mobile photo application. These scenarios can be used as the basis of a structured data collection tool, focus groups or role-playing studies. Mitchell's mobility mapping technique combined the three contexts with social network analysis of who was communicating with whom and where activities took place.

In the case study by Bellotti *et al.* (2008), they needed to gain an understanding about the leisure activities of teenagers. The aim of the project was to supply new service information in order to recommend particular activities. They conducted six different types of research focusing on the questions:

- How do young Japanese spend their leisure time?
- What resources do they use to support leisure time?
- What needs exist for additional support that might be provided by a new kind of media technology?

They report on their methods as follows. This demonstrates the importance of using a variety of methods so that data can be verified and so that different understanding will be provided through different methods of research and requirements.

Interviews and mock-ups (IM): Twenty semi-structured interviews with 16–33-year-olds and a further 12 interviews with 19–25-year-olds examined routines, leisure activities and resources used to support them. We first asked for accounts of recent outings and then for feedback on *Magitti* concept scenarios and a mock-up.

Online survey: We conducted a survey on a market research website to get statistical information on specific issues. We received 699 responses from 19–25-year-olds.

Focus groups: We ran three focus groups of 6–10 participants each, concentrating on mobile phone use. In these we presented a walkthrough of the *Magitti* mock-up and its functions to gather detailed feedback on the concept.

Mobile phone diaries (MPD): To get a picture of the daily activities of 19–25-year-olds, we conducted two mobile phone diary studies, first with 12 people for one Sunday, and then with 19 participants for a seven-day week.

Street activity sampling (SAS): We conducted 367 short interviews with people who appeared to be in our target age range and at leisure in about 30 locations in Tokyo and surrounding areas at different times and days of the week. We asked people to report on three activities from their day, choose one as a *focal activity,* classify it into one of a number of pre-determined types and characterize it in terms of planning, transportation, companionship, information requirements, familiarity with the location, and so on.

Expert interviews: We interviewed three experts on the youth market in the publishing industry to learn about youth trends in leisure, and information commonly published to inform and support their activities.

Informal observation: Finally, we 'hung out' in popular Tokyo neighborhoods observing young adults at leisure. SAS interviewees reported going out on average 2–3 times a week. Average commutes to leisure took 20 to 30 minutes, but it was not unusual to commute for an hour or more.

Challenge 19.1

You have been asked to develop a mobile device and application for people who go running or jogging. How would you go about the understanding process? What research would you do and how would you do it?

19.4 Designing for mobiles

Most of the major suppliers of mobile devices supply useful guidelines for interface and interaction design, and system development kits (SDKs) to ensure consistent look and feel of applications. Apple, Nokia, Google, BlackBerry and Microsoft compete with one

← Interface guidelines are also discussed in Chapter 12

another to offer the best designs, applications and services. Microsoft, for example, have guidelines for developing applications for pocket PCs, such as:

- Make the text for menu commands as short as possible
- Use an ampersand rather than the word 'and'
- Use dividers to group commands on a menu
- Keep the delete command near the bottom of the menu.

Figure 19.5 Windows mobile 6 professional

(Source: Lancelhoff.com)

Even with these guidelines, anyone who has used a pocket PC application will know that menus can get long and unwieldy. The task flow on mobiles is particularly important as the screen quickly gets cluttered if there are several steps that need to be undertaken to achieve a goal. Other useful general guidelines include 'design for one-handed use' and 'design for thumb use'.

Development environments are a useful aid to developers. For example, Visual Studio from Microsoft is used to develop mobile as well as desktop applications. It provides a pocket PC emulator, so that designers can see what the design will look like on the small screen of a pocket PC (Figure 19.5). The problem with developing applications on a full-sized PC, however, is that it does have a big keyboard, it is not portable, it is high-performance with lots of storage and memory and it uses a mouse for pointing rather than a stylus or one of the various navigation buttons, jog-wheels, thumb scanners and so on. These differences can make the use of pocket PC applications quite different from the simulation, or emulator, on a PC.

Jones and Marsden (2006) discuss the concept of mobile information ecologies. This concerns the contexts within which mobile technologies need to operate. They point out that mobile devices have to fit in with other devices such as desktop computers, televisions and other home entertainment systems. Increasingly they have to fit in with public technologies such as ticket machines, checkouts and other self-service systems. Mobiles need to fit in with display devices such as big screens and data projectors. Mobile devices have to fit in with physical resources and other technologies such as radio-frequency identification (RFID) and near field communications (NFC). They need to work with network availability and different communication standards such as Bluetooth and Wi-Fi. The mobile has to contend with varying spaces of interaction, from sitting in a café to walking briskly through a park. And they have to fit into the multiple contexts of use that computing on the move has to deal with. An iPhone behaves quite differently in the searing heat of the summer in India than it does in the cold of Finland. And try using a Nokia S60 whilst wearing gloves!

Jones and Marsden (2006) also provide a thorough discussion of the issues raised by designing for small screens.

The Magitti case

Returning to the case study from Bellotti *et al.* (2008), the Magitti's Main Screen is shown in Figure 19.6. They describe the design and their design rationale as follows:

The main screen [Figure 19.6] shows a scrollable list of up to 20 recommended items that match the user's current situation and profile. As the user walks around, the list updates automatically to show items relevant to new locations. Each recommendation

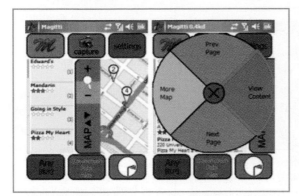

Figure 19.6 Magitti interface design

(Source: Bellotti, V. *et al.* (2008) Activity-based serendipitous recommendations with the Magitti mobile leisure guide, *Proceedings of the Twenty-sixth Annual SIGCHI Conference on Human Factors in Computing Systems*, 5–10 April, Florence, Italy. © 2008 ACM, Inc. Reprinted by permission)

Figure 19.7 Magitti screen

(Source: Bellotti, V. *et al.* (2008) Activity-based serendipitous recommendations with the Magitti mobile leisure guide, *Proceedings of the Twenty-sixth Annual SIGCHI Conference on Human Factors in Computing Systems*, 5–10 April, Florence, Italy. © 2008 ACM, Inc. Reprinted by permission)

is presented in summary form on the Main Screen, but users can tap each one to view its Detail Screen [Figure 19.7, right]. This screen shows the initial texts of a description, a formal review, and user comments, and the user can view the full text of each component on separate screens. The Detail Screen also allows the user to rate the item on a 5-star scale.

To locate recommended items on the Main Screen, users can pull out the Map tab to see a partial map [Figure 19.7, right], which shows the four items currently visible in the list. A second tap slides the map out to full screen. The minimal size and one-handed operation requirements have a clear impact on the UI. As can be seen from Figures 1 and 2 [reproduced here as Figures 19.7 and 19.6], large buttons dominate the screen to enable the user to operate Magitti with a thumb while holding the device in one hand. Our design utilizes marking menus on touch screens to operate the interface, as shown in the right side of [Figure 19.7]. The user taps on an item and holds for 400ms to view the menu; then drags her thumb from the center X and releases over the menu item. As the user learns commands and their gestures, she can simply sweep her thumb in that direction without waiting for the menu to appear. Over time, she learns to operate the device without the menus, although they are available whenever needed.

Challenge 19.2

Find a novel application on your mobile and discuss the design with a colleague. Is it usable? Is it fun to use?

19.5 Evaluation for mobile computing

The evaluation of mobile applications offers its own challenges. One method is to use paper prototypes of designs physically stuck onto the face of a mobile device. Yatani *et al.* (2008) used this technique to evaluate the different design of icons for providing navigation support, as illustrated in Figure 19.8. Bellotti *et al.* (2008) used questionnaires and interviews to evaluate the success of their Magitti system.

Figure 19.8 Paper prototypes of icon designs

(Source: Yatani *et al.* (2008) Escape: a target selection technique using visually-cued gestures. *Proceedings of the Twenty-sixth Annual SIGCHI Conference on Human Factors in Computing Systems, 5–10 April, Florence, Italy.* © 2008 ACM, Inc. Reprinted by permission)

Navigation in a wireless sensor network

In order to illustrate the use of mobiles within a ubiquitous computing environment such as a wireless sensor network (WSN) and demonstrate an approch to evaluation, we have included work by Matthew Leach, a PhD student at Edinburgh Napier University. This related to work on navigation discussed in Chapter 25 and work on ubicomp environments discussed in Chapter 18.

← Specknet WSNs are described in Chapter 18

Matthew Leach evaluated a mobile virtual soundscape that would allow people to gain an overview of data distributed in a simulated 'Specknet' WSN. He was interested in how people could gain an overview of the regions of interest generated in Specknets, in order to prioritize their interaction. Recall that a Specknet is a wireless network of tiny computational devices known as 'specks'. A key feature about moving through Specknets is that the specks cannot be seen and they do not have their own display. Moreover, they do not have any representation of the physical world. The tools required to navigate in such an environment need to support gaining an overview of an environment and the types of object that were in that environment. The person needs to understand the spread of objects in an environment, their significance and the distance and direction they are from the current location.

The scenario chosen for the evaluation was a chemical spillage. Specks would be spread over the area of the spillage and would register whether the chemical was a liquid or a powder. An investigator would use a mobile device to interrogate the Specknet. The variables of distance, direction and significance can be presented in a number of modalities, with a few examples presented in Table 19.1. An individual may be surrounded by data in 360 degrees and three dimensions. Therefore the options presented in Table 19.1 aim to minimize the use of screen space, while providing a 360 degree overview.

The visual option represents a peripheral display where the edge of a screen appears to glow if a region of interest is off to that side, with a bright glow indicating close proximity, and a colour scale used to convey significance. The tactile option imagines a set of vibrotactile motors arranged around the edge of the interaction device where the choice of motor activated could convey direction, the strength of vibration could convey distance, and pulse tempo could convey significance (using the Geiger counter metaphor). The audio is in effect an audible version of the tactile option, but with the option for spatialized sound to convey direction.

Table 19.1 Modalities of gaining an overview

	Visual	**Tactile**	**Audio**
Distance	Brightness	Strength	Volume
Direction	Screen edge	Motor activation	3D sound
Significance	Colour	Pulse tempo	Repetition tempo

Not presented in Table 19.1, but of vital importance, is that mixed types of specks may be present in the network. This information would be important in prioritizing regions of interest; for example, in a situation where two types of chemical were spilt, high concentrations of either may be of importance, but also a region where both are present may be of higher importance (if their combination created a more dangerous chemical). Inclusion of this information matches the model of data-flow in Specknets, which identified that representation of data must convey both type and value.

← This model is presented in Section 18.5

Ultimately it was decided to use sound as the method for gaining an overview, because the sense of hearing is our natural omni-directional sense (Hoggan and Brewster, 2007). The choice of audio also allowed a method for conveying the type of speck through the choice of sound. Although it has potential benefits, sonification also has limitations (Hoggan and Brewster, 2007). These were considered to ensure that they do not compromise the intended goal of the tool:

1 *The sense of hearing provides less detail than the sense of sight.* The sounds will only be used as an overview, identifying areas that warrant closer inspection visually, and so only need to convey limited information.
2 *Systems of generating virtual sounds through headphones are primitive compared to real-world sounds.* Previous experiments have established that headphone representations are adequate for localizing sounds and interpreting data although the accuracy of both at the same time is less well established.
3 *Human hearing is well equipped for discerning the azimuth of a source, but poor at determining elevation.* Additional features may be required if the system is to be used in an environment with a range of elevations (e.g. a multi-storey building), but as an initial investigation this study will assume all sources are on a horizontal plane.

Different types of specks will be represented by different sounds. Pitch can then be used to indicate value: higher pitch means higher value. To convey direction it was decided to use the spatial rendering of sounds, but to reinforce it with another dynamic system. The chosen mappings are shown in Table 19.2.

Table 19.2 Sound study final audio encoding choice

Information	**Type**	**Value**	**Distance**	**Direction**
Encoding	Sound	Pitch	Volume	Sequence and spatialized

The design of the dynamic direction system is shown in Figure 19.9. An arc continuously sweeps around the participant, with a unique (in the audio interface) sounding when the sweep passes directly in front of the direction in which participants are facing. The principal task for participants in an evaluation experiment was to listen to an audio environment, and to then draw a map of the specks distribution (location and type). Each participant performed this task twice, once with an environment containing six objects, and once with an environment containing ten objects.

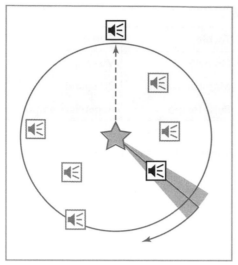

Figure 19.9 Sound study final dynamic system

The evaluation criteria are:

- To what extent did the tool allow people to gain an overview of the data? – To be assessed by asking study participants to produce maps of the data distribution, and determining their accuracy. Comparison between maps will allow trends to be identified, and any failings to be identified.
- Were people able to prioritize information? – To be assessed by tasking study participants with selecting the highest values present in the datasets. The number of actual correct selections will be compared against the probability of doing so by chance.
- Did participants identify any issues in the usability of the tools? – To be assessed through questionnaire, probing users' confidence in use and opinions of features.

Figures 19.10 to 19.13 show an analysis of the distribution maps drawn by participants. The coloured circles represent the location, value (radius) and type (red for powder blue for liquid) for the chemical sounds. The representation uses the same scaling as the training images that participants were exposed to. Lines represent errors between where participants marked sound locations and their actual locations. General trends in the errors were the marking of sound locations counter-clockwise to their true locations, seen most notably in Figure 19.11, and a tendency to place the sounds closer to the centre. Both complex sets included a pair of liquid sounds placed in close proximity. Participants using complex set 1 (Figure 19.12) did not distinguish between these two sounds, only marking one, while those using complex set 2 (Figure 19.13) did identify two separate sounds. When using the complex sets some participants failed to identify low-value sounds at a distance, specifically the bottom-right liquid value.

Discussion

The sweeping arc in effect negated the need for participants to move their head, since it explored the soundscape for them. Participants reported confidence in identifying distance and direction; the confidence for direction was higher than that for distance.

Use of pitch to convey value did not greatly increase confidence in recognizing regions of high and low concentration. Success in selecting high values in the soundscape was also relatively low, being in the order of 37.5 per cent for full success, and 62.5 per cent for partial success (when a graphical aid was not used). The consistency between results suggests that difference in participants may play a larger role than the number of items being sonified. To increase the robustness of the system, the method

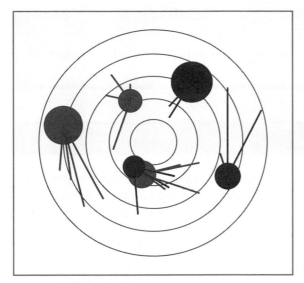

Figure 19.10 Basic set 1 – audio maps

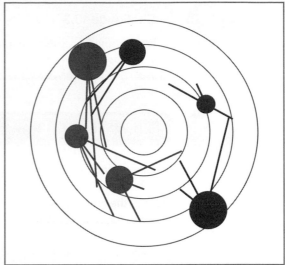

Figure 19.11 Basic set 2 – audio maps

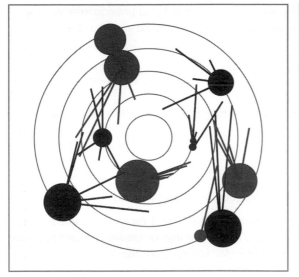

Figure 19.12 Complex set 1 – audio maps

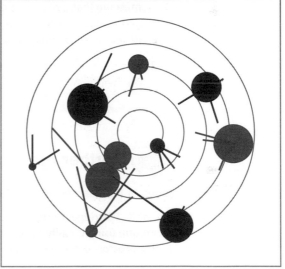

Figure 19.13 Complex set 2 – audio maps

of choosing different pitch values for different levels could be adjusted. For example, since in this case the highest values were important, pitch may be scaled higher at high concentration values, using a logarithmic scale.

The diagrams produced by participants were relatively accurate considering that they had limited exposure to *ideal* maps. As the sound density increases, the potential for interference between them becomes an issue. In the current system, sounds at a distance are particularly vulnerable, with participants failing to differentiate two close-proximity sounds (while other participants could differentiate equivalent sounds when closer to centre – and thus louder), and only 1 in 5 identifying a low-value sound masked by a higher-valued one. However, if the aim is to identify the highest values in a sonification, then a full understanding of distribution may not be required.

Overall the sonification of data demonstrated potential in providing an overview of its distribution, offering an omni-directional representation without visual attention, in environments where people would be surrounded by data and are mobile.

Challenge 19.3

What methods of evaluation would you use if you were asked to evaluate a prototype iPhone app?

Summary and key points

Mobile computing offers particular challenges for designers as the context makes it hard to understand how people use mobiles in the first place and how they might like to use them in the future. Design is constrained by the features of the target device. Evaluation needs to focus on key issues.

Exercises

1 You have been commissioned to develop an application for an outdoor museum that visitors can download onto their mobiles to provide information and guidance as they go around the museum. How would you plan the development of this project?

2 Design an application for students that provides relevant information to them on their mobile device.

Further reading

Jones, M. and Marsden, G. (2006) *Mobile Interaction Design.* Wiley, Chichester.

Yatani K. Partridge, K., Bern, H. and Newman, M.W. (2008) Escape: a target selection technique using visually cued gestures. *CHI'08: Proceedings of the SIGCHI Conference on Human Factors in Computing Systems.* ACM Press, New York, pp. 285–94.

Getting ahead

Bellotti, V. Begole, B., Chi, E.H., Ducheneaut, N., Fang, J., Isaacs, E., *et al.* (2008) Activity-based serendipitous recommendations with the Magitti mobile leisure guide. *CHI'08: Proceedings of the SIGCHI Conference on Human Factors in Computing Systems.* ACM Press, New York, pp. 1157–66.

Web links

The accompanying website has links to relevant websites. Go to
www.pearsoned.co.uk/benyon

Comments on challenges

Challenge 19.1

I would start with a PACT analysis (see Chapter 2) to scope out the design space. You will need to understand all the different technologies that are available from manufacturers such as Nike (look at their website). You probably want to measure speed, distance and location. People might want to meet up with others, so would want mobile communications possibilities and awareness of where others are. You would interview runners, join a running club and survey their members. Prototype ideas and evaluate them. Chapter 7 has many techniques for understanding and requirements generation.

Challenge 19.2

There is no answer for this, but refer back to Chapter 5 on experience design and Chapter 4 on usability for some things you should consider.

Challenge 19.3

Refer to Chapter 10 for general material on evaluation, but also think about the particular issues of evaluation in a mobile environment. You might add some software to the iPhone to record what people are doing with the application. You can try to observe them using it, or interview them directly after they have used the application.

Chapter 20
Wearable computing

Contents

Aims

The next wave of interactive materials promises to bring another major change to interaction design. There will be new forms of interaction as we poke, scrunch, pat and stroke materials with different textures. Gestures and movement will become a natural part of our interaction with digital content. Interacting with wearable computing will be the most multimodal of interactions.

This chapter introduces recent developments in textiles and other materials that are able to manipulate digital content. There are new flexible display devices and new fabrics that have electronic thread woven in. These developments mean that interactive systems are now entering the world of fashion and design and are no longer confined to desktop or mobile devices.

After studying this chapter you should understand:

- The particular relationships between people and technologies that wearable computing brings
- The options available to interactive systems designers that new materials offer
- The changing nature of interactive systems development
- The issues of interactive implants.

20.1 Introduction

Wearable computing refers both to computers that can be worn – on a wrist, say – and to the new forms of interactive technologies made available through new materials. These range from the simple addition of interactive features such as light-emitting diodes (LEDs) into regular clothing to the complex technologies of e-textiles where computing power is woven into a fabric. In this chapter we will push the idea one stage further and discuss not just wearable computing, but also interactive technologies that are implanted into people.

→ Presence is discussed in Chapter 24

One example of a wearable technology is the Nike+ system which allows you to track your time, distance, pace and calories via a sensor in the shoe (Figure 20.1). Another example of an innovative wearable is Google glasses (Figure 20.2). These combine innovative displays with some novel gestural movements for the interaction. The glasses are used to follow where the user is looking, so that a longer gaze at an item will select it. Raising or nodding the head also helps to control the glasses.

Figure 20.1 Nike+
(Source: Nike)

Figure 20.2 Google glasses
(Source: Google UK)

Human–Computer Confluence

Human–Computer Confluence is a research programme funded by the European Union that investigates the coming together (confluence) of people and technologies. For example you could imagine having a direct link to Facebook implanted into a tooth so that you would be immediately aware of any status changes. There are many other futuristic scenarios you could imagine. Two large projects are currently funded by the programme:

- **CEEDS** – the Collective Experience of Empathic Data Systems (CEEDS) project aims to develop novel, integrated technologies to support human experience, analysis and understanding of very large datasets.
- **VERE** (www.vereproject.eu) – this project aims at dissolving the boundary between the human body and surrogate representations in immersive virtual reality and physical reality. The work considers how people can feel present in a distant representation of themselves, whether that representation is as an avatar in a virtual world or as a physical object such as a robot in the real world.

FURTHER THOUGHTS

BOX
20.1

Vuman

The Vuman project (Figure 20.3) has been developing wearable computers to help the US army undertake vehicle inspections. Previously the inspectors had to complete a 50-page checklist for each vehicle – making the inspection, coming out from underneath the vehicle, then writing down the results. The Vuman wearable computing was developed to deal specifically with this domain and included a novel wheel-based interface for navigating the menu. Inspections and data entry can now be carried out together, saving 40% on overall inspection time.

Figure 20.3 Vuman
(Source: Kristen Sabol, Carnegie Mellon/QoLT Center; location courtesy of Voyager Jet, Pittsburgh)

→ Implants are described in Section 20.4

There are a lot of applications of wearable computing and as sensors continue to evolve and technologies mature we can expect to see many more. One active area for wearable computing is the medical domain. Here sensors for checking blood pressure, heart rate and other bodily functions can be attached to the body to provide monitoring of a person's health. There are also many medical implants such as muscle stimulators, artificial hearts and even replacement corneas. However, such devices are primarily non-interactive. It is when we have interactive implants and wearables that things get interesting.

Spacesuits and the military and emergency services demonstrate the most advanced examples of wearable computing. The ongoing Future Force Warrior project in the USA has visions for what the soldier in 2020 will be wearing. Firefighters may have protective clothing with built-in audio, GPS and head-up displays (where information is displayed on the visor of the protective helmet) to show the plans of buildings, for example.

Wearable computers have actually been around in a variety of experimental and prototype forms since the 1960s – see Figure 20.4. In one early project (dating from the mid-1960s) at Bell Helicopter Company, the head-mounted display was coupled with an infra-red camera that would give military helicopter pilots the ability to land at night in rough terrain. An infra-red camera, which moved as the pilot's head moved, was mounted on the bottom of a helicopter.

A further early example of a wearable computer was the HP-01 (Figure 20.5). This was Hewlett-Packard's creation of a wristwatch/algebraic calculator; its user interface combined the elements from both. The watch face had 28 tiny keys. Four of these were raised for easy finger access. The raised keys were D (date), A (alarm), M (memory) and T (time). Each of these keys recalled the appropriate information when pressed alone or, when pressed after the shift key, stored the information. Two more keys were recessed in such a way that they would not be pressed accidentally but could still be operated by

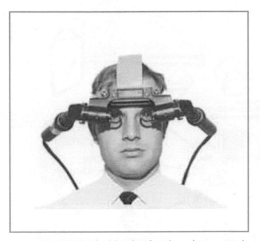

Figure 20.4 (Probably) the first head mounted display (HMD), dating from 1967

(Source: www.sun.com/960710/feature3/alice.html
© Sun Microsystems. Courtesy of Sun Microsystems, Inc.)

Figure 20.5 The HP-01 algebraic watch

(Source: The Museum of HP Calculators.
www.hpmuseum.org.)

finger. These were the R (read/recall/reset depending on mode) and S (stopwatch) keys. The other keys were meant to be pressed with one of two styluses that came with the watch. One of these was a small unit that snapped into the clasp of the bracelet.

Steve Mann continues to be a pioneer in the field of wearable and has compiled a long list of examples that he has developed over two decades (Mann, 2013). He identified what he calls the six informational flow paths associated with wearable computing (Mann, 1998). These informational flows are essentially the key attributes of wearable computing (the headings are Mann's):

1 *Unmonopolizing of people's attention.* That is, they do not detach the wearer from the outside world. The wearer is able to pay attention to other tasks while wearing the kit. Moreover, the wearable computer may provide enhanced sensory capabilities.
2 *Unrestrictive.* The wearer can still engage with the computation and communication powers of the wearable computer while walking or running.
3 *Observable.* As the system is being worn, there is no reason why the wearer cannot be aware of it continuously.
4 *Controllable.* The wearer can take control of it at any time.
5 *Attentive to the environment.* Wearable systems can enhance environmental and situational awareness.
6 *Communicative to others.* Wearable systems can be used as a communications medium.

Spacesuits

Perhaps the ultimate wearable computer is the spacesuit. Whether this is the genuine article as used by astronauts or something more fanciful from science fiction, the spacesuit encompasses and protects the individual while providing (at least) communication with the mother ship or with command and control. While the Borg in *Star Trek* may have enhanced senses, today's spacesuits are actually limited to a single-line text display and a human voice relay channel. These limitations reflect the practical issues of power consumption and the demands of working in a vacuum. NASA and its industrial collaborators are trying to create extra-vehicular activity – EVA (space walk) – support systems using head-up displays (mounted in the helmet), wrist-mounted displays and modifications of

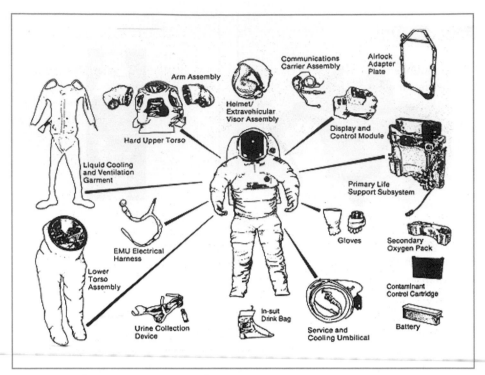

Figure 20.6 The major components of a spacesuit

(Source: http://starchild.gsfc.nasa.gov/docs/StarChild/spce_level2/spacesuit.html)

the current chest-mounted display and control system. The work continues to balance the requirements of utility, reliability, size and mass. Figure 20.6 is an illustration of some of the key components of this particular type of wearable computer system or spacesuit.

Designers of wearable systems also need to worry about things like communications and power consumption and how different components come together into an integrated system. Siewiorek *et al.* (2008) recommend a framework called UCAMP to help designers focus on the key issues. This stands for

- *Users*, who must be consulted early on in the design process to establish their needs and the constraints of the job that they have to do.
- *Corporal*. The body is central to wearable computing and the designers need to think about weight, comfort, location for the computer and novel methods of interaction.
- *Attention*. Interface should be designed to take account of the user's divided attention between the real and digital worlds.
- *Manipulation*. Controls should be quick to find and simple to manipulate.
- *Perception*, which is limited in many domains where wearable computers are used. Displays should be simple, distinct and quick to navigate.

They propose a human-centred methodology for the design of wearable computers that uses paper prototyping and storyboarding early on to get the conceptual design right before building the physical wearable computer.

Challenge 20.1

Think about the design of wearable computers for firefighters. What would you include? What modalities for input and output would be appropriate? Discuss with a colleague.

20.2 Smart materials

There continue to be many new developments in the area of new materials for interaction. For example a number of flexible multitouch displays were announced in 2012, thus bringing in a new era of curved displays (Figure 20.7) and the ability to easily add a touch-sensitive display to any object, For example we can add a flexible display to an item of clothing.

Figure 20.7 Samsung OLED display

(Source: Curved OLED TV, http://www.samsungces.com/keynote.aspx)

Smart materials are materials that react to some external stimulus and change as a result of this interaction. For example, shape memory alloys can change shape in response to changes in temperature or magnetic field. Other materials change in response to changes in light or electricity. Materials may simply change colour, or they may change shape, or transmit some data as a result of changing shape.

The problem for the interactive system designer is that there are such a huge number of opportunities that knowing when to use which one can be difficult.

Some smart materials

BOX 20.2

- **Piezoelectric materials** produce a voltage when stress is applied. Since this effect also applies in the reverse manner, a voltage across the sample will produce stress within the sample. Suitably designed structures made from these materials can therefore be made that bend, expand or contract when a voltage is applied.
- **Shape-memory alloys** and **shape-memory polymers** are materials in which large deformation can be induced and recovered through temperature changes or stress changes (pseudoelasticity). The large deformation results from martensitic phase change.
- **Magnetostrictive** materials exhibit change in shape under the influence of magnetic field and also exhibit change in their magnetization under the influence of mechanical stress.

- **Magnetic shape memory alloys** are materials that change their shape in response to a significant change in the magnetic field.
- **pH-sensitive polymers** are materials that change in volume when the pH of the surrounding medium changes.
- **Temperature-responsive polymers** are materials which undergo change with temperature.
- **Halochromic materials** are commonly used materials that change their colour as a result of changing acidity. One suggested application is for paints that can change colour to indicate corrosion in the metal underneath them.

Source: http://en.wikipedia.org/wiki/Smart_material

Plush Touch from International Fashion Machines is a fabric in which electronic yarn is woven with other fabrics to produce touch-sensitive fabrics. This could be used, for example, in a ski jacket to control an MP3 player. Another example of smart material is the dress that changes colour (Figure 20.8).

Figure 20.8 Smart-material dress that changes colour
(Source: Maggie Orth)

The e-motion project is looking at combinations of emotion and fashion. Look at the e-motion project and discuss different types of interactivity (Figure 20.9, see also http://www.design.udk-berlin.de/Modedesign/Emotion).

Example 1: Garment-based body sensing

A group of researchers from Dublin in Ireland describe the development of a sensor for detecting movement based on a foam sensor (Dunne *et al.*, 2006). Their research concerns identifying which sensors are best to use in wearable computing applications so that they do not make the wearer uncomfortable, but the sensors do provide a level of accuracy that is useful in providing the interactivity.

The authors' work aims to ensure that the properties of textiles (how soft it is, how it stretches and so on) are maintained when the sensing technology is introduced. For example if a fabric is treated with a sensing material, or if an electronic thread is added to an existing textile, the texture may be compromised, making the garment less attractive to people. If the interactive

Figure 20.9 E-motion. Human feelings emerge from an accumulation of sensations which contribute to a conglomerate of senses. The garment finds its emotional expression in the transformation of the hood by utilising integrated sensors and shape memory alloys. No specific emotion is represented, but a further repositioning of the hood is created which generates an awareness with the wearer who can evaluate his or her feelings in a novel way.

(Source: institut für experimentelles bekleidungs Copyright design: Max Schath, in cooperation with the Frauenhofer IZM, Photo: Özgür Albayrak. e-motion, an interdiscplinary project at the Institute of Fashion and Textile design (IBT), Berlin University of the Arts (UdK), Germany during wintersemester 2008 / 2009, Prof. Valeska Schmidt-Thomsen and Prof. Holger Neuman)

features of the textile are to be very accurate, then this may require a form of clothing, such as a skin-tight suit that people would find socially unacceptable. The usability and acceptability of interactive fabrics must not be compromised if people are going to be happy wearing them.

← See Chapter 4 on usability and acceptability

The sensor that they were investigating was a foam based on PPy (polymer polypyrrole) in which a tiny electrical current is monitored. Any change in the foam will be detected by the sensor, so the foam can be woven with other fabrics. The researchers point out that this type of sensor is useful in detecting repetitive movements such as breathing or walking and in detecting the specific movements such as that an elbow has been bent or the person has shrugged. These simple switch-like actions can be used in a variety of ways. The sensor can also be used to monitor things such as breathing by placing it close to the skin.

The researchers undertook a number of experiments and concluded that the sensor was able to reliably detect the shrugging movement and to some extent could detect the extent of that movement (a big shrug or a smaller one). Combined with the fact that the foam could be included in other fabrics and that it was washable, inexpensive and durable (all desirable features of wearable sensors) made this a good choice for a wearable sensor.

Graphene

Even before the pioneers of graphene were given the Nobel Prize in 2011, this material was already being proclaimed as 'the next big thing'. Graphene is not just one material but a huge range of materials (similar to the range of plastics). It is seen both as an improvement on, and a replacement for silicon, and is said to be the strongest material ever measured, in addition to being the most conductive material known to man. In short, its properties have created a real stir. One scientist commented, 'It would take an elephant, balanced on a pencil, to break through a sheet of graphene the thickness of Saran Wrap [cling film].' The way in which this material can be used is as astonishing as its properties, as it can be used for anything from composite materials (just like how carbon-fibre is used now) to electronics.

Source: Based on http://news.bbc.co.uk/1/hi/programmes/click_online/9491789.stm

FURTHER THOUGHTS

Challenge 20.2

Think of some innovative uses for smart clothing that can react to changes in people's physical characteristics. You can have some fun with this. For example, how about a shirt that changes colour in response to changes in someone's heart rate? Discuss the possible social issues of such technologies. (You might want to revisit the different types of sensors in Chapter 2.)

→ See Chapter 22
on emotion

20.3 Material design

Mikael Wiberg and his colleagues (Wiberg, 2011; Robles and Wiberg, 2011) argue that the significant changes that are happening as a result of wearable computing and tangible user interfaces mean that it is no longer sensible to distinguish atoms and bits: the physical world and the digital world are brought together. Instead they talk about 'computational compositions' and creating a composition of unified texture. Texture is how an underlying infrastructure is communicated to an observer and materiality is the relationship between people and things.

They refer to this as the 'material turn' in interaction design. The concept of texture is used both metaphorically and literally to think about the new forms of interaction that are opening up. Interaction design becomes designing the relationships between architecture and appearance. Texture is the concern for properties, structures, surfaces and expression. Thus design is composition (like a musical composition), to do with the aesthetics of textures.

**BOX
20.3**

Somaesthetics

Somaesthetics is a philosophical position developed by Richard Shusterman (2013), foregrounding the importance of the body and taking a holistic approach to life and the self. Aesthetics is concerned with notions of beauty, appreciation and balance and of experiencing the whole in the context of your purposeful existence. Somaesthetics looks to train people in an understanding of the role of the body in philosophy drawing upon Eastern and Western philosophical traditions. It has only recently been applied to interaction design, but in the context of the developments that wearable computing will bring, the body will become increasingly important to how we feel about interactive experiences.

HCI theories

Mikael Wiberg's invocation of a 'turn to the material' reflects the changing nature of how we see, or frame, HCI and interaction design. Yvonne Rogers in her recent book on HCI theory (Rogers, 2012) traces a number of turns that the discipline has taken since the original 'turn to the social' that ushered in the study of HCI in context that happened at the start of the 1990s. Rogers identifies:

**FURTHER
THOUGHTS**

● The turn to *design* – where HCI theorists have brought in ideas from design and design philosophy to HCI thinking that started in the mid-1990s

- The turn to *culture* – is a more recent development (Bardzell, 2009) where theorists and practitioners have brought critical theory to bear on interaction design. Coming from different perspectives such as Marxism, feminism, literary criticism, film theory and so on, the turn to culture is about critical, value-based interpretations of people and technologies.
- The turn to *the wild* – looks back to the important book *Cognition in the Wild* (Hutchins, 1995) and to the host of interventions and studies that focus on interaction design for everyday activities, and for people fitting technologies into their everyday lives.
- The turn to *embodiment* – stresses the importance of our bodies to the way humans think and act, the importance of the objects and people in our environment to the meanings that we make of, and in, the world.

This notion of interaction design as composition develops all the various issues to do with personalization of devices, using interaction 'in the wild', mobility, ubiquitous computing and all the difficulties and complexities of these design situations. Wearable computing makes use of tangible user interfaces (TUIs) and all the other modalities such as movement, gesture, speech and non-speech audio.

← For TUI and GUI see Chapter 13

The tight coupling of the physical and the digital opens up wholly new form of interaction. Fabrics can be stroked, scrunched, pinched, pulled, tugged, poked and ruffled. There are hand gestures, arm movements and head movements. People can jump, kick, point, jog, walk and run. All of these have the potential to cause some computation to happen whether that is jumping over an imaginary wall in a computer game, to controlling the volume on an MP3 player, to uploading a photo to Facebook.

Recall the idea of interaction patterns introduced earlier (in Chapter 9). Interaction patterns are regularities used in interaction such as 'pinch to zoom' on the iPad, 'swipe right' to go to the next item on Android phones, or 'click the select button' to chose an item from a list in Windows 8. What are the interaction patterns going to be in wearable computing? There are no standards such as those of Apple, Google or Microsoft and the inherent variety of different fabrics and different types of clothing and different types of application mean that material design is a very *ad hoc* affair.

Challenge 20.3

Draw up a list of gestures that are used on Kinect or Wii.

Designers can just rely on the approaches and techniques of human-centred design, developing personas and scenarios, prototyping with the intended users, or representative users and evaluation to help them develop effective designs.

For example, Sarah Kettley developed some interactive jewellery (Figure 20.10) using focus groups and interactive prototyping to explore how the jewellery affected the interaction of a small group. Markus Klann (Klann, 2009) worked with French firefighters to develop new wearable equipment and Oakley and colleagues (2008) undertook controlled experiments to explore different methods of interactive pointing gestures in the development of their wearable system.

Figure 20.10 Interactive jewellery

(Source: Sarah Kettley Design)

20.4 From materials to implants

It is not difficult to imagine the inevitable movement from wearable computers to implanted computers. Simple devices such as RFID tags have been implanted into people and can be used to automatically open doors and turn on lights when the tag is detected. There are also night clubs where club-goers can have implants to jump the queue, or pay for drinks.

There are already many examples of brain–computer interfaces (BCI) where EEG signals from the brain are used to interact with some other device (Figure 20.11). However, BCI has not lived up to its original hype and is still only useful for limited input. For example, an EEG cap can detect a person concentrating on 'right' or 'left' and turn a remote vehicle right or left, or make other simple choices from a menu.

Direct neurological connections are routine in some areas such as retinal implants, but are still rare for interactive functionality. Kevin Warwick at Reading University has conducted some experiments with direct neurological implants into his arm. He was able to learn to feel the distance from objects and directly link to other objects that were on the Internet. In one experiment his arm movements are used to control the colour of interactive jewellery and in another he is able to control a robotic hand over the Internet. In the final experiment of his Cyborg 2.0 project he linked his arm with his wife's, thus feeling what her arm was doing. The artist Stelarc has undertaken similar connections in his work (Figure 20.12).

The final destination for this work is the idea of cyborgs such as the Borg (Figure 20.13) who figured in episodes of *Star Trek* or the film *Terminator*. Of course there are tremendous medical benefits to be had from implants, but there are also huge ethical issues concerned with invading people's bodies with implanted technology. Fortunately, perhaps, the interaction designer of today does not have to worry too much about designing implants, but will need to be aware of the possibilities.

Challenge 20.4

Reflect on the changes that will come about as implants become more common and move from medical to cosmetic usage. What human characteristics might people want to enhance? How might that change the nature of interaction between people and between people, objects and spaces?

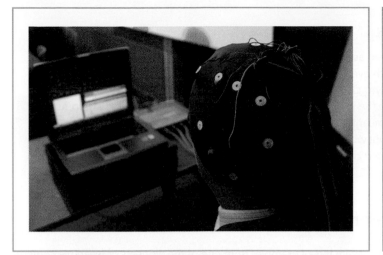

Figure 20.11 Brain–computer interface
(Source: Stephane de Sakutin/AFP Getty Images)

Figure 20.12 Stelarc
(Source: Christian Zachariasen/Sygma/Corbis)

Figure 20.13 Borg
(Source: Peter Ginter/Science
Faction/Corbis)

Summary and key points

Wearable computing offers a new set of challenges for the interaction designer. It brings together many of the issues of tangible user interfaces with new forms of interaction gestures such as stroking, scrunching and so on.

- Designers will need to know about different materials and their properties, about how robust they are and about what they can sense and with what accuracy. Designers will be crafting new experiences.
- Wearable computers need to be designed with the human body in mind so that they are confortable and suitable for the domain in which they will be used
- New computational materials will be developed that can make use of different sensors to bring about change and interact with people
- Interaction designers need to appreciate the aesthetics of the new forms of interaction that wearables bring.

Exercises

1 You have been asked to design gym clothing for busy executives who need to keep in touch even when they are working out in the gym. What functionality would this gym clothing have, how could it be manufactured and how would it interact with the gym equipment, with the Internet and with other people?

2 Imagine the near future when you can have interactive evening wear to put on for an evening out with friends. Develop some scenarios for the interaction of people, places and their clothing and the new experiences that could be produced.

Further reading

There is a long chapter with lots of examples from one of the pioneers of wearable computing, Steve Mann, at: www.interaction-design.org/encyclopedia/wearable_computing.html

Getting ahead

Robles, E. and Wiberg, M. (2011) From materials to materiality: thinking of computation from within an Icehotel, *Interactions* **18(1):** 32–7

Wiberg. M. and Robles, E. (2010) Computational compositions: aesthetics, materials and interaction design, *International Journal of Design* **4(2):** 65–76

Web links

The accompanying website has links to relevant websites. Go to
www.pearsoned.co.uk/benyon

Comments on challenges

Challenge 20.1

Firefighters wear special suits to protect them from heat and smoke, of course, and many of these are enhanced with extra sensors and effectors. Sound is a very effective medium for firefighters and they often cannot see where they are going. A head-up display showing the schematics for buildings might be useful.

Challenge 20.2

This is a chance to brainstorm opportunities for future clothing. Review the range of different sensors that are available, such as heart monitor, galvanic skin response, and other measures of arousal, and think how they could change the colour of a shirt from white to red, getting redder the more aroused a person becomes! The social consequences of such technologies should be discussed. Fabrics could react to all manner of other contexts such as how many e-mails you have received, how many of your friends are nearby or how many messages your colleagues have left at a particular location.

Challenge 20.3

There are thousands of gestures used by games that make use of devices such as the Wii or the Kinect. Many of them depend on the context and content of particular games. There are throwing gestures, fishing gestures, jumping gestures, ducking and weaving gestures and so on. There are also more general gestures for waves, sweeps, pointing and selecting and moving objects. Discuss how these can be used in the context of interacting with other people and with objects and how gestures interact with fabrics.

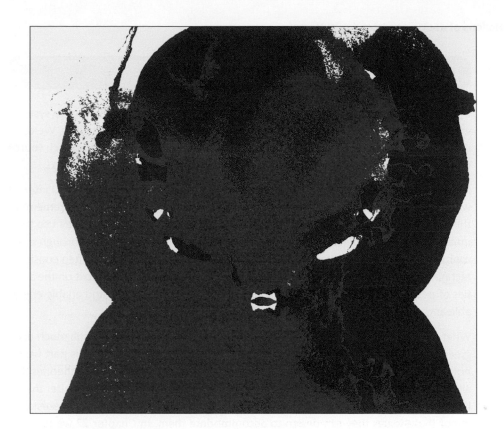

PART IV

Foundations of designing interactive systems

Introduction to Part IV

In this part the main fundamental theories that underlie designing interactive systems are brought together. These theories aim to explain people and their abilities. We draw upon theories of cognition, emotion, perception and interaction to provide a rich source of material for understanding people in the context of interactive systems design.

People have tremendous abilities to perceive and understand the world and to interact with it. But they also have inherent limitations. For example, people cannot remember things very well. They get distracted and make mistakes. They get lost. They use their innate abilities of understanding, learning, sensing and feeling to move through environments. In the case of interactive systems design, these environments often consist of technologies, or have technologies embedded in them. In this part we focus on the abilities of people so that designers can create appropriate technologies and enable enjoyable and engaging interactive experiences.

What is perhaps most surprising about these foundations is that there is still much disagreement about how, exactly, people do think and act in the world. In this part we do not proclaim a single view that explains it all. Instead we present competing theories that allow readers to discuss the issues. Chapter 21 deals with how people remember things, how people forget and why people make mistakes. If designers have a deep understanding of these issues they can design to accommodate them. In Chapter 22 we turn our attention to emotion and to the important role that this has to play in interactive systems design. Emotion is a central part of being human, so designers should aim to design for emotion rather than trying to design it away. Chapter 23 is concerned with thinking and how thinking and action work together. The chapter explores a number of views on cognition and action. In Chapter 24 we move from looking at people as individuals and consider how we operate in groups. The chapter considers how we interact with one another and how we form our identity with our culture. Finally in Chapter 25 we look at how people interact with the world that surrounds them: how we perceive and navigate a complex world.

Case studies

Most of the material in this part is theoretical and so there are not many case studies included. There are lots of examples of novel systems in Chapter 22.

Teaching and learning

There is a lot of complex material in this part that takes time to study and understand. Much of the material would be suitable for psychology students, and in many ways the material here constitutes a course in psychology: psychology for interactive systems design. The best way to understand the material in this part is through focused study of small sections. This should be placed in the context of some aspect of interaction design, and the list of topics below should help to structure this. Alternatively these five chapters would make a good in-depth course of study.

The list of topics covered in this part is shown below, each of which could take 10–15 hours of study to reach a good general level of understanding, or 3–5 hours for a basic appreciation of the issues. Of course, each topic could be the subject of extensive and in depth study.

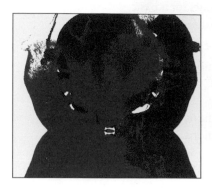

Chapter 21
Memory and attention

Contents

Aims

Memory and attention are two key abilities that people have. They work together to enable us to act in the world. For interactive systems designers there are some key features of memory and attention that provide important background to their craft. Some useful design guidelines that arise from the study of memory and attention are presented in Chapter 12 and influence the design guidelines in Chapter 3. In this chapter we focus on the theoretical background.

After studying this chapter you should be able to describe:

- The importance of memory and attention and their major components and processes
- Attention and awareness; situation awareness, attracting and holding attention
- The characteristics of human error and mental workload and how it is measured.

21.1   Introduction

It is said that a goldfish has a memory that lasts only three seconds. Imagine this were true of you: everything would be new and fresh every three seconds. Of course, it would be impossible to live or function as a human being. This has been succinctly expressed by Colin Blakemore (1988):

> without the capacity to remember and to learn, it is difficult to imagine what life would be like, whether it could be called living at all. Without memory, we would be servants of the moment, with nothing but our innate reflexes to help us deal with the world. There could be no language, no art, no science, no culture.

Memory is one of the main components of a psychological view of humans that aims to explain how we think and act. It is shown in Figure 21.1 along with awareness, motivation, affect and attention (and other unnamed functions). These subjects are covered in the next few chapters. In introducing memory we begin with a brief discussion of what memory is *not* and in doing so we hope to challenge a number of misconceptions.

There are several key issues about memory. First, it is not just a single, simple information store – it has a complex, and still argued over, structure. There are differences between short-term (or working) memory and long-term memory. Short-term memory is very limited but is useful for holding such things as telephone numbers while we are dialling them. In contrast, long-term memory stores, fairly reliably, things such as our names and other biographical information, the word describing someone who has

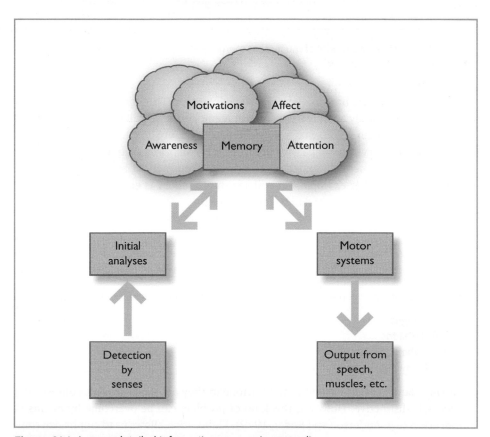

Figure 21.1 A more detailed information processing paradigm

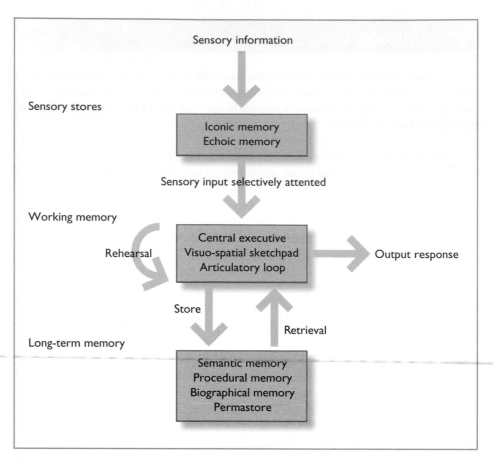

Figure 21.2 A schematic model of multi-store memory
(Source: After Atkinson and Shiffrin, 1968)

lost their memory, and how to operate a cash dispenser. This common-sense division reflects the most widely accepted structure of memory, the so-called multi-store model (Atkinson and Shiffrin, 1968) that is illustrated here (Figure 21.2).

Secondly, memory is not a passive repository: it comprises a number of active processes. When we remember something we do not simply file it away to be retrieved whenever we wish. For example, we will see that memory is enhanced by deeper or richer processing of the material to be remembered.

Thirdly, memory is also affected by the very nature of the material to be remembered. Words, names, commands or images for that matter which are not particularly distinctive will tend to interfere with their subsequent recognition and recall. Game shows (and multiple-choice examination questions) rely on this lack of distinctiveness. A contestant may be asked:

For 10,000 can you tell me . . . Bridgetown is the capital of which of the following?

    (a) Antigua
    (b) Barbados
    (c) Cuba
    (d) Dominica

As the islands are all located in the Caribbean they are not (for most contestants) particularly distinctive. However, this kind of problem can be overcome by means of **elaboration** (e.g. Anderson and Reder, 1979). Elaboration allows us to emphasize similarities and differences among the items.

Fourthly, memory can also be seen as a **constructive process**. Bransford *et al.* (1972) were able to show that we construct and integrate information from, for example, individual sentences. In an experiment they presented a group of people with a series of thematically related sentences and then presented them with a second set of sentences, asking 'Have you seen this sentence before?'. They found that most people estimated that they had seen approximately 80 per cent of these sentences before. In fact *all* of the sentences were new. Bransford *et al.* concluded that people are happy to say that they recognized sentences they have not seen providing they are *consistent* with the theme of the other sentences.

Finally, many researchers would now argue that memory cannot be meaningfully studied in isolation, as it necessarily underpins all other aspects of cognition (thinking). For example, object recognition relies on memory; the production and understanding of language relies on some form of internal lexicon (or dictionary); finding our way about town relies on an internal representation of the environment, sometimes described as a cognitive map (Tversky, 2003); the acquisition of skills often begins with internalizing and remembering instructions.

Memory is related to attention and these two are related to making mistakes, having accidents or doing things unintentionally. Memory, attention and error are also related to emotion. In this chapter we discuss the first three of these, devoting the next chapter to looking at emotion, or 'affect'.

21.2 Memory

Memory is usually divided into a set of **memory processes** and a number of different types of **memory store**. Table 21.1 is a summary of the main memory stores and their sub-components and associated processes. Figure 21.1 is an illustration of this multi-store model of the memory (note the role of attention).

Memory stores: working memory

As we have already noted, working memory, first identified and named by Baddeley and Hitch (1974), is made up from three linked components, namely a **central executive**, a **visuo-spatial sketchpad** and an **articulatory loop** (also called the phonological loop). The central executive is involved in decision making, planning and related activities. It is also closely linked to managing our ability to perform more than one thing at a time (see the section below which discusses the role of attention). The articulatory or phonological loop can be thought of as behaving like a loop of audio tape. When we are trying to dial an unfamiliar telephone number or repeating a phrase in a foreign language, we tend to repeat the string of numbers (or words) either out loud or silently to ourselves. This process is called **rehearsal**. When we are doing this we are making use of the articulatory loop, which can also account for our experience of the **inner voice**. The analogy of the audio tape is useful as it allows us to see that the articulatory loop is limited in both capacity and duration.

The visuo-spatial sketchpad (also called the scratchpad) is the visual and spatial information equivalent of the articulatory loop and has been linked to our **mind's eye**. We use our mind's eye to visualize a route through a town or building or for the mental rotation of figures (visualize a coin and then rotate it to see what is on the other side). The visuo-spatial sketchpad is also limited in capacity and duration unless refreshed

Table 21.1 A summary of the structure of memory

Main components	Key processes associated with this particular store
Sensory stores The **iconic** store (visual) and the **echoic** store (auditory) are temporary stores where information is held before it enters working memory.	The contents of these stores are transferred to working memory within a fraction of a second.
Working memory (WM) Working memory is made up from three key elements: the **central executive,** the **articulatory loop** and the **visuo-spatial sketchpad**. The central executive is involved in decision making, the articulatory loop holds auditory information and the visuo-spatial sketchpad, as the name suggests, holds visual information.	**Rehearsal** is the process of refreshing the contents of WM, such as repeating aloud a phone number. The contents of WM are said to **decay** (are lost/forgotten) if they are not rehearsed. Another way of forgetting from WM is **displacement** which is the process by which the current contents of WM are pushed out by new material.
Long-term memory (LTM) Long-term memory comprises the following: **Semantic** memory. This holds information related to meaning. **Procedural** memory. This stores our knowledge of how to do things such as typing or driving. **Episodic** and/or **autobiographical** memory. This may be one or two different forms of memory that are related to memories personal to an individual such as memories of birthdays, graduation or getting married. **Permastore**. This has been suggested by Bahrick (1984) as the name for the part of LTM which lasts for our lifetime. It stores the things you never forget.	**Encoding** is the process by which information is stored in memory. **Retrieval** is the means by which memories are recovered from long-term storage. **Forgetting** is the name of a number of different possible processes by which we fail to recover information.

by means of rehearsal. Finally, the capacity of working memory itself is approximately three or four items (e.g. MacGregor, 1987; LeCompte, 1999) where an item may be a word or a phrase or an image. It should be noted that older textbooks and papers suggest that the limit of short-term memory is 7 ± 2 items, sometimes called the *magical number* 7: this is now known to be incorrect.

BOX 21.1

Distinguishing between short-term and working memory

In their multi-store model of memory, Atkinson and Shiffrin (1968) distinguish between short- and long-term memory (reflecting William James's primary and secondary memory division 70 years earlier). While the term short-term memory (STM) is still widely used, we have chosen to employ the term working memory (WM) instead. STM is usually characterized by a limited, temporary store for information before it is transferred to long-term memory, while WM is much more flexible and detailed in structure and function. Our use of WM instead of STM also better reflects our everyday experience.

Memory stores: long-term memory

Long-term memory has an effectively unlimited capacity and memories stored there may last as long as an individual's lifetime. The coding (the internal representation) of the information held by it is primarily semantic in nature, that is, it is stored in terms of its meaning, e.g. knowledge of facts and the meaning of words (contrast this with the binary encoding of information in a computer). However, research has indicated that other forms of encoding are present too: for example, memories of music or the bark of a dog are encoded as auditory information, and similarly haptic (touch) encoding allows us to remember the feeling of silk and the sting of a cut. Finally, olfactory (smell) and gustatory (taste) encoding allows us to recognize and distinguish between the smell and taste of fresh and rotten food.

In addition to semantic memory, long-term memory includes other kinds of memories such as **episodic** or **autobiographical** memory (memory of our personal history, for example our first kiss, graduation day, the death of a parent) and **procedural memory** (e.g. the knowledge of how to ride a bike, type, play the euphonium). This neat three-way division of long-term memory into component parts – semantic, episodic and procedural – has been questioned by Cohen and Squire (1980) who argued that the real distinction is between 'knowing that' (declarative memory) and 'knowing how' (procedural memory), but in practice there is little between these two accounts.

Challenge 21.1

Contrast listing the components of a bicycle (e.g. frame, wheels, etc.) with knowing how to ride a bicycle (e.g. sitting on the saddle and pedalling) and with your memory of the first time you rode a bicycle (e.g. How old were you? What sort of day was it? Who else was there?). Which is hardest to describe?

How do we remember?

In everyday English, to remember means both to retrieve information ('I think her birthday is the 18th of June') and to store information in memory ('I'll remember that'). To remove this ambiguity we will use the terms **store** and **encode** to mean place in memory, and **retrieve** and **recall** to mean bring back from memory.

If what we want to store is not too complex (that is, it does not exceed the capacity of working memory), we will typically rehearse it, that is, repeat the string of words either aloud or using our inner voice. This is useful for remembering unfamiliar names or strings of numbers or words such as a foreign phrase, for example '*Dos cervezas, por favor*'. This technique exploits the articulatory loop of working memory. Similar strategies are also used to remember, for a short time, the shape of an object or a set of directions. The capacity of working memory can effectively be enhanced by chunking the material to be remembered first. Chunking is the process by which we can organize material into meaningful groups (chunks). For example, an apparently random string of numbers such as 00441314551234 may defeat most people unless it is chunked. This particular number may be seen to be a telephone number made up from the code for international calls (0044), the area code for Edinburgh (131) and the prefix for Edinburgh Napier University (455), leaving only 1234 to remember. Thus the string of numbers has been reduced to four chunks.

So how do we remember things for longer periods? One answer is **elaboration** which has been developed as an alternative view of memory in itself. The **levels of processing**

(LoP) model proposed by Craik and Lockhart (1972) argues that rather than focusing on the structural, multi-store model of memory we should emphasize the memory processes involved. The LoP model recognizes that any given stimulus (piece of information) can be processed in a number of different ways (or levels) ranging from the trivial or shallow all the way through to a deep, semantic analysis. Superficial processing may involve the analysis of the stimulus's surface features such as its colour or shape; a deeper level of analysis may follow which may test for such things as whether the stimulus (e.g. cow) rhymes with the word 'hat'. The final and deepest level of analysis is the semantic, which considers the stimulus's meaning – does the word refer to a mammal?

Finally, we are able to retrieve stored information by way of **recall** and/or **recognition**. Recall is the process whereby individuals actively search their memories to retrieve a particular piece of information. Recognition involves searching our memory and then deciding whether the piece of information matches what we have in our memory stores.

How and why do we forget?

There are numerous theories of forgetting. However, before we discuss their strengths and weaknesses, we begin with another key distinction, namely the difference between **accessibility** and **availability**. Accessibility refers to whether or not we are able to retrieve information that has been stored in memory, while the availability of a memory depends on whether or not it was stored in memory. The metaphor of a library is often used to illustrate this difference. Imagine you are trying to find a specific book in a library. There are three possible outcomes:

(a) you find the book (the memory is retrieved);
(b) the book is not in the library (the memory is not available); or
(c) the book is in the library but has been misfiled (not accessible).

There is, of course, a fourth possibility, namely that someone else has borrowed the book, which is where the metaphor breaks down!

As we described earlier, information is transferred from working memory to long-term memory to be stored permanently, which means that availability is the main issue for working memory while accessibility is the main (potential) problem for long-term memory.

Challenge 21.2

Demonstrating recency and the serial order effect. The serial position curve is an elegant demonstration of the presence of (a) a short/long-term divide in memory and (b) the primacy and recency effects in forgetting. This is easily demonstrated. First, create a list of, say, 20 to 30 words. Present them in turn (read them or present them on a screen – try using PowerPoint) to a friend, noting the order in which the words were presented. At the end of the list, ask them to recall as many of the words as they can. Again note the order of the words. Repeat this process with another 6–10 people. Plot how many words presented first (in position 1) were recalled, then how many in positions 2, 3, 4, etc., up to the end of the list.

Forgetting from working memory

The first and perhaps oldest theory is **decay theory,** which argues that memory simply fades with time, a point which is particularly relevant to working memory which maintains memories for only 30 seconds or so without rehearsal. Another account is

displacement theory, which has also been developed to account for forgetting from working memory. As we have already seen, working memory is limited in capacity, so it follows that if we were to try to add another item or two to this memory, a corresponding number of items must be squeezed out.

Forgetting from long-term memory (LTM)

We turn now to more widely respected theories of forgetting from long-term memory. Again psychology cannot supply us with one, simple, widely agreed view of how we forget from LTM. Instead there are a number of competing theories with varying amounts of supporting evidence. Early theories (Hebb, 1949) suggested that we forget from *disuse*. For example, we become less proficient in a foreign language learned at school if we never use it. In the 1950s it was suggested that forgetting from LTM may simply be a matter of decay. Perhaps memory engrams (= memory traces) simply fade with time, but except in cases of explicit neurological damage such as Alzheimer's disease no evidence has been found to support this.

A more widely regarded account of forgetting is **interference theory,** which suggests that forgetting is more strongly influenced by what we have done before or after learning than the passage of time itself. Interference takes two forms: **retroactive interference** (RI) and **proactive interference** (PI).

Retroactive interference, as the name suggests, works backwards. That is, newer learning interferes with earlier learning. Having been used to driving a manual-shift car, spending time on holiday driving an automatic may interfere with the way one drives after returning home.

In contrast to RI, proactive interference may be seen in action in, for example, moving from word processor v1 to v2. Version 2 may have added new features and reorganized the presentation of menus. Having learned version 1 interferes with learning version 2. Thus earlier learning interferes with new learning. However, despite these and numerous other examples of PI and RI, there is surprisingly little outside the laboratory to support this theory.

Retrieval failure theory proposes that memories cannot be retrieved because we have not employed the correct retrieval cue. Recalling the earlier library metaphor, it is as if we have 'filed' the memory in the wrong place. The model is similar to the tip-of-the-tongue phenomenon (Box 21.2). All in all, many of these theories probably account for some forgetting from LTM.

The tip-of-the-tongue phenomenon

BOX
21.2

Researchers Brown and McNeill (1966) created a list of dictionary definitions of unfamiliar words and asked a group of people to provide words that matched them. Not surprisingly, not everyone was able to provide the missing word. However, of those people who could not, many were able to supply the word's first letter, or the number of syllables or even words that sounded like the missing word itself. Examples of the definitions are:

- Favouritism, especially governmental patronage extended to relatives (nepotism)
- The common cavity into which the various ducts of the body open in certain fish, birds and mammals (cloaca).

21.3 Attention

Attention is a pivotally important human ability and is central to operating a machine, using a computer, driving to work or catching a train. Failures in attention are a frequently cited reason for accidents: car accidents have been attributed to the driver using their mobile phone while driving; aircraft have experienced 'controlled flight into terrain' (to use the official jargon) when the pilots have paid too much attention to the 'wrong' cockpit warning; and control room operators can be overwhelmed by the range and complexity of instruments to which they must attend. Clearly we need to be able to understand the mechanism of attention, its capabilities and limitations, and how to design to make the most of these abilities while minimizing its limitations.

Attention is an aspect of cognition that is particularly important in the design and operation of safety-critical interactive systems (ranging from the all too frequently quoted control room operator through to inspection tasks on mundane production lines). While there is no single agreed definition of attention, Solso (1995) defines it as 'the concentration of mental effort on sensory or mental events', which is typical of many definitions. The problem with definitions in many ways reflects how attention has been studied and what mental faculties researchers have included under the umbrella term of attention. However, the study of attention has been split between two basic forms, namely **selective attention** and **divided attention**. Selective (or focused) attention generally refers to whether or not we become aware of sensory information. Indeed, Cherry (1953) coined the term **the cocktail party effect** to illustrate this (Box 21.3).

BOX 21.3

The cocktail party effect

Cherry (1953), presumably while at a cocktail party, had noticed that we are able to focus our attention on the person we are talking to while filtering out everyone else's conversation. This principle is at the heart of the search for extra-terrestrial intelligence (SETI), which is selectively listening for alien radio signals against the background of natural radio signals.

Studies of selective attention have employed a *dichotic* listening approach. Typically, participants in such experiments are requested to shadow (repeat aloud) one of the two voices they will hear through a set of headphones. One voice will be played through the right headphone while another is played through the left – hence *dichotic*. In contrast to selective attention, divided attention recognizes that attention can be thought of in terms of mental resources (e.g. Kahneman, 1973; Pashler, 1998) that can in some sense be divided between tasks being performed simultaneously (commonly referred to as *multi-tasking*). For example, when watching television while holding a conversation, attention is being split between two tasks. Unless an individual is very well practised, the performance of two simultaneously executed tasks would be expected to be poorer than attending to just one at a time. Studies of *divided* attention might employ the same physical arrangements as above but ask the participant to attend (listen to) both voices and, say, press a button when a keyword is heard spoken in either channel.

The Stroop effect

Stroop (1935) showed that if a colour word such as 'green' is written in a conflicting colour such as red, people find it remarkably difficult to name the colour the word is written in. The reason is that reading is an automatic process which conflicts with the task of naming the colour of the 'ink' a word is written in. The Stroop effect has also been shown to apply to suitably organized numbers and words.

Try saying aloud the colour of the text – not the word itself:

Column 1	*Column 2*
RED	RED
GREEN	GREEN
BLUE	**BLUE**
RED	RED
GREEN	GREEN
RED	**RED**

You should find that saying the *colour* of each word in column 1 is slower and more prone to error owing to the meaning of the word itself. The word 'red' interferes with the colour (green) it is printed in and vice versa.

How attention works

To date, there have been a number of different accounts or models of attention. The earliest date from the 1950s and are characterized by likening attention to a bottle-neck. Later theories have concentrated on an allocation model that treats attention as a resource that can be spread (or allocated) across a number of different tasks. Other views of attention have concentrated on the automatic/controlled processing divide and on sequential/parallel processing. As in most aspects of psychology, there is no single account of attention; instead there is a mosaic of complementary views.

'Bottleneck' theories of attention

We begin with Donald Broadbent's single-channel theory of attention (Broadbent, 1958). He proposed that information arriving at the senses is stored in short-term memory before being **filtered** or selected as being of interest (or being discarded), which in practice means that we attend to one particular channel and ignore others. This information (this channel) is then processed by a limited-capacity processor. On being processed, instructions may be sent to motor effectors (the muscles) to generate a response. The presence of short-term memory, acting as a temporary buffer, means that information which is not selected is not immediately discarded either. Figure 21.3 is an illustration of Broadbent's model. Broadbent realized that we might be able to attend to this information stored in the short-term memory, but switching between two different channels of information would be inefficient. (It has been observed by a number of researchers that Broadbent's thinking reflects the technology of his day, as in many ways this single-channel model of attention is similar to the conventional model of a computer's central processing unit (CPU), which also has a single channel and is a serial processing device – the *von Neumann* architecture.) This original single-channel model (sometimes referred to as a bottle-neck account of attention) was refined and developed by Broadbent's co-workers and

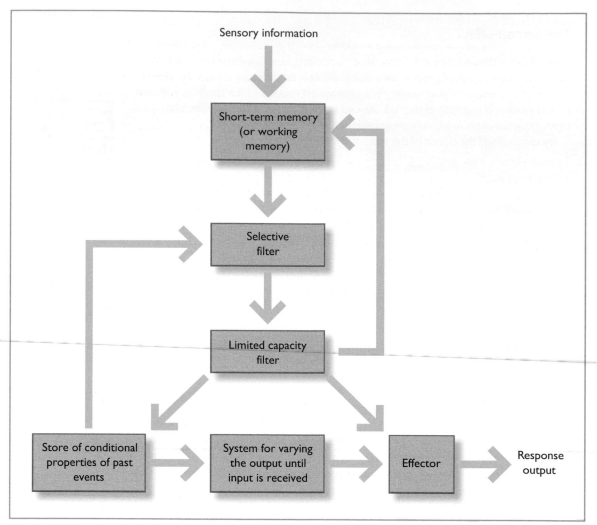

Figure 21.3 Broadbent's single-channel model of attention

others (Triesman, 1960; Deutsch and Deutsch, 1963; Norman, 1968) but remained *broadly* similar.

Triesman argued for the **attenuation** of the unattended channel, which is like turning down the volume of a signal, rather than an on–off switch. In Triesman's model, competing information is analysed for its physical properties, and for sound, syllable pattern, grammatical structure and meaning, before being attended. The later Deutsch and Deutsch (1963) and Deutsch–Norman (Norman, 1968) models completely rejected Broadbent's early selection model, instead arguing for a **later-selection** filter/**pertinence** account. Selection (or filtering) only occurs after all of the sensory inputs have been analysed. The major criticism of this family of single-channel models is their lack of flexibility, particularly in the face of a competing allocation model discussed below. It has also been questioned as to whether any single, general-purpose, limited-capacity processor can ever account for the complexity of selective attention. The reality of everyday divided attention presents even greater problems for such accounts. As we have just discussed, models of selective attention assume the existence of a limited-capacity filter capable of dealing with only one information channel at a time. However, this is at odds with both everyday experience and experimental evidence.

Attention as capacity allocation

Next, we briefly discuss an example of a group of models of attention which treat attention as a limited resource that is allocated to different processes. The best known is Kahneman's **capacity allocation** model (Kahneman, 1973). Kahneman argued that we have a limited amount of processing power at our disposal and whether or not we are able to carry out a task depends on how much of this capacity is applied to the task. Of course, some tasks require relatively little processing power and others may require more – perhaps more than we have available. This intuitively appealing account does allow us to explain how we can divide our attention across a number of tasks depending upon how demanding they are and how experienced we are in executing them. However, there are a number of other variables that affect the ways in which we allocate this attentional capacity, including our state of arousal and what Kahneman describes as enduring dispositions, momentary intentions and the evaluation of the attentional demands. Enduring dispositions are described as the rules for allocating capacity that are not under voluntary control (e.g. hearing your own name spoken), and momentary intentions are voluntary shifts in attention, such as responding to a particular signal. There is a further variable that is how aroused we are. Arousal in this context may be thought of as how awake we are. Figure 21.4 is a diagram of the capacity allocation model in which we can see the limit capacity; the central processor has been replaced by an allocation policy component that governs which of the competing demands should receive attention. While Kahneman portrays attention as being more flexible and dynamic than the single-channel models, he is unable to describe how attention is channelled or focused. Similarly, he is unable to define the limits of what is meant by 'capacity'.

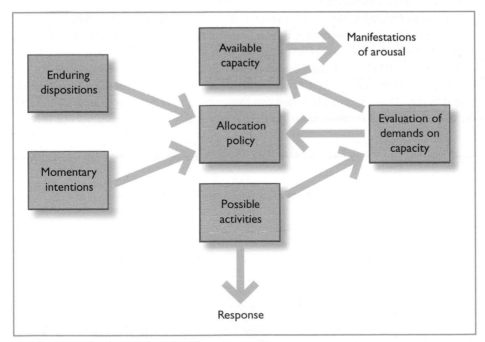

Figure 21.4 Kahneman's capacity allocation model

Automatic and controlled processing

In contrast to the foregoing models of attention, Schneider and Shiffrin (1977) observed that we are capable of both automatic and controlled information processing. We generally use **automatic processing** with tasks we find easy (and this, of course, is dependent upon our expertise in this task) but use **controlled processing** on unfamiliar and difficult tasks.

Schneider and Shiffrin distinguish between controlled and automatic processing in terms of attention as follows. Controlled processing makes heavy demands on attention and is slow, limited in capacity and involving consciously directing attention towards a task. In contrast, automatic processing makes little or no demand on attention, is fast, unaffected by capacity limitations, unavoidable and difficult to modify, and is not subject to conscious awareness.

Schneider and Shiffrin found that if people are given practice at a task, they can perform it quickly and accurately, but their performance is resistant to change. An example of apparent automaticity in real life occurs when we learn to drive a car. At first, focused attention is required for each component of driving, and any distraction can disrupt performance. Once we have learnt to drive, and as we become more experienced, our ability to attend simultaneously to other things increases.

Moving from this very brief treatment of models of attention, we now consider how a wide range of internal and external factors can affect our ability to attend.

Factors affecting attention

Of the factors that affect our ability to pay attention to a task, stress is the most important. Stress is the effect of external and psychological stimuli on us and directly affects our level of arousal. Arousal is different from attention in that it refers to a general increase or decrease in perceptual and motor activity. For example, sexual arousal is typified by heightened levels of hormonal secretions, dilation of the pupils, increased blood flow and a whole range of mating behaviours.

Stressors (stimuli which cause stress) include such things as noise, light, vibration (e.g. flying through turbulence) and more psychological factors such as anxiety, fatigue, anger, threat, lack of sleep and fear (e.g. think about the days before an examination). As long ago as 1908, Yerkes and Dodson found a relationship between performance of tasks and level of arousal. Figure 21.5 is an illustration of this relationship – the so-called Yerkes–Dodson law. There are two things to note about this relationship. First, for both simple and complex tasks there is an optimal level of arousal. As our level of

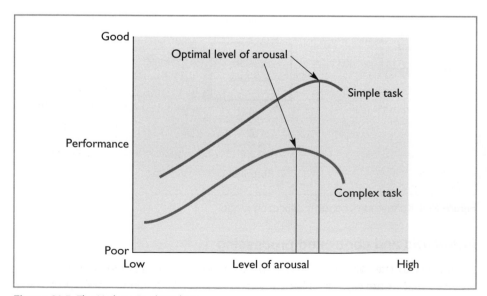

Figure 21.5 The Yerkes–Dodson law

arousal increases, our ability to execute a task increases until we reach a point when we are too aroused and our performance falls off sharply. Secondly, simple tasks are more resistant to increased levels of arousal than are complex tasks. The other aspect of this is the skill of the individual involved. A simple task to a highly skilled individual is likely to be seen as complex by a less skilled or able individual.

→ Arousal is also important to the study of emotion, described in Chapter 22

Vigilance

Vigilance is a term applied to the execution of a task wherein an individual is required to monitor an instrument or situation for a signal. Perhaps the classic example of a vigilance task is being on watch on board a ship. During the Second World War mariners were required to be vigilant in scanning the horizon for enemy ships, submarines, aircraft or icefloes. Wartime aside, vigilance is still an important element of many jobs – consider the role of the operator of a luggage X-ray machine at an airport, or a safety inspector checking for cracks or loose fittings on a railway track.

Attention drivers!

Wikman *et al.* (1998) have reported differences in the performance of inexperienced (novice) and experienced drivers when given a secondary task to perform while driving. The drivers were asked to do such things as changing a CD, operating the car radio or using a mobile (cell) phone. Unsurprisingly, the novice drivers were distracted more (allocated their attention less effectively) than the experienced drivers. Experienced drivers took their eyes off the road for less than three seconds, while novice drivers were found to weave across the road.

BOX 21.5

In-car systems

The use of spoken messages in-car, particularly for satellite navigation (satnav) systems, is now becoming commonplace. The challenge for the designers of these systems is

(a) to attract the attention of the driver without distracting him or her, and
(b) to avoid habituation – that is, the driver learning to ignore the nagging voice.

The choice of voice is also critical. Honda have decided upon 'Midori' – the name given to the voice of an unnamed bilingual Japanese actress whose voice is 'smooth as liqueur'. In contrast, Italian Range Rovers are equipped with a voice which is argumentative in tone, and Jaguar (the English motor manufacturer) retains British colloquialisms to reinforce their brand image. These brand images aside, manufacturers have found that drivers tend to listen to female voices more than male voices.

Other issues in in-car HCI concern the design of devices such as phones and satellite navigation systems that require complex operation and hence result in divided attention (Green, 2012).

FURTHER THOUGHTS

Mental workload

Mental workload addresses issues such as how busy the user or operator is and how difficult are the tasks assigned to him or her – will he or she be able to deal with an additional workload? A classic example of this occurred in the 1970s when it was decided to remove the third crew member from a flight team on board a medium to large passenger jet. The Federal Aviation Administration now requires measures of the mental workload on the crew prior to the certification of a new aircraft or new control system.

Turning now to design issues in respect of mental workload, the first observation is that a discussion of mental workload does not necessarily equate workload with overload. Indeed, the reverse is often true: just consider the potential consequences of operator/user boredom and fatigue (Wickens and Hollands, 2000, p. 470). There are a number of different ways in which workload can be estimated, one of which is the NASA TLX scale. This scale (Table 21.2) is a subjective rating procedure that provides an overall workload score based on a weighted average of ratings on six sub-scales.

Table 21.2 Measuring workload

Title	Endpoints	Description
Mental demand	Low/end	How much mental and perceptual activity was required (e.g. thinking, deciding, etc.)? Was the task easy or demanding, simple or complex?
Physical demand	Low/high	How much physical effort was required (e.g. pushing, pulling, etc.)? Was the task easy or demanding, slack or strenuous, restful or laborious?
Temporal demand	Low/high	How much time pressure did you feel due to the rate or pace at which the tasks or task elements occurred? Was the pace slow and leisurely or rapid and frantic?
Performance	Perfect/failure	How successful do you think you were in accomplishing the goals of the task set by the experimenter (or yourself)? How satisfied were you with your performance in accomplishing these goals?
Effort	Low/high	How hard did you have to work (mentally and physically) to accomplish your level of performance?
Frustration level	Low/high	How insecure, discouraged, irritated, stressed and annoyed as opposed to secure, gratified, content, relaxed and complacent did you feel during your task?

Source: Wickens, Christopher D.; Hollands, Justin G., *Engineering Psychology and Human Performance, 3rd*, © 2000. Printed and Electronically reproduced by permission of Pearson Education, Inc., Upper Saddle River, New Jersey.

Visual search

Visual search has been researched extensively by psychologists and ergonomists and refers to our ability to locate particular items in a visual scene. Participants in a visual search study, for example, may be required to locate a single letter in a block of miscellaneous characters. Try to find the letter 'F' in the matrix in Figure 21.6.

This is a good example of how perception and attention overlap and an understanding of the issues involved in visual search can help in avoiding interactive systems such as that shown in Figure 21.7.

Research has revealed that there is no consistent visual search pattern which can be predicted in advance. Visual search cannot be presumed to be left to right, or clockwise rather than anti-clockwise, except to say that searching tends to be directed towards where the target is expected to be. However, visual attention will be drawn towards features which are large and bright and changing (e.g. flashing, which may be used for warnings). These visual features can be used to direct attention, particularly if they have a sudden onset (i.e. a light being switched on, or a car horn sounding). Megaw and Richardson (1979) found that physical organization can also have an effect on search patterns. Displays or dials organized in rows tended to be scanned from left to right (just as in reading Western languages, but raising the question of cultural bias – would the same be true for those cultures who read from right to left or from top to bottom?). Parasuraman (1986) has reported evidence of an **edge effect** wherein during supervisory tasks (that is, the routine scanning of dials and displays) operators tended to concentrate on the centre of the display panel and tended to ignore the periphery. As Wickens and Hollands (2000) note, research into visual scanning behaviour has yielded two broad conclusions. First, visual scanning reveals much about the internal expectancies that drive selective attention. Secondly, these insights are probably most useful in the area of diagnostics. Clearly those instruments which are most frequently watched are likely to be the most important to an operator's task. This should guide design decisions to place the instruments in prominent locations or to locate them adjacent to one another.

E	E	E	E	E	E	E	E
E	E	E	E	E	E	E	E
E	E	E	E	E	E	E	E
E	E	E	E	E	E	E	E
E	E	E	E	E	E	E	E
E	E	E	E	E	E	E	E
E	E	E	E	E	E	F	E
E	E	E	E	E	E	E	E

Figure 21.6 A matrix of letters

Figure 21.7 A practical example of the challenge of visual search
(Source: www.HavenWorks.com)

BOX
21.6

Just how long is it reasonable to wait?

It is generally accepted that delays of less than 0.1 second are taken to be effectively instantaneous, but delays of a second or two may be perceived by the user of an interactive system as being an interruption in the free flow of his or her interaction. Delays of more than 10 seconds present problems for people. Minimizing delay is important in the design of websites for which numerous, often contradictory, guidelines have been published. Here are two perfectly reasonable suggestions:

● The top of your page should be meaningful and fast.
● Simplify complex tables as they display more slowly.

Signal detection theory

It is late at night. You are asleep alone in your apartment. You are awoken by a noise. What do you do? For many people the first thing to do is to wait and see (as it were) whether they hear the noise again. Here we are in the domain of **signal detection theory** – was there really a signal (e.g. the sound of breaking glass by the local axe-murderer) and if so, are we to act on it – or was it just the wind or a cat in the dustbin? Signal detection theory (SDT) is applicable in any situation in which there are two different, non-overlapping states (i.e. signal and noise) that cannot be easily discriminated – that is, for example, did a signal appear on the radar screen, did it move, has it changed size or shape? In such situations we are concerned with signals which must be detected, and in the process one of two responses may be produced – e.g. 'I detected the presence of a signal, so I shall press the stop button', or 'I failed to see anything, so I shall continue to watch'. This may vary in importance from the trivial, e.g. recognizing that a job has been printed (the printer icon has disappeared from the application's status bar), through to the safety-critical, e.g. a train driver spotting (or not) a stop light.

The following compelling examples of the importance of SDT have been identified by Wickens and Hollands (2000): the detection of a concealed weapon by an airport security guard; the identification of a malignant tumour on an X-ray plate by a radiologist; and a system malfunction detected by a nuclear plant supervisor. Their list goes on to include identifying critical incidents in the context of air traffic control, proofreading, detecting lies from a polygraph (lie detector) and spotting hairline cracks in aircraft wings, amongst other things. SDT recognizes that an individual faced with such a situation can respond in one of four ways: in the presence of a signal, the operator may detect it (hit) or fail to detect it (miss); in the absence of a signal, the operator may correctly reject it (correct rejection) or incorrectly identify it (false alarm). This is illustrated in Table 21.3.

Table 21.3 SDT decision table

Response	State	
	Signal	*Noise*
Yes	Hit	False alarm
No	Miss	Correct rejection

The probability of each response is typically calculated for a given situation and these figures are often quoted for both people and machines. So, a navigational aid on board an aircraft (e.g. ground collision radar) might be quoted as producing false alarms (also called false positives) at a rate of less than 0.001 – one in a thousand. Similar figures are quoted as targets for medical screening operators (e.g. no more than 1 in 10,000 real instances of, say, breast cancer should be missed while 1 in 1000 false alarms are acceptable).

Transcript from Apollo XIII: barber-poles and the Moon

The Apollo flights to the Moon in the late 1960s and early 1970s are excellent examples of both user-centred design and brilliant and innovative ergonomic design. One of the innovations can be found in the design of the Apollo spacecraft which used barber-poles to provide status information to the astronauts. A barber-pole is a striped bar signalling that a particular circuit or function is active (for example, the communication system – the talkback system), or, as can be seen in the transcript below, measures of liquid helium and the state of the electrical systems. In the transcript we see that Jim Lovell reports to Mission Control that main bus *'B is barber poled and D is barber poled, helium 2, D is barber pole'*:

55:55:35 – Lovell: *'Houston, we've had a problem. We've had a main B bus undervolt.'*
55:55:20 – Swigert: *'Okay, Houston, we've had a problem here.'*

. . .

55:57:40 – DC main bus B drops below 26.25 volts and continues to fall rapidly.
55:57:44 – Lovell: *'Okay. And we're looking at our service module RCS helium 1. We have – B is barber poled and D is barber poled, helium 2, D is barber pole, and secondary propellants, I have A and C barber pole.'* AC bus fails within 2 seconds.

Interestingly, the use of a barber-pole can be found in modern operating systems. For example, the OS X system uses barber-poles (Figure 21.8).

Figure 21.8 Barber-pole, OS X

21.4 Human error

Human error is studied in a wide variety of ways. Some researchers conduct laboratory investigations while others investigate the causes of major accidents after the event. A typical example of a laboratory study is that by Hull *et al.* (1988) who asked 24 ordinary men and women to wire an electric plug. They found that only 5 succeeded in doing so safely, despite the fact that 23 of the 24 had wired a plug in the previous 12 months. In analysing the results of this study it was found that a number of different factors contributed to these failures, including:

← Chapter 2 discusses mental models

- Failure to read the instructions
- Inability to formulate an appropriate mental model
- Failure of the plug designers to provide clear physical constraints on erroneous actions. This last point was regarded as the most significant.

Unhappily, error is an inescapable fact of life. Analysis of the causes of major accidents has found that human error is primarily responsible in 60–90 per cent of all major accidents (Rouse and Rouse, 1983; Reason, 1997). This figure is consistent with the findings of commercial organizations: for example, Boeing, the aircraft manufacturer, estimate that 70 per cent of all 'commercial airplane hull-loss accidents' are attributable to human error.

Understanding action slips

Research conducted by Reason (1992) has given insight into everyday errors. In one study he asked 36 people to keep a diary of action slips (i.e. actions which have deviated from what they intended) for a period of four weeks. Analysis of the reported 433 slips revealed that storage failures (e.g repeating an action which has already been completed) were the most frequently reported. Figure 21.9 summarizes the key findings of this study and Table 21.4 describes each type of action slip (the miscellaneous errors are too diverse to discuss).

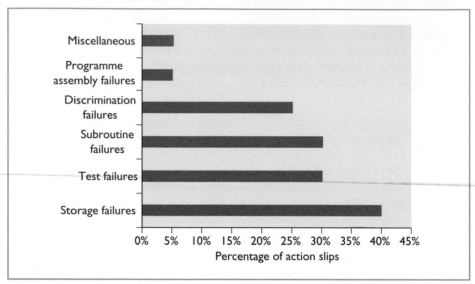

Figure 21.9 Five categories of action slips

(Source: After Reason, 1992, Fig. 15.24)

Table 21.4 Action slips

Type of action slip	Description
Storage failures	These were the most common and involved errors such as repeating an action which has already been completed, e.g. sending the same e-mail twice.
Test failures	These refer to forgetting what the goal of the action was, owing to failing to monitor the execution of a series of actions, e.g. starting to compose an e-mail and then forgetting to whom you are sending it.
Subroutine failures	These errors were due to omitting a step in the sequence of executing an action, e.g. sending an e-mail and forgetting to attach the attachment.
Discrimination failures	Failure to discriminate between two similar objects used in the execution of an action resulted in this category of error, e.g. intending to send an e-mail and starting Word instead by mistake.
Programme assembly failures	This was the smallest category, accounting for only 5 per cent of the total. They involved incorrectly combining actions, e.g. saving the e-mail and deleting the attachment instead of saving the attachment and deleting the e-mail.

Each of these slips (and there are other classifications of errors, e.g. Smith *et al.* (2012)) presents challenges for the interactive systems designer. Some can be reduced or managed, others cannot.

Reducing action slips

Designers should design to minimize the chance of slips. For example, 'wizards' prompt people for, and help them recall, the steps which need to be undertaken to complete a task, such as installing a printer. In the image of the sequence in Figure 21.10 the system prompts to obtain information to allow the operating system to install a printer. The advantage of this approach is that only relatively small amounts of information are required at any one time. It also has the advantage of an error correction system (i.e. use of the *Back* and *Next* steps).

Figure 21.10 Using a Microsoft wizard to prompt a user to supply information one step at a time

One of the most demanding tasks in the work of an academic is marking course-work and examination scripts and tabulating the results without making mistakes. Figure 21.11 is a snapshot of a spreadsheet designed by Professor Jon Kerridge of the School of Computing, Edinburgh Napier University, to help reduce errors in this process. It is an example of good practice in this kind of manual tabulation of data as it employs a number of semi-automated checks (with corresponding error messages): in the column labelled *Checked* is a *note* indicating that an error message will appear if 'either the mark inserted for a question is more than the maximum mark obtainable for that question or . . . '. The author of the system has annotated the spreadsheet using *comments* and has used a series of *if statements* to check the inputted data. So, for example, marks should be entered for three questions only and an error is signalled if this number is exceeded.

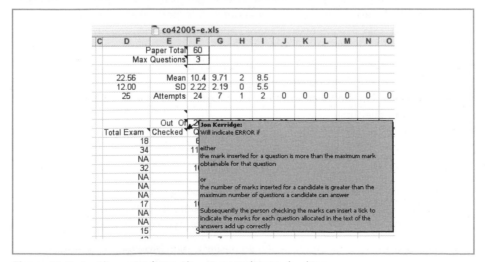

Figure 21.11 Avoiding mistakes with automated error checking

(Source: Courtesy of Jon Kerridge)

Challenge 21.3

What is wrong with the error message in Figure 21.12? How would you reword it?

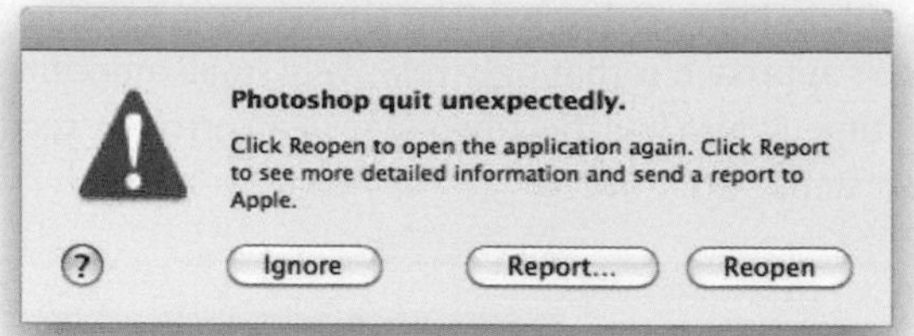

Photoshop quit unexpectedly.

Click Reopen to open the application again. Click Report to see more detailed information and send a report to Apple.

(?)   (Ignore)   (Report...)   (Reopen)

Figure 21.12 An unexpected error message

Summary and key points

We have seen that memory is divided into a number of different stores, each of different size, make-up and purpose. Information arriving at the senses is held very briefly in the *sensory stores* before moving on to *working memory*. Working memory (the modern equivalent of short-term memory) holds three or four items for up to 30 seconds unless *rehearsed*. Information may subsequently be stored in the *long-term memory* store with additional processing. The contents of long-term memory last a long time (minutes, hours, days, even years) and are held in several different types of memory, including memory for skills (*procedural memory*), *semantic memory* which holds the meaning of words, facts and knowledge generally, *autobiographical memory* which holds our personal experiences, and finally *perma-store* which holds information which literally may last a lifetime.

In terms of design these limitations and capabilities translate into two important principles: the need to *chunk* material to reduce the load on working memory; the importance of designing for *recognition* rather than *recall*.

Attention can be thought of in terms of being *divided or selective*. Divided attention refers to our ability to carry out more than one task at a time, though our ability to carry out multiple tasks also depends upon our skill (expertise) and the difficulty of the task. In contrast, selective attention is more concerned with focusing on particular tasks or things in the environment. It should come as no surprise that we make errors while using interactive devices. These errors have been classified and described by a range of researchers, *storage failures* being the most common. While all errors cannot be prevented, measures can be taken to minimize them, using devices such as *wizards* and automated error checking.

Exercises

1 As wizards can be used to prevent action slips being made, does it make good sense to use them for all dialogues with the system or application? When would you *not* use an error-preventing dialogue style such as wizards?

2 Compare and contrast how you would design a Web browser for recall as compared to one for recognition. What are the key differences?

3 (Advanced) – You are responsible for designing the control panel for a nuclear reactor. Operators have to monitor numerous alerts, alarms and readings which (thankfully) indicate normal operating conditions almost all the time. If and when an abnormal state is indicated, the operator must take remedial action immediately. Discuss how you would design the control panel to take into account the qualities of human attention.

4 (Advanced) – How far (if at all) does psychological research into the mechanisms of human memory support the effective design of interactive systems? Give concrete examples.

 ## Further reading

Reason, J. (1990) *Human Error.* Cambridge University Press, Cambridge. *Perhaps a little dated now but a highly readable introduction to the study of error.*

Wickens, C.D. and Hollands, J.G. (2000) *Engineering Psychology and Human Performance,* **3rd edn**. Prentice-Hall, Upper Saddle River, NJ. *One of the definitive texts on engineering psychology.*

Getting ahead

Baddeley, A. (1997) *Human Memory: Theory and Practice*. Psychology Press, Hove, Sussex. *An excellent introduction to human memory.*

Ericsson, K.A. and Smith, J. (eds) (1991) *Towards a General Theory of Expertise*. Cambridge University Press, Cambridge. *This is an interesting collection of chapters written by experts in expertise.*

 ## Web links

The accompanying website has links to relevant websites. Go to
www.pearsoned.co.uk/benyon

 ## Comments on challenges

Challenge 21.1
The most difficult of these to describe is usually the procedural knowledge of how to ride a bicycle. Most people find the other two aspects reasonably easy. Procedural knowledge is notoriously difficult to articulate – hence the advisability of having users *show* you how they perform particular tasks rather than try to *tell* you.

Challenge 21.2
The plot should resemble Figure 21.13. Words presented first, second, third,... are recalled well, as are the last four or five words. The twin peaks represent recall from long-term (*primacy*) and working memory (*recency*), respectively. This is a well-known effect and explains why, when asking directions or instructions, we tend to remember the beginning and end but are very vague about what was said in the middle.

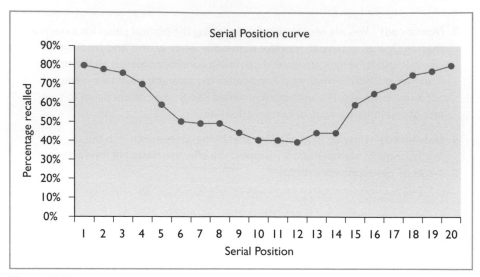

Figure 21.13

Challenge 21.3

This error message violates a number of good practice guidelines. 'Critical' sounds scary. 'Can't start program' is not helpful – what is the user supposed to do next? How does the user avoid the error in the future? See the guidelines above. Perhaps a better form of wording might be 'System problem encountered. Please restart application'.

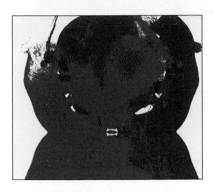

Chapter 22
Affect

Contents

Aims

In a special issue of an academic journal devoted to affective computing, Rosalind Picard quotes a MORI survey that found three-quarters of people using computers admit to swearing at them (Picard, 2003). This chapter focuses on the role of emotions (often termed **affect** in this context) in interactive systems design. We first introduce theories of human emotion and demonstrate their application in technologies that respond to emotion, or can generate 'emotions' themselves.

After studying this chapter you should be able to describe:

- The physical and cognitive accounts (models) of emotion
- The potential for **affective computing** in interactive systems design
- Applications of affective computing
- Sensing and recognizing human affective/emotional signals and understanding affective behaviour
- Synthesizing emotional responses in interactive devices.

22.1   Introduction

Affect is concerned with describing the whole range of emotions, feelings, moods, sentiment and other aspects of people that might be considered non-cognitive (not aiming to describe how we come to know and understand things) and non-conative (not aiming to describe intention and volition). Of course, affect interacts with the cognitive and conative in complex ways. In particular, a person's level of arousal and stress impacts on what they know, what they can remember, what they are attending to, how good they are at doing something and what they want to do!

There are basic emotions such as fear, anger and surprise (discussed further below) and there are longer-term emotions such as love or jealousy that may be built up over years. People can be in different moods at different times. Moods tend to be longer lasting and slower to develop than emotions. Affect interacts with both cognitive and conative aspects of people. For example, if you are afraid of something it will affect the attention you pay to it. If you are in a positive frame of mind, it might affect how you perceive some event. If an event has a strong emotional impact, you are more likely to remember it.

Affective computing concerns how computing devices can deal with emotions. There are three basic aspects to consider: getting interactive systems to recognize human emotions and adapt accordingly; getting interactive systems to synthesize emotions and hence to appear more engaging or desirable; designing systems that elicit an emotional response from people or that allow people to express emotions.

A good example of getting computers to recognize human emotions and react accordingly might be the use of a sensor in a motor car to detect whether or not the driver is angry or stressed. Sensors could be used to pick up on the fact that the driver is perspiring, is holding the steering wheel in a vice-like grip or has elevated blood pressure or heart rate. These are physiological signs of arousal. As statistics show that stress and anger are major contributory factors in road accidents, the car may then offer counselling, refuse to start (or something equally infuriating) or phone ahead to the emergency services. Another couple of examples, suggested by Picard and Healey (1997), are (a) the creation of an intelligent Web browser which responds to the wearer's degree of interest in a topic that the wearer found interesting, until it detected the interest fading, and (b) an affective assistant agent that could intelligently filter your e-mail or schedule, taking into account your emotional state or degree of activity.

Synthesizing emotion is concerned with giving the impression of computers behaving or reacting with emotion. Here an example might be a machine showing signs of distress when a system crash has just destroyed several hours' work. The notion permeates much science fiction. A classic instance here is HAL, the onboard computer on the spaceship in Arthur C. Clarke's novel *2001: A Space Odyssey* (Clarke, 1968). In Stanley Kubrick's film version HAL's voice eloquently expresses fear as Dave, the astronaut, considers switching 'him' off. HAL's 'death' is agonizingly slow and piteous:

> *'Dave, stop. Stop, will you? Stop, Dave. Will you stop, Dave? Stop, Dave. I'm afraid. I'm afraid, Dave. Dave, my mind is going. I can feel it. I can feel it. My mind is going. There is no question about it. I can feel it. I can feel it. I can feel it. I'm afraid.'*

In the film the dialogue is particularly poignant when contrasted with the unchanging expression of HAL's 'eye'.

Designing interactive systems that communicate or evoke human emotions is another key aspect of affective computing. Designing for pleasure is one aspect of this – and commercially crucial for small consumer devices such as phones – but others include devices which allow people to communicate affect at a distance, and the creation of virtual environments which support the treatment of phobias or attempt to evoke the feelings associated with particular places.

← Chapter 5 covers designing for pleasure

Whether or not computers could ever actually feel emotion is beyond this discussion, but science fiction novels such as *Do Androids Dream of Electric Sheep?* by Philip K. Dick (1968) offer interesting discussions of such themes. At first sight, the idea of 'giving' computers emotion seems to be counter-intuitive. Computers are the epitome of logic and the idea of acting emotionally has strong negative connotations – just think of *Star Trek's* Mr Spock, or the android Data. There is no denying that emotion (affect) has traditionally had a bad press.

The other side of the argument is the recognition that emotions are part of day-to-day human functioning. Emotion plays a significant part in decision making, social interaction and most aspects of what we would describe as cognition, such as problem solving, thinking and perception.

Increasingly, these human activities and functions are supported by interactive systems, so an understanding of how emotion works can help us design systems that recognize, synthesize or evoke emotions. Or computers with affective capabilities might be more effective than conventional technology in making decisions with incomplete data – circumstances where affect helps human beings to respond quickly. Needless to say, we must now turn to what psychologists have concluded over the years. Be warned that the research findings are less well agreed than many other aspects of human behaviour.

Challenge 22.1

Is it ethical to attempt to manipulate people's emotions through technology? Do new technologies differ from older media such as films in this respect?

22.2 Psychological theories of emotion

What are the basic human emotions? Ekman *et al.* (1972) are widely quoted researchers who identified six basic emotions, namely, fear, surprise, disgust, anger, happiness and sadness. These are generally regarded as being universal – that is, recognized and expressed (facially at least) in the same way in all cultures. Ekman and Friesen (1978) went on to develop the 'facial action coding system' (FACS) which uses facial muscle movements to quantify emotions; an automated version of FACS has also been produced (Bartlett *et al.*, 1999). FACS is still the most widely used method of detecting emotion from facial expression.

Similar work has been undertaken by Plutchik (1980) who has argued for eight pairs of basic or primary emotions that can be combined to produce secondary emotions. In Figure 22.1 we can see that disgust and sadness combine to give the experience of remorse.

But what do we mean by basic or primary emotions? For Ekman this means that they have adaptive value (that is, they have evolved for some purpose), they are, as we have already said, common to everyone irrespective of culture and individual differences,

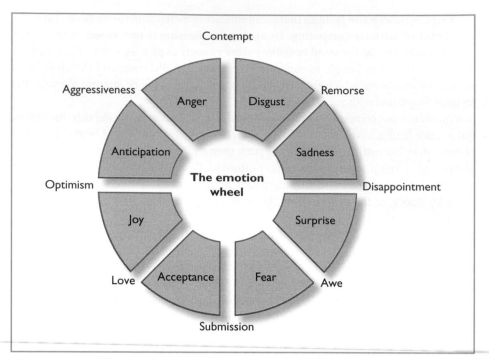

Figure 22.1 The 'emotion wheel'

(Source: After Plutchik, Robert, *Emotion: A Psychoevolutionary Synthesis, 1st,* © 1979. Printed and Electronically reproduced by permission of Pearson Education, Inc., Upper Saddle River, New Jersey.)

and finally, they all have a quick onset – that is, they appear or start quickly. There is indeed some evidence of different patterns of activity in the ANS (the autonomic nervous system, which links organs such as the heart and stomach to the central nervous system embodied in the brain and spinal cord) for some of the basic emotions. Clearly it would be useful for the designers of affective systems if there is indeed a relatively small number of basic emotions to recognize or simulate.

However, the idea of basic emotions has been challenged, largely because of methodological issues. The main flaw, it is argued, is that the experiments of Ekman and others required participants to make a 'forced choice' between the eight emotions when identifying facial expressions rather than having a completely free choice of emotion terms. Instead of the eight emotions model, Russell and his colleagues propose that variations in just two dimensions – greater or lesser degrees of pleasure (or 'valence') and arousal – can describe the range of affective facial expressions (Russell and Fernandez-Dols, 1997). For example, 'happy' and 'content' lie at the pleasure end of the pleasure/displeasure dimension and entail slightly positive and slightly negative degrees of arousal respectively.

Both the Ekman and Russell approaches continue to be used in affective computing research and development. In particular, the Russell wheel lays out a large number of emotions in the two-dimensional space described by an *x*-axis of valence and a *y*-axis of arousal.

It is generally agreed that emotions have three components:

- The *subjective experience* or feelings of fear and so on.
- The associated *physiological changes* in the ANS and the endocrine system (glands and the hormones released by them). We are aware of some but not all of these (e.g trembling with fear) and have little or no conscious control of them.
- The *behaviour* evoked, such as running away.

Virtual environments

Consideration of these three aspects of emotions can be seen in the evaluation of virtual environments, as discussed in Chapter 10. Researchers evaluating the impact of a 'precipice' in the virtual environment might capture data on people's reported experience through questionnaires and interviews, their physiological changes through various sensors, and behaviour through observation. In convincing virtual environments, reports of fear, increases in heart rate and retreat from the 'precipice' have all been found. In this context the self-report measures are often termed 'subjective', and behavioural and physiological measures 'objective'. However, as we shall see from this chapter, the so-called objective measures require a degree of interpretation by researchers, thereby introducing a substantial degree of subjectivity.

Beyond the simple cataloguing of emotion and its components are the various attempts to account for them. This, until relatively recently, was the province of philosophers until the early psychologists decided to try their hands at it. Probably the first of these were James and Lange.

The James–Lange theory

This theory, which dates from the 1890s, argues that action precedes emotions and the brain interprets the observed action or actions as emotions. So, for example, we see an axe-wielding maniac walking towards us: in response our pulse rate rises, we begin to sweat and we quicken our step – we run for our lives. These changes in the state of our body (increased pulse, sweating and running) are then interpreted as fear. Thus from interpreting the state of our bodies we conclude that we must be afraid.

This is summarized in Figure 22.2 but is obviously a rather crude model. What bodily state, for example, corresponds to the emotional state 'mildly disappointed but amused'?

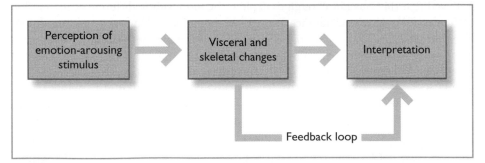

Figure 22.2 The James–Lange theory of emotion

The Cannon–Bard theory

Two psychologists working in the 1920s, Cannon and Bard, disagreed with the James–Lange theory and argued that when an emotion-arousing stimulus is first perceived, actions follow from cognitive appraisal. They also noted that the same visceral changes occur in a range of different emotions. In their view, the thalamus (a complex structure in the brain) plays a central role by interpreting an emotional situation while simultaneously sending signals to the autonomic nervous system (ANS) and to the cortex that interprets the situation. The ANS is responsible for the regulation of unconscious functions like heart rate and the secretion of hormones such as adrenaline. This is shown in Figure 22.3.

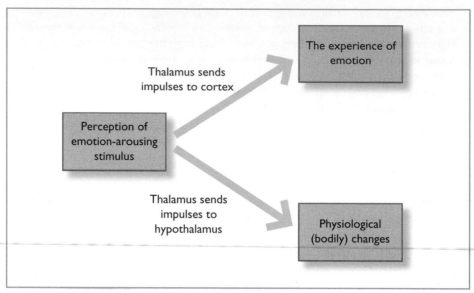

Figure 22.3 The Cannon–Bard theory

Cognitive labelling and appraisal theories: Schachter–Singer and Lazarus

On a more contemporary note, Schachter and Singer conducted a series of experiments in the 1960s, basically working along the same lines as James and Lange. However, Schachter and Singer favoured the idea that the experience of emotions arises from the **cognitive labelling** of physiological sensation. However, they also believed that this was not enough to explain the more subtle differences in emotion self-perception, i.e. the difference between anger and fear. Thus, they proposed that, once the physiological symptoms or arousal have been experienced, an individual will gather information from the immediate context and use it to modify the label they attach to the sensation. Figure 22.4 is an illustration of the Schachter and Singer model of emotion.

In a series of classic experimental studies they tested these ideas. The most famous of their studies was the adrenaline experiment (Schachter and Singer, 1962). In this experiment they told the participants that they would receive an injection of a vitamin (adrenaline is not a vitamin) and then test to see whether it had affected their vision. They also divided the participants into four groups:

Group A   These people were given accurate information as to the effect of the 'vitamin', that is, sweating, tremor, feeling jittery.

Group B   They were given false information as to the effect of the 'vitamin', namely, itching and headaches.

Group C   These people were told nothing.

Group D   This group served as a control and were actually injected with saline (which has no side effects) and were also told nothing.

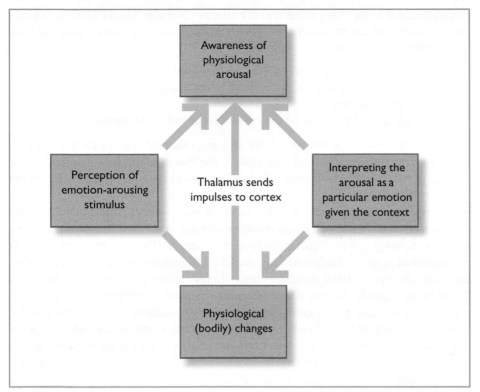

Figure 22.4 The Schachter–Singer theory

Before the (fake) vision test, the experimenters exposed everyone to an emotion-arousing stimulus that in practice was invoked by a stooge – a laughing, happy individual who fooled around or an angry, bad-tempered person who was seen to rip up a questionnaire. The participants were then asked to rate to what degree they had joined in with the stooge's behaviour and to report on how they felt. As expected, groups A and D said that they felt less likely to join in, while groups B and C said that they shared the stooge's apparent emotional state.

There have been several criticisms and qualifications of the theory arising from later research:

- The situation in the experiment is atypical, in that there is usually much less ambiguity about what is happening.
- We base our labelling of the emotion not just on the behaviour of others, but on our own past experiences and many other sources of information.
- Unexplained emotional arousal tends to be experienced as negative – for example, a vague sense of unease – thus indicating that the nature of emotional experience is not entirely determined by cognitive labelling.

Cognitive labelling theory has been developed further by Lazarus (1982), who proposed the notion of **cognitive appraisal**. According to cognitive appraisal theory, some degree of evaluation of the situation (appraising the situation) always precedes the affective reaction, although this can be unconscious and does not prevent the immediacy of the sensation. Zajonc (1984), however, argues that some emotional responses do precede any cognitive processing.

In conclusion, it is generally believed that some cognitive evaluation, or appraisal, occurs in the experience of emotion, but there is no overall agreement about the relative dominance and order of cognition and the affective reaction. Sherer (2005) proposes that appraisal consists of four checks that are carried out by people in assessing their environment. They consider:

- The relevance and implication of events for their well-being
- The relevance and implication of events for long-term goals
- How well they can cope with the situation
- The significance of the event for their self-concept and social norms.

Emotion is defined as the changes in the ANS and other subsystems such as the central nervous system. For our work as designers, the 'take-home message' is that it is not enough to induce emotional arousal, but the context of the arousal must support the identification of the particular emotion that it is intended to evoke.

As a concrete instance of this, we return to the design issues for virtual environments. Many experiments have shown that events or features in the environment can engender some sensation of anticipation, or fear, or whatever. However, those feelings can be attenuated or labelled differently because of the knowledge that one is experiencing the world through an HMD (head-mounted display) within a laboratory. Moreover, it is (we hope) unlikely that one's colleagues have created a situation that is genuinely dangerous. Computer games minimize this problem by creating a strong narrative (or story) and a good deal of interaction, both of which help to reduce the influence of the real world beyond the virtual one. It is necessary to use similar stratagems in the design of virtual worlds intended to evoke an emotional response, whether this is for entertainment, therapy, training or some other purpose.

BOX 22.2

The EMMA project

In the EU-funded EMMA project researchers were investigating the relationship between presence (the sense of 'being there') and emotions. EMMA uses tools such as virtual reality, intelligent agents, augmented reality and wireless devices to provide ways of coping with distressing emotions for users, including people with psychological problems. Emotions are stimulated through engagement with a virtual park, which changes in accordance with the emotion involved. Figure 22.5 shows the winter view of the park, designed to evoke sadness.

Figure 22.5 The 'sad' park development in the EMMA project

(Source: www.psychology. org/The%20EMMA%20 Project.htm. Courtesy of Mariano Alcañiz)

Source: http://cordis.europa.eu/search/index.cfm?fuseaction-proj.document&PJ_RCN-5874162

Challenge 22.2

Use Sherer's four checks to evaluate your response to someone leaping out at you and shouting 'boo!' very loudly.

22.3 Detecting and recognizing emotions

If technologies are to act upon human emotions, the first step is to recognize different affective states. As we have already seen from the psychology of emotion, human emotional states have physiological, cognitive and behavioural components. Behavioural and (some) physiological changes are, of course, most apparent to the outside world, unless we deliberately choose to disguise our feelings. Some signs of our affective state are more easily detected than others, however, as shown in Table 22.1. But while some of the physiological changes are obscure to other people, unless they are extremely physically close or have special monitoring equipment, they are virtually all accessible to a computer armed with the appropriate sensors.

However, detecting changes and attributing them to the correct emotion are two radically different problems. The second is much more intractable than the first, and one which causes much misunderstanding between people as well as potentially between people and machines. This area is also known as social signal processing. A good source of material on this is at http://sspnet.eu.

What if boredom couldn't be disguised?

BOX 22.3

We are, of course, capable of disguising the more overt symptoms of socially unacceptable emotions. Writing in the *Observer* newspaper of 7 September 2003, the columnist Victoria Coren speculates thus: 'What if (just as you blush when you're embarrassed or shiver when you're cold) you automatically removed your trousers when you were bored? The world of polite feigned interest would be dead and gone. You could smile all you liked as the boss made small talk – but no use, the trousers would be off. Everyone would have to try harder and waffle less. As things stand, boredom is too easily disguised, but we have tamed our wilder instincts.'

Table 22.1 Forms of sentic modulation

Apparent to other people	Less apparent to other people
Facial expression	Respiration
Voice intonation	Heart rate, pulse
Gesture, movement	Temperature
Posture	Electrodermal response, perspiration
Pupillary dilation	Muscle action potentials
	Blood pressure

Source: Adapted from Picard, Rosalind W. *Affective Computing*, Table 1.1, © 1997 Massachusetts Institute of Technology, by permission of The MIT Press

Basic capabilities for recognizing emotion

Technologies that successfully recognize emotion need to draw upon techniques such as pattern recognition and are likely to need to be trained to individual people – as for voice input technologies. The list below is reproduced from Picard (1997, p. 55) and sets out what capabilities a computer requires to be able to discriminate emotions.

- *Input*. Receiving a variety of input signals, for example face, hand gestures, posture and gait, respiration, electrothermal response, temperature, electrocardiogram, blood pressure, blood volume, and electromyogram (a test that measures the activity of the muscles).
- *Pattern recognition*. Performs feature extraction and classification on these signals. For example, analyzes video motion features to discriminate a frown from a smile.
- *Reasoning*. Predicts underlying emotion based on knowledge about how emotions are generated and expressed. This reasoning would require the system to reason about the context of the emotion and a wide knowledge of social psychology.
- *Learning*. As the computer 'gets to know' someone, it learns which of the above factors are most important for that individual, and gets quicker and better at recognizing his or her emotions.
- *Bias*. The emotional state of the computer, if it has emotions, influences its recognition of ambiguous emotions.
- *Output*. The computer names (or describes) the recognized expressions and the likely underlying emotion.

Progress has been made on many of these dimensions. Sensors and software that detect physiological changes such as heart rate, skin conductivity and so forth have long been available. However, there are practical issues with relying on this sort of data alone. The sensors themselves are too intrusive or awkward for most everyday uses, and the data requires expert analysis – or intelligent systems – to interpret the significance of changes. Also, individual physiological signs tend to indicate a general increase in arousal rather than specific emotions, and the same combinations of physiological signs can belong to different emotions – the signs of disgust and amusement are very similar, for example. Hence the need for the detection of other physical signs and/or pattern recognition to support computers in recognizing emotions.

BOX 22.4

StartleCam

StartleCam is a wearable video camera, computer and sensing system, which enables the camera to be controlled via both conscious and preconscious events involving the wearer. Traditionally, a wearer consciously hits 'record' on the video camera, or runs a computer script to trigger the camera according to some prespecified frequency. The system described here offers an additional option: images are saved by the system when it detects certain events of supposed interest to the wearer. The implementation described here aims to capture events that are likely to get the user's attention and to be remembered. Attention and memory are highly correlated with what psychologists call arousal level, and the latter is often signalled by skin conductivity changes; consequently, StartleCam monitors the wearer's skin conductivity. StartleCam looks for patterns indicative of a 'startle response' in the skin conductivity signal. When this response is detected, a buffer of digital images, recently captured by the wearer's digital camera, is downloaded and optionally transmitted wirelessly to a Web server. This selective storage of digital images creates a 'flashbulb' memory archive for the wearable which aims to mimic the wearer's own selective memory response. Using a startle detection filter, the StartleCam system has been demonstrated to work on several wearers in both indoor and outdoor ambulatory environments.

Source: StartleCam (1999)

Recognizing emotions in practice

Pattern recognition was exploited in work by Picard and her team which was designed to explore whether a wearable computer could recognize a person's emotions over an extended period of time (Picard *et al.,* 2001). Over a period of 'many weeks', four sensors captured

- an electromyogram (indicating muscle activity)
- skin conductance
- blood volume pulse (a measure of arousal)
- respiration rate.

By using pattern recognition algorithms, eight emotions were distinguishable at levels significantly higher than chance. This does not mean, however, that computers can recognize people's emotions with reliable accuracy – the main reason being that the recognition software was constrained to a forced choice among the eight defined emotions. But as Picard notes, even partial recognition can be helpful – provided that the wrong emotion is not positively identified. Elsewhere at MIT, work has been targeted at identifying rather more diffuse emotions such as 'the state you are in when all is going well with the computer', as contrasted with 'the state you are in when encountering annoying usability problems' (Picard, 2003). There is clear value here for developing applications that mitigate user frustration.

Tracking changes in facial expression offers another means of extending the data from physiology. In one experiment, for example, Ward *et al.,* (2003) used a commercially available facial tracking package. The software works by tracking facial movements detected from a video of the face. The findings suggested the following:

- Facial expressions change in response to even relatively minor interaction events (in this case low-key surprising and amusing events, where the latter produced a weaker reaction).
- These changes were detected by the tracking software.

The authors concluded that the approach has potential as a tool for detecting emotions evoked by interacting with computers, but best performance in recognizing emotions (rather than simply tracking physical changes) is likely to be more successful with a combination of data sources.

Most applications of computer recognition of emotion lie in the development of systems that moderate their responses to respond to user frustration, stress or anxiety. However, there are worthwhile applications in domains beyond computing *per se*. One of the most significant of these is healthcare, where taking account of affective state is a vital element of patient care. In tele-healthcare, however, the clinician's scope for doing this is rather limited. Tele-healthcare is used for such applications as collecting 'vital signs' such as blood pressure, checking that medication has been taken or compliance with other medical directions. Lisetti *et al.* (2003) report early work on an application designed to improve affective information in this context. The system models the patient's affective state using multiple inputs from wearable sensors and other devices such as a camera. The identified emotions are then mapped on to intelligent agents which are embodied as avatars. The personal avatar is then able to 'chat' to the patient to confirm the emotions identified, and also to reflect this state in supplementing textual communication between patient and clinician (Figure 22.6).

Preliminary results showed 90 per cent success in recognizing sadness, 80 per cent success for anger, 80 per cent for fear and 70 per cent for frustration.

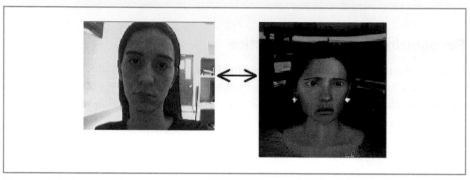

Figure 22.6 An avatar mirroring a user's sad state

(Source: Reprinted from *International Jounal of Human–Computer Studies*, 59, Lisetti, C. *et al.*, Developing multimodal intelligent affective interfaces for tele-home health care, pp. 245–55. Copyright 2003, with permission from Elsevier)

Affective wearables

← Wearables are discussed in Chapter 20

'An affective wearable is a wearable system equipped with sensors and tools that enables recognition of its wearer's affective patterns' (Picard, 1997, p. 227). Wearable computers are not merely portable like a laptop or a Walkman but can be used whether we are walking, standing or travelling. Wearables are also always on (in every sense). At present, a wide range of prototypes of affective wearables already exists, though they are far from complete or polished and require regular attention/maintenance. One of the clear advantages to the design and use of affective wearables is that they can supply information on affect naturalistically. Affective wearables provide an opportunity to study and test theories of emotion. Currently, the most common examples of affective wearables are affective jewellery.

Figure 22.7 is an illustration of a piece of affective jewellery, in this instance an earring that also serves to display the wearer's blood volume pressure using photoplethysmography. This involves using an LED to sense the amount of blood flow in the earlobe. From this reading both the heart beat and constriction of the blood vessel can be determined. In practice, the earring proved to be very sensitive to movement but future applications might include being able to gauge the wearer's reaction to consumer products.

Figure 22.8 is a further example of a system that can sample and transmit biometric data to larger computers for analysis. The data is sent by way of an infra-red (IR) link.

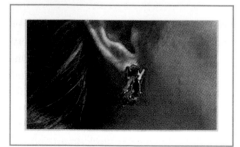

Figure 22.7 The Blood Volume Pressure (BVP) earring

(Source: Courtesy of Frank Dabek)

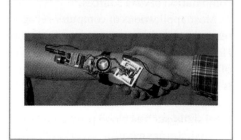

Figure 22.8 Sampling biometric data with a wearable device

(Source: Courtesy of Frank Dabek)

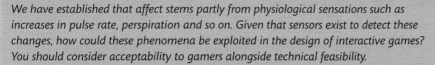

Challenge 22.3

We have established that affect stems partly from physiological sensations such as increases in pulse rate, perspiration and so on. Given that sensors exist to detect these changes, how could these phenomena be exploited in the design of interactive games? You should consider acceptability to gamers alongside technical feasibility.

Whether computers could ever be said to *experience* emotions has long been a matter for debate and is largely beyond the scope of this chapter, but in some ways this fascinating question does not fundamentally affect thinking on how to design for affect. We now move on to investigate what it means for a computer – or any other interactive system – to express emotion.

22.4 Expressing emotion

This is the other side of the affective computing equation. As we have seen, humans express emotions through facial expressions, body movements and posture, smaller-scale physiological changes and changes in tone of voice – which can be extended to the tone and style of written communications. With interactive systems, there are several aspects to consider:

- How computers that apparently express emotion can improve the quality and effectiveness of communication between people and technologies.
- How people can communicate with computers in ways that express their emotions.
- How technology can stimulate and support new modes of affective communication between people.

Can computers express emotion?

There is little argument that computers can *appear* to express emotion. Consider the expressions of the Microsoft Office Assistant – in Figure 22.9 he is 'sulking' when ignored by the author. Whether such unsophisticated anthropomorphism enhances the interactive experience is debatable at best. As well as the irritation provoked in many users, there is a risk that people may expect much more than the system can provide.

Many of the more visible outward expressions of emotion introduced in Section 22.3 can be mimicked by computing applications. Even very simple facial models have been found capable of expressing recognizable emotions. A representative instance of this strand of research is reported by Schiano and her colleagues (Schiano *et al.*, 2000). The experiment tested an early prototype of a simple robot with 'a box-like face containing eyes with moveable lids, tilting eyebrows, and an upper and lower lip which could be independently raised or lowered from the center'. The face was made of metal and had a generally cartoon-like appearance – most of the subtle changes in facial folds and lines that characterize human emotions were missing. Despite these limitations, human observers were able to identify the emotions communicated successfully.

The impact of even limited emotional expression is illustrated again by an experimental application at MIT, the 'relational agent' (Bickmore, 2003). This was designed to sustain a long-term relationship with people who were undertaking a programme to enhance exercise levels. The agent asked about, and responded to, their emotions and expressed concern by modifying text and bodily expression where appropriate. The computer did not disguise its limited empathetic skills, nor were people really convinced of the reality of the 'feelings' displayed, but nevertheless the agent was rated significantly higher for likeability, trust, respect and feelings that it cared for them than a standard interactive agent.

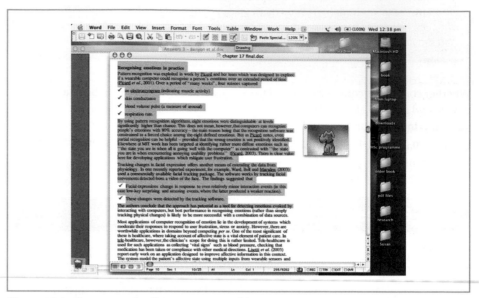

Figure 22.9 The Microsoft Office Assistant 'sulking'

By contrast, 'Kismet' (Figure 22.10), an expressive robot developed at MIT, provides a much more complex physical implementation. It is equipped with visual, auditory and proprioceptive (touch) sensory inputs. Kismet can express apparent emotion through vocalization, facial expression, and adjustment of gaze direction and head orientation.

← See also Chapter 17 on avatars and companions

Figure 22.10
The Kismet
robot

(Source: Sam Ogden/Science Photo Library)

Affective input to interactive systems

So, if computers can express apparent emotions to humans, how can humans express emotions to computers, aside from swearing or switching off the machine in a fit of pique? We have already seen in Section 22.3 that computers can detect affective states. Interactive systems such as those described in that section generally aim to monitor human affective signs unobtrusively so as to identify current emotions. But what if the human wants to communicate an emotion more actively, perhaps to influence the actions of her character in a game?

The affective, tangible user interface developed in the SenToy project (Paiva *et al.*, 2003) affords an imaginative treatment of this type of input problem. Manipulating the SenToy doll (Figure 22.11) so that it performs pre-specified gestures and movements allows people to modify the 'emotions' and behaviour of a character in a game. People can express anger, fear, surprise, sadness, gloating and happiness through gestures which are picked up by the doll's internal sensors and transmitted to the game software. Sadness, for example, is expressed through bending the doll forwards, while shaking it with its arms raised denotes anger. Actions carried out by the game character reflect the emotion detected.

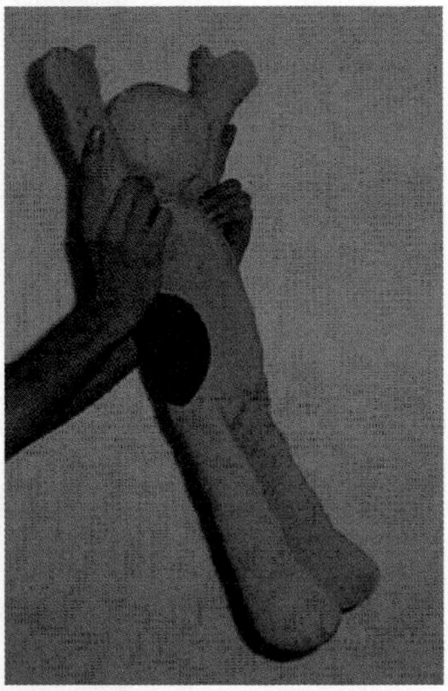

In preliminary trials with adults and children, sadness, anger and happiness were easily expressed without instruction, while gloating – requiring the doll to point and perform a little dance – was particularly difficult. In playing the game itself, this time with instructions for the gestures, all the emotions except surprise were expressed effectively. People became very involved with the game and the doll, and generally enjoyed the experience.

Figure 22.11 The SenToy affective interface

(Source: Reprinted from *International Journal of Human–Computer Studies*, 59(1–2), Paiva, A. *et al.*, SenToy: an effective sympathetic interface. Copyright 2003, with permission from Elsevier)

Enhancing human affective communication

Researchers have also turned their attention to enhancing emotionally toned communication between people. Developments fuse highly creative conceptual design with (sometimes very simple) technology. Sometimes the idea is to convey a particular emotion – generally a positive one – but more often the aim is to foster emotional bonds through feelings of connection. Like much else in the affective computing field, these innovations are very much in their infancy at the time of writing, with few realized in their final form.

A representative set of examples, designed for 'telematic emotional communication', is described by Tollmar and Persson (2002). Rather unusually in this domain, the inspiration behind the ideas comes not only from the designers or technologists, but also from ethnographic studies of households and their use of artefacts to support emotional closeness.

They include '6th sense' (Figure 22.12), a light sculpture which senses body movement in the vicinity. If there is continuous movement for a time, the lamp sends this information to its sister lamp in another household. This lights up, indicating someone's presence in the first household – an unobtrusive way of staying in touch with the movements of a friend or family member.

Figure 22.12 6th Sense

(Source: Tollmar and Persson (2002)
Understanding remote presence,
*Proceedings of the Second Nordic
Conference on Human–Computer
Interaction*, Aarhus, Denmark, 19–23
October, Nordi CHI'02, vol. 31. ACM,
New York, pp. 41–50. © 2002 ACM,
Inc. Reprinted by permission. http://
doi.acm.org/10.1145.572020.572027)

22.5 Potential applications and key issues for further research

Table 22.2 is a list of potential 'areas of impact' for affective computing. 'Foreground' applications are those in which the computer takes an active, usually visible, role; in 'background' applications the computer is a more backstage presence.

Despite lists such as that in Table 22.2 which identify a compelling range of *potential* applications, affective computing is still a developing area. There are fundamental issues which remain to be clarified. Perhaps the most salient for interactive systems designers are:

- In which domains does affective capability make a positive difference to human–computer interaction, and where is it irrelevant or even obstructive?
- How precise do we need to be in identifying human emotions – perhaps it is enough to identify a generally positive or negative feeling? What techniques best detect emotional states for this purpose?
- How do we evaluate the contribution of affect to the overall success of a design?

Table 22.2 Potential 'areas of impact' for affective computing

	Human–human mediation	Human–computer interaction
Foreground	Conversation • Recognizing emotional states Wireless-mobile devices • Representing–displaying emotional states Telephones • Speech-synthetic affect and voice Video teleconferences • Affective iconics	Graphical user interface • Adaptive response based on physiological detection Wearable computers • Remote sensing of physiological states Virtual environments • Emotional capture and display Decision support • Affective elements of decision-making
Background	Portholes (video/audio links between offices or other spaces) • Affective interchanges – adaptive monitoring Electronic badges • Affective alert and display systems Avatars • Creation of personality via synthetic emotional content	Smart house technology • Sensors and affective architectures Ubiquitous computing • Affective learning Speech recognition • Monitoring voice stress Gaze systems • Movements and emotion detection Intelligent agents • Social and emotional intelligence

Source: Reprinted from *International Journal of Human–Computer Studies*, 59 (1–2), McNeese, M.D., New visions of human–computer interaction: making affect compute, copyright 2003, with permission from Elsevier

FURTHER THOUGHTS

Is affective computing possible or desirable?

Writing in the 2003 Special Issue on Affective Computing of the *International Journal of Human–Computer Studies,* Eric Hollnagel argues thus:

> Emotions can provide some kind of redundancy that may improve the effectiveness of communication. The affective modality of communication can furthermore be expressed by different means such as the grammatical structure (a polite request versus an order), the choice of words, or the tone of voice (or choice of colours, depending on the medium or channel). Yet neither of these represents affective computing as such. Instead the style of computing – or rather, the style of communication or interaction – is effectual. It does not try to transmit emotions as such but rather settles for adjusting the style of communication to achieve maximum effectiveness.
>
> In work, people are generally encouraged to be rational and logical rather than affective and emotional. Indeed, every effort in task design, ergonomics, procedures and training goes towards that. From the practical perspective the need is therefore not to emulate emotions but to be able to recognize and control emotions. (This goes for human–human communication as well as human–machine interaction.) In cases where emotions are considered an advantage, they should be amplified. But in cases where they are a disadvantage (which include most practical work situations), they should be dampened. All work, with or without information technology, aims to produce something in a systematic and replicable manner – from ploughing a field to assembling a machine. Affects and emotions usually do not contribute to the efficiency of that but are more likely to have a negative influence. In contrast, art

does not aim to produce identical copies of the same thing and emotions or non-logical (not replicable) procedures and thinking are therefore valuable.

In conclusion, affective computing is neither a meaningful concept nor a reasonable goal. Rather than trying to make computers (or computing) affective, we should try to make communication effectual. Rather than trying to reproduce emotions we should try to imitate those aspects of emotions that are known to enhance the effectiveness of communication.

Source: Reprinted from *International Journal of Human–Computer Studies,* 59 (1–2), Hollnagel, E., Is affective computing an oxymoron?, p.69, copyright 2003, with permission from Elsevier.

Kristina Höök *et al.* (2008) express similar views in arguing for an interactionist view of emotion. We should not be trying to guess people's emotions and adapting systems based on this guess; we should be designing systems that let people express emotion when and how they want to.

Summary and key points

In this chapter we have explored the theory of emotions and seen how this has been applied to the developing field of affective computing. We have discussed what is required for technologies to display apparent emotion, to detect and respond to human emotions and to support human affective communication – potentially a very diverse and technically advanced set of capabilities – but we have suggested that an approximate identification and representation of emotion may suffice for many purposes. Applications have been identified which range from affective communication to supporting telemedicine to interacting with games.

Exercises

1 How far is it necessary to understand the theory of human emotions in order to design affective technologies? Illustrate your answer with examples.

2 Develop a storyboard showing the proposed use of an affective operating system designed to respond when it detects frustration and tiredness in its user.

 ## Further reading

International Journal of Human–Computer Studies, **no. 59 (2003)** – special issue on Affective Computing. *Includes review papers, opinion pieces, theoretical treatments and applications and so provides an excellent snapshot of the state of affective computing in the early twenty-first century.*

Norman, D.A. (2004) *Emotional Design: Why We Love (or Hate) Everday Things.* Basic Books, New York. *A very readable account of the relationship between emotions and design.*

Picard, R.W. (1997) *Affective Computing.* MIT Press, Cambridge, MA. *A stimulating discussion of the theoretical and technological issues grounded in (then) state-of-the-art research at MIT.*

Getting ahead

Brave, S. and Nass, C. (2007) *Emotion in Human–Computer Interaction*. In *Sears A. and Jacko, J.A. (eds) The Handbook of Human–Computer Interaction: Fundamentals, Growing Technologies and Emerging Applications,* **2nd edn.** Lawrence Erlbaum Associates, Mahwah, N.J.

 **Web links**

The HUMAINE project at **http://emotion-research.net**

The accompanying website has links to relevant websites. Go to
www.pearsoned.co.uk/benyon

Comments on challenges

Challenge 22.1

There are many possible arguments here. Our view on this is that it is probably acceptable as long as people can choose whether to use the technology, they are aware that the technology has affective aspects and they can stop using it at any point. Among the differences from older media are the interactive nature of new technologies and the possibility that giving technology reactions and expressions which mimic human emotions may mislead people into inappropriately trustful behaviour.

Challenge 22.2

1 The relevance and implication of events for your well-being will probably initially induce fear.
2 The relevance and implication of events for long-term goals will help you understand that this is a temporary thing.
3 How well they can cope with the situation will probably make you jump and then laugh.
4 The significance of the event for their self-concept and social norms will make you angry if you have looked foolish in the presence of others.

Challenge 22.3

It would be possible, for example, to detect that a games player's state of arousal had remained unchanged since starting the game and step up the pace accordingly, or conversely to slow things down to provide a calmer interlude after a sustained period of high arousal readings. I would guess that people might prefer not to wear (and fix, and calibrate) physical sensors, so perhaps non-contact monitoring, e.g. of facial expression, might be an acceptable solution.

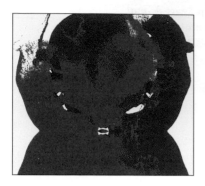

Chapter 23
Cognition and action

Contents

Aims

Perhaps surprisingly, there is no single theory about how people think and reason (cognition) and what relationships there are between thought and actions. In this chapter we look at a number of different views. Cognitive psychology tends to focus on a disembodied view of cognition: 'I think therefore I am' in the famous phrase of René Descartes. Embodied cognition recognizes that we have physical bodies which have evolved and are adapted to a range of activities that take place in the world. Distributed cognition argues that thinking is spread across brains, artefacts and devices and is not simply processed in the brain. Situated action points to the importance of context in deciding what we do and activity theory focuses on action in pursuit of objectives.

After studying this chapter you should be able to understand:

- Cognitive psychology and in particular the idea of humans as information processors
- The importance of context in the design of interactive systems and as a major part of determining the range and type of actions we take
- The importance of the body to thinking and taking action
- Two more views of cognition and action – distributed cognition and activity theory.

23.1 Human information processing

In 1983, Card *et al.* published *The Psychology of Human–Computer Interaction*. In the preface to this, one of the first and certainly the most celebrated book on psychology and HCI, we find this earnest hope expressed:

> The domain of concern to us, and the subject of this book, is how humans interact with computers. A scientific psychology should help us in arranging the interface so it is easy, efficient and error free – even enjoyable.
>
> Card *et al.* (1983), p. vii

The book has at its core the Model Human Processor which is a simplified model of human information processing from the perspective of (a) the psychological knowledge at that time and (b) a task-based approach to human–computer interaction. Task-based approaches to HCI are concerned with looking at people trying to achieve a specific goal (they are discussed in Chapter 11). The human information processing paradigm characterizes or simplifies people's abilities into three 'blocks' or subsystems: (a) a sensory input subsystem, (b) a central information processing subsystem and (c) a motor output subsystem. This is, of course, remarkably similar to how we generally partition the main elements of a computer. Figure 23.1 is an illustration of this relation between people and computers. In this view of HCI, humans and computers are functionally similar and form a closed loop.

In this model, all of our cognitive abilities have been grouped into a box labelled 'Human Information Processing' which is a great oversimplification. For example in previous chapters we have discussed the role of memory, attention and affect in understanding how people think and act. In this representation of humans and computers

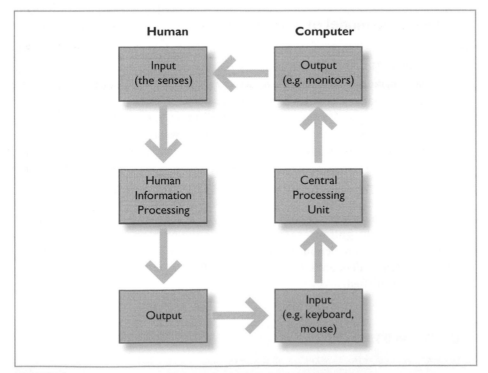

Figure 23.1 The information processing paradigm (in its simplest form)

the outside world is reduced to stimuli, which can be detected by the senses, so the model effectively *decontextualizes* human beings. There are more complex and empirically tested models of humans (see Box 23.1) and there are many accounts at the neurological level of how the brain is organized and how it processes signals. As researchers, academics and designers we are interested in understanding and predicting the use of interactive systems and, for many of us, this is best done using an underlying theory such as cognitive psychology. But human beings are very complex, so we have to simplify our view of human cognitive abilities in order to make them manageable.

BOX 23.1

Cognitive models

Cognitive models or cognitive architectures were once the flagships of both cognitive psychology and HCI. Cognitive models (or architectures) such as SOAR and ACT–R have been developed by research teams to accommodate a range of what Newell has called micro-theories of cognition. ACT–R (http://act-r.psy.cmu.edu/about/) stands for 'The Adaptive Control of Thought – Rational' and is strictly speaking a cognitive architecture. ACT–R is broader than any particular theory and can even accommodate multiple theories within its framework. It has been developed to model problem solving, learning and memory. ACT–R looks and behaves like a programming language except that it is based on constructs based on human cognition (or what its creators believe to be the elements of human cognition). Using ACT–R the programmer/psychologist or cognitive scientist can solve or model problems such as logic puzzles, or control an aircraft and then study the results. These results might give insights into the time to perform tasks and the kinds of errors which people might make in doing so. For example, see Barnard (1985).

Other cognitive architectures work in similar ways.

A seven-stage model of activity

One celebrated psychologist who has been involved in psychology and HCI since the 1970s is Donald Norman. Figure 23.2 is a representation of Norman's seven-stage model of how an individual completes an activity (Norman, 1988). Norman argues that we begin with a **goal,** e.g. checking sports results on the Web, or phoning a friend. Our next step is to form a set of **intentions** to achieve this goal, e.g. finding a computer with a browser, or trying to remember which jacket we were wearing when we last used our mobile phone. This is then translated into a sequence of actions which we then execute, e.g. go to a computer lab or Internet café, then log on to a PC, double-click on a Web browser, type in the URL, hit return, read sports results. At each step on the way we perceive the new state of the world, interpret what we see, and compare it against what we intended to change. We may have to repeat these actions if our goals were not met.

In Figure 23.2, the **gulf of execution** refers to the problem of how an individual translates intentions into action. The **gulf of evaluation** is the converse and refers to ← We encountered these how an individual understands, or evaluates, the effects of actions and knows when his gulfs briefly in Chapter 2 or her goals are satisfied.

Challenge 23.1

Identify instances of the gulf of execution and the gulf of evaluation in devices or systems which you (or other people) have difficulty using.

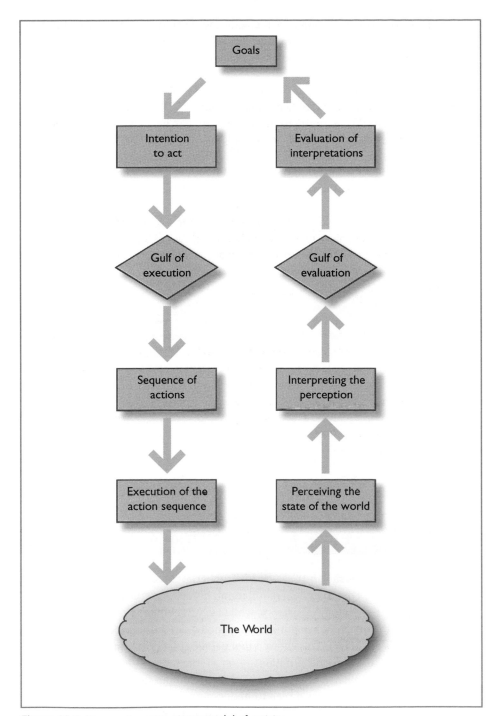

Figure 23.2 Norman's seven-stage model of activity

(Source: After Norman, 1988)

Why HIP is not enough

While the human information processing (HIP) account of cognition proved to be popular both within psychology and in the early years of HCI, this popularity has diminished dramatically in recent years, for the following reasons:

● It is *too simple*. We are much more complex and cannot be represented meaningfully as a series of boxes, clouds and arrows. Human memory is not a passive receptacle; it is not analogous to an SQL database. It is active, with multiple, concurrent and evolving goals, and is multimodal. Visual perception has very little in common with a pair of binocular cameras connected to a computer. Perception exists to guide purposive action.

- *HIP arose from laboratory studies*. The physical and social contexts of people are many and varied and conspicuous by their absence from these diagrams.
- *HIP models assume that we are alone in the world*. Human behaviour is primarily social and hardly ever solitary. Work is social, travel is usually social, playing games is often social, writing a document (e-mail, assignment, book, text message, graffiti) is social as it is intended to be read by someone else. Where are these people represented in the block and arrow models of cognition?

These models are very clearly *incomplete* as they omit important aspects of human psychology such as affect (our emotional response); they also fail to notice that we have bodies.

FURTHER THOUGHTS

Creativity and cognition

Human abilities of creativity offer something of a challenge to cognition. Where do new ideas come from? How do we make the jump in thinking that is characteristic of being creative? There are, of course, many views on this and it is most likely that emotion, social interaction, intention and volition all have a part to play. One distinction that has been made is between convergent and divergent thinking (Guilford, 1967). Convergent thinking is directed at finding the best solution to a problem whereas divergent thinking is concerned with bringing diverse ideas together and exploring many unusual ideas and possibilities. (Many design techniques for encouraging divergent thinking such as brainstorming are described in Chapters 7 and 9.)

23.2 Situated action

The late 1980s and 1990s saw the rise of criticisms of the classic cognitive psychological accounts such as HIP. For example, Liam Bannon argued for studying people outside the confines of the psychology laboratory, while Lucy Suchman criticized the idea that people follow simple plans in her ground-breaking book *Plans and Situated Actions* in 1987 (second edition, 2007). This showed that people respond constructively and perhaps unpredictably to real-world situations.

In 1991 Bannon published a paper entitled 'From human factors to human actors' (Bannon, 1991). The paper was a plea to understand the people using collaborative systems as empowered, problem-solving, value-laden, cooperative individuals rather than mere subjects in an applied psychology experiment. In adopting this new perspective we necessarily move out of the laboratory and into complex real-world settings. The argument highlights the differences in perception between treating people as merely a set of cognitive systems and subsystems (which is implied by the term *human factors*) and respecting people as autonomous participants, actors, with the capacity to govern their own behaviour. From this point Bannon explores the consequences of this change in perspective. He argues that it involves moving from narrow experimental studies of individual people working on a computer system to the social setting of the workplace. This too would require changes in techniques, from a cognitive and experimental approach to less intrusive techniques with perhaps an emphasis on the observational. Once in the workplace we should study experts and the obstacles they face in improving their practice or competence. There is a need to shift from snapshot studies to extended longitudinal studies. Finally, Bannon argues that we should adopt a design approach that places people at the centre of the design process through participative design approaches.

← There is more about participative design in Chapter 7

It is said that Lucy Suchman's *Plans and Situated Actions* is the book most widely quoted by researchers of collaborative system design. The book is a critique of some of the core assumptions of artificial intelligence (AI) and cognitive science, specifically the role of plans in behaviour, but in doing so it opened the door to ethnomethodology and conversation analysis in HCI. Suchman's starting point – before refuting the planning approach – is to identify the role of planning in AI and the belief of cognitive psychology that this is true of human behaviour too. Simply put, both human and artificially intelligent behaviour can be modelled in terms of the **formulation** and **execution** of **plans**. A plan is a **script,** a sequence of actions.

← See also the discussion of collaboration in Chapter 16

'Going for a curry' script

BOX 23.2

As the national dish of the UK is said to be chicken tikka masala (a kind of creamy curry), let us think about how the British enjoy this dish.

The scene is a Saturday night in any city in the UK. Our potential curry enthusiasts (let's call them *students* for the sake of argument) meet and then drink a great deal of lager which creates an irresistible desire for a curry. The second step is to locate an Indian restaurant. Having gained entry to the restaurant one of the students will ask a waiter for a table. The waiter will guide the party to a table, offering to take their coats as they go. Next the waiter will give each student a copy of the menu, suggesting that they might like to have a lager while choosing from the menu. The students then decide what they want to eat and order it from the waiter, stopping only to argue over how many poppadums, chapattis or naan breads they want (these are common forms of Indian breads eaten prior to or with a curry). The curry is then served and consumed. Everyone being sated, one of the students asks for the bill. After 20 minutes of heated argument about who had ordered what, the students finally settle the bill and hurry home to ensure that they have a good night's sleep.

Researchers Schank and Abelson (1977) were the first to identify scripts as being a credible means by which we organize our knowledge of the world and, more importantly, as a means of directing our behaviour (i.e. planning). The advantage of scripts is that they can be adapted to other situations. The above Indian restaurant script is readily adapted for use in a Thai, Chinese or Italian restaurant (i.e. find restaurant, get table, read menu, order food, eat food, pay for meal) and easily adapted to, for example, hamburger restaurants (the order of get table and order food is simply reversed).

Plans are formulated through a set of procedures beginning with a goal, successive decomposition into subgoals and into primitive actions. The plan is then executed. A goal is the desired state of the system.

→ Chapter 25 on navigation also criticizes the traditional view of plans

The problems with the planning model as identified by Suchman included the observations that the world is not stable, immutable and objective. Instead it is dynamic and interpreted (by us) and the interpretation is contextual or 'situated'. Thus plans are not executed but rather they are just one resource which can shape an individual's behaviour.

> **Challenge 23.2**
>
> *How do the current generation of graphical user interfaces support behaviour that does not rely on planning?*

23.3 Distributed cognition

On 20 July 1969, astronauts Neil Armstrong and Buzz Aldrin landed on the Moon. At Mission Control, Charlie Duke followed the process closely (along with 600,000,000 other people listening on radio and watching on TV). What follows is a transcript of the last few seconds of the landing of the Lunar Module (LM).

Aldrin: *'4 forward. 4 forward. Drifting to the right a little. 20 feet, down a half.'*
Duke: *'30 seconds.'*
Aldrin: *'Drifting forward just a little bit; that's good.'*
Aldrin: *'Contact Light.'*
Armstrong: *'Shutdown.'*
Aldrin: *'Okay. Engine Stop.'*
Aldrin: *'ACA out of detent'*
Armstrong: *'Out of detent. Auto.'*
Duke: *'We copy you down, Eagle.'*
Armstrong: *'Engine arm is off. Houston, Tranquillity Base here. The Eagle has landed.'*
Duke: *Roger, Tranquillity. We copy you on the ground. You got a bunch of guys about to turn blue. We're breathing again. Thanks a lot.'*

The question is, who landed the spacecraft? History records that Neil Armstrong was the mission commander while Buzz Aldrin was the LM pilot. While Armstrong operated the descent engine and control thrusters, Aldrin read aloud the speed and altitude of the LM ('4 forward', that is, we are moving forward at 4 feet per second), while 250,000 miles away back on Earth, Duke confirms the quantity of fuel remaining (30 seconds). So who landed the LM? In a very real sense they all did: it was a joint activity.

Ed Hutchins has developed the theory of **distributed cognition** to describe situations such as this (Hutchins, 1995). The theory argues that both the cognitive process itself and the knowledge used and generated are often distributed across multiple people, tools and representations. Everyday examples would include:

- A driver and passenger navigating a foreign city using maps and road signs
- The homely task of shopping with the aid of a list and the reminders presented by the supermarket shelves
- Colleagues rationalizing a project budget using an Excel spreadsheet and some unintelligible printouts from Finance.

Internal and external representation

In distributed cognition, resources include the **internal representation** of knowledge (human memory, sometimes called knowledge in the head) and **external representations** (knowledge in the world). This is potentially anything that supports the cognitive activity, but instances would include gestures, the physical layout of objects, notes, diagrams, computer readings and so forth. These are just as much part of the activity as cognitive processes, not just memory aids (Zhang and Norman, 1994). Hutchins has studied distributed cognition in a range of team-working situations, from Pacific islanders wayfinding between far distant islands to the navigation of US naval ships to aircraft cockpits. In a study of how pilots control approach speeds (aircraft landing speeds), Hutchins (1995) suggests that the cockpit system as a whole in a sense 'remembers' its speed. He argued that the various representations in the cockpit, their physical location and the way in which they are shared between pilots make up the cockpit system as a whole (Figure 23.3).

Figure 23.3 A typical example of distributed cognition in an aircraft cockpit
(Source: Mike Miller/Science Photo Library)

The representations employed by the pilots include what they say, charts and manuals, and the cockpit instruments themselves. There is also a whole host of implicit information in aircraft cockpits, such as the relative positions of airspeed indicators and other dials. Hutchins also notes that the various representational states change with time and may even transfer between media in the course of the system's operation. These transformations may be carried out by an individual using a tool (artefact) while at other times representational states are produced or transformed entirely by artefacts.

Different ways in which processes might be distributed

When these principles are applied in the wild, three different kinds of distribution emerge:

← Chapter 18 discusses distributed information

- Cognitive processes may be distributed across the members of a social group
- Cognitive processes may involve coordination between internal and external structures
- Processes may be distributed through time in such a way that the products of earlier events can transform the nature of later events.

All in all, distributed cognition offers an excellent means of describing how complex systems operate which is well supported by empirical evidence. However, translating these descriptions into the design of interactive systems remains problematic. Hollan *et al.* (2000) showed how insights from a distributed cognition perspective have guided the design of their PAD++ system, but such examples remain few.

23.4 Embodied cognition

James Gibson is best known in HCI design circles as the man who gave us the concept of **affordance**. An affordance is a resource or support that the environment offers an animal; the animal in turn must possess the capabilities to perceive it and to use it.

> The affordances of the environment are what it offers animals, what it provides or furnishes, for good or ill.
>
> (Gibson, 1977)

Examples of affordances include surfaces that provide support, objects that can be manipulated, substances that can be eaten and other animals that afford interactions of all kinds. This all seems quite remote from HCI, but if we were able to design interactive systems which immediately presented their affordances then many, if not all, usability issues would be banished: people would perceive the opportunities for action as simply as they recognize they can walk through a doorway.

← Affordance is one of the usability principles described in Chapter 4

The properties of these affordances for animals are specified in stimulus information. Even if an animal possesses the appropriate attributes and equipment, it may need to learn to detect the information and to perfect the activities that make the affordance useful – or dangerous if ignored. An affordance, once detected, is meaningful and has value for the animal. It is nevertheless objective, inasmuch as it refers to physical properties of the animal's niche (environmental constraints) and to its bodily dimensions and capacities. An affordance thus exists, whether it is perceived or used or not. It may be detected and used without explicit awareness of doing so. This description was revised in 1986 when Gibson wrote

> An affordance cuts across the dichotomy of subjective–objective and helps us to understand its inadequacy. It is equally a fact of the environment and a fact of behavior. It is both physical and psychical, yet neither. An affordance points both ways, to the environment and to the observer.
>
> (Gibson, 1986, p. 129)

So affordances are (confusingly) neither and both in the world and in the mind of the observer. Figure 23.4 is an illustration of a door. Opening a door is probably the most widely cited example of an affordance in action. The argument is that we 'see' that we can either push or pull open the door from the affordances of the door itself. This might work well for doors, but does it apply to the design of interactive systems?

Challenge 23.3

Find some more affordances in everyday objects. How is the affordance 'presented'? Also try to identify apparent affordances that are misleading.

Donald Norman, who was instrumental in introducing the concept of affordance to HCI, recognized that Gibson's formulation of the concept needs some revision. He has argued that we need to replace the original biological–environmental formulation

Figure 23.4 An affordance in the world
(Source: Phil Turner)

with a definition that is at one remove, namely perceived affordance (Norman, 1988). He has suggested that the concept of affordances can be extended to a weaker formulation: people are said to perceive the intended behaviour of the interface widgets such as the knobs and dials of a range of software applications. These intended and perceived behaviours are usually very simple, including sliding, pressing and rotating. He continues,

> real affordances are not nearly as important as perceived affordances; it is perceived affordances that tell the user what actions can be performed on an object and, to some extent, how to do them. [Perceived affordances are] often more about conventions than about reality.
> (Norman, 1999, p. 123)

He gives a scrollbar as an example of such a convention. Figure 23.5 is a screenshot with a number of perceived affordances present. The slider labelled 'Dock Size' affords sliding; the radio buttons ('Position on screen') afford selecting; but does the checkbox 'Animate opening applications' really afford checking? What does 'checking' really mean? Are these really affordances or just conventions?

Despite the difficulties in precisely stating what an affordance is, as a concept it is enormously popular amongst researchers. The use of the term *affordance* in anthropology is not unusual (e.g. Cole, 1996; Wenger, 1998; Hollan *et al*., 2000). However, what may be surprising is the extravagant use of the term, going well beyond Gibson's modest conceptualization. Cole (1996), for example, identified a range of affordances offered by a variety of mediating artefacts including the life stories of recovering alcoholics in an AA meeting (affording rehabilitation), patients' charts in a hospital setting (affording access to a patient's medical history), poker chips (affording gambling) and 'sexy' clothes (affording gender stereotyping). Cole notes that mediating artefacts embody their own 'developmental histories' that are a reflection of their use. That is, these artefacts have been manufactured or produced and continue to be used as part of, and in relation to, intentional human actions.

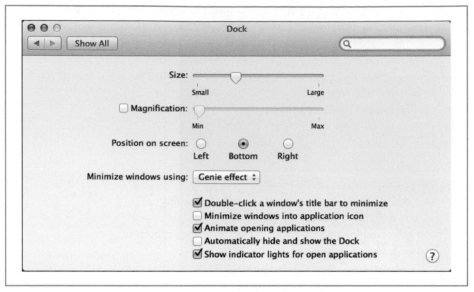

Figure 23.5 A perceived affordance at the user interface

In *Where the Action Is* Paul Dourish develops his ideas on the foundations of embodied interaction (Dourish, 2001). The embodied interaction perspective considers interaction 'with the things themselves'. Dourish draws on the phenomenological philosophy of such writers as Heidegger, Husserl and Merleau-Ponty and recent developments in tangible computing and social computing to develop a theory of embodied interaction. For Dourish, phenomenology is about the tight coupling of action and meaning.

BOX 23.3

Enactive interaction

The close coupling of the perception–action loop is a key characteristic of enactive interfaces. Enactive interaction is direct, natural and intuitive, based on physical and social experiences with the world. Bruner describes three systems or ways of organizing knowledge and three corresponding forms of representation of the interaction with the world: enactive, iconic and symbolic (Bruner, 1966, 1968). Enactive knowledge is constructed on motor skills, enactive representations are acquired by doing, and doing is the means for learning in an enactive context. Enactive interaction is direct, natural and intuitive. In order to give rise to believable experiences with enactive interfaces it is necessary to respect certain conditions of the interaction with the real world, such as the role played by action in the shaping of the perceptual content, the role of active exploration and the role of perception in the guidance of action. The close coupling of the perception–action loop is hence a key characteristic of enactive interfaces.

Embodied interaction is concerned with two main features: meaning and coupling. Meaning may be about ontology, inter-subjectivity or intentionality. Ontology is concerned with how we describe the world, with the entities and relationships with which we interact. Inter-subjectivity is about how meaning can be shared with others. This involves both the communication of meaning from designers to other people, so that the system can reveal its purpose, and the communication between people through the system. The third aspect of meaning is intentionality. This is to do with the directedness of meaning and how it relates one thing to another.

Actions take on meaning for people. Coupling is concerned with making the relationship between actions and meaning effective. If objects and relationships are coupled then effects of actions can be passed through the system. Dourish uses the familiar example of a hammer (also used by Heidegger) to illustrate coupling. When you use a hammer it becomes an extension to your arm (it is coupled) and you act through the hammer onto the nail. You are engaged in the activity of hammering.

From this theory of embodied interaction – 'not just how we act *on* technology, but how we act *through* it' (Dourish, 2001, p. 154) – Dourish goes on to develop some high-level design principles:

- Computation is a medium
- Meaning arises on multiple levels
- Users, not designers, create and communicate meaning
- Users, not designers, manage coupling
- Embodied technologies participate in the world they represent
- Embodied interaction turns action into meaning

An embodied view of cognition is also central to the ideas of George Lakoff and Mark Johnson (Lakoff and Johnson, 1981, 1999). They have argued that language and thought are based on a limited number of fundamental, conceptual metaphors. Metaphor was much more than a literary trope, it was central to how humans thought. Many metaphors were not recognized as metaphors because they had been so entrenched into our ways of thinking and talking that we no longer saw them at all. They gave examples such as 'knowing is seeing' (e.g. I see what you mean), 'up is good' (e.g. he is climbing the ladder of success). Computing examples such as 'cut', 'paste' or 'menu' would not be recognized as metaphors by many; they are what we do with computers.

The discovery of the systematic embedding of metaphors was accompanied by another key insight. These metaphors were based on *embodied* experience. These fundamental, conceptual metaphors derive from the fact that we are people living in the world:

> three natural kinds of experience—experience of the body, of the physical environment, *and* of the culture—are what constitute the basic source domains upon which metaphors draw.
> (Rohrer, 2005, p. 14)

In many ways this philosophical movement brings together distributed cognition and embodied cognition as it emphasizes that cognition is embodied and embedded in the world. We see people as thinking and acting in a physical and cultural medium. (These ideas of metaphors and blends were also discussed in Chapter 9.)

23.5 Activity theory

Activity theory is a body of work that stems from the work developed from the ideas of the Soviet psychologist LevVygotsky (1896–1934), Vygotsky (1978) and his students Luria and Leont'ev. From its origins in psychology and education, activity theory has recently gained ground in many other domains, including the study of work (e.g. Engeström, 1995, 1999), information systems and CSCW (e.g. Christiansen, 1996; Heeren and Lewis, 1997; Hasan *et al.*, 1998; Turner and Turner, 2001, 2002) and organizational theory (e.g. Blackler, 1993, 1995).

Engeström and others have extended the original philosophy and ideas to include a model of human activity and methods for analysing activity and bringing about change.

Most authors would agree that the core features of activity theory, more fully described as CHAT – Cultural Historical Activity Theory – comprise a recognition of the role and importance of culture, history and activity in understanding human behaviour. Other authors do, of course, emphasize different aspects of activity theory, variously reflecting their individual research needs and the dynamic, evolving nature of activity theory.

CHAT – a modern formulation of activity theory

The flavour of activity theory employed here draws primarily upon the contemporary work of Engeström which has been adopted and elaborated by many Scandinavian (e.g. Bødker and Christiansen, 1997; Bardram, 1998), American (e.g. Nardi, 1996), Australian (e.g. Hasan *et al.*, 1998) and British researchers (e.g. Blackler, 1993, 1995). Engeström's account of activity theory is probably the dominant formulation in use in the study of information systems, HCI and CSCW research. In such research there is perhaps a greater focus on the role of activity *per se* rather than history and culture. Reflecting this, Engeström has formulated three basic principles, building on the work of earlier activity theorists, which are widely used and cited within the activity theory community:

(a) activities as the smallest meaningful unit of analysis (originally identified by Leont'ev);
(b) the principle of self-organizing activity systems driven by contradictions; and
(c) changes in activities (and by extension the organization hosting them) as instantiations of cycles of expansive learning.

The structure of an activity

Central to activity theory is the concept that all purposive human activity can be characterized by a triadic interaction between a *subject* (one or more people) and the group's *object* (or purpose) mediated by *artefacts* or tools. In activity theory terms, the subject is the individual or individuals carrying out the activity, the artefact is any tool or representation used in that activity, whether external or internal to the subject, and the object encompasses both the purpose of the activity and its product or output. Subsequent developments of activity theory by Engeström and others have added more elements to the original formulation: *community* (all other groups with a stake in the activity), the *division of labour* (the horizontal and vertical divisions of responsibilities and power within the activity) and *praxis* (the formal and informal rules and norms governing the relations between the subjects and the wider community for the activity). These relationships are often represented by an *activity triangle*. Thus activities are social and collective in nature. The use of activity triangles is widespread in the activity theory literature but it must be remembered that this is only a partial representation of an activity. The triangle should be regarded as a nexus, existing as it does in a continuum of development and learning and in turn masking its internal structure. Within the activity are the individual *actions* by which it is carried out. These are each directed at achieving a particular goal mediated by the use of an artefact. Actions, in turn, are executed by means of *operations*: lower-level steps that do not require conscious attention. Thus activities are social and collective in nature (see Figure 23.6).

The internal structure of an activity

Activities are realized by way of an aggregation of *mediated actions*, which, in turn, are achieved by a series of low-level operations. This structure, however, is flexible and may change as a consequence of learning, context or both (Figure 23.7).

By way of example, consider the process of learning to use a complex interactive device such as a motor car. The object of the activity is probably quite complex, ranging

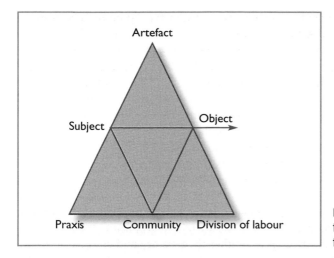

Figure 23.6 An activity triangle (sometimes called the activity schema)

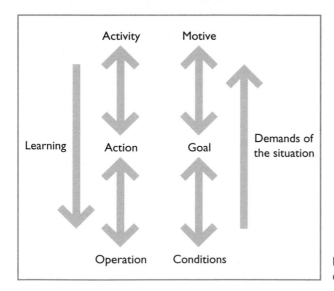

Figure 23.7 Structure of an activity

from and probably including the need to be able to drive because of work commitments, the need to attract the opposite sex, because of peer pressure, because an indulgent parent has given you a car, or the need to participate in a robbery. The activity is realized by means of an aggregation of actions (i.e. obtain driving licence; insure car; take driving lessons; learn the Highway Code; get a job to pay for the petrol and so on). These individual actions in their turn are realized by a set of operations (i.e. get driving licence application form, complete form, write out cheque for the licence, send off licence, . . .). This, of course, is an incomplete, *static* description of the activity whereas humans are constantly learning with practice, so when first presented with the intricacies of the gear lever (manual gear shift) it is likely that the process of disengaging the engine, shifting gear and re-engaging the engine are under conscious control (thus the action of changing gear is realized by the following operations: depress clutch, shift to the top left, release clutch). Thus the focus of attention is at the operations level but with practice attention will tend to slide down the hierarchy as the action becomes automatic. Over time, actions become automatic and the activity itself is effectively demoted to that of an action – unless circumstances change. Such changes might include driving on the right (the British drive on the left), changing the make of motor car or driving a lorry, or being faced with the possibility of a collision. In such circumstances consciousness becomes refocused at the level demanded by the context.

Thus, this alternative formulation of the nature and structure of an activity is of interest for a number of reasons. First, this theory of activity has, at its heart, a hierarchical task-like structure. Secondly, it introduces the ideas of consciousness and motivation at the heart of the activity. Leont'ev (2009) offers a mechanism by which the focus (and locus) of consciousness moves between these various levels of abstraction – up and down the hierarchy depending on the demands of the context.

Activity theory is perhaps unique among accounts of work in placing such a strong emphasis on the role of individual and group or collective learning. Vygotsky's work on developmental learning has been a major influence on the thinking of Engeström, who extended the idea to encompass collective learning which he termed *expansive learning* (Engeström, 1987). Engeström has demonstrated the usefulness of expansive learning with its cycles of internalization, questioning, reflection and externalization in the development of activities in a variety of domains (see, for example, Engeström, 1999). The drivers for these expansive cycles of learning and development are *contradictions* within and between activities. While this is something of a departure from Vygotsky, it has proved particularly valuable to HCI and CSCW researchers. We now consider contradictions in more detail.

Engeström's description of contradictions

Activities are dynamic entities, having their roots in earlier activities and bearing the seeds of their own successors. They are subject to transformation in the light of contradictions. Those contradictions found within a single node of an activity are described as *primary* contradictions. In practice, this kind of contradiction can be understood in terms of breakdowns between actions or sets of actions that realize the activity. These actions are typically poly-motivated, i.e. the same action is executed by different people for different reasons, or by the same person as a part of two separate activities, and it is this poly-motivation that may be at the root of subsequent contradictions. The next category of contradictions is those that occur between nodes and are described as *secondary* contradictions. *Tertiary* contradictions may be found when an activity is remodelled to take account of new motives or ways of working. Thus they occur between an existing activity and what is described as a 'culturally more advanced form' of that activity. A culturally more advanced activity is one that has arisen from the resolution of contradictions within an existing activity and may involve the creation of new working practices (praxis) or artefacts or division of responsibilities. Finally, those occurring between different coexisting or concurrent activities are described as *quaternary* contradictions. From this, it can be seen that a complex and continuing evolving web of contradictions may emerge (Figure 23.8). Primary and secondary contradictions in an activity may give rise to a new activity which in turn spawns a set of tertiary contradictions between it and the original activity, and this may be compounded by quaternary contradictions with coexisting activities.

Concrete examples of contradictions

Table 23.1 holds a set of sample contradictions that might exist within a modern university. A university can be thought of as an activity system, that is, a university can be thought of as the sum of its activities. Put *very* simply, a university comprises teaching, research and (by far the biggest) administration activities. Table 23.1 details a number of potential contradictions that may exist within and between these activities.

A contradictions analysis such as the one above can be used to direct the evaluation of new interactive systems. (It should also be noted that a contradictions analysis also closely resembles the creation of a rich picture – see Chapter 3 and Checkland and Scholes, 1999.)

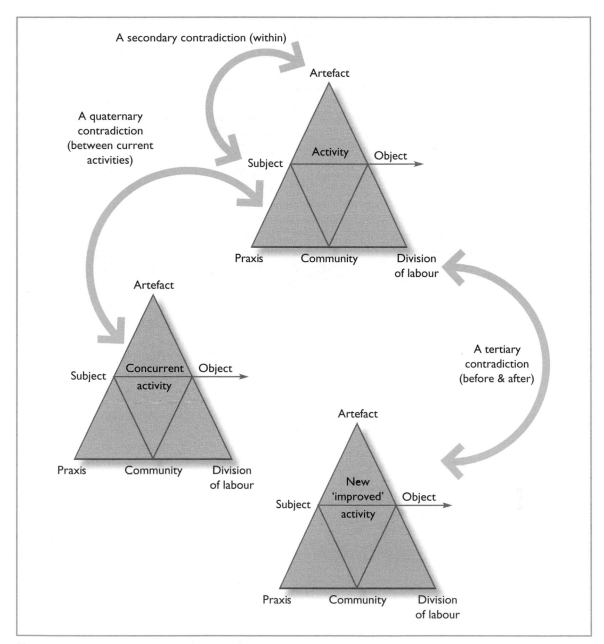

Figure 23.8 An activity system and potential contradictions

Activity theory in practice

In a study between the School of Computing at Edinburgh Napier University and the Gastrointestinal (GI) Unit at the Western General Hospital Trust in Edinburgh a wireless network of personal digital assistants (PDAs) has been created. The specific benefits of using such a wireless network of PDAs in the GI unit are expected to be:

- Delivering patients' records, key test results and clinical histories directly into the hands of the clinician and enabling direct data entry at the point of care
- Requesting medical tests
- Access to the GI unit on-line guidelines and drug manuals
- Synchronization with other computers, that is, being able to mutually update files and other materials which the clinician has on his or her desktop

Table 23.1 Sample contradictions

Type of contradiction	
Primary	The set book for the HCI module is outdated and a new one is required. This would be symptomatic of breakdown in the artefact node of the teaching activity.
Secondary	Within the teaching activity, the number of students studying HCI has risen (or dropped) dramatically, which changes the staff–student ratio from the target 20:1 to 50:1. The contradiction (or breakdown) lies between the subject and object nodes.
Tertiary	Tertiary contradictions occur between currently formulated activities and new versions of those activities. So if a Web-based student enrolment system was introduced to replace the academic-based manual system, contradictions may arise from having accurate student numbers. Having accurate student numbers would make for more accurate timetabling. Not all contradictions are negative.
Quaternary	Quaternary contradictions occur between different activities. In all universities (probably without exception) the only reliable growth area is administration, which necessarily causes problems for the other activities of teaching and research.

- Portable e-mail, allowing clinicians to read their e-mail on their PDAs off-line at home
- An enhanced means of managing patients both within the hospital context and between general practitioners and hospitals. This work has been partially supported by the Electronic Clinical Communications Implementation (ECCI) project which itself is looking at improving communications between general practitioners and the hospitals.

In order to determine whether or not these benefits are achieved, it is important to evaluate the usefulness and usability of the network. Activity theory allows us to organize this evaluation effort. Figure 23.9 is a hierarchically organized evaluation framework created for this task.

A fuller account of the evaluation of the PDAs in this clinical setting may be found in Turner *et al.* (2003).

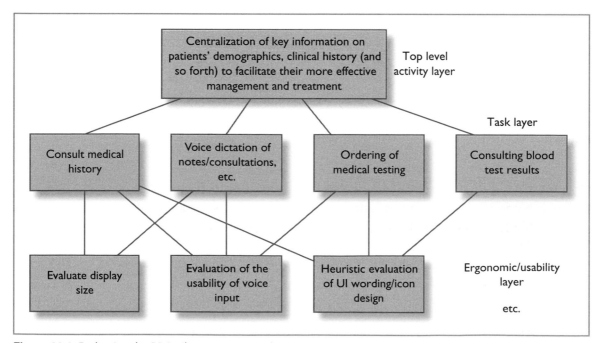

Figure 23.9 Evaluating the PDA pilot using activity theory

Summary and key points

Early views of cognition and action concentrated on the human as an 'information processor' with people engaged in simple goal-focused tasks where people followed a plan to achieve their objective. This view was challenged in the 1980s both in respect of planning and in respect of the over-simplified view of cognition. Embodied interaction recognizes the role and importance of the body in understanding and in determining actions. In particular, the idea of affordances arises from bodies.

- Distributed cognition argues that cognitive processing is not confined to the individual mind, but is distributed between mind and external artefacts.

- Distributed cognition exists between the minds of cooperating human actors and artefacts, which is best understood as a unified cognitive system with a particular goal, e.g. using a calculator, a shopping list, or navigating and driving in a foreign city.

- Embodied cognition emphasizes the importance of embodiment – people are physical and social beings – in cognition.

- Activity theory has its origins in Soviet psychology and places emphasis on society and community, not the isolated individual. It also asserts that human activity itself is the context as people pursue the object of the activity.

Exercises

1 Embodied interaction as a way of thinking about designing interactive systems is currently in vogue, but what would disembodied interaction imply? While it is possible to imagine usable systems and unusable systems and aesthetically pleasing and plain ugly designs, what would a disembodied design look like? Is embodied interaction tautological? Or is it emphasizing an aspect of design which is usually ignored?

2 As we have seen, the concept of affordance was originally applied to simple real-world situations. Then Norman suggested that user interface widgets provided perceived affordances (e.g. sliders afford scrolling through a document). But is a perceived affordance just a convention? (We have all learned to use GUIs such as Windows, and a widget such as a slider is just a way one scrolls through a document. These are conventions, not affordances.)

 **Further reading**

Embodied interaction

Dourish, P. (2001) *Where the Action Is: The Foundations of Embodied Interaction*. MIT Press, Cambridge, MA.

Winograd, T. and Flores, F. (1986) *Understanding Computers and Cognition: a New Foundation for Design*. Ablex Publishing, Norwood, NJ.

Affordance

Gibson, J.J. (1977) The theory of affordances. In Shaw, R. and Bransford, J. (eds), *Perceiving, Acting and Knowing*. Wiley, New York, pp. 67–82.

Gibson, J.J. (1986) *The Ecological Approach to Visual Perception*. Lawrence Erlbaum Associates, Hillsdale, NJ.

Norman, D. (1988) *The Psychology of Everyday Things*. Basic Books, New York.

Situated action

Schank, R. and Abelson, R. (1977) *Scripts, Plans, Goals and Understanding*. Lawrence Erlbaum Associates, Hillsdale, NJ.

Suchman, L. (1987) *Plans and Situated Actions*. Cambridge University Press, New York.

Distributed cognition

Hollan, J., Hutchins, E. and Kirsh, D. (2000) Distributed cognition: toward a new foundation for human–computer interaction research. *ACM Transactions on Computer–Human Interaction*, 7(2), 174–96.

Hutchins, E. *(1995) Cognition in the Wild*. MIT Press, Cambridge, MA.

Activity theory

Engeström, Y. (1987) *Learning by Expanding: an Activity-Theoretical Approach to Developmental Research*. Orienta-Konsultit, Helsinki.

Hasan, H., Gould, E. and Hyland, P. (eds) (1998) *Information Systems and Activity Theory: Tools in Context*. University of Wollongong Press, Wollongong, New South Wales.

Kaptelinin, V., Nardi, B.A. and Macaulay, C. (1999) The Activity Checklist: a tool for representing the 'space' of context. *Interactions*, 6(4), 27–39.

Monk, A. and Gilbert, N. (eds) (1995) *Perspectives on HCI – Diverse Approaches*. Academic Press, London.

Nardi, B. (ed.) (1996) *Context and Consciousness: Activity Theory and Human–Computer Interaction*. MIT Press, Cambridge, MA.

Vygotsky, L.S. (1978) *Mind in Society: the Development of Higher Psychological Processes* (English trans. ed. M. Cole). Harvard University Press, Cambridge, MA.

Getting ahead

Carroll, J. (ed) (2002) *HCI in the New Millennium*. Addison-Wesley, Harlow.

Rogers, Y. (2012) *HCI Theories: Classical, Modern, and Contemporary*. Morgan & Claypool, San Rafael, CA.

 **Web links**

The accompanying website has links to relevant website. Go to
www.pearsoned.co.uk/benyon

 Comments on challenges

Challenge 23.1

Taking the state of technology at the time of writing, you will probably have observed that the size and layout of many phone keys are too small and cramped for easy and quick operation for anyone with normal-sized fingers. Thus the physical gulf of execution is making sure you press the right button. The design is a shifting compromise between ergonomics and style, where designers have decided that style is a more important marketing point. You can find similar trade-offs in many consumer products.

Challenge 23.2

For example, some computer systems provide 'wizards' which step people through a sequence of actions without the requirement for planning that sequence. The context-sensitive cornucopia of icons and other widgets presented by most graphical user interfaces also help to suggest what we might do. Most websites – especially e-commerce sites – encourage browsing as well as goal-directed activities.

Challenge 23.3

There is a multitude of possible examples. An easy one, leading on from the door handle example, is the near-universal provision of handles on objects designed to be picked up. A counter-affordance is illustrated by door handles such as those pictured on doors designed for *pushing*: not uncommon and very tedious.

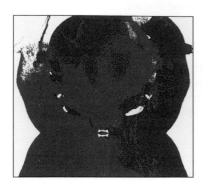

Chapter 24
Social interaction

Contents

Aims

Human beings are generally social creatures and an understanding of the social side of interactions is a necessary part of designing interactive systems. Designers should always consider the social impact that their designs will have. Disciplines contributing to understanding social issues include (social) anthropology, sociology and social psychology. These disciplines tend to use different methods and to focus on different aspects of the social. For example, anthropology has pioneered ethnographic approaches to understanding social settings, psychology tends to favour controlled experiments, while sociology takes a stance often focused more towards the needs of societies as a whole. The aim of this chapter is to see people as living within cultures and participating with others.

After studying this chapter you should be able to:

- Understand the main issues in human communication
- Understand issues concerned with participating in groups
- Understand presence
- Understand the main issues of identity and culture.

24.1 Introduction

The discipline of social psychology brings together the psychological and sociological. A classic definition of social psychology states that it is:

> an attempt to understand and explain how the thoughts, feelings and behaviors of individuals are influenced by the actual, imagined, or implied presence of others.
>
> Allport (1968)

With the rise of social networking websites and on-line communities such as Second Life or World of Warcraft, social interaction is an increasingly important part of designing interactive systems. People need to be able to work with others. (Much of the discussion in Chapters 15 and 16 concerned group working and support of social networking.) Another aspect that will become increasingly important is knowing where you are and who you are! Augmented and virtual reality systems aim to make you feel present somewhere else. The sense of presence is 'being there', whether present in a place or in the presence of other people. As people have multiple identities through their on-line 'selves', so issues of culture and identity also become increasingly important.

In this chapter we are not going to be able to explore the whole of the world's accumulated knowledge of social issues. However, we can look at four key aspects of people engaged in social interaction: human communication; participating in groups; issues of presence; and culture and identity.

24.2 Human communication

Social interaction begins with the ability to communicate. Understanding communication is usually traced back to theories of semiotics and how we exchange signs through some communication channel. Ferdinand de Saussure expressed many of the ideas as related to language, but others such as Umberto Eco have broadened out semiotic theories of communication to all manner of signs. O'Neil (2008) discusses the role of semiotics in new media and Sickiens de Souza (2005) develops a design method based on a semiotic approach.

Semiotics, or semiology, is the study of signs and how they function. Signs can take a variety of forms such as words, images, sounds, gestures or objects. A sign consists of a signifier and the signified. The two always travel together, which is why Eco prefers the term 'sign vehicle' (Figure 24.1). Signs are transmitted from a transmitter to a receiver along a communication channel. Words are transmitted through speech along the auditory communication channel or through writing using the visual channel. The signifier is the concrete representation and the signified is the abstract concept that is denoted by the signifier. Signs will frequently have wider interpretations, the connotations.

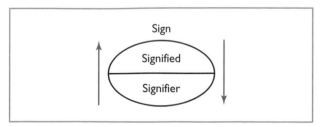

Figure 24.1 A sign consists of a signifier and signified

Semiotics is a very general theory of communication. In terms of human–human communication there are two key components to be considered: a linguistic element (i.e. what is said) and a non-verbal element. The non-verbal element of communication is more popularly known as 'body language' or non-verbal communication (NVC). NVC includes movement and body position, eye gaze, touch and gesture. It also includes aspects of the environment in which any communication takes place, including the distance between the people communicating. Thirdly, NVC deals with paralinguistic features of a communication such as prosody (tone, pitch and rhythm of speech) and the use of linguistic acts such as humour and sarcasm. Whilst it is generally argued that NVC is a vital part of communication, there is still no definitive view on how big a part it plays. Communication is necessary if people are to form relationships with each other. Communication is also central to how those relationships are perceived, bringing in issues of trust, negotiation, persuasion and establishing shared and agreed understandings ('common ground'). Communication needs to be seen both in the short term and in the long term. In the context of interactive systems design, communication is often mediated by technologies; the effectiveness of the communication depends on how the technologies are designed.

Speech and language

Clearly, much communication between people takes place through the use of language, both spoken and written. There is still some controversy concerning whether language is an innate human ability or whether it is something that is learned. Noam Chomsky was an early pioneer of language understanding, though his work is not very accessible, ingrained in the philosophy of mind of the period that was dominated by the HIP view of people.

← Chapter 23 discusses HIP

Most recently, Steven Pinker, a philosopher at Harvard, argues that language is central to the way we are and the way we think and Nass and Brave have published *Wired for Speech,* a book that presents a huge body of empirical research showing how innate the ability of speech and language is (Nass and Brave, 2005).

Speech has many characteristics other than just the words. Prosody concerns the rhythm, stress and intonation of speech. Variations in pitch and the tone of speech and the speed of delivery all contribute to the meanings that are conveyed. Prosody is very important for conveying emotions, and subtle variations of meaning that can be lost in written language. We all know how written forms of communication such as e-mail can cause difficulties because of the lack of non-verbal signals. Of course, written language has long used italic, bold and other typographic cues to indicate emphasis. More recently, things such as emoticons (Figure 24.2) have been developed in order to add some of these additional cues to written communication.

BOX 24.1

Analysing discourse

There is a considerable body of knowledge concerned with understanding written and verbal communication. Discourse analysis and conversation analysis are two examples of how communication can be analysed. Discourse analysis looks at the various speech acts that are involved in a communication. For example, 'Hello' is a greeting and 'How are you?' is a question. In conversation analysis more emphasis is put on turn-taking and how the conversation flows.

Figure 24.2 Emoticons

(Source: © Geo Icons/Alamy Images)

Non-verbal communication

Non-verbal communication refers to the host of signs that are used in communication, whether intentionally or not, outside of the spoken channel. There are a number of different forms of NVC.

Facial expressions

A very important component of NVC is our range of facial expressions – indeed, significant proportions of the brain are thought to be involved in understanding each other's expressions (Figure 24.3).

← FACS – the facial coding system was discussed in Chapter 22

Facial expressions concern changes in the eyes, mouth, cheeks and other facial muscles. Companies such as Sensory Logic exploit this to infer and manage emotional aspects of situations.

Figure 24.3 Female face robot: smiling third-generation female face robot. Inside this robot's head is a CCD camera which it uses to gather visual stimuli. It will react to stimuli with a facial expression based on one of six basic emotions (anger, fear, disgust, happiness, sadness, surprise). Unlike previous generations, this robot can interact with humans in real-time. Previous generations had taken too long to form and lose a facial expression. This robot face was developed at the Laboratory of Fumio Hara and Hiroski Kobayashi at the Science University, Tokyo, Japan.

(Source: Peter Menzel/Science Photo Library)

Gesture

Another key aspect of NVC for many people is the role of gesture. When we speak we move our hands, head and body. This is often used to display the structure of the utterance by enumerating elements or showing how they are grouped, pointing at people or objects for emphasis, a disambiguating gesture, and to give an illustration of shapes, sizes or movements. Gestures can be very effective methods of communication (particularly at a distance) to indicate placement or movement. They are becoming increasingly important as communication methods within interactive systems.

Gestures are not limited to hand movements: whole-body movements are often used to clarify the target of a speech reference – as in the case of someone turning towards a whiteboard when discussing its contents.

Challenge 24.1

Find someone else to do this with. First, take turns to explain to each other (1) directions to the exit from the building, and (2) the plot of a film (preferably with lots of action) that you have enjoyed recently. You should do this in a standing position and must not use gesture. Secondly, note approximately how far apart you have chosen to stand.

Body language

Body posture and movement expresses attitudes and moods and the whole range of stronger emotions. Bodily posture itself is also revealing of our attitude and emotional state. Confident people are erect and square with shoulders back. A positive attitude to others is expressed by leaning forward towards them, together with smiling and looking. Bodily contact for most people is confined to shaking hands, patting each other on the back (found frequently among politicians and senior academics), and kissing; it is governed by strict rules – some of these are legally binding, others are a matter of good taste. Social anthropologists often classify cultures into contact and non-contact cultures.

Reading body language and what it really means is a popular pastime for the press, particularly with respect to politicians or famous couples (Figure 24.4). Handshakes are often given as an example of the power balance in a relationship. Folding the arms is seen as putting a barrier between two discussants. Eye contact is important to engender trust and conviction whereas shifting the eyes or looking down conveys insecurity. Mirroring is an interesting phenomenon in which people will unconsciously copy the body movements of those they are interacting with. It often happens at meetings where people lean forward one after the other, and then one by one lean back. Personal space is another aspect of body language.

BOX 24.2

First impressions

Evidence is mounting to support the intuitive idea that first impressions are highly significant in forming an opinion of someone. A study by Tricia Prickett found that observers could predict whether an applicant would be offered a job by watching the first 15 seconds of a recording of an interview. The popular book *Blink* by Malcolm Gladwell is one of

Figure 24.4 Body language: Prince Charles and Princess Diana pictured together in 1992
(Source: © Trinity Mirror/Mirrorpix/Alamy Images)

several that present the ideas of 'think slicing': our unconscious ability to see familiar patterns of behaviour based on narrow slices of experience. To some extent we are all expert at weighing up people and situations and our quickly formed first impressions are often right (Gladwell, 2000).

Proxemics

The term proxemics was coined by Edward Hall (1966) to describe the study of our use of space and how various differences in that use can make us feel more relaxed or anxious. Proxemics applies to two main contexts: (a) physical territory, such as why desks face the front of a classroom rather than towards a centre aisle, and (b) personal territory, which may be thought of as a 'bubble' of space which we maintain between ourselves and others. Physical distances between people indicate intimacy and friendship. There are major cross-cultural differences in spatial behaviour: for example, Arabs and Latin Americans prefer to get up close whereas the Swedes and the Scots require a good deal more personal space. But how far apart do we stand? Proxemics tells us that the intimate distance for embracing or whispering is perhaps 15–50 cm (and occasionally even closer), the personal distance for conversations among good friends is 50–150 cm, the social distance for conversations among acquaintances is 1–3 metres, and the public distance used for public speaking is 3+ metres. If these spatial norms are violated, we may do one or more of the following:

- Shift position
- Decrease eye contact
- Change orientation (turn away from the other person)
- Decrease duration of responses
- Give fewer 'affiliative' responses.

However, there is some contrary evidence that if we spend more time in such situations, then we perceive the other person as warmer and more persuasive.

Common ground

A study of synchronous, co-located work (that is, working together at the same time in the same place) conducted by Gary and Judith Olson and reported in 2000 involved observing the work of people in nine corporate sites. The Olsons found that the people they observed all normally share office space. Table 24.1 summarizes their findings and is reproduced from Olson and Olson (2000). If we look at the fifth row down, Shared local context, people sharing a common space are all aware of the time of day (nearly lunchtime, working late) and the consequences of this knowledge – it is the end of the week, it is payday, the next working day is a week away because of the local holiday. All of this is quite unremarkable until thought is given to supplying this background, contextual information by means of technology to people who are not present.

← Chapter 7 discusses ethnography

Moving from what might be described as an ethnographic study of nine corporate sites, the Olsons turned their attention to the adequacy of existing technology to support the creation of the common ground which the above co-workers enjoy. Table 24.2 summarizes these reflections.

Table 24.1 Strengths and advantages of sharing the same space synchronously

Characteristic	Description	Implications
Rapid feedback	As interaction flows, feedback is rapid	Quick corrections possible
Multiple channels	Information from voice, facial expression, gesture, body posture, etc., flows among participants	There are many ways to convey a subtle or complex message (provides redundancy)
Personal information	The identity of the contributors to conversation is usually known	The characteristics of the person can help the interpretation of meaning
Nuanced information	The kind of information that flows is often analogue (continuous) with many subtle dimensions (e.g. gesture)	Very small differences in meaning can be conveyed; information can easily be modulated
Shared local context	Participants have a similar situation (time of day, local events)	Allows for easy socializing as well as mutual understanding about what is on each other's mind
Information 'hall' time before and after	Impromptu interactions take place among participants upon arrival and departure	Opportunistic information exchanges and social bonding
Co-reference	Ease of joint reference to objects	Gaze and gesture can easily identify the referent deictic terms
Individual control	Each participant can freely choose what to attend to	Rich, flexible monitoring of how the participants are reacting
Implicit cues	A variety of cues as to what is going on are available in the periphery	Natural operations of human attention provide access to important contextual information
Spatiality of reference	People and work objects are located in space	Both people and ideas can be referred to spatiality: 'air boards'

Source: Olson and Olson (2000), p. 149, Fig. 3

Table 24.2 Achieving common ground

	Co-presence	Visibility	Audibility	Co-temporality	Simultaneity	Sequentiality	Reviewability	Revisability
Face-to-face	✓	✓	✓	✓	✓	✓		
Telephone			✓	✓	✓	✓		
Video-conferencing		✓	✓	✓	✓	✓		
Two-way chat				✓	✓	✓	✓	✓
Answering machine			✓				✓	
E-mail							✓	✓
Letter							✓	✓

Source: After Olson and Olson (2000), p. 160, Fig. 8

These characteristics are defined by the Olsons as follows. Co-presence implies access to the same artefacts to support the conversation. Co-presence also implies shared reference and shared context. **Co-temporality** leads to understanding of the same 'circadian' context (the participants know whether or not it is morning, lunchtime, evening or just much too late). **Visibility** and **audibility** provide 'rich clues' to the situation. **Simultaneity** and **sequentiality** 'relieve the person of having to remember the context of the previous utterance when receiving the current one'. **Reviewability** and **revisability** are the means by which people can review and revise carefully what they mean and have opportunities to make sense of what is being communicated to them. (We return to ideas of co-presence, and other forms of presence in Section 24.4.)

Physical distance can make a difference to how we perceive other people and interact with them in situations involving trust, persuasion and cooperation. A study by Bradner and Mark (2002) set out to investigate this. The researchers had students work in pairs with a 'confederate' (someone working for the researchers who pretended to be just an ordinary participant). The details of the experimental set-up were as follows:

- Each pair undertook tasks designed to investigate deceptive, persuasive and cooperative behaviour.
- The pairs communicated either by instant messaging or by video-conferencing (only one medium per pair).
- Some of the participants were told their co-worker was in the same city, others that they were 3000 miles away – in reality, the confederate was just in the next room.
- The researchers checked the participants' perceptions of the confederate's location by having them sketch their relative locations – two examples are shown in Figure 24.5.

Those who were told their colleague was in a distant city were more likely to deceive, were less persuaded by their colleague, and initially cooperated less with them than those who believed that they were in the same city. The different media made no difference to the effect. Why should this have been so?

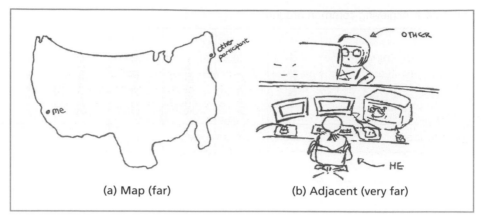

(a) Map (far)   (b) Adjacent (very far)

Figure 24.5 Participants' sketches of the location of self and others

(Source: Bradner and Mark (2002) pp. 226–35. © 2002 ACM, Inc. Reprinted by permission)

Bradner and Mark suggest that social impact theory may be the main explanation for the results. Essentially, people are more likely to be influenced by, and less likely to deceive, others who are located nearby. The study also reinforces other findings that adding video does not make much difference to interpersonal interaction. They conclude that designers of technology need to be concerned with 'bridging social distance, as well as geographic distance'.

24.3 People in groups

The behavior towards one another of two or more persons who have convergent interests (positive interdependence). Each perceives that progress towards his own goal will be enhanced by the progress of the other person or persons as well and each expects reciprocation.

Raven and Rubin (1976)

As you can see from this, cooperation is not an unselfish behaviour, but depends on the recognition of mutual benefits. Studies of cooperation are cross- and multi-disciplinary, including anthropological and naturalistic animal studies (especially primatology), experimental and social psychology, and studies from mathematics.

For example, Axelrod (1984, revised edition 2006) has studied cooperation in the real world in many different domains, from international politics to computer chess, and has concluded that tit-for-tat is a successful model of the observed behaviour. Tit-for-tat is a strategy that starts with explicit cooperation and follows by doing what the other party did last.

A view from primatology

The idea that cooperation during hunting led to the evolution of human social and moral behaviour has received recent support. Capuchin monkeys have been observed to pay one another for the work done in getting food. US primatologists discovered that, after a collaborative hunting effort, the monkey left holding the spoils willingly shared out the food. One of the team noted: 'Tit-for-tat is essential in our economies, and even our morality emphasizes how one good turn deserves another. Our lives depend on our ability to co-operate with one another and to reciprocate for the help of others.'

BOX
24.3

The Swiss at play

Swiss psychologists have been trying to work out why human beings have evolved to cooperate rather than act in a mostly selfish manner. They invented a laboratory game in which volunteers passed money to each other. The rules prevented a player from directly returning the favour to the donor – they had to give their cash to a third party. As the game developed, the researchers noticed that the most generous players actually began to accumulate the most money. The researchers conclude that doing good deeds increases the likelihood that someone else will treat you better.

Group formation

Groups do not just pop into existence, they need to be formed. Studies by social psychologists suggest that most groups (larger than two people – which is a special case) go through a series of predictable phases. Figure 24.6 showing these phases and their characteristics is derived from the work of Tuckerman (1965) and other authors – note that 'decay' is not always regarded as a phase in the life of a group. You might be familiar with the ideas since they are often used – and misused – by people leading group activities of various sorts.

Challenge 24.2

Think of groups you have been part of. At what stages in the group's life could you have used (or did you use) technologies to support the communication process?

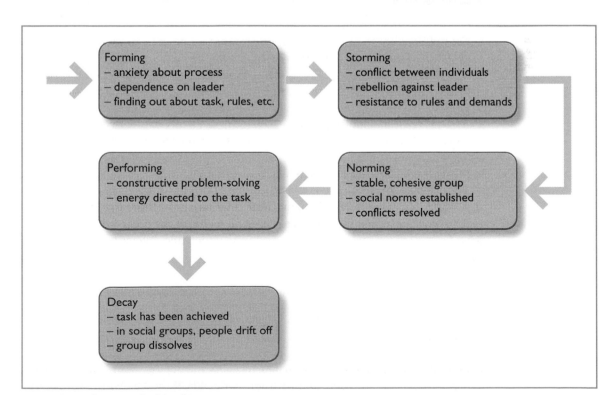

Figure 24.6 Phases in the life of a group
(Source: After Tuckerman, 1965)

Jenny Preece and Howard Rheingold are two people who have investigated the emergence of on-line communities where the same processes of group formation, normalization and decay can be found (Rheingold, 2000, 2003; Preece, 2000). On-line communities need to have some shared interests and goals and need the active participation of their members. Shared social conventions, languages and protocols evolve and are more or less adhered to. In some situations the groups evolve more highly specialized and nuanced shared views, in which case they become 'communities of practice' (Wenger, 1998). However, the Web is also littered with examples of very short-lived groups.

On-line communities can be significantly helped if there is a moderator who oversees the group's activities. The moderator needs to facilitate discussions, keeping them on-topic and stopping any aggressive behaviours, weeding discussions to remove old or irrelevant material and promoting and generally managing the community.

BOX 24.4

Social network analysis

Social network analysis (SNA) is the study of people's social relationships. Sociograms are network diagrams that can be used to show how people are linked to each other and the strength of different relationships. Zaphiris *et al.* (2012) describe how SNA can be used to look at the ties between people in a network, the composition of the network, roles, density and distance between people. Cliques can be identified and illustrated through sociograms.

Social norms

Social norms affect the way people interact in groups. A classic study was carried out at the Hawthorne Works of the Western Electric Company in the late 1920s and early 1930s. The original intention was to investigate how improved working conditions might improve productivity in the factory's 'Bank Wiring Room'. The variables that the researcher manipulated were the temperature, lighting, humidity and length of working day (including such things as rest periods). The workers were placed in a separate experimental room where each of these factors was varied one by one. It was found that each change increased productivity. As a final test, all of the improvements were removed, yet productivity remained at the same high level. Much thought has been given as to why this should be. One popular conclusion was that the workers in the experimental room felt that because their supervisor had been replaced by an observer they were freer to talk to each other and were more cheerful. Alongside this, social norms – what is considered acceptable behaviour – changed: absenteeism had fallen, morale had increased, hard work was the norm. When these experiments were re-analysed, it was suggested that the reason that behaviour changed was more to do with the fact that the workers knew they were being monitored. In general, the phenomenon that an observer changes the behaviour of what is being observed is known as the Hawthorne Effect.

Compliance

Haney *et al.* (1973) were interested in how we adopt roles in a group. If we are assigned a role, to what extent do we comply with the demands of the role itself, regardless of how arbitrary or unreasonable they may seem? (Note: this is more usually known as the Zimbardo study, after one of the most well known of the researchers.)

Eighteen male undergraduates from Stanford University were selected from a group of volunteers. The 18 were tested to ensure they were 'normal' using interviews and question-naires (i.e. they had no serious emotional problems). Then a coin was flipped to divide the group into nine guards and nine prisoners. Each student had previously said that they would prefer to be a prisoner.

Day 1: With the cooperation of the local police (and as a surprise) the prisoners were arrested, cuffed, stripped, de-loused and given a smock to wear. They were then herded into 6' × 9' cells. The guards were given khaki uniforms, mirrored shades, a club and a whistle. They were told not to use physical violence.

After 2–3 days: Everyone had adopted their roles. The guards denied prisoners bathing and sleep, and made them do push-ups. The prisoners became compliant and passive, and began to call each other by number rather than by name.

After 6 days (of 14): The prisoners began to show signs of significant emotional stress – bouts of crying, rashes and depression. At this point the experiment was terminated.

What had happened to the participants? Haney and colleagues concluded that they had ceased to behave as individuals and had complied with group norms, which in turn were being reinforced by others' compliant behaviour.

A modified version of the experiment was recently staged by BBC television in the UK. In the later stages, prisoners and guards rebelled against their imposed roles and briefly collaborated with each other as a 'commune'. However, the structure and organization imposed by the designers of the experiment did not allow sufficient autonomy for the commune to function effectively. After a short time, the group polarized again, the guards proposing an even more severe regime for the prisoners. As in Haney's original version, the experiment was terminated before its planned end-date.

Group think

Group thinking refers to the effect that working in a group – particularly a tight-knit group – can have on people's thoughts and decision making. According to this view, groups adopt more extreme views than individuals – views which may be highly risky or highly cautious.

Groups will often accept a higher degree of risk than individuals: this has been found in many experimental studies, of which Stoner (1961) was the first. Evidence of the effect can be found in many everyday occurrences, but usually only comes to light in cases of disaster or near disaster. The astronauts of Apollo XI, for example, are reported to have accepted a risk of 50:50 that they would not make it back from the Moon. Explanations for this effect include the theory that people who lead or dominate groups tend to be risk-takers and that the group brings with it a diffusion of personal responsibility.

Conformity

Early, classic work by Asch (1951, 1956) and later studies investigated different dimensions of conformity and cross-cultural comparisons. In the classic study Asch asked participants to decide which of three comparison lines of different lengths matched a standard line. To summarize briefly, participants almost always made the right decision when tested on their own. When placed in groups with people who had been coached to give the wrong answer, 32 per cent of individuals agreed with the majority – although there were wide individual differences and some people never conformed. Reasons given included:

- Didn't want to upset the experiment by disagreeing
- Thought their eyesight might be faulty

- Not aware of giving the wrong answer
- Didn't want to 'appear different'.

The number of people who could be induced to conform varied according to group size and the degree of unanimity, task difficulty and whether answers were given in private. Many later studies have found conflicting results, and among the reasons for this cultural factors are significant. A high proportion of the studies were carried out with students (easy to find, easy to persuade away from other tasks) and in the years of campus revolts lower conformity rates were observed. As well as cultural changes over time, there are well-established differences between ethnic and national cultures. To take a couple of extreme examples, the Japanese and Americans are among the most conformist nations and the French and Portuguese among the least (according to the evidence from conformity studies, which do have their limitations).

Groups and technology

These findings may be diverting insights into our own behaviour, but how might the theory help us to understand the effects of computer technologies on groups working together? One area of research has focused on the claim that group decision support systems (GDSS) help to remedy undesirable aspects of group decision making, such as the effects of conformity. More specifically, researchers have investigated whether the 'social distance' and anonymity enforced by interacting through technology as disembodied entities overcome these effects.

In a typical study, Sumner and Hostetler (2000) compared students using computer conferencing (e-mail) with those holding face-to-face meetings to complete a systems analysis project. Those in the computer condition made better decisions: more group members participated, a wider range of opinions were generated, and more rigorous analysis was carried out. They also felt at a greater psychological distance from each other and took longer to arrive at a decision. However, the effect of anonymity is less clear-cut. Postmes and Lea (2000) conducted a meta-analysis of 12 independent studies. The only reliable effect of anonymity was to lead to more contributions, especially critical ones. They argue that performance in decision making is influenced by the strength of group identity and social norms as well as by system characteristics such as anonymity. It is suggested that this is because anonymity affects two rather different social processes – depersonalization and accountability. Some thinkers believe that new Web and communication technologies are radically changing the way people work together and the impact this will have on the world (Rheingold, 2003).

Group productivity and social loafing

It is well established (e.g. Harkins and Szymanski, 1987; Geen, 1991) that people tend to under-exert themselves in groups. Typically, for example, the output of brainstorming groups tends to be less than that of the same number of individuals working in isolation. This effect has been named **social loafing** and tends to occur more frequently when it is hard for individual effort to be identified, or when there is weak group identity, or when the group is not very cohesive. However, some individuals may work harder – **social compensation** – to make up for their lazier colleagues if the group is important to them. Another phenomenon that can decrease group productivity is **production blocking** – where one person's contribution simply gets in the way of another's, principally by causing the second person to forget what they were about to say. It has been suggested that communicating via computers may help to avoid social loafing and production blocking. McKinlay *et al.* (1999) investigated this in their laboratory study of undergraduates. We report this in a reasonable amount of detail so you can appreciate how this type of experiment is carried out.

The groups carried out brainstorming and decision-making tasks, working in groups of three. One set of groups worked under normal face-to-face conditions and a second set used computer-conferencing software. The remaining groups were 'nominal groups' only – that is, they worked individually, but their outputs were aggregated to provide a comparison with that of the true groups. Two main hypotheses (or ideas) were tested:

Hypothesis 1. The nominal groups would produce more ideas. This was what previous research had suggested. The relative output from the groups' brainstorming confirmed this. (The groups had to come up with lists of the advantages and disadvantages of an extra thumb.) But it did not seem that production blocking accounted for the difference, since both the computer-mediated and face-to-face groups could 'jot down' ideas as they occurred to them.

Hypothesis 2. There would be less social compensation in the computer-mediated group than in the face-to-face group. This was based on the theory that the computer group would be less socially cohesive. These groups worked with a scenario about surviving an accident in the Arctic or the desert and had to prioritize a list of items of equipment according to their survival value. The discussion took place either around a table or by text-conferencing. A degree of social loafing was deliberately introduced by including a confederate (someone acting under instructions without the knowledge of the others) as one of the three people. Each confederate either contributed constructively or 'loafed'. It was found that when a social loafer was present, people spoke more in face-to-face groups, but less in computer-mediated groups.

What did the researchers conclude from these results? First, they wondered whether the computer-mediated groups were really less cohesive or whether it was simply more difficult to identify that someone was apparently being lazy. Examining the transcripts of the sessions suggested that the computer group worked more individually, so this suggests that the loafers may have escaped undetected. The text-conferencing medium in real life may be sufficiently social to allow loafing to happen, but not to foster compensatory behaviour. It is suggested that the computer technology may need to be supplemented by activities which enhance group identity if groups are to work together effectively in such media.

In summary: the social psychology of groups

- People behave differently in groups.
- Social psychology tells us much about the change in behaviour from individuals to groups.
- Technology has the potential to mitigate or enhance some of these effects.
- Predicting social effects in computer-mediated groups requires careful thought to identify the real issues.
- Finally, there are individual differences to take into account. We have not strayed into this area so as to keep this material to a manageable length, but you should be aware that factors such as personality, gender and so forth will also affect how individuals work in groups.

Challenge 24.3

Think of groups you have been part of. How did the group work out?

24.4 Presence

The sense of presence is a key component of social interaction. Exactly what presence is is still a philosophically charged issue. Part of the problem with the term is that it is used both as a philosophical construct and as shorthand when talking about telepresence. These two meanings often get confused in discussions.

Telepresence is the use of technology to give people the feeling that they are in another place. (It is discussed in Section 13.1 in terms of mixed reality systems and in Chapter 16 in the context of collaborative virtual environments.) Figure 24.7 shows a system for telepresence.

Figure 24.7 Telepresence
(Source: Marmaduke St. John/Alamy)

Presence has been described in various ways, as the sense of 'being there', or as 'the illusion of non-mediation' (Lombard and Ditton, 1997) by which they mean that the technology in an interaction seems to disappear. As with much discussion of presence, the issue of whether the interaction is mediated or not becomes critical. A high degree of presence is achieved if the medium through which a person experiences something appears to disappear.

Although presence is normally thought of with respect to high-fidelity, high-technology communication devices – telepresence – it can apply to any medium. For example, a person may achieve a high sense of presence when reading a book. They may feel transported to another land depicted in the book, or may feel close to a character in a book. The same is true of radio drama and TV, and becomes more so in the more immersive media such as cinema. Even in a cinema, your sense of presence can be broken by the sight of a person coming in late. In full virtual reality (VR) the very vivid displays cut out any other peripheral sights, and the sights you have are controlled by moving your head. This more immersive experience should make the medium vanish. Unfortunately, the weight and awkwardness of much of today's equipment does not quite achieve the ideal effect.

The psychology of well-being

The way in which we live and socialize has a huge impact on how we feel. The psychology of well-being is a serious academic discipline looking at the factors that make people feel fulfilled, satisfied and well. There is also a lot of 'pop' psychology and easy fixes for striving for well-being. Interaction designers should pay attention to this work as, arguably, part of their job is to increase the opportunities for well-being. Emotion research, psychology, presence, attitudes, financial and career security. There are many factors contributing to well-being.

FURTHER THOUGHTS

A philosophical treatment is given by Riva *et al.* (2004). They argue that humans are social beings, pre-programmed to prioritize the presence of others. The sense of presence of the other arises from the integration of information about three levels of being of the sensed person, all arrived at from the observation of the physical cues inherent in actions: the *physical,* the *physiological* and the *psychological* (Figure 24.8).

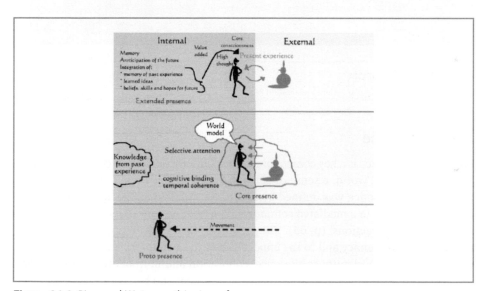

Figure 24.8 Riva and Waterworth's view of presence
(Source: Riva, G. *et al.* (2004))

They take a three-level view of presence. At the physical level, people either confirm that the patterns of bodily movements are those of a recognized person, or they register those of an unknown person. At the physiological level, people infer the emotional state of the person from how they are behaving. At the psychological level, people interpret their observations in terms of the likely mode of cognition of the other person.

Presence can be described as the feeling of being somewhere, and co-presence that of being somewhere with someone else. When presence is mediated by technologies, the sense of presence experienced through a communication channel is a combined function of the extent to which the person is addressed on the three levels: the sensorimotor (does the system respond appropriately – how and on what timescale – to body movements), the perceptual (for example, the quality of sound and visual presentations), and the conceptual. Things such as 'cyber-sickness' may cause a break in presence.

High fidelity is not always associated with high presence, especially the co-presence with others that is our focus. The conceptual level of co-presence is largely generated by the information exchanged between the participants, as in a conversation. It is more or less important to overall presence depending on the activity.

A high degree of presence is necessary to control things at a distance such as with tele-medicine, or controlling the Mars lander (Figure 24.9).

Figure 24.9 Mars lander
(Source: NASA/JPL-Caltech/Solar System Visualization Project)

Social presence

The sense of presence is a key component of social interaction. This sense includes feelings of being in the world, a sense of being in a place and a sense of being with other people. Social presence was defined by Short *et al.* in 1976 as the 'degree of salience of the other person in a mediated communication and the consequent salience of their interpersonal interactions' (p. 65). They refer this idea back to previous concepts of immediacy and intimacy and to the importance of these to interpersonal interactions. Biocca *et al.* (2001) identify co-presence, co-location and mutual awareness as facets of social presence along with psychological involvement and behavioural engagement. Awareness has been important in the field of Computer Supported Cooperative Work (CSCW) for a long time, with novel technological solutions being proposed that allow people to be aware of what others are doing in remote locations (see Chapter 16). There are several technologies that are helping to achieve a high level of social presence, most notably the new video-conferencing facilities such as Cisco's telepresence and HP's Halo (Figure 24.7). These systems use life-size displays, with careful design and a mirroring of meeting room layout to create a real sense of being with other people who are remote.

Another view of social presence relates it to connectedness. Smith and Mackie (2000) argue that the pursuit of connectedness is a fundamental need that drives the search for social relationships and belonging to community. Connectedness is something that can be provided with relatively light and mobile technologies. For example, the hug-me T-shirt provides the wearer a light squeeze when the actuators are activated from a remote device. Another device connects a ring on one lover to an earring on the other. Rubbing the ring makes the earring warm. Figure 24.10 illustrates the Stress OutSourced project which is described as 'crowdsourcing' massage. People connected

Figure 24.10 A prototype massage module attached to an SOS member's jacket

(Source: MIT Media Lab, Tangible Media Group)

to the wearer over the Internet can send a massage to a stressed individual using their wearable module.

A sense of connectedness can be provided though e-mail, the phone, instant messaging and so on. There is little awareness offered by these technologies (the person on the other end of the phone could be doing anything), but there is some sense of presence. Clear areas of advance include notions of network presence where people see themselves as part of a large network, not simply connected one-to-one. With more effective tools to enable people to feel more present in their social networks, economic and social benefits will be derived.

The challenges that lie ahead for technological supporting of social presence include both technological issues and design issues. Technologies need to become lighter and less intrusive (see also Section 2.4). High degrees of presence are only enabled through high-tech solutions such as the Halo system above. Similarly, connecting people through virtual environments is still relatively slow and cumbersome and these restrictions affect the sense of really being with another person. Certainly some work in the Presenccia project has shown that people react to avatars in some ways that are similar to how they react in a real situation (e.g. people have been embarrassed if an attractive female avatar comes too close). This demonstrates a degree of social presence. As avatars become more and more lifelike, people will feel more present with them (Figure 24.11).

Much more needs to be done, however, before avatars become effective virtual humans. Technologies should fit more easily into people's lives both at home (e.g. with large displays embedded in walls) and on the move. Technologies need to be designed to better match the social activities of people and this will provide new forms of social presence and new ways of connecting people.

Figure 24.11 Avatars are becoming more lifelike

(Source: © Image Source Pink/Alamy Images)

Challenge 24.4

How important is social presence and what is the importance of physical presence?

24.5 Culture and identity

In the globalized world we live in, issues of culture and identity are increasingly important. People are concerned that globalization leads to a world dominated by the attitudes and values of big (usually American) organizations. It is sometimes referred to as the McDonaldization of the world. Furthermore, it is a thoroughly intertwined world, with the Internet joining cultures in new ways.

Many people see this as a threat to the diversity of cultures, and see diversity of cultures as a key component of the vitality of ideas and thoughts. If everyone gets their definitions of ideas from Wikipedia, where is the argument and debate that fuels new ideas and new perspectives? Besides national and ethnic cultures, there is a need to consider subcultures and the things that social groups identify with.

Marcus and Gould (2012) discusses globalization, internationalization (preparing systems so that they can be made available for an international distribution) and localization (the process of adapting systems for particular cultures). He gives advice on ensuring that metaphors, icons, language, appearance and other aspects of a system are able to be localized to cultural mores.

Cultural differences

Designers of interactive systems should be sensitive to the values of different cultures and subcultures. The best-known analysis of (national) cultural differences comes from Geert Hofstede (1994). Since the late 1970s Hofstede and his co-workers have been developing theories of cultural differences and have created an industry advising businesses on how to approach doing business with people from different cultures. His theories arose out of a detailed analysis of interviews with IBM employees across 53 countries. He described the patterns of thinking, feeling and acting of these cultures in terms of five dimensions.

Power Distance concerns the extent to which a country centralizes power through strong hierarchical structures or distributes it across people in a more equitable, heterarchical way. This difference affects the way people perceive and approach expertise, authority, security certification and so on. Aaron Marcus gives the example of the difference between a Malaysian university website and a Dutch one. Malaysia is much higher on the Power Distance scale and this is reflected in the site's design. An important consideration for designers is how to present their designs. Will people respect a design if it embodies very different attitudes?

Individualism versus Collectivism is another dimension that divides cultures around issues of individual challenge, honesty, truth and privacy against society support for training and collective harmony.

Masculine versus Feminine differentiates cultures that are at the assertive, competitive and tough end of the scale from those that are at the family, tender and people-oriented end.

Uncertainty Avoidance concerns the extent to which a culture embraces an expressive, active and emotional stance against one that focuses on clarity, simplicity and reducing errors.

Long-term or Short-term perspective is the fifth dimension, concerning cultures that perceive themselves as having a long tradition against those that identify with a shorter timescale.

There are some surprising differences between cultures. For example, Marcus and Gould (2012) suggests that Chinese and North American people organize their homes differently. Different typography, aesthetics and colours also need to be considered.

Identity

Another important area that is being changed through interactive technologies is the idea of identity. As individuals we are shaped by the cultures that we live in and the values that we hold. In the globalized world of the 'information age' these values are shaped, not just by our immediate surroundings and our basic needs to work, eat and play, but also by global trends and influences. As we now have multiple identities, such as in Second Life (Figure 24.12), will we become confused?

Figure 24.12 Second Life
(Source: http://secondlife.com, Linden Lab)

Manuel Castells has written a trilogy of books (1996, 1997, 1998) analysing the changes that the post-industrial age is bringing. As the Internet becomes increasingly dominant, so those who are excluded from the dominant set of values may react badly to this exclusion. For the rest of us, the images and ideas that dominate may lose the appropriate moral background that we have had in the past. Cassells sees a growing juxtaposition of individualism and communalism. We are a world of individuals with our profiles on Facebook or MySpace and with our own set of preferred websites and RSS feeds. On the other hand we join on-line communities and feel identified with different groups and collections of individuals. The Internet makes this much easier to do.

For the students of the future he emphasizes just how important education is – but it is education that allows people to adapt, to learn to learn. People need flexible personalities in order to cope with the rapid nature of change in the twenty-first century.

Another key writer on identity and cyber-culture is Sherry Turkle (2005). She writes on the changes to how we come to know ourselves through participation in on-line communities and games such as MMORGs (massively multi-player on-line role-playing games). These various virtual environments allow us to have multiple personalities and identities, to role-play and to explore different aspects of ourselves. The sense of immersion one gets from these environments is very much a factor of the degree of presence we feel. People can become completely absorbed in games, even when quite low-tech. Turkle does not necessarily see this as a bad thing, as culture can hold people back through its values as well as support them. She also writes on cyber-companionship, and how people identify with and form relationships with robots, cyber-pets and other artificial companions.

Summary and key points

Human beings are generally social creatures and an understanding of the social side of interactions is a necessary part of designing interactive systems. Designers should always consider the social impact that their designs will have.

- The study of the social side of interaction is an important part of interactive systems design.
- Designers need to be aware of the social effects that their designs may have on people.
- Understanding both verbal and non-verbal communication is important
- People often work together in groups and these go through typical phases of forming, storming, 'norming' and performing.
- The sense of presence, the feeling of 'being there', is an important aspects of interaction design.
- Designers need to be aware of cultural differences and to understand the importance of identity.

Exercises

1   Think about what it means to be in the same place as another person. For example are the people in the back row of a large lecture theatre in the same place as those in the front row? Will a good audio system help them feel as if they are in the front row, or is video required as well? Is this the same at a rock concert or in a cinema?

2   What are the cultural differences that affect group formation and other aspects of being with others? For example, the English like to queue, whereas people from India tend to cluster. Italians get closer to each other than Dutch. Are these ridiculous stereotypes or genuine cultural differences?

 Further reading

IJsselsteijn, W.A. and Riva, G. (2003). Being There: The experience of presence in mediated environments. In: Riva, G., Davide, F., and IJsselsteijn, W.A. (eds), *Being There – Concepts, Effects and Measurements of User Presence in Synthetic Environments.* IOS Press, Amsterdam, pp. 3–16.

Lombard, M. and Ditton, T. (1997). At the heart of it all: the concept of presence. *Journal of Computer-Mediated Communication*, **3(2)**. Available at www.ascusc.org/jcmc/vol3/issue2/lombard.html

Getting ahead

Marcus, A. and Gould, E.W. (2012) Globalization, localization, and cross-cultural user-interface design. In Jacko, J.A. (ed) *Handbook of Human–Computer Interaction: Fundamentals, Evolving Technologies and Emerging Applications*, **3rd edn**. CRC Press, Taylor and Francis, Boca Raton, FL, pp. 341–66.

 **Web links**

The international Society for Presence Research is at **http://ispr.info**

There is an interesting site on 'smart mobs' at **www.smartmobs.com**

The accompanying website has links to relevant websites. Go to
www.pearsoned.co.uk/benyon

Comments on challenges

Challenge 24.1

Most people find it very hard to resist the urge to gesture. NVC is an essential part of the communication process. The next but one subsection below talks about proxemics: how far we stand apart.

Challenge 24.2

There are some related ideas on this in Chapter 15 and in Chapter 16 where we discuss Web 2.0 and CSCW. Technologies allow us to connect in different ways and this gives us different views on the world. See the Web link to smart mobs.

Challenge 24.3

You have probably been part of many groups that have folded and some that keep going and develop. My old football (soccer) support group struggles on. It used to be a regular newsletter, then we moved to e-mail, then to a Facebook group. It is the love of the team that keeps it going.

Challenge 24.4

Presence is a fundamental part of communication and central to allowing us to build relationships. In particular, social presence is the sense of being with other people and of engaging with their emotions, social attitudes and psychological state. Physical presence is perhaps less important owing to the improvement in telepresence technologies.

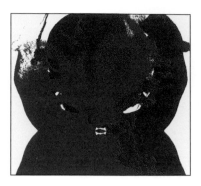

Chapter 25
Perception and navigation

Contents

Aims

Perception and navigation are two important abilities that people have. Perception is concerned with how we come to know an environment through our senses. Navigation is concerned with how we move through environments. Until now the study of perception and navigation concentrated primarily on the physical world. Now that we are introducing interaction in information spaces and interaction through novel devices the world is becoming a more complex and media-rich place.

In this chapter we look at issues of perception – how we can sense what is going on – and navigation – how we move through environments. After studying this chapter you should be able to:

● Understand various theories of visual perception

● Understand other forms of perception

● Understand how we navigate in physical environments

● Understand navigation in information spaces.

25.1 Introduction

How we perceive, understand and make our way through the world is critical to our existence as people. The physical environment has to be sensed for us to know it is there, what is there and how we can move from location to location. Nowadays the physical world is often computationally enabled (see Chapter 18). Thus we need to know not just what things there are in the environment, but what those things can do and what information content they may provide for us.

Moreover, this mixed reality world is highly dynamic. Whilst many aspects of the physical world are relatively static (such as roads, buildings and other geographic features), the world of information content is not. The movement of people and traffic through streets and public spaces is also highly dynamic. Sensing and navigating, adjusting to changes and evaluating the changing world are essential skills for a human living in an environment.

In terms of interactive systems design, understanding human perceptual abilities is important background for the design of visual experiences and provides background for some of the advice on design discussed in Chapter 12 and the guidelines in Chapter 4. Hearing and haptics are important background for the design of multimodal and mixed reality systems provided in Chapter 13. Navigation is central to the development of any information space, including mobile and ubiquitous environments, websites and collaborative environments.

25.2 Visual perception

Visual perception is concerned with extracting meaning (and hence recognition and understanding) from the light falling on our eyes. Visual perception allows us to recognize a room and the people and furniture therein, or to recognize the Windows XP 'start' button, or the meaning of an alert. In contrast, vision is a series of computationally simpler processes. Vision is concerned with such things as detecting colour, shapes and the edges of objects.

Normally sighted people perceive a stable, three-dimensional, full-colour world filled with objects. This is achieved by the brain extracting and making sense of the sensory data picked up by our eyes. The study of visual perception is often divided into a number of interwoven threads, namely theories of visual perception (accounts of how we perceive the world and how these can be explained), including depth perception, pattern recognition (including such things as how we recognize each other) and developmental aspects (how we learn to perceive, or how our perceptual abilities develop).

Richard Gregory has presented (e.g. in Gregory, 1973, among many related works) a good example of a constructivist account of visual perception. He has argued that we *construct* our perception of the world from *some* of the sensory data falling on our senses. His theory is based on the nineteenth-century thinking of Helmholtz who had concluded that we perceive the world by means of a series of unconscious inferences. Gregory has drawn on numerous practical examples of the constructive/interpretative processes to support his theory. Of this supporting evidence we shall consider perceptual constancies and so-called visual illusions (actually better described as perceptual illusions). A red car appears red in normal daylight because it reflects the red elements of (white) light. Yet the same car will appear red at night or parked under a yellow street light. This is an example of a **perceptual constancy** – in this instance, colour constancy. Similarly, a coin always appears coin-shaped (that is, disc-shaped) no matter how it is held in one's hand. This too is an example of another constancy – shape constancy. This ability to perceive an object or a scene in an unchanged fashion, despite changing illumination, viewpoint and so forth affecting the information arriving at our senses, is described as perceptual constancy.

Visual (perceptual) illusions are studied because they are thought to be very revealing of how perception works by understanding what happens when perception does not work! The argument goes like this. Perception is seamless and, as it works very well, it is almost impossible to find a way into the process unless we study it when it does not work. When perception is faulty we can, so to speak, lift a corner and peek underneath and see how it works. Figure 25.1 is an illustration of the Müller–Lyer illusion. The central shaft of the upper figure looks longer despite being exactly the same length as the one below. Gregory explains this illusion by suggesting that our knowledge of the real world causes us to infer (incorrectly) that the upper figure must have a longer shaft. Figure 25.2 is an image of the corner of a door in a corridor. A vertical Müller–Lyer 'arrow' can be seen, made up from the door frame and the wall. A vertical Müller–Lyer 'arrow' points away from the viewer and thus appears to be longer than an equivalent 'arrow' pointing towards the viewer.

Figure 25.1 The Müller–Lyer illusion

Figure 25.3 illustrates a pair of Necker cubes. The Necker cube illustrates **hypothesis testing** very effectively. Gregory has argued that when we are faced with an ambiguous figure such as a Necker cube we unconsciously form a hypothesis that the cube is, say, facing to the right or left. But if we gaze for a few more seconds at the figure it appears to turn inside-out and back again as we try to make sense of the figure. We make unconscious inferences.

Gregory has produced an interesting and engaging account of visual perception that is supported by numerous examples.

Figure 25.2 The Müller–Lyer illusion in the world

(Source: Phil Turner)

However, the central weakness of his argument lies with the question – how do we get started? If visual perception relies on knowledge of the world, how do we bootstrap the process? We can only acquire (visual) knowledge of the world from visual perception, which relies on knowledge of the world.

Direct perception

In sharp contrast to Gregory's work is that of J.J. Gibson. Gibson's work on visual perception dates back to the Second World War (Gibson, 1950) and his work for the US military in improving the training of aircraft pilots, particularly during taking off and

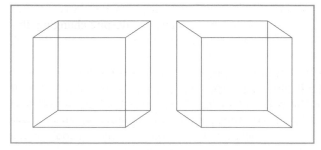

Figure 25.3 A pair of Necker cubes

landing. He observed that a pilot sitting in the fixed point (the pilot's seat at the front of the aircraft) experiences the world apparently flowing past him. Gibson called this flow of information the **optic array**. This optic flow supplies *unambiguously* all information relevant to the position, speed and altitude of the aircraft to the pilot. So there is no need for unconscious inference or hypothesis testing. Figure 25.4 is an illustration of the flow of the optic array. As we drive down a road the environment appears to flow out and past us as we move. What is actually happening is that the **texture** of the environment is expanding.

Texture gradients provide important depth information. Examples of texture gradients include such things as pebbles on a beach or trees in a wood. As we approach a beach or a forest the texture gradient expands as individual pebbles or trees reveal themselves against the higher density of pebbles and trees of the beach or forest. Equally, as we retreat from a scene the texture gradient is seen to condense. Thus Gibson argued (e.g. Gibson, 1966, 1979) that the environment provides all of the information we require to experience it. Gibson also introduced the idea of **affordance** (Gibson, 1977), which has been a recurring concept in HCI design for many years.

← Ideas of affordance and enactive thinking are discussed in Chapter 23

In practice, many psychologists believe that there is merit in both theories: Gibson offers an account for optimal viewing conditions, Gregory for sub-optimal (or restricted) conditions.

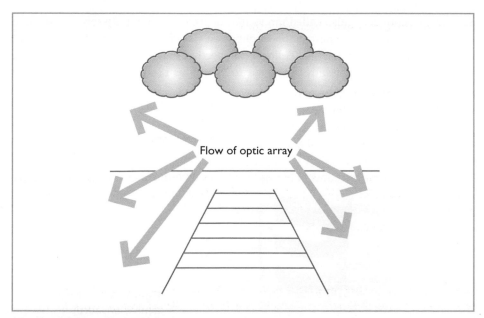

Flow of optic array

Figure 25.4 Flow of optic array

Depth perception

While understanding how we perceive depth is not particularly relevant to everyday office applications, it is often essential to the effective design of games, multimedia applications and virtual reality systems. When designing to give the impression of three-dimensionality (a sense of depth and height) we need to understand how we pick up information from the environment which we interpret as height and depth. Depth perception is usually divided into the role of primary (relevant to immersive virtual reality systems) and secondary depth cues (more important to non-immersive applications such as games). We begin with the primary depth cues and their key application in virtual reality systems.

Primary depth cues

The four key primary depth cues are retinal disparity, stereopsis, accommodation and convergence. A **cue** is a means or mechanism that allows us to pick up information about the environment. Two of these four cues make use of the two different retinal images we have of the world; the other two rely on the muscles that control the movement and focusing of our eyes.

- *Retinal disparity*. As our eyes are approximately 7 cm apart (less if you are a child, more if you have a big head), each retina receives a slightly different image of the world. This difference (the retinal disparity) is processed by the brain and interpreted as distance information.
- *Stereopsis* is the process by which the different images of the world received by each eye are combined to produce a single three-dimensional experience.
- *Accommodation*. This is a muscular process by which we change the shape of the lens in our eyes in order to create a sharply focused image. We unconsciously use information from these muscles to provide depth information.
- *Convergence*. Over distances of 2–7 metres we move our eyes more and more inwards to focus on an object at these distances. This process of convergence is used to help provide additional distance information.

Secondary depth cues

Secondary depth cues (also called monocular depth cues – i.e. they rely on only one eye) are the basis for the perception of depth on flat visual displays. These secondary depth cues are light and shade, linear perspective, height in the horizontal plane, motion parallax, overlap, relative size and texture gradient (the order in which they are discussed is not significant).

- *Light and shade*. An object with its attendant shadow (Figure 25.5) improves the sense of depth.

Figure 25.5 A three-dimension teacup

(Source: Steve Gorton/DK Images)

- *Linear perspective*. Figure 25.6 illustrates some examples of the use of linear perspective to give an impression of depth.

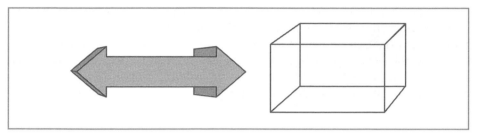

Figure 25.6 Examples of linear perspective, using 'shadow' and wire frame

- *Height in horizontal plane*. Distant objects appear higher (above the horizon) than nearby objects. Figure 25.7 is a screenshot of a chessboard which uses height in the horizontal plane to give the impression of the black pieces being further away than the white.

Figure 25.7 Use of height in the horizontal plane to give an impression of depth

- *Motion parallax*. This cannot be demonstrated in a static image as it depends upon movement. It is perhaps best seen when looking out through a window in a fast-moving train or car. Objects such as telegraph poles that are nearby are seen to flash past very quickly while, in contrast, a distant building moves much more slowly.
- *Overlap*. An object which obscures the sight of another is understood to be nearer. Figure 25.8 illustrates this point with an image of three overlapping windows.

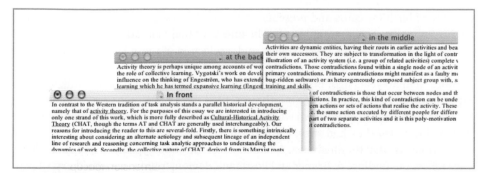

Figure 25.8 Overlapping documents

● *Relative size*. Smaller objects are usually seen as being further away, particularly if the objects in the scene are of approximately the same size (Figure 25.9).

Figure 25.9 Relative size

● *Texture gradient*. Textured surfaces appear closer; irregularities tend to be smoothed out over distance (Figure 25.10).

Figure 25.10 Texture gradient
(Source: Phil Turner)

Factors affecting perception

Perceptual set refers to the effect of such things as our expectations of a situation, our state of arousal and our past experiences on how we perceive others, objects and situations. For example, as children we all interpreted every sound on our birthdays as the delivery of birthday cards and presents; to nervous fliers, every noise is the sound of engine failure or the wings falling off. The effects of these situations and other stimuli have long been studied by psychologists and a selection of these factors can be seen in Figure 25.11.

More than 50 years ago, Bruner and Postman (1949) demonstrated a link between expectation and perception. They briefly presented the sentences in Box 25.1 and asked a number of people to write down what they had seen. People reliably wrote down what they had *expected* they had seen, e.g. Paris in the spring, rather than Paris in *the the* spring which is what they had seen. A similar demonstration appears in Box 25.1 where, if we follow the findings of Bruner and Postman's demonstration, we would expect people to write down 'patience is a virtue' rather than 'patience is *a a* virtue'.

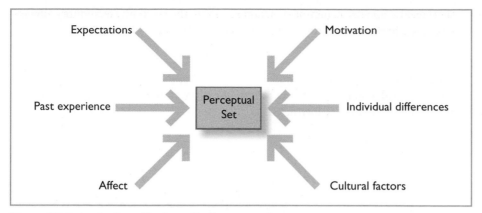

Figure 25.11 A selection of factors affecting perception

(Source: *Psychology: The Science of Mind and Behaviour* (Gross, R. 2001) p. 221, Copyright © 2001 Richard Gross. Reproduced by permission of Hodder Education)

Effects of expectation of perception

PATIENCE	PRIDE COMES	THE END
IS A	BEFORE A	JUSTIFIES THE
A VIRTUE	A FALL	THE MEANS

Source: Based on Bruner and Postman (1949), pp. 206–23

BOX 25.1

The Gestalt laws of perception

The Gestaltists were a group of psychologists working in the early years of the twentieth century who identified a number of 'laws' of perception that they regarded as being **innate** (i.e. we are born with them). While they did not create a theory of visual perception as such, their influence is still widely regarded as important. Indeed, despite their age, these laws map remarkably well onto a number of modern interface design features, as described in Chapter 12.

Proximity

The law of proximity refers to the observation that objects appearing close together in space or time tend to be perceived together. For example, by the careful spacing of objects they will be perceived as being organized into either columns or rows (Figure 25.12).

Figure 25.12 Proximity

This law also applies to auditory perception, where the proximity of auditory 'objects' is perceived as a song or a tune.

Continuity

We tend to perceive smooth, continuous patterns rather than disjoint, interrupted ones. Figure 25.13 will tend to be seen as a continuous curve rather than the five semi-circles from which it was actually constructed.

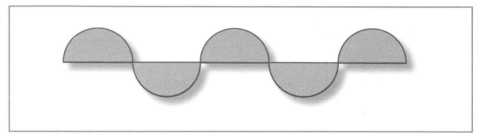

Figure 25.13 Continuity

Part–whole relationships

This is an example of the classic 'law' – the whole is greater than the sum of its parts. Figure 25.14(a) is made up from the same number of H's as Figure 25.14(b): same parts – different whole(s).

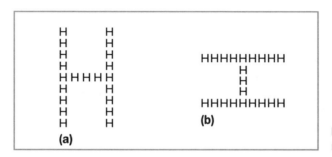

Figure 25.14 Part–whole relationships

Similarity

Similar figures tend to be grouped together. Figure 25.15 is seen as two rows of circles with a single row of diamonds sandwiched between them.

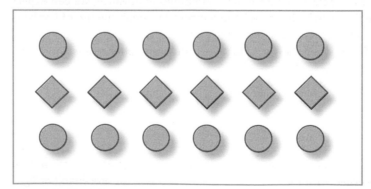

Figure 25.15 Similarity

Closure

Closed figures are perceived more easily than incomplete (or open) figures. This feature of perception is so strong that we even supply missing information ourselves to make a figure easier to perceive. Figure 25.16 is either four triangles or a Maltese cross.

Figure 25.16 Closure

Colour perception

At the back of each eye is the retina, which contains two types of light-sensitive cells called rods and cones. The rods (which are rod-shaped) number approximately 120 million and are more sensitive than the cones (which are cone-shaped). However, they are not sensitive to colour. The 6 or 7 million cones provide the eye's sensitivity to colour. The cones are concentrated in the part of the retina called the *fovea* which is approximately 0.3 mm in diameter. The colour-sensitive cones are divided into 'red' cones (64 per cent), 'green' cones (32 per cent) and 'blue' cones (2 per cent). The 'colour' of these cones reflects their particular sensitivity. The cones are also responsible for all high-resolution vision (as used in such things as reading), which is why the eye moves continually to keep the light from the object of interest falling on the fovea.

25.3 Non-visual perception

In addition to visual perception, people are endowed with other ways of sensing the external environment. These are usually identified as our other four senses: taste, smell, touch and hearing. However, this classification disguises a number of subtleties that exist within each of these senses. As technology continues to advance, we can expect our abilities to sense things to be improved and enhanced through the use of implants that can sense additional phenomena in the environment. For example, we could imagine a scenario in the future when the ability to sense radiation might become important. At present, we sense radiation only after it has done us damage (e.g. through a change in skin colour). With a suitable sensor implanted in our body and connected directly to the brain we could sense it at a distance.

Auditory perception

The first distinction to be made is between *hearing* and *audition* (*auditory perception*). Just as vision is concerned with the physiological and neurological processing of light (with visual perception being the extraction of meaning from the patterns of light), hearing is the processing of variations in air pressure (sound) and auditory perception is the extraction of meaning from the patterns of sound, for example recognizing a fire alarm or holding a conversation.

Sound comes from the *motion* (or vibration) of an object. This motion is transmitted through a *medium* (such as air or water) as a series of *changes in pressure*. Figure 25.17 is an illustration of a single (pure) sound wave. The height of the wave is a measure of the sound's loudness: the time from peak to peak is its frequency (or pitch).

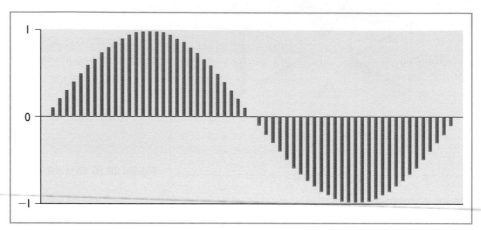

Figure 25.17 A pure sound wave

Loudness

The heights of the peaks (and the depths of the troughs) indicate how loud the sound is. Loudness is measured in decibels (dB). On the decibel scale, the smallest audible sound (near total silence) is 0 dB. The decibel scale is logarithmic, which means that a sound of 40 dB is 10 times louder than the same sound at 30 Db

It should be noted that prolonged exposure to any sound above 85 dB will cause hearing loss.

Near total silence	0 dB
A whisper	15 dB
Normal conversation	60 dB
A car horn	110 dB
A rock concert	120 dB

Frequency

The frequency of the sound wave is the pitch of the sound – low-frequency sounds like the rumble of an earthquake have a very low pitch, while high-frequency sounds like those of screaming children have a high pitch. Human hearing is quite limited in terms of the range of frequencies we can detect, and as we get older we tend to lose the ability to hear higher-pitched sounds. So while children may be able to hear a dog whistle or the sound of a bat's echo location, adults usually cannot. (The pipistrelle bat emits its echo-location signals at about 45 kHz, whereas the noctule bat uses a lower frequency of about 25 kHz or so.) The range of hearing for a typical young person is 20 to 20,000 hertz.

How do we hear?

The outer part of the ear (or *pinna*) is shaped to capture sound waves. If a sound is coming from behind or above the listener, it will reflect off the pinna in a different way from if it is coming from in front of or below the listener. The sound reflection changes the pattern of the sound wave that is recognized by the brain and helps determine where the sound has come from. From the pinna, the sound waves travel along the ear canal to the tympanic membrane (the *eardrum*). The eardrum is a thin, cone-shaped piece of skin about 10 mm wide. The movement of the eardrum is then amplified by way of *ossicles* (a small group of tiny bones). The ossicles include the *malleus* (hammer), the *incus* (anvil) and the *stapes* (stirrup). This amplified signal (approximately 22*) is then passed on to the *cochlea*. The cochlea transforms the physical vibrations into electrical signals.

The cochlea is a snailshell-shaped structure, and is made up from a number of structures including the scala vestibuli, the scala media, the basilar membrane and the organ of Corti. Each of these structures contributes to the transduction of the sound waves into complex electrical signals which are transmitted by way of the cochlear nerve to the cerebral cortex, where the brain interprets them. The structure is shown in simplified form in Figure 25.18.

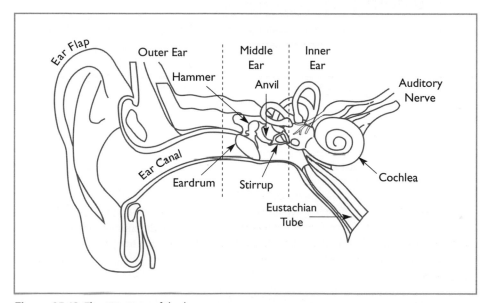

Figure 25.18 The structure of the human ear

Haptic perception

Haptic perception has become in recent years an area of significant research. Again we distinguish between the *sense* of touch and haptic *perception,* which is the interpretation of this sense (see Figure 25.19). Haptic perception starts with touch, which is sensed by receptors lying both beneath the skin surface (cutaneous receptors) and in the muscles and joints (kinaesthetic receptors). This sense provides the data about objects and surfaces in contact with the individual. It should also be remembered that heat and vibration can also be sensed from a source with which we are not in direct contact. Haptic perception provides a rich 'picture' of an individual's immediate surroundings and is essential to manipulating objects.

In HCI, the term haptics refers to both sensing and manipulating through the sense of touch (Tan, 2000). The keyboard and mouse are haptic input devices. Tan divides haptics into two components – *tactile sensing,* that is, sensing via the outsides of our bodies (skin, nails and hair), and *kinaesthetic sensing,* which concerns the knowledge we have of our body's position. As I type, I am aware of my forearms resting on the table, the crick in my neck and the looseness of my shoes on my feet – this information is provided by the **proprioceptic** nerves. Unlike visual perception and audition which can be thought of as input systems, the haptic system is *bidirectional*. Activities such as the reading of Braille text by blind people require the use of both the sensing and manipulation aspects of the haptic system. Tan notes that, historically, work on haptic systems display has been driven by the need to develop 'sensory-substitution systems for the visually or hearing impaired'.

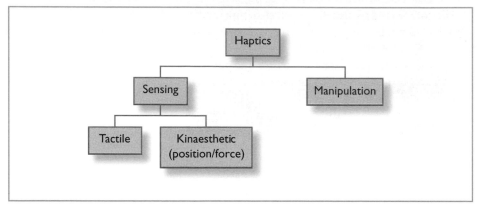

Figure 25.19 Defining haptics

(Source: After Tan (2000), pp. 40–1. © 2000 ACM, Inc. Reprinted by permission)

BOX 25.2

Key terms for haptics

Haptic	Relating to the sense of touch.
Proprioceptive	Relating to sensory information about the state of the body (including cutaneous, kinaesthetic and vestibular sensations).
Vestibular	Pertaining to the perception of head position, acceleration and deceleration.
Kinaesthetic	The feeling of motion. Relating to sensations originating in muscles, tendons and joints.
Cutaneous	Pertaining to the skin itself or the skin as a sense organ. Includes sensation of pressure, temperature and pain.
Tactile	Pertaining to the cutaneous sense but more specifically the sensation of pressure rather than temperature or pain.
Force feedback	Relating to the mechanical production of information sensed by the human kinaesthetic system.

Source: After Oakley *et al.* (2000)

Taste and smell

Taste, or gustation, and smell, or olfaction, are two senses that have not been used much in interactive systems, primarily because they have not been digitized. The systems that are available for making smells rely on releasing chemicals into the air, or on enclosing smells in some container that can be scratched or otherwise disturbed to release the smell. A secondary problem with smell is that it is difficult to disperse. So, for highly interactive experiences it is difficult to provide one smell at one moment and another at the next moment. Smell has been used in the cinema, but without any great success, and was a part of the all-round sensory experience in the 1950s, the Sensorama (Figure 25.20).

Taste is experienced through the taste buds in the mouth and in Western views was originally considered to have four states – sweet, salty, sour and bitter – but Eastern traditions have included a fifth, umami, which translates roughly as savoury, or brothy.

← See also the discussion in Chapter 13

Figure 25.20 Sensorama
(Source: www.telepresence.org)

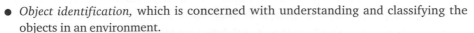

Challenge 25.1

We developed a visual virtual environment for a botanical garden. When people tried it, what do you think they missed from the real experience?

25.4 Navigation

Perception is how we sense the environment; navigation is concerned with finding out about, and moving through, the environment. Navigation includes three different but related activities:

- *Object identification,* which is concerned with understanding and classifying the objects in an environment.
- *Exploration,* which is concerned with finding out about a local environment and how that environment relates to other environments.
- *Wayfinding,* which is concerned with navigating towards a known destination.

Although object identification is somewhat akin to exploration, its purpose is different. Exploration focuses on understanding what exists in an environment and how the things are related. Object identification is concerned with finding categories and clusters of objects spread across environments, with finding interesting configurations of objects and with finding out information about the objects.

Navigation is concerned both with the location of things and with what those things mean for an individual. How many times have you been told something like 'turn left at the grocer's shop, you can't miss it', only to drive straight past the supposed obvious landmark? Objects in an environment have different meanings for different people.

A lot of work in psychology has been done on how people learn about environments and with the development of 'cognitive maps', the mental representations that people are assumed to have of their environment (Tversky, 2003). Barbara Tversky points out that people's cognitive maps are often inaccurate because they are distorted by other factors. The city of Edinburgh is actually further west than the city of Bristol, but people distort this because they assume that the UK lies north–south. In a similar way people think Berkeley is east of Stanford.

← Chapter 23 discusses distributed cognition

Mental map representations are rarely wholly complete or static. Ecological considerations are concerned with the cues that people draw from the immediate environment as they interact with it. People develop knowledge of the space over time and through the experience of interacting with and within a space. There is still much debate about how much knowledge is 'in the head' and how much is 'in the world'. Hutchins (1995) considered the different forms of mental 'maps' in developing his ideas on distributed cognition when he looked at Polynesian navigators and the different perceptions and methods that they appear to have for navigation.

Wayfinding is concerned with how people work out how to reach their destination. For Downs and Stea (1973) and Passini (1994) the process involves four steps: orienting oneself in the environment, choosing the correct route, monitoring this route, and recognizing that the destination has been reached. To do this people use a variety of aids, such as signposts, maps and guides. They exploit landmarks in order to have something to aim for. They use 'dead reckoning' at sea or elsewhere when there are no landmarks. With dead reckoning you calculate your position by noting the direction you have headed in, the speed of travel and the time that has passed. This is usually correlated with a landmark whenever possible.

Learning to find one's way in a new space is another aspect of navigation considered by psychologists (Kuipers, 1982; Gärling et al., 1982). First, we learn a linked list of items. Then we get to know some landmarks and can start relating our position with regard to these landmarks. We learn the relative position of landmarks and start building mental maps of parts of the space between these landmarks. These maps are not all complete. Some of the 'pages' are detailed, others are not, and more importantly, the relations between the pages are not perfect. Some may be distorted with respect to one another.

In the 1960s the psychologist Kevin Lynch identified five key aspects of the environment: nodes, landmarks, paths, districts and edges (Lynch, 1961). Figure 25.21 shows an example of one of his maps.

Districts are identifiable parts of an environment that are defined by their edges. Nodes are smaller points within the environment; those with particular significance may be seen as landmarks. Paths connect nodes. These concepts have endured, though not without criticism. The main issue is to what extent are features of the environment objectively identified. Other writers (e.g. Barthes, 1986) have pointed out that the identification of these features is much more subjective. It is also important to consider the significance and meanings that are attached to spaces by people. Different people see things differently at different times. Shoppers see shopping malls in a different way from skateboarders. A street corner might feel very different in the middle of the day from how it does at night. There are different conceptions of landmarks, districts, etc., depending on cultural differences such as race, gender or social group. The ship's captain can see

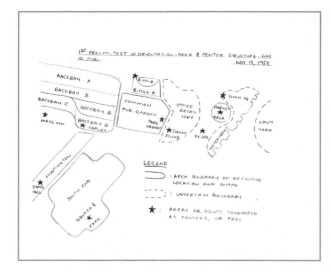

Figure 25.21 Sketch from Kevin Lynch's original survey of Boston

(Source: from Massachusetts Institute of Technology, Kevin Lynch papers, MC 208, box 2. Massachusetts Institute of Technology, Institute Archives and Special Collections, Cambridge, Massachusetts.)

many more different landmarks in the ebb and flow of a river than the novice. Navigation in a wilderness is a wholly different activity from navigation in a museum.

FURTHER THOUGHTS

Space syntax

An interesting approach to architectural understanding is provided by the space syntax theory of Hillier (1996). This theory looks at the connectivity of nodes in a space: how closely connected one node is to another through the paths that link them. Hillier uses the theory to explore issues of legibility of a space – how easy it is to understand the connections and how visible different connections are. By concentrating on people's movement through space, many of the features of the space are revealed. Using the theory, social phenomena such as burglary rates and house prices can be predicted. Chalmers (2003) adapts and applies the theory to the design of information spaces

In addition to the five features identified by Lynch, it is generally assumed that there are three different types of knowledge that people have of an environment: landmark, route and survey knowledge (Downs and Stea, 1973). Landmark knowledge is the simplest sort of spatial knowledge in which people just recognize important features of the environment. Gradually they will fill in the details between landmarks and form route knowledge. As they become more familiar with the environment they will develop survey knowledge, the 'cognitive map' of the environment.

Challenge 25.2

Write down your journey from home to work or college. Identify where you have a clear and detailed cognitive map and where you have only sketchy knowledge. Identify the main landmarks on your route and distinguish where you have just route knowledge against where you have survey knowledge. Give examples of where ecological decisions are made (i.e. where you rely on knowledge in the world). List the nodes, paths, edges and districts on your route. Discuss this with a colleague and identify areas of agreement/disagreement.

Designing for navigation

The essential thing about designing for navigation is to keep in mind the different activities that people undertake in a space – object identification, wayfinding and exploration – and the different purposes and meanings that people will bring to the space. Of course, designing for navigation has been the concern of architecture, interior design and urban planning for years and many useful principles have been developed that can be applied to the design of information spaces.

The practical aim of navigation design is to encourage people to develop a good understanding of the space in terms of landmark, route and survey knowledge. However, another aim is to create spaces that are enjoyable and engaging. Design (as ever) is about form and function and how these can be harmoniously united.

One commentator on the aesthetics of space is Norberg-Schulz (1971), another is Bacon (1974). Bacon suggests that any experience we have of space depends on a number of issues. These include:

- Impact of shape, colour, location and other properties on the environment
- Features that infuse character
- Relationships between space and time – each experience is based partly on those preceding it
- Involvement.

These all have an impact on navigation. Too much similarity between different areas of an environment can cause confusion. The design should encourage people to recognize and recall an environment, to understand the context and use of the environment and to map the functional to the physical form of the space. Another important design principle from architecture is the idea of gaining gradual knowledge of the space through use. Designers should aim for a 'responsive environment', ensuring the availability of alternative routes, the legibility of landmarks, paths and districts and the ability to undertake a range of activities.

Gordon Cullen developed a number of urban design principles known as 'serial vision'. Cullen's theory (1961) was based on the gradually unfolding nature of vistas as one walked through an environment (see Gosling, 1996). Figure 25.22 illustrates this.

Benyon and Wilmes (2003) applied this theory to the design of a website.

Signage

Good, clear signposting of spaces is critical in the design of spaces. There are three primary types of sign that designers can use:

- *Informational signs* provide information on objects, people and activities and hence aid object identification and classification.
- *Directional signs* provide route and survey information. They do this often through sign hierarchies, with one type of sign providing general directions being followed by another that provides local directions.
- *Warning and reassurance signs* provide feedback or information on actual or potential actions within the environment.

Of course, any particular sign may serve more than one purpose, and an effective signage system will not only help people in getting to their desired destination but also make them aware of alternative options. Signage needs to integrate aesthetically with the environment in which it is situated, so that it will help both good and poor navigators. Consistency of signage is important, but so is being able to distinguish different types of sign (Figure 25.23).

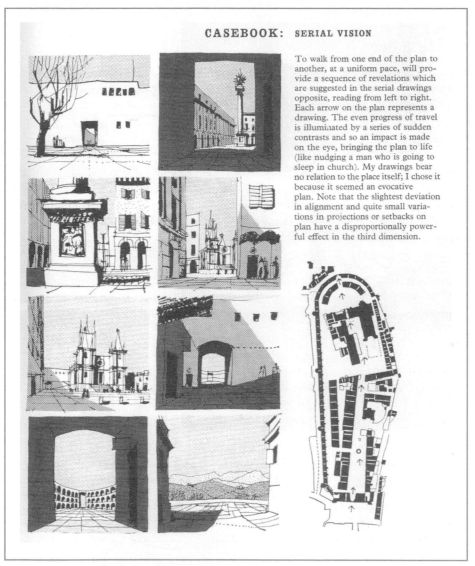

CASEBOOK: SERIAL VISION

To walk from one end of the plan to another, at a uniform pace, will provide a sequence of revelations which are suggested in the serial drawings opposite, reading from left to right. Each arrow on the plan represents a drawing. The even progress of travel is illuminated by a series of sudden contrasts and so an impact is made on the eye, bringing the plan to life (like nudging a man who is going to sleep in church). My drawings bear no relation to the place itself; I chose it because it seemed an evocative plan. Note that the slightest deviation in alignment and quite small variations in projections or setbacks on plan have a disproportionally powerful effect in the third dimension.

Figure 25.22 Gordon Cullen's serial vision
(Source: Cullen, 1961)

Maps and guides

Maps can be used to provide navigational information. Supplemented with additional detail about the objects in the environment, they become guides. There are many different sorts of map, from the very detailed and realistic to the highly abstract schematic. We have already seen examples of schematic maps such as the map of the London Underground (Chapter 12). We have also seen site maps in websites that show the structure of the information and how it is classified and categorized.

Maps are social things – they are there to give information and help people explore, understand and find their way through spaces. They should be designed to fit in with the signage system. Like signs, there will often be a need for maps at different levels of abstraction. A global map which shows the whole extent of the environment will need to be supplemented by local maps showing the details of what is nearby. Figure 25.24 shows some different sorts of map.

Figure 25.23 Signage in London

(Source: Philip Enticknap/DK Images)

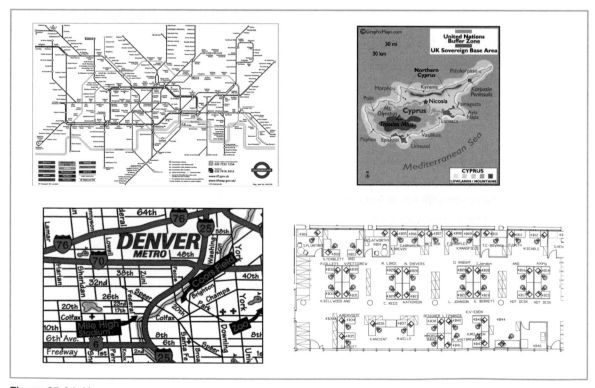

Figure 25.24 Maps

(Sources: London Underground Map, 2009. © TfL from the London Transport Museum collection; http://worldatlas.com; http://graphicmaps.com; PearsonEducation)

Challenge 25.3

How can we adapt these ideas to the design of information spaces such as websites?

Social navigation

A well-designed environment with good signage and well-designed navigational aids such as maps will be conducive to good navigation, but even in the best-designed environment people will often turn to other people for information on navigation rather than use more formalized information artefacts. When navigating cities people tend to ask other people for advice rather than study maps. Information from other people is usually personalized and adapted to suit the individual's needs. Even when we are not directly looking for information we use a wide range of cues, both from features of the environment and from the behaviour of other people, to manage our activities. We might be influenced to pick up a book because it appears well thumbed, we walk into a sunny courtyard because it looks attractive, or we might decide to see a film because our friends enjoyed it. We find our way through spaces by talking to or following the trails of others. The whole myriad of uses that people make of other people, whether directly or indirectly, is called *social navigation*.

← Chapter 15 on social media uses some of these ideas

Navigation is an important, and very general, activity for people to undertake. Navigation requires people to explore, wayfind and identify objects in an environment. In Chapter 18 this general model was applied to ubiquitous computing environments where a more functional description of 'overview, wayfind, interpret' was adopted. Elsewhere we see similarities with Shneiderman's mantra for visualization: 'overview first, zoom and filter, and details on demand'.

Summary and key points

Perception relies on our five senses and how we interpret the signals we receive. It is a constructed process that involves us making inferences from these sometimes ambiguous signals. Navigation concerns how we move through environments and make sense of the objects that are in the environment. We can learn much from studying navigation in geographical spaces and indeed apply design principles from urban planning and architecture to the design of information spaces.

- Perception is concerned with how we get to know about an environment and how we monitor our interaction with an environment.
- Good design will help people obtain a survey knowledge of the environment.
- Navigation is concerned with the three key activities of wayfinding, exploration and object identification.

Exercises

1 Take a small electronic space such as a mobile (cell) phone, a tablet, or even a car radio/cassette/CD player. Look at the signs, maps and other items that are there to help you find your way through the space. Consider the design

in terms of landmarks, nodes, districts, etc. How well designed is it? Do you always know 'where you are' and how to get to where you want to go?

2 Find a large website such as the Amazon.co.uk site in Figure 15.6. Write down the various navigational features that have been included in terms of local and global navigation, searching and labelling. Critique the information design of the site (perhaps reverse-engineer the wireframes for different pages).

 Further reading

Passini, R. (1994) *Wayfinding in Architecture*. Van Nostrand, New York. *The most approachable book on navigation in geographical spaces.*

Getting ahead

Bacon, E.N. (1974) *Design of Cities*. Thomas Hudson, London.

Gibson, J.J. (1986) *The Ecological Approach to Visual Perception*. Lawrence Erlbaum Associates, Hillsdale, NJ.

Lynch, K. (1961) *The Image of the City*. MIT Press, Cambridge, MA.

 Web links

The accompanying website has links to relevant websites. Go to
www.pearsoned.co.uk/benyon

 Comments on challenges

Challenge 25.1

People missed the smell of an exotic garden, the heat of the tropics, the sounds of birds and the feel of the earth. In short, people missed all the non-visual features of a botanical garden. As soon as these are removed from a scene, the power of the visual image is diminished.

Challenge 25.2

There is not much that can be said in general here about what you know about where you live and work! There are some interesting points about knowledge in the world, however. When we reflect for an exercise such as this, we 'run a mental model'; that is, we visualize the journey in our 'mind's eye'. This may mean that we attend to more detail than we would do when we are really navigating the route when our minds might be on something else. In such cases we may rely much more on ecological issues than we think we do.

Challenge 25.3

Navigation design is a central part of designing for websites, but also in designing ubiquitous computing environments. Websites have local and global navigation bars. They include menus (signposts) and have page titles to tell you where you are. There are many examples of navigation in information spaces that are similar to navigation in geographical spaces.

References

Abed, M., Tabary, D. and Kolski, C. (2004) Using formal specification techniques for the modeling of tasks and the generation of human–computer user interface specifications. In Diaper, D. and Stanton, N. (eds), *The Handbook of Task Analysis for Human–Computer Interaction*. Lawrence Erlbaum Associates, Mahwah, NJ.

Ackerman, M. (2000) The intellectual challenge of CSCW: the gap between social requirements and technical feasibility. *Human–Computer Interaction,* 15(2–3), 181–205.

Ahlberg, C. and Shneiderman, B. (1994) Visual information seeking: tight coupling of dynamic query filters with starfield displays. *CHI '94: Proceedings of the SIGCHI Conference on Human Factors in Computing Systems.* ACM Press, New York, pp. 313–317.

Alexander, C. (1979) *The Timeless Way of Building*. Oxford University Press, New York.

Alexander, I. and Maiden, N. (2004) *Scenarios, Stories, Use Cases Through the Systems Development Life Cycle*. John Wiley, Chichester.

Allport, G.W. (1968) *The Person in Psychology: Selected Readings*. Bacon Press, Boston, MA.

Anderson, C. (2008) *The Long Tail: Why the Future of Business Is Selling Less of More*, Revised and updated edition. Hyperion, New York.

Anderson, J.R. and Reder, L. (1979) An elaborate processing explanation for depth of processing. In Cermak, L.S. and Craik, F.I.M. (eds), *Levels of Processing in Human Memory*. Lawrence Erlbaum Associates, Hillsdale, NJ.

Annett, J. (2004) Hierarchical task analysis. In Diaper, D. and Stanton, N. (eds), *The Handbook of Task Analysis for Human–Computer Interaction*. Lawrence Erlbaum Associates, Mahwah, NJ.

Antunes, P. and Costa, C.J. (2003) From genre analysis to the design of meetingware. *Proceedings of Group '03 Conference,* Sanibel Island, FL, 9–12 December. ACM Press, New York, pp. 302–310.

ARGO (2007, 6 September) *Project Homepage*. Retrieved 19 September 2007 from http://www.argo.ucsd.edu/.

ARToolkit (2007, 7 February) *Project homepage*. Retrieved 19 September 2007 from http://www.hitl.washington.edu/artoolkit/.

Asch, S.E. (1951) Effects of group pressure upon the modification and distortion of judgement. In Guetzkow, H. (ed.), *Groups, Leadership and Men*. Carnegie Press, Pittsburgh, PA.

Asch, S.E. (1956) Studies of independence and conformity: A minority of one against a unanimous majority. *Psychological Monographs,* 70 (whole no. 416).

Ashbrook, D. and Starner, T. (2010) MAGIC: a motion gesture design tool. *CHI '10: Proceedings of the SIGCHI Conference on Human Factors in Computing Systems.* ACM Press, pp. 2159–2168.

Atkinson, R.C. and Shiffrin, R.M. (1968) Human memory: a proposed system and its control processes. In Spence, K.W. and Spence, J.T. (eds), *The Psychology of Learning and Motivation,* vol. 2. Academic Press, London.

Axelrod, R. (2006) *The Evolution of Cooperation* (rev. edn). Perseus Books Group, New York.

Azuma, R.T. (1997) A survey of augmented reality. *Presence: Teleoperators and Virtual Environments,* 6(4), 355–358.

Bacon, E.N. (1974) *Design of Cities*. Thomas Hudson, London.

Baddeley, A. (1997) *Human Memory: Theory and Practice*. Psychology Press, Hove, Sussex.

Baddeley, A.D. and Hitch, G. (1974) Working memory. In Bower, G.H. (ed.), *Recent Advances in Learning and Motivation,* vol. 8. Academic Press, New York.

Badre, A.N. (2002) *Shaping Web Usability: Interaction Design in Context*. Addison-Wesley, Boston, MA.

Bahrick, H.P. (1984) Semantic memory content in permastore: fifty years of memory for Spanish learned in school. *Journal of Experimental Psychology: General*, 113(1), March: 1–29.

Baillie, L. (2002) *The Home Workshop: a method for investigating the home*. PhD Thesis, School of Computing, Napier University, Edinburgh.

Baillie, L. and Benyon, D.R. (2008) Place and technology in the home. *Computer Supported Cooperative Work,* 17(2–3), 227–256.

Baillie, L., Benyon, D., MacAulay, C. and Petersen, M (2003) Investigating design issues in household environments. *Cognition Technology and Work,* 5(1), 33–44.

Balbo, S., Ozkan, N. and Paris, C. (2004) Choosing the right task modeling notation: a taxonomy. In Diaper, D. and Stanton, N. (eds), *The Handbook of Task Analysis for Human–Computer Interaction*. Lawrence Erlbaum Associates, Mahwah, NJ.

Bannon, L.J. (1991) From human factors to human actors: the role of psychology and human–computer interaction studies in system design. In Greenbaum, J. and Kyng, M. (eds), *Design at Work: Cooperative Design of Computer Systems*. Lawrence Erlbaum Associates, Hillsdale, NJ, pp. 25–44.

Bannon, L.J. and Schmidt, K. (1991) CSCW: four characters in search of context. In Bowers, J.M. and Benford, S.D. (eds), *Studies in Computer Supported Collaborative Work*. Elsevier North-Holland, Amsterdam.

Bardram, J.E. (1998) Designing for the dynamics of cooperative work activities. *Proceedings of CSCW '98 Conference,* Seattle, WA, 14–18 November. ACM Press, New York, pp. 89–98.

Bardzell, J. (2009) Interaction criticism and aesthetics. *CHI '09: Proceedings of the SIGCHI Conference on Human Factors in Computing Systems.* ACM Press, New York, pp. 2357–2366.

Barnard, P.J. (1985) Interacting cognitive subsystems: a psycholinguistic approach to short term memory. In Ellis, A. (ed.), *Progress in the Psychology of Language,* vol. 2. Lawrence Erlbaum Associates, London, pp. 197–258.

Barthes, R. (1986) Semiology and the urban. In Gottdiener, M. and Lagopoulos, A.P. (eds), *The City and the Sign.* Columbia University Press, New York.

Bartlett, M.S., Hager, J.C., Ekman, P. and Sejnowski, T.J. (1999) Measuring facial expressions by computer image analysis. *Psychophysiology,* 36, 253–263.

Beaudouin-Lafon, M. and Mackay, W. (2012) Prototyping tools and techniques. In Jacko, J. A. (ed.), *The Human—Computer Interaction Handbook: Fundamentals, Evolving Technologies and Emerging Applications* (3rd edn). CRC Press, Taylor and Francis, Boca Raton, FL, pp. 1081–1104.

Beck, K. and Andres, C. (2004) *Extreme Programming Explained: Embrace Change* (2nd edn). Addison-Wesley, Boston, MA.

Bellotti, V., Begole, B., Chi, E.H., *et al.* (2008) Activity-based serendipitous recommendations with the Magitti mobile leisure guide. *CHI '08: Proceedings of the SIGCHI Conference on Human Factors in Computing Systems.* ACM, New York, pp. 1157–1166

Benda, P. and Sanderson, P. (1999) New technology and work practice: modelling change with cognitive work analysis. In Sasse, M. and Johnson, C. (eds), *Proceedings of INTERACT '99.* IOS Press, Amsterdam, pp. 566–573.

Benford, S., Fraser, M., Reynard, G., Koleva, B. and Drozd, A. (2002) Staging and evaluating public performances as an approach to CVE research. *Proceedings of CVE '02 Conference,* Bonn, Germany, 30 September–2 October ACM Press, New York, pp. 80–87.

Benford, S., Giannachi, G., Koleva, B. and Rodden, T. (2009) From interaction to trajectories: designing coherent journeys through user experiences. *CHI '09: Proceedings of the SIGCHI Conference on Human Factors in Computing Systems.* ACM, New York, pp. 709–718.

Benford, S., Snowdon, D., Colebourne, A., O'Brien, J. and Rodden, T. (1997) Informing the design of collaborative virtual environments. *Proceedings of Group '97 Conference,* Phoenix, AZ, 16–19 November. ACM Press, New York, pp. 71–80.

Benyon, D. and Mival, O. (2008) Landscaping personification technologies. *CHI '08: Proceedings of the SIGCHI Conference on Human Factors in Computing Systems.* ACM Press, New York, pp. 3657–3662.

Benyon, D.R. and Murray, D.M. (1993) Adaptive systems; from intelligent tutoring to autonomous agents. *Knowledge-based Systems,* 6(4), 197–219.

Benyon, D.R. and Skidmore, S. (eds) (1988) *Automating Systems Development.* Plenum, New York.

Benyon, D.R. and Wilmes, B. (2003) The application of urban design principles to navigation of web sites. In O'Neill, E., Palanque, P. and Johnson, P. (eds), *People and Computers XVII – Proceedings of HCI 2003 Conference.* Springer-Verlag, London, pp. 105–126.

Benyon, D.R., Crerar, A. and Wilkinson, S. (2001) Individual differences and inclusive design. In Stephanidis, C. (ed.), *User Interfaces for All: Concepts, Methods and Tools.* Lawrence Erlbaum Associates, Mahwah, NJ.

Benyon, D.R., Green, T.R.G. and Bental, D. (1999) *Conceptual Modelling for Human–Computer Interaction, Using ERMIA.* Springer-Verlag, London.

Benyon, D., Smyth, M., O'Neill, S., McCall, R. and Carroll, F. (2006). The place probe: exploring a sense of place in real and virtual environments. *Presence: Teleoperators and Virtual Environment* 15(6), 668–687.

Benyon, D.R., Mival, O. and Ayan, S. (2012) Designing blended spaces. *BCS–HCI '12: Proceedings of the 26th Annual BCS Interaction Specialist Group Conference on People and Computers.* British Computer Society, Swindon, 398–403.

Benyon, D., O'Keefe, B., Riva, G. and Quigley, A. (2013a) Presence and digital tourism. *Journal of AI and Society,* in press.

Benyon, D.R., Mival, O. and O'Keefe, B. (2013b) Blended spaces and digital tourism. *Proceedings of CHI2013 Workshop on Blended Interaction Spaces,* 28 April, Paris.

Bertin, J. (1981) *Graphics and Graphic Information Processing.* Walter de Gruyter, Berlin.

Beyer, H. and Holtzblatt, K. (1998) *Contextual Design.* Morgan Kaufmann, San Francisco, CA.

Bickmore, T. (2003) *Relational agents: Effecting change through human–computer relationships.* PhD thesis, MIT Media Arts and Science.

Bickmore T. and Picard R. (2005) Establishing and maintaining long-term human–computer relationships. *ACM Transactions on Computer–Human Interaction* (TOCHI), 12(2), 293–327.

Biocca, F., Harms, C., Burgoon, J. and Stoner, M. (2001) Criteria and Scope Conditions for a Theory and Measure of Social Presence. *Presence 2001, 4th Annual International Workshop on Presence,* Philadelphia, PA, 21–23 May.

Blackler, F. (1993) Knowledge and the theory of organiz-ations: organizations as activity systems and the reframing of management. *Journal of Management Studies,* 30(6), 863–884.

Blackler, F. (1995) Activity theory, CSCW and organizations. In Monk, A.F. and Gilbert, N. (eds), *Perspectives on HCI – Diverse Approaches.* Academic Press, London.

Blackwell, A. and Green, T. (2003) Notational systems – the cognitive dimensions of notations framework. In Carroll, J.M. (ed.), *HCI Models, Theories and Frameworks.* Morgan Kaufmann, San Francisco, CA.

Blackwell, A.F. (2006) The reification of metaphor as a design tool. *ACM Transactions on Computer–Human Interaction (TOCHI),* 13(4), 490–530.

Blakemore, C. (1988) *The Mind Machine*. BBC Publications, London.

Blandford, A., Green, T., Furniss, D. and Makri, S. (2008) Evaluating system utility and conceptual fit using CASSM. *International Journal of Human–Computer Studies*, 66(6), 393–409.

Blast Theory (2007) *Blast Theory Website*. Retrieved 14 August 2007 from http://www.blasttheory.co.uk/.

Blattner, M., Sumikawa, D. and Greenberg, R. (1989) Earcons and icons: their structure and common design principles. *Human–Computer Interaction*, 4(1), 11–44.

Blauert, J. (1999) *Spatial Hearing*. MIT Press, Cambridge, MA.

Bødker, S. (2006) When second wave HCI meets third wave challenges. *Proceedings of the Fourth Nordic Conference on Human—Computer Interaction* (Oslo, Norway, 14–18 October 2006). NordiCHI '06. ACM Press, New York, pp. 1–8.

Bødker, S. and Buur, J. (2002) The Design Collaboratorium: a place for usability design. *ACM Transactions on Computer–Human Interaction (TOCHI)*, 9(2), 152–169.

Bødker, S. and Christiansen, E. (1997) Scenarios as springboards in CSCW design. In Bowker, G.C., Star, S.L., Turner, W. and Gasser, L. (eds), *Social Science, Technical Systems and Cooperative Work: Beyond the Great Divide*. Lawrence Erlbaum Associates, Mahwah, NJ, pp. 217–234.

Bødker, S., Ehn, P., Kammersgaard, J., Kyng, M. and Sundblad, Y. (1987) A UTOPIAN experience: on design of powerful computer-based tools for skilled graphical workers. In Bjerknes, G., Ehn, P. and Kyng, M. (eds), *Computers and Democracy – A Scandinavian Challenge*. Avebury, Aldershot, pp. 251–278.

Boehner, K., Sengers, P. and Warner, S. (2008) Interfaces with the ineffable: meeting aesthetic experience on its own terms. *ACM Transactions on Computer–Human Interaction (TOCHI)*, 15(3), pp. 1–29.

Bolt, R.A. (1980) 'Put-that-there': Voice and gesture at the graphics interface. *Proceedings of the 7th annual conference on Computer graphics and interactive techniques*, Seattle, WA. ACM Press, New York, pp. 262–270.

Borges, J.L. (1999) Essay: 'The Analytical Language of John Wilkins'. Retrieved 17 August 2009 from http://www.alamut.com/subj/artiface/language/ johnWilkins.html.

Bowers, J., Pycock, J. and O'Brien, J. (1996) Talk and embodiment in collaborative virtual environments. *CHI '96: Proceedings of the SIGCHI Conference on Human Factors in Computing Systems*. ACM Press, New York, pp. 58–65.

Bradner, E. and Mark, G. (2002) Why distance matters: effects on cooperation, persuasion and deception. *Proceedings of CSCW '02 Conference*, New Orleans, LA, 16–20 November. ACM Press, New York, pp. 226–235.

Bransford, J.R., Barclay, J.R. and Franks, J.J. (1972) Sentence memory: a constructive versus interpretative approach. *Cognitive Psychology*, 3, 193–209.

Brave, S. and Nass, C. (2007) Emotion in human-computer interaction. In Sears, A. and Jacko, J.A. (eds), *The Human–Computer Interaction Handbook: Fundamentals, Evolving Technologies and Emerging Applications* (2nd edn). Mahwah, NJ: Lawrence Erlbaum Associates.

Brems, D.J. and Whitten, W.B. (1987) Learning and preference for icon-based interface. *Proceedings of the Human Factors and Ergonomics Society 31st Annual Meeting*, 19–22 October, New York, pp. 125–129.

Brewster, S. (1998) Using non-speech sounds to provide navigation cues. *ACM Transactions on Computer–Human Interaction (TOCHI)*, 5(3), 224–259.

Brewster, S.A., Wright, P.C. and Edwards, A.D.N. (1993) An evaluation of earcons for use in auditory human–computer interfaces. *Proceedings of INTERCHI '93*. ACM Press, New York, pp. 222–227.

Brinck, T., Gergle, D. and Wood, S.D. (2002) *Designing Web Sites that Work: Usability for the Web*. Morgan Kaufmann, San Francisco, CA.

Broadbent, D.E. (1958) *Perception and Communication*. Pergamon, Oxford.

Brown, R. and McNeill, D. (1966) The 'tip-of-the-tongue' phenomenon. *Journal of Verbal Learning and Verbal Behaviour*, 5, 325–327.

Browne, D.P., Totterdell, P.A. and Norman, M.A. (1990) *Adaptive User Interfaces*. Academic Press, London.

Bruner, J. (1966) *Toward a Theory of Instruction*. Belknap Press of Harvard University Press, Cambridge, MA.

Bruner, J. (1968) *Processes of Cognitive Growth: Infancy*. Clark University Press, Worcester, MA.

Bruner, J. and Postman, L. (1949) On the perception of incongruity: a paradigm. *Journal of Personality*, 18, 206–223.

Brusilovsky, P. (2001) Adaptive hypermedia. *User Modeling and User-adapted Interaction*, 11(1–2), 87–110.

Bullivant, L. (2006) *Responsive Environments Architecture, Art And Design*. V&A Publications, London.

Burrell, J., Broke, T. and Beckwith, R. (2004) Vineyard computing: sensor networks in agricultural production. *IEEE Pervasive Computing*, 3(1), 38–45. IEEE Computer Society Press, Washington, DC.

Bush, V. (1945) As we may think, *The Atlantic Monthly*, 11 July.

Cairns, P. and Cox, A.L. (2008) *Research Methods for Human–Computer Interaction*. Cambridge University Press, Cambridge.

Card, S. (2012) Information visualization. In Jacko, J.A. (ed.), *The Human—Computer Interaction Handbook: Fundamentals, Evolving Technologies and Emerging Applications* (3rd edn). CRC Press, Taylor and Francis, Boca Raton, FL, pp. 515–548.

Card, S., Mackinlay, S. and Shneiderman, B. (1999) *Information Visualization: Using Vision to Think*. Morgan Kaufmann, San Francisco, CA.

Card, S.K., Moran, T.P. and Newell, A. (1983) *The Psychology of Human–Computer Interaction*. Lawrence Erlbaum Associates, Hillsdale, NJ.

Carroll, J.M. (ed.) (1995) *Scenario-based Design*. Wiley, New York.

Carroll, J.M. (2000) *Making Use: Scenario-based Design of Human–Computer Interactions*. MIT Press, Cambridge, MA.

Carroll, J.M. (2002) *HCI in the New Millennium*. Addison-Wesley, Harlow.

Carroll, J.M. (ed.) (2003) *HCI Models, Theories and Frameworks*. Morgan Kaufmann, San Francisco, CA.

Cassell, J. (2000) Embodied conversational interface agents. *Communications of the ACM, 43*(4), 70–78.

Castells, M. (1996) *The Information Age: Economy, Society and Culture. Volume 1. The Rise of the Network Society*. Blackwell, Oxford.

Castells, M. (1997) *The Information Age: Economy, Society and Culture. Volume 2. The Power of Identity*. Blackwell, Oxford.

Castells, M. (1998) *The Information Age: Economy, Society and Culture. Volume 3. End of Millennium*. Blackwell, Oxford.

Chalmers, M. (2003) Informatics, architecture and language. In Höök, K., Benyon, D.R. and Munro, A. (eds), *Designing Information Spaces: The Social Navigation Approach*. Springer-Verlag, London, pp. 315–342.

Checkland, P. (1981) *Systems Thinking, Systems Practice*. Wiley, Chichester.

Checkland, P. and Scholes, J. (1999) *Soft Systems Methodology in Action* (paperback edn). Wiley, Chichester.

Cheok, A.D., Fong, S.W., Goh, K.H., Yang, X., Liu, W. and Farbiz, F. (2003) Human Pacman: a mobile entertainment system with ubiquitous computing and tangible interaction over a wide outdoor area. In Chittaro, L. (ed.) *Human–Computer Interaction with Mobile Devices and Services – 5th International Symposium – Mobile HCI 2003*, 8–11 September, Udine, Italy. Springer, New York, pp. 209–223.

Cheok, A.D., Weihua, W., Yang, X., Prince, S., Wan, F-S., Billinghurst, M. and Kato, H. (2002) Interactive theatre experience in embodied + wearable mixed reality space. *International Symposium on Mixed and Augmented Reality* (ISMAR'02). IEEE Computer Society Press, Washington, DC, p. 317.

Cherry, E.C. (1953) Some experiments on the experiments on the recognition of speech with one and two ears. *Journal of the Acoustical Society of America, 26*, 554–559.

Christiansen, E. (1996) Tamed by a rose. In Nardi, B.A. (ed.), *Context and Consciousness: Activity Theory and Human–Computer Interaction*. MIT Press, Cambridge, MA, pp. 175–198.

Clarke, A.C. (1968) *2001: A Space Odyssey*. New American Library, New York.

Cockton, G. (2009) Getting there: six meta-principles and interaction design. *CHI '09: Proceedings of the SIGCHI Conference on Human Factors in Computing Systems*. ACM Press, New York, pp. 2223–2232.

Cockton, G., Woolrych, A., Hornbæk, K. and Frøkjær, E. (2012) Inspection-based evaluations. In Jacko, J.A. (ed.), *The Human–Computer Interaction Handbook: Fundamentals, Evolving Technologies and Emerging Applications* (3rd edn). CRC Press, Taylor and Francis, Boca Raton, FL, pp. 1279–1298.

Cohen, N.J. and Squire, L.R. (1980) Preserved learning and retention of pattern-analysing skills in amnesia: dissociation of knowing how from knowing that. *Science, 210*, 207–210.

Cole, M. (1996) *Cultural Psychology*. Harvard University Press, Cambridge, MA.

Constantine, L.L. and Lockwood, L.A.D. (2001) Structure and style in use cases for user interface design. In van Harmelen, M. (ed.), *Object Modeling and User Interface Design: Designing Interactive Systems*. Addison-Wesley, Boston, MA.

Cooper, A. (1999) *The Inmates are Running the Asylum*. SAMS, Macmillan Computer Publishing, Indianapolis, IN.

Cooper, A., Reiman, R. and Cronin, D. (2007) *About Face 3: The Essentials of Interaction Design*. Wiley, Hoboken, NJ.

Coutaz, J. and Calvary, G. (2012) Human–computer interaction and software engineering for user interface plasticity. In Jacko, J.A. (ed.), *The Human—Computer Interaction Handbook: Fundamentals, Evolving Technologies and Emerging Applications* (3rd edn). CRC Press, Taylor and Francis, Boca Raton, FL, pp. 1195–1220.

Cowan, N. (2002) The magical number four in short-term memory: a reconsideration of mental storage capacity. *Behavioural and Brain Sciences, 24*(1), 87–114.

Craik, F.I.M. and Lockhart, R. (1972) Levels of processing. *Journal of Verbal Learning and Verbal Behaviour, 12*, 599–607.

Crampton-Smith, G. (2004) From material to immaterial and back again. *Proceedings of Designing Interactive Systems (DIS) 2004*. Cambridge, MA, p. 3.

Csikszentmihalyi, M. (1990) *Flow: The Psychology of Optimal Experience*. Harper & Row, New York.

Cullen, G. (1961) *The Concise Townscape*. Van Nostrand Reinhold, New York.

Davenport, E. (2008) Social informatics and sociotechnical research – a view from the UK. *Journal of Information Science, 34*(4), 519–530.

Dennett, D. (1989) *The Intentional Stance*. MIT Press, Cambridge, MA.

DeSanctis, G. and Gallupe, B. (1987) A foundation for the study of group decision support systems. *Management Science, 33*(5), 589–609.

Desmet, P.M.A. (2002) *Designing Emotions*. Delft University of Technology, Delft.

Deutsch, J.A. and Deutsch, D. (1963) Attention: some theoretical considerations. *Psychological Review, 70*, 80–90.

Dew, P., Galata, A., Maxfield, J. and Romano, D. (2002) Virtual artefacts to support negotiation within an augmented collaborative environment for alternate dispute resolution. *Proceedings of CVE '02 Conference*, Bonn, Germany, 30 September–2 October. ACM Press, New York, pp. 10–16.

Diaper, D. (2004) Understanding task analysis for human–computer interaction. In Diaper, D. and Stanton, N. (eds), *The Handbook of Task Analysis for Human–Computer Interaction*. Lawrence Erlbaum Associates, Mahwah, NJ.

Diaper, D. and Stanton, N. (eds) (2004a) *The Handbook of Task Analysis for Human–Computer Interaction*. Lawrence Erlbaum Associates, Mahwah, NJ.

Diaper, D. and Stanton, N. (2004b) Wishing on a star: the future of task analysis. In Diaper, D. and Stanton, N. (eds), *The Handbook of Task Analysis for Human–Computer Interaction*. Lawrence Erlbaum Associates, Mahwah, NJ.

Dick, P.K. (1968) *Do Androids Dream of Electric Sheep?* Doubleday, New York.

Dietrich, H., Malinowski, U., Kühme, T. and Schneider-Hufschmidt, M. (1993) State of the art in adaptive user interfaces. In Schneider-Hufschmidt, M., Kühme, T. and Malinowski, U. (eds), *Adaptive User Interfaces*. North-Holland, Amsterdam.

Dix, A. (2012) Network-based interaction. In Jacko, J.A. (ed.), *The Human—Computer Interaction Handbook: Fundamentals, Evolving Technologies and Emerging Applications* (3rd edn). CRC Press, Taylor and Francis, Boca Raton, FL, pp. 237–272.

Doubleday, A., Ryan, M., Springett, M. and Sutcliffe, A. (1997) A comparison of usability techniques for evaluating design. *Proceedings of DIS '97 Conference,* Amsterdam, Netherlands. ACM Press, New York, pp. 101–110.

Dourish, P. (2001) *Where the Action Is: The Foundations of Embodied Interaction*. MIT Press, Cambridge, MA.

Dourish, P. and Bly, S. (1992) Portholes: supporting awareness in a distributed work group. *CHI '92: Proceedings of the SIGCHI Conference on Human Factors in Computing Systems*. ACM Press, New York, pp. 541–547.

Dowell, J. and Long, J. (1998) A conception of human–computer interaction. *Ergonomics,* 41(2), 174–178.

Downs, R. and Stea, D. (1973) Cognitive representations. In Downs, R. and Stea, D. (eds), *Image and Environment*. Aldine, Chicago, IL, pp. 79–86.

Dumas, J. and Fox, J. (2012) Usability testing. In Jacko, J.A. (ed.), *The Human—Computer Interaction Handbook: Fundamentals, Evolving Technologies and Emerging Applications* (3rd edn). CRC Press, Taylor and Francis, Boca Raton, FL, pp. 1221–1242.

Dunne, L.E., Brady, S., Tynan, R., Lau, K., Smyth, B., Diamond, D. and O'Hare, G.M.P. (2006) Garment-based body sensing using foam sensors. In Piekarski, W. (ed.), *Proceedings Seventh Australasian User Interface Conference (AUIC2006)*. Australian Computer Society, Sydney, pp. 165–171.

Eason, K.D., Harker, S.D. and Olphert, C.W. (1996) Representing socio-technical systems options in the development of new forms of work organization. *European Journal of Work and Organizational Psychology,* 5(3), 399–420.

Economou, D., Mitchell, L.W., Pettifer, R.S. and West, J.A. (2000) CVE technology development based on real world application and user needs. *Proceedings of WET ICE '00 Conference,* Gaithersburg, MD, 14–16 June. IEEE Computer Society Press, Washington, DC, pp. 12–20.

Eggen, B., Hollemans, G. and van de Sluis, R. (2003) Exploring and enhancing the home experience. *Cognition Technology and Work,* 5(1), 44–54.

Ehn, P. and Kyng, M. (eds) (1987) *Computers and Democracy – A Scandinavian Challenge*. Avebury, Aldershot, pp. 251–278.

Ekman, P. and Friesen, W.V. (1978) *The Facial Action Coding System*. Consulting Psychologists' Press, Palo Alto, CA.

Ekman, P., Friesen, W.V. and Ellsworth, P. (1972) *Emotion in the Human Face*. Pergamon, New York.

Elrod, S., Bruce, R., Gold, R., Goldberg, D., Halasz, F., Janssen, W., Lee, D., McCall, K., Pederson, E., Pier, K., Tang, J. and Welch, B. (1992) Liveboard: a large interactive display supporting group meetings, presentations and remote collaboration. *CHI '92: Proceedings of the SIGCHI Conference on Human Factors in Computing Systems*. ACM Press, New York, pp. 599–607.

Engeström, Y. (1987) *Learning by Expanding: an Activity-Theoretical Approach to Developmental Research*. Orienta-Konsultit, Helsinki.

Engeström, Y. (1995) Objects, contradictions and collaboration in medical cognition: an activity-theoretical perspective. *Artificial Intelligence in Medicine,* 7, 395–412.

Engeström, Y. (1999) Activity theory and individual and social transformation. In Engeström, Y., Miettinen, R. and Punamaki, R.-L. (eds), *Perspectives on Activity Theory*. Cambridge University Press, Cambridge, pp. 19–38.

Erickson, K.A., Smith, D.N., Kellogg, W.A., Laff, M., Richards, J.T. and Bradner, E. (1999) Socially translucent systems: social proxies, persistent conversation, and the design of 'Babble'. *CHI '99: Proceedings of the SIGCHI Conference on Human Factors in Computing Systems*. ACM Press, New York, pp. 72–79.

Erickson, T. (2003) http://www.pliant.org/personal/Tom_Erickson/InteractionPatterns.html, accessed 5 January 2004.

Erickson, T. and Kellogg, W.A. (2003) Social translucence: using minimalist visualisations of social activity to support collective interaction. In Höök, K., Benyon, D.R. and Munro, A. (eds), *Designing Information Spaces: The Social Navigation Approach*. Springer-Verlag, London, pp. 17–42.

Ericsson, K.A. and Simon, H.A. (1985) *Protocol Analysis: Verbal Reports as Data*. MIT Press, Cambridge, MA.

Ericsson, K.A. and Smith, J. (eds) (1991) *Towards a General Theory of Expertise*. Cambridge University Press, Cambridge.

Fauconnier, G. and Turner, M. (2002) *The Way We Think: Conceptual Blending and the Mind's Hidden Complexities*. Basic Books, New York.

Fiebrink, R., Morris, D. and Morris, M.R. (2009) Dynamic mapping of physical controls for tabletop groupware. *CHI '09: Proceedings of the SIGCHI Conference on Human Factors in Computing Systems*. ACM Press, New York, pp. 471–480.

Fischer, G. (1989) Human–computer interaction software: lessons learned, challenges ahead. *IEEE Software,* 6(1), 44–52.

Fischer, G. (2001) User modelling in human–computer interaction. *User Modeling and User-adapted Interaction,* 11(1–2), 65–86.

Fjermestad, J. and Hiltz, S.R. (2000) Case and field studies of group support systems: an empirical assessment.

Proceedings of HICSS '00 Conference, Maui, Hawaii, 4–7 January. IEEE Computer Society Press, Washington, DC.

Flach, J. (1995) The ecology of human–machine systems: a personal history. In Flach, J., Hancock, P., Caird, J. and Vicente, K. (eds), *Global Perspectives on the Ecology of Human–Machine Systems.* Lawrence Erlbaum Associates, Hillsdale, NJ, pp. 1–13.

Fogg, B., Cuellar, G. and Danielson, D. (2007) Motivating, influencing and persuading users: an introduction to captology. In Sears, A. and Jacko, J.A. (eds), *The Human–Computer Interaction Handbook: Fundamentals, Evolving Technologies and Emerging Applications* (2nd edn). Lawrence Erlbaum Associates, Mahwah, NJ, pp. 1265–1275.

Fogg, B.J. (2003) *Persuasive Technologies: Using Computers to Change What We Think and Do.* Morgan Kaufman, Amsterdam.

Forlizzi, J. and Batterbee, K. (2004) Understanding experience in interactive systems. *Proceedings of Designing Interactive Systems (DIS) 2004.* Cambridge, MA, pp. 261–268.

Forsythe, D.E. (1999) It's just a matter of common sense: ethnography as invisible work. *Computer Supported Cooperative Work,* 8(1/2), 127–145.

Friedman, B. and Kahn, P.H. (2007) Human values, ethics and design. In Jacko, J.A. and Sears, A. (eds), *The Human–Computer Interaction Handbook: Fundamentals, Evolving Technologies and Emerging Applications* (2nd edn). Lawrence Erlbaum Associates, Mahwah, NJ.

Gärling, T., Böök, A. and Ergesen, N. (1982) Memory for the spatial layout of the everyday physical environment: different rates of acquisition of different types of information. *Scandinavian Journal of Psychology,* 23, 23–35.

Garrett, J.J. (2003) *The Elements of User Experience.* New Riders, Indianapolis, IN.

Gaver, W., Dunne, T. and Pacenti, E. (1999) Cultural probes. *Interactions,* 6(1), 21–29.

Geen, R. (1991) Social motivation. *Annual Review of Psychology,* 42, 377–399.

Gibson, J.J. (1950) *The Perception of the Visual World.* Houghton Mifflin, Boston, MA.

Gibson, J.J. (1966) *The Senses Considered as Perceptual Systems.* Houghton Mifflin, Boston, MA.

Gibson, J.J. (1977) The theory of affordances. In Shaw, R. and Bransford, J. (eds), *Perceiving, Acting and Knowing.* Wiley, New York, pp. 67–82.

Gibson, J.J. (1979) *The Ecological Approach to Human Perception.* Houghton Mifflin, Boston, MA.

Gibson, J.J. (1986) *The Ecological Approach to Visual Perception.* Lawrence Erlbaum Associates, Hillsdale, NJ.

Gladwell, M. (2000) The new-boy network: what do job interviews really tell us? *The New Yorker,* 29 May. See also www.gladwell.com/

Glaser B.G. and Strauss A. (1967) *Discovery of Grounded Theory. Strategies for Qualitative Research.* Sociology Press, Mill Valley, CA.

Gosling, D. (1996) *Gordon Cullen: Visions of Urban Design.* Academy Editions, London.

Gould, J.D. and Lewis, C. (1985) Designing for usability: key principles and what designers think, *Communications of the ACM* 28(3), 300–311.

Gould, J.D., Boies, S.J., Levy, S., Richards, J.T. and Schoonard, J. (1987) The 1984 Olympic Message System: a test of behavioral principles of system design. *Communications of the ACM,* 30(9), 758–769.

Graham, C., Rouncefield, M., Gibbs, M., Vetere, F., and Cheverst, K. (2007). How probes work. *Proceedings of the 19th Australasian Conference on Computer-Human Interaction: Entertaining User Interfaces* (Adelaide, Australia, 28–30 November 2007). OZCHI '07, vol. 251. ACM Press, New York, pp. 29–37.

Graham, I. (2003) *A Pattern Language for Web Usability.* Addison-Wesley, Harlow.

Green, P. (2012) Motor vehicle-driver interfaces. In Jacko, J.A. (ed.), *The Human—Computer Interaction Handbook: Fundamentals, Evolving Technologies and Emerging Applications* (3rd edn). CRC Press, Taylor and Francis, Boca Raton, FL, pp. 749–770.

Green, T.R.G. and Benyon, D.R. (1996) The skull beneath the skin: entity–relationship modelling of information artefacts. *International Journal of Human–Computer Studies,* 44(6), 801–828.

Gregory, R.L. (1973) *Eye and Brain* (2nd edn). World Universities Library, New York.

Gross, M. (1996) The Electronic Cocktail Napkin – a computational environment for working with design diagrams. *Design Studies,* 17(1), 53–69.

Gross, R. (2001) *Psychology: the Science of Mind and Behaviour.* Hodder Arnold, London.

Grudin, J. (1988) Why CSCW applications fail: problems in the design and evaluation of organization interfaces. *Proceedings of CSCW '88 Conference,* Portland, OR, 26–28 September. ACM Press, New York, pp. 85–93.

Grudin, J. (1994) Groupware and social dynamics: eight challenges for developers. *Communications of the ACM,* 37, 93–105.

Grudin, J. and Poltrock, S.E. (1997) Computer-supported cooperative work and groupware. In Zelkowitz, M.V. (ed.), *Advances in Computing.* Academic Press, New York, pp. 269–320.

Guilford, J.P. (1967) *The Nature of Human Intelligence.* McGraw-Hill, New York.

Gutwin, C., Roseman, M. and Greenberg, S. (1996) A usability study of awareness widgets in a shared workspace groupware system. *Proceedings of CSCW '96 Conference,* Boston, MA, 16–20 November. ACM Press, New York, pp. 258–267.

Hall, E.T. (1966) *The Hidden Dimension.* Doubleday, New York.

Haller, M., Leitner, J., Seifried, T., Wallace, J., Scot, S., Richter, C., Brandl, P., Gokcezade, A. and Hunter, S. (2010) The NiCE discussion room: integrating paper and digital media to support co-located group meetings. *CHI '10: Proceedings of the SIGCHI Conference on Human Factors in Computing Systems.* ACM Press, pp. 609–618.

Haney, C., Banks, W.C. and Zimbardo, P.G. (1973) Interpersonal dynamics in a simulated prison. *International Journal of Penology and Criminology,* 1, 69–97.

Harkins, S. and Szymanski, K. (1987) Social loafing and social facilitation: new wine in old bottles. In Hendrick, C. (ed.), *Review of Personality and Social Psychology: Group Processes and Intergroup Relations,* vol. 9. Sage, London, pp. 167–188.

Harper, R.H.R. (1992) Looking at ourselves: an examination of the social organisation of two research laboratories. *Proceedings of CSCW '92 Conference,* Toronto, 1–4 November. ACM Press, New York, pp. 330–337.

Hartman, J., Sutcliffe A. and de Angeli, A. (2008) Investigating attractiveness in web user interfaces. *CHI '08: Proceedings of the SIGCHI Conference on Human Factors in Computing Systems.* ACM Press, New York, pp. 387–396.

Hasan, H., Gould, E. and Hyland, P. (eds) (1998) *Information Systems and Activity Theory: Tools in Context.* University of Wollongong Press, Wollongong, New South Wales.

Hassenzahl, M. (2007) Aesthetics in interactive products: Correlates and consequences of beauty. In Schifferstein, H.N.J. and Hekkert, P. (eds), *Product Experience.* Elsevier, Amsterdam, pp. 287–302.

Hayward, V., Astley, O., Cruz-Hernandez, M., Grant, D. and Robles-De-La-Torre, G. (2004) Haptic interfaces and devices. *Sensor Review,* 24(1), 16–29. Retrieved 14 September 2007 from http://www.clm.mcgill.ca/ ~ haptic/pub/ VH-ET-AL-SR-04.pdf.

Heath, C. and Luff, P. (2000) *Technology in Action.* Cambridge University Press, Cambridge.

Hebb, D.O. (1949) *The Organization of Behavior.* Wiley, New York.

Heeren, E. and Lewis, R. (1997) Selecting communication media for distributed communities. *Journal of Computer Assisted Learning,* 13, 85–98.

Herring, S.R., Chang, C-C., Krantzler, J. and Bailey, B.P. (2009) Getting inspired!: understanding how and why examples are used in creative design practice. *CHI '09: Proceedings of the SIGCHI Conference on Human Factors in Computing Systems.* ACM Press, New York, pp. 87–96.

Hill, J. and Gutwin, C. (2003) Awareness support in a groupware widget toolkit. *Proceedings of Group '03 Conference,* Sanibel Island, FL, 9–12 December. ACM Press, New York, pp. 258–267.

Hillier, B. (1996) *Space is the Machine.* Cambridge University Press, Cambridge.

Hoffman, T. (2003, 24 March) Smart dust: mighty motes for medicine, manufacturing, the military and more. *Computer World.* [Electronic Version]. Retrieved August 12, 2007 from http://www.computerworld.com/ mobile topics/mobile/story/0,10801,79572,00.html.

Hofstede, G. (1994) *Cultures and Organisations.* HarperCollins, London.

Hoggan, E. and Brewster, S. (2012) Nonspeech auditory and crossmodal output. In Jacko, J.A. (ed.), *The Human—Computer Interaction Handbook: Fundamentals, Evolving Technologies and Emerging Applications* (3rd edn). CRC Press, Taylor and Francis, Boca Raton, FL, pp. 211–236.

Hollan, J., Hutchins, E. and Kirsh, D. (2000) Distributed cognition: toward a new foundation for human–computer interaction research. *ACM Transactions on Computer–Human Interaction (TOCHI),* 7(2), 174–196.

Hollnagel, E. (1997) Building joint cognitive systems: a case of horses for courses? *Design of Computing Systems: Social and Ergonomic Considerations, Proceedings of HCI '97 International Conference.* Elsevier, New York, vol. 2, pp. 39–42.

Hollnagel, E. (2003) Is affective computing an oxymoron? *International Journal of Human–Computer Studies,* 59(1–2), 65–70.

Holmquist, L.E. *et al.* (2004) Building intelligent environments with Smart-Its. *IEEE Computer Graphics and Applications,* 24(1), 56–64.

Holtzblatt, K. (2012) Contextual design. In Jacko, J.A. (ed.), *The Human—Computer Interaction Handbook: Fundamentals, Evolving Technologies and Emerging Applications* (3rd edn). CRC Press, Taylor and Francis, Boca Raton, FL, pp. 983–1002.

Höök, K. (2000) Seven steps to take before intelligent user interfaces become real. *Interacting with Computers,* 12(4), 409–426.

Höök, K., Benyon, D.R. and Munro, A. (2003) *Designing Information Spaces: The Social Navigation Approach.* Springer-Verlag, London.

Höök, K., Ståhl, A., Sundström, P. and Laaksolaahti, J. (2008) Interactional empowerment. *CHI '08: Proceedings of the SIGCHI Conference on Human Factors in Computing Systems.* ACM Press, New York, pp. 647–656.

Horton, W. (1991) *Illustrating Computer Documentation: The Art of Presenting Graphically on Paper On-line.* John Wiley, Toronto.

Hoschka, P. (1998) CSCW research at GMD-FIT: from basic groupware to the social Web. *ACM SIGGROUP Bulletin,* 19(2), 5–9.

Howe, J. (2006) The rise of crowdsourcing, *Wired,* Issue 14.06, June.

Hudson, W. (2012): Card sorting. In Soegaard, M. and Dam, R.F. (eds), *Encyclopedia of Human–Computer Interaction.* The Interaction Design Foundation, Aarhus, Denmark. Available online at www.interaction-design.org/ encyclopedia/card_sorting.html.

Hughes, C.E., Stapleton, C.B., Micikevicius, P., Hughes, D.E., Malo, S. and O'Connor, M. (2004) *Mixed Fantasy: An Integrated System for Delivering MR Experiences.* Paper presented at VR Usability Workshop: Designing and Evaluating VR Systems, Nottingham, England, 22–23 January.

Hulkko, S., Mattelmäki, T., Virtanen, K. and Keinonen, T. (2004) Mobile probes. *Proceedings of the Third Nordic Conference on Human–Computer Interaction* (Tampere, Finland, 23–27 October 2004). NordiCHI '04, vol. 82. ACM Press, New York, pp. 43–51.

Hull, A., Wilkins, A.J. and Baddeley, A. (1988) Cognitive psychology and the wiring of plugs. In Gruneberg, M.M., Morris, P.E. and Sykes, R.N. (eds), *Practical Aspects of Memory: Current Research and Issues, vol. 1: Memory in Everyday Life.* Wiley, Chichester, pp. 514–518.

Hutchins, E. (1995) *Cognition in the Wild*. MIT Press, Cambridge, MA.

IJsselsteijn, W.A. and Riva, G. (2003) Being there: the experience of presence in mediated environments. In Riva, G., Davide, F. and IJsselsteijn, W.A. (eds), *Being There – Concepts, Effects and Measurements of User Presence in Synthetic Environments*. IOS Press, Amsterdam, pp. 3–16.

Imaz, M. and Benyon, D.R. (2005) *Designing with Blends: Conceptual Foundations of Human Computer Interaction and Software Engineering*. MIT Press, Cambridge, MA.

Insko, B.E. (2001) *Passive haptics significantly enhance virtual environments*. Doctoral Dissertation, University of North Carolina at Chapel Hill, NC.

Insko, B.E. (2003) Measuring presence: subjective, behavioral and physiological methods. In Riva, G., Davide, F. and IJsselsteijn, W.A. (eds), *Being There: Concepts, Effects and Measurement of User Presence in Synthetic Environments*. IOS Press, Amsterdam.

It's Alive (2004, July) *Company website: Botfighters 2*. Retrieved 18 July 2005 from http://www.itsalive.com/page.asp.

Iwata, H., Yano, H., Uemura, T. and Moriya, T. (2004) Food simulator: a haptic interface for biting. *Proceedings of the IEEE Virtual Reality 2004 (Vr'04)*. IEEE Computer Society Press, Washington, DC.

Jacobson, R. (ed.) (2000) *Information Design*. MIT Press, Cambridge, MA.

Jameson, A. (2007) Adaptive interfaces and agents. In Sears A. and Jacko, J.A. (eds), *The Human–Computer Interaction Handbook: Fundamentals, Evolving Technologies and Emerging Applications* (2nd edn). Lawrence Erlbaum Associates, Mahwah, NJ.

Jetter, H.-C., Geyer, F., Schwarz, T. and Reiterer, H. (2012) Blended interaction – toward a framework for the design of interactive spaces. *Workshop Designing Collaborative Interactive Spaces* DCIS, at AVI 2012, Human-Computer Interaction Group, Univ. of Konstanz, May 2012, http://hci.uni-konstanz.de/downloads/dcis2012_Jetter.pdf. AVI Workshop, Capri, 25 May.

JLH Labs (2006, 22 January) *Company website: Hardware profiles*. Retrieved 19 August 2007 from http://www.jlhlabs.com/.

John, B. (2003) Information processing and skilled behaviour. In Carroll, J.M. (ed.), *HCI Models, Theories and Frameworks*. Morgan Kaufmann, San Francisco, CA.

Jones, M. and Marsden, G. (2006) *Mobile Interaction Design*. Wiley, Chichester.

Jordan, P.W. (2000) *Designing Pleasurable Products*. Taylor & Francis, London.

Jungk, R. and Müllert, N. (1987) *Future Workshops: How to Create Desirable Futures*. Institute for Social Inventions, London.

Kahneman, D. (1973) *Attention and Effort*. Prentice-Hall, Englewood Cliffs, NJ.

Kane, S., Shulman, J., Shockley, T. and Ladner, R. (2007) A web accessibility report card for top university web sites. *Proceedings of the 2007 International Cross-Disciplinary conference on Web accessibility (W4A)*. ACM International Conference Proceeding Series. ACM Press, New York, pp. 148–156.

Kaptelinin, V., Nardi, B.A. and Macaulay, C. (1999) Methods and tools: the Activity Checklist: a tool for representing the 'space' of context. *Interactions,* 6(4), 27–39.

Kay, A. (1990) User interface: a personal view. In Laurel, B. (ed.), *The Art of Human–Computer Interface Design*. Addison Wesley, Reading, MA.

Kay, A. and Goldberg, A. (1977) Personal dynamic media. *IEEE Computer*, 10(3), 31–44.

Kay, J. (2001) Learner control. *User Modeling and User-adapted Interaction,* 11(1–2), 111–127.

Kelley, D. and Hartfield, B. (1996) The designer's stance. In Winograd, T. (ed.), *Bringing Design to Software*. ACM Press, New York.

Kelley, H. (1983) Epilogue: An essential science. In Kelly, H., Berscheid, A., Christensen, J. *et al.* (eds) *Close Relationships*. Freeman, New York, pp. 486–503.

Kellogg, W. (1989) The dimensions of consistency. In Nielsen, J. (ed.), *Coordinating User Interfaces for Consistency*. Academic Press, San Diego, CA.

Kelly, G. (1955) *The Psychology of Personal Constructs*. Vol. I, II. Norton, New York (2nd printing: 1991, Routledge, London, New York).

Kemp, J.A.M. and van Gelderen, T. (1996). Co-discovery exploration: an informal method for the iterative design of consumer products. In Jordan, P.W., Thomas, B., Weerdmeester, B.A. and McClelland, I.L. (eds) *Usability Evaluation in Industry*. Taylor and Francis, London, pp. 139–146.

Kieras, D. (2004) GOMS models for task analysis. In Diaper, D. and Stanton, N. (eds), *The Handbook of Task Analysis for Human–Computer Interaction*. Lawrence Erlbaum Associates, Mahwah, NJ.

Kieras, D. (2012) Model-based evaluation. In Jacko, J. (ed.) *The Human—Computer Interaction Handbook: Fundamentals, Evolving Technologies and Emerging Applications* (3rd edn). CRC Press, Taylor and Francis, Boca Raton, FL, pp. 1299–1318.

Kieras, D.E. and Bovair, S. (1984) The role of a mental model in learning to operate a device. *Cognitive Science,* 8, 255–273.

Klann, M. (2009) Tactical navigation support for firefighters: the LifeNet ad-hoc sensor-network and wearable system. In *Mobile Response,* LNCS 5424. Springer-Verlag, Berlin, pp. 41–56.

Kobsa, A. and Wahlster, A. (1993) *User Models in Dialog Systems*. Springer-Verlag, Berlin.

Konstan, J.A. and Riedl, J. (2003) Collaborative filtering: supporting social navigation in large, crowded infospaces. In Höök, K., Benyon, D.R. and Munro, A. (eds), *Designing Information Spaces: The Social Navigation Approach*. Springer-Verlag, London, pp. 43–82.

Kruger, R., Carpendale, S., Scott, S.D. and Tang, A. (2005) Fluid integration of rotation and translation. *CHI '05:*

Proceedings of the SIGCHI Conference on Human Factors in Computing Systems. ACM Press, New York, pp. 601–610.

Kuipers, B. (1982) The 'map in the head' metaphor. *Environment and Behaviour,* 14, 202–220.

Kuniavsky, M. (2003) *Observing the User Experience – a Practitioner's Guide to User Research.* Morgan Kaufmann, San Francisco, CA.

Lakoff, G. and Johnson, M. (1981) *Metaphors We Live By.* Chicago University Press, Chicago, IL.

Lakoff, G. and Johnson, M. (1999) *Philosophy of the Flesh.* Basic Books, New York.

Lapham, L.H. (1994) Introduction to the MIT Press edition. In McLuhan, M. (ed.), *Understanding Media: The Extensions of Man* (new edn). MIT Press, Cambridge, MA.

Laurel, B. (ed.) (1990a) *The Art of Human–Computer Interface Design.* Addison-Wesley, Reading, MA.

Laurel, B. (1990b) Interface agents. In Laurel, B. (ed.), *The Art of Human–Computer Interface Design.* Addison Wesley, Reading, MA.

Lavie, T. and Tractinsky, N. (2004) Assessing dimensions of perceived visual aesthetics of web sites. *International Journal of Human–Computer Studies,* 60(3), 269–298.

Lawson, B. (2001) *The Language of Space.* Architectural Press, Oxford.

Lazarus, R.S. (1982) Thoughts on the relations between emotion and cognition. *American Psychologist,* 37, 1019–1024.

Lazzaro N. (2012) Why we play: affect and the fun of games – designing emotions for games, entertainment interfaces, and interactive products. In Jacko, J. (ed.) *The Human—Computer Interaction Handbook: Fundamentals, Evolving Technologies and Emerging Applications* (3rd edn). CRC Press, Taylor and Francis, Boca Raton, FL, pp. 725–748.

Leach, M. and Benyon, D.R. (2008) Navigating in a speckled world: interacting with wireless sensor networks. In P. Turner and S. Turner (eds), *The Exploration of Space, Spatiality and Technology.* Springer, Amsterdam.

LeCompte, D. (1999) Seven, plus or minus two, is too much to bear: three (or fewer) is the real magic number. *Proceedings of the Human Factors and Ergonomics Society 43rd Annual Meeting,* 27 September–1 October, Houston, TX, pp. 289–292.

Lee, H., Gurrin, C., Jones, G. and Smeaton, A.F. (2008) Interaction design for personal photo management on a mobile device. In Lumsden, J. (ed.), *Handbook of Research on User Interface Design and Evaluation for Mobile Technology.* IGI Global, Hershey, PA, pp. 69–85.

Lei, P. and Wong, A. (2009) The multiple-touch user interface revolution. *IT Pro,* 42–49.

Leontiev, A.N. (2009) *The Development of Mind,* a reproduction of the Progress Publishers 1981 edition, plus 'Activity and consciousness', originally published by Progress Publishers, 1977, published by Erythros Press, see Erythrospress.com

Lessiter, J., Freeman, J., Keogh, E. and Davidoff, J.D. (2001) A cross-media presence questionnaire: the ITC sense of presence inventory. *Presence: Teleoperators and Virtual Environments,* 10(3), 282–297.

Lester, J.C., Converse, S.A., Kahler, S.E., Barlow, S.T., Stone, B.A. and Bhogal, R.S. (1997) *CHI '97: Proceedings of the SIGCHI Conference on Human Factors in Computing Systems.* ACM Press, New York, pp. 359–366.

Lewis, C., Polson, P., Wharton, C. and Rieman, J. (1990) Testing a walkthrough methodology for theory-based design of walk-up-and-use interfaces. *CHI '90: Proceedings of the SIGCHI Conference on Human Factors in Computing Systems.* ACM Press, New York, pp. 235–242.

Licklider, J.C.R. (2003) http://memex.org/licklider.html, accessed 7 November 2003.

Lieberman, H. (1995) Letizia: an agent that assists Web browsing. *Proceedings of 14th International Joint Conference on Artificial Intelligence,* Montreal, August. Morgan Kaufmann, San Francisco, CA, pp. 924–929.

Lieberman, H. and Selker, T. (2000) Out of context: Computer systems that adapt to, and learn from, context. *IBM Systems Journal,* 39(3, 4). [Electronic version]. Retrieved 15 August 2007 from http://www.research.ibm.com/journal/sj/393/part1/lieberman.html.

Lieberman, H., Fry, C. and Weitzman, L. (2001) Exploring the Web with reconnaissance agents. *Communications of the ACM,* 44(8), 69–75.

Likert, R. (1932) A technique for the measurement of attitudes. *Archives of Psychology,* 140, 1–55.

Lim, K.Y. and Long, J. (1994) *The MUSE Method for Usability Engineering.* Cambridge University Press, Cambridge.

Lim, Y-K., Stolterman, E. and Tenenberg, J. (2008) The anatomy of prototypes: Prototypes as filters, prototypes as manifestations of design ideas. *ACM Transactions on Computer–Human Interaction (TOCHI),* 15(2), 7.

Lisetti, C., Nasoz, F., LeRouge, C., Ozyer, O. and Alvarez, K. (2003) Developing multimodal intelligent affective interfaces for tele-home health care. *International Journal of Human–Computer Studies,* 59, 245–255.

Lombard, M. and Ditton, T. (1997) At the heart of it all: the concept of presence. *Journal of Computer-Mediated Communication,* 3(2), 1–39.

Lucero, A. (2009) *Co-Designing Interactive Spaces for and with Designers: Supporting Mood-Board Making.* PhD Thesis, Eindhoven University of Technology.

Lucero, A., Aliakseyeu, D. and Martens, J.-B. (2008) Funky wall: presenting mood boards using gesture, speech and visuals. In Levialdi, S. (ed.), *Proceedings AVI '08 Working Conference on Advanced Visual Interfaces.* ACM Press, New York, pp. 425–428.

Lundberg, J., Ibrahim, A., Jönsson, D., Lindquist, S. and Qvarfordt, P. (2002) 'The snatcher catcher': an interactive refrigerator. *Proceedings of the Second Nordic Conference on Human–Computer Interaction* (Aarhus, Denmark, 19–23 October 2002). NordiCHI '02, vol. 31. ACM Press, New York, pp. 209–212.

Lutters, W.G. and Ackerman, M.S. (2007) Beyond boundary objects: collaborative reuse in aircraft technical support. *Computer Supported Cooperative Work,* 16(3), pp. 341–372.

Lynch, K. (1961) *The Image of the City*. MIT Press, Cambridge, MA.

MacGregor, J.N. (1987) Short-term memory capacity: limitation or optimization? *Psychological Review,* 94(1), 107–108.

Mackay, W., Ratzer, A. and Janecek, P. (2000) Video artifacts for design: bridging the gap between abstraction and detail. In Boyarski, D. and Kellogg, W. (eds), *Proceedings of DIS '00*. ACM Press, New York, pp. 72–82.

MacLean, A., Young, R., Bellotti, V. and Moran, T. (1991) Questions, options and criteria: elements of design space analysis. *Human–Computer Interaction,* 6, 201–251.

Macleod, E. (2002) *Accessibility of online galleries*. Unpublished MSc Dissertation, Napier University, Edinburgh.

Maes, P. (1994) Agents that reduce work and information overload. *Communications of the ACM,* 37(7), 30–41.

Majaranta, P., Ahola, U. and Špakov, O. (2009) Fast gaze typing with an adjustable dwell time. *CHI '09: Proceedings of the SIGCHI Conference on Human Factors in Computing Systems*. ACM Press, New York, pp. 357–360.

Mann, S. (1998) Wearable computing as a means for personal empowerment. Keynote address, *First International Conference on Wearable Computing,* ICWC-98, Fairfax, VA, 12–13 May.

Mann, S. (2013) Wearable computing. In M. Soegaard and R.F. Dam (eds), *The Encyclopedia of Human–Computer Interaction,* 2nd edn. The Interaction Design Foundation, Aarhus, Denmark. Available online at www.interaction-design.org/encyclopedia/wearable_computing.html.

Marcus, A. (1992) *Graphic Design for Electronic Documents and User Interfaces*. ACM Press, New York.

Marcus, A. and Gould, E.W. (2012) Globalization, localization, and cross–cultural user–interface design. In Jacko, J. (ed.) *The Human—Computer Interaction Handbook: Fundamentals, Evolving Technologies and Emerging Applications* (3rd edn). CRC Press, Taylor and Francis, Boca Raton, FL, pp. 341–366.

Marcus, A. and Chen, E. (2002) Designing the PDA of the future. *Interactions,* 9(1), 34–44.

Martin, D., Rodden, T., Rouncefield, R., Sommerville, I. and Viller, S. (2001) Finding patterns in the fieldwork. In Prinz, W., Jarke, M., Rogers, Y., Schmidt, K. and Wull, V. (eds), *Proceedings of ECSCW '01 Conference*. Bonn, Germany, 16–20 September. Kluwer, Dordrecht, pp. 39–58.

Mayhew, D. (1999) *The Usability Engineering Lifecycle: a Practitioner's Handbook for User Interface Design*. Morgan Kaufmann, San Francisco, CA.

Mayhew, D. and Follansbee, T.J. (2012) User experience requirements analysis within the usability engineering lifecycle. In Jacko, J. (ed.) *The Human—Computer Interaction Handbook: Fundamentals, Evolving Technologies and Emerging Applications* (3rd edn). CRC Press, Taylor and Francis, Boca Raton, FL, pp. 945–954.

McCarthy, J. and Wright, P. (2004) *Technology as Experience*. MIT Press, Cambridge, MA.

McCullough, M. (2002a) *Abstracting Craft: The Practiced Digital Hand*. MIT Press, Cambridge, MA.

McCullough, M. (2002b) Digital ground: fixity, flow and engagement with context. *Archis,* no. 5 (special 'flow issue', Oct/Nov); also on Doors of Perception website, www.doorsofperception.com.

McKinlay, A., Proctor, R. and Dunnett, A. (1999) An investigation of social loafing and social compensation in computer-supported cooperative work. In Hayne, S.C. (ed.), *Proceedings of Group '99 Conference*. ACM Press, New York, pp. 249–257.

McLuhan, M. (1964) *Understanding Media*. McGraw-Hill, New York. Reprinted 1994, MIT Press, Cambridge, MA.

McNeese, M.D. (2003) New visions of human–computer interaction: making affect compute. *International Journal of Human–Computer Studies,* 59, 33–53.

Meehan, M. (2001) *Physiological reaction as an objective measure of presence in virtual environments*. Doctoral Dissertation, University of North Carolina at Chapel Hill, NC.

Megaw, E.D. and Richardson, J. (1979) Target uncertainty and visual scanning strategies. *Human Factors,* 21, 303–316.

Microsoft (2008) *Being Human: Human–Computer Interaction in the Year 2020*. Retrieved 18 August 2009 from http://research.microsoft.com/en-us/um/cambridge/projects/hci2020/default.html.

Milgram, P., Takemura, H., Utsumi, A. and Kishino, F. (1994) Augmented reality: a class of displays on the reality–virtuality continuum. In Das, H. (ed.), *Proceedings of Telemanipulator and Telepresence Technologies*. Boston, MA. *SPIE,* 2351, pp. 282–292.

Miller, G.A. (1956) The magical number seven, plus or minus two: some limits on our capacity for processing information. *Psychological Review,* 63, 81–97.

Miller, S. (1984) *Experimental Design and Statistics* (2nd edn), Routledge, London.

Mitchell, V. (2005) *Mobile Methods: Eliciting User Needs for Future Mobile Products*. Unpublished PhD thesis, Loughborough University, UK.

Mitchell, W. (1998) *City of Bits*. MIT Press, Cambridge, MA.

Mival, O. (2004) Crossing the chasm: developing and understanding support tools to bridge the research design divide within a leading product design company. In Marjanovic, D. (ed.), *Proceedings of Design 2004,* Faculty of Mechanical Engineering and Naval Architecture, Zagreb, pp. 61–73.

Moggridge, B. (2007) *Designing Interactions*. MIT Press, Cambridge, MA.

Monk, A. and Gilbert, N. (eds) (1995) *Perspectives on HCI – Diverse Approaches*. Academic Press, London.

Monk, A. and Howard, S. (1998) The rich picture: a tool for reasoning about work context. *Interactions,* 5(2), 21–30.

Monk, A., Wright, P., Haber, J. and Davenport, L. (1993) *Improving Your Human–Computer Interface: a Practical Technique*. BCS Practitioner Series, Prentice-Hall, New York and Hemel Hempstead.

Morville, J. and Rosenfeld (2006) *Information Architecture for the World Wide Web* (3rd edn). O'Reilly, Sebastopol, CA.

Muller, M.J. (2001) Layered participatory analysis: new developments in the CARD technique. *CHI '01: Proceedings of the SIGCHI Conference on Human Factors in Computing Systems.* ACM Press, New York, pp. 90–97.

Muller, M.J., Matheson, L., Page, C. and Gallup, R. (1998) Methods and tools: participatory heuristic evaluation. *Interactions,* 5(5), 13–18.

Mumford, E. (1983) *Designing Human Systems.* Manchester Business School, Manchester.

Mumford, E. (1993) The participation of users in systems design: an account of the origin, evolution and use of the ETHICS method. In Schuler, D. and Namioka, A. (eds), *Participatory Design: Principles and Practices.* Lawrence Erlbaum Associates, Hillsdale, NJ, pp. 257–270.

Myst (2003) www.riven.com/home.html, accessed 7 November 2003.

Nardi, B. (ed.) (1996) *Context and Consciousness: Activity Theory and Human–Computer Interaction.* MIT Press, Cambridge, MA.

Nardi, B. and O'Day, V. (1999) *Information Ecologies.* MIT Press, Cambridge, MA.

Nass, C. and Brave, S. (2005) *Wired For Speech. How voice activates and advances the human–computer relationship.* MIT Press, Cambridge, MA.

Negroponte, N. (1995) *Being Digital.* Knopf, New York.

Nelson, T. (1982) *Literary Machines.* Mindful Press, New York.

Newell, A. (1995) Extra-ordinary human–computer interaction. In Edwards, A.K. (ed.), *Extra-ordinary Human–Computer Interaction: Interfaces for Users with Disabilities.* Cambridge University Press, New York.

Newell, A. and Simon, H. (1972) *Human Problem Solving.* Prentice-Hall, Englewood Cliffs, NJ.

Newell, A., Carmichael, A., Gregor, P., Alm, N., Waller, A., Hanson, V.L., Pullin, G. and Hoey, J. (2012) Information technology for communication and cognitive support. In Jacko, J. (ed.) *The Human—Computer Interaction Handbook: Fundamentals, Evolving Technologies and Emerging Applications* (3rd edn). CRC Press, Taylor and Francis, Boca Raton, FL, pp. 863–892.

Newlands, A., Anderson, A.H. and Mullin, J. (1996) Dialog structure and cooperative task performance in two CSCW environments. In Connolly, J.H. and Pemberton, L. (eds), *Linguistic Concepts and Methods in CSCW.* Springer-Verlag, London, pp. 41–60.

Nielsen, J. (1993) *Usability Engineering.* Academic Press, New York.

Nielsen, J. and Mack, R.L. (eds) (1994) *Usability Inspection Methods.* Wiley, New York.

Nilsen, T., Linton, S. and Looser, J. (2004) Motivations for AR gaming. *Proceedings Fuse '04, New Zealand Game Developers Conference.* ACM Press, New York, pp. 86–93.

Norberg-Schulz, C. (1971) *Existence, Space, Architecture.* Studio Vista, London.

Norman, D. (1968) Towards a theory of memory and attention. *Psychological Review,* 75, 522–536.

Norman, D. (1981) The trouble with UNIX: the user interface is horrid. *Datamation,* 27(12), 139–150.

Norman, D. (1983) Some observations on mental models. In Gentner, D. and Stevens, A.L. (eds), *Mental Models.* Lawrence Erlbaum Associates, Hillsdale, NJ, pp. 7–14.

Norman, D. (1986) Cognitive engineering. In Norman, D.A. and Draper, S. (eds), *User-centred System Design: New Perspectives on Human–Computer Interaction.* Lawrence Erlbaum Associates, Hillsdale, NJ, pp. 31–61.

Norman, D. (1988) *The Psychology of Everyday Things.* Basic Books, New York.

Norman, D. (1993) *Things That Make Us Smart.* Addison-Wesley, Reading, MA.

Norman, D. (1998) *The Design of Everyday Things.* Addison-Wesley, Reading, MA.

Norman, D. (1999) *The Invisible Computer: Why Good Products Can Fail.* MIT Press, Cambridge, MA.

Norman, D. (2004) *Emotional Design: Why We Love (or Hate) Everyday Things.* Basic Books, New York.

Norman, D. (2007) The next UI breakthrough: command lines. *Interactions,* 14(3), 44–45.

Norman, D. and Draper, S. (eds) (1969; 1986) *User-centred System Design: New Perspectives on Human–Computer Interaction.* Lawrence Erlbaum Associates, Hillsdale, NJ.

Oakley, I., Sunwoo, J. and Cho, I.-Y. (2008) Pointing with fingers, hands and arms for wearable computing. *CHI EA '08: Extended Abstracts on Human Factors in Computing Systems.* ACM Press, New York, pp. 3255–3260.

Oakley, I., McGee, M.R., Brewster, S. and Gray, P. (2000) Putting the feel in 'look and feel'. *CHI '00: Proceedings of the SIGCHI Conference on Human Factors in Computing Systems.* ACM Press, New York, pp. 415–422.

Obendorf, H. and Finck, M. (2008) Scenario-based usability engineering techniques in agile development processes. *CHI EA '08: Extended Abstracts on Human Factors in Computing Systems.* ACM Press, New York, pp. 2159–2166.

Olson, G. and Olson, J. (2007) Collaboration technologies. In Jacko, J. (ed.) *The Human—Computer Interaction Handbook: Fundamentals, Evolving Technologies and Emerging Applications.* CRC Press, Taylor and Francis, Boca Raton, FL, pp. 549–564.

Olson, G.M. and Olson, J.S. (2000) Distance matters. *Human–Computer Interaction,* 15, 139–179.

Olson, J.S., Olson, G.M., Storrøsten, M. and Carter, M. (1992) How a group editor changes the character of a design meeting as well as its outcome. *Proceedings of CSCW '92 Conference,* Toronto, 1–4 November. ACM Press, New York, pp. 91–98.

O'Neil, S. (2008) *Interactive Media: The Semiotics of Embodied Interaction.* Springer, London.

Oppenheim, A.N. (2000) *Questionnaire Design, Interviewing and Attitude Measurement* (new edn). Continuum, London.

Osgood, C.E., Suci, G. and Tannenbaum, P. (1957) *The Measurement of Meaning.* University of Illinois Press, Urbana, IL.

Paiva, P., Costa, M., Chaves, R., Piedade, M., Mourão, D., Sobrala, D., Höök, K., Andersson, G. and Bullock, A. (2003) SenToy: an affective sympathetic interface. *International Journal of Human–Computer Studies,* 59, 227–235.

Parasuraman, R. (1986) Vigilance, monitoring, and search. In Boff, K.R., Kaufman, L. and Thomas, J.P. (eds), *Handbook of Human Performance, vol. 2: Cognitive Processes and Performance*. Wiley, Chichester.

Pashler, H.E. (1998) *The Psychology of Attention*. MIT Press, Cambridge, MA.

Passini, R. (1994) *Wayfinding in Architecture*. Van Nostrand, New York.

Payne, S. (2007) Mental models in human—computer interaction. In Jacko, J. (ed.) *The Human—Computer Interaction Handbook: Fundamentals, Evolving Technologies and Emerging Applications*. CRC Press, Taylor and Francis, Boca Raton, FL, pp. 41–54.

Payne, S.J. (1991) A descriptive study of mental models. *Behaviour and Information Technology, 10, 3–21*.

Pekkola, S., Kaarilahti, N. and Pohjola, P. (2006) Towards formalised end-user participation in information systems development process: bridging the gap between participatory design and ISD methodologies. *Proceedings of the Ninth Conference on Participatory Design: Expanding Boundaries in Design, 1–5 August , Trento, Italy*.

Pender, T. (2003) *UML Bible*. John Wiley & Sons, Chichester.

Persson, P., Espinoza, F., Fagerberg, P., Sandin, A. and Cöster, R. (2003) GeoNotes: a location-based information system for public spaces. In Höök, K., Benyon, D.R. and Munro, A. (eds), *Designing Information Spaces: The Social Navigation Approach*. Springer-Verlag, London, pp. 151–174.

Petersen, M., Madsen, K. and Kjaer, A. (2002) The usability of everyday technology – emerging and fading opportunities. *ACM Transactions on Computer–Human Interaction (TOCHI), 9(2), 74–105*.

Pew, R.W. (2003) Introduction: Evolution of human–computer interaction: from Memex to Bluetooth and beyond. In Jacko, J.A. and Sears, A. (eds), *The Human–Computer Interaction Handbook: Fundamentals, Evolving Technologies and Emerging Applications*. Lawrence Erlbaum Associates, Mahwah, NJ.

Philips (2005) *Philips Research Technology* magazine, issue 2 3, May. www.research.philips.com/password/download/password_23.pdf

Picard, R. (1997) *Affective Computing*. MIT Press, Boston, MA.

Picard, R.W. (2003) Affective computing: challenges. *International Journal of Human–Computer Studies, 59(1–2), 55–64*.

Picard, R.W. and Healey, J. (1997) Affective wearables. *Proceedings of First International Symposium on Wearable Computers, ISWC '97*, Cambridge, MA, 13–14 October. IEEE Computer Society Press, Washington, DC, pp. 90–97.

Picard, R.W., Vyzas, E. and Healey, J. (2001) Toward machine emotional intelligence: analysis of affective physiological state. *IEEE Transactions on Pattern Analysis and Machine Intelligence, 23(10), 1175–1191*.

Piper, B., Ratti, C. and Ishii, H. (2002) Illuminating Clay: a 3-D tangible interface for landscape analysis. *CHI '02: Proceedings of the SIGCHI Conference on Human Factors in Computing Systems*. ACM Press, New York, pp. 355–362.

Pirolli, P (2003) Exploring and finding information. In Carroll, J. (ed.), *HCI Models, Theories and Frameworks*. Morgan Kaufmann, Boston, MA.

Plaue, C., Stasko, J. and Baloga, M. (2009) The conference room as a toolbox: technological and social routines in corporate meeting spaces. *Proceedings C&T 2009*. ACM Press, New York, 95–104.

Plutchik, R. (1980) *Emotion: A Psychobioevolutionary Synthesis*. Harper and Row, New York.

Postmes, T. and Lea, M. (2000) Social processes and group decision making: anonymity in group decision support systems. *Ergonomics, 43(8), 1252–1274*.

Prasolova-Førland, E. and Divitini, M. (2003) Collaborative virtual environments for supporting learning communities: an experience of use. *Proceedings of Group '03 Conference,* Sanibel Island, FL, 9–12 December. ACM Press, New York, pp. 58–67.

Preece, J. (2000) *Online Communities: Designing Usability, Supporting Sociability*. John Wiley, Chichester.

Pycock, J. and Bowers, J. (1996) Getting others to get it right: an ethnography of design work in the fashion industry. *Proceedings of CSCW '96 Conference*, Boston, MA, 16–20 November. ACM Press, New York, pp. 219–228.

Pylyshyn, Z.W. (1984) *Computation and Cognition*. MIT Press, Cambridge, MA.

Randell, C., Phelps, T. and Rogers, Y. (2003) Ambient wood: demonstration of a digitally enhanced field trip for school children, *Adjunct Proc. UbiComp 2003,* 12–15 October, Seattle, WA, pp. 100–104.

Rasmussen, J. (1986) *Information Processing and Human–Machine Interaction*. Elsevier North-Holland, Amsterdam.

Rasmussen, J. (1990) Mental models and their implications for design. In Ackermann, D. and Tauber, M.J. (eds), *Mental Models and Human—Computer Interaction*. North Holland, Amsterdam, 41–69.

Raven, B.H. and Rubin, J.Z. (1976) *Social Psychology*. Wiley, New York.

Read, J.C. and MacFarlane, S.J. (2000) Measuring Fun – Usability Testing for Children. *Computers and Fun 3,* York, England, BCS HCI Group.

Reason, J. (1990) *Human Error*. Cambridge University Press, Cambridge.

Reason, J. (1992) Cognitive underspecification: its variety and consequence. In Baars, B.J. (ed.), *Experimental Slips and Human Error: Exploring the Architecture of Volition*. Plenum Press, New York.

Reason, J. (1997) *Managing the Risks of Organizational Accidents*. Ashgate, Brookfield, VT.

Reeves, B. and Nass, C. (1996) *The Media Equation: How People Treat Computers, Television and New Media Like Real People and Places*. Cambridge University Press, New York.

Relph, E. (1976) *Place and Placelessness*. Pion Books, London.

Rheinfrank, J. and Evenson, S. (1996) Design languages. In Winograd, T. (ed.), *Bringing Design to Software*. ACM Press, New York.

Rheingold, H. (2000) *The Virtual Community: Homesteading on the Electronic Frontier*. MIT Press, Cambridge, MA.

Rheingold, H. (2003) *Smart Mobs. The Next Social Revolution*. Perseus Books, Cambridge, MA.

Rich, E. (1989) Stereotypes and user modelling. In Kobsa, A. and Wahlster, W. (eds), *User Models in Dialog Systems*. Springer-Verlag, Berlin.

Riva, G., Waterworth, J.A. and Waterworth, E.L. (2004) The layers of presence: a bio-cultural approach to understanding presence in natural and mediated environments. *Cyberpsychology and Behavior*, 7(4), 402–416.

Robertson, S. and Robertson, J. (1999) *Mastering the Requirements Process*. Addison-Wesley, Harlow.

Robles, E. and Wiberg, M. (2011) From materials to materiality: thinking of computation from within an Icehotel. *Interactions*, 18(1), 32–37.

Robson, C. (1993) *Real World Research: A Resource for Social Scientists and Practitioner–Researchers*. Blackwell, Oxford.

Robson, C. (1994) *Experiment, Design and Statistics in Psychology*. Penguin, London.

Rogers, Y. (2012) *HCI Theories: Classical, Modern, and Contemporary*. Morgan & Claypool, San Rafael, CA.

Rogers, Y. and Bellotti, V. (1997) Grounding blue-sky research: how can ethnography help? *Interactions*, 4(3), 58–63.

Rogers, Y., Lim, Y., Hazelwood, W. and Marshall, P. (2009) Equal opportunities: do shareable interfaces promote more group participation than single user displays? *Human–Computer Interaction*, 24(2), 79–116.

Rohrer, T. (2005) Image schemata in the brain. In Hampe, B. and Grady, J. (eds), *From Perception to Meaning: Image Schemas in Cognitive Linguistics*. Mouton de Gruyter, Berlin, pp. 165–196.

Romer, K. and Mattern, F. (2004) The design space of wireless sensor networks. *IEEE Wireless Communications*, 11(6), 54–61. IEEE Computer Society Press, Washington, DC.

Rosenfeld, L. and Morville, P. (2002) *Information Architecture for the World Wide Web*. O'Reilly, Sebastopol, CA.

Ross, P.R., Overbeeke, C.J., Wensveen, S.A.G. and Hummels, C.C.M. (2008) A designerly critique on enchantment. *Personal and Ubiquitous Computing*, 12(5), 359–371.

Rosson, M.-B. and Carroll, J. (2002) *Usability Engineering*. Morgan Kaufmann, San Francisco, CA.

Rosson, M-B and Carroll, J. (2012) Scenario-based design. In Jacko, J. (ed.) *The Human—Computer Interaction Handbook: Fundamentals, Evolving Technologies and Emerging Applications* (3rd edn). CRC Press, Taylor and Francis, Boca Raton, FL, pp. 1105–1124.

Rouse, W.B. and Rouse, S.H. (1983) Analysis and classification of human error. *IEEE Transactions on Systems, Man, and Cybernetics*, SMC-13, 539–549.

Rowley, D.E. and Rhoades, D.G. (1992) The cognitive jogthrough: a fast-paced user interface evaluation procedure. *CHI '92: Proceedings of the SIGCHI Conference on Human Factors in Computing Systems*. ACM Press, New York, pp. 389–395.

Rudd, J., Stern, K. and Isensee, S. (1996) Low vs. high fidelity prototyping debate. *Interactions*, 3(1), 76–85.

Russell, J.A. and Fernandez-Dols, J.M. (1997) *The Psychology of Facial Expression*. Cambridge University Press, New York.

Saffer, D. (2008) *Designing Gestural Interfaces*. O'Reilly, Sebastopol, CA.

Saffer, D. (2009) *Designing for Interaction* (2nd edn). New Riders, Indianapolis, IN.

Schachter, S. and Singer, J.E. (1962) Cognitive, social and physiological determinants of emotional state. *Psychological Review*, 69, 379–399.

Schank, R. and Abelson, R. (1977) *Scripts, Plans, Goals and Understanding*. Lawrence Erlbaum Associates, Hillsdale, NJ.

Schiano, D.J., Ehrlich, S.M., Rahardja, K. and Sheridan, K. (2000) Face to InterFace: facial affect in (hu)man and machine. *CHI '00: Proceedings of the SIGCHI Conference on Human Factors in Computing Systems*. ACM Press, New York, pp. 193–200.

Schneider, W. and Shiffrin, R.M. (1977) Controlled and automatic human information processing: 1. Detection, search and attention. *Psychological Review*, 84, 1–66.

Schoenfelder, R., Maegerlein, A. and Regenbrecht, H. (2004) TACTool: freehand interaction with directed tactile feedback. *Proceedings of Beyond Wand and Glove Based Interaction*, Workshop at IEEE VR2004, Washington. IEEE Computer Society Press, Washington, DC, pp. 13–15.

Schütte, S. (2005) *Engineering Emotional Values in Product Design – Kansei Engineering in Development*. PhD Thesis, Institute of Technology, Linköping.

Shackel, B. (1959) Ergonomics for a computer. *Design*, 120, 36–39.

Shackel, B. (1990) Human factors and usability. In Preece, J. and Keller, L. (eds), *Human–Computer Interaction: Selected Readings*. Prentice Hall, Hemel Hempstead.

Sharpe, W.P. and Stenton, S.P. (2003) Information appliances. In Jacko, J.A. and Sears, A. (eds), *The Human–Computer Interaction Handbook: Fundamentals, Evolving Technologies and Emerging Applications*. Lawrence Erlbaum Associates, Mahwah, NJ.

Shedroff, N. (2001) *Experience Design 1*. New Riders, Indianapolis, IN.

Shen, C., Ryall, K., Forlines, C., Esenther, A., Vernier, F.D., Everitt, K., Wu, M., Wigdor, D., Morris, M.R., Hancock, M. and Tse, E. (2006) Informing the design of direct-touch tabletops. *IEEE Computer Graphic and Application*, 26(5), 36–46.

Sherer, K. (2005) What are emotions? How can they be measured? *Social Science Information*, 44(4), 695–729.

Shneiderman, B. (1980) *Software Psychology: Human Factors in Computer and Information Systems*. Winthrop, Cambridge, MA.

Shneiderman, B. (1982) The future of interactive systems and the emergence of direct manipulation. *Behaviour and Information Technology,* 1(3), 237–256.

Shneiderman, B. (1998) *Designing the User Interface* (3rd edn). Addison-Wesley, Reading, MA.

Short, J., Williams, E. and Christie, B. (1976) *The Social Psychology of Telecommunications.* John Wiley, London.

Shusterman, R. (2013) Somaesthetics. In M. Soegaard and R.F. Dam (eds), *The Encyclopedia of Human–Computer Interaction,* 2nd edn. The Interaction Design Foundation, Aarhus, Denmark. Available online at www.interaction-design.org/encyclopedia/somaesthetics.html

Sickiens de Souza, C. (2005) *The Semiotic Engineering of Human–Computer Interaction.* MIT Press, Boston, MA.

Siewiorek, D., Smailagic, A. and Starner, T. (2008) *Application Design for Wearable Computing.* Morgan & Claypool, San Rafael, CA.

Simonsen, J. and Kensing, F. (1997) Using ethnography in contextual design. *Communications of the ACM,* 40(7), 82–88.

Sinclair, P.A.S., Martinez, K., Millard, D.E. and Weal M.J. (2002) Links in the palm of your hand: tangible hypermedia using augmented reality. *Proceedings of the Thirteenth ACM Conference on Hypertext and Hypermedia: Next-Gen Open Hypermedia.* ACM Press, New York, pp. 127–136.

Slater, M. (1999) Measuring presence: a response to the Witmer and Singer questionnaire. *Presence,* 8(5), 560–566.

Smith, D.C., Irby, C., Kimball, R., Verplank, B. and Harslem, E. (1982) Designing the Star user interface. *BYTE,* 7(4), 242–282.

Smith, E. and Mackie D. (2000) *Social Psychology* (2nd edn). Psychology Press, New York.

Smith, P.J., Beatty, R., Hayes, C.C., Larson, A., Geddes, N.D. and Domeich, N.C. (2012) Human–centred design of decision–support systems. In Jacko, J. (ed.) *The Human—Computer Interaction Handbook: Fundamentals, Evolving Technologies and Emerging Applications* (3rd edn). CRC Press, Taylor and Francis, Boca Raton, FL, pp. 589–622.

Snyder, C. (2003) *Paper Prototyping: The Fast and Easy Way to Design and Refine User Interfaces.* Morgan Kaufmann, San Francisco, CA.

Solso, R.L. (1995) *Cognitive Psychology* (4th edn). Allyn & Bacon, Boston, MA.

Sommerville, I. and Sawyer, P. (1997) *Requirements Engineering: a Good Practice Guide.* Wiley, Chichester.

Spence, R. (2001) *Information Visualization.* ACM Press/Addison-Wesley, New York.

Spencer, R. (2000) The streamlined cognitive walkthrough method, working around social constraints encountered in a software development company. *CHI '00: Proceedings of the SIGCHI Conference on Human Factors in Computing Systems.* ACM Press, New York, pp. 353–359.

SRI International (2003, 5 February) *Wireless Micro- Sensors Monitor Structural Health.* [Electronic version]. Retrieved 9 August 2007 from http://www.sri.com/rd/microsensors.pdf.

Ståhl, O., Wallberg, A., Söderberg, J., Humble, J., Fahlén, L.E., Bullock, A. and Lundberg, J. (2002) Information exploration using The Pond. *Proceedings of CVE '02 Conference,* Bonn, Germany, 30 September–2 October. ACM Press, New York, pp. 72–79.

Stanton, N. (2003) Human error identification in human–computer interaction. In Jacko, J.A. and Sears, A. (eds), *The Human–Computer Interaction Handbook: Fundamentals, Evolving Technologies and Emerging Applications.* Lawrence Erlbaum Associates, Mahwah, NJ.

StartleCam (1999) http://vismod.media.mit.edu/tech-reports/TR-468/node3.html.

Stephanidis, C. (ed.) (2001) *User Interfaces for All: Concepts, Methods and Tools.* Lawrence Erlbaum Associates, Mahwah, NJ.

Stewart, J. (2003) The social consumption of information and communication technologies (ICTs): insights from research on the appropriation and consumption of new ICTs in the domestic environment. *Cognition Technology and Work,* 5(1), 4–14.

Stoner, J.A.F. (1961) *A comparison of individual and group decisions involving risk.* Unpublished Master's Thesis, MIT, Cambridge, MA.

Streitz, N.A., Geissler, J., Holmer, T., Konomi, S., Müller-Tomfelde, C., Reischl, W., Rexroth, P., Seitz, P., Steinmetz, R. (1999) i-LAND: an interactive landscape for creativity and innovation. *CHI '99 Proceedings of the SIGCHI conference on Human Factors in Computing Systems.* ACM New York, pp. 120–27

Streitz, N.A., Geissler, J., Holmer, T. (1998) Roomware for cooperative buildings: integrated design of architectural spaces and information spaces. *Proceedings of CoBuild' 1998. Cooperative Buildings: Integrating Information, Organization and Architecture.* LNCS 1370, Springer, Heidelberg, pp. 4–21.

Streitz, N.A., Rexroth, P. and Holmer, T. (1997) Does 'roomware' matter? Investigating the role of personal and public information devices and their combination in meeting room collaboration. *Proceedings of ECSCW '97 Conference,* Lancaster, UK, 7–11 September. Kluwer, Dordrecht, pp. 297–312.

Stroop, J.R. (1935) Studies in inference in serial verbal reactions. *Journal of Experimental Psychology,* 18, 643–662.

Suchman, L. (1987) *Plans and Situated Actions.* Cambridge University Press, New York (2nd edn, 2007).

Sumner, M. and Hostetler, D. (2000) A comparative study of computer conferencing and face-to-face communications in systems design. *Proceedings of SIGCPR '00 Conference,* Chicago, IL, 6–8 April. ACM Press, New York, pp. 93–99.

Sutcliffe, A. (2007) Multimedia user interface design. In Jacko, J. (ed.) *The Human—Computer Interaction Handbook: Fundamentals, Evolving Technologies and Emerging Applications.* CRC Press, Taylor and Francis, Boca Raton, FL, pp. 387–404.

Symon, G., Long, K. and Ellis, J. (1996) The coordination of work activities: cooperation and conflict in a hospital context. *Computer Supported Cooperative Work,* 5, 1–21.

Tan, H.Z. (2000) Perceptual user interfaces: haptic interfaces. *Communications of the ACM,* 43(3), 40–41.

Tang, J.C. and Isaacs, E. (1993) Why do users like video? *Computer Supported Cooperative Work,* 1, 163–196.

Taylor, B. (1990) The HUFIT planning, analysis and specification toolset. *Proceedings of INTERACT '90 Conference,* Cambridge, UK, 27–31 August. North-Holland, Amsterdam, pp. 371–376.

Thomas, B., Close, B., Donoghue, J., Squires, J., De Bondi, P., Morris, M. and Piekarski, W. (2000) ARQuake: an outdoor/indoor augmented reality first person application. *Proceedings of 4th International Symposium on Wearable Computers,* Atlanta, GA, October, pp. 139–146. [Electronic Version]. Retrieved 10 June 2004 from http://www.tinmith.net/papers/thomas-iswc-2000.pdf.

Tiger, L. (1992) *The Pursuit of Pleasure.* Little, Brown & Co., Boston, MA.

Tollmar, K. and Persson, J. (2002) Understanding remote presence. *Proceedings of the Second Nordic Conference on Human—Computer Interaction* (Aarhus, Denmark, 19–23 October 2002). NordiCHI '02. ACM Press, New York, pp. 41–49.

Triesman, A.M. (1960) Contextual cues in selective listening. *Quarterly Journal of Experimental Psychology,* 12, 242–248.

Tuckerman, B.W. (1965) Development sequence in small groups. *Psychological Bulletin,* 63, 316–328.

Tudor, L.G., Muller, M.J., Dayton, T. and Root, R.W. (1993) A participatory design technique for high-level task analysis, critique and redesign: the CARD method. *Proceedings of the Human Factors and Ergonomics Society 37th Annual Meeting,* Seattle, WA, 11–15 October, pp. 295–299.

Tufte, E.R. (1983) *The Visual Display of Quantitative Information.* Graphics Press, Cheshire, CT.

Tufte, E.R. (1990) *Envisioning Information.* Graphics Press, Cheshire, CT.

Tufte, E.R. (1997) *Visual Explanations.* Graphics Press, Cheshire, CT.

Turkle, S. (2005) *The Second Self: Computers and the Human Spirit,* Twentieth Anniversary Edition. MIT Press, Boston, MA.

Turner, P. and Turner, S. (2001) Describing Team Work with Activity Theory. *Cognition, Technology and Work,* 3(3), 127–139.

Turner, P. and Turner, S. (2002) Surfacing issues using activity theory. *Journal of Applied Systems Science,* 3(1), 134–155.

Turner, P., Milne, G., Turner, S. and Kubitscheck, M. (2003) Towards the wireless ward: evaluating a trial of networked PDAs in the National Health Service. In Chittaro, L. (ed.), *Human–Computer Interaction with Mobile Devices and Services, Proceedings of Mobile HCI 2003 Symposium,* Udine, Italy, 8–11 September. Lecture Notes in Computer Science Proceedings Series, Springer-Verlag, Berlin, pp. 202–214.

Tversky, B. (2003) Structures of mental spaces: how people think about space. *Environment and Behavior,* 35, 66–80.

Ullmer, B. and Ishii, H. (2002) Emerging frameworks for tangible user interfaces. In Carroll, J.M. (ed.), *Human–Computer Interaction in the New Millennium.* ACM Press, New York.

Usoh, M., Arthur, K., Whitton, M.C., Bastos, R., Steed, A., Slater, M. and Brooks, F.P. (1999) Walking > walking-in-place > flying, in virtual environments. *Proceedings of SIGGRAPH '99 Conference.* ACM Press, New York, pp. 359–364.

Usoh, M., Catena, E., Arman, S. and Slater, M. (2000) Using presence questionnaires in reality. *Presence,* 9(5), 497–503.

Van der Veer, G.C., Tauber, M., Waern, Y. and van Muylwijk, B. (1985) On the interaction between system and user characteristics. *Behaviour and Information Technology,* 4(4), 284–308.

van Harmelen, M. (ed.) (2001) *Object Modeling and User Interface Design: Designing Interactive Systems.* Addison-Wesley, Boston, MA.

Venkatesh, A., Kruse, E. and Chuan-Fong Shih, E. (2003) The networked home: an analysis of current developments and future trends. *Cognition, Technology and Work,* 5(1), 23–32.

Vera, A.H. and Simon, H.A. (1993) Situated action: a symbolic interpretation. *Cognitive Science,* 17, 7–48.

Verplank, W. (2007) *Designing Interactions.* MIT Press, Boston, MA.

Vertelney, L. (1989) Using video to prototype user interfaces. *ACM SIGCHI Bulletin,* 21(2), 57–61.

Vicente, K.J. (1999) *Cognitive Work Analysis: Toward Safe, Productive, and Healthy Computer-based Work.* Lawrence Erlbaum Associates, Mahwah, NJ.

Vicente, K.J. and Rasmussen, J. (1992) Ecological interface design: theoretical foundations. *IEEE Transactions in Systems, Man and Cybernetics,* 22(4), 589–605.

Viller, S. and Sommerville, I. (1998) *Coherence: an approach to representing ethnographic analyses in systems design.* CSEG Technical Report, CSEG/7/97, Lancaster University, UK, available at ftp://ftp.comp. lancs.ac.uk/pub/reports/1997/CSEG.7.9.

Viller, S. and Sommerville, I. (2000) Ethnographically informed analysis for software engineers. *International Journal of Human–Computer Studies,* 53(1), 169–196.

Vredenburg, K., Mao, J.-Y., Smith, P.W. and Carey, T. (2002) A survey of user-centred design practice. *CHI '02: Proceedings of the SIGCHI Conference on Human Factors in Computing Systems.* ACM Press, New York, pp. 471–478.

Vygotsky, L.S. (1978) *Mind in Society: The Development of Higher Psychological Processes* (English trans. ed. M. Cole). Harvard University Press, Cambridge, MA.

Ward, R., Bell, D. and Marsden, P. (2003) An exploration of facial expression tracking in affective HCI. In O'Neill, E., Palanque, P. and Johnson, P. (eds), *People and Computers XVII – Proceedings of HCI 2003 Conference.* Springer-Verlag, London, pp. 383–399.

Warr, A. and O'Neill, E. (2007) Tool support for creativity using externalizations. *Proceedings of the 6th ACM SIGCHI Conference on Creativity and Cognition.* ACM Press, New York, pp. 127–36.

Weiser, M. (1991) The computer of the 21st century. *Scientific American,* 265(9), 66–75.

Weiser, M. (1993) Some computer science issues in ubiquitous computing. *Communications of the ACM,* 36(7), 75–84.

Wenger, E. (1998) *Communities of Practice: Learning Memory and Identity.* Cambridge University Press, Cambridge.

Wexelblat, A. (2003) Results from the Footprints project. In Höök, K., Benyon, D.R. and Munro, A. (eds), *Designing Information Spaces: The Social Navigation Approach.* Springer-Verlag, London, pp. 223–248.

Wharton, C., Rieman, J., Lewis, C. and Polson, P. (1994) The cognitive walkthrough method: a practitioner's guide. In Nielsen, J. and Mack, R.L. (eds), *Usability Inspection Methods.* Wiley, New York.

Wiberg, M. (2011) Making the case for 'architectural informatics': a new research horizon for ambient computing? *International Journal of Ambient Computing and Intelligence,* 3(3), 1–7.

Wickens, C.D. and Hollands, J.G. (2000) *Engineering Psychology and Human Performance* (3rd edn). Prentice-Hall, Upper Saddle River, NJ.

Wikman, A.-S., Nieminen, T. and Summala, H. (1998) Driving experience and time-sharing during in-car tasks on roads of different width. *Ergonomics,* 41, 358–372.

Willcocks, L. and Lester, S. (1998) *Beyond the IT Productivity Paradox: Assessment Issues.* Wiley, Chichester.

Williams, J., Bias, R. and Mayhew, D. (2007) Cost justification. In Sears, A. and Jacko, J.A. (eds), *The Human–Computer Interaction Handbook: Fundamentals, Evolving Technologies and Emerging Applications* (2nd edn). Lawrence Erlbaum Associates, Mahwah, NJ, pp. 1265–1275.

Wilson, A. (2012) Sensor- and recognition-based input for interaction. In Jacko, J. (ed.) *The Human—Computer Interaction Handbook: Fundamentals, Evolving Technologies and Emerging Applications* (3rd edn). CRC Press, Taylor and Francis, Boca Raton, FL, pp. 133–156.

Winograd, T. (ed.) (1996) *Bringing Design to Software.* ACM Press, New York.

Winograd, T. and Flores, F. (1986) *Understanding Computers and Cognition: A New Foundation for Design.* Ablex Publishing, Norwood, NJ.

Witmer, B.G. and Singer, M.J. (1998) Measuring presence in virtual environments: a presence questionnaire. *Presence,* 7(3), 225–240.

Wixon, D. and Ramey, J. (eds) (1996) *Field Methods Casebook for Software Design.* Wiley, New York.

Wobbrock, J.O., Morris, M.R. and Wilson, A.D. (2009) User-defined gestures for surface computing. *CHI '09: Proceedings of the SIGCHI Conference on Human Factors in Computing Systems.* ACM Press, New York, pp. 1083–1092.

Wodtke, C. (2003) *Information Architecture: Blueprints for the Web.* New Riders, Indianapolis, IN.

Wodtke, C. and Govella, A. (2009) *Information Architecture: Blueprints for the Web* (2nd edn). New Riders, Indianapolis, IN.

Won, S.S., Jin, J. and Hong, J.I. (2009) Contextual web history: using visual and contextual cues to improve web browser history. *CHI '09: Proceedings of the SIGCHI Conference on Human Factors in Computing Systems.* ACM Press, New York, pp. 1457–1466.

Wood, J. and Silver, D. (1995) *Joint Application Development.* Wiley, New York.

Woolrych, A. and Cockton, G. (2000) Assessing heuristic evaluation: mind the quality, not just percentages. In Turner, S. and Turner, P. (eds), *Proceedings of British HCI Group HCI 2000 Conference,* Sunderland, UK, 5–8 September. British Computer Society, London, vol. 2, pp. 35–36.

Woolrych, A. and Cockton, G. (2001) Why and when five test users aren't enough. In Vanderdonckt, J., Blandford, A. and Derycke, A. (eds), *Proceedings of the IHM–HCI '01 Conference.* Cepadeus, Toulouse, Vol. 2, pp. 105–108.

Wright, P.C., Fields, R.E. and Harrison, M.D. (2000) Analyzing human–computer interaction as distributed cognition: the resources model. *Human–Computer Interaction,* 15(1), 1–42.

Wurman, R.S. (1991) *New Road Atlas: US Atlas.* Simon and Schuster, New York.

Wurman, R.S. (1997) *Information Architects.* Printed in China through Palace Press International, distributed by Hi Marketing, London.

Wurman, R.S. (2000) *Understanding USA.* TED Conferences, Menlo Park, CA.

Yatani, K., Partridge, K., Bern, M. and Newman, M.W. (2008, April) Escape: a target selection technique using visually-cued gestures. *CHI '08: Proceedings of the SIGCHI Conference on Human Factors in Computing Systems.* ACM Press, New York, pp. 285–294.

Yerkes, R.M. and Dodson, J.D. (1908) The relation of the strength of stimulus to rapidity of habit formation. *Journal of Comparative Neurological Psychology,* 18, 459–482.

Zajonc, R.B. (1984) On the primacy of affect. *American Psychologist,* 39, 117–123.

Zaphiris, P., Ang, C.S. and Laghos, A. (2007) Online communities. In Jacko, J. (ed.) *The Human—Computer Interaction Handbook: Fundamentals, Evolving Technologies and Emerging Applications.* CRC Press, Taylor and Francis, Boca Raton, FL, pp. 623–642.

Zhang, J. and Norman, D.A. (1994) Representations in distributed cognitive tasks. *Cognition Science,* 18, 87–122.

Zimmerman, J. (2009) Designing for the self: making products that help people become the person they desire to be. *CHI '09: Proceedings of the SIGCHI Conference on Human Factors in Computing Systems.* ACM Press, New York, pp. 395–404.

Index